Labor Markets and Employment Relationships

Joyce Jacobsen: To Bill, Catherine, and Kenneth
Gilbert Skillman: To Sue and my parents

LABOR MARKETS AND EMPLOYMENT RELATIONSHIPS
A Comprehensive Approach

JOYCE P. JACOBSEN *and* **GILBERT L. SKILLMAN**

Blackwell
Publishing

350 Main Street, Malden, MA 02148-5020, USA
108 Cowley Road, Oxford OX4 1JF, UK
550 Swanston Street, Carlton, Victoria 3053, Australia

First published 2004 by Blackwell Publishing Ltd

Library of Congress Cataloging-in-Publication Data

Jacobsen, Joyce P.
Labor markets and employment relationships : a comprehensive approach
/ Joyce P. Jacobsen and Gilbert L. Skillman.
p.   cm.
Includes bibliographical references and index.
ISBN 0-631-20836-4 (cloth : alk. paper)
1. Labor market.   2. Industrial relations.   3. Labor economics.
I. Skillman, Gilbert L.   II. Title.
HD5706.J33   2004
331 – dc22

2003023829

A catalogue record for this title is available from the British Library.

Set in 10/12 Book Antique
by SNP Best-set Typesetter Ltd, Hong Kong
Printed and bound in the United Kingdom
by TJ International, Padstow, Cornwall

For further information on
Blackwell Publishing, visit our website:
http://www.blackwellpublishing.com

CONTENTS

LIST OF FIGURES

LIST OF BOXES

LIST OF TABLES

PREFACE

The study of labor markets and employment relationships is among the most exciting and dynamic fields of inquiry in the discipline of economics. As such, it has given rise to a number of ongoing debates concerning matters of fundamental importance to the human condition, including the organization of work, the distribution of income, the nature, incidence and causes of unemployment, and the appropriate functions of the state and the market in the determination of economic outcomes. These debates have prompted in turn the development of new methods of theoretical analysis, new means of assessing competing hypotheses, and new sources of relevant data.

However, it is difficult for students to appreciate the significance and vitality of these debates without the perspective offered by an analytical framework broad enough to encompass all sides of prevailing controversies in the field. Start with the presumption that labor markets are perfectly competitive or virtually so, for example, and it becomes arbitrarily easy to dismiss the possibility of persistent unemployment in the absence of government intervention in the labor market. Conversely, categorical rejection of competitive market analysis or other formal theoretical treatments of labor market phenomena raises the risk of losing insights yielded by these approaches which remain relevant even if their premises are not strictly satisfied.

Our primary motive in writing this text has been to develop an analytical approach to the subject matter of labor economics that is versatile enough to accommodate competing positions in most of the major controversies and lines of inquiry animating the contemporary discipline, yet tractable enough to be understood by new students of the field who have some background in the larger discipline of economics. In keeping with this goal, the text begins on the familiar turf of competitive market theory, but presents this material so as to promote critical awareness of the core assumptions undergirding this approach and of labor market conditions that may clash with these assumptions. We then use this critical perspective to motivate the introduction of a broader theoretical framework that is nonetheless recognizably grounded in the methods of economic analysis most students learn in their introductory and intermediate economic theory courses.

The key to this more general framework lies in the observation that institutions of exchange, particularly those manifested in labor market transactions, are generally premised on individual efforts devoted to searching for and pairing with prospective trading partners, negotiating terms of trade with selected partners, and ensuring that negotiated terms of trade are carried out; and that these economic activities, like all others, incur costs. The presence of significant mobility or transaction costs undercuts the economic logic of the perfectly competitive model, and gives rise to conditions of market power or imperfect contracting that may yield outcomes that are fundamentally at odds with the model's standard predictions and normative claims. Therefore, allowing for various configurations of these costs (including their virtual absence) makes it possible to investigate a much broader array of labor market phenomena, while maintaining the familiar tenets of optimization and equilibrium that give structure to the simpler theory.

While this approach owes an obvious debt to "transaction cost economics," associated with the influential work of Oliver Williamson, it differs from that construct in at least two significant ways. One difference is a matter of scope: while the main focus of transaction cost analysis concerns the organizational implications of factors giving rise to contractual incompleteness, the approach outlined in this text also embraces forms of exchange costs that give rise to wage-setting power and that create incentives for monitoring of effort or the provision of signals about unseen characteristics. A second difference is methodological, in that the strategic analysis of costly labor exchange presented in this text is grounded more explicitly in the basic framework of noncooperative game theory.

The analytical material in the text, including its game-theoretic foundation, is presented in verbal and graphical form with occasional mathematical supplements placed in chapter appendices. While the theoretical analysis is entirely self-contained, students familiar with the notions of indifference and isoquant maps will find the going easier, especially in the early chapters. Accordingly, the text is intended primarily for use in upper-level undergraduate courses in economics or in masters' programs in economics, industrial relations, and public policy.

Every topic addressed in the text is motivated and illustrated by reference to contemporary and historical empirical trends. However, given the rapidity with which labor market conditions change, it is impossible for any text to provide completely up-to-the minute data, and we have not attempted to do so. We encourage instructors to supplement the empirical information in the text as desired with additional readings or web-based sources.

Some additional suggestions for using this text: first, most instructors will find it difficult at best to cover the entire book in a single semester course, and therefore it will generally be necessary to decide beforehand which chapters to omit, which to cover partially or in broad outline, and which to give special attention. We consider the introductory chapter plus chapters 1 through 8, comprising parts I and II, to provide the foundation for the analytical approach developed in the text. Instructors might therefore consider spending the first half of the semester on these "core" chapters, depending on the preparation levels of their students.

The topics to be covered in the second half of the semester will depend on the particular focus of the course being taught. Courses emphasizing the nature and operation of labor market institutions might therefore concentrate on the chapters in part III, which address various features of the employment relationship, plus chapters 15 and 16, dealing respectively with discrimination and the hypothesis of labor market segmentation. A more traditional survey course might wish to skip part III entirely except for the chapter 11 discussion of on-the-job training, and focus instead on the chapters of part IV concerning labor market divisions, in particular those concerning variations in working conditions (chapter 13) and formal educational attainment (chapter 14).

The end-of-chapter questions are designed to promote students' hands-on understanding of the material, either by suggesting concrete applications of abstract analytical material or pursuing extensions of ideas and results suggested in the text. Instructors can obtain suggested answers to these questions by contacting the authors.

The authors would like to acknowledge the contributions of several people who helped make this text a reality. We thank Blackwell's Al Bruckner for encouraging this project at its inception and Elizabeth Wald for able and good-natured editorial advice and assistance, especially in the final stages. Seth Ditchik took over Al's editorial role in the project and provided steady oversight as the material began to take shape. Paul Stringer cheerfully steered us through the tortuous final stages of copy-editing. We especially thank the anonymous reviewers of the text's early drafts for their helpful comments and reactions. We are also grateful for the feedback, research, and production assistance provided by the following Wesleyan undergraduates: Ambika Ahuja, Michael Aylward, Bryan Bissell, Derek Chung, David Ehrenberg, Wei Kwan, Nuanphan Maithongdee, Rachel Mandal, Te-ling Nai, James Pearce, Emily Weissman, Kingston Wong, and Huan Yu. And we are particularly grateful to several years' worth of Wesleyan students in our labor economics courses who served as test subjects for earlier drafts of the text.

Coauthor Skillman would further like to thank his wife, Sue Augustyniak, for her steadfast support over the course of writing this text, and his family for their patience in the face of persistently discouraging replies to the repeated query, "Is the book done yet?" Coauthor Jacobsen thanks her husband, Bill Boyd, and children Catherine and Kenneth, for generally desisting from asking if the book was done yet.

INTRODUCTION: LABOR ECONOMICS AND THE POLITICAL ECONOMY OF LABOR

This chapter introduces the study of labor economics by briefly considering the nature, significance, and historical development of its primary
subject matter, and then tracing the field's intellectual heritage. This will
lead to a preview of the central issues and themes to be addressed in this
text. The chapter's argument starts with a basic question: Why should a
specialized field of economic inquiry be devoted to the study of labor?

THE ECONOMIC SIGNIFICANCE OF LABOR

Labor economics might broadly be defined as the branch of this social science that
studies the allocation of time across competing purposes. This definition has the
advantage of being comprehensive, in that it encompasses all human activities,
remunerated or otherwise, that might count as labor, as well as its principal alternatives. Defined in this way, however, it is difficult to see how labor economics is
anything more than simply applied microeconomics. This is in fact how the field's
subject matter was understood before it became a distinct subdiscipline.

A tighter definition posits labor economics as an inquiry into *the nature and allocation of paid work in market economies*. The narrower focus suggested by this definition is justifiable if there is something about the particular activity of *paid* work
that merits special study. Why might this be the case? At first glance the answer
to this question may seem obvious. Work is an essential aspect of the human condition, the activity through which nature is transformed to meet human needs
and wants. Most people engage in paid labor of some form, spend a major chunk
of their lives working, and depend for their livelihoods on the income secured
through labor.

Table I.1   Labor force, absolute and relative sizes, for ten industrialized countries, 2000

	Absolute size	Relative size
United States	140 863 000	0.67
Japan	66 990 000	0.62
Germany	39 750 000	0.57
United Kingdom	29 450 000	0.63
France	25 980 000	0.56
Italy	23 340 000	0.48
Canada	15 789 000	0.66
Australia	9 678 000	0.65
Netherlands	8 050 000	0.63
Sweden	4 489 000	0.64

Source: US Department of Labor, Bureau of Labor Statistics, Office of Productivity and Technology, *Comparative Civilian Labor Force Statistics: Ten Countries, 1959–2001* (March 2002): tables 1 and 2; website: <http://www.bls.gov/fls/flslforc.pdf>. The Civilian Labor Force for each country is determined on the basis of the US definition.

Employment and labor income

Consider some of the ways in which the scope and significance of labor is mani-fested in modern industrialized economies. First, note that most adults have or seek remunerated work in these economies. Table I.1 reports the size of the *labor force*, that is, people counted as performing paid labor or actively seeking paid work in 2000, both in absolute terms and as a percentage of the civilian working-age population (generally defined as persons over age sixteen), for ten industri-alized economies. It is interesting to note, though, how widely the degree of labor force participation varies across countries. Why might this be the case?

Note second that not all those who seek paid work find it – or at least not imme-diately. Table I.2 indicates the proportion of the labor force that is *unemployed*, that is, jobless but seeking work, in 1985, 1989, 1993 and 1999 for a selection of coun-tries. As you can see from the table, the rate of unemployment – the ratio of unem-ployed to total labor force – varies dramatically over time and across economies. Over this 15-year period, some countries have rising unemployment rates, some have falling rates, and some changed direction. Almost no country stays about the same.

Third, labor income, defined specifically as "employee compensation," is by far the largest category of compensation in national income accounts, representing about 60 percent of aggregate income in the US. Most households derive the lion's share of their income from paid employment. A similar pattern holds for other industrialized economies.

These data suggest why paid work as an economic activity is important to study, but not why this investigation requires a special branch of economics. Com-

Table I.2   Unemployment rates for various countries, 1985, 1989, 1993, and 1999

	1985[1]	1989[1]	1993[1]	1999[2]
Argentina	5.3	7.3	10.1	12.8[3]
Denmark	9.1	9.5	12.2	5.7
France	10.2	9.4	12.5	11.9
Germany	9.2	8.0	7.2	8.8
Israel	6.7	8.9	10.0	8.9
Japan	2.6	2.3	2.5	4.7
Singapore	4.1	2.2	2.6	4.6
Sweden	2.8	1.5	8.2	5.6
Turkey	11.2	8.5	7.9	7.3
United Kingdom	11.2	7.2	10.2	6.0
United States	7.2	5.3	6.8	4.2

Source:
[1] United Nations, *Statistical Yearbook*, 41st issue.
[2] United Nations, *Statistical Yearbook*, 46th issue, 2002.
[3] Data from 1998.

puters play an increasingly important role in economic life, for example, but this has not prompted the creation of "computer economics" as a separate subdiscipline with its own methods, research agenda, and academic journals. Is there something about paid work, other than its pervasiveness and prominence in the national income accounts, that demands a customized body of inquiry?

Possible clues to answering this question can be found lurking behind the statistics presented above. First, it is clear from table I.1 that not everyone in the population is in the labor force. For example, in the US, over 65 million people of working age were not in the labor force. What are they doing instead, and how do they manage to stay alive if they are not being remunerated for their labor?

Second, what does it mean that large numbers of people who say they are seeking employment cannot find it, as indicated in table I.2? Why are people unemployed, and why does the rate of unemployment vary so widely across time and place? Does the existence of unemployment suggest that exchanges for labor don't work in the same way as those in other types of market?

Third, a subtle but potentially important issue underlies the distinction between income from "employment" and from "self-employment" in the income accounts. Given that the services of "self-employed" individuals are often engaged by firms, one might be tempted to consider the affected workers as employees of those firms. What is the basis for making this distinction?

Whatever the reason, this distinction goes well beyond national income accounting practices, arising as well in the areas of tax and labor law. The primary basis for distinguishing *employment* from the provision of services by self-employed workers appears to be who has ultimate authority for overseeing or directing the work involved: in the former case, *employers* fill this role, while service providers counted as self-employed largely determine the manner in which their tasks are performed. For example, the neighborhood pre-teen hired to mow your parents' lawn provides a service; so does the plumber who fixes your sink or the mechanic who repairs your automobile. And although such service transactions directly involve expenditures of labor, they are not typically counted as *employment* transactions. However, if a service supplier – an electrician, say – hires an assistant to help her in the general performance of her duties, that would typically constitute a labor market transaction.

The immediate question is whether this distinction reflects something fundamental about the economic logic of transactions involving labor. The question gains salience once it is noted that, with the possible exception of mercenary labor, employment relationships in the sense just defined did not become pervasive prior to significant institutional changes associated with the emergence of capitalism in Western Europe roughly five hundred years ago. Thus, inasmuch as labor economics studies markets for labor services offered by the suppliers of those services, it concerns a relatively recent pattern of widespread economic interaction. This point can be illustrated with a brief look at the historical evolution of transactions for labor.

Labor exchange in economic history

As just noted, it is only relatively recently in economic history – specifically, within the last half-millennium – that markets in which individuals offered their own working capacities for hire became significant means of allocating labor for any society. In particular, markets for the products of labor flourished long before markets for self-supplied labor did, and the latter did not attain equal prominence until the social and economic changes wrought by the Industrial Revolution of the eighteenth century.

There are a number of interrelated reasons for that disparity. First, in the primarily agrarian world economy that preceded this economic watershed, most people sustained themselves through subsistence farming. There was small-scale urban industry and commerce, certainly, but this economic sector was generally very small in relative terms. Second, in those historical instances where large-scale enterprises demanded significant additional labor resources, such as the Roman *latifundia* or ancient Egyptian copper mines, most of the required human muscle power was supplied by slaves. Third, the economic primacy of agriculture was reflected in social and political strictures that tied workers to the land and thus sharply limited their economic mobility. An example of this is seen in the feudal institution of *serfdom*. While feudal lords could not buy or sell serfs, they could command a significant portion of their labor, and these workers were bonded to the estate or fief on which they lived.

In the case of both slavery and serfdom, labor markets in their modern form were impossible, as workers did not typically enjoy the right to offer for hire their own capacity for labor. In western Europe, these restrictions began to disintegrate toward the end of the feudal era with the rise of cities and towns, intermittent shortages of labor occasioned by famine and plague, and the increasing role of money and trade. However, the creation of a legally free labor force did not take place without considerable time and social change. Nor did the dissolution of feudal bonds immediately lead to employment relationships as we now recognize them. Two examples serve to illustrate this point.

First, urban *craft guilds* which flourished in medieval Europe and until more recent times in India, Japan, and several Islamic countries, banded together artisans in branches of industry such as cloth-making and weaving. While the guilds, like many modern firms, were characterized by hierarchical organization, they were based on levels of professional mastery (apprentice, journeyman, and master) rather than the relationship of employers to employees. After successfully serving their apprenticeships, guild workers could expect to advance to journeyman and eventually master status upon completion of a "masterpiece."

The second example, intriguing because of its similarity in many respects to modern labor market conditions, involves the case of early post-feudal manufacturing, termed *proto-industrialization*. A key proto-industrial structure was the *putting-out system*, in which merchants provided rural "cottage industry" producers with raw materials and paid them for their output, which was then collected and sold in domestic and international markets. Thus, as in modern manufacturing, this system was premised on a relationship between capital suppliers and unbonded workers.

However, it also differed from its more recent counterpart in two respects: workers in this system rather than the merchants who supplied them typically owned the characteristic tools and machines of their craft, such as spinning wheels or weaving looms. Second, they produced without direct oversight by capital suppliers or their proxies, who instead motivated productive effort through *piece rates*, that is, payment per unit of output. Interestingly, in some areas such proto-industrial forms persisted alongside the factory system that eventually superceded them, in some cases well into the nineteenth century.

It can be seen from this short historical overview that the emergence of forms of labor exchange now taken for granted required drastic changes in existing political and economic structures. However, these changes did not automatically give rise to relationships of *employment* in the modern sense. Intriguingly, there are recent indications in the US economy of a partial return to labor exchanges which echo earlier proto-industrial forms.

Specifically, some evidence suggests that manufacturing firms have begun to rely increasingly on *externally contracted* labor rather than in-house employees. In such cases, work is contracted out to temporary workers. While the actual numbers are still relatively small, the popular press has made much of the increased economic insecurity associated with the apparently reduced emphasis on long-term employment relationships. To understand the basis for such phenomena, it will be necessary to look more closely at the nature of labor as an economic good in private ownership economies.

Labor exchange in capitalist economies

As discussed above, the institution of market exchange is consistent with a number of different means for procuring labor services, including slavery, serfdom, and bonded apprenticeships.

Capitalism is a shorthand term for the form of market system in which the means of production are also privately owned and freely exchangeable; in particular, workers retain the right to hire out their own labor. Firm owners must thus secure the needed means of production through market transactions with those who own them. Restaurant owners, to take one example, must engage the services of managers, chefs, waiters, and cleaning staff in addition to buying ingredients, serving supplies, equipment, and if necessary renting a building in which to operate.

There are, however, at least two important differences between labor and other inputs acquired in capitalist input markets. First, unlike the case for material inputs like bread and meat, tools such as knives and skillets, and machines such as microwave ovens and computers, labor, or rather the capacity to labor, is not produced by commercial enterprises. To put this in the standard terminology of economics, labor is supplied by *households* rather than *firms*. This fact is so deeply embedded in our culture that it may be difficult to imagine how it could be otherwise – we must look to dystopian novels like Aldous Huxley's *Brave New World* to supply alternative visions in which future workers are produced outside of the family.

The economic significance of this is that the provision of labor through market exchange may not be governed by the same motives that drive commercial enterprises. Economists typically assume that capitalist firms produce in order to make a profit, that is, a pecuniary return in excess of the direct and imputed costs of production. It seems much less plausible to suppose that family members are driven only or even primarily by this consideration in deciding whether, where, and how much to work.

Labor economists must therefore address the possibility that the supply of labor is determined by fundamentally different purposes than those which presumably govern the supply of commercial goods. Particularly interesting in this regard is the economic logic of wage determination in the *long run*, i.e. the time horizon allowing for mobility into and out of the labor force. The standard competitive theory of market behavior by profit-seeking firms suggests that supply increases in the long run in response to *extranormal* profits, and shrinks if existing prices do not permit attainment of even a *normal* rate of profit. Is there a meaningful analogue in markets for labor, and if so, what market outcomes drive labor supply choices?

A second fundamental difference between labor and other "factors of production" has to do with the *inalienability* of labor from its supplier. In the case of material inputs such as tools and machines, it is possible to separate the factor supplier from the factor supplied after the input transaction has taken place: the buyer may simply purchase the good in question and, if the conditions of the exchange prove to be fully satisfied, need never deal with that input supplier again. Not so with labor: since the capacity to labor is necessarily embodied in workers themselves, the latter must be physically present wherever and whenever their work is performed.

The inalienability of labor has a number of potentially important consequences for the nature of labor exchange. One is that by engaging in production a worker must also "consume" aspects of the production environment, such as temperature, ambient pollution and noise levels, and location. These conditions thus presumably influence a worker's labor supply choices. Second, just as performing labor will affect a worker's life experience, a worker's life experience may have an impact on his or her capacity to perform labor. For example, the skill a worker brings to a given set of tasks may increase as the result of training, or simply by practicing those tasks repeatedly.

Third, the expenditure of labor in production always involves an exercise of the conscious will of the worker. The productive properties of a tool can be elicited by situating it at the production site and wielding it appropriately. However, the productive properties of labor do not similarly derive automatically from bringing the worker to the production site and somehow setting him or her in motion. The worker must know what to do and how to do it, and must be willing to expend effort toward accomplishing the designated tasks. Thus, questions of *motivation* and *direction* of work effort necessarily arise in employment relations.

A related consequence of the inalienability of labor is that work is typically performed in a social context. Although effective labor per person can vary in length, intensity and skill, individuals are often handicapped in the performance of large-scale tasks. Individual workers can't be in two places at once, can't see out the back of their heads, and can't use more than one brain each to innovate a coherent plan of productive activity. Developments in automation and computer technology serve to minimize the extent of this consequence, but rarely, if ever, eliminate it entirely. Thus workers, especially those in large-scale enterprises, must work together in achieving given production goals; not only must their efforts be individually motivated and directed in this social context, but they must be *coordinated* as well.

In sum, the economics of labor markets and employment relations merits specialized study because transactions involving labor are both quantitatively significant and, in some respects, qualitatively unique. It is particularly intriguing to consider possible connections between the unique characteristics of labor as a productive input and labor market outcomes. For example, do these characteristics have any bearing on the existence of such problematic labor market phenomena as employment relationships and unemployment? The next section considers the different ways in which the discipline has historically confronted these issues.

THE FOUNDATIONS AND HISTORICAL
DEVELOPMENT OF LABOR ECONOMICS

Classical foundations of labor economics

Many if not most of the issues addressed by contemporary labor economists can be traced to the ideas of the *classical* school of economics, articulated in the eighteenth and nineteenth centuries, and in particular to those of its two most prominent exponents, Adam Smith and Karl Marx. While Smith and Marx shared certain precepts, including the presumption that society is divided into economic classes, they differed fundamentally on basic questions concerning how markets function and to what effect.

In his magisterial *Inquiry into the Nature and Causes of the Wealth of Nations*, published in 1776, Adam Smith was chiefly concerned to explain how the emerging capitalist order could possibly translate the countless independent actions of self-interested individuals into a coherent social order. He argued that in the absence of government interference, the "invisible hand" of competitive market forces could not only impose this order, but promote a pattern of economic activity which greatly increased the general level of material well-being. Behind Smith's advocacy of laissez-faire lay a vision of the market as a self-regulating system of "natural liberty."

In his three-volume masterwork *Capital*, published in installments over the last third of the nineteenth century (mostly after his death), Marx took fundamental exception to Adam Smith's economic vision. Where Smith saw capitalism as a system of natural liberty with no necessary end, Marx understood capitalism as a historically contingent economic system subject to eventually fatal contradictions. Where Smith saw markets mediating competing interests in a coherent and mutually beneficial fashion, Marx found just a new conduit for the expression of ongoing class conflict. Finally, while Smith championed the market system, Marx argued for its complete overthrow in favor of planned production and distribution.

Two specific points of difference in Smith's and Marx's analyses are of particular relevance to contemporary debates in labor economics. The first concerns the consequences of labor inalienability. To Smith, the primary significance of labor's inalienability from its supplier lay in accounting for persistent variations in wage rates across industries. He argued first that labor in disagreeable or dangerous jobs would be compensated with a higher wage rate. Since the supplier of the labor will directly bear these unpleasant aspects of work, he or she must be induced by pecuniary means to perform that labor. Relatedly, Smith maintained that, other things equal, wages would vary with the difficulty and expense of learning the skills intrinsic to given occupations. In explaining this point, Smith compared the costs of skill acquisition to investments in machines or "capital stock," thus anticipating contemporary use of the term "human capital" to represent an individual's capacity to labor as a durable and improvable asset.

In contrast, Marx associated the inalienability of labor with a *qualitative* difference in the logic of labor exchange. Specifically, Marx argued that the difference between *labor power*, or the capacity to labor, and labor itself, created a strategic problem for firms in ensuring profitable levels of effort from the workers they engaged. In the language of contemporary economic theory, Marx insisted in effect that labor market exchanges were mediated by imperfect contracting conditions, such that capital suppliers were unable to specify the labor services they desired so that the terms of labor exchange could be legally enforced.

A related and equally salient point of difference between Smith and Marx concerns the internal organization of the capitalist workplace. Smith saw the division of labor within firms as promoting labor productivity to the significant benefit of "the wealth of nations," while Marx saw the internal organization of the firm as an expression of the power of firm owners contributing directly and indirectly to the exploitation of workers. Marx argued that supervision of work and technical modifications in the process of production were required to guarantee the desired levels of labor, given the strategic problem of extracting desired levels of labor from suppliers of labor capacity. Marx was thus among the first economists to posit production relations in the firm as a strategic response to what would now be termed imperfect contracting conditions.

Three eras of labor economics

The classical school of economic thought gave way to the *neoclassical* framework of Alfred Marshall and marginal utility theorists soon after *Capital* was published. This framework is more or less the one typically studied in introductory microeconomics classes. However, questions pertaining to the primary significance of labor inalienability, the nature of employment relationships, and the social desirability of unregulated market processes have animated economic debates since Smith and Marx, and in particular have informed subsequent developments in labor economics. But the presumptive answers to these questions have taken very different forms over the course of this development, since the methods and chief concerns of labor economics itself have changed dramatically since its birth as a distinct field in the first half of the twentieth century.

Broadly speaking, one may say that there have been three overlapping eras in the development of labor economics since it first emerged as a distinct field in the 1930s. These eras are distinguished by the chief analytical concerns that shaped their corresponding research agendas, and these agendas can be associated in turn with, on the one hand, particular forms of theoretical analysis, and on the other, with characteristic forms, sources, and analyses of economic data. Unsurprisingly, the theoretical and empirical programs of a given research framework are interrelated, with new analytical methods prompting searches for new sources of data, and advances in data collection and analysis prompting the development of new hypotheses.

The first era of labor economics as a distinct field arose partly in response to claims that the study of labor market outcomes constituted a simple extension of the analytical agenda of the parent discipline – in other words, that labor economics was simply a branch of applied microeconomic analysis. The first self-conscious practitioners of the new subdiscipline retorted that standard economic principles could not hope to account for the distinctive quantitative and qualitative aspects of labor market transactions, pointing to the prevalence of complex structures governing internal relations within firms, as well as to anomalous market outcomes such as unemployment and wage differentials among workers with apparently similar skills and experience.

In the words of one early labor economist, Clark Kerr, the theoretical framework applied by this first wave of labor economists was that of "institutionally informed neoclassical economics,"[1] although it might as legitimately be termed "neoclassically informed institutional economics." The theory developed by these economists was less formally elegant than the neoclassical model of market exchange, and more extensively descriptive in its treatment of labor market-specific institutions and practices, but it understood these phenomena within the neoclassical context of rational self-interested behavior and the market forces of supply and demand, broadly conceived. The primary emphasis of the new labor economists, relative to their pure-theory counterparts, was to document and explain the distinctive features of real-world labor market phenomena as fully as possible, even if it meant departing from a strict application of the neoclassical paradigm.

The corresponding agenda for empirical analysis emphasized *case studies* of individual labor markets as a vehicle for identifying and classifying labor market institutions and practices. The data emerging from these investigations were descriptively rich and at least suggestive of a wide array of hypotheses about labor market behavior. But while they convincingly challenged any comfortable presumptions about the universal capacity of pure neoclassical theory to account for economic phenomena, they also were too limited in scope to support theoretical generalizations concerning the logic underlying market outcomes peculiar to exchanges for labor.

The next phase in the development of labor economics, emerging in the 1950s, can be read in part as a critical reaction to the theoretical eclecticism of the institutionalist era and the limited and idiosyncratic empirical base for its chief conclusions. This new phase was fueled by the establishment of new and more extensive sources of data as well as efforts to extend the formal language of neoclassical economics to incorporate the specific economic features of labor first identified by Adam Smith. Its focus was specifically on labor market outcomes rather than industrial institutions and practices, and its chief concern was to account for such phenomena strictly in terms of suitably modified principles of supply and demand.

The analytical framework which characterized this phase was termed *human capital theory*, harking back to Smith's analysis of the impact of training on wage levels. Where institutionally minded labor economists were concerned to provide as comprehensive a representation of labor transactions as possible, both in the market and within firms, exponents of the human capital school surrendered strict fidelity to institutional detail in return for greater rigor in generating testable economic hypotheses from given axioms and greater power in econometric assessments of these hypotheses. This era has been especially notable for efforts undertaken to identify and extend the range of valid inferences that can be drawn from statistical analysis of large-scale data sets, as well as to develop new and tractable sources of data.

Finally, the last two decades have witnessed the emergence of a new phase of labor economics in which the still vital methods and concerns of the human capital school have been complemented by an approach to understanding labor market transactions that once again emphasizes the significance of contracting difficulties and the central relevance of organizational responses to contractual failures. This approach has gained impetus from a number of sources within and without the economics mainstream. As detailed below, neoclassical theory was augmented by models of strategic interaction under imperfect informational and contracting conditions. Marxist economists criticized human capital theory for being unable to address issues of power in workplace relations and blind to significant and systematic differences in labor market experiences of people with nominally similar skill and backgrounds. New strains of institutionalist theory probed more deeply into the logic of organizational responses to given transactional failures. A new generation of labor economists brought sophisticated econometric techniques and more extensive microdata sets to the analysis of these issues as well as the concerns of the original labor institutionalists.

This new approach to the study of labor market phenomena is grounded in the analysis of *strategic exchange* conditions. In terms of formal theoretical tools, advances in game theory and the theory of economic behavior in the presence of imperfect information have made possible rigorous and insightful explorations of transactional arrangements that could only be treated discursively by the earlier generation of institutional labor economists. New sources of data describing behavior *within* firms and households have increased the scope for empirical assessment of hypotheses generated within this new theoretical framework. As discussed in later chapters, the strategic exchange approach often yields explanations for familiar labor market phenomena such as wage differentials and unemployment that differ fundamentally from those of the human capital school, and it renews the analytical focus on institutions which complement and shape the operation of labor markets.

In one sense, then, the discipline of labor economics has come full circle since its inception over 65 years ago, with its renewed emphasis on institutions and practices idiosyncratic to labor market exchange. In another sense, however, this circle is more like an upward spiral, characterized by a deeper and more fully articulated theoretical basis for comprehending labor market phenomena, richer and more extensive sources of data, and more definitive and powerful means of assessing the hypotheses generating by these approaches.

Consequently, the primary goal of this text will be to construct a comprehensive view of the competing analytical positions within modern labor economics, as well as to indicate their relative contributions and the ongoing controversies that persist among them. The controversies are unlikely ever to be fully resolved; however, this is less important than that they continue to generate new insights into the logic of social interaction governing the allocation of paid work.

CENTRAL ISSUES IN CONTEMPORARY LABOR ECONOMICS

Part I of the text presents the supply and demand model of labor market outcomes, augmented by the basic tenets of human capital theory. This model serves as the foundation for much of the research currently being done in the field, and as a useful point of reference for alternative analytical approaches. Part II of the text then offers a unifying framework for the analysis of labor market behavior under imperfectly competitive conditions, based on the nature and possible strategic implications of *exchange costs*. Elements of game theory, which provides the analytical vocabulary and orientation of this framework, are introduced in chapter 6 and applied in the succeeding two chapters to the analysis of bargaining and imperfect contracting in labor exchange.

Proceeding from this foundation, the remaining chapters of the text take up the fundamental issues in labor economics as well the ongoing controversies arising from investigation of these issues. These issues, and the continuing debates they engender, are anticipated here via a preview of the standard model of supply and demand in perfectly competitive markets, familiar to all students of introductory economics. The supply and demand model is potentially revealing both for what it says and for what it omits from the depiction of labor market outcomes.

Figure I.1 presents a standard supply and demand graph for a hypothetical labor market. The behavior of buyers in this market (that is, of firm owners seeking labor inputs in order to produce for profit) is represented by a downward-sloping demand curve, indicating that quantity demanded is inversely related to the going wage level. The behavior of households supplying labor inputs in this market is summarized by an upward-sloping supply curve. It is assumed that market equilibrium occurs uniquely at the wage rate that equates quantities supplied and demanded, indicated by W_E at the intersection of the two curves.

This model is used to generate both *positive* and *normative* claims about market outcomes. You may recall that positive statements are those that can in principle be assessed by reference to facts, while normative statements involve value judgments. A prediction about market outcomes is an example of a positive statement, since its truth can in principle be assessed by reference to actual behavior under the conditions presumed by the hypothesis. Alternatively, economic outcomes are assessed on normative grounds by evaluating them on the basis of some standard of desirability.

The supply and demand model depicted in figure I.1 can be made to yield potentially testable hypotheses by adducing two additional components to the

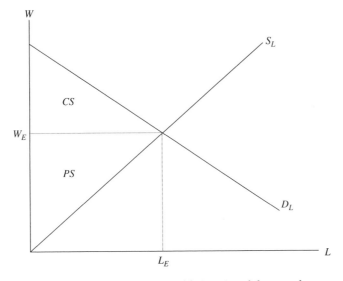

Figure I.1 Competitive equilibrium in a labor market.

model: first, factors that cause the supply or demand curve to shift in specified directions, and second, an assumption that the market wage rate will always adjust to the unique market-clearing level after any such shift.

Using these assumptions, it is possible to predict the implications for equilibrium wage rates and quantities of any given changes in conditions underlying market demand and supply. For example, as discussed in chapter 2, a technical innovation leading to an increase in (marginal) labor productivity might be expected to increase the demand for labor, leading in turn, other things being equal, to an increase in the equilibrium levels of wage and labor hired.

Normative claims about market outcomes on the basis of the simple supply and demand model of figure I.1. are generally made on the basis of "social welfare" measured as the sum of *consumer surplus* and *producer surplus*, represented in the figure by the areas marked respectively by CS and PS. In graphical terms, consumer surplus is defined as the area between demand and the market price up to the quantity exchanged, while producer surplus is defined as the area between the supply curve and the market price up to the quantity exchanged. One might on this interpretation of social welfare argue against governmental interventions in the form of a legislated minimum wage, on the ground that the resulting market outcome lowers the sum of producer and consumer surplus. This result is shown in figure I.2, where an effective wage floor is shown to reduce equilibrium quantity exchanged. The resulting reduction in social welfare is indicated by the area marked "deadweight loss" (DWL).

Using this supply and demand model of labor market outcomes as a reference point, one can identify four issues that arise persistently in the contemporary study of labor economics.

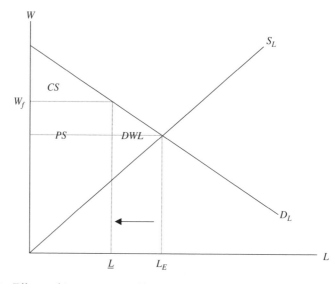

Figure I.2 Effects of imposing an effective wage floor in a competitive labor market.

Is employment simply an exchange relationship?

To use the supply and demand model of competitive markets is to presume, at least implicitly, that prices and quantities are the essential economic variables requiring explanation. These are, after all, the only variables explicitly represented in the model. To put the point another way, representing labor market outcomes on the basis of the supply and demand model described above is tantamount to presuming that all matters of economic interest in transactions governing paid labor can be represented by quantitative terms of *exchange*, and thus that nothing of essential interest is lost by ignoring aspects of the employment relationship that arise after the terms of exchange are determined.

This should not be taken to imply that differences in the *quality* of exchanged goods are ignored in the supply and demand model. Supply and demand curves are defined for goods with *given* characteristics, including quality level. Determining the market effects of variations in quality is therefore tantamount to comparing equilibria in distinct markets. Quality differences are reflected in equilibrium price or quantity differentials between otherwise similar goods, as will be explained in more detail below.

Rather, the focus on terms of exchange neglects other aspects of the relationship between firms and workers, such as the manner in which employees' labor efforts subsequent to being hired are structured, coordinated, and motivated. This neglect is arguably justifiable if *all* of the relevant terms of a labor exchange can be easily specified in an appropriate contract and strictly enforced by an external agency (i.e., the judicial system) at no cost to the transactors. For example, if the structure or sequence of subsequent production tasks matter to prospective employees, these and their corresponding levels of compensation can be negotiated beforehand and written into the employment contract with the confident expectation that these terms will be carried out.

However, it is not generally the case that all relevant terms of a labor exchange can be costlessly specified and enforced via the use of contracts. Absent this condition, the structure of relations within the workplace matters. First and most fundamentally, the allocation of *ownership rights* in given productive assets may be significant in determining who can make what decisions about the use of those assets. Second, in order to provide work incentives, decision-making powers may be supplemented by the use of specialized compensation schemes such as piece rates, bonuses or promotion ladders combined with systematic if imperfect monitoring of work performance. Third, the content or sequence of production tasks themselves might be altered in order to make it easier for firm owners to determine which production outcomes have taken place.

The exchange problems engendered by imperfect contracting conditions are investigated in chapter 8. Part III of the text then analyzes various aspects of the employment relationship as organizational and behavioral responses to difficulties encountered in using contracts to specify and enforce terms of labor exchange. Taken together, these chapters offer reasons why employment might appropriately be thought of as more than simply an exchange relationship.

Do wage disparities represent compensating differentials?

If labor markets are perfectly competitive, so that outcomes in each market are determined by the intersection of supply and demand, and labor market participants can move freely among markets, then persistent differences in individual wage levels can only be explained by the presence of factors which affect *both* the supply and the demand for given types of labor. More specifically, as discussed in chapter 3, two workers will receive unequal equilibrium wage rates under these market conditions only if the services offered by the high-wage worker are distinguished by a feature which is both beneficial to employers (thus increasing the demand for workers with that feature) and costly for workers to supply.

The wage disparity resulting from such conditions is known as a *compensating differential*. Thus, if labor markets are perfectly competitive, then persistent differences in individual wage levels can only be explained on the basis of compensating differentials. (A partial exception is if workers possess a certain feature that is *absolutely* scarce, leading to a supply curve that eventually turns vertical. But this can be interpreted as a case of *infinite* marginal cost for the trait in question.) For example, higher educational attainment generates a compensating differential for a worker under competitive conditions if it makes the worker more revenue productive and it is costly for the worker to achieve.

The same market conditions that generate compensating differentials also ensure that labor services with identical qualities command the same wage rate. This corollary is an instance of the so-called "law of one price." The economic intuition for this "law" should be clear: if labor services of equal quality were offered at unequal wages, potential buyers would flock toward the lower-cost alternative, driving up its relative wage until the disparity is eliminated.

This "law" has empirical meaning only if there is a measurable sense in which labor services provided by different workers can be judged of equal quality. But human capital theory offers just such an unambiguous statement about the comparability of labor services, i.e. in terms of their marginal contributions to firm profitability. Therefore workers that can make equal contributions to firm profitability should command the same wage rate.

There are two distinct reasons why the hypothesis of compensating wage differentials and its corollary, the law of one wage, might not obtain in actual labor markets. One possibility is that transactional difficulties of the sort discussed above affect labor markets unequally, so that wages fail to adjust toward market-clearing levels in some markets. For instance, as can be seen from figure I.2 above, such "stickiness" creates a situation of excess supply if the wage is stuck above its market-clearing level. Workers fortunate enough to find employment in such markets receive the high wage, while workers shut out from the market – even otherwise identical counterparts to market "insiders" – receive a smaller alternative wage.

Second, since the existence of labor supply and demand curves is premised on the condition that all market participants take the wage rate as *given*, the compensating wage differential hypothesis might be violated in the presence of *wage-setting power* enjoyed by actors on one or both sides of the market. In that event, the distribution of gains from trade is not necessarily determined by the intersection of supply and demand curves, and furthermore, one or both of these curves can't meaningfully be defined in the first place.

If buyers and sellers *both* enjoy some degree of wage-setting power, then a situation of *bilateral monopoly* (or more generally, *bilateral oligopoly*, meaning few competitors on each side of the market) is said to exist. In this case demand or supply curves cannot be used to represent any group's market behavior, and equilibrium wages and quantities are instead typically determined by *bargaining* over the terms of labor exchange. Nothing guarantees that equilibrium bargaining outcomes in this scenario will take place along either market demand or market supply curves.

The implications of unilateral wage-setting power at the market level are addressed in chapter 4, which contrasts the effects of labor monopoly and monopsony with outcomes in perfectly competitive labor markets. This chapter also considers evidence concerning the presence of wage-setting power in real-world labor markets. The consequences of bilateral wage-setting power in a single labor exchange relationship are studied in chapter 7.

The determinants of persistent wage differentials among workers are discussed in part IV. Some such differentials are consistent with the compensation hypothesis. But in other cases, persistent wage differentials are not as easily explained on this basis, suggesting the influence of imperfect transactional or mobility conditions.

Can significant unemployment persist in unregulated labor markets?

The immediate implication of flexible wage adjustment in the supply and demand model is that the equilibrium wage rate must equate quantities of labor demanded and supplied; in other words, a situation such as that shown in figure I.2 cannot persist unless dictated by forces external to the market (e.g., government wage controls). A corollary of this result is that unemployment, defined earlier in the chapter as a situation in which people are jobless but are willing and able to work, cannot exist in market equilibrium. Some workers may be *non*-employed, that is, choose not to work at the going wage rate, but this implies that they freely choose to stay out of the labor force.

This assessment is apparently at odds with the fact that the reported unemployment rate is positive in every country that measures it, and sometimes significantly so. Most market economies experienced devastatingly high unemployment rates in the Great Depression of the 1930s. The countries of western Europe have experienced average unemployment rates significantly in excess of those in the United States since the 1960s. After enjoying years of relatively low unemployment, the Japanese economy has recently been mired in a persistent recession with relatively high unemployment.

Why does such unemployment exist? One possibility is that it is costly for labor market participants to locate appropriate exchange partners, implying that they must spend some period of time in searching for an appropriate employment match. During this period of search, would-be workers are registered as being unemployed, that is, willing and able to work but still without a job. Another possibility is that there are obstacles to flexible wage adjustment that keep markets from clearing immediately. Consider this possibility a bit further.

Undergirding the hypothesis of flexible wage adjustment is the premise that all mutually beneficial exchanges in a given market setting are ultimately realized. This means that potential exchange partners always recognize each other's existence, and having done so, are able to negotiate and implement mutually desirable terms of trade to the point where all potential gains from trade are realized: for example, someone who is willing and able to work but cannot find a job at the going wage rate can offer labor services at a lower wage rate until suitable employment is offered.

There are, however, a number of potential obstacles to exhausting all possible gains from exchange. Their common source is the existence of significant costs of transacting mutually beneficial exchanges. Such *transaction costs* may preclude objectively desirable exchanges from being realized. In the above scenario, for example, the would-be employee may find it impossible to guarantee that he or she won't reduce work effort in response to receiving a smaller wage rate than initially sought. As a result, potential employers might be put off by the risk of hiring a disgruntled or underperforming worker.

Alternatively, suppose that employers want to minimize turnover in their labor forces due to the costs of finding, screening, and training new workers. Given that involuntary servitude is illegal, employers can't address the turnover problem by insisting that their workers sign contracts binding them to their incumbent firms. An alternative approach would be to make continued employment attractive by raising the wage rate above its market-clearing level, thus creating unemployment. Competition might not drive down the wage rate in this case, since unemployed workers may have no effective way of guaranteeing that they won't seek alternative jobs subsequent to being hired at the market-clearing wage level.

Note that in the above example, the relevant transaction cost is effectively infinite, since employers are simply unable to write contractual provisions preventing their workers from leaving. The most economically significant transaction costs may thus be those that are never incurred and thus never actually observed. Note second that transaction costs (in the form of contractual difficulties) also figured in the foregoing discussion of possible *qualitative* dimensions of employment relations. This is no accident; a central theme of the text is that labor markets may not clear for the same reasons that employment is not similar to other forms of market exchange.

Do unregulated labor markets yield the best economic outcomes?

The final issue persistently confronted by labor economists is a normative one concerning the appropriate role for government vis-à-vis private economic activity in labor markets. The traditional case for a laissez-faire governmental policy with respect to market activity – that is, one in which government does no more than define and enforce property rights – is built on the well-known efficiency properties of markets that satisfy ideal exchange conditions. You saw this in comparing the market outcomes shown in figures I.1 and I.2 above, which indicated a reduction in social welfare (and the consequent existence of dead-weight loss) due to government intervention in the form of an effective wage floor.

This case for such a hands-off stance vis-à-vis labor markets by governments might thus be challenged at either of its two foundations, its exclusive commitment to the norm of efficient allocation or its vision of how markets function. You have seen in the foregoing discussion how the latter challenge might proceed. Realistic departures from ideal exchange conditions establish *potential* grounds for government involvement in or replacement of market functions, as in the case of macroeconomic policies to reduce the magnitude of unemployment. The grounds are only potential in that the fact of market failure does not of itself ensure government success.

Parts IV and V of the text devote particular attention to the prospects for government intervention to improve the efficiency of labor market outcomes. However, inefficiency is not the only basis on which one might argue against the unfettered operation of market forces. The latter might be objectionable on alternative normative grounds as well. For example, labor market outcomes might be efficient and yet involve discrimination against certain workers on the basis of gender, race, ethnicity, age, or sexual orientation. If one rejects efficiency considerations as a legitimate basis for defending such practices, then government intervention might be justified to discourage discriminatory practices.

In some cases, departures from ideal market conditions that threaten efficiency may infringe on other values as well. For example, if it is costly for workers to find alternatives for unsatisfactory working conditions, exit, or "voting with one's feet," may be an unreliable way of ensuring that worker concerns are addressed in the market. In this case, the same value judgments that argue for democratic representation in political systems may also dictate that workers have a collective voice in the organization and function of the workplace.

A possible policy response to this situation is to modify private property rights of firm owners so as to ensure that workers can effectively exercise their powers of voice without threat of retribution. Examples of such policies are those that ensure workers rights of collective bargaining over the terms of pay and working conditions or rights of participation in the executive decisionmaking process in firms, as in the case of the German "codetermination" laws (see discussion box). These possibilities are considered in more detail in chapter 12.

Try to keep these four questions in mind as you work your way through the text. They might help to organize your thinking about the wide range of labor market phenomena discussed herein. The first question raises an issue about the necessary *scope* of an adequate theory of labor market outcomes; it asks if what we need to know as economists about employment relations can be reduced to a matter of prices and quantities exchanged. Granting that this might be the case, the next two questions raise the *positive* issue as to whether the competitive supply and demand model best explains the determination of wages and (un)employment. Finally, the fourth question concerns the *normative* issue of what might be done to improve given labor market outcomes.

The ensuing chapters will introduce you to tools of positive and normative analysis suitable for exploring the issues enumerated above. The overarching goal of the text is not to insist on a particular set of "correct" conclusions about labor market phenomena, but rather to provide a framework for posing and evaluating coherent positions with respect to these concerns.

WHY ARE NATIONAL EMPLOYMENT SYSTEMS SO DIFFERENT?

In economies based on private ownership of the means of production, labor markets are the predominant social mechanism for allocating work performed outside the home. Beyond this common denominator, however, there are significant national variations in the institutional framework within which labor markets are embedded, as reflected in given configurations of laws, organizations, and customs pertaining to employment and the conditions of work. These differences in national employment systems are typically reflected in varying patterns of job stability, wage inequality, and unemployment.

An important dimension along which national employment systems vary concerns the process of *wage determination*, particularly respecting the degree to which the process is centralized. At one extreme are the practices of several northern European countries, in which wage bargaining often occurs at the industry or supra-industry level (Iverson and Pontusson, 2000); at the other is the United States, where wage negotiations are typically between firms and their respective individual employees. The centralization of wage bargaining is reflected in relative levels of *union density*, that is, the percentage of employed workers in a given economy who belong to unions. Among member countries of the Organization for Economic Cooperation and Development (OECD), this figure ranges from highs of 90.5% for Sweden and 80.5% for Finland to lows of 8.8% for France and 15.3% for the US (Iversen and Pontusson, table 1.1, p. 9).

A second dimension of variation concerns the degree to which the security of workers' jobs is protected by either legislation or concerted efforts on the part of employers to avoid layoffs and dismissals. Some countries, such as Spain and Germany, have passed laws requiring employers to give advance notice of, and justification for, proposed layoffs. In Japan, dismissals are discouraged by custom and case law rather than by statute (Brown *et al.*, 1997). In contrast, the US has generally avoided legislative measures to promote job security, even in the form of advance notification laws. These formal and informal structural differences are reflected in very different average levels of job tenure in the respective countries.

The longevity of employment attachments is to some degree reflected in corresponding national differences in provisions for worker training on the job. As discussed in chapter 11, firms tend to provide more training in economies featuring longer job tenure. This is particularly so in the case of Japan, which leads other OECD nations in training provided to first-year employees.

Finally, national employment systems vary in the extent of provisions made for employee involvement in workplace decision making. At one extreme, German codetermination laws mandate worker representation on the supervisory boards of large corporations, and works councils generally have the right to veto certain managerial decisions. However, all western European economies with the exception of Ireland and the United Kingdom have legislative provisions for some form of systematic worker involvement in firm-level decisionmaking.

Although no such formal provisions are in place in the United States, the incidence of firm-level worker participation programs has increased dramatically since the 1980s.

One researcher has characterized different national approaches to organizing labor exchange according to the binary classification of *liberal* vs *coordinated* market economies, with the former tending to avoid government interventions in market processes, and the latter tending to favor them (Soskice, 2000). By this classification, Germany, Sweden, Denmark and the Netherlands are exemplars of the coordinated approach, while the US, New Zealand, and the United Kingdom have adhered more closely to the liberal model (Iversen and Pontusson, p. 3).

What sense can be made of these and related differences in national employment systems? From the standpoint of the perfectly competitive market model, the significance of these differences is primarily political, having to do with the redistribution of gains from labor exchange. However, in this perspective, all government interventions have the effect of reducing social welfare, relative to a laissez-faire policy of enforcing property rights and otherwise staying out of the way.

In contrast, the presence of significant frictions in labor exchange raises the prospect that selective government intervention might improve the efficiency of market outcomes. One possibility that arises under such exchange conditions is the existence of *multiple* market equilibria, some of which are superior to others on welfare grounds. In this context, government policies have a potential role in promoting the selection of mutually beneficial outcomes. Whether government policies actually have this effect is, of course, a matter for empirical political and economic analysis.

Related discussion question:
1. Concerning Soskice's distinction between *liberal* and *coordinated* market economies: Laissez-faire theorists since Adam Smith have argued that unregulated markets coordinate economic activity in a socially desirable way. Under what conditions, if any, might government interventions usefully supplement or replace the coordination functions of labor markets?

Related references:
Clair Brown, Yoshifumi Nakata, Michael Reich and Lloyd Ulman, *Work and Pay in the United States and Japan* (Oxford: Oxford University Press, 1997).

continued

Torben Iversen and Jonas Pontusson, "Comparative Political Economy: A Northern European Perspective," in Torben Iversen, Jonas Pontusson, and David Soskice (eds) *Unions, Employers and Central Banks: Macroeconomic Coordination and Institutional Change in Social Market Economies* (Cambridge: Cambridge University Press, 2000).

David Soskice, "Macroeconomic Analysis and the Political Economy of Unemployment," in Torben Iversen, Jonas Pontusson, and David Soskice (eds) *Unions, Employers and Central Banks: Macroeconomic Coordination and Institutional Change in Social Market Economies* (Cambridge: Cambridge University Press, 2000).

Study Questions

1. In what ways are labor markets different from other markets (in particular, product markets, and also financial markets)? How might these differences lead us to analyze labor markets differently from other markets?
2. Describe some ways in which you or other members of your family have been involved in paid labor markets. Then describe some ways in which you and other members of your family have been involved in unpaid labor. How are these activities different, if at all, from those described in your first response?
3. Why do firms typically rely on long-term employees, rather than just hiring labor on a daily basis to fill their immediate productive and administrative needs?

Note

1   Clark Kerr, "The Neoclassical Revisionists in Labor Economics (1940–1960) – R.I.P.," in Bruce E. Kaufman (ed.), *How Labor Markets Work*, (Lexington, MA: D.C. Heath & Co, 1988).

Suggestions for Further Reading

Maxine Berg, *The Age of Manufactures 1700–1820* (New York: Oxford University Press, 1986).

Richard B. Freeman, "Does the New Generation of Labor Economists Know More than the Old Generation?" in Bruce E. Kaufman (ed.) *How Labor Markets Work* (Lexington, MA: D.C. Heath and Co, 1988).

Karl Polanyi, *The Great Transformation* (Boston: Beacon Press, 1957).

PART ONE

LABOR SUPPLY AND DEMAND

The text's study of labor markets and the relationships they encompass begins with an overview of the theoretical model of *perfectly competitive* labor exchange. This representation of how markets function is relatively simple, often intuitive, and has the added advantage of being familiar to most students of economics. It is the framework most appropriate to the invocation of "supply and demand" analysis in investigating labor market behavior.

However, the relevance of this model stems primarily from its utility as a framework for investigating the logic of labor market interactions and outcomes. Consequently, the overview provided in these first four chapters is a critical one; the goal is to convey not only the range of phenomena the model is adept at explaining, but also the intrinsic limitations in its analytical reach. A fuller appreciation of these limitations flows from a close look at the assumptions required to make the competitive model "work" when applied to the analysis of labor markets.

The importance of gaining a critical understanding of competitive market theory can be gleaned in light of the often-repeated claim that labor markets obey the "laws" of supply and demand. Despite the implicit suggestion to the contrary, these "laws" do not hold in the same categorical sense as, say, the law of gravity. Their relevance depends rather on certain assumptions respecting individual behavior and market structure that may not be realized in practice. Indeed, the assumptions on which the theory is built are almost certainly never completely satisfied in real-world exchange relations.

If the ideal of perfectly competitive markets is unlikely to be fully attained in practice, then why study it? There are at least three compelling answers to this question. First, even if the assumptions of the model are

continued

not fully met, they may be closely enough approximated in given empiri-cal contexts to justify its use in parsing labor market outcomes. In other words, the competitiveness of labor markets might plausibly thought of as a matter of degree, such that the ideal representation of market competi-tion constitutes a legitimate simplification of a more complex economic reality.

Second, and at least as importantly for the concerns of this text, the com-petitive market model serves as a useful point of reference in investigating given deviations from the ideal case it depicts. Since there are a number of distinct ways in which labor markets might diverge from this ideal, it will prove extremely helpful to contrast alternative market scenarios with a well-understood "base case" in order to assess the consequences of specific departures from this standard. If the goal is to achieve a full understand-ing of how labor markets function, it is not enough to say that labor markets don't operate according to the laws of supply and demand; it is necessary to determine what specific factors keep these "laws" from operating, and why.

Third, but not least, it is important to understand the logical and empiri-cal basis for the competitive model because it has provided the theoretical foundation for most of the research undertaken to date in the field of labor economics, especially as supplemented by the premises of human capital theory. Thus, one cannot follow the major developments in the field without a firm grasp of the competitive framework. And if one wishes to criticize the theory of perfectly competitive markets, it is most persuasive to do so from a position of thorough understanding.

CHAPTER ONE

LABOR SUPPLY

This chapter constructs a theory of labor supply premised on the optimizing market behavior of rational households. The main purpose of this effort is to establish a theoretical basis for the derivation of labor supply curves and determination of factors that influence their position and slope. When combined with a parallel analysis of labor demand developed in chapter 2, this will provide a foundation for explaining labor market outcomes under conditions of perfect competition.

The chapter takes up the following questions regarding household labor supply in competitive markets. First, assuming that a representative household elects to work for pay, how does its labor supply respond to changes in market conditions? In particular, are labor supply curves upward-sloping in the wage rate, and if so, how responsive is quantity supplied to wage variations? Second, what other factors influence a household's labor supply decisions? Finally, how do households allocate their total labor time between paid and unpaid activities, and when are they willing to acquire more skill or expend greater labor effort when these activities are costly?

Understanding the nature and determinants of labor supply is important for a number of reasons. Labor supply analysis may help to explain a number of intriguing empirical phenomena such as the dramatic increase in women's labor force participation rates beginning in the 1960s. Moreover, the responsiveness of labor supply to changed market conditions influences the impact of a number of government policies, including income taxation, income transfers, and unemployment compensation.

A BASIC MODEL OF HOUSEHOLD LABOR SUPPLY

In typical markets for labor, firms are the buyers and households the suppliers. Under competitive exchange conditions, the intended market behavior of a household or set of households can be summarized by a labor supply function, represented graphically by a labor supply curve. The purpose of this and the following section is to show how this function is derived from the premise that wage-taking households make optimizing choices among alternative bundles of leisure and other goods. Within this framework one can then analyze the slope and responsiveness of labor supply in terms of the *substitution* and *income effects* of given wage changes on households' consumption decisions.

There are four dimensions or aspects of individual labor supply decisions. The first concerns the binary decision of whether or not to participate in the labor market. The second is the *extensive* dimension of labor supply, or the number of hours to be worked per given time period, if any. The third dimension of choice is *intensive*, involving the degree of labor effort or intensity per hour worked. The final dimension concerns the *quality* of labor provided, corresponding to the level of relevant aptitude or skills brought to bear by labor suppliers. The following discussion begins with the extensive dimension of labor supply, taking as given the intensity and skill with which labor is supplied. The impact of variations in labor effort and acquirable skills is considered later in the chapter; however, it should be remembered that the construction of labor supply curves is built on the premise that these other dimensions can be taken as given.

Elements of the basic model

In order to construct labor supply curves for individuals or markets, it is necessary to begin with the assumption that households take the wage rate as *given*, instead of enjoying the capacity to influence its level through their market participation (say, through their ability to bargain). Without this assumption, the wage rate cannot coherently be understood as an independent variable in household decisionmaking, and thus labor supply functions cannot generally be said to exist. Therefore, it is presumed throughout the chapter that households are wage-takers rather than wage-setters.

The second critical element of the model concerns the basis on which households make choices about their labor supply. This is captured by the assumption, elaborated below, that households have well-defined preferences over alternative bundles of leisure (understood initially as time not spent in paid labor) and income, and that household labor decisions are driven by a rational assessment of alternative market opportunities. Any such representation of preferences is based on the necessary assumption that households are always *able* to supply labor, whether or not they choose to do so.

Other assumptions are less fundamental to the argument, and serve primarily to give structure to the optimal choice problem attributed to a representative household. The consequences of relaxing several of these assumptions are considered later on in the chapter. Initially, the household is treated as a single decisionmaker. In addition, the household is first assumed to make consumption and supply decisions within a single period, abstracting from labor supply decisions over time. In that period, the household is assumed to have a fixed time endowment of hours (the total hours in a day, perhaps) to allocate between labor and leisure. As indicated above, the effort and skill dimensions of household labor are initially taken as given.

Next, assume that the representative household derives its income both from labor and from some source (however minor) of non-labor income, and that each household engages in only one type of employment. Finally, assume that labor supply is perfectly divisible, meaning that the household is free to work for any portion of its available time. Building on these assumptions, the next step is to specify the two key elements of the theory of individual labor supply: the household's budget frontier and indifference map.

The household's budget frontier

The first and easiest step in constructing this theory is to derive the *budget frontier* over bundles of leisure and total income for a household facing a given wage rate and a given level of non-labor income. By definition, a budget frontier depicts the consumption bundles a household can just afford given its endowment and relative prices. In this case, the household's endowment consists of both its non-labor income and the time it has available for work and leisure, and the relative price in question is the wage rate relative to the "price" of a unit of pecuniary income, which is effectively equal to one.

The budget frontier defined for given time endowment T, non-labor income N, and initial wage rate W_1 is shown by the solid line labeled F_1 in figure 1.1. Leisure hours, denoted by H, are measured along the horizontal axis and total income I along the vertical axis. The horizontal intercept is T, the maximum possible quantity of leisure, attained when no hours are devoted to work. At this level of leisure, total household income just equals N, the height of the budget frontier at point T. The slope of the budget frontier is equal to $-W_1$, since each hour of sacrificed leisure increases income by the wage rate. This indicates that the wage can be thought of as the price or opportunity cost of an hour of leisure.

Note two additional implications of this construction. First, the vertical intercept of the budget frontier equals $N + W_1 \cdot T$, since this is the money income attainable by the household if no hours at all are allotted to leisure activity. Second, an increase in non-labor income N shifts the budget frontier parallel upward, resulting in a higher vertical intercept with no change in the horizontal intercept. Third, as indicated by the dotted line, an increase in the market wage rate to W_2 rotates

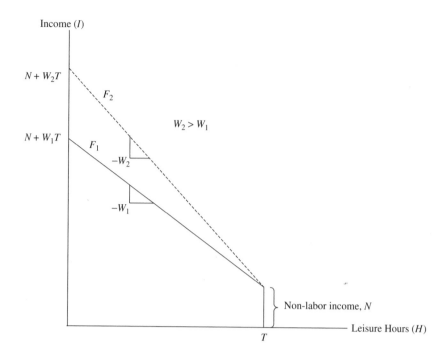

Figure 1.1   The household's budget frontier over bundles of leisure and money income.

the household's budget line upward to frontier F_2, with a steeper slope corresponding to the same horizontal intercept.

Household preferences:
the utility function and the indifference map

Suppose that the representative household has a _preference ranking_ over alternative bundles of leisure H and pecuniary income I. Labor economists do not typically investigate the possible psychological or social origins of such rankings, but it is necessary for the coherence of the theory to assume that the set of rankings over available bundles is determined independently of market wages or non-labor income. Beyond that, it is useful to add some plausible conditions ensuring the regularity and internal consistency of preference orderings.

If these regularity assumptions are satisfied, it is possible to represent the household's preference ranking completely by a _utility function_ that maps consumption bundles into arbitrarily measured utility levels. This function, written $U = u(I, H)$, has the property that strictly preferred consumption bundles yield strictly higher levels of utility, while consumption bundles among which the

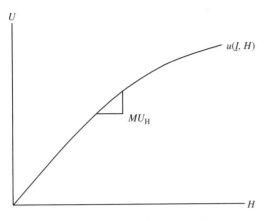

Figure 1.2(a)   Marginal utility of leisure.

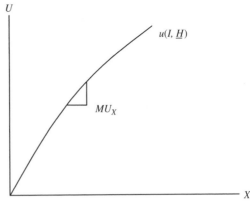

Figure   1.2(b)   Marginal   utility   of income.

individual is indifferent yield equal levels of utility. Note that in all these comparisons the absolute magnitude of utility – the specific number generated by the function when particular consumption levels are plugged in – is unimportant, if not meaningless; the purpose of the utility function is rather to provide a convenient way of summarizing *ordinal* or *relative* preferences.

Given a utility function summarizing the household's preference rankings, one can define the *marginal utility* (MU) of a particular consumption item as the change in the household's utility level associated with a small increase in its consumption of that item, holding the consumption of all other items constant. The household's marginal utility of leisure, for example, can thus be expressed as $MU_H = \dfrac{\Delta U}{\Delta H}\Big|_I$, where the notation " $|_I$" is read "given that money income I is held constant." In similar fashion, the household's marginal utility of income is expressed as $MU_I = \dfrac{\Delta U}{\Delta I}\Big|_H$. (Note that marginal utilities can be interpreted as *partial derivatives* of the utility function if it is differentiable and the indicated changes are infinitesimally small. As depicted in figures 1.2(a) and (b), marginal utilities can be thought of as the slopes of the utility function in its respective arguments.)

It follows that marginal utilities are positive for economic *goods* and negative for economic *bads* such as air pollution. Hereafter it is assumed that both leisure and money income are always goods, so that their respective marginal utilities are strictly positive. In this case it is said that preferences are *strictly monotonic* in leisure and income. This assumption is made primarily for the sake of analytical convenience; it isn't a necessary condition for expressing household preferences in terms of a utility function.

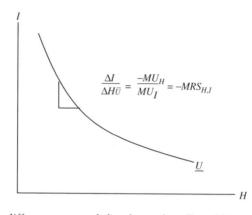

Figure 1.3(a)   Indifference curve defined over bundles of leisure and money income.

$$\frac{\partial u}{\partial H} = \Delta I$$
$$\frac{\partial u}{\partial I} = \overline{\Delta H}$$

A standard way of representing household preferences graphically is with an indifference map. A constituent element of this map, called an *indifference curve*, depicts the set of consumption bundles that yield equal utility, so that all such bundles satisfy the expression $\overline{U} = u(I, H)$ for a given level of utility $\overline{U}$. If the utility function were differentiable and, as assumed, the marginal utility of income is not zero, then the indifference curve is also differentiable, and its slope at each point is just equal to the ratio $-MU_H/MU_I$, assuming that the indifference curve is graphed with leisure on the horizontal axis, as shown in figure 1.3(a). Note that an indifference curve must therefore be negatively sloped if leisure hours and money income are both economic goods.

The absolute value of the indifference curve's slope, given by the ratio of marginal utilities, reflects the household's *marginal rate of substitution* between leisure and income (denoted $MRS_{H,I}$), understood as the rate at which the household is *just willing* to trade off leisure for income, since doing so leaves utility unchanged. Contrast this with the slope of the budget frontier, which indicates the rate at which the market *compels* the household to trade off leisure for income, given that the household is a wage-taker.

The *indifference map* is, in principle, a *complete* representation of the household's preferences, meaning all possible indifference curves; but since this is impractical, indifference maps generally just show a subset of the household's indifference curves sufficient to indicate the structure of its preferences, as in figure 1.3(b). As a second consequence of assuming that leisure and money income are both goods, note that bundles with greater amounts of leisure or income, but no less of either, generate higher levels of utility. Thus, as shown in figure 1.3(b), indifference curves further up and to the right, or "to the northeast," correspond to higher levels of household utility.

Note further that, as drawn, all indifference curves are bowed in the direction of increasing utility and are thus convex relative to the origin. This depiction reflects the additional assumption of *strictly convex* preferences, meaning that the

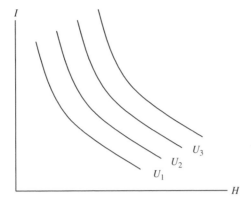

Figure 1.3(b) Indifference map defined over leisure and money income.

household prefers weighted averages of any two bundles that yield equal utility to either bundle. Another way of phrasing this assumption is that the household prefers "moderation" (represented by the weighted averages of any two bundles yielding equal utility) to "extremes." Strictly convex preferences imply a diminishing marginal rate of substitution as one moves from left to right along any given indifference curve, because the curve gets flatter as the good measured along the horizontal axis (leisure, in this case) is increased.

In sum, the representative household is assumed to have an exogenously given set of preference rankings over bundles of money income and leisure hours. Under certain regularity and consistency conditions, these preferences can be conveniently summarized with a utility function. Beyond this, it is also helpful to assume that preferences are strictly monotonic (implying strictly positive marginal utilities) and strictly convex (reflected in indifference curves that are bowed in the direction of increasing utility).

The household's optimal labor choice

Theoretical predictions about a representative household's labor supply choices are derived by combining its budget frontier and indifference map with the assumption that the household will select the bundle that maximizes its utility level, given its budget. The nature of this choice is made clear in figure 1.3(c), in which the household's budget frontier has been superimposed on its indifference map. The *optimization* assumption just described can be translated visually as the premise that the household will choose the bundle on the highest attainable indifference curve, consistent with staying on its budget frontier. This outcome corresponds to the bundle marked (I^*, H^*) in figure 1.3(c). The household's optimal labor choice L^* is then just equal to the distance $(T - H^*)$, as shown.

b/c T=max

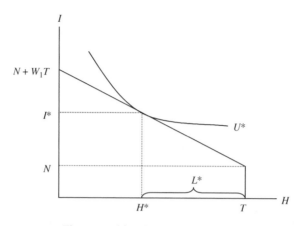

w = MRS

optimal pt.

Figure 1.3(c)   Optimal labor choice.

Note as an immediate implication of the outcome depicted in figure 1.3(c) that if the household chooses strictly positive quantities of both labor and leisure, then its optimal bundle necessarily occurs at a point of tangency between its budget frontier and its highest attainable indifference curve. This implies in turn that, at the optimal bundle, the rate at which the household is *compelled* to trade off leisure for income (reflected by the market wage rate) is equal to the rate at which it is *just willing* to make this same tradeoff (as reflected by the household's marginal rate of substitution). If this equality were not attained, then the household could always increase its utility by altering its consumption choice along the budget line until a point of tangency is achieved.

The derivation of household labor choice for a given wage rate and level of non-labor income is theoretically coherent, given its underlying assumptions, but doesn't provide much guidance in assessing actual household labor supply decisions. Since indifference curves can't be seen, there is no way to infer from observed market outcomes whether households are acting in accordance with the theory. If the theory is to be of use in the empirical analysis of labor supply, it must therefore be capable of generating testable hypotheses concerning the *response* of household supply decisions to *changes* in wage rates or non-labor income. These relationships are considered next.

IMPLICATIONS OF THE BASIC MODEL

Labor force participation

The most basic labor supply decision of the household concerns whether or not to supply any market labor at all. Labor economists refer to this as a decision concerning *labor force participation*. Individuals who either have a job or are actively

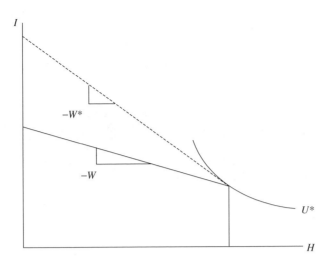

Figure 1.4 Optimal non-participation in the labor force.

looking for work are classified as being in the labor force, while those who are neither employed nor looking for employment are defined as being out of the labor force.

Given the availability of some source of non-labor income, it is plausible to imagine that a household might not supply any labor at all, even if the wage rate were positive. This situation is illustrated in figure 1.4, where the household is seen to reach its highest level of utility by spending all of its time endowment in leisure. Other things equal, this outcome would tend to arise for households with a relatively high marginal rate of substitution of leisure for consumption goods purchased with labor income (implying relatively steep indifference curves). Conversely, households that respond to a given configuration of wage rate and non-labor income by supplying labor have relatively low marginal valuations of leisure.

Another way of stating this point in light of the basic optimization model is as follows: for any household, there is some threshold level of the wage rate (not necessarily zero) at which that household is just indifferent between supplying labor and not doing so. This is represented by wage W^* in figure 1.4. For any lower wage rate, it will elect to supply no labor at all to the market. Furthermore, there is some wage rate above that threshold level for which the household will always choose to supply *some* labor to the market.

Assuming, therefore, that there is a certain probability distribution of marginal rates of substitution across all economies in the labor force (and thus a corresponding distribution of threshold wage levels), it follows that, first, the probability that any given household will enter the labor force if it hasn't done so already is increasing in the wage rate, and second, that *aggregate* labor force participation among households in the economy must increase with the market wage rate. For reasons considered next, it is less clear how labor force participation decisions will vary with changes in non-labor income, or how a household's labor hours will vary with wages once it has elected to enter the labor force.

WHY HAS WOMEN'S LABOR FORCE PARTICIPATION INCREASED SO DRAMATICALLY?

The US economy experienced a steady and dramatic increase in women's labor force participation over the second half of the twentieth century, with the most dramatic increase occurring among married women. In 1960, not quite 38% of all women, and about 32% of married women, over the age of 16 were counted as in the labor force. In the year 2000, the corresponding numbers were just over 60 and 61%, respectively. Moreover, the aggregate data obscure even larger increases within specific age groups. Among married women over the same time period, the labor force participation of those aged 25 through 34 increased from just under 29% to just over 70%, while that for women in the 35 through 44 age group more than doubled, from 37.2% to 74.8%. Over the same span, the labor force participation rate of married men dropped from 89.2% to just over 77%.

What factors account for this dramatic increase in labor force participation, particularly among married women? Melford (1999) reviewed the existing literature addressing this question and supplemented it with her own empirical results based on newer data and additional econometric tests. Her work reinforced prior findings that the single most important explanatory variable, in terms of both statistical significance and estimated positive impact on women's labor force participation, was the divorce rate. The US divorce rate more than doubled in the period from the mid-1960s to 1980. She also found a strong negative impact of having children, but only for the 35–44 age group.

Melford differed from much of the earlier literature in finding less consistent support for economic variables such as female earnings level, male income and the unemployment rate. Unlike earlier studies, she found that the level of female earnings had no discernible effect except for married women aged 45–54, for whom the impact was *negative*, contrary to hypothesis. The impact of male income level, if statistically discernible, was sometimes positive and sometimes negative, depending on age group, while the impact of the unemployment rate was negative, but not for all age groups.

Other statistically significant relations found in the literature include: (a) a negative impact of the price of child care, (b) a positive impact of the labor force status of a married woman's sister-in-law, and (c) a negative impact of relative male income, measured as male income divided by income of the parents' age cohort.

Some of the empirical results reviewed here can be straightforwardly interpreted in terms of the theory developed in this chapter. For example, the price of child care can be understood as reflecting the tradeoff between home production and market income, and a higher divorce rate plausibly reduces at least the expected level of income not directly derived from a woman's labor supply. Other results, such as the apparently inconsistent impact of male income and female earnings, merit further investigation.

Related discussion questions:
1. Do you expect women's labor force participation to continue to rise over the next twenty years? Why or why not?
2. Do you think the invention of various labor-saving devices for use in the home (e.g., dishwashers, clothes washers) have had an effect on women's labor force participation? Why or why not?

Related references:
Genevieve G. Melford, *An Empirical Investigation of the Causes of Female Labor Force Participation in the United States after World War II*. Unpublished thesis, Wesleyan University (1999).
US Census Bureau, *Statistical Abstract of the United States* (2000, 2001).

Household labor supply

Generally speaking, the ultimate purpose of the theoretical framework constructed here is to specify household labor decisions as a *function* of observable economic variables. Toward this end, define a household's *quantity supplied* of labor as the amount it is *willing and able* to offer. This corresponds to the optimal labor choice L^* described earlier. Then the household's *labor supply function* indicates how its quantity of labor supplied is linked to given levels of independent variables such as the market wage rate.

A standard way of illustrating the supply function is the *supply curve*, which, as shown in figure 1.5, depicts the relationship between quantity supplied and the wage level, holding constant the values of other independent variables in the supply function. A movement along a given supply curve, occasioned by a change in the going wage rate, is referred to as a *change in quantity supplied*, as distinguished by a shift in the entire supply curve, which is called a *change in supply*. Note that the latter can only result from a change in some independent variable *other* than the wage rate. Not also that the supply curve in figure 1.5 is drawn to reflect the "law of supply," the premise that quantity supplied increases (or, more generally, does not decrease) with the wage rate.

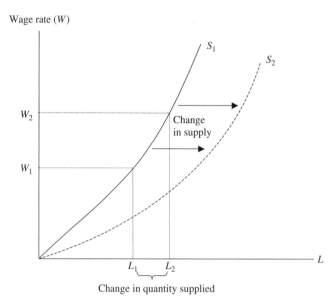

Wage rate (W)

Figure 1.5 The household's labor supply curve.

For some analytical purposes, it is useful to determine not only the *direction* in which a household's labor supplied responds to changes in market conditions, but also the *degree* of response. The standard measure of responsiveness used in economic analysis is called *elasticity*, understood as the ratio of *percentage* changes in given dependent and independent variables in the functional relationship under study. Percentage rather than absolute changes are analytically useful because they eliminate variations in magnitude stemming from arbitrary choices in the unit of measurement, such as measuring wage rates in cents rather than dollars.

The *wage elasticity* of labor supply, written E_{LW}^S, is thus defined as the ratio of percentage change in quantity supplied to the corresponding percentage change in the wage rate, and this formula can be expressed in turn by the product $\left(\dfrac{\Delta L_s}{\Delta W} \cdot \dfrac{W}{L_s}\right)$, where the first ratio is the inverse of the slope of the supply curve and the second represents the ratio of wage rate to quantity supplied at a given point on the supply curve. Note that this measure must be positive if the supply curve is upward-sloping, so that "more wage-elastic supply" translates as "bigger positive number" so long as the law of supply holds.

Of course, it has not yet been established whether labor supply curves generated by the theory now under study obey the law of supply, or are even consistent with it. Nor is it yet clear what determines the magnitude of wage elasticity of a given household's labor supply. These questions are taken up below, after considering the role of the other basic economic factor affecting household labor supply decisions.

The effect of non-labor income on labor supply

It will prove convenient to consider the impact of increasing non-labor income on labor supply before taking up the more involved implications for optimal labor choice of a change in the wage rate. Therefore, consider figure 1.6, which depicts a possible consequence of increasing the level of non-labor income received by a representative household. At the initial level of non-labor income, denoted N_1, the household chooses to supply L_1 units of labor, as shown in the upper panel of figure 1.6.

Since this is the amount of labor that this household is *willing and able* to supply at the going wage rate W, it therefore corresponds to a point on the household's initial labor supply curve S_1, as illustrated in the lower panel of the figure. Note

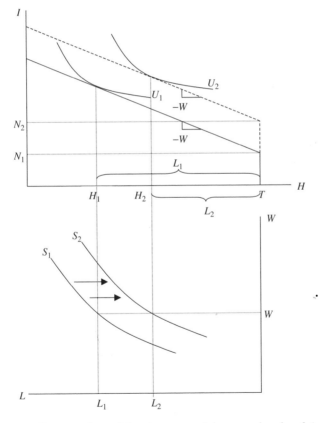

Figure 1.6   Impact of increased non-labor income on labor supply when leisure is a normal good.

that since labor and leisure are inversely related, the quantity supplied of labor measured along the horizontal axis in the lower graph increases as leisure decreases in the upper graph, and vice versa; also, the origin on the lower graph is reached when all T hours of the household's time endowment are devoted to leisure. Again, the supply curve is drawn on the hypothesis, as yet unsupported, that household labor choices obey the "law of supply."

Now suppose the household's non-labor income increases to N_2. As shown in the upper panel of the figure, this results in a parallel upward shift in the budget frontier. A necessary consequence is that the household is now able to achieve higher levels of utility. Microeconomists refer to this as an increase in *real* (as opposed to *pecuniary*) income, on the premise that what matters to the household is not the magnitude of income in pecuniary terms, but the level of well-being it can attain.

What is the impact of this increase in real income on the household's labor supply decision? It depends. Increasing real income can in general change a household's labor supply in either direction (or not at all), depending on the economic nature of leisure as a consumption good. Specifically, a good is defined as *income-normal* (or simply *normal*, if the context is unambiguous) if its consumption increases with a household's real income, other things equal, and *income-inferior* (or simply *inferior*) if its consumption is inversely related to the household's real income level. Goods for which household consumption is invariant to changes in real income are termed *(income-)neutral.*

The impact of increased non-labor income on the quantity of labor supplied thus depends on whether leisure is viewed by the household as a normal or an inferior good. If leisure were a normal good, then other things equal an increase in non-labor income will lead the household to consume more leisure and thus must shift the household labor supply curve down. This is the scenario depicted in figure 1.6.

If leisure were an inferior good, however, the opposite would occur: an increase in non-labor income leads to an *increase* in the household's supply of labor. Finally, an increase in non-labor income has no effect on labor supply if leisure is a neutral good. It's left to you to illustrate these two cases. Which of the three possible cases obtains in practice is primarily an empirical matter. The standard economic model of household labor choice, at any rate, has nothing to say concerning the determination of income effects.

As with the relationship between quantity supplied and the wage rate, it is possible to express the impact on labor supply of changes in non-labor income in elasticity terms. Define the *income elasticity of labor supply* as the ratio of the percentage change in quantity supplied of labor to the corresponding percentage change in income that occasioned it. For this purpose, it doesn't matter whether "income" is measured in pecuniary (N) or real (U) terms, so income elasticity of labor supply can be expressed as $E_{LI}^S = \%\Delta L_S / \%\Delta N = \%\Delta L_S / \%\Delta U^*$, where U^* is interpreted as highest utility level attainable by the household given N. Note that this elasticity measure is positive if leisure is normal, negative if inferior, and zero in the case that leisure is income-neutral.

DOES "HITTING IT BIG" REDUCE LABOR SUPPLY?

If leisure were a normal good, it might be expected that offspring in afflu-ent families who receive a substantial inheritance would reduce their labor supply in response, perhaps even to the extent of leaving the labor market entirely. Indeed, the wealthy industrialist Andrew Carnegie made this pre-diction some hundred years ago. His prediction recently received strong support from a study based on an analysis of US tax returns for the period 1982–5 of over four thousand people who received inheritances in 1982 or 1983 (Holtz-Eakin *et al.*, 1993).

The study showed that a person was more likely to reduce labor force participation the higher was his or her inheritance. For example, an indi-vidual inheriting more than $150,000 was found to be four times more likely to stop working than someone receiving less than $25,000. In addition, high-inheritance individuals that continued to supply some labor experienced lower growth in earnings than did their low-inheritance counterparts. Fur-thermore, the negative effect on labor supply typically lasted for the full three years covered by the study.

Lottery winners also respond to their good fortune by reducing labor supply. A study of Massachusetts lottery winners found that this form of unearned income reduced labor earnings significantly, with the largest effects being registered for individuals near retirement age (Imbens *et al.*, 2001).

Related discussion questions:
1. If you knew you were going to inherit a substantial amount eventually, would you reduce your work in the years before inheriting it?
2. Why would someone who had a major lottery win or gained a sub-stantial inheritance continue to work at all?

Related references:
Douglas Holtz-Eakin, David Joulfaian, and Harvey Rosen, "The Carnegie Conjec-ture: Some Empirical Evidence," *Quarterly Journal of Economics* 108 (May 1993): 415–35.
Guido W. Imbens, Donald B. Rubin, and Bruce I. Sacerdote, "Estimating the Effect of Unearned Income on Labor Earnings, Savings, and Consumption: Evidence from a Survey of Lottery Players," *American Economic Review* 91 (September 2001): 778–94.

Derivation of the household's labor supply curve

Turn now to the derivation of the household's labor supply curve. In the upper panel of figure 1.7, the scenario depicting the household's optimal leisure choice for an arbitrary initial wage rate is reproduced. As before, it is presumed that the household will choose a positive quantity supplied of labor, here denoted L_1, for a given initial wage W_1. This choice is represented by the point (L_1, W_1) in the graph in the lower panel.

Now suppose that the market wage rate increases from W_1 to W_2, resulting in the steeper budget frontier in the upper panel of figure 1.7. How will the household's quantity supplied of labor respond to the increase? The answer is determined by drawing the optimal bundle corresponding to the new, steeper budget line. In the scenario illustrated in figure 1.7, this results in a higher level of quantity supplied, denoted L_2. This new bundle is represented by the point (L_2, W_2) in the lower graph.

The segment of the household's labor supply curve corresponding to this span of wage rates is then established by drawing a line "connecting the dots" in the lower graph. To see the labor supply curve in its standard representation, as in figure 1.5, simply imagine flipping around the horizontal axis so that labor supply increases to the right. The result is the familiar-looking, upward-sloping supply curve for the representative household.

This exercise demonstrates that the "law of supply" – the notion that quantity supplied increases with the market wage rate – is at least *consistent* with the assumption of optimizing behavior by rational, wage-taking households with exogenously given preferences satisfying the axioms reviewed earlier. But does this "law" follow *necessarily* from these assumptions? Could it ever be the case that a household satisfying all of the foregoing assumptions might *reduce* its quantity supplied of labor if offered a higher wage rate? This question cannot be answered fully without introducing an additional theoretical distinction in the model spelled out above.

Income and substitution effects of a wage change

A change in the market wage rate can be regarded as having two economically distinct impacts on a household's optimal labor decision. On one hand, an increase in the wage rate increases the effective price of leisure, other things equal, making it a more expensive good and thus reducing its relative desirability. This is reflected in the fact that the budget line becomes steeper with a wage increase, putting aside for a moment what it does to the vertical intercept. The change in quantity supplied corresponding to this feature is termed the *substitution effect* of a wage change.

In addition, as shown in the upper graph of figure 1.7, an increase in the wage rate rotates the household's budget frontier upward, thus making more

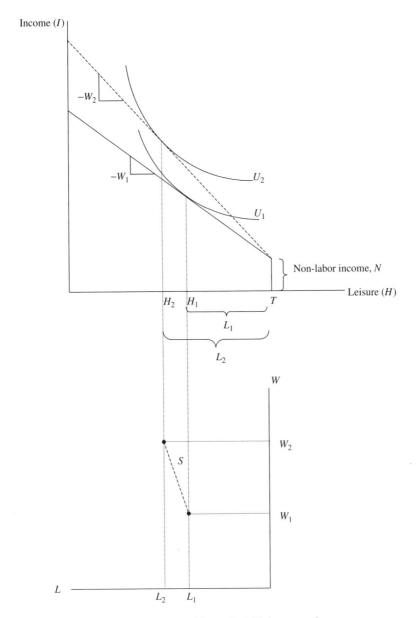

Figure 1.7 Derivation of household labor supply curve.

consumption bundles affordable and permitting a higher level of utility to be reached, just as with the case of increased non-labor income discussed above. The change in consumption resulting specifically from this increase in attainable utility or real income is correspondingly called the *income effect* of the wage change.

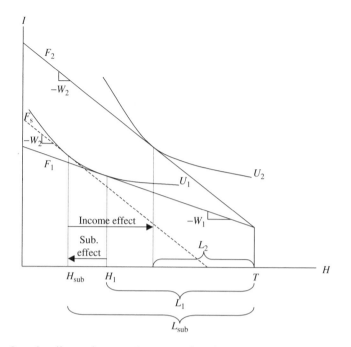

Figure 1.8 Supply effects of a wage increase when leisure is normal and the income effect dominates the substitution effect.

Adding together the two effects determines the total impact of a change in the wage rate on a household's quantity supplied of labor.

To see how these effects combine to determine the slope of a household's labor supply curve, consider again the steps involved in generating a labor supply curve for the representative household, and examine figure 1.8. As before, the household is assumed to choose labor hours L_1 given wage rate W_1, corresponding to a point of tangency between budget frontier F_1 and indifference curve U_1. Now again suppose that the market wage rate increases to W_2, creating the new, steeper budget frontier labeled F_2. The purpose now is to decompose the household's supply response into the separate substitution and income effects of this change in the market wage rate.

To isolate the substitution effect, draw an *imaginary* budget frontier F_s parallel to the actual *new* budget line, but just tangent to the *original* indifference curve U_1. This procedure captures the higher *relative* price of leisure, reflected in the steeper slope of the hypothetical frontier, while holding the household's attainable utility constant (and thus netting out the income effect). Note that a new point of tangency is established between the imaginary budget frontier F_s and the original indifference curve U_1 at a lower level of leisure H_{sub}, and correspondingly, a higher level of labor hours L_{sub}.

The substitution effect of the wage change on labor supplied, denoted $\left.\dfrac{\Delta L_s}{\Delta W}\right|_{\bar{U}}$,

is then just equal to the difference between L_{sub} and L_1. Thus, expressed as the ratio of change in labor supplied to the change in wages that caused it, the substitution effect is seen to be *positive* (or, stated more generally, non-negative) given the standard assumptions of strictly convex and monotonic preferences. Equivalently, the substitution effect of a wage change on quantity of *leisure* hours is always negative (more generally, non-positive).

Now, to capture the corresponding income effect of the wage change, one simply compares L_{sub} to the quantity of labor established by the point of tangency between the *true* new budget frontier F_2 and the higher indifference curve newly attainable with this frontier. But where should that new point of tangency be drawn? Equal to L_{sub}, or somewhere to the left or to the right of that quantity? And in the latter cases, *how far* to the left or right does the new point of tangency occur? Here we encounter literally the same degree of indeterminacy as with the effects of changing non-labor income, and for the same reason: the answers depend on the nature of leisure as a consumption good.

Note, however, in this case that, since the income effect results from the *indirect* impact of a wage increase on the household's attainable utility, rather than a *direct* increase in absolute income, it is best expressed as a product of *two* ratios,

$\dfrac{\Delta L_s}{\Delta U^*} \cdot \dfrac{\Delta U^*}{\Delta W}$. The sign of the second ratio is always positive, since increasing the

wage rate always rotates the household's budget frontier upward. The sign of the former ratio, as before, depends on the economic nature of leisure.

What does all of this have to do with the slope of the household labor supply curve? Note that if leisure were an inferior good, the income effect of a wage change would work *in the same direction* as the corresponding substitution effect, implying unambiguously that quantity supplied increases with the wage rate. If instead leisure were an *income-neutral* good, then the income effect is zero, so that the supply curve is upward-sloping so long as the substitution effect is not zero (a case considered in one of the end-of-chapter questions). Thus, the only serious challenge to the "law of supply" arises in the event that leisure is a *normal* good, that is, that households tend to consume more leisure as their income increases.

Furthermore, an anomalous outcome only arises from this scenario if leisure is income-normal *and* the income effect is larger in absolute value than the substitution effect of a wage change. This scenario is depicted in figure 1.8. Given these two assumptions, the final quantity supplied of labor, denoted L_2, is smaller in magnitude than L_{sub}, so that an increase in the wage rate from W_1 to W_2 is associated with a strict *decrease* in the household's quantity supplied of labor. You should be able to establish that in this case the corresponding supply curve is *downward-sloping* over the relevant range of wages. This result confirms that the standard assumptions about household preferences and behavior do not suffice to ensure that the "law of supply" obtains for labor supply curves.

Greater insight into the factors that determine the shape of household labor supply curves can be gained by expressing the slope of the supply curve just derived in elasticity terms. Specifically, that the household's wage elasticity of labor supply can be decomposed into the substitution and income effects of a given wage change, expressed as elasticities. The relevant formula is $E_{LW}^{S} = E_{LW}^{sub} + Z \cdot E_{LU^*}$, where E_{LW}^{S} denotes the household's elasticity of labor supply, E_{LW}^{sub} represents the substitution effect elasticity, and E_{LU^*} is interpreted as the "pure" income elasticity of labor supply – that is, the responsiveness of household labor supply to an increase in real income, holding the wage rate constant. Finally, Z represents the share of labor income, expressed by WL, in the household's *total* pecuniary income, $N + WL$.

A number of insights can be gleaned from this expression. First, note that it confirms the previously stated conclusion that the slope of the household's labor supply curve is, as a general matter, indeterminate if leisure is a normal good. As discussed in the previous section, in this case the substitution effect and income effect move in opposite directions, so that the sign of the elasticity of labor supply – and thus the slope of the supply curve – is given by the sum of a positive and a negative number. Without more information, it is impossible to tell which effect dominates.

One can, however, make some general statements about the overall shape of a typical household supply curve given this formula. To see this, note that the wage elasticity of labor supply is strictly increasing in the substitution effect elasticity, strictly increasing in the income effect elasticity and wage share if leisure is inferior, and strictly decreasing in each of the latter two elements if leisure is normal.

With these relationships in mind, consider the impact on wage elasticity as one moves from low to high market wage levels. Presumably, at sufficiently low wage rates (in particular, zero), the representative household will supply no labor, and thus the income elasticity term will disappear from the right-hand side of the above formula. Assuming that the substitution effect is strictly positive, the household's supply curve must thus be strictly positively sloped for sufficiently low wage rates, no matter what the sign of the income effect. For households in which leisure is always an inferior good, the supply curve will remain upward-sloping for all other wage rates. A less definitive statement can be made if the household treats leisure as a normal good: for a given value of the substitution effect elasticity, so long as the income elasticity of labor supply and the wage share of total household income are not perfectly inversely related, it must be the case that the household labor supply curve becomes less elastic as the wage increases.

Whether or not labor supply ever becomes backward-bending depends on the magnitude of the income effect elasticity at higher wage levels. Although the standard economic model of household choice offers no predictions about this, it seems at least plausible to suggest that leisure becomes strongly normal for sufficiently high levels of income, and thus that labor supply curves *eventually* "bend backward." But even then it can't be determined at what wage this would take place.

There is a large literature devoted to the problem of estimating labor supply elasticities. It is the general practice in this literature to estimate these elasticities separately for male and female workers in the labor force. These studies generally find a very low (i.e., highly wage-inelastic) supply response for males of "prime" working years (ages 25–54), and higher, albeit still wage-inelastic, supply responses for prime-age women. Indeed, when the income effect of wage changes is included, men are generally found to have slightly backward-bending labor supply. The difference in estimates for male and female supply elasticities may simply be due to the fact that, on average, men earn a higher wage, and are thus "further up" on a given backward-bending supply curve than women.

Knowing the shape of representative supply curves has potentially important implications for the effectiveness of various government policies. For example, as addressed in one of the end-of-chapter questions, the impact of income tax rate changes on labor supply depends critically on the slope of typical labor supply curves at the point of policy impact. This analysis can also be applied in studying the effects on labor supply of anti-poverty income transfers. We consider this issue and accompanying evidence in chapter 19, noting for now that the key question for empirical analysis is the effective income "cutoff" at which non-labor income begins to reduce quantity supplied of labor.

Aggregating household supply curves

The theory just constructed is premised on the optimizing behavior of a hypothetical representative household. In most empirical applications of the theory, however, labor economists are interested in the labor supply behavior of particular *groups* of people, defined for example by demographic category (race, gender, age, and so on) or the particular type of labor being supplied. Thus it is important to consider how *aggregate* supply curves are derived from the individual supply curves of the households constituting the group under study.

This is most readily done in the case that the members of the group in question are easily defined, either through direct observation or indirectly due to the nature of economic circumstance under consideration. An example of the latter might be the set of all workers *currently* supplying a certain type of labor, or the set of women currently in the labor force within a given economy. In that case, to derive the corresponding aggregate supply curve for the indicated group, one simply adds together the labor supply curves for all individuals in the group. Visually speaking, in terms of the standard labor supply graph, this means adding individual supply curves *horizontally*, or summing quantities supplied corresponding to each possible value of the market wage rate. This procedure is illustrated in figure 1.9. Note that it is therefore not possible to determine in general what would be the slope of the aggregate labor supply curve thus derived, since it would depend on the slopes of individual curves.

However, a more definitive statement about the slope of aggregate labor supply can be made if the number of households joining the group under study (for

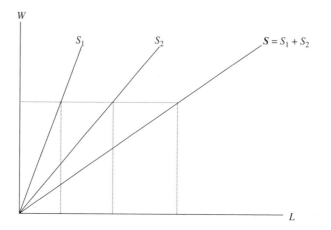

Figure 1.9   Derivation of an aggregate labor supply curve.

instance, the group of individuals supplying labor in the market for a certain type of labor) is an increasing function of the relevant wage rate. For example, it might be that people are willing to commute, or even migrate, longer distances to join a given geographically defined labor market at wage rates sufficiently higher than the going level. In that case it can in general be said that the aggregate supply curve that allows for such additions to a particular group will be more elastic than the corresponding aggregate curve defined for the set of suppliers *presently* in the group under study (for example, presently supplying labor in a specified market). This is so because in the former case, unlike the latter, the slope of the aggregate curve is informed by the changing numbers of suppliers in the market in addition to the given slopes of the individual household supply curves.

EXTENSIONS OF THE BASIC
MODEL OF HOUSEHOLD LABOR SUPPLY

Now that you've seen how the basic model of optimal choice can be used to derive labor supply curves, let's return to the list of simplifying assumptions and consider the theoretical implications for labor supply of relaxing some of the key ones.

Household production

Related to the role of non-labor income is the possibility that a significant portion of a household's income comes from *household production* – that is, direct production of consumption goods within the home, done by household members. Examples of household production include home-cooked meals, child care, gardening, and home repairs and improvements. Given this possibility, household members must decide how to allocate their time across three activities – market labor, household labor, and leisure. The goal is to determine what impact this has on the household's market labor supply curve.

Once again the analysis starts with the household's budget frontier. The simplest way to model the effect of household production is to assume that wages and household output are measured in the same units. It can also reasonably be assumed that household production is characterized by diminishing marginal returns throughout, and involves essentially the same type of labor as that supplied in the market. Finally, and purely for the sake of simplicity, assume that the household receives no non-labor income.

Based on these simplifying assumptions, the consumption opportunities made possible by home production can be represented by an *individual production possibilities frontier* (IPPF) linking household labor inputs to output produced in the home. As shown in figure 1.10(a), the IPPF starts at point T on the horizontal axis and increases to the left in a concave fashion, reflecting diminishing marginal returns. For each hour of labor, then, the household must decide whether to produce along its IPPF or supply that hour to the market at wage rate W. Assuming the labor activity is essentially the same in any case, and produces the same good, the model of optimal choice implies that the household would choose the activity with the greatest return.

Suppose for the sake of argument that home production initially yields the highest marginal return, as indicated by a slope at the base of the IPPF that is higher in absolute value than the market wage rate. Therefore, if the household chooses to expend that first hour in labor rather than leisure, that labor hour will

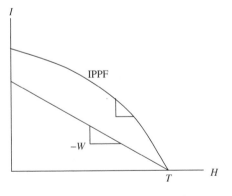

Figure 1.10(a) Individual production possibilities frontier (IPPF) for household production.

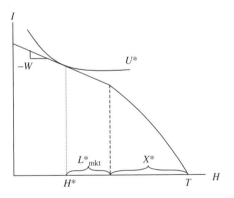

Figure 1.10(b) Optimal time allocation with household production.

be directed to household production. This will continue to be true for successive hours of labor so long as the marginal product of home production (indicated by the absolute value of the IPPF's slope) exceeds the market wage rate. Once that marginal product begins to fall below the market wage, any additional labor hours would be devoted to wage labor, since – given diminishing marginal returns – the market wage will thereafter exceed marginal household product.

The composite budget frontier resulting from this construction is illustrated in figure 1.10(b). Note that its right-most portion is strictly concave, corresponding to the lower portion of an IPPF with diminishing returns, and the left-most portion is linear, with a slope equal in absolute value to the market wage rate. The vertical dotted line indicates where home production stops and market labor starts, as you move to the left from intercept T.

The household's optimizing bundle of leisure and income is found by locating the point on the budget frontier that yields the highest possible utility. If this bundle involves a mix of labor and leisure hours, it will correspond to a point of tangency between the budget frontier and an indifference curve, as illustrated in figure 1.10(b). However, in this case any such point will potentially involve a *three-way* allocation of household time: so long as the tangency is achieved along the linear portion of the budget frontier, the hours to the left of the dotted line marking this point represent leisure (H^*), the hours between the dotted and dashed vertical lines represent market labor (L^*), and the hours between the dashed line and the endowment T represent labor time devoted to home production (denoted X^*).

Of course, this three-way allocation of hours is not the only logical possibility. There are two possible outcomes in which, respectively, either no leisure or only leisure is chosen by the household, and if the utility-maximizing point occurs along the concave portion of the budget frontier, the household will choose only leisure and home production labor, thus supplying no labor to the market. We leave it to you to diagram these scenarios.

The presence of household production affects the household labor supply curve in two ways, one qualitative and one quantitative. The qualitative impact is that it increases the scope for viable non-participation in the labor market, since the household in this case has an alternative to the market for generating "income." (Note that this conclusion holds whether or not one includes positive non-labor income N.) In quantitative terms, the presence of household production increases the wage elasticity of labor supply, other things equal, assuming some labor is supplied prior to the wage change.

To see why this is so, refer to figure 1.11, which shows a representative household supplying L_1 units of market labor at an initial wage rate W_1. Now suppose the wage rate increases to W_2. As in the case without household production, the linear portion of the budget frontier becomes steeper, corresponding to the higher wage rate received.

But something else happens as well: since the wage rate is higher, it now exceeds the marginal product of labor devoted to household production for a greater portion of the household's given IPPF. Therefore the dotted vertical line marking the transition point from household to market labor shifts to the right,

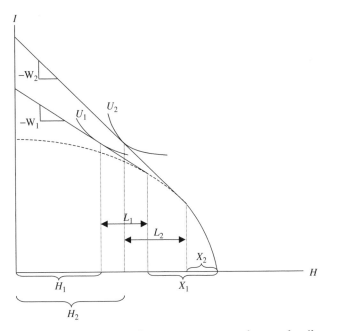

Figure 1.11 Impact of increasing the wage rate on the market/home production boundary.

resulting in an increase in market labor supplied by the household (net of the substitution and income effects of the wage change that would arise in any case). Therefore, whatever the net impact of the latter effects, the resulting household supply curve is more responsive to wage changes. A corollary of this result is that the time devoted to household production falls as the wage rate increases.

Skill acquisition and labor expenditure

The chapter's analysis of labor supply has to this point been based on the simplifying assumption that the intensive and quality dimensions of labor are given. This may also be a realistic assumption with respect to the working conditions for certain forms of employment. For example, some jobs (positions on an assembly line, perhaps?) may dictate a specific stream of effort, or require a certain set of skills for their performance. However, even in that event households are presumably able to choose among alternative jobs with different effort or skill requirements. Therefore it is relevant to treat these dimensions of labor supply as variable, and consider how the choice of effort or skill level factors into household labor supply decisions.

At least two theoretical issues arise in this connection. One concerns the logic of household choices respecting levels of skill attainment and effort expenditure on the job. It is possible to explore this issue using appropriately modified versions of the analytical framework laid out earlier in the chapter, and on that basis to derive hypothetical supply functions for these dimensions of labor supply. The logic of these derivations is considered in the end-of-chapter questions, but not pursued in detail until later in the text.

The issue of more immediate relevance to the analysis presented in this chapter concerns the impact of variations in costly effort or skill on the household's supply of labor hours. These cannot be interpreted simply as a matter of shifting a given supply curve, as in the case of variations in non-labor income, since any such curve is constructed on the premise that the labor supplied is of a given quality or type. But since skill acquisition or increased effort presumably enhances the quality of labor supplied (in an economic sense to be explored further in the next chapter), labor hours performed on the basis of different skill or effort levels might best be thought of as being supplied in separate labor markets. Under that interpretation, the relevant issue concerns household choices among alternative markets defined by skill or effort levels.

Consider first the nature of a household's choice to supply labor in markets defined by differences in skill requirements. Assume for the sake of simplicity that skill acquisition is costly in (only) pecuniary terms and is instantaneous, so that any wage increase corresponding to the attainment of greater skill is realized immediately. Suppose further that the representative household may choose between (just) two markets, one requiring "low-skill" and the other "high-skill" labor. Given these assumptions, the nature of the household's choice can be framed in the following way: what wage rate, if any, would render the household just indifferent between supplying labor in the two markets?

To address this question, consider figure 1.12. Panel (a) of the figure depicts the household's optimizing labor supply choice in the low-skill market, distinguished by wage rate W_1. As indicated, this choice corresponds to utility level U_1.

Suppose now that the skills required for participation in market 2 are acquired at some strictly pecuniary cost C to be subtracted from the household's non-labor income. As indicated in figure 1.12(a), this implies that the budget frontier corresponding to the household's participation in the high-skill labor market has a shorter vertical portion than the frontier for the low-skill market.

Now pose the following question: what level of W_2, the wage rate in the high-skill labor market, would render this household *just indifferent* between supplying labor in each of the two markets? To answer this, it is necessary to complete the budget frontier for market 2 by drawing a negatively sloped line tangent to indifference curve U_1 and reaching height $(N–C)$ at the time endowment point T. This frontier, with corresponding wage rate W_2, is depicted in figure 1.12(b).

This exercise yields two implications. First, it should be clear that higher wages must be offered in the high-skill market in order to attract any labor supply at all from the household. If wage rates were the same in the two markets, for example,

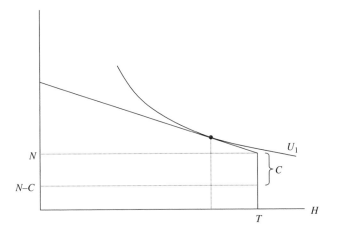

Figure 1.12(a) Household optimization in the low-skill labor market.

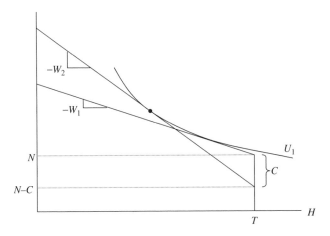

Figure 1.12(b) Compensating wage differential for provision of costly skill.

this household would be made strictly better off by supplying labor only to the low-skill market. Second, the high-skill wage derived in figure 1.12(b) has the property that it *just* compensates the household for the expenses it would incur in acquiring the skills required in market 2, since it renders the household indifferent between the two markets. Labor economists thus refer to the disparity between W_2 and W_1 as a *compensating wage differential* corresponding in the unequal skill requirements of the two markets.

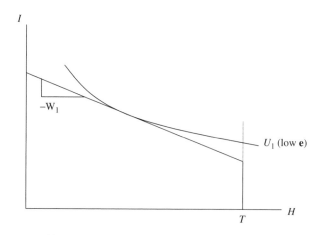

Figure 1.13(a)   Household optimization in the low-effort labor market.

Using the analytical framework established in this chapter, a wage differential can similarly be derived for the provision of different levels of labor *effort*. Labor economists typically assume that households find it costly to supply additional effort, at least beyond a certain point (i.e., the onset of physical or mental strain). The key difference from the scenario involving skill acquisition is that these costs are usually interpreted as *psychic* rather than *pecuniary* in nature. In the terms of the theory presented in this chapter, variations in effort affect the household's indifference map rather than its budget frontier.

Therefore suppose, for the sake of illustration, that greater effort expenditure by the household both lowers total utility and raises the marginal utility of leisure, on the premise that this expenditure raises the desirability of working less. Assume further, however, that labor effort is only expended if labor hours are supplied. Given these assumptions, different effort levels translate into different indifference maps defined over bundles of money income and leisure. Specifically, for any given combination of income and leisure such that some labor is supplied, the indifference curve running through that point which is associated with higher labor effort must be both steeper (reflecting a higher marginal rate of substitution of leisure for income) and representative of a lower level of utility (reflecting the psychic cost of expending greater effort). A corollary of this is that any two indifference curves representing the same utility must intersect when total leisure hours equal the time endowment T, since in that case no effort is expended.

With these assumptions in mind, examine figure 1.13. Panel (a) shows the household's optimal labor choice if its only option were to supply labor in the low-effort market, characterized by wage rate W_1. Let U_1 denote the household's utility at this point.

Suppose now that the household had the alternative option of supplying labor in the high-effort market. Per the preceding assumptions, the indifference curve

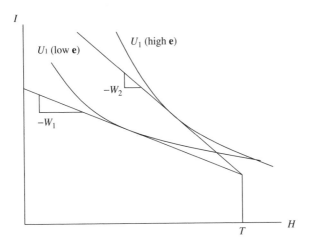

Figure 1.13(b) Compensating wage differential for provision of additional costly labor effort.

corresponding to the same level of utility, but premised on the higher effort expenditure, must be steeper, and rise above the other one for all positive levels of labor supplied. Given these conditions, the wage rate in the high-effort market that is just sufficient to render the household indifferent between supplying labor in either of the two markets must strictly exceed the wage rate offered in the low-effort labor market. The higher wage rate, labeled W_2 in figure 1.13(b), has the property that it renders the high-effort budget frontier just tangent to the indifference curve corresponding to the greater level of effort expenditure required in market 2.

As in the case of costly skill acquisition, then, the household's willingness to supply additional costly labor effort requires the existence of at least a compensating differential in the wages offered in the two markets. What differential actually obtains in the two markets cannot be determined without more details about competitive conditions in the respective markets. These features are considered in more detail beginning in chapter 3.

Finally, this analysis could also be extended to incorporate the effects of other variables that might affect the cost to households of supplying labor hours. For example, one would expect rational households to require a higher wage rate, other things equal, to supply labor in a risky or unpleasant working environment.

CONCLUSION

This chapter develops a theory of household labor supply on the premise of rational utility-maximizing choice. Given exchange conditions (as yet unspecified) ensuring that households take market wages as given, it is possible to derive individual and aggregate supply curves and identify economic factors affecting their position and shape. Using the same framework, it is possible to make predictions about the conditions minimally necessary to influence variations in dimensions of labor supply such as effort or skill.

The theory of labor supply developed here can be used to inform empirical research into a number of issues, such as the responsiveness of labor supply to changes in market wage rates, the determinants of labor force participation for specific demographic groups, and the impact of government policies on labor supply. As indicated in one of the study questions, for example, this model can generate testable hypotheses concerning the impact of income taxes and transfer payments on household labor supply decisions.

However, a comprehensive analysis of labor market outcomes will require development of the companion theory of labor demand. Competitive market outcomes can then be interpreted in terms of the interaction of these two forces. This second component of the competitive model is taken up in the next chapter.

Study Questions

1. Suppose that a firm pays an *overtime wage premium* for all labor hours supplied in excess of some threshold (say, an 8-hour working day). Illustrate the corresponding budget frontier for a household supplying labor to this firm. Would a household supplying the threshold number of hours in the absence of this premium increase or decrease its hours in response?

2. Suppose that a per-unit tax t were imposed on labor income. Indicate the impact on the budget frontier of a representative household. (Hint: what's the *net* wage rate received by the household?) Under what conditions would a reduction in the per-unit tax lead to an increase in labor hours, assuming that changing the tax rate had no effect on the market wage level? Given the same assumption, would these conditions ensure that a fall in the tax *rate* leads to an increase in total taxes, the product of tax rate times total income subject to the tax? (Hint: think in terms of the wage elasticity of labor supply.)

3. Illustrate a scenario under which the substitution effect of a wage change is zero. What does this scenario indicate about the relationship between leisure and income as consumption goods? Can you think of a reason that such a relationship would hold?

4. The study quoted in the chapter concerning the effects of inheritance on labor supply suggests that the absolute magnitude of the income effect increases with the level of household income. If this were typically the case, what does it suggest about the shape of a representative house-

hold's labor supply curve, compared to the case in which income elasticity of labor supply does not vary with income?

5. Labor economists standardly assume that labor effort constitutes an economic *bad*, at least beyond some minimum level. Given this assumption, derive the household's indifference map over bundles of labor effort and pecuniary income, assuming a constant wage rate per unit of effort supplied. Then use this framework to derive a household supply curve for labor effort. Is this supply curve necessarily upward-sloping?

6. The model of labor supply with household production developed in the chapter did not consider how households would allocate market and non-market labor among its individual members. Assuming this were done so as to maximize potential household income from all sources (that is, from labor in the home and in the market), what considerations would determine which household member did what kind of labor? Is it reasonable to assume that household members would each act so as to maximize the total income received by the household? Explain.

Suggestion For Further Reading

Mark R. Killingsworth, *Labor Supply* (Cambridge: Cambridge University Press, 1983).

CHAPTER TWO

LABOR DEMAND

This chapter develops a theory of the demand for labor by profit-maximizing firms. The theory yields testable hypotheses about the behavior of such firms in competitive markets, but more importantly, it provides, along with the companion theory of labor supply, the foundation for characterizing labor market outcomes under perfectly competitive exchange conditions.

The discussion in this chapter is organized along lines parallel to the previous one. A basic model of labor demand is first introduced and its key implications summarized, along with some observations about the assumptions required to make the theory work. The consequences of relaxing certain of these key assumptions are then examined.

THE BASIC MODEL OF LABOR DEMAND

Many households employ labor intermittently, for example when hiring a plumber to fix the sink or a neighborhood kid with a snow shovel to clear the front steps and sidewalk. Many fewer households hire employees, such as servants or gardeners, on a long-term basis. But in most economies, the primary buyers of labor services are *firms*. Therefore the basic model of labor demand is a story about the market behavior of these economic actors. As such, the model is built on three elements: the market conditions under which firms operate, the nature and economic goals of firms, and the production opportunities they face. Consider each in turn.

The firm's market environment

As with the theory of household labor supply, the derivation of labor demand curves requires the assumption that firms, whatever they are or want to accomplish, take the market wage as given, rather than something that can effectively be influenced through the exercise of market power. It is not necessary for the theory, but it will prove convenient to assume in addition that firms are price-takers in all other input and output markets in which they participate, as well. Wage- and price-taking behavior is a feature of markets described as *perfectly competitive*, a scenario that will be specified more fully in the next chapter. Unlike in the theory of household labor supply developed in the previous chapter, however, market conditions have implications beyond individuals' ability to influence market prices. As discussed next, the economic goals of firms depend closely on the market environment in which they operate.

The nature and goals of firms

It is descriptively accurate, at least, to define a *firm* as an economic entity that hires inputs in order to produce commodities for sale. But as discussed in the previous chapter, households engage in buying, selling, and (in a certain sense) production as well, so it is not immediately clear what fundamental distinction is signaled by this definition. Economists have typically distinguished firms from households on the basis of the goals they are understood to pursue, but this qualification merely relocates the puzzle rather than resolving it, since whatever firms are, in private ownership economies they are always owned by households. Presumably, then, the economic nature of firms in such economies should be derivable from the goals of the households that own them. In the language of the first chapter, the goals imputed to firms should therefore be consistent with the premise of utility-maximizing households.

This turns out to be the key to resolving the puzzle. Under certain market conditions, the utility of firm-owning households is maximized, other things equal, if the firms they own act so as to maximize *profit*, defined as the difference between the revenues received and costs incurred by firms. These conditions will be examined in more detail in chapter 9. But since they are consistent with the theory of perfectly competitive markets being developed in these first three chapters, for now it will simply be assumed that firms always seek to maximize profits.

The firm's production possibilities

Production can be defined as the transformation of given materials or conditions into forms more suited to particular human wants. It can be as simple as picking fruit from trees or as complex as manufacturing lunar landing modules, but in every case it requires the purposive application of human time and effort. Labor is therefore the fundamental input in production. From the standpoint of any given productive activity, there are at least four dimensions along which labor input might vary: number of laborers, hours worked per laborer, effort expended per hour, and the competence or skill with which labor is expended.

In all production processes save the most primitive, moreover, labor is combined with outputs of prior production, called *intermediate goods*, which serve to boost the productivity or output per unit of given labor inputs. Intermediate goods can take the form of materials (such as flour used in the baking of bread), tools, or machines. Besides being the outputs of prior production activity, in market economies these goods also have the characteristic of being purchased for use in production. Thus, they are commodities used in the production of other commodities. In the theory now under study, they are known as *capital* goods to distinguish them from labor inputs.

Production by firms, then, involves the purchase of labor and capital inputs for the purpose of producing outputs for sale. In the basic theory of labor demand, the specific methods by which given inputs are translated into outputs are taken for granted; the production process itself is thus treated as a "black box" within which inputs are translated into outputs. The quantitative relation between inputs and outputs is then typically summarized by a *production function*, a mathematical expression that associates given combinations of inputs with the *maximum possible* output they can generate, on the basis of existing technical knowledge. This stipulation, together with the parallel requirement that any given level of output be created by the smallest possible input bundle, is termed *technical efficiency*. Without this condition or something like it, the link between given inputs and the resulting output is ambiguous, since it is always possible to reduce output below the maximum possible level by using inputs wastefully.

Assuming technical efficiency, the production technology available to a firm can be summarized as a function linking the quantity of output to particular sets of inputs. Two conventions are typically invoked in defining a production function for a given labor process. First, it simplifies matters considerably to represent only inputs that are *scarce* in the economic sense, i.e., those that would command a positive price if exchanged in a market economy. For example, air is required for all production processes, if only to keep its participants alive, but it is not necessary to remind ourselves of this basic fact of human existence at every step.

Second, it may be appropriate in particular applications to represent explicitly only a subset of the inputs required for producing a given output. As indicated above, a comprehensive representation of the labor input in a given production activity would typically specify at least four variables, including the number of people working in a given period, the hours per worker day spent in labor, the effort expended per labor hour, and the level of skill exercised in working. For given analytical purposes it may nonetheless be appropriate to represent only one or two dimensions of labor explicitly, as long as it is not forgotten that the other dimensions are implicitly present. For example, production typically depends on the existence of given *social* capital goods like roads, bridges, communication systems, and the like. Ignoring this dependence may lead people to overestimate their economic self-sufficiency, but it may not matter in applications for which the social context of production is not at issue.

Given these conventions, a basic production function for a representative firm might be written $X = f(L, K)$, where L and K are respectively the magnitudes of labor and capital inputs, measured in specific dimensions, taking the magnitudes of other dimensions of input as given. The labor input, for example, might be measured in number of workers or number of person-hours employed, while K might most easily be thought of as a machine of a given size rented by the firm under study. Problems raised by the existence of *heterogeneous* capital goods are discussed later in the chapter.

Production in the short run

The properties of production and labor demand are typically investigated under two scenarios corresponding to distinct decision horizons faced by firm owners or their agents. The *short run* refers to the decision horizon in which the magnitude of at least one productive input is fixed, and that of at least one other input is variable. In the case of the two-input production function specified above, it is typical (and plausible) to assume that the capital input is fixed. The short-run production function might thus be written $X = f(L, \overline{K})$, where $\overline{K}$ indicates the fixed capital input. In contrast, the *long run* decision horizon is defined as that in which firms take all factors as variable. Production possibilities in this decision horizon are considered further below.

Short-run production possibilities for a firm can be represented with *product curves*. To see how these are constructed, imagine the relationship obtaining between quantities of labor input and output X given that the capital input is fixed. The graph of this relationship for a *particular* fixed quantity of capital is called a *total product curve* for labor, or simply the *total product of labor*, denoted TP_L. An example is illustrated in the upper panel of figure 2.1.

From this parent concept two useful subsidiary notions can be derived. The *average product of labor* (AP_L) is defined as total product divided by the labor input that produced it, that is $AP_L = \dfrac{TP_L}{L}$. When economists and journalists speak of trends in labor productivity, they are referring to some version of this measure applied to the entire economy. In some cases, it is also possible to derive the *marginal product of labor*, written MP_L and defined as the *change* in total product that results from a small increase in the labor input, holding all other inputs fixed. This is written $MP_L = \dfrac{\Delta TP_L}{\Delta L}\Big|_{\overline{K}}$ where the symbol "$\overline{K}$" can be read as "given a capital input fixed at $\overline{K}$." If the production function is differentiable, then MP_L corresponds to the partial derivative of total product with respect to labor, and thus represents the slope of total product at any given point. The related AP_L and MP_L curves are shown in the lower panel of figure 2.1.

What considerations inform the shapes of the product curves just drawn? The key one is known as the *law of diminishing marginal returns*, which necessarily arises in some form whenever there are both fixed and variable factors in production. This "law" states that if a variable factor is increased relative to a fixed factor in

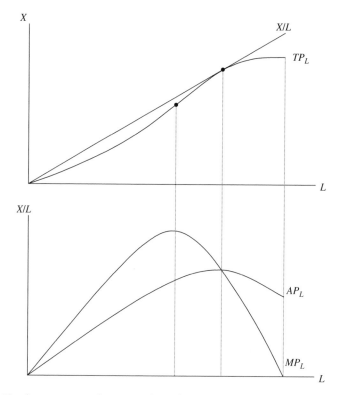

Figure 2.1 Total, average, and marginal product of labor curves exhibiting diminishing marginal returns.

a given production process, the marginal product of the variable factor eventually declines, and then does not increase again.

Note how the law is manifested in figure 2.1. Diminishing marginal returns to labor shows up in two places, most obviously in the downwardly sloped portion of the marginal product curve. But since marginal product corresponds to the slope of the total product curve, diminishing returns are also indicated by the portion of the total product curve in which the slope decreases with more labor input, that is, the region in which the total product curve is concave downward.

Notice that the law does not require that diminishing returns set in immediately, so as indicated in the figure, marginal product may be initially increasing, or what amounts to the same thing, the total product curve may be convex relative to the horizontal axis for relatively low labor inputs, and then concave thereafter. Alternatively, one of the study questions at the end of the chapter poses a realistic scenario in which *constant* returns to the variable input obtain until a capacity constraint determined by the firm's existing capital stock is reached.

Production in the long run

By definition, all inputs to a firm's production process are variable in its long-run decision horizon. Applying this principle in practice, it may be necessary to acknowledge that some inputs, whether or not explicitly represented in the production function, are essentially invariable. For example, the capacity of the atmosphere to absorb pollutants resulting from production does not vary just because the firm can build a differently-sized plant. In the basic model under construction, however, these difficulties are put aside for convenience.

To represent the firm's long-run production possibilities, then, it is necessary to allow the possibility that all inputs are variable, and thus that the production function is written $X = f(L, K)$. Correspondingly, one can in principle derive total, average, and marginal product curves for *capital* inputs, holding the level of the labor input hypothetically fixed. The "marginal product" of capital simply reflects the idea that the ability to use "more capital," however measured, increases labor productivity. As noted in the application box, though, it's not entirely clear how to measure such an increase when capital goods are heterogeneous.

A handy way of representing long-run production possibilities is through the use of an *isoquant map*. The constituent element of this map is an *isoquant*, defined as the locus of all input combinations that yield a constant level of output, thus satisfying the equation $\overline{X} = f(L, K)$ for some fixed quantity of output $\overline{X}$. The isoquant illustrated in figure 2.2(a) has two features of immediate interest: it is negatively sloped and convex relative to the origin.

What accounts for these features? First, assuming the production function is differentiable, it can readily be shown that the slope of the isoquant for any given input combination is just equal to the negative ratio of marginal products for labor and capital ($-MP_L/MP_K$), assuming that MP_K is not zero. But note that marginal products of both labor and capital will generally be positive so long as the condition of technical efficiency is met. Thus, the isoquant is negatively sloped in the region that the marginal products of both inputs are strictly positive. The absolute

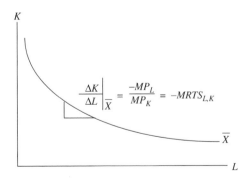

$$\frac{\Delta K}{\Delta L}\bigg|_{\overline{X}} = \frac{-MP_L}{MP_K} = -MRTS_{L,K}$$

Figure 2.2(a) An isoquant defined over labor and capital inputs.

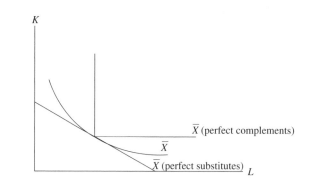

Figure 2.2(b) Different degrees of factor complementarity (substitutability).

value of the isoquant's slope at any point, equal to the ratio of the marginal product of labor to the marginal product of capital, is called the *marginal rate of technical substitution* of capital for labor (denoted $MRTS_{L,K}$), because it indicates how much of one input can be given up when another is increased, holding output constant.

Second, the curvature of the isoquant reflects the degree to which one factor can be *substituted* for the other in producing a given level of output. The standard measure of factor substitutability, known as the *elasticity of substitution*, is given by the forbidding mathematical expression $\sigma = (\%\Delta (K/L))/(\%\Delta MRTS)$, that is, the proportionate change in the capital–labor ratio, starting from some point on an isoquant, relative to a given proportionate change in the (absolute value of the) slope starting from the same point.

One element in the determination of factor substitutability is the *complementarity* of inputs. Two factors of production are said to be *complements* in production if increasing the use of one input increases the marginal productivity of the other input. Other things equal, the greater the degree of complementarity between two inputs with positive marginal products, the more *convex relative to the origin* is the corresponding isoquant. Notice this is not the same thing as saying that factor complementarity implies isoquant convexity, which is not generally true.

Various degrees of factor substitutability are illustrated in figure 2.2(b). The straight-line isoquant depicts the case in which inputs L and K are *perfect substitutes* in production. The right-angled isoquant represents the opposite extreme of *perfect complementarity*, in which increasing either input alone cannot increase output, once the two inputs are present in a given proportion. For example, production of a ditch may require one person using one shovel for an hour. Once this ratio has been achieved, increasing either input alone (having two shovels available for one person, for example) does no good. The third, smoothly curved isoquant represents the intermediate case in which some finite degree of factor substitutability is present. Thus one can say that factor substitutability generically corresponds to a case of *diminishing MRTS* as the horizontal-axis input increases.

WHAT ABOUT HETEROGENEOUS CAPITAL GOODS?

One of the most famous debates in the history of economics (between the "Cambridge school," led by British economist Joan Robinson, and two universities located in "the other Cambridge" – Harvard and MIT) concerns the depiction of capital – input K – as a homogeneous input in production. The difficulty stems from the fact that, in most labor processes, production is carried out with the aid of a variety of distinct tools and machines. For example, modern office work uses computers as well as telephones, pencils, staplers, and hole punches. Hence aggregation is as problematic for capital as it is for labor. For instance, suppose one approach to producing a given quantity of output requires a computer, two photocopiers, and two office workers, while an alternative approach requires three office workers, two typewriters, and one photocopier. In what sense can it be said that the latter process uses "less capital"?

Three different approaches for addressing this problem have been employed in the economics literature. One has been to ignore the problem completely. A second approach has been to aggregate dissimilar capital goods by weighting quantities according to their respective purchase or rental prices. This is problematic as it mixes together price and quantity; hence the aggregate value of capital can rise either because more capital is being used or because prices rise. One consequence of this is that the quantity demanded of "capital" measured in this way may not vary as expected with the "price of capital," as proxied by the real interest rate.

The third and most theoretically coherent approach is to acknowledge the fundamental heterogeneity of capital goods and treat them as distinct inputs in production, just as different dimensions of labor input might be separately represented in the production function. But coherence comes at the cost of simplicity in analyzing the nature and determinants of labor demand. Consequently, despite the fact that capital aggregation problems are routinely encountered in economic analysis, they are rarely resolved to everyone's satisfaction.

Related discussion questions:
1. For a job you have had, try to list all the capital equipment that you utilized in order to perform that job. Were any of the pieces of equipment substitutable for any of the others?
2. On what grounds might it be said that the second process described in the box uses less capital?

Related reference:
Marjorie S. Turner, *Joan Robinson and the Americans* (Armonk, NY: M.E. Sharpe, 1989).

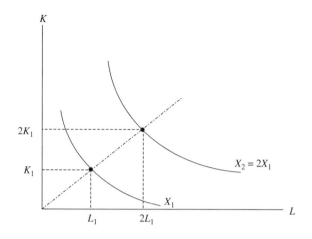

Figure 2.3(a) An isoquant map with constant returns to scale.

Note that factor substitutability or complementarity only applies in describing input combinations yielding a *constant* level of output. But it is typically the case that a given production process can yield a range of output levels. This possibility is represented by drawing isoquants corresponding to different output levels, creating an *isoquant map* for a given production technology. Examples are shown in figure 2.3. Note that isoquants representing successively higher levels of output are further "to the northeast" in the graph, reflecting the assumption that marginal products of both inputs are positive in the indicated range.

Isoquant maps can be used to illustrate the other "long-run" aspect of production considered here, *returns to scale*. The phenomenon of returns to scale concerns the relationship between proportional variations in *all* inputs and the resulting changes in output. For example, suppose that all inputs were doubled. If output doubles as well in response, *constant returns to scale* are said to obtain. If instead output more than doubles, *increasing returns to scale* are said to exist over that range of inputs, and if it falls short of doubling, *decreasing returns to scale* obtain.

The first two of these cases are illustrated in figure 2.3(a). Panel (a) depicts a case of constant returns: when the input combination (L_1, K_1) is doubled, output doubles, moving from X_1 to $X_2 = 2X_1$. In panel (b), however, the same doubling of inputs is associated with more than twice the original output. The case of decreasing returns to scale is left for you to illustrate as an exercise.

Finally, the basic model of labor demand is built on the simplifying assumptions that labor and capital inputs are *homogeneous*, that is, of given, identical quality per unit consumed in production, and that number of workers and hours per worker are *perfect substitutes* in each firm's profit function. The latter assumption makes it possible to measure the labor input simply in labor hours, without having to specify who is supplying those hours. The former assumption says that

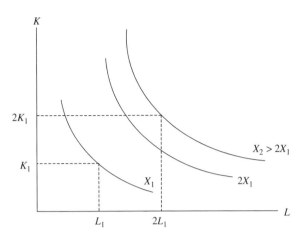

Figure 2.3(b)   An isoquant map with increasing returns to scale.

the *quality* of labor and capital inputs is constant. In the case of labor inputs, this implies that the levels of skill and effort exercised in production are given. These assumptions are relaxed later in the chapter.

Profit maximization conditions

Building on the foregoing assumptions, short- and long-run labor demand curves are derived from the maintained hypothesis that, given the production technology, firms choose inputs (and thus output) so as to maximize profit. Before constructing this derivation, it is useful to spell out how profits are defined in terms of input levels in light of the assumptions of the basic model.

Given the firm's production function and the assumption that it acts as a wage- and price-taker in the related markets, its profit is represented by the expression $\Pi = P \cdot f(L, K) - WL - RK$, where P is the firm's selling price determined in its product market, $f(L, K)$ is the firm's production function with labor L and capital stock K as inputs, and W and R are, respectively, the wage rate and rental rate of capital. The product $P \cdot f(L, K)$, or price times output, is referred to as the firm's *total revenue product*, or more specifically its *value of total product* (VTP) when, as in the present case, output price is taken as given. The sum $WL + RK$, in contrast, represents the firm's *total cost* of input use. Thus, profit can be interpreted as the difference between the firm's total revenue and the total cost associated with its input use. An example of this function, graphed over labor units, is depicted in the upper panel of figure 2.4.

In general, a given quantity of labor (and capital, if variable) hired by the firm must satisfy three conditions if it is to maximize profit. It will serve the subse-

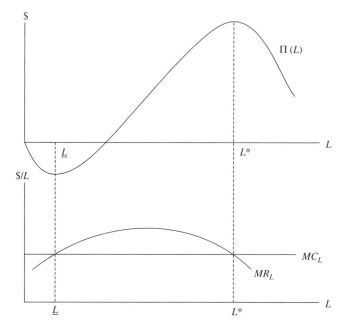

Figure 2.4 The profit function and the marginal conditions for profit maximization.

quent analysis of firm-level labor demand to state these conditions up front. Once these general conditions are understood, they can be tailored to specific scenarios depending on the nature of the labor choice problem under study.

The first profit maximization condition is that the slope of the profit function must be zero if the firm elects to hire a positive amount of labor. This holds true at the point marked L^* in figure 2.4. If the slope at the optimal point *weren't* zero, then it must be that the firm can achieve higher profits by altering its labor choice, and thus its profits aren't yet maximized. Furthermore, since profit is just equal to total revenue minus total cost, a zero slope for the profit function implies in turn that *marginal* revenue minus *marginal* cost equals zero, that is, the firm's MR and MC curves (to be specified below) must be equated, as shown in the lower panel of figure 2.4.

Note from the figure, however, that while equating marginal revenue and marginal cost of hiring labor is *necessary* for maximizing profit, it is clearly not *sufficient*, since this condition also obtains at the point of *minimum* profit, shown at quantity of labor $\underline{L}$ in the upper panel of figure 2.4. To rule out the latter possibility, an additional restriction is added: where the marginal revenue and marginal cost curves are equated, the latter curve must intersect the former from below. This is equivalent to stating that the profit function is *concave* rather than *convex* in the neighborhood of the point where its slope is zero, which uniquely occurs at point L^* in figure 2.4.

However, even these two conditions are not enough to guarantee that the corresponding positive level of labor input maximizes profit. This is because they do not rule out the possibility that the firm could do better by producing *nothing at all*, and thus hiring no labor inputs. Note that by producing nothing the firm incurs only *fixed* costs, that is, costs associated with the use of fixed inputs. By instead choosing to produce positive output, and thus to use positive levels of the variable factor, the firm incurs *variable* costs from hiring labor and other inputs in addition to its fixed costs.

Therefore, in order for the firm to gain profit from hiring workers, it must be that the total revenue thus generated is at least as great as the *total variable cost* incurred. This is equivalent to saying that the *average revenue* associated with employing workers must be at least as much as its *average variable cost*. This is known as the *shutdown condition*. The condition applies in both the short and long run, noting that *all* costs are variable in the long run. In figure 2.4, point L^* clearly satisfies the shutdown condition, since profit is strictly positive.

The general conditions for the firm's profit-maximizing labor choice, assuming it is greater than zero, can thus be summarized as follows: hire labor inputs to the point at which (1) the marginal revenue and marginal costs associated with hiring labor are equated, provided that (2) the marginal cost curve intersects the marginal revenue curve from below, and (3) the average revenue associated with hiring labor is at least as great as its average variable cost. In the next section, these general conditions are adapted to the firm's two decision horizons.

IMPLICATIONS OF THE BASIC MODEL

The main purpose of developing the basic model of firm labor choice is to derive the *labor demand function* for a representative firm, illustrated graphically by a *labor demand curve*. To grasp these notions, begin by defining the firm's *quantity demanded of labor* as the amount that it is just *willing and able* to hire. Then the firm's labor demand function is simply its quantity demanded stated as a function of its theoretical determinants, such as the wage rate. The demand curve associated with this function graphs the relationship between quantity demanded and the wage rate, for given levels of all other arguments in the function. One example of an individual demand curve is graphed in figure 2.5. Note that it reflects the (as yet theoretically unsupported) "law of demand," the hypothesis that the quantity demanded of labor is decreasing (or more generally, not increasing) in the wage rate.

In many cases, it is useful to know the relative *magnitude* as well as the direction of a wage change's impact on quantity of labor demanded. For example, assuming labor markets are competitive, the effect on employment of increasing the legislated level of a minimum wage will depend on how responsive is quantity demanded to given wage changes. The appropriate measure of demand responsiveness is termed the *wage elasticity of demand*.

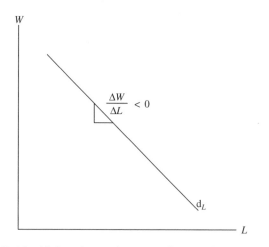

Figure 2.5 An individual labor demand curve reflecting the "law of demand".

The generic expression for wage elasticity of demand is the ratio of percentage change in labor demanded to the corresponding percentage change in the wage rate, written $E_{LW} = \frac{\%\Delta L_d}{\%\Delta W}$. If the "law of demand" holds, then the wage elasticity of labor demand is negative (or at least non-positive). As with the elasticity of labor supply discussed in the previous chapter and the elasticity of factor substitution described above, *percentage* changes are used in the definition so that the measure of demand responsiveness does not depend on the arbitrary choice of measurement units.

The more negative is the number (that is, the larger is the ratio in absolute value), the more elastic is a firm's labor demand. An elasticity less than − 1 is considered *elastic* or relatively responsive, while an elasticity between − 1 and 0 is termed *inelastic*, or relatively unresponsive to a change in the wage. Note that in the latter case the absolute magnitude of the percentage change in labor demanded is smaller than the corresponding percentage change in the wage rate.

The measure of wage elasticity of demand at a given point on the demand curve can be expressed as $\frac{\Delta L_d}{\Delta W} \cdot \frac{W}{L_d}$, where the first ratio denotes the inverse slope of the demand curve when it is depicted (as in figure 2.5) with the wage rate (the independent variable) measured along the vertical axis. Thus, for a given wage–quantity combination, the flatter the slope of the demand curve as drawn, the higher is its inverse, $\frac{\Delta L_d}{\Delta W}$, and thus the more elastic is labor demand. Conversely, for a given slope, the higher the level of quantity demanded for any given wage rate, the lower is the ratio $\frac{W}{L_d}$, and thus the less elastic is demand.

Key questions to be addressed by the theory of labor demand are thus, first, how does the quantity of labor demanded by profit-maximizing firms under competitive market conditions respond to changes in the wage rate – in particular, do labor demand curves typically obey the "law of demand?" Second, if so, what determines the *magnitude* or elasticity of these responses? These questions are addressed by deriving labor demand curves in the short and long run with the assumptions previously stated.

The firm's short-run labor demand

It is easiest to derive the firm's labor demand in the short run, when its capital input is fixed. Given this restriction, the shape of the firm's demand curve is informed primarily by the law of diminishing returns. To establish this point, it is necessary to derive the relevant revenue and cost curves for this scenario.

Consider first the marginal revenue associated with hiring an additional laborer, given that the capital input is fixed. Since total labor input increases, one would expect the firm's value of total product (*VTP*) to increase. However, since the firm is a price-taker in its product market, the only component of *VTP* that changes is total product itself, so the marginal revenue associated with hiring labor is just equivalent to the *value marginal product* of labor (VMP_L), defined as $VMP_L = P{\cdot}MP_L$, or the marginal product of labor evaluated at the going output price.

As the VMP_L is thus simply the marginal product of labor multiplied by a constant, it must have the same shape as the firm's marginal product curve, an example of which is reproduced in figure 2.6(a). Here it's drawn so that there are initially increasing returns to labor use before diminishing marginal returns kick in, but this is not the only possibility; diminishing returns might instead hold for all levels of labor hired, or there may be constant returns until the firm's output capacity is reached. Remember that this curve is always drawn assuming a particular level of capital input.

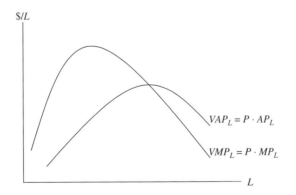

Figure 2.6(a)   The firm's short-run labor revenue curves.

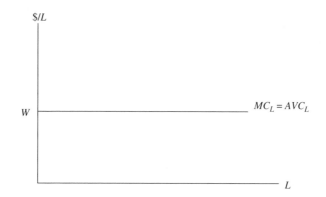

Figure 2.6(b)   The firm's short-run labor cost curves.

By similar reasoning, the average revenue from hiring labor is in this case equal to the *value average product* (VAP$_L$), defined as $VAP_L = P{\cdot}AP_L$, or the average product of labor evaluated at the going price. This curve is also illustrated in figure 2.6(a); note by comparison to figure 2.1 that it has the same relationship to VMP$_L$ as AP$_L$ has to MP$_L$.

Now consider the cost curves associated with hiring labor in the short run. The marginal cost of labor is the change in the firm's total cost when it hires one more unit of labor. As the firm's hiring decisions cannot affect the going wage rate, the cost of an additional unit of labor just equals the wage rate W. This result is illustrated in figure 2.6(b).

What are the average variable costs associated with a given labor choice? In the short run, as specified above, *only* labor costs are variable, so in this case $AVC_L = \dfrac{TVC}{L} = \dfrac{W \cdot L}{L} = W$, the market-determined wage rate. Thus, as indicated in figure 2.6(b), in the short run the marginal and average variable costs associated with hiring a given amount of labor are identical.

The firm's labor demand curve is determined by applying the general profit maximization conditions stated above to the specific revenue and cost curves just derived. This is done with the aid of figure 2.7(a), in which the firm's revenue and cost curves associated with hiring labor are superimposed. Given these conditions, how much labor will a price-taking, profit-maximizing firm choose to hire at alternative wage rates?

To answer this question, suppose that the market wage rate faced by the firm is initially set at W_1. By the argument given above this magnitude also represents the firm's marginal cost and average variable cost associated with hiring labor. Now consider the point where $W_1 = MC_L^1$ intersects the VMP$_L$ curve, at labor input L_1. Does this constitute a point on the firm's short-run labor demand curve? The $MR = MC$ condition of profit maximization is satisfied. So is the condition that

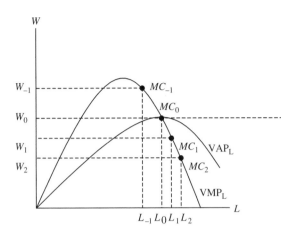

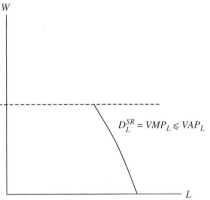

Figure 2.7(a) Derivation of the firm's short-run demand for labor.

Figure 2.7(b) The firm's short-run labor demand curve.

MC intersects MR from below, since this is how MC_L^1 and VMP_L relate in the graph. Finally, since W_1 is by construction strictly below VAP_L at L_1, the shutdown condition is also met.

It has thus been established that (L_1, W_1) is a point on the firm's short-run labor demand curve; this point represents the quantity of labor the firm is *willing and able* to hire at that wage rate. By the same logic, points such as (L_2, W_2) and (L_3, W_3) must also lie on the firm's short-run demand curve, since they also satisfy all three profit maximization conditions. In fact, all points on the VMP_L curve equal to or below the VAP_L are on the firm's short-run demand curve.

What happens when the wage rate equals W_{-1} in figure 2.7(a)? Since the corresponding marginal cost is MC_L^{-1}, the point (L_{-1}, W_{-1}) satisfies the first two conditions for profit maximization. However, since W_{-1}, corresponding to the firm's average variable cost of labor, exceeds the average revenue from hiring labor at that point, it does not satisfy the shutdown condition. Thus it is not a point on the firm's demand curve. The firm would produce nothing and hire no labor at this or any higher wage rate. W_0, which marks the intersection of the firm's VMP_L and VAP_L curves, thus represents the highest wage at which the firm would have non-zero labor demand.

The foregoing argument demonstrates that the firm's short-run labor demand curve, labeled d_L^{sr}, is represented by the portion of its VMP_L curve equal to or beneath its VAP_L curve. This is illustrated in figure 2.7(b). The law of diminishing marginal returns is reflected in the shape of the demand curve, specifically in its downward slope.

Note, however, a subtle but important shift in interpretation in reading this portion of the VMP_L curve as the firm's labor demand curve: while for the VMP_L

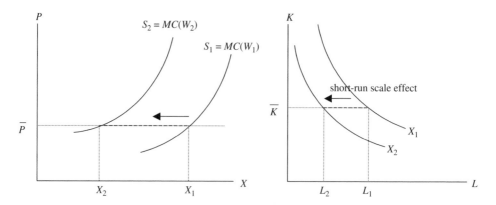

Figure 2.8(a) Short-run scale effect of wage change on output supply.

Figure 2.8(b) Short-run scale effect of wage change on labor demanded.

curve the labor input L is the independent variable, and the value marginal product of labor, represented (for example) in euros per unit of labor, is the dependent variable, the opposite is true for the firm's demand curve. Here, since the firm takes wages as given, the wage rate is the *independent* variable and labor demanded is the *dependent* variable. Thus it is more accurate to say that the firm's short-run labor demand curve is equivalent to the *inverse* of its VMP_L curve.

It will prove useful for the subsequent discussion of long-run demand to consider a second view of the logic behind the firm's short-run demand curve, from the perspective of the firm's *output* choice. This is done with the aid of figure 2.8. This approach traces the impact of a change in the market wage on labor demanded through the more immediate effect on the firm's desired output. This is known as the *scale effect* of a change in the wage rate, which corresponds to the income effect discussed in the previous chapter's analysis of household labor supply decisions.

Suppose that for an initial wage W_1 the firm chooses output X_1 along its supply curve given market price P, as shown in figure 2.8(a). This choice corresponds to the firm being on isoquant X_1 in figure 2.8(b). Suppose that the firm initially chooses labor input L_1 along this isoquant (the basis on which it does so is discussed below).

You may recall from introductory microeconomics that the firm's output supply curve is derived from its marginal cost curve, in a fashion exactly parallel to that in which its labor demand curve is derived from the VMP_L curve. The immediate consequence of an increase in the wage rate is therefore to increase the firm's marginal cost of production, as increased output can be attained only by hiring now more expensive labor inputs. This leads in turn to a *decrease* in the output supply curve of a price-taking firm, and thus a reduction in output at the going market price to X_2. This is indicated by the leftward shift in output supply from S_1 to S_2 in figure 2.8(a).

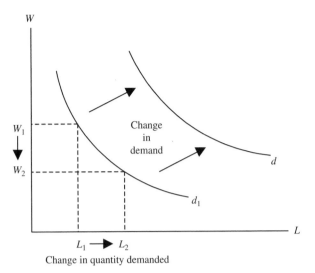

Figure 2.9 Change in demand and change in quantity demanded.

This reduction in output also implies that the firm shifts to a new, lower iso-quant corresponding to X_2, as shown in figure 2.8(b). However, in the short run the firm's capital input is fixed at some level $\overline{K}$, so the only adjustment in input use the firm can make is to reduce its labor input. The decrease from L_1 to L_2 is thus the scale effect mentioned earlier, and this effect is the sole basis for the firm's input adjustment in the short run in response to a change in the wage rate.

What does the basic model imply about the determinants of a firm's short-run demand for labor? First, the analysis establishes that a firm's labor demand curve obeys the law of demand, at least in the short run, due to the effects of the law of diminishing marginal returns. Note, though, that the overall prospect of diminishing returns does not rule out the possibility that the demand curve might also be horizontal for some range of labor hired.

A movement along a given demand curve, which can only be induced by changes in the market wage rate, is called a *change in quantity demanded*. Changes in non-wage variables affecting labor demand, in contrast, shift the entire curve, leading to a *change in demand*. This distinction is illustrated in figure 2.9. The basic model can also be used to identify the factors that cause the firm's entire labor demand curve to shift.

First, an increase in the output price P faced by the firm must shift the VMP_L curve upward, and thus lead to an increase in its labor demand, represented as an increase in the firm's quantity of labor demanded *at each wage level* for which demand is positive. Second, and similarly, if labor and capital are complementary factors of production, then an increase in the fixed level of capital must increase the marginal productivity of labor and thus increase the firm's demand curve.

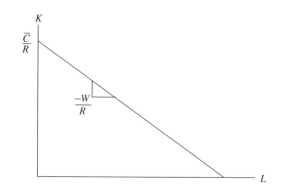

Figure 2.10(a)　An isocost curve defined over labor and capital inputs.

Finally, an improvement in the firm's technology that increases the marginal productivity of labor must increase the firm's demand for labor.

The firm's long-run labor demand

Now consider the economic logic underlying a firm's *long-run* labor demand curve, and the relationship of that curve to its short-run counterpart. Since the firm has more flexibility in adjusting its inputs, labor demand should in general be more elastic in the long run.

As a first step in deriving the firm's long-run labor demand curve, return to the profit maximization conditions described earlier. As in the short run, the first condition of profit maximization requires, given the other assumptions of the basic model, that the firm equate the market-determined wage rate to VMP_L. This condition is just as in the short run, with the important difference that the capital input – and therefore the *particular* VMP_L to be equated to the wage rate – is not fixed, but rather chosen by the firm.

What level of capital input will the firm choose in the long run? The answer to this question comes from the same general profit maximization condition that marginal revenue must be equated to marginal cost. Applied to the choice of capital input in light of the given assumptions, this leads to the parallel result that the firm must equate the *rental* rate R to the value of marginal product of *capital*, that is, $R = VMP_K = P \cdot MP_K$. Notice this condition must hold simultaneously with that for the profit-maximizing labor choice.

Another way of answering this question is to break the economic logic into two distinct steps. First, for any given output, a profit-maximizing firm will choose the combination of capital and labor inputs that minimizes its cost of producing that quantity. Second, given its cost-minimizing input choices, the firm will then choose the output level that maximizes profit.

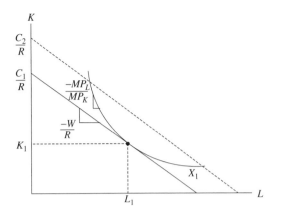

Figure 2.10(b) Cost-minimizing input choice for given output X_1.

To see how the first step is determined, examine figure 2.10. Panel (a) of this figure introduces a new concept called the *isocost curve*. This curve represents the locus of input combinations that achieve a certain cost level, given the market-determined input prices; in other words, it represents the set of (L, K) bundles for which $W \cdot L + R \cdot K = \overline{C}$, for some fixed cost level $\overline{C}$. Solving this expression for K as a function of L and the constants yields a straight line with slope $-W/R$, as indicated in the graph.

The associated input cost-minimization condition is illustrated in panel (b) of figure 2.10. For given output level X_1, the associated cost-minimizing input combination (L_1, K_1) attains the lowest isocost curve consistent with being on the X_1 isoquant. In the absence of a corner solution, this implies in turn a point of tangency between the isoquant of choice and the lowest attainable isocost curve. Since the absolute value of the isocost curve's slope is always the input price ratio $\dfrac{W}{R}$, this tangency condition is equivalent to the requirement that $\dfrac{W}{R} = \dfrac{MP_L}{MP_K}$; in words, the rate at which the firm is *compelled* by input prices to trade off inputs L and K is equated to the rate at which the firm is just willing to trade them off.

Thus, in the long run, a profit-maximizing firm will always respond to a wage change by adjusting all of its inputs so as to minimize the cost of output, which of course it can't do in the short run. That is, in the long run the firm responds to a wage change not only by adjusting output, but also by substituting away from the inputs made relatively more expensive by the wage change. This *substitution effect* accounts for the difference between the firm's short- and long-run labor demand curves.

To demonstrate this, once again begin with the scenario in which the firm maximizes profits given an initial array of input prices, as shown in figure 2.11. These figures replicate the setting examined in figure 2.8, with two significant

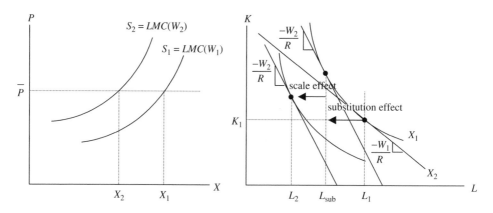

Figure 2.11 Long-run scale and substitution effects of a wage increase.

differences: first, the preferred level of labor input L_1 is depicted explicitly in panel (b) as resulting from the firm's cost-minimizing response to the rental rate R and initial wage rate W_1. Second, the firm's long-run marginal cost/output supply curve in panel (a) is represented as being more elastic than its short-run counterpart.

Put aside the latter difference for a moment and focus on the implications of cost-minimizing behavior in the long run. Suppose as before that the market wage rate increases to W_2. Even if the firm didn't change its output from X_1, it would want to adjust its inputs to minimize costs in response to the new input price ratio. This adjustment is shown occurring along isoquant X_1 in panel (b), as the firm moves from the initial tangency condition to a new point corresponding to the isocost curve with the steeper slope $-\dfrac{W_2}{R}$.

Note that as a result the firm reduces its desired labor input for producing X_1 from L_1 to L_{sub}. This is the *substitution effect* of the wage change, which can only occur in the long run. Expressing the substitution effect as a ratio of the change in labor demanded to the change in the wage rate that occasioned it, written $\left.\dfrac{\Delta L_d}{\Delta W}\right|_{\bar{X}}$, one sees that the substitution effect is negative: an increase in the wage rate leads to a decline in labor demanded, other things equal. Put more generally, the substitution effect is *non-positive*, since it may also be zero under certain conditions.

Furthermore, just as in the short run, the firm will wish to adjust its output in response to a wage change. The qualitative logic for this is the same as before: an increase in the wage rate leads to an increase in the firm's marginal cost curve, which corresponds to a downward shift in its supply curve, leading in turn to a lower output at the going output price. However, the degree of the supply

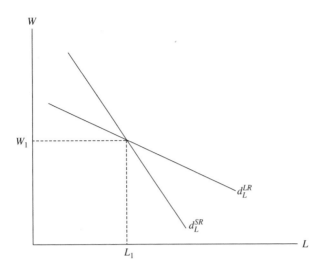

Figure 2.12 The firm's long-run labor demand is more elastic than its short-run counterpart.

response is typically stronger, and this is where the second difference between short-run and long-run labor demand mentioned above comes into play.

The firm's *long-run* marginal cost curve and therefore its long-run output supply curve are more elastic than their short-run counterparts. This is because of the firm's increased flexibility in adjusting its inputs, which implies in the typical case that the firm's costs increase more slowly with output. But as you can see from figure 2.11(a), a given upward shift in a flatter marginal cost curve leads to a bigger *leftward* shift in the supply curve, and therefore a bigger reduction in desired output. This implies that the *scale effect* $\dfrac{\Delta L_D}{\Delta W}\bigg|_{\left(\frac{\overline{W}}{R}\right)}$, shown in figure 2.11(b) as the movement from L_s on isoquant X_1 to L_2 on isoquant X_2, is typically larger than in the short run, other things equal.

The total effect of a given wage change on a firm's quantity of labor demanded in the long run is just the sum of the substitution and scale effects. But since these effects work in the same direction, and the scale effect is at least as large in the long run as in the less flexible time horizon, it follows that the firm's long-run labor demand curve d_L^{lr} is generally *more elastic* than its short-run counterpart, as shown in figure 2.12.

The comparative static predictions with respect to the long-run demand curve are qualitatively the same as in the short run, with increases in output price and improvements in technology leading to corresponding increases in the long-run demand for labor. But now there is an additional consideration: since capital inputs are no longer fixed, changes in the rental rate of capital can also be expected to affect the firm's profit-maximizing choice of labor.

The new comparative static prediction is that an increase in the rental rate shifts the firm's long-run demand curve leftward so long as labor and capital are complements in production, such that an increase in the use of one input increases the marginal productivity of the other. By an argument parallel to that given above in establishing the demand curve for labor, an increase in the rental rate leads to a reduction in the firm's quantity demanded of capital. But since capital and labor are complementary inputs, this reduction shifts down the VMP_L curve, and thus other things equal leads to a lower desired level of labor.

Aggregate short-run and long-run demand curves for labor

Insofar as economics is a social science, its primary interest is in the behavior of groups of people, rather than of individuals. Therefore the analytical trail must eventually lead from individual demand curves to labor demand curves defined for some aggregate of prospective buyers of labor. For macroeconomic analysis, this aggregate may be all employers in a given economy. In labor economic analysis at the micro level, however, the relevant aggregates are given *markets* for labor, where markets may be defined by worker characteristics or geographic location. In that case, the task is thus to derive short- or long-run *market* demand curves.

Defining labor demand curves at this level of aggregation introduces a new complication. While the assumption of competitive behavior in product markets dictates that *individual* firms take output prices as given, it is not necessary or even plausible to suppose that output market prices will stay fixed when the costs of all firms in the market increase. As illustrated above in figures 2.8 and 2.11, varying the wage rate also shifts each firm's marginal cost curve, and thus the market supply curve in affected output markets. Therefore, while a first approximation to the actual labor demand curve can be made by assuming output prices constant, the full representation must take into account the effect of wage changes on output prices.

Consider first the simpler derivation of short-run demand. Recall that at least one factor of production is fixed in this decision horizon, implying that firms are not free to move into new lines of production requiring different types of labor. Therefore the number of firms in a given labor market is fixed in the short run, although some or all firms may choose, given market conditions, to shut down and thus hire no labor at all.

Since the number of firms is effectively fixed in the short run, a first approximation of the aggregate demand curve in a given labor market can be made simply by adding the labor demand curves of the firms operating in that market. This procedure is illustrated in figure 2.13 for the simple case of a market with just two firms. Note that the addition is *horizontal*, that is, individual quantities demanded of labor are added together at each wage rate, resulting in the short-run market demand curve denoted D_L^{sr}.

As indicated in the figure, individual demand curves need not look alike, even if the technology of producing a particular good is shared by all firms in that

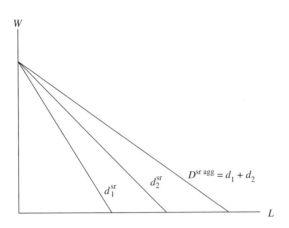

Figure 2.13 Derivation of short-run market labor demand: First approximation.

product market. This is because firms operating in the same *labor* market need not be in the same *product* market. For example, custodians are hired by both telephone companies and retail motorcycle shops, and market conditions for telephones and motorcycles are very different.

Assuming that all firms producing in a given output market also hire labor in the same labor market, however, it must be that changes in the wage rate affect the marginal cost and thus the output supply curves of each firm. Consequently, a change in the wage rate will generally have an impact on output price, to an extent determined by the *price elasticity of demand* in the affected output markets. The more price-elastic is output demand in absolute value, the more elastic is labor demand. If output demand were *perfectly* price-elastic, then output price could not change, and the first approximation derived above would give an exact representation of wage elasticity of market labor demand. In the opposite polar case of perfectly inelastic output demand, however, labor demand would also be perfectly inelastic.

What about the derivation of the long-run market demand curve for labor? It might be tempting to argue by analogy to the short-run case that, at least in the first approximation, the long-run market curve is derived by horizontally summing the corresponding long-run demand curves for firms operating in a given labor market. However, this doesn't work, because in the long run the number of firms in the market is not necessarily fixed. If entry and exit are possible, firms will enter the market if it is profitable to do so, and firms will eventually exit if losses are incurred.

Consequently, the long-run market demand curve must be defined and derived in a different manner. To see how, suppose that in fact the long-run market demand were determined in the same manner as its short-run counterpart. Then the first approximation of the long-run curve would be equal to the summation of long-run demand curves for the firms currently in the labor market, as

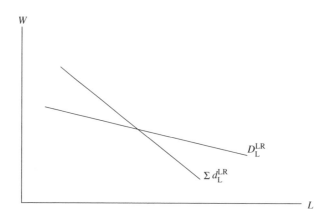

Figure 2.14   The long-run market demand curve is more elastic than the horizontal summation of individual demand curves for firms currently in the market.

represented in figure 2.14. Suppose further that the going market wage rate is W_1, corresponding to an initial quantity demanded of L_1.

Then what happens if the wage rate falls, say to W_2? For the firms currently in the market, this implies a movement along the initial demand curve, leading to an increase in quantity demanded to $\hat{L}_2$, as shown. But as discussed above, this fall in wages also reduces the cost of production relative to the output price. If this makes it profitable for more firms to enter their respective product markets, it will lead to more firms entering the labor market, and a rightward shift in the horizontal summation of labor demand curves for firms currently in the market. As a result, there will be a larger total increase in quantity demanded, to L_2, corresponding to the wage change.

This argument can be run in reverse for the case of a wage increase. The higher wage raises production costs, creating economic losses for some firms, which then exit the labor market and thereby cause the horizontal summation of individual demand curves to shift left, resulting in a greater fall in quantity demanded than is indicated by the movement along the original curve. Putting these two results together suggests the general conclusion that the long-run market demand curve will be in general more elastic than the horizontal summation of long-run labor demand curves for firms currently in the labor market, as indicated by curve D_L^{lr}.

But again, a completely accurate determination of long-run labor demand at the *market* level must take into account the impact of varying wages on product price in the affected output markets. This impact can be stated most succinctly for the special case that all firms in the labor market produce in the same output market characterized by constant returns to scale production. In this case, the long-run wage elasticity of labor demand for the market can be expressed as $E_{LW}^{L-R} = \Omega \cdot E_{XP} - (1 - \Omega) \Sigma_{LK}$, where E_{XP} denotes the price elasticity of output demand, $\Omega = W \cdot L / P \cdot X$ represents the ratio of labor cost to firms' total revenues, and Σ_{LK} represents the elasticity of substitution between capital and labor, defined earlier.

This equation therefore gives precise expression for the previously stated conclusion, that the long-run impact of wage changes on labor demand divides into a scale effect (the magnitude of which is given by $\Omega \cdot E_{XP}$) and a substitution effect (indicated by $-(1 - \Omega) \Sigma_{LK}$).

In summary, the elasticity of short-run demand depends solely on the scale effect, which is directly related to the absolute value of output demand elasticity if the impact of wages on output price is admitted. A somewhat different logic underlies the long-run market demand curve. Assuming entry and exit are possible, its derivation is driven by the double condition that firms substitute labor for capital and enter or leave the labor market depending on the changing opportunities for profitable production created by variations in the wage rate. The net result is that the long-run market demand curve is more elastic than the curve given by the horizontal summation of long-run demand curves of firms currently in the market. In at least one scenario, long-run wage elasticity can be understood as the weighted average of scale and substitution effects of a wage change.

EXTENSIONS OF THE BASIC MODEL OF LABOR DEMAND

This section considers the theoretical implications of relaxing two of the simplifying assumptions used in building the basic model of labor demand. The first extension examined here has to do with the implications for firm demand of variations in labor effort or skill. The second addresses the somewhat more complex matter of imperfect substitutability between number of workers hired and hours performed per worker hired.

Variations in skill and work effort

The derivation of labor demand curves discussed earlier in the chapter was based on the assumption that each labor hour was of a given quality. But as a practical matter this need not be the case. On one hand, workers in a given firm may undergo training in job-relevant skills, making them more productive for each hour they work. On the other, firms may require their incumbent workers to expend greater effort, or else induce greater productive efforts through the use of incentive devices of the sort discussed in chapter 10. What are the consequences of allowing for these variations?

In either case, the result is to increase the productivity (average, marginal and total) associated with *each* hour of labor performed. For example, a skilled worker may commit fewer mistakes performing a complex task, resulting in more defect-free products per hour of work. Thus, other things equal, the labor demand of a wage-taking, profit-maximizing firm would *increase* (that is, shift to the right) in response to either an increase in work effort or the skill that workers bring to their tasks. Figure 2.15 illustrates this effect for the short-run horizon, but the result holds for both short-run and long-run demand curves.

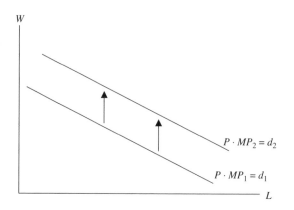

Figure 2.15 The impact of increased effort or skill on the firm's labor demand.

Since labor hours performed with more skill or intensity are more productive, why wouldn't firms *always* favor workers offering greater quantities of these goods, when given the choice? Other things equal, of course, they would. But as discussed in the previous chapter, it is precisely the case that "other things" won't be equal, so long as job-relevant skills are costly for workers to acquire, or work effort is personally costly for them to perform.

Finally, it should be emphasized that the foregoing construction of labor demand curves was premised on the notion that levels of skill, innate ability or effort are *given*. If for some reason this is not the case, for instance because firms cannot observe effort in order to specify desired levels, then the firm and market demand functions may behave differently – for example, variations in the wage rate may cause shifts in demand as well as movements along given curves. This point will be explored more fully beginning in chapter 4.

Imperfect substitutability of workers and hours per worker

The basic model of labor demand is built on the premise that number of workers and hours per worker are perfect substitutes in the firm's profit function. One way of looking at the economic logic of this condition is in terms of the firm's goal of minimizing the cost of acquiring a certain total quantity of labor input L, defined as the product of hours per worker H times number of workers hired N. As in the standard cost minimization analysis, the optimal input combination will involve a relationship between isoquants and isocost curves.

In this case the isoquants in question represent quantities of total labor input L generated by alternative combinations of workers N and hours per worker H, given that $L = NH$. By what should now be familiar analytical steps, the slope of

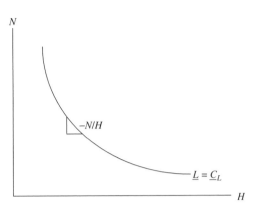

Figure 2.16   Perfect substitutability of worker numbers (N) with hours per worker (H).

a given L-isoquant can be shown to equal $-\dfrac{N}{H}$, resulting in isoquants that are convex to the origin, as illustrated in figure 2.16.

In the cases analyzed so far, the cost to the firm of a given quantity of labor L is simply $C_L = WL = WNH$. The slope of any given labor isocost curve $\underline{C}_L$ is therefore equal to negative the ratio of the marginal cost of labor hours, given a certain number of workers hired, to the marginal cost of workers, given a certain number of hours per worker, or $-\dfrac{WN}{WH}$, which simplifies to $-N/H$, the same slope as the isoquant. In other words, isocost and isoquant curves perfectly overlap under these conditions. Consequently, as noted earlier in the chapter, firms are in this case indifferent as to which mix of workers and hours per worker is used to generate a given quantity of labor.

But suppose instead that workers and hours per worker are *not* perfect substitutes in production. Beyond some quantity of total hours worked this is *necessarily* the case, of course, since any one worker can supply at most twenty-four hours in a given day. But suppose that substitutability is limited even short of this extreme. One possibility is that effective labor input is not linear in one or the other of its two components. For example, suppose that total labor input is instead equal to number of workers N times some *function* $A(H)$ of hours, where the function A exhibits first increasing and then decreasing returns to hours H. This specification suggests that there are initial "startup costs" in gearing up for work (including, perhaps, time spent in getting that first cup of coffee, settling down at one's desk, and turning on the computer), and that workers eventually get progressively less productive later in the work day.

The chief consequence of this modification, as shown in figure 2.17, is that *labor* isoquant and isocost curves no longer overlap, implying that profit-

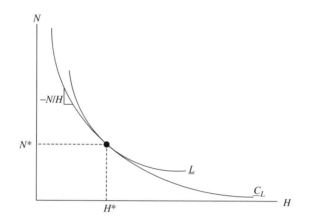

Figure 2.17   Imperfect substitutability of N and H.

maximizing firms are not indifferent among various combinations of workers and
hours per worker yielding a given effective labor input. In fact, since neither the
slope of the isocost curve nor the slope of the isoquant depends on the wage rate,
it follows that under these conditions a firm would desire a particular quantity
of hours per worker that is independent of the wage rate. Furthermore, this
quantity of hours is the same for any level of the L-isoquant, so it is also unaffected by the firm's choice of output.

   A corollary of this outcome is that firms under such circumstances would not
be content to let employees choose their utility-maximizing work hours at going
wage rates, since except by accident this choice will be at odds with the firm's
preferences. Instead of taking individual labor supply choices as well as the wage
rate as given, as predicted by the basic model of labor demand, firms in this
context will want to dictate the hours worked by each of its employees. But since
the workday lengths are generally no longer than those that are freely chosen by
the employees, firms will typically have to pay workers more to compensate them
for the extra hours performed beyond their desired levels. Therefore, denote the
wages paid to any given employee by the strictly increasing function $W(H)$. This
construction is used in the next scenario.

   An alternative, and empirically significant, basis for imperfect substitutability
of workers and hours per worker in the profit function is the presence of *quasi-
fixed labor costs*, that is, costs that vary with the number of workers hired rather
than the number of hours worked. These may include search, hiring and training
costs, both direct and implicit, as well as expenses of equipping employees with
needed equipment and personal spaces (clothes lockers, for example). In this case
total labor costs are given by the expression $(C_N + W(H)) \cdot N$, where C_N is the level
of quasi-fixed labor cost and $W(H)$ is the function defined above.

   How does the presence of quasi-fixed labor costs affect the firm's labor choices?
To determine this we return to the firm's cost minimization problem, allowing for

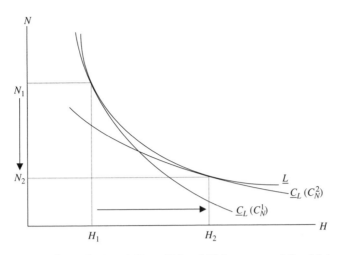

Figure 2.18   Imperfect substitutability of N and H due to quasi-fixed labor costs C_N.

the presence of quasi-fixed labor costs but assuming as before that workers and hours per worker are perfect substitutes in production, so that $L = NH$. As before, the slope of the isoquant at each point is just equal to $-N/H$. In the presence of the quasi-fixed cost, however, the isocost curve is once again not identical to the labor isoquant, as shown in figure 2.18. Thus, in this scenario as in the previous one, the firm will not be indifferent concerning the mix of number of workers and hours per worker.

The key difference from the previous scenario lies in the role of quasi-fixed costs. Since increasing quasi-fixed cost C_N raises the marginal cost of hiring an additional worker, but not the marginal cost of having each worker supply more hours, it must render each isocost curve *flatter*, leading to a cost-minimizing adjustment in which the firm increases hours per worker and reduces the number of workers required to produce a given level of L, as shown in figure 2.18.

EMPLOYEE BENEFITS AS A PERCENTAGE OF TOTAL COMPENSATION

Employee *benefits*, or non-pecuniary forms of compensation, are a potential form of quasi-fixed labor costs. In the US, employee benefits, including employer-sponsored health insurance, retirement plan contributions, and paid leave, among many other categories, accounted for about 28% of total employee compensation (US Department of Labor, 2002). Of these benefits, about 8% were legally required benefits; the rest were employer-optional.

continued

By definition, employee benefits constitute quasi-fixed costs only to the extent that they vary with the number of workers rather than hours worked per employee, implying that benefit costs per hour are higher for part-time than for full-time employees. For example, the quasi-fixity of benefit costs is mitigated if employers provide benefits only to full-time workers, as is often the case in US labor markets. Examining data on benefits provided by US firms, Michael Lettau and Thomas Buchmueller (1999) concluded that only health insurance benefits constitute a true quasi-fixed cost to employers.

Consistently with this assessment, a study of child-care workers found that as the level of fringe benefits, especially health and dental insurance, paid by a particular child care center rose (holding wages and other establishment characteristics constant), the number of hours of work by part-time workers fell significantly (Montgomery and Cosgrove, 1993). This result is also in line with the argument put forth in the text regarding the effect of quasi-fixed costs on labor demand.

Related discussion questions:
1. Why would employee benefits be rising as a percentage of total compensation over time?
2. Quasi-fixed labor costs can also affect labor supply decisions. For example, commuting costs generally vary with number of days worked rather than with hours per day. Can you think of other examples of quasi-fixed costs that might affect a person's decision as to whether or not to work, and how to organize their worktime (e.g., preferring to work fewer days for more hours)?

Related references:
Michael K. Lettau and Thomas C. Buchmueller, "Comparing Benefit Costs for Full- and Part-Time Workers," *Monthly Labor Review* 122, no. 3 (March 1999): 30–5.
Mark Montgomery and James Cosgrove, "The Effect of Employee Benefits on the Demand for Part-Time Workers," *Industrial and Labor Relations Review* 47, no. 1 (October 1993): 87–98
US Department of Labor, *Employee Costs for Employment Compensation*, December 11, 2002 (updated quarterly).

CONCLUSION

This chapter has derived a theory of labor demand for wage-taking, profit-maximizing firms. Three central themes emerge from this exploration. First, since the demand for any given type of labor is a *derived* demand, generated by the desire of firms to produce for profit, it will necessarily be related to the market demand for goods produced by firms hiring that form of labor. Thus, the higher is output price, other things equal, the higher the demand for labor, and the wage elasticity of labor demand similarly increases with the price elasticity of output demand.

Second, in the long run it is possible to substitute labor for other inputs and vice versa. Consequently, the long-run wage elasticity of demand is influenced by the ease with which firms can make these substitutions, as measured by the elasticity of substitution. If hourly wages are the only source of labor costs and there are constant returns to scale, the wage elasticity of long-run market demand for labor is determined by a weighted average of the price elasticity of output demand and the elasticity of substitution of capital for labor.

Third, these results are premised on the notion that workers and hours per worker are perfect substitutes in the production process. If this is not the case, then the firm will typically wish to dictate the hours worked by each employee, with the general result that changing the wage rate will also alter the firm's allocation of total hours among workers.

Study Questions

1. Suppose that a firm owner supplies labor to the firm but does not pay herself a wage or salary. Why should her wage nonetheless be counted in the firm's cost, and what measure of the cost of her labor should be used?

2. Illustrate the respective cases in which (a) the substitution effect of a wage increase on labor hired is zero and (b) the scale effect of a wage increase on labor hired is zero.

3. By analogy with household indifference curves, a short-run *isoprofit* curve for a firm can be defined as the set of all combinations of wage rate and labor hired that yield a positive profit, so that for the short-run profit function $\Pi = P \cdot f(L, \overline{K}) - W \cdot L - R \cdot \overline{K}$ (where $P \cdot f(L, \overline{K})$ represents the total value product of labor for fixed capital level $\overline{K}$, and (P, W, R) are respectively the output price, wage rate, and capital rental rate, taken as given by the firm) and fixed profit level $\overline{\Pi}$, the slope of a given short-run isoprofit curve is easily shown to equal $\dfrac{dW}{dL}\Big|_{\overline{\Pi}} = \dfrac{VMP_L - W}{L}$.

   Given this result, show how the firm's isoprofit map is positioned with respect to its short-run labor demand curve.

4. Given the formula for wage elasticity of labor demand discussed in the chapter, demonstrate the following results:
   a) Wage elasticity varies continuously as one moves up a negatively sloped straight-line demand curve, from a value of 0 at the horizontal intercept toward a value of negative infinity as one approaches the vertical intercept.
   b) The wage elasticity of demand is always equal one in absolute value at the midpoint of a negatively sloped straight-line demand curve.

continued

    c)   A parallel rightward shift in demand results in lower wage elasticity of demand measured at a given wage rate.

    d)   The flatter of two demand curves drawn through a single point is more wage-elastic at that point.

5.   For a job you have had, try to list all the capital equipment that you utilized in order to perform that job. Were any of the pieces of equipment substitutable for any of the others?

6.   Draw the VMP_L and VAP_L curves for the case of a *fixed coefficient* technology, and indicate the corresponding short-run demand curve for labor.

Suggestions for Further Reading

Daniel S. Hamermesh, *Labor Demand* (Princeton, NJ: Princeton University, 1993).

David Donaldson and B. Curtis Eaton, "Person-Specific Costs of Production: Hours of Work, Rates of Pay, Labor Contracts," *Canadian Journal of Economics* 17, no. 3 (August 1984): 441–9.

CHAPTER THREE

PERFECTLY COMPETITIVE LABOR MARKETS

Labor supply and demand functions, and the assumptions enabling their derivation, are elements of a broader theoretical vision of market function that goes back at least to the writings of Adam Smith and continues to inform research in labor economics. The purpose of this chapter is to offer a careful examination of a theory that implements this vision, the economic model of *perfectly competitive* labor markets: its core assumptions, hypotheses, and implications for the appropriate roles of markets and government in the allocation of labor services.

In order to provide the first step toward a critical understanding of the competitive model of labor market outcomes, the overview begins with some definitions and a basic statement of the theory's core assumptions. The model is then applied to the respective contexts of a single labor market and multiple interconnected markets to illustrate its capacity for yielding testable hypotheses and evaluation criteria for given market outcomes. The chapter closes by considering what is involved in empirical testing of hypotheses generated by the theory.

BASIC DEFINITIONS AND ASSUMPTIONS OF THE COMPETITIVE MODEL

As mentioned in the introductory chapter, labor market outcomes can be analyzed in *positive* or *normative* terms. *Positive* claims have to do with statements of fact, and consequently an important purpose of positive theory is to generate hypotheses about economic phenomena that can be assessed for relevance or likelihood by reference to empirical data. An example of such a positive claim is the assertion that workers with more years of formal schooling earn higher wage rates on average.

In contrast, the essential purpose of *normative* analysis is to *evaluate* alternative economic outcomes. The validity of normative claims about economic outcomes cannot be determined by appeals to any given set of facts, but instead must be premised on some value system. To continue with the schooling example, it might additionally be claimed that paying higher wages to workers with more formal schooling is justified on the basis of norms of merit or efficiency.

The positive theory of perfectly competitive labor markets is built on five primary assumptions. These assumptions are interrelated, but none can be wholly derived from the others. Three of the assumptions concern the behavior of labor market participants and have already been encountered, directly or indirectly, in the preceding two chapters. They provided a basis for deriving labor supply and demand functions. The two remaining positive assumptions have to do with the scope and fluidity of labor market processes and are used to translate the specification of demand and supply functions into potentially observable market outcomes.

The behavioral assumptions of the competitive model concern the economic goals of labor market actors, their capacity for pursuing these goals, and the basis on which they make decisions with respect to their interests. To review briefly, the first assumption asserts that the economic ends of these actors can be summarized by objective functions defined on the basis of market prices and quantities exchanged. For firms, as buyers of labor services, the relevant objective function is profit defined in terms of inputs and input prices, while for each labor-supplying individual, preferences for tangible goods and leisure are represented by a utility function constrained by a budget frontier.

A corollary of this assumption is that the model of perfectly competitive labor markets offers a theory concerning the determination of the *quantitative* terms of exchange, that is, what magnitudes of given types of labor are traded and at what wage rates. To put the point another way, representing market outcomes on the basis of the competitive model is tantamount to presuming that all matters of economic interest in market transactions are summarized by these quantitative terms of exchange. For example, perfectly competitive market theory could not be used to account for, or evaluate, the allocation of decision-making powers regarding production or the relative use of different compensation schemes such as piece rates or bonuses.

The second of the core behavioral assumptions asserts that labor market participants act as if to maximize their respective objective functions based on a rational calculation of available opportunities. This is not to say that people are necessarily certain as to the precise consequence of their decisions, although the model has not been yet been complicated by elements of risk or uncertainty in labor market outcomes. Rather, it says that if uncertainty exists, individuals are fully aware of the risks they face, and make rationally optimizing decisions in light of such risks.

According to the third core assumption of the competitive model, all market participants are understood to take the market wage rate as *given* when they choose their respective quantities to trade, rather than as a magnitude that they can or wish to influence. This implies in turn that no one enjoys a significant share of the trade in a given labor market, such that their marginal decisions about exchange quantities influence the going price. Perhaps less obviously, this assumption also dictates that the quality of the goods being exchanged (e.g., the revenue productivity of labor hours or the level of workplace amenities) can be determined independently of the wage rate. If this weren't true, individual actors might wish to alter the going wage rate so as to increase the gains realized from a given labor market transaction.

As demonstrated in the preceding chapters, these three assumptions make it possible to summarize the behavior of buyers and sellers in the labor market by demand and supply functions, respectively. These functions are represented in turn by market demand and supply curves for labor, as illustrated in figures 3.1(a) through 3.1(c). The demand curve is drawn in figure 3.1(a) to reflect the "law of demand," understood as the hypothesis that quantity demanded is decreasing (or, to put it in the most general terms, not increasing) in the wage rate: the higher the going wage rate, the less labor that purchasers are willing and able to buy.

In parallel fashion, the labor supply curve in figure 3.1(b) reflects the "law of supply," understood as the hypothesis that quantity supplied is increasing (or, more generally, not decreasing) in the wage rate. Note with respect to both graphs that, contrary to the standard practice in mathematics but traditional in economics, the independent variable (wage rate) is placed on the vertical axis and the dependent variable (quantity of labor) on the horizontal.

Of itself, the specification of supply and demand functions for a given labor market does not suffice to yield predictions about the wage rate and quantities exchanged occurring in that market. Such predictions are possible only if it is known how supply and demand curves interact to determine an *equilibrium* position for the labor market. This issue is addressed by the two remaining positive assumptions of the perfectly competitive model.

First consider figure 3.1(c), where the labor supply and demand curves have been superimposed within a single diagram. What might it mean to assert that a market represented by these curves is in "equilibrium"? Virtually any veteran of introductory economics would presume that market equilibrium is achieved at the wage rate for which demand and supply intersect, that is, at which quantities demanded and supplied are equated (wage rate W_E in figure 3.1(c), corresponding to a quantity exchanged of L_E). But what is the economic sense underlying this presumption?

To answer this question, it is useful to distinguish *weak* and *strong* notions of equilibrium. A *weak*, that is, minimum requirement for equilibrium is that, given the wage rate, the intentions of all market participants are realized. This clearly occurs in figure 3.1(c) at W_E, in the sense that quantities demanded and supplied are equated at this wage rate: both buyers and sellers are exchanging the

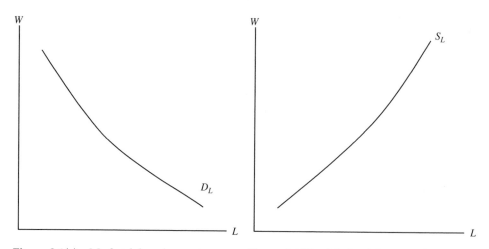

Figure 3.1(a)   Market labor demand curve.   **Figure 3.1(b)**   Market labor supply curve.

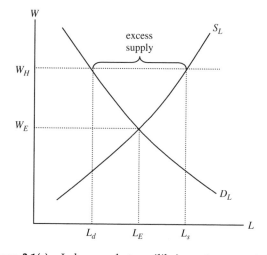

Figure 3.1(c)   Labor market equilibrium at wage rate W_E.

quantities they desire, contingent on the wage level. The wage rate in this event is said to "clear the market."

But economists often intend something stronger by the assertion that a given price corresponds to a market equilibrium position. Applied to labor markets, this *strong* notion of equilibrium asserts in addition that the wage rate will tend to adjust toward the market-clearing level if it hasn't yet been attained; i.e., that somehow the "forces" of supply and demand will drive the wage rate to the market-clearing level. This notion, posited as the fourth positive assumption of the perfectly competitive model, is thus sometimes referred to as *flexible-price* (or, in the context of labor markets, *flexible-wage*) equilibrium.

In figure 3.1(c), wage rate W_H fails to clear the labor market: at that wage rate, quantity supplied strictly exceeds quantity demanded, creating a situation of excess supply. (This also corresponds to the economic condition known as *involuntary unemployment*, for reasons discussed in more detail in the final section of the text. But see the related study question at the end of this chapter.) Under the scenario of flexible-wage equilibrium, it is assumed that the wage rate will therefore automatically adjust downward to W_E.

The analysis to follow is premised on this stronger notion of equilibrium, albeit with the caution that its economic logic demands further investigation. Note, for instance, the seeming inconsistency between the notion that the wage rate automatically adjusts toward its market-clearing level and the prior assumption that all market participants are wage-takers: if everyone takes the going wage as given, who is it that adjusts the wage rate when it fails to clear the market? To resolve the seeming inconsistency, it will be necessary to take a closer look at the economic sense of the premise that buyers and sellers take the wage rate as given. This task is pursued in the next chapter.

Potentially testable hypotheses about the determination of labor market outcomes can be generated by combining the equilibrium condition with the theories of market demand and supply behavior constructed in the previous chapters. Taken together, these elements make it possible to predict how differences in non-wage explanatory variables might influence observed wage or quantity levels. This can be done in two ways.

The most basic method studies changes in equilibrium within a single labor market. Specifically, a change in some non-wage variable affecting either demand or supply is introduced in the model, and then it is determined how the corresponding market equilibrium responds to the shift. This is known as *comparative static* analysis, since it involves the comparison of distinct static equilibria within the market, ignoring the dynamic path involved in moving from the old equilibrium to the new.

The nature and degree of market responses to given disturbances depends in part on the ability of prospective traders to enter or leave the market under study. This capacity bears in particular on the specification of *long-run* demand and supply. The fifth core assumption of the perfectly competitive model asserts that there exists *free* entry into, or exit from, the market. This assumption of *free entry and exit* implies, among other things, that firms earn zero economic profit in the market's long-run equilibrium.

Entry and exit conditions are also relevant in the second approach for yielding predictions on the basis of the competitive model. In this latter approach, testable hypotheses are derived by comparing equilibria between markets for distinct but related types of labor. That is, suppose that the labor supplied in two markets is distinguished by a single factor, such as the amount of training received by labor sellers. Then without assuming that any non-wage explanatory variable actually changes, it is possible to make predictions about the market effects of differences in any such variable *across* the two labor markets.

Testable predictions flow from assessing the impact of experiencing different levels of the non-wage variable in question in the two markets. If qualified market participants encounter no obstacles specific to moving among markets, then any persistent differences in market outcomes must derive in turn from differences in non-wage variables that distinguish the quality of labor offered in the two markets. This approach to yielding testable hypotheses is known as *compensating differential* analysis.

Besides yielding predictions about market outcomes, the perfectly competitive model is also used to evaluate alternative market outcomes, for example those resulting from the effects of government policies. Labor market outcomes might be evaluated on a number of alternative normative grounds, but in the context of the competitive market model this evaluation is generally based on some measure of the economic well-being of individuals affected by those outcomes. This normative approach is called *welfare analysis*.

The first normative assumption underlying welfare analysis, then, is that market outcomes are evaluated on the basis of an appropriate aggregate measure of the welfare of labor market participants (itself represented by individual profit and utility functions). As will be discussed below, this *hedonic* assumption is implemented by calculating measures of *consumer* and *producer surplus* corresponding to given market outcomes.

In order for these surplus measures to be understood as giving a precise indication of the net *social* benefit deriving from given labor market outcomes, a final assumption is needed. The above understanding only holds if the benefit to buyers from consuming each additional unit represents in addition the full *social* benefit of such consumption, with the parallel stipulation that prices along the supply curve reflect the *full* cost to sellers of offering successive units of labor for exchange. That is, there can be no costs or benefits that are not reflected in the demand and supply curves, and are thus "external" to the buyers and sellers exchanging these services. It cannot be, for example, that anyone but the buyers of labor services benefits from having those services provided without paying for them. Label this final assumption the *no-externality* condition.

In sum, five positive assumptions support the use of the perfectly competitive model to generate testable hypotheses about labor market outcomes, and two additional assumptions are required in order for the theory to provide assessments of these outcomes on the basis of welfare analysis. Are the positive assumptions undergirding the perfectly competitive model realistic? In terms of pure description of labor market realities, surely not: firms or workers often enjoy bargaining power in the determination of wages, it is generally costly to enter or leave particular markets, wage adjustments may be somewhat "sticky" rather than perfectly flexible, and so on. The operational question, though, is whether these distinctions make a qualitative difference with respect to the determination and assessment of labor market outcomes. And to address this question, it is necessary to understand what the competitive model has to say on these matters.

EQUILIBRIUM IN A SINGLE LABOR MARKET

This section reviews how positive and normative claims are derived on the basis of studying equilibrium outcomes in a single perfectly competitive labor market. In this context, positive analysis is based on the comparative static method for generating testable hypotheses about market outcomes, while normative assessments are constructed in terms of the preferences of market participants. These procedures are illustrated by considering the effects of certain government policies vis-à-vis labor markets.

Comparative static analysis of labor market outcomes

As this is the aspect of competitive market analysis that is probably most familiar to students of economics, its recap here will be relatively brief. Two issues arise in comparative static analysis, concerning, respectively, the *direction* of changes in equilibrium wages and quantities of labor hired in response to either demand or supply shifts or government interventions in the labor market, and the *magnitude* of those changes. The latter are reflected in the wage elasticity of labor demand or supply.

First, examine the qualitative effects of a shift in the labor demand curve. The analysis of the previous chapter identified a number of independent variables that might affect the position of the demand curve in a particular labor market, including firms' output price, the level of capital stock, or the level of worker effort or skill, if the quantity of labor demanded is measured in terms of number of workers or total hours. Suppose for the sake of illustration, then, that all workers in this market complete a training program, resulting in their increased marginal productivity and a consequent increase in demand for their services. This is depicted in figure 3.2a. Given that the supply curve is upward-sloping, as shown, the result of an increase in labor demand is an increase in the market wage rate and an increase in the equilibrium quantity of labor hired.

This argument can also be run in reverse. If for some reason demand were to decline – say, because firms' output price declined – then both the equilibrium wage and quantity of labor hired would decrease, assuming once again that the market supply curve obeyed the law of supply. (The first of the end-of-chapter questions asks you to explore the implications of abandoning this assumption.)

Alternatively, suppose that the market supply of labor were to increase relative to a given demand curve that embodies the law of demand. In light of the theory of labor supply developed in chapter 1, this might occur for a number of reasons, including an increase in the number of workers trained to provide a certain type of labor or a general decrease in household non-labor income (assuming leisure is normal). This scenario is illustrated in figure 3.2(b), with an increase in the supply curve from S_1 to S_2. As shown, the consequence is an increase in the equilibrium quantity of labor hired, but a *reduction* in the equilibrium wage rate, as

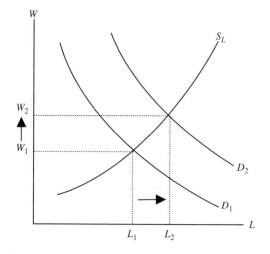

Figure 3.2(a)   Comparative static effects of an increase in labor demand.

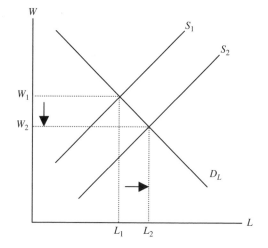

Figure 3.2(b)   Comparative static effects of an increase in labor supply.

labor has become relatively more plentiful. The consequences of a decline in supply can be gleaned from the graph by simply switching the labels of the two supply curves.

It is also possible in this framework to yield predictions about the effects of given *combinations* of shifts in supply and demand. However, when both the supply and demand curves shift, it will typically be the case that the change in

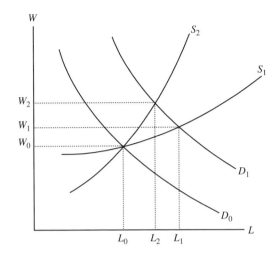

Figure 3.3 The impact of a given shift in demand varies with the elasticity of labor supply.

one equilibrium magnitude is ambiguous, because the supply and demand changes have offsetting effects. In that case one would need information about the relative magnitudes of the respective curve shifts in order to eliminate the ambiguity.

For example, suppose that the result of a new training program is to increase both the demand for labor (because workers are now more productive) and the supply (because there are now more workers with improved skills). It is evident that the result must be an increase in the equilibrium quantity of labor hired, since both the demand and the supply shifts would contribute to that result. However, it is impossible to determine, without further information, what is the net impact of these shifts on the equilibrium wage rate.

In some cases, it is useful to determine not only the *direction* of changes in market outcomes driven by curve shifts or policy interventions, but also the relative *magnitude* of such changes. For example, to continue the earlier example, an effective training program would increase the productivity, and consequently the wages, of a given set of workers in a market. How much wages increase for a given shift in market demand will depend on the elasticity of labor supply. This assessment is illustrated in figure 3.3, which shows two labor supply curves going through an initial equilibrium point, the flatter one being more elastic. As shown, the more elastic supply curve, labeled S_1 in the graph, supports a smaller equilibrium wage increase.

Knowledge of labor supply and demand elasticities is of particular importance in the assessment of government policies affecting labor market outcomes, since in general the impact of such policies will depend on the magnitude of these elasticities. For example, the effectiveness of reducing marginal tax rates in inducing individuals to work more will depend on the wage elasticity of labor supply. In principle, at least, empirical studies based on the competitive model can be used to inform the selection of appropriate policies. This leads to the question of what constitutes an "appropriate" policy.

Welfare analysis of labor market outcomes

As mentioned earlier, labor market outcomes can be analyzed in *normative* as well as *positive* terms. The point of the former type of analysis is to rank alternative outcomes according to some desired goal. The premise of economic welfare analysis is that the relevant goal is to achieve the maximum possible aggregate well-being associated with the operation of labor markets. In the context of a single market, "social welfare" is measured by the sum of *producer* and *consumer surplus* accrued in equilibrium.

These measures can be defined as corresponding to designated areas in the supply and demand graph. Thus, *consumer surplus*, which is meant to represent the net gain to buyers from participating in the labor market, is defined as the net area between the market demand curve and the market wage rate, up to the quantity of labor exchanged. This corresponds to the area marked CS in figure 3.4.

Similarly, *producer surplus* in a given labor market, meant to be understood as the net benefit enjoyed by sellers in this market, corresponds to the net area between the market supply curve and the market wage rate, up to the quantity of labor exchanged. This is illustrated by the area marked PS in figure 3.4. Note that in the context of labor markets, the "producers" are individual labor suppliers, while the "consumers" are typically firms. Given these constructions, the

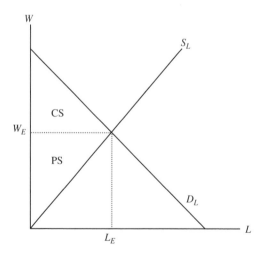

Figure 3.4 Consumer and producer surplus associated with competitive labor market equilibrium.

"social welfare" delivered by a given labor market outcome is then understood as the sum of consumer and producer surplus.

An immediate implication of surplus analysis is that social welfare is *maximized* at the competitive market equilibrium, so long as externalities do not exist. To see this, examine figure 3.5. Given the no-externality assumption, the social welfare flowing from the competitive equilibrium point (L_1, W_1) corresponds to the large triangle equal to the sum of areas marked CS_1 and PS_1.

But now consider an alternative, non-equilibrium point such as (L_2, W_2), which is characterized by excess demand since the wage rate is below its market-clearing level. The sum of the corresponding areas CS_2 and PS_2 falls short of the original measure of social welfare by the area marked DWL, representing the "dead-weight loss" in social welfare as a result of not being at the competitive labor market equilibrium. Furthermore, any other departure from the competitive equilibrium quantity would yield a similar decline in social welfare as measured by the sum of producer and consumer surplus.

This is the simplest possible demonstration of the reasoning that leads many economists and policy analysts to believe that "markets work" and should thus be left free of government intervention. By this reasoning, government policies can alter market outcomes, and change the *distribution* of economic benefits flowing from exchange as a consequence, but can't help but reduce the size of the total surplus to be distributed.

Is this a valid assessment? Given the assumptions of the model, yes, although with one additional caveat: these stringent conditions must also obtain for every other market in the economy, not simply the single labor market under study, in order to ensure the general conclusion that social welfare is maximized when the sum of producer and consumer surplus are maximized in a given market. The

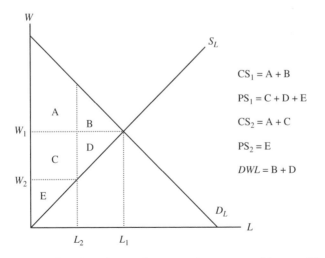

Figure 3.5 Welfare loss due to departure from competitive equilibrium.

reason for this is that global social optimality requires that the effects of non-competitive conditions in any one market must be countered by offsetting adjustments in other markets, in much the same way that optimizing households must respond to changes in market conditions by adjusting their market behavior. If conditions of the competitive model aren't realized for all markets, then *total* social welfare is not necessarily maximized at the competitive equilibrium, and there is no general rule for what departure from that point will achieve social optimality.

Effects of government policies

In addition to gauging the effects of given changes in demand and supply, competitive analysis can be used to assess both the positive and normative effects of given government interventions in the labor market. Examples of such interventions are wage controls (that is, wage floors and wage ceilings and regulations with respect to wage increases), quantity controls such as quotas with respect to the minimum number of workers hired, taxes on labor income or on payrolls, and employment subsidies.

Consider first the predicted impact of imposing an effective wage floor – that is, one that strictly exceeds the going wage rate – on a competitive labor market in equilibrium. This is, for example, the intended effect of "minimum wage" or "living wage" laws, though it is not necessarily the case that the legislated minimums remain above wage levels the market would attain in the absence of such a policy. The scenario of an effective wage floor is depicted in figure 3.6.

As shown, the predicted effect of raising the wage rate from its equilibrium value W_E to $\underline{W}$ is to reduce employment from L_E to $\underline{L}$. The reason for this is that

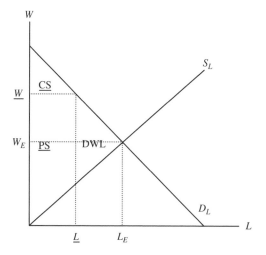

Figure 3.6 Impact of an effective wage floor in a perfectly competitive labor market.

buyers can't be forced to hire labor they don't want, and the effect of raising the wage rate is to reduce their willingness to hire. Consequently the quantity exchanged under the wage floor is determined only by the demand curve. Thus, assuming that the market demand curve is downward-sloping and that labor quantities are measured in number of workers hired (rather than, say, hours per worker), the effect of imposing a minimum wage on worker incomes is dichotomous – workers who remain employed enjoy higher labor incomes, while those who are disemployed receive no labor income.

In addition, the imposition of an effective wage floor in an otherwise perfectly competitive labor market reduces social welfare. Compared to the competitive equilibrium benchmark, consumer surplus declines by more than producer surplus increases, and so total social welfare represented by the sum of these measures declines by the area designated by DWL.

The magnitude of the disemployment effect of the wage floor – and that of the corresponding loss in social welfare – is directly related to the wage elasticity of demand. To take two polar cases, an effective wage floor would cause the entire market to shut down if market demand were perfectly elastic (i.e., horizontal), while there would be no disemployment – or welfare loss – if market demand were vertical (perfectly inelastic).

DO "LIVING WAGE" LAWS IMPROVE THE WELFARE OF WORKERS?

Living wage laws generally specify that covered employers pay a wage at which a full-time worker could be self-supporting, generally a level significantly above current market wage levels. Living wage laws have caught the attention of labor economists, several of whom have examined data on wages and employment for potentially covered workers in a number of urban areas and come up with varying conclusions regarding the laws' effects. Neumark (2002) found results consistent with the competitive labor market model, namely that wages increase for covered workers while employment opportunities for all workers in the target markets decrease. Notably, he found relatively large numbers of people to be affected positively by these ordinances, and relatively substantial wage increases, holding out some promise that living wage laws could lift some families out of poverty. Hence policymakers deciding whether such policies are desirable must weigh the tradeoff of higher earnings for some low-wage workers against reduced employment opportunities for similar potential workers. Another group of economists, using the same data, take issue with his assessment of the laws' negative effects, making this an active area of debate within the profession (Brenner *et al.*, 2002).

continued

While both authors cited here used national data and compared areas with living wage ordinances to areas without such ordinances to assess the effects of these policies, another approach is to do a case study of a particular area (usually a city) to compare labor market results before and after the ordinance comes into effect. The first such study was done for Baltimore in 1996, and numerous other studies have followed for other areas (see the Internet web site of the Living Wage Resource Center for a list of studies and links to many of them). Many of these studies find relatively limited effects on wages and employment, and evidence of widespread noncompliance with these ordinances.

Related discussion questions:
1. How do high noncompliance rates relate to findings of limited effects?
2. How do local living wage ordinances potentially differ from a national rise in the minimum wage?

Related references:

Mark D. Brenner, Jeannette Wicks-Lim, and Robert Pollin, "Measuring the Impact of Living Wage Laws: A Critical Appraisal of David Neumark's *How Living Wage Laws Affect Low-Wage Workers and Low-Income Families*," University of Massachusetts–Amherst Economics Department Working Paper No. 43 (2002).

David Neumark, *How Living Wage Laws Affect Low-Wage Workers and Low-Income Families*, Public Policy Institute of California Report No. 156 (2002).

Living Wage Resource Center: http://www.livingwagecampaign.org/impact.php.

Second, examine the case of employment quotas. For the sake of specificity, imagine that an effective minimum quota on labor hired, L_Q, is imposed on buyers in a given labor market. As shown in figure 3.7, the consequence of this required increase in the number of workers hired is to raise the wage rate received by all workers; imposing a quota is thus equivalent in effect to rendering the market demand curve vertical at L_Q, and thus affecting equilibrium wages in a manner equivalent to an outward shift in market demand.

Determining the welfare consequences of a quota is a somewhat more complex task than for the case of a wage floor. To see the basis of this calculation, recall that consumer surplus is defined as the *net* area between the wage rate and the (original) market demand curve, up to the actual quantity exchanged (in this case, L_Q). It should be clear enough that producer surplus goes up due to the quota, since the wage rate increases, but that consumer surplus declines by more than this amount due to the *negative* magnitude (i.e., negative distance between the demand curve and the market wage) corresponding to the areas marked A, B, and C in the graph. Net social welfare therefore declines by the area marked A, correspond to the dead-weight loss created by the quota.

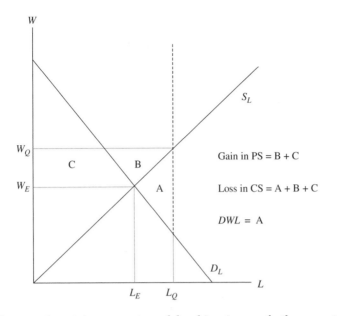

Figure 3.7 Impact of a minimum quota on labor hires in a perfectly competitive market.

The perfectly competitive model, then, offers one interpretation of Adam Smith's famous claim that the self-serving actions of individuals are made to serve the social interest through the "invisible hand" of market forces. If one accepts social welfare as measured by consumer and producer surplus as the appropriate representation of "the social interest," then endorsement of a "laissez-faire" or non-interventionist policy with respect to labor markets follows. This normative conclusion may not be supported, of course, if all of the conditions of the perfectly competitive model are not met, or if some goal other than maximizing the sum of producer and consumer surplus is emphasized.

EQUILIBRIUM ACROSS LABOR MARKETS

Equilibrium wage differentials

In many cases, workers and employers can choose among alternative labor markets, distinguished by particular qualities of the job being performed or the labor being provided. For example, firms may choose to employ workers with greater or less skill in the exercise of particular tasks, or workers may choose to work in settings with more or less non-wage amenities. In such cases, competitive market theory might be used to predict how equilibrium wage differentials arise across such markets.

To see how this might be done, initially imagine that markets for labor are distinguished on the basis of some visible characteristic – call it Z – that is possessed by all labor suppliers in the second of the two markets. Imagine further that this characteristic can be acquired by any supplier who wants it, although possibly at some cost. One may ask whether this distinction bears implications for the equilibria achieved in the two markets.

The key to answering this question lies with the *free entry and exit* condition discussed earlier. That is, assume that both buyers and sellers can move freely from one market to the other, providing only that sellers entering the second market have, or acquire, characteristic Z. This assumption entails, at minimum, that market participants are fully aware of the alternative market opportunities and requirements; incur no costs in simply moving from one market to the other, independently of the cost (if any) of acquiring characteristic Z; and are not hindered in entering or leaving a market through the exercise of government or monopoly power. A corollary of the latter is that anyone who wishes can acquire characteristic Z, and at the same cost, if there is any.

Given the entry and exit condition, when would it be the case that equilibrium wage rates differ across the two markets? As a point of reference, consider the case in which neither demand nor supply is a function of Z; that is, the acquisition of Z does not cause the supply of labor to shift, and the demand for a market full of workers with characteristic Z is no different than the demand for workers without this characteristic. Given the theories of labor supply and demand considered in the foregoing chapters, this is tantamount to saying that acquisition of Z neither adds to the opportunity cost of individuals supplying Z nor contributes to the profitability of prospective employers.

If that is the case, then the presence or absence of Z makes no economic difference, and thus the equilibrium wage rate should be the same in both markets. If this were not the case, then it would be in the interest of sellers in the low-wage market and buyers in the high-wage market to move, which by assumption they can do without incurring any losses. The resulting shifts in supply and demand in the two markets would continue until the wage rate were equalized.

Now suppose instead that, although the presence of Z conveys no incremental benefit to buyers, it is costly for labor sellers to acquire. Given that some sellers bear this characteristic initially, would this be a basis for an equilibrium wage differential between the two markets? The answer is no. Since the presence of characteristic Z offers no incremental benefits to buyers, they would be unwilling to pay a higher wage rate to labor suppliers with this characteristic, even though bearers of Z previously incurred some cost in acquiring it. Labor suppliers with Z may thus wish they could command a wage bonus for this characteristic, but competition would preclude them from doing so. Alternatively, if no supplier had yet acquired Z, no one would have any incentive to do so, and thus only non-Z labor suppliers would exist in equilibrium.

Conversely, suppose that the presence of Z increased the benefit to buyers of consuming incremental labor services, but was costless for sellers to acquire. Would an equilibrium wage differential arise in this case? Again, no: in this sce-

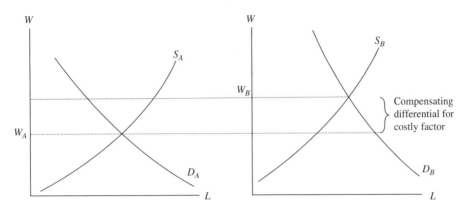

Figure 3.8   A compensating wage differential between competitive labor markets.

nario, sellers would strictly prefer workers with characteristic Z, but since it is costless to acquire, all workers would therefore choose to possess the characteristic, and thus any basis for paying an equilibrium wage differential would disappear.

Thus, in order for an equilibrium wage differential to arise, it must be the case that the presence of characteristic Z *simultaneously* shifts the labor supply curve down and the labor demand curve up. Given the economic logic of labor supply and demand functions, this is equivalent to saying that it is *both* costly for sellers to acquire Z, and beneficial to buyers to hire workers with that characteristic. Furthermore, given the assumption of free entry and exit, the magnitude of the differential can *only* be attributed to the cost to sellers of acquiring the characteristic. This is the logic behind referring to the difference in equilibrium wage rates in the two markets as a *compensating differential* – the higher equilibrium wage in the second market just offsets the cost to the marginal worker of acquiring the desirable characteristic. This outcome is illustrated in figure 3.8.

According to human capital theory, optional variations in formal schooling among individual workers establish a basis for compensating wage differentials. The fundamental tenet of the theory is that schooling contributes to workers' productivity by imparting job-relevant skills. Extra schooling is also generally costly either in pecuniary terms or indirectly in terms of the opportunity costs of time spent in acquiring additional education. Thus, in the context of perfectly competitive labor markets, human capital theory predicts that wages increase with formal schooling levels.

Note that an exactly parallel story to the above could have been told if Z were interpreted as an acquirable characteristic of jobs offered by labor *buyers*, such as a workplace safety device. In that case, assuming that the device were costly for buyers to attain and that workers valued safety, then one would predict that the equilibrium wage rate will be lower in the market in which the safety device is employed; buyers would thus be "compensated," in the form of a lower wage rate, for the cost of acquiring the device.

Not all wage differentials arising under competitive equilibrium represent compensations for the acquisition of desirable but costly characteristics, however. An alternative basis for equilibrium differentials arises when some factor affecting the gains to be had from labor exchange is *absolutely* scarce, meaning that its supply can't be varied at the margin simply by incurring the relevant costs of producing it. Obvious examples of absolutely scarce factors are exceptional talents and unreproducible workplace amenities, such as those associated with specific and very well-favored geographic locations (Hawaii, say).

In such cases, wage differentials corresponding to these factors (wage premiums in the case of special talents, wage deductions in the case of unreproducible amenities) will clearly not correspond to the marginal cost of supplying them, but rather to their degrees of scarcity relative to existing demand. In keeping with the foregoing logic, however, one might represent such cases as ones in which the marginal cost of supplying the good in question becomes *infinite*.

Government policies and market wage differentials

Government interventions in the operation of otherwise perfectly competitive labor markets may also affect wage differentials across markets, either modifying existing differentials or else creating a differential where none existed. As an example of the former, suppose that the government offered workers a subsidy for the acquisition of characteristic Z in the foregoing scenario of compensation differentials. The effect of this subsidy would be to reduce the net cost to workers of acquiring Z, and thus would entice more workers to acquire the characteristic and gain the higher wage in the second market. This shifts the supply curve in the second market to the right until the wage differential just equals the new, lower net cost of acquiring Z.

Alternatively, government policies might create a wage differential where none would otherwise exist by establishing effective barriers to movement across markets, compromising free entry and exit and thus inhibiting any long-run tendencies toward wage equalization that might otherwise occur. Consider, for example, the scenario depicted in figure 3.9. In the initial market equilibrium without government intervention, it is supposed that the same wage rate, W_E, is attained in both markets; thus, there might not initially be any effective difference in the labor supplied in them. But now suppose that the government imposes an effective wage floor $\underline{W}$ on employers in market A. This creates a disparity between the wage floor in market A and the lower wage rate W_E initially still offered in market B.

But the wage differentiation caused by the government intervention may not end there. Noting that the wage floor in market A creates a situation of excess supply, it may be the case that some of the disappointed labor sellers from market

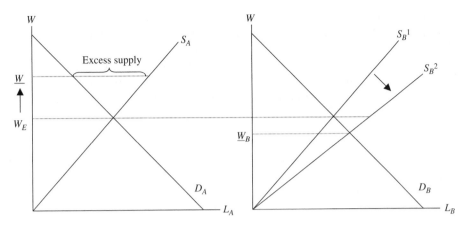

Figure 3.9 Spillover effects of an effective wage floor in market A.

A seek employment in market B, shifting the supply curve in that market to the right and thus driving the wage rate down to $\underline{W}_B$. The latter outcome is termed a *spillover effect* on market B wages of the policy intervention in market A, resulting in an even larger equilibrium wage differential across the two markets.

In both of these scenarios, the resulting outcome is inefficient (that is, results in lower social welfare) so long as perfectly competitive conditions obtain in all affected markets. In the first case, government policy creates inefficiency by rendering the cost of acquiring Z artificially low, leading to a greater supply of this characteristic than would be justified by an efficient tradeoff of its true costs and benefits. In the latter case, the effective minimum wage creates inefficiencies by obstructing wage adjustment toward a market-clearing equilibrium.

DO LABOR MARKETS OBEY THE LAWS OF SUPPLY AND DEMAND?

That is, are labor market outcomes successfully accounted for by the predictions of the competitive model? This is a big question; in one sense, it is the task of this entire text to provide grounds for a comprehensive answer to it. A first step toward this goal is taken here by exploring how labor economists attempt to address the question.

Briefly put, there are four steps involved in assessing the empirical relevance of a given theory: deriving a prediction about potentially observable market phenomena from the model; augmenting the predicted relationship by an assumed structure of random variation; collecting data relevant to the hypothesis; and evaluating the "fit" of the data to the hypothesis, given the assumptions about the behavior of the random element. These steps are most easily illustrated in terms of compensating differential analysis, since this approach yields very sharp predictions about the determination of a specific dependent variable, the wage rate paid in given markets or to specific groups of individuals.

Generally speaking, there are five variables that meet the dual requirement of affecting the determination of both the relevant labor demand and the labor supply functions. These variables reflect the levels of job-related education and training received (in other words, acquired abilities); work experience (a source of acquired job-relevant ability that is not instantaneously reproducible), innate ability, work effort, and workplace disamenities. As defined, increases in each of these variables would be expected to increase the relevant wage rate, other things equal.

Consequently, the theory of wage determination in perfectly competitive labor markets could be summarized by a function relating these independent variables to the wage rate:

$$W = F(Ed, Exp, Ab, Ef, Dis),$$

where the arguments of the function respectively denote magnitudes of education and training, experience, innate ability, labor effort, and workplace disamenities, each of which is assumed to have a positive impact on the wage level.

Recall, however, that this relationship is postulated on the assumption that all other factors are equal – the famous, and ubiquitous, *ceteris paribus* assumption in economic theory. Of course, all other factors are never equal in actual economies, and in economics as in other social sciences it is difficult to emulate the natural sciences in designing experiments to eliminate variations in factors not under immediate study. (Difficult but not impossible, as witnessed by the growing subfield of experimental economics, in which the choices and strategies of selected test subjects – usually college students – are studied in the context of carefully designed economic settings.)

If there are other factors that *systematically* affect the wage level, then in principle these should be incorporated in the theoretical model, and failure to do so will tend to produce inaccurate assessments of the impact of included independent variables. Putting aside the possibility of other systematic influences on the wage rate, there may still be a myriad of unidentifiable and idiosyncratic individual variations that cancel out when averaged over a large enough target group. The standard approach is to accommodate such real-world complexities by assuming that the functional relationship under study is *stochastic* rather than *deterministic*, meaning that observed wage levels in the economy are understood to be influenced by both the theoretically generated variables (education, ability, and so on) and a *random* variable whose incidence is governed by some probability distribution.

Correspondingly, the set of assumptions underlying the theoretical model is then augmented with assumptions about the structure of the probability distribution for the *error term*, that is, the random component of the model to be subjected to empirical test.

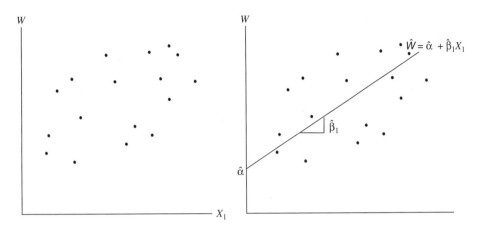

Figure 3.10(a) Scatter diagram for given labor market data.

Figure 3.10(b) Estimated regression line for scatter diagram.

Given the augmented set of assumptions, the hypothesized relationship between wage levels and the five explanatory variables might be written

$$W = F(Ed^+, Exp^+, Ab^+, Ef^+, Dis^+, \varepsilon),$$

indicating that the wage rate W is some theoretically determined function of the five independent variables, as well as the random component ε. The superscripts on the theoretically determined variables are meant to indicate the hypothesized impact of changes in each on the wage level, holding constant the value of the other arguments.

After deriving the theoretical relationship and augmenting it with an assumed error structure, labor economists must then gather data linking labor incomes, educational attainments, ability, experience and effort levels, and the incidence of workplace disamenities. In principle, the specificity of such data should be appropriate to the hypothesis under study. For example, the theory reviewed in this chapter concerns market aggregates, so that the relevant data would concern average wage rates and, say, average levels of training and safety in specified labor markets.

Once the statistical model has been specified and the data collected, the empirical applicability of the hypothesized functional relationship is then assessed. Given that the wage relationship is stochastic, the fit between data and prediction is in general a matter of degree, so that one must make a judgment as to whether the empirical connection is strong enough to be accepted as consistent with the theory. For example, data on the relationship between educational attainment and the wage rate can typically be represented in the form of a *scatter diagram* such as that shown in figure 3.10(a), which is derived on the basis that the value of other independent variables is held constant.

Note that while there seems to be a general upward trend in the empirical relationship between levels of education and W exhibited in figure 3.10(a), consistent with the initial hypothesis, this relationship does not hold universally: sometimes low values of education are associated with relatively high values of W and vice versa. Consequently the empirical analyst has two tasks: first, to identify a deterministic functional relationship that best "summarizes" the apparently stochastic relationship presented by the data, and second, to determine if this summary relationship is strong enough to be accepted as legitimate evidence in favor of the relationship predicted by the theory. The statistical methodology used by economists to address these tasks is called *econometrics*.

More specifically, the econometric method generally employed by empirical economists in addressing these two tasks is a statistical technique known as *multiple regression analysis*. The technique has two main components. First, the relationship between dependent and independent variables suggested by the straight line that minimizes, in a certain sense, the sum of divergences of the data points from the line. An example of this is shown in figure 3.10(b), where the estimated linear relationship is shown with positive intercept $\hat{\alpha}$ and positive slope $\hat{\beta}_r$.

The next step in this statistical procedure is to determine, based on one's assumptions about the probability distribution for the random variable, the likelihood that the estimated slope is sufficiently different from zero to warrant the conclusion that the empirical results are consistent with the hypothesized relationship. If this is found to be so, the estimated relationship is said to be *statistically significant*. Note that statistical significance should not be taken to imply that the relationship thus estimated is quantitatively important; for example, the estimated relationship could be statistically significant even if each percentage increase in the independent variable yields only one-hundredth of a percentage point increase in the dependent variable.

Note further that finding a statistically significant empirical relationship consistent with the hypothesized one cannot be interpreted as "proving" the truth of the hypothesis or the economic theory that generated it. Conversely, the inability to establish that the hypothesized relationship is statistically significant does not necessarily mean that the theory is false. Broadly speaking, there are four distinct bases for this indeterminacy:

1) *The nature of the statistical test*   Given the presence of a random element in the determination of market outcomes, there is always the possibility that a given empirical test will give a false reading on the true state of affairs. This can happen in either of two ways. First, there is some probability, given the random element in the wage relationship, that an empirical outcome consistent with the hypothesized deterministic relationship will fail to obtain, even though it is true (e.g., in terms of the example, the test finds no statistically significant relationship between values of X_1 and wage levels, even though the model is correct). This is known as an instance of *Type I error*.

Conversely, *Type II error* refers to the symmetrically false outcome of finding statistical grounds for a hypothesized relationship that is false. Furthermore, the probabilities of committing the respective errors are inversely related, so that in adjusting the test to reduce the chance of committing one error, the empirical analyst increases the risk of committing the other. Assuming a correct imputation of the probability structure of the error term, it is possible to compute the probabilities of Type I and Type II errors, and thus to choose in advance the most acceptable combinations of error risks.

2)   *The quality of available data*   Ideally, the data collected to test given economic theories would be readily available, precise, and perfectly representative of the variables featured in the economic theory under study. However, as a practical matter this is rarely the case. There may be random measurement errors in the collection of the data, or more seriously for the validity of the econometric test, there may be systematic biases in the way in which the data were collected. Alternatively, data may simply not exist for some of the variables central to the theoretical model. This is a real danger in labor economics, since for example certain aspects of labor such as work effort or worker ability are by their nature very difficult to observe directly. In such cases, methods must be devised to accommodate data limitations. These have proved such a standard problem for empirical analysis in labor economics that this field has been an important source of innovations in methods of addressing that problem.

3)   *Assumptions concerning the structure of random errors*   As noted earlier, the undertaking of any econometric investigation requires that a number of assumptions be made about the probability distribution of random factors influencing economic outcomes. Of course, nothing guarantees that the assumed conditions obtain in practice. If these conditions are violated, a finding of statistical significance may be reached in error, or else the estimated relationship between a given independent variable and the wage rate may be biased upward or downward. Econometricians have developed statistical tests to determine the robustness of these assumptions, and corresponding techniques for addressing violations of these assumptions, but of course the tests are not infallible, and accommodating observed violations typically diminishes the power of the resulting econometric tests.

4)   *Assumptions underlying the economic model*   Finally, there is always the possibility that the theoretical model does not essentially reflect economic reality. Most simply, this may imply that the true functional relationship between dependent and independent variables is different from the predicted one. The more serious danger is that the economic logic generating labor market outcomes is fundamentally different from that posited by the assumptions of the theoretical model.

Of course, it is precisely the purpose of the econometric testing procedure reviewed above to confront this possibility. An interesting difficulty arises, however, in the event that the functional relationship generated by a given theory is also consistent with another theory altogether, in which case one might assert with at least equal justification that the empirical results support the alternative account. Indeed, this scenario has become the case with increasing frequency as the set of coherent theoretical perspectives available to labor economists has expanded.

In such situations the competing theories are said to be *observationally equivalent* with respect to given economic relationships. For example, certain of the predictions of competitive market theory may hold even if labor markets prove not to satisfy all of the conditions required for this theory to be manifested in practice. What is to be done in this case? In order to distinguish the competing theories, it would be necessary to identify auxiliary hypotheses, dealing with relationships other than those for which the theories are observationally equivalent, that obtain under one theory but not the other. The need for undertaking this further analysis would not be evident, however, unless the possibility of outcomes outside of the realm of one's given theory were acknowledged. Thus the most rigorous test of the perfectly competitive model requires development of alternative hypotheses based on given departures from the competitive ideal.

What does all of this have to do with the conformity of labor market outcomes to the laws of supply and demand? Each of the hypothesized influences on observed wages rates will be discussed in much greater detail in part IV of the text. However, to speak very broadly, some of the empirical relationships hypothesized by the perfectly competitive model – in particular, the relationship between formal schooling and wages – have been strongly and consistently borne out by the data. Other hypotheses, such as that concerning the wage impact of workplace disamenities, have enjoyed less consistent empirical support. In addition, empirical labor market analysis has identified regularities that are at best difficult to explain in terms of the logic of the competitive model.

How should this mixed record of empirical success be interpreted? It should be clear from the foregoing discussion that there is room for legitimate disagreement on this issue. On the one hand, it is logically defensible to presume that the competitive model is essentially valid, and thus to ascribe any anomalous empirical results to limitations in the data or ongoing uncertainty about the behavior of the random component in an otherwise valid theoretical model. On the other, it is also legitimate to argue that the anomalies uncovered raise fundamental questions about the applicability of the competitive model, questions that demand serious investigation of alternative theories of market behavior.

It should also be clear from the preceding discussion that no single econometric test can coherently be understood as "proving" or "disproving" a given economic theory. It is more appropriate to assess an economic theory in terms of its capacity for supporting a fruitful *program* of empirical research. A theory may be judged successful to the extent it proves capable of generating interesting and relevant hypotheses about social phenomena that are found more often than not to be consistent with available data.

Finally, it can perhaps be appreciated in this context why it is important to understand the assumptions undergirding a given economic theory such as the competitive model of labor market outcomes. Considering possible departures from these assumptions gives rise to alternative hypotheses that can be used to test the robustness of a theory's predictions, or to point the way to the construction of a more successful alternative.

CONCLUSION

The model of perfectly competitive labor markets has provided a foundation for a broad-based and still quite vigorous program of empirical research in labor economics. In particular, the competitive market framework has provided the primary analytical platform for the "human capital" paradigm, which emphasizes the role of education and other sources of investment in labor productivity in determining levels and rates of growth in wages. Grounds for the continued vibrancy of this analytical framework seem assured, if for no other reason than that it is difficult to imagine that supply and demand considerations are categorically irrelevant to a wide range of labor market phenomena. However, there may be compelling reasons to consider augmenting the theory on the basis of economic considerations that fall outside the reach of the competitive model. Some motivations for this assessment are introduced beginning in the next chapter.

Study Questions

1. Suppose that the supply curve in a particular labor market is "backward-bending" above a certain wage rate. Why would this be the case? How do the comparative static predictions of the competitive model change if market demand intersects supply in its backward-bending region?

2. If labor and capital stock are perfect complements in production for all firms in a given labor market, the short-run demand curve is horizontal at some positive wage rate up to a limit set by the fixed capital stock of firms, and zero thereafter, creating a discontinuity in the market demand at the upper limit of labor demanded. Suppose the market supply curve runs through this discontinuity. What are the equilibrium wage and quantity exchanged in this case? What are the magnitudes of consumer and producer surplus? What would be the effect on all of these measures of a slight upward shift in supply?

3. Suppose that the going wage rate in a labor market exceeds the market-clearing level, creating excess supply. The assumption of flexible wage adjustment implies that the wage would therefore fall until the market-clearing level is reached. Is this consistent with the assumption that all participants in the labor market take wages as given?

4. British economist John Maynard Keynes defined *involuntary unemployment* as a scenario in which some workers are willing and able to work, but unable to find a job even at a wage rate *slightly below* the current

continued

level. Show that the scenario of excess supply described in the previous question satisfies this definition. What is the significance of the latter criterion? In particular, can you illustrate a scenario in which workers without jobs are willing and able to work at the going wage rate, but not at any lower wage rate? Why might this not count as involuntary unemployment?

5. In the context of labor markets, what exactly does "consumer surplus" measure? Does the meaning of this "surplus" differ in the short and long run? (Hint: think of the shutdown condition for profit-maximizing firms.)

6. If "producer surplus" is a valid measure of the net benefit accruing to workers from supplying labor in a particular market, it must represent the gain in utility enjoyed by suppliers from receiving the market wage rate rather than the lower "reservation" wage rate measured by the supply curve. Is this generally the case? (Hint: does the individual demand curve resulting from both income and substitution effects reflect, at each level of quantity supplied, the wage rate *just sufficient* to keep the worker's utility constant?)

7. The overarching normative criterion for welfare analysis is *Pareto-optimality*. An economic allocation is said to be *Pareto-optimal* (or *Pareto-efficient*) if it is impossible to reallocate goods so as to make someone better off without making at least one person worse off. Similarly, reallocations that make everyone better off are called *Pareto-superior*. Given these definitions, is it necessarily the case that any change in market outcomes that increases the sum of producer and consumer surplus is Pareto-superior?

8. Illustrate the impact of each of the following government policies with respect to the short-run equilibrium of a perfectly competitive labor market:
   a) An effective wage ceiling
   b) A per-unit subsidy to firms for each worker employed
   c) An increase in immigration quotas

Suggestions for Further Reading

Peter Kennedy, *A Guide to Econometrics*, 5th edn (Cambridge, MA: The MIT Press, 2003).

Andrew Schotter, *Microeconomics: A Modern Approach*, 3rd edn (Reading, MA: Addison-Wesley, 2001): chapters 13 and 15.

CHAPTER FOUR

IMPERFECTLY COMPETITIVE LABOR MARKETS

The previous chapter considered how markets for labor services would function under perfectly competitive exchange conditions. The "laws" of supply and demand hold sway in this world, yielding potentially testable hypotheses about market behavior as well as a generally negative assessment of the net benefits of government intervention in the process of labor exchange. The theory also has the benefit of comparative simplicity: although the optimization analyses underlying it are technically detailed, the supply and demand framework itself is relatively easy to apply and has straightforward positive and normative implications.

However, the theory's simplicity comes at a cost, in that it makes no allowance for significant social interactions in the process of labor exchange. In effect, the world of perfectly competitive labor markets is one in which all buyers and sellers are fully aware of all matters affecting their interests in given transactions; in which, despite encompassing all such matters, negotiations are always trivially simple and immediately concluded; and in which agreed-upon terms of exchange are faithfully implemented without exception. No one has the power to influence the equilibrium wage rate, there is never any basis for strikes or lockouts, incentive pay is unnecessary, and persistent unemployment is impossible in the absence of government intervention.

As demonstrated in this chapter, it is possible to address some of these phenomena while remaining consistent with the supply and demand framework. Ironically, this is accomplished by going from one behavioral extreme to another: instead of assuming that all labor market participants are wage-takers, the scenario of *imperfect competition* is addressed by allowing one side of the labor market *complete* power to select the going wage rate from the range of market possibilities. This scenario is studied in three

continued

possible manifestations: *monopsony, monopoly,* and *wage-dependent gains from trade.*

This approach to the scenario of imperfectly competitive labor markets is able to account for some of the phenomena alluded to above, as you'll see. But since it still does not articulate a comprehensive account of possible departures from ideal market conditions, or incorporate a theory of social interaction among prospective market participants, its analytical reach remains severely limited. In particular, there is no basis *internal to the theory* for determining in which of multiple alternative ways forms of imperfect competition might be manifested. Moreover, while the assumption that there is *no* competition on the wage-setting side of the market can be relaxed, this is only achieved at the cost of assuming that competitors do not act rationally, thus contradicting the basic premise of the underlying theoretical approach. Finally, the theory is unable to generate unambiguous hypotheses in the case of *bilateral monopoly,* in which both sides of the labor market enjoy wage-setting power.

Addressing these deficiencies will require a more thorough examination of possible departures from the perfectly competitive ideal and their implications for the scope of *strategic* behavior among market actors. This investigation is begun in the next part of the text. As a prelude to that investigation, and in order to motivate the subsequent approaches to imperfect competition, the chapter's analysis begins by examining the economic logic of two core assumptions of the competitive model, wage-taking behavior and flexible wage adjustment.

BEHIND THE WAGE ASSUMPTIONS OF THE COMPETITIVE MODEL

Wage-taking behavior

The problem of out-of-equilibrium wage adjustments is considered below. Therefore, consider the assumption of wage-taking behavior on the premise that the labor market is in equilibrium.

Even in equilibrium, why would presumably self-interested labor market actors take the wage rate as given, as required in the perfectly competitive model? It's not generally the case that labor buyers and sellers are physically or legally precluded from altering the going wage rate; given freedom of contract, any terms of trade mutually agreed upon by the exchanging parties are feasible. Moreover, every market actor would seem to have a potential interest in altering the wage rate: other things equal, profit-seeking firms would want to pay a lower price for labor inputs, and utility-maximizing households would benefit from higher pay for their work. At the least, one might therefore expect wage *haggling* rather than wage *taking* to be the behavioral norm. And indeed, formal or informal wage bargaining is a common feature of labor markets.

In terms of economic logic, then, the assumption of wage-taking behavior must assert something about the particular market conditions that buyers and sellers find themselves in, rather than their literal incapacity or indifference with respect to changing the wage rate. In effect, the assumption posits conditions of market competition that make it undesirable for any actor to attempt raising *or* lowering the going wage rate. In other words, at least when the market is in equilibrium, each trader is able to exchange as much as desired at the going wage rate, and is unable to exchange at all at any otherwise favorable alternative rate. Why might this be the case?

For the sake of illustration, consider this question in terms of the situation faced by a profit-maximizing firm seeking to hire workers in a given labor market. This firm would be strictly better off if it could hire workers at less than the going wage rate, but it would find itself unable to do so if there were other prospective employers who were offering essentially the same jobs at the going wage rate and were immediately available. In that case the workers would rationally refuse to work for the firm at anything less than the going wage rate. By the same reasoning, any worker in the firm's incumbent labor force could effectively refuse a wage cut.

Conversely, under what conditions would the firm have no interest in offering a wage *higher* than the going rate? Generally speaking, the firm must find itself able to buy as much labor as it wishes – and thus potentially more than it actually purchases in market equilibrium – and of equal quality, at the going wage rate. Think of this condition as the polar case of a situation in which the firm would find itself swamped with prospective employees of equal revenue productivity were it to raise its wage offer even incrementally above the going rate.

In sum, the assumption of wage-taking behavior translates into a set of market conditions such that the firm would lose all of its employees were it to lower its wage offer even slightly below the going rate, and would gain more employees of equal quality than it could profitably utilize if it even slightly raised its wage offer. Clearly, an exactly parallel interpretation can be given for the economic sense of the wage-taking assumption as applied to labor suppliers.

The required market conditions are twofold. The first is a generalization of the assumption of *free entry and exit* to movements *within* as well as *across* markets. Specifically, it must be the case that each market actor's potential trading partners can *immediately* and *costlessly* gain access to substitute partners. Second, these partners must be of equal quality, so that variations in the offered wage rate have no implications for the gains from exchange to be realized with prospective exchange partners. This is ensured in turn by a strict interpretation of the assumption that the *quality* of services being exchanged is independent of the wage rate.

A corollary of this conclusion is that violation of either of these latter assumptions raises the prospect of wage-setting power in the labor market. *Monopsony* power arises to the extent that potential competitors for a given labor buyer find their entry inhibited for whatever reason, while *monopoly* power arises to the extent that entry is difficult for prospective competitors with a given labor seller. Finally, even otherwise competitive buyers and sellers may have an incentive to alter the going wage rate if the total gains realizable from exchange are dependent on the level of the wage offer. These scenarios are explored in the remainder of the chapter.

Flexible wage adjustment

The considerations introduced above help to resolve a puzzle advanced early in the previous chapter: if all labor market participants take the wage rate as given, how does the wage rate adjust when it's not at its market-clearing level? The outlines of a coherent answer to this question can be seen when the wage-taking hypothesis is translated as the dual statement that market actors can trade as much as they wish at the going wage rate and lose all of their existing or prospective trading partners if they attempt to alter their wage offer in a nominally self-serving direction. Clearly, when the existing wage rate does not clear the market, then traders on one side of the market find to the contrary that they *cannot* exchange as much as they'd like at the going rate.

In that event, there is at least no *necessary* contradiction with the wage-taking assumption, appropriately understood. Since traders on the "long" side of the market at the non-market clearing wage can't exchange as much as they'd like, they have at least a potential incentive to alter the wage rate so as to attract more trading partners, and this incentive will persist so long as the wage rate is not at its competitive equilibrium level.

Whether or not this potential would be translated into practice by gain-seeking market participants depends, like the wage-taking assumption, on the condition that the total gains to be had from exchange are not influenced by the level of the wage rate. To see this, consider again the situation faced by a typical profit-seeking firm, this time in a market scenario of excess supply. Suppose, in this scenario, that unemployed workers offer their labor services to the firm at a wage rate below the going level. If for whatever reason (as yet unexplained) the lower wage rate is accompanied by a diminution in the revenue productivity of these workers, then the firm may rationally reject these offers even though they offer an immediate advantage in terms of reduced labor costs. Consequently, even though market actors are capable of altering the going wage rate, alternative wage offers are not accepted, and the wage could not then adjust toward its market-clearing level. Excess demand or supply would not only persist in this scenario, but would constitute a point of equilibrium, in the sense that no rational gain-seeking market actor is both willing and able to alter this condition.

The assumptions of wage-taking behavior and flexible wage adjustment are thus both now seen to rely in part on the postulate that the total gains from labor exchange are independent of the wage rate. The economic significance of this assumption, and the possible consequences of relaxing it, are considered later in the chapter.

MONOPSONY IN THE LABOR MARKET

Pure monopsony

Strictly speaking, monopsony is defined as a market setting in which there is only one buyer for a particular type or set of labor services offered by perfectly competitive sellers. More generally, it refers to situations of wage-setting market power resulting from limited competition among buyers. In all such cases, the expression of this power has potential implications for the distribution of available surplus, as well as for the efficiency of labor market outcomes, and thus the total magnitude of that surplus available for distribution.

First consider the case of pure monopsony power, in which there is only one buyer in an otherwise competitive labor market. As a point of departure, consider the situation depicted in figure 4.1. It shows a market supply curve for labor, S_L, and the aggregate value marginal product of labor (VMP_L) curve for all firms operating in the market. As discussed in the previous chapter, for given output prices this VMP_L function corresponds to the market demand curve if labor buyers are wage-takers, and the intersection of S_L and VMP_L thus determines the equilibrium wage rate W_c and quantity exchanged L_c in a perfectly competitive labor market. The magnitude and distribution of welfare gains in this equilibrium are indicated by the areas marked A (representing consumer surplus) and B (representing producer surplus).

But now suppose that the demand side of the market is represented by a single profit-maximizing firm with no outside threat of competition. To make the two scenarios directly comparable, imagine that somehow the many employers

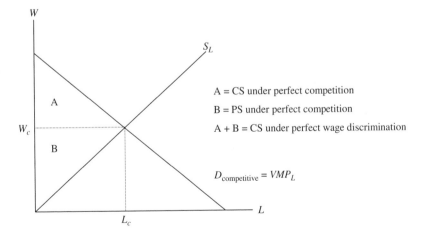

Figure 4.1 Employment and distribution under perfect competition and perfect wage discrimination.

participating in a competitive labor market, each operating a single factory, are taken over by a single firm which continues to operate all existing production facilities. How would this firm use the market power thus acquired?

If the existence of monopsony is understood as the *only* deviation from otherwise competitive exchange conditions, so that market participants are fully informed about all conditions affecting potential gains from trade, the monopsonist will wish to practice *wage discrimination*, defined as a situation in which wages vary independently of the revenue productivity of the units of labor hired. Indeed, absent any legal or other obstacle, profit maximization entails that the monopsonist will practice *perfect* or *first-degree* wage discrimination, that is, offer the lowest possible wage rate for *each incremental unit* of labor hired, as indicated by the market supply curve. This implies that the market supply curve corresponds exactly to the monopsonist's marginal cost of hiring labor.

But then by the first profit-maximization condition, the monopsonist chooses the employment level that equates its marginal cost with its VMP_L. Consequently, first-degree wage discrimination just leads to the competitive equilibrium level of labor hired, since it is at that point that the wage paid by the monopsonist to the marginal worker (indicated by the supply curve) is equal to the marginal revenue product of hiring labor (corresponding to the market demand curve under perfectly competitive conditions). The market outcome achieved by a perfectly wage-discriminating monopsonist is therefore economically efficient.

There are, however, two important and related ways in which the scenario of perfect monopsonistic wage discrimination deviates from the perfectly competitive outcome. First, and most evidently, different workers (or different hours of work by the same workers) are paid different wage rates, with some being paid much lower than the competitive equilibrium wage rate. Second, and concomitantly, the perfectly wage-discriminating employer appropriates *all* of the welfare gains from this market – that is, it gets a net benefit equal to the *sum* of producer and consumer surplus that would obtain under perfect competition.

It is unlikely that an instance of *perfectly* wage-discriminating monopsony has ever arisen. Clearly, the informational requirements alone for exercising such power are extreme. To accomplish this outcome, a monopsonist would have to know the exact shape of the market supply curve and, more to the point, where each potential employee lies along it. Otherwise it wouldn't know how low a wage rate to offer for each successive unit of labor engaged, and of course its potential employees have no incentive to volunteer this information.

Therefore, suppose instead that the employer does not know the supply prices of each potential employee. The consequence is that even with pure monopsony power the firm may be unable to impose the perfectly wage-discriminating outcome. It may still, to the extent feasible and allowed by law, practice a less refined version of wage discrimination in which only a few different wage rates are offered to potential employees.

To see how this works, first consider the polar opposite case of a *single*-wage-setting monopsonist before addressing the intermediate case of imperfect wage discrimination. Suppose that for practical or legal reasons, the monopsonist is

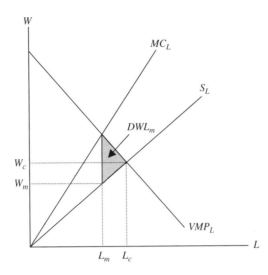

Figure 4.2 Inefficient employment by a single-wage setting monopsony.

unable to undertake *any* degree of wage discrimination. What combination of wage rate and quantity of labor hired will it then choose?

In this setting, the monopsonist encounters a tradeoff: if it faces an upward-sloping supply curve, as shown in figure 4.2, then it must offer higher wage rates to secure successively more labor input. Furthermore, since wage discrimination is ruled out by assumption, it must pay the higher wage rate commanded by the marginal worker hired to *all* of its employees, including those who would have settled for a lower wage rate if fewer workers were engaged. The consequence of this tradeoff is that the firm's marginal cost of hiring labor, denoted MC_L, is strictly higher than the wage rate. In the case of an affine (straight-line) supply curve, such as that depicted in figure 4.2, the associated MC_L curve has the same vertical intercept but double the slope.

The profit-maximizing equilibrium that results is also shown in figure 4.2. Consistent with the general conditions for profit-maximizing behavior, the monopsonist will hire workers up to the point where $MC_L = VMP_L$, indicated by L_m. The wage rate corresponding to this quantity of labor supplied is, as expected, given by the supply curve, so that the resulting monopsony wage is W_m.

Note three major features of this equilibrium scenario. First, the quantity of labor hired is less than under perfect competition. To see this, note that by construction the monopsonist's marginal benefit curve VMP_L corresponds to the market demand curve for a set of competitive labor buyers operating the same number of plants. Therefore, the amount of labor hired when this market is in competitive equilibrium is L_c, corresponding to the market-clearing wage rate W_c.

Second, the monopsony wage rate is also lower than the perfectly competitive level. This divergence of wage from marginal revenue productivity is referred to

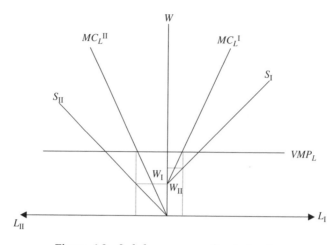

Figure 4.3   3rd-degree wage discrimination.

as *monopsonistic exploitation*. A frequently used measure of monopsonistic exploitation is $E = (VMP_L - W)/W$, or the proportional divergence of wage from workers' value marginal product.

It is not difficult to show (see the related study question at the end of the chapter) that for a profit-maximizing monopsonist, this measure just equals the reciprocal of the elasticity of the firm's labor supply evaluated at the point on the upward-sloping supply curve chosen by the monopsonist. In other words, the relative ability of a firm to drive the wage below its competitive level is strictly decreasing in the elasticity of the labor supply curve it faces. This should make intuitive sense: high wage elasticity of supply implies that prospective employees enjoy close substitutes for working in this firm, either by working elsewhere or taking leisure.

Finally, as a consequence of the interaction of imperfect competition and the monopsonist's incomplete information concerning the reservation wage levels of its potential employees, there arises dead-weight loss corresponding to the deviation from competitive wage and quantity conditions. Thus, although the firm's consumer surplus increases due to its exercise of monopsony power, producer surplus flowing to workers declines by a greater amount, leading to a net reduction in market social welfare, measured by the area marked DWL in figure 4.2.

Armed with these theoretical results for the case of a single-wage-setting monopsonist, now return to the scenario of partial wage discrimination under conditions of incomplete information. Continue to suppose that the monopsonist does not know the supply price of any labor supplier (or for any hour of labor supplied) it considers hiring, but imagine that the firm has enough information to partition the market supply curve into two constituent supply curves distinguished by their degree of wage elasticity. This scenario is illustrated in figure 4.3, where the respective submarkets are labeled I and II. As drawn, supply curve S_I

is more elastic at each wage level than its counterpart S_{II}. Assume for simplicity that the monopsonist's VMP_L curve is horizontal.

If the monopsonist sets a single wage rate in each submarket, then the theoretical conclusions derived above can be applied in each of the sub-markets I and II. The consequences of profit-maximizing firm behavior are thus indicated by the respective quantity and wage pairs (L_1, W_1) and (L_{II}, W_{II}). The key prediction of this model of *third-degree* wage discrimination is that, other things equal, the monopsonist offers a lower wage rate in the sub-market with lower wage elasticity of supply. The intuition behind this result is that higher supply elasticity means that workers have superior market mobility, and can thus more readily escape low wages.

There are a number of potentially fruitful applications of this analysis. First, this model offers a possible explanation as to why equally productive employees might yet receive different wage rates for the same work. This result will therefore be discussed in more depth in chapter 15 on wage variations across worker demographic groups. Monopsonistic wage discrimination is also a potential basis for the phenomenon of *market segmentation*, examined in chapter 16.

Second, the exercise of monopsony power establishes a potential basis for welfare-improving government intervention in the labor market. This is a corollary of the theoretical finding that if perfect or *first-degree* wage discrimination is not possible, the expression of monopsony power generically results in subcompetitive levels of employment and consequent dead-weight loss. One possibility, of course, is that governments might act to prohibit or otherwise restrict the attainment of monopsony power, and thus avoid any attendant efficiency problems directly.

Second, the negative effects of monopsony might be mitigated through the judicious use of legislated wage floors. Recall from the previous chapter that the imposition of an effective minimum wage under perfectly competitive conditions and downward-sloping demand must reduce the quantity of labor time hired (although it may increase the actual number of workers employed in the market in the presence of quasi-fixed labor costs) and reduce social welfare. These consequences need not arise in a labor market with a single wage-setting monopsonist. Indeed, it is possible that imposing an effective minimum wage in the scenario of figure 4.2 would both raise the number of workers hired by a monopsonist and lower the dead-weight loss associated with monopsony power. This outcome is demonstrated in figure 4.4, which represents the imposition of an effective wage floor W_f.

The key to this seemingly contrary result is that imposing a binding wage floor alters the monopsonist's MC_L curve. Since the wage rate cannot fall below W_f, the monopsonist can no longer set wages along the portion of the labor supply curve that falls below this wage rate. This also eliminates the lower portion of the original MC_L curve shown in figure 4.4, leading to the new, discontinuous MC_L curve shown in figure 4.4. The discontinuity occurs at the "kink" in the monopsonist's new effective supply curve, where it shifts from the horizontal portion established by the minimum wage to the original upward-sloping curve. As shown, this new

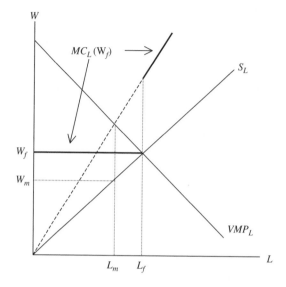

Figure 4.4 Positive employment and efficiency effects of a wage floor in a monopsony market.

MC_L curve intersects with VMP_L at the competitive employment level L_f. Since the efficient competitive equilibrium is thus attained, the wage rate is increased and dead-weight loss is eliminated.

The foregoing analysis suggests that informational or legal limitations on a monopsony's power to discriminate in setting wage rates leads, other things equal, to a reduction in equilibrium employment and the creation of dead-weight loss. However, these limitations would also mitigate the extreme distributional consequences of first-degree wage discrimination, since any monopsonistic wage-setting practice short of this extreme will generally imply that labor sellers accrue some producer surplus.

RECENT CONTROVERSY OVER MINIMUM WAGE LAW EFFECTS

The effects of minimum wage laws is a contentious topic within and without economics. Economists David Card and Alan Krueger published a study showing that a higher state minimum wage in New Jersey was associated with either no effect on employment or slightly positive effects in a sample of fast food restaurants in that state (Card and Krueger, 1994) as compared to Pennsylvania, a neighboring state with a lower minimum wage. This finding, which is counter to the prediction of lowered employment that comes from the competitive labor market model, unleashed a storm of controversy within the economics profession. Two other economists subsequently carried out another study in the same two states (using administrative payroll records obtained from a sample of fast food chain restaurants, including Burger King, Wendy's, Roy Rogers, and Kentucky Fried Chicken outlets), and argued the opposite result for their sample (namely lowered employment, consistent with the competitive model) (Neumark and Wascher, 2000). Card and Krueger then analyzed Neumark's and Wascher's data set and argued that it in fact did not overturn their original finding.

While this controversy was notable within the profession in part because of the central role of differing interpretations of the available data, it was also notable that many economists dismissed Card's and Krueger's finding simply because it was at odds with the competitive labor market model. Yet this result is perfectly in keeping with the predictions of the monopsony model discussed in the body of the text.

Related discussion questions:
1. Can you think of other explanations as to why this particular industry would have had rising employment even as the minimum wage was raised in New Jersey?
2. What options do managers of fast food restaurants have if they want to reduce their use of low-wage labor?

Related references:
David Card and Alan Krueger, "Minimum Wages and Employment: A Case Study of the Fast-Food Industry in New Jersey and Pennsylvania," *American Economic Review* 84, no. 4 (September 1994): 772–93.
David Card and Alan Krueger, "Minimum Wages and Employment: A Case Study of the Fast-Food Industry in New Jersey and Pennsylvania: Reply," *American Economic Review* 90, no. 5 (December 2000): 1397–420.
David Neumark and William Wascher, "A Case Study of the Fast-Food Industry in New Jersey and Pennsylvania: Comment," *American Economic Review* 90, no. 5 (December 2000): 1362–96.

Oligopsony: the case of limited buyer-side competition

Historical instances of purely monopsonistic labor markets are rare. However, it is at least plausible to suppose that employers might enjoy wage-setting power even if there were more than one labor buyer in a given labor market, so longer as the numbers weren't so great as to induce perfectly competitive exchange conditions. The more general case of buyer-side wage-setting power is therefore *oligopsony*, defined as a setting in which there are only a few buyers.

Oligopsonistic competition raises a new possibility that is not encountered in the scenarios of perfect competition or pure monopsony. Since there are multiple buyers in the labor market, but not so many that prospective employers simply take the wage rate as given, the decisions of each buyer will generally have a noticeable impact on the profitability of its competitors. Other things equal, for example, if one firm raises its wage offer, its competitors will find it harder to attract employees. If buyers are rational, they will take this interdependence of profits into account, and their optimization conditions will tend to be *interactive*, meaning that each employer must consider the actions of its competitors when deciding what market actions to take.

This scenario creates a problem for the supply and demand framework in that, as noted previously, the latter does not incorporate a theory of interactive decision-making. It is possible to modify the pure monopsony model to accommodate the presence of multiple competitors, but absent a theory of social interaction it is only possible to do so, within the confines of the present model, by assuming a special form of irrationality such that each competitor assumes that the actions of others are fixed, and maintains this assumption even if it is demonstrably false. Therefore, satisfactory treatment of this scenario awaits the introduction of elements of game-theoretic analysis in chapter 6. For now, it is sufficient to note the typical result of such an analysis that increasing the number of competitors tends to move the monopsony outcome toward the competitive level and thus to increase the share of economic surplus received by labor sellers.

Mobility barriers and monopsony power

The analysis to this point suggests that imperfect demand-side competition in a labor market is likely to increase rents enjoyed by employers, with the likelihood and/or magnitude of surplus appropriated increasing as the number of competitors declines. In view of this result, it might be asked how monopsony power is maintained in the face of potential competitors presumably eager to share the spoils of dominating the labor market.

Why might this competition not arise? The generic answer to this question is that since unimpeded mobility allows effective competition, there must exist barriers to entry by potential competitors. Obstacles to entry may arise from several sources. The simplest one is geographic distance. For example, earlier in the previous century, Eastern Kentucky coal miners faced a single mine owner as the only local employer. Changing employers would have meant leaving the region and uprooting families, a presumably daunting prospect to many workers.

Relatedly, search costs can create obstacles to potential competition. For instance, some labor economists explain unemployment as the outcome of workers' voluntarily refraining from current employment in order to search for better jobs. However, the fact that search is costly means that employers enjoy a corresponding degree of monopsony power with regard to their incumbent workers, since these workers cannot secure equivalent employment conditions without incurring search costs.

Alternatively, government intervention may promote monopsony power as the cost of addressing some other deviation from perfectly competitive conditions. For example, many countries encourage innovation by granting patent rights in the economic use of inventions. However, the resulting monopoly might also give the patentee monopsony power in related labor markets.

Finally, it may be that the monopsonists themselves take action to deter entry by potential competitors, in order to preserve the economic rents flowing from their wage-setting power. The motive for them to do so is clear; what's perhaps less obvious is how they would go about deterring the entry of firms which would presumably like to share in those rents. This problem is considered in somewhat more detail in chapter 6.

MONOPSONY IN THE NURSING MARKET

Markets for the services of registered nurses (RNs) would seem to provide a textbook case for the existence of monopsony power. Hospitals provide the biggest single source of employment for RNs, and the combination of high overhead costs and difficulties of market entry and exit creates some degree of natural monopoly conditions in local markets for hospital care. Many if not most towns and small cities in the US feature at most a single hospital within their borders.

Furthermore, these labor markets appear to exhibit many of the classic features of monopsony. Reports of nursing shortages are persistent and widespread, consistent with the prediction that employment by single-wage-setting monopsonists is less than corresponding competitive levels. There are also tenacious interregional wage differentials for RNs, suggesting the possibility of significant geographical mobility barriers.

That said, however, it has proved surprisingly difficult to establish robust empirical estimates of the degree of monopsony power expressed in markets for RNs, not to mention other types of labor market. Researchers encounter at least two difficulties in generating these measures. First, in a real-world setting one must allow for both short-run and long-run supply responses to given wages, since mobility frictions imply that entry and exit take place over time. In the relevant multi-period context, it can be shown that the rate of exploitation is equal to a weighted average of the short- and long-run supply elasticities for the given market, such that the weight on the latter is increasing in the prevailing interest rate. (Recall that labor supply is typically more elastic in the long run.) Thus, to provide fully accurate measures of the rate of exploitation in RN labor markets, one must estimate both short- and long-run supply responses.

continued

This leads to the second point. Whether monopsonistic exploitation is measured directly or indirectly, it is necessary to control statistically for factors affecting the revenue productivity of nursing labor. This is necessarily true in estimating E, since VMP_L is part of its definition. But one must also do so when estimating supply elasticities, in order to distinguish movements *along* a given supply curve for RN labor (induced by shifts in VMP_L) from shifts in labor supply.

Many studies have found significant monopsony effects on nursing salaries, which may explain persistent reports of nursing shortages. But these studies have encountered difficulties in distinguishing true monopsony effects from other factors that might influence wages. For example, urban areas tend to have more hospitals than more sparsely populated areas, and thus would be deemed more competitive markets. But the corresponding population density of urban areas may also increase the revenue productivity of hospital nursing labor, leading to higher wages independently of the pro-competitive effects of having more employers. And as it turns out, the observed effect of hospital market concentration on nursing wages is typically offset or eliminated when population density is included in the relevant regression equations.

A recent study by Douglas Staiger, Joanne Spetz and Ciaran Phibbs attempts to get around the problem of controlling for VMP by taking advantage of a "natural experiment" resulting from an increase in wages for registered nurses (RNs) that has no evident connection to variations in labor productivity. The basis of this experiment was a legislated change in wage policies for hospitals run by the US Department of Veteran's Affairs (VA), allowing them to pay RNs on the basis of local wage surveys rather than a uniform national scale. This resulted in wage increases at roughly two-thirds of all VA hospitals.

Based on a model of spatial differentiation among hospitals, Staiger *et al.* derive expressions relating exogenous wage adjustments to changes in a hospital's RN employment levels and to the wages of progressively more distant (and thus putatively less strategically interdependent) non-VA hospitals. They find that VA wage changes have successively less impact on more distant non-VA hospitals, consistent with the hypothesis that geography creates mobility frictions. Their results concerning employment consequences of exogenous wage increases are consistent with the existence of monopsony power in markets for RNs, and suggest further that average short-run labor supply elasticity to VA hospitals is around 0.1, an order of magnitude lower than the typical estimate of previous studies.

This elasticity value suggests a rate of exploitation equal to 10 if long-run supply elasticity is ignored. As mentioned earlier, estimates for long-run elasticity should properly be included in calculating the degree of monopsonistic exploitation, and (as the authors note), long-run elasticities are likely to be considerably greater, so that their inclusion would push the estimated value of exploitation significantly lower. However, the data used in this study did not permit estimation of long-run supply elasticities.

Related discussion questions:
1. If nursing shortages are created by monopsony power in markets for medical services, why might this power *not* also result in physician shortages?
2. Would the provision of government subsidies for training new nurses be an effective policy response to nursing shortages? Explain.

Related references:
William M. Boal and Michael R. Ransom, "Monopsony in the Labor Market," *Journal of Economic Literature* 35, no. 1 (March 1997): 86–112.
Douglas Staiger, Joanne Spetz and Ciaran Phibbs, "Is There Monopsony in the Labor Market? Evidence from a Natural Experiment," NBER Working Paper No. 7258 (July 1999).

UNIONS AS LABOR MONOPOLIES

Wage effects for unionized workers

In principle, wage-setting power on the supply side of labor markets could be analyzed in a manner exactly parallel to the preceding discussion. Thus, one could compare different degrees of wage discrimination as practiced by monopoly sellers, discuss the added impact of asymmetric information about buyer preferences on the efficiency of monopoly wage-setting, and contrast models of oligopoly wage-setting in order to gauge the potential impact of "competition of the few" among labor sellers. You are invited to consider how the relevant models would look when buyers behave competitively and sellers enjoy wage-setting power.

However, there are a number of practical considerations that must be taken into account in attempting to develop relevant theories of supply-side power in labor markets. These considerations stem from the fact that *unions* rather than *firms* (or cartels of firms) provide the typical organizational basis for exercising wage-setting power in labor markets. It is not necessarily the case that unions have the same goals or powers as firms in capitalist economies.

First, the power of unions to act on behalf of workers in setting or influencing wages is often legally guaranteed, especially in the developed economies of Western Europe and North America. In the United States, for example, the right to be represented by a union is ensured by the Wagner Act, which became law in 1935. However, union density, defined as the proportion of employed workers represented by unions, varies dramatically among these countries, from below

25% for France, the United States, and Spain, to above 75% for Denmark, Finland, and Sweden. Moreover, there is remarkable divergence in national time paths of union density, with the US and France experiencing sharp proportionate declines in unionization, and Finland and Spain showing strong proportionate increases, since 1970.[1]

When unionization rights are invoked for all workers in a given market, they may also impart some degree of monopoly power by shielding the workers from non-unionized competitors. Legal protections can thus be interpreted as a form of entry barrier into affected labor markets. However, this does not imply that there are *no* challenges to a union's wage setting power; firms can move their production operations to a locale where workers aren't unionized. For example, automobile plants in northern US states such as Michigan, Ohio, and New York typically unionized, while those in the South and in Mexico generally are not.

In addition, in some countries it is not unionization *per se* that is protected by law, but the right of workers to *vote* for union representation. In the US, for example, workers must first request a certification election for a given union. Assuming this election is won, a majority of employees in a given workplace must opt to be represented by the nominated union. Employees may also vote to *decer-tify* an existing union. Firms can thus fight against unions by discouraging orga-nizing efforts, persuading workers not to vote for unions, or providing inducements to give up union status once it is achieved.

A second issue that arises in analyzing unions as agents of supply-side market power concerns the identification of union objectives. Even granting that unions exercise wage-setting power, it is not at all clear toward what ends this power is generally directed. In particular, it is doubtful on both theoretical and empirical grounds that unions mirror firms in pursuing a simple objective such as maxi-mizing profits.

Assuming that a single union objective could be identified, what could it plau-sibly be? Since workers don't have property rights in unions, they can't sell these rights, and therefore, unlike firm owners, they have no necessary interest in max-imizing the economic value of the organization. It makes sense to say that workers care about higher wages, but it is reasonable to assume that they also care about such matters as the prospects for continued employment, the riskiness of their labor income, the form in which compensation is paid, and job safety.

A final complication concerning the scope of union power should be noted. Specifically, to what extent can unions dictate the terms of labor exchange in exer-cising market power? Unions with market power should be able to influence or even set wage rates and the form of worker compensation, but can they also deter-mine employment levels or working conditions? Answers to these questions are critical in assessing the impact of union power on labor market outcomes.

The issues raised here overlap with those encountered in the analysis of monopsonistic wage discrimination, in that the ability of unions to dictate the terms of exchange may be limited by problems of asymmetric information. For example, suppose a union tries to set both the wage rate and the quantity of labor

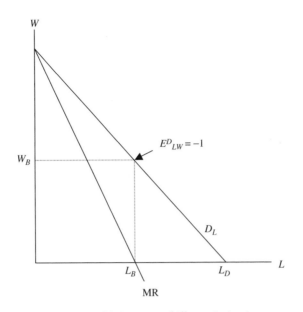

Figure 4.5 Union wage bill maximization.

employed in a firm. Firm owners might argue, on the basis of information available only to them, that this mix is economically infeasible given the firm's cost and revenue streams. The union in this case has no way of knowing whether the firm is bluffing, and attempting to "call its bluff" may prove very costly to the union's constituents.

For this reason, it is appropriate to consider alternative models of union actions, particularly with respect to the tradeoff between wage and employment levels. Two scenarios seem particularly relevant: one in which unions are understood to set wages "along the market demand curve," and one in which they bargain "on the contract curve." Each scenario is considered in turn.

First, suppose that informational or legal restrictions are such that unions can only set wage rates, leaving firms the freedom to adjust employment levels optimally in response. This suggests that in effect unions choose points along firms' labor demand curves, since these tell how profit-maximizing firms will set employment for given wage rates. Granting this is the case, the question remains what unions attempt to accomplish in setting wage rates.

One hypothesis is that unions act to maximize the *wage bill*, that is, the total wages paid to their members. This hypothesis yields a very specific implication when unions set wages along the demand curve. Refer to figure 4.5, which depicts the demand curve for a market in which workers are unionized. If the union in question can perfectly wage discriminate, equilibrium employment levels can then be determined in a manner parallel to that for the case of perfect monopsonistic wage discrimination. Since the union charges the highest wage that firms in the market are willing to pay for *each successive* unit of labor hired, beginning with the first one, firms are indifferent between hiring or not hiring each unit for which marginal profits are zero, and can therefore be induced to move to the point where the demand curve crosses the horizontal axis at L_D. In this case, the union extracts the entire consumer surplus.

But now suppose that informational or legal restrictions prevent wage discrimination. In this case the union sets a single wage rate along the demand curve. Now it faces a dilemma in attempting to maximize the total wages: if it raises the wage rate, it reduces the quantity of labor hired in the market, and if it wants to get more workers hired, it must reduce the wage rate. Furthermore, since it can only set one wage rate, it must lower the rate charged for *all* units of labor, even those for which firms in the market would have a higher willingness to pay.

The result of this restriction is that the curve representing *marginal* return to the total wage bill lies *below* the market demand curve. It is easily established that in the case of an affine market demand curve, the relevant marginal return curve, labeled MR in figure 4.5, shares the same vertical intercept but has double the slope of the market demand curve. Consequently, it intersects the horizontal intercept at a point exactly halfway between 0 and L_D, labeled L_B.

Since L_B is the point where marginal return to the wage bill is zero, it is also the point where the wage bill is maximized, and thus is chosen by the union under the present hypothesis. This corresponds to the wage rate W_B, which is located at the exact midpoint of the market demand curve, where the wage elasticity of labor demand equals one in absolute value. The wage bill hypothesis thus yields a very sharp prediction about wage and employment levels.

One problem with the microeconomic logic of this hypothesis is that it neglects the opportunity costs of union members, who can in general secure non-union employment elsewhere in the economy. Assume for simplicity that the wage rate thus afforded by alternative, non-union employment is W_N. Neglecting this opportunity cost of unionized employment is equivalent to asserting that firms seek to maximize total revenue rather than profit. Nothing in the logic of this model, for example, guarantees that the maximizing wage W_B exceeds workers' alternative wages.

A related but somewhat more sophisticated hypothesis would therefore be that unions attempt to maximize the *rents* earned by their members, represented by the product $(W - W_N) \cdot L$, where W_N represents the non-union wage and L is the total employment in the unionized market. This scenario is depicted in figure 4.6, which depicts workers' opportunity cost of remaining in the unionized market by the horizontal line corresponding to W_N.

This scenario is exactly analogous to that of a profit-maximizing monopoly firm facing constant average and marginal cost. If the union can perfectly wage discriminate, it will charge the highest wage firms are willing to bear for each additional unit of labor until the marginal wage rate just equals W_N, which occurs at a quantity L_N of labor hired. If instead the union can only set a single wage rate, it chooses the point where MR just equals marginal opportunity cost W_N, at employment level L_R and wage W_R. This no longer corresponds to the point of

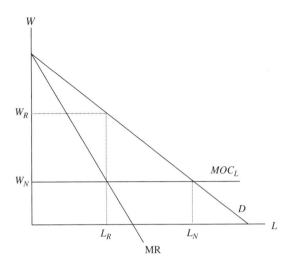

Figure 4.6   Union rent maximization.

unitary wage elasticity, but must instead occur where labor demand is wage-elastic. The degree of demand elasticity at the equilibrium point will typically vary with the level of the non-union wage.

An obvious generalization of this model would be to allow the marginal opportunity cost of supplying labor to increase with the total level of labor supplied, allowing for either heterogeneity in worker preferences toward leisure and income or increasing relative disutility of labor for the representative union member. In this case, workers' preferences with respect to labor supply would be summarized by an upward-sloping marginal opportunity cost curve. Illustration of this more general case is left to you as an exercise. It should be readily determined that this more general scenario reproduces the simpler model's predictions regarding the wage elasticity of labor demand at the union's optimal wage-employment point.

How do the foregoing hypotheses square with the available evidence? Empirical studies of union behavior have tended to reject *both* the wage bill and rent maximization hypotheses. That is, they do not find that estimated wage elasticities of demand are unitary at the union wage rate, or that union wage rates vary closely with estimated wage elasticities. Empirical findings suggest that while unions do raise wages above non-union levels, union members also prefer forms of compensation that do not vary significantly with random economic changes – for example, hourly wages rather than piece rates – and favor higher proportions of in-kind compensation (such as health insurance) relative to non-union workers. These results reinforce the earlier suggestion that unionized workers do not seek simply to maximize the "value" of the union.

There is a more general problem with any theory based on the premise that unions choose points along the market demand curve, especially if wage discrimination is ruled out on legal, informational, or other grounds. It is then

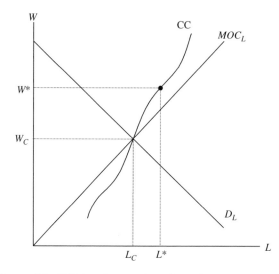

Figure 4.7   Efficient bargaining along the contract curve.

generally the case that monopoly wage setting relative to the market demand curve is inefficient, as can be seen from the fact that dead-weight loss is generated at any wage and quantity combination along the demand curve that diverges from the competitive equilibrium point. In principle, then, for any other point on the demand curve, *both* workers and firms would favor alternative terms of labor exchange.

The notion that unions seek these alternative terms is called the *efficient bargaining hypothesis*. Since all efficient wage-employment combinations save for that corresponding to competitive equilibrium diverges from the market demand curve (as well as the market supply curve, in the case of monopsony), articulation of this hypothesis must await theoretical developments pursued in subsequent chapters. In anticipation of these developments, a possible set of efficient bargaining points is shown by the curve marked CC (for "contract curve") in figure 4.7. Note that, whatever the shape of this curve, it must go through the point of intersection of the market demand and union members' marginal opportunity cost curve. Note in addition that efficient bargaining may entail employment in excess of the competitive level (say, at point (L^*, W^*)).

Do unions bargain along the contract curve rather than the demand curve (or some other reference line)? The available evidence is mixed. In some studies labor economists have been unable to reject the hypothesis of contract curve bargaining on the basis of the statistical evidence, although a particular *shape* of the contract curve (specifically, vertical) is consistently ruled out by the data. Again, the empirical findings make it difficult to insist on the primacy of any *one* set of union objectives and capabilities, contrary to the hypothesis that unions act like profit-maximizing monopolists.

Finally, there is a number of other empirical corollaries of collective bargaining that are not readily explained by the monopoly model of union behavior. For example, labor economists have found that union representation, besides raising wage rates, tends to increase the proportion of compensation devoted to in-kind benefits and to reduce pay inequalities among workers. In addition, there is significant evidence that unionization frequently promotes worker morale and productivity. These facets of collective bargaining are discussed more thoroughly in chapter 12 on representation of employee interests in the workplace.

Labor spillover and threat effects of union wage gains

If union wage-setting does not in fact satisfy the efficient bargaining hypothesis, then higher wages of unionized workers will tend to be accompanied by lower aggregate employment, the degree of which would be determined by the wage elasticity of labor demand. But in that case, the wage differential between unionized and non-unionized workers is not fully captured by the wage increases achieved in unionized markets. There are at least two reasons for this.

First, placing the effects of unions in a more general market context, the possibility arises that workers directly or indirectly disemployed as a result of inefficient union wage-setting would shift their labor supply to other markets (or to the non-unionized portion of the same labor market), shifting out the aggregate supply curves and lowering the equilibrium wages in those markets, and thereby increasing the union/non-union wage differential. This phenomenon, referred to as the *labor spillover* effect of union wage setting, is illustrated in figure 4.8. As shown, the effect of raising the wage rate from W_C to W_U in the unionized market is to shift the supply curve in the non-unionized market to the right, thus driving down the wage rate for non-unionized workers.

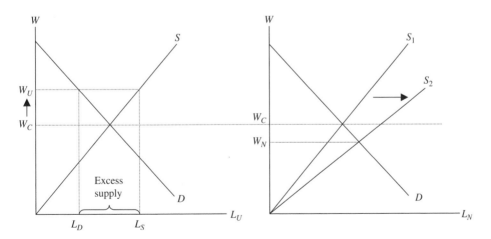

Figure 4.8 Spillover effects of a union wage increase.

Empirical studies of union/non-union wage differentials do not tend to find a substantial labor spillover effect. To the contrary, most studies that consider the matter tend to find that the degree of unionization in a particular labor market is *positively* related to the wages received by non-unionized workers in the same or adjacent markets. Why might this be the case? One possibility is known as the *threat effect* of prospective unionization: employers may rationally raise the wages they pay in order to reduce the incentive of workers in their labor force to vote for a collective bargaining agreement. If this effect were broad enough in scope, then union wage gains would tend to be disseminated, rather than limited to the set of unionized workers.

THE PROBLEM OF BILATERAL MONOPOLY

The supply and demand framework can be applied to scenarios in which only one side of the market has wage-setting power because they do not necessarily involve significant social interactions of the sort that the theory is not equipped to handle. Rather than taking the wage rate as given, the side of the market enjoying wage-setting power takes the market behavior (reflected in the market supply, demand, or contract curve, depending on context) of the other side as given, and then acts accordingly. This approach can yield unambiguous behavioral hypotheses and normative assessments concerning the impact of market power once one selects a particular model of wage-setting behavior, but is unable to provide *theoretical* criteria for choosing among multiple models.

Not even this level of precision is attained in the model of *bilateral monopoly*, which addresses the scenario in which *both* sides of the labor market enjoy wage-setting power. The pure case of bilateral monopoly obtains literally only when a monopolist seller negotiates with a monopsonist buyer, as when a completely unionized labor force faces an industry cartel, but it arises to a lesser degree whenever both sides incur costs of exiting a given labor exchange relationship. All such instances raise the prospect of *bargaining* between the parties to the exchange.

The theory of bilateral monopoly based on the supply and demand framework is at best incomplete because it does not offer a theory of relative bargaining power. Instead, it simply combines the predictions of the monopoly and monopsony models, yielding generally inconsistent and therefore ambiguous results. To see this, examine figure 4.9, in which the scenarios of single-wage-setting monopoly and monopsony have been superimposed. The curves labeled "S_L" and "D_L" correspond respectively to market supply and demand curves only in a figurative sense, since neither party is a wage-taker in this scenario.

However, within the theory, these curves serve as necessary points of reference for determining the hypothesized behavior of the two actors. Following the standard theory of monopoly, a marginal revenue curve (labeled MR_L in the graph) for the monopolist labor seller is derived from the value of marginal product (VMP_L) schedule that would correspond to the market demand curve under competitive conditions. Again following the standard theory, this marginal revenue

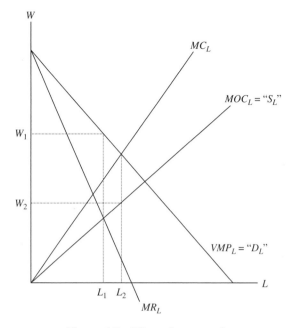

Figure 4.9 Bilateral monopoly.

curve is equated to the "S_L" curve, reflecting the marginal opportunity cost of sellers, to yield the monopolist's desired quantity of labor sold, L_1. The corresponding point on the VMP_L curve yields the monopolist's desired wage rate (according to this approach), W_1.

Parallel reasoning from the perspective of the monopsonist treats the marginal opportunity cost curve for supplying labor, labeled "S_L," as the market labor supply curve, and derives from it the monopsonist's marginal cost of *hiring* labor, labeled MC_L. The profit-maximizing labor buyer equates MC_L to its VMP_L to yield L_2, which corresponds to its preferred wage rate W_2 on the surrogate labor supply function.

In general, as indicated in figure 4.9, the respective preferred outcomes of the monopolist and monopsonist are not mutually consistent, so the model yields no determinate prediction about the wage or employment levels resulting from a scenario of bilateral monopoly in the labor market. Worse, the respective preferred outcomes cannot meaningfully even be considered as "boundary cases" for possible outcomes, since they are derived from supply and demand curves that cannot coherently be said to exist in this economic scenario. The supply and demand framework consequently breaks down when confronted with a situation that centrally involves social interaction among market participants.

This problem could be addressed in part by assuming that bilateral monopolists bargain efficiently, negotiating over points along a contract curve such as that depicted in figure 4.8 above. But even if the contract curve were known, the theory would still fail to provide any indication as to *which point* might be chosen along this curve. A broader theoretical canvas is therefore needed to accommodate more complex economic settings of this sort. The task of developing this more broad-based framework is begun in the next chapter.

WAGE-DEPENDENT GAINS FROM LABOR EXCHANGE

Under the conditions of the perfectly competitive model, the wage level determines only the *division* of the gains from labor exchange between the transacting parties, not the total magnitude of those gains. In effect, all market participants are fully aware of the benefits to be had from prospective exchanges and presume that these benefits will be fully realized, subject to payment or receipt of the market-determined wage rate. Consequently, the gains from exchange are determined independently of the wage level. Why might it ever be otherwise?

To anticipate the argument developed in subsequent chapters, the gains from exchange may be influenced by the wage rate whenever there are costs to the activity of exchange itself, in addition to the activities yielding the goods to be exchanged. To take the simplest possible scenario, firms may be reluctant to alter their going wage offers because broadcasting these changes to prospective employees incurs significant cost. A possible consequence of such *menu costs* is that wages may not flexibly adjust even though they fail to clear the market.

A second possibility has to do with possible connections between the wage rate and the quality of particular labor services or job characteristics being offered in exchange. To see this, recall from the chapters on labor supply and demand that there are multiple dimensions along which the quantity of labor may vary, including intensity and skill in addition to number of workers and hours per worker. Furthermore, given the inalienability of labor from the persons supplying it, workers will generally care about the conditions under which they perform labor. If all of these potential dimensions of labor exchange can be dictated in advance, then their determination is independent of the wage rate, although the converse is not true: other things equal, workers would demand higher pay in return for contributing more skill or greater effort, while competitive firms would require wage concessions in return for the provision of workplace amenities.

Suppose, however, that certain elements of importance to the labor exchange cannot be dictated in advance because of the costs involved in doing so. Then the possibility arises that the gains from trade related to these unstipulated elements may depend on the level of the wage rate provided. To take a single and very simple instance of this phenomenon, suppose that firms dislike turnover in their incumbent labor force because it compels them to incur significant costs of searching for, hiring, and training replacements. If incumbent workers can be dissuaded from leaving through the payment of a premium above the going wage rate, then the *net* revenue productivity of a given labor force is increasing in the wage rate, other things equal.

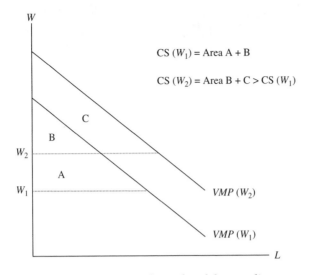

Figure 4.10   Wage-dependent labor quality.

In any such scenario, the wage rate determines the *level* of the relevant market curve as well as the position *along* that curve. In the foregoing example, the market demand curve of profit-maximizing firms, based in general on the net marginal productivity of labor, would shift upward with increases in the market wage rate. As a result, even otherwise competitive firms would have an incentive to offer wages in excess of the going rate.

This possibility is depicted in figure 4.10, which shows a representative firm's VMP_L curve shifting up in response to an increase in the wage rate. Suppose for the sake of argument that other firms maintain the going market wage rate; would this firm necessarily do so? This would necessarily be the case under perfectly competitive conditions, since raising the wage rate would only serve to raise the firm's labor costs without any offsetting benefit. In the scenario of figure 4.10, however, the net revenue productivity of the firm's employees increase with the wage rate. In response to this setting, a profit-maximizing firm would choose the wage rate that maximizes its consumer surplus – the area between the wage rate offered by the firm and its corresponding VMP_L curve – even if this rate is strictly above that offered by all other firms in the market.

A general implication of wage-dependent gains from labor exchange is that wages need not adjust to market-clearing levels, and even if they do, these do not ensure efficient provision of gains from exchange. As a consequence, this scenario creates a *potential* basis for welfare-improving government interventions in the market, although the realization of that potential will depend on the specific conditions giving rise to this scenario.

DOES LABOR PRODUCTIVITY INCREASE WITH WAGE LEVELS IN DEVELOPING ECONOMIES?

The assumption that gains from labor exchange are independent of the wage level rules out, among other things, a scenario in which workers' basic capacity to engage in arduous productive activities is compromised by not having enough to eat. This assumption may be appropriate for the analysis of labor markets in developed economies, where the average level of labor incomes and the presence of social welfare programs may ensure that most workers receive more than enough nutrition to live and work on. (Though this is hardly a foregone conclusion even in the United States, where income transfer programs have been sharply scaled back and food kitchens have done a thriving business, even in the boom times of the 1990s.) But it is much more problematic with respect to the situation of workers in poorer economies.

This issue was raised almost fifty years ago by Harvey Leibenstein, who pointed to a number of studies establishing, on one hand, a strong positive correlation between income levels and calorie consumption, and on the other, that the average caloric intake of workers in many developing economies fell well below the levels considered minimally necessary for continued health and working strength. These connections were reinforced, Leibenstein argued, by both physiological and "human engineering" studies showing a significant positive relationship between calorie consumption and labor productivity in physically demanding tasks. His conclusion? Labor markets in less-developed economies might be prone to a "low-productivity trap" in which market-clearing wages permit insufficient calorie consumption. The consequent inefficiency might be ameliorated, Leibenstein suggested, by institutional arrangements encouraging "over-employment" of workers relative to the labor hours actually demanded, so that general wage levels would be higher. The resulting supra-competitive wage rate is a special case of the *efficiency wage*, discussed more thoroughly in chapter 9.

Related discussion questions:
1. Why couldn't underfed workers in poorer economies simply borrow money to finance better nutrition for themselves and their families, and then repay the loans with interest out of their subsequently higher wages?
2. Under the efficiency wage hypothesis discussed by Leibenstein, employers benefit by paying their incumbent workers higher wages because labor productivity is raised thereby. Why might individual employers nonetheless raise wages to less than the socially desirable level, even if these productivity effects occur?

Related reference:
Harvey Leibenstein, "The Theory of Underemployment in Densely Populated Backward Areas," *Economic Backwardness and Economic Growth* (New York: Wiley & Sons, 1963): chapter 6.

CONCLUSION

This chapter takes the supply and demand framework about as far as it can go in accommodating phenomena inconsistent with the model of perfectly competitive labor markets. The possibility of wage-setting power is most easily and consistently handled by allowing one and only one side of the labor market complete power to set wages consistent with existing demand or supply conditions. The possibility that gains from labor exchange are dependent on the wage level can similarly be represented by allowing one side of the market freedom to adjust wages so as to make optimal use of this dependency.

Some common themes emerge from this exercise. The main one is that departures from competitive market conditions bear consequences for both the distribution of economic surplus and its total magnitude, except in the polar cases of perfect wage discrimination; in the latter scenarios, the consequence of market power is purely redistributive. In every other case, the corresponding equilibrium involves some efficiency loss.

The second major theme is methodological. The theoretical applications pursued in this chapter expose fundamental limitations in the reach of the supply and demand framework, generally related to the absence of a meaningful account of social interaction within the confines of the theory. As a consequence, the framework itself can provide no guidance about the degree of wage discrimination practiced, if any, by actors with wage-setting power; the impact of degrees of competition that fall short of the perfectly competitive ideal; the logic of wage determination in settings of bilateral monopoly; or alternative motives for unionization, given evidence casting doubt on the pure monopoly theory of union behavior. These limitations suggest the need for a broader analytical framework for studying labor market phenomena.

Study Questions

1. Illustrate two conditions in which even a single-wage-setting monopsony will *not* create dead-weight loss at its profit-maximizing employment level.
2. Illustrate the difference between *monopsonistic* exploitation, defined in the body of the chapter, and *Marxian* exploitation, which might be approximately defined as the divergence of the wage rate from the value *average* product of labor (VAP_L). Does Marxian exploitation require the existence of monopsony power? What rate of profit and rental rate of capital inputs is required for the elimination of exploitation defined in the Marxian sense?
3. Illustrate and explain conditions under which a profit-maximizing monopsonist earns zero economic profit in equilibrium.

continued

4. If the labor supply curve faced by a firm is written in inverse form as $W(L)$, that is, the wage rate the firm has to pay as a function of the amount of labor it hires, then the marginal cost of hiring additional units of labor can be expressed as $MC_L = W \cdot (1 + 1/E_{LW})$, where E_{LW} denotes the wage elasticity of labor supply. Use this fact and the marginal condition for profit-maximizing employment of labor to show that the rate of monopsonistic exploitation E (defined in the chapter) is just equal to $1/E_{LW}$.

5. The presence of persistent job vacancies is sometimes cited as evidence for the existence of monopsony power. However, this need not be the case. What other economic explanations might be given for this phenomenon?

6. If the labor market demand curve faced by a rent-maximizing union is written in inverse form as $W(L_d)$, with wage specified as a function of the quantity of labor demanded, then the marginal revenue to the union can be written $MR_L = W \cdot (1 + 1/E_{LW}^d)$, where E_{LW}^d denotes the wage elasticity of market demand (a negative number, assuming the demand curve is downward-sloping). Assuming that workers' opportunity cost of supplying labor in the unionized market is constant at W_N, demonstrate that the union wage premium expressed as a percentage, $(W_R - W_N)/W_R$, is just equal to the inverse of the absolute value of E_{LW}^d. Use this result to demonstrate (a) that the union will only choose points in the elastic range of market demand, and (b) the union wage premium increases, the more inelastic is the market demand for labor. Given this result, what labor market setting would be most prone to unionization, given this theory of union behavior?

7. The exercise of wage-setting power by unionized workers does not create market inefficiencies so long as negotiated wages and employment levels correspond to points on the contract curve. However, the existence of union practices such as *featherbedding* (demanding the presence of more employees than are required for the work to be performed) suggest that union bargaining may not be efficient. Supposing that is true, what keeps unions and employers from presumably mutually agreeable movements toward the contract curve (e.g., by trading off unnecessary jobs for higher compensation)?

Note

1 Torben Iversen and Jonas Pontusson, "Comparative Political Economy: A Northern European Perspective," in *Unions, Employers and Central Banks: Macroeconomic Coordination and Institutional Change in Social Market Economies* (Cambridge: Cambridge University Press, 2000): 9, table 1.1.

Suggestions for Further Reading

George A. Akerlof and Janet L. Yellen (eds) *Efficiency Wage Models of the Labor Market* (Cambridge: Cambridge University Press, 1986).

Barry T. Hirsch and John T. Addison, *The Economic Analysis of Unions: New Approaches and Evidence* (Boston: Allen & Unwin, 1986).

Alan Manning, *Monopsony in Motion: Imperfect Competition in Labor Markets* (Princeton: Princeton University Press, 2003).

PART TWO

THE LABOR EXCHANGE

Supply and demand analysis of labor market outcomes is premised on the assumptions of wage-taking behavior and flexible wage adjustment. Without the former, supply and demand curves could not be defined in the first place, and without the latter, there is no reason to believe that market equilibrium is determined by the intersection of supply and demand curves. However, as explained in the previous chapter, the plausibility of these assumptions depends on the absence of significant costs of exchange.

Chapter 5 introduces the contrary hypothesis that labor exchange itself typically incurs costs. If the activities required to engage in labor exchange are costly, then labor market transactions are unlikely to have the seamless, anonymous character presumed in the model of perfect competition. Prospective exchange partners are not perfectly substitutable when it is costly to locate and pair with them, and mutually acceptable terms of employment may not be executable if there are significant direct or indirect costs of contract enforcement. For many analytical purposes, the appropriate unit of analysis under such conditions is the labor exchange itself, represented with the aid of Edgeworth box diagrams.

Labor exchange costs raise the prospect of various forms of strategic behavior by one or both parties to a given labor exchange. Attempts to understand such behavior are facilitated by the analytical language of game theory, introduced in chapter 6. This language is then applied in chapters 7 and 8 to the study of two phenomena that frequently arise in labor exchange relationships: respectively, bargaining under conditions of bilateral wage-setting power, and imperfect contracting due to costs of identifying, specifying, or enforcing relevant terms of exchange. Analytical results of these chapters then form the foundation for the text's subsequent study of employment relationships and labor market outcomes under exchange conditions that may be less than ideal.

CHAPTER FIVE

THE STRUCTURE OF LABOR EXCHANGE

Markets, whether for labor or for any other good, are arenas for the economic activity of exchange. In the theory of perfectly competitive markets, however, that activity is rendered so trivial as to be virtually invisible. Were the conditions of perfect competition to obtain precisely in practice, this obscuration would be justifiable at least for the sake of simplicity, since nothing about the activity would then be problematic: people could exchange as much as they want at terms that have been predetermined, and it wouldn't matter who they traded with. Furthermore, the given terms of trade would unfailingly be carried out.

The evidence that exchange, particularly labor exchange, doesn't generally proceed in this seamless fashion is both abundant and recurrent. The ubiquity of unemployment and job vacancies suggests that finding suitable labor exchange partners is neither immediate nor automatic. Strikes and lockouts indicate that the path to agreement on the terms of labor exchange does not always run smooth. Employee dismissals "for cause" and lawsuits for wrongful termination appear to reflect serious conflict over the implementation of given labor agreements. Relatedly, the widespread incidence of extensive legislation and legal regulations pertaining to all of these phenomena suggests either an intrinsic desire of governments to influence the course of otherwise unproblematic labor exchange – worthy of study in its own right, if so – or an attempt to respond to systematic concerns about the performance of labor markets as a means for allocating productive activity.

It may be that these phenomena imply no fundamental violation of the core predictions or normative assessments of the perfectly competitive model. But they may instead portend that some other theory of labor market function would offer a better explanation of the relevant facts, and

continued

this could not be adequately determined until an alternative theoretical framework is spelled out. This chapter begins the task of developing a more broad-based analytical foundation for the analysis of labor market phenomena grounded in a consideration of the nature and scope of social interactions intrinsic to labor exchange.

This approach posits individual labor market transactions as the fundamental unit of analysis, and investigates the process by which such transactions are initiated and carried through. The analysis begins with a review of some basic features of exchange as an economic activity, after which the *Edgeworth box* is introduced as a visual basis for thinking about the *distributional* and *efficiency* issues that arise in transactions for labor. The next step in the analysis is to identify the constituent activities of exchange and the institutions that support them, leading to the hypothesis that exchange outcomes depend closely on the magnitude and incidence of exchange costs.

ELEMENTAL FEATURES OF LABOR EXCHANGE

Property rights and labor exchange

In the simplest sense, an *exchange* is a mutual transfer of tangible possessions, as in the case of barter. However, this is clearly not an appropriate rubric for thinking about transactions for labor that do not involve slavery. In developed market economies, it is useful to think of exchange more generally as involving mutual transfers of *property rights* with respect to particular assets. Three types of property rights with respect to an asset can be distinguished: the right to use and exclude or regulate others' use; the right to income derived from use of the asset; and the right to transfer ownership to others. However, an exchange need not involve transfer of *all* property rights in a given asset. An apartment lease, for example, extends the right of use to others but not always the right to generate income from this use (so that subletting the apartment may be forbidden), and never involves an outright transfer of ownership.

In exchanges governing the performance of labor, the asset in question is "human capital," i.e. the capacity for work. In slave-owning societies, *all* of the above-mentioned property rights were involved in transactions for labor; it was often even the case that free workers could sell themselves or family members into slavery, for instance to pay a debt. In contrast, in modern market economies, the capacity to labor is legally as well as physically inalienable: individuals are forbidden to sell themselves or others into slavery, or to acquire slaves.

Exchanges for labor in these economies are consequently like leasing arrangements, in the sense that ownership in one's capacity to work is never transferred. Rather, a delimited use of someone's capacity for labor is exchanged for a consideration, usually in monetary form. The limitation on other parties' use of one's capacity to labor may be in terms of duration (a work day, for example) or more narrowly a specific set of services to be performed.

The scope for cooperation and conflict in labor exchange

The structure of a given labor exchange – the scope of the transaction, the magnitude of potential gains from exchange, and the division of these gains between the trading parties – can be depicted with the aid of an *Edgeworth box* defined over the relevant dimensions of the exchange. An Edgeworth box for two prospective trading partners is derived by counterposing their indifference maps in the same diagram, as shown in figure 5.1c. In this scenario, the trading parties are respectively a profit-seeking firm and a household whose preferences over bundles of income and leisure are represented by a utility function. The present analysis of their choices differs in the key respect that the wage rate is treated as a potential variable for these parties, rather than as dictated by market conditions.

Accordingly, figures 5.1a and 5.1b depict the preferences of a representative firm and household over combinations of the wage rate and quantity of labor supplied by the household to the firm. Since the firm seeks profits rather than utility, its preferences are represented by an *isoprofit map*. The constituent element of this map, called an *isoprofit curve*, is defined in this context as the locus of all combinations of wage rates and quantities of labor supplied by the household to the firm that yield a constant level of profit. The firm's isoprofit map is shown in figure 5.1a.

The isoprofit map has several key features. First, the slope of any given isoprofit curve is given by the negative ratio of the marginal profit contribution of labor hours and the marginal contribution to profits of the wage rate, or $-M\pi_L/M\pi_W$. This translates into the expression $(VMP_L - W)/L_D$, where L_D is the *total* labor hired by the firm. Note two implications of this formula for the slope: first, isoprofit curves are positively sloped for any wage and labor combination that falls below the firm's VMP_L curve, and negatively sloped for any wage and labor bundle above it; second, and relatedly, each isoprofit curve reaches a peak on the VMP_L curve, as shown. Note finally that the firm's profit level increases down and to the right in the graph, since other things equal, more labor contributes to and higher wages subtract from profit.

The household's indifference map over combinations of wage rate and quantity of labor supplied to the firm is shown in figure 5.1b. The slope of a given indifference curve is expressed by $(MRS_{H,I} - W)/L_S$, where $MRS_{H,W} = MU_H/MU_I$ denotes the household's marginal rate of substitution between leisure and income and L_S represents the *total* labor supplied by the household (assumed for convenience to exceed the quantity supplied to the present firm). In the special case that the household's MRS is defined independently of the wage rate, the MRS curve can be thought of as the household's net marginal utility cost of supplying labor hours. Given this condition, it thus serves as the reference for determining the slope of

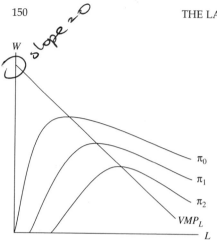

Figure 5.1(a)   The firm's isoprofit map over household labor hours and wage rate.

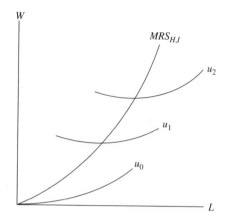

Figure 5.1(b)   Household's indifference map over hours worked for firm and wage rate.

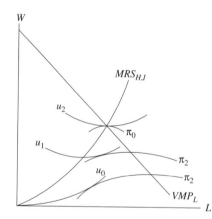

Figure 5.1(c)   The Edgeworth box over labor hours and wage rate.

each indifference curve: negative for wage and labor combinations above the MRS curve, positive for points below it, and zero along the MRS curve. Consequently, each indifference curve attains its minimum on the MRS curve, as shown in panel b. As drawn, household utility increases generally upward, indicating that higher wage rates unambiguously raise utility. The net effect of increasing labor hours on utility varies, however, since doing so both increases income and reduces leisure.

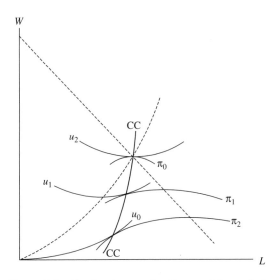

Figure 5.2   Contract curve for firm and household.

The two preference maps are brought together in figure 5.1c to create an Edge-worth box over wage and labor quantity combinations for the firm and house-hold. Although not all isoprofit and indifference curves are drawn, it should be remembered that each point in the box corresponds to a particular utility and profit combination. Points along the horizontal axis represent the quantity of labor supplied by this household to this firm, so the origin can be interpreted as the point at which no labor exchange takes place between these two parties. Every other point represents a possible trade of labor hours for wages.

The Edgeworth box exhibits two key features of labor exchange. First, both parties stand to gain from trading with each other. By construction, the firm enjoys some initial profit level π_0 and the household some utility level U_0 at the point of no exchange. All points within the area enclosed by these two curves represent exchange outcomes that make both parties *strictly* better off compared to the no-exchange position.

Second, mutual gains can be reaped from exchange until the firm and house-hold reach the *contract curve*, depicting the points of tangency between pairs of indifference and isoprofit curves. The contract curve corresponding to the Edge-worth box in figure 5.1c is illustrated in figure 5.2. Note that it goes through the point of intersection of the firm's VMP and the household's MRS curves. Once the exchange partners reach the contract curve, it is impossible to make both parties better off by further adjustments of wages or quantities. Consequently, the curve represents the set of *Pareto-efficient* exchanges of wages for labor performed, defined as allocations such that it is impossible to make one party better off without making the other worse off.

However, this Edgeworth box is constructed on the premise that all other aspects of labor exchange relevant to the interests of these parties are held fixed. These would include the degree of labor effort and skill exercised by the household and the levels of relevant workplace amenities offered by the firm. Were these additional features of the labor exchange taken into account, it would be necessary to construct Edgeworth boxes in each of these dimensions, showing the attainable combinations of wage rate and, respectively, effort, skill, and amenities. Achievement of Pareto-efficiency in labor exchange would then require attainment of the contract curve in every box, that is, with respect to all relevant dimensions of labor exchange.

There are two implications of these features. One is that exchanges for labor may in general involve very complex and multifaceted transactions with many dimensions of concern. Workers not need just one skill but a particular array of capabilities, and correspondingly may be asked to expend effort in a number of distinct tasks. "Workplace amenities" may summarize a long list of conditions including location, convenience, safety, identity of coworkers, and so on.

A second implication of these features is that every scenario of labor exchange raises the prospect of both cooperation and conflict. Cooperation, because it is possible for both parties to gain by engaging in exchange. Conflict, because once the contract curve is achieved, more for one party necessarily means less for the other. Thus, a fundamental question posed by this analytical perspective concerns the relative manifestation of cooperative and conflictual behavior in given labor market exchanges.

Very broadly speaking, the realized mix of cooperation and conflict in actual labor exchanges depends strongly on the structure of exchange conditions within which prospective trading partners operate. The theoretical conditions of perfect competition impose a very tight and specific structure that eliminates the scope for distributional conflict. This is due to the assumption that all labor market participants take the wage rate as given.

This aspect of perfect competition is illustrated in figure 5.3, which superimposes a constant market wage rate over all possible quantities of labor in the Edgeworth box. Since this wage rate W_C is taken as given by perfectly competitive market actors, the horizontal line corresponding to this wage rate constitutes the "budget frontier" of both the firm and the household over wage and labor combinations. Consequently, each actor would choose a point of tangency along this frontier in order to optimize with respect to the relevant preferences.

If the wage rate also corresponds to an equilibrium for this firm and household, their tangencies will occur at the *same point* on the frontier, implying that the respective optimal indifference and isoprofit curves are tangent to each other. This simultaneous tangency occurs at point E in figure 5.3. As a corollary, any labor market equilibrium achieved under perfectly competitive conditions must also be on the contract curve. This consequence is the analog, in the Edgeworth box framework, of the result in supply and demand analysis that the sum of consumer

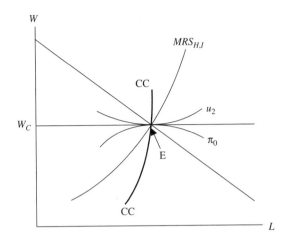

Figure 5.3 Competitive equilibrium in the Edgeworth box.

and producer surplus is maximized at the point of competitive equilibrium. Furthermore, since market forces, as expressed in the wage rate, dictate a unique point of equilibrium on the contract curve, no scope remains for conflict over the distribution of this surplus.

These results need not obtain when perfectly competitive exchange conditions are not realized. As discussed in the previous chapter, the wage-taking and flexible wage adjustment conditions required for the attainment of perfectly competitive labor market outcomes depend on highly restrictive exchange conditions related to the degree of mobility enjoyed by market participants and their ability to ensure that given terms of labor exchange are realized. The next step in the argument is to consider how the structure of labor market exchange affects the attainment of these conditions, and how labor market institutions influence this relationship.

EXCHANGE COSTS AND LABOR MARKET INSTITUTIONS

In private ownership economies, the allocation of goods and services is accomplished primarily through the institution of exchange. Systematic exchange entails in turn three types of microeconomic activity, here termed *matching, negotiation,* and *enforcement*. These activities, and particularly the costs of undertaking them, play a key role in determining the structure and content of.labor exchange relations. Generally speaking, the presence of exchange costs has implications for both the total realized gains from exchange and the distribution of those gains between employers and workers. Consequently, the costs of these activities are reflected in the existence of a number of prominent labor market institutions that serve to mitigate these costs or alter their relative incidence among labor buyers and sellers.

Matching

Matching refers to the set of activities involved in bringing together prospective transaction partners. It entails learning about the existence of suitable exchange partners and arranging the necessary form of contact or interaction between them. In some forms of exchange, this contact may require no more than an electronic interface, as when equity shares are bought and sold on line. In others, particularly those involving exchange for labor, the required contact may be more direct, requiring physical relocation by one or more party to the exchange. This necessity is dictated by the embodied nature of the capacity to labor: it's pointless to engage the services of a worker who cannot be present to deliver them.

This requirement of physical relocation is suggested in the related terms *mobility* and *entry and exit*. These concepts, used frequently in discussing the microeconomic structure of labor markets, suggest the idea that traders must be prepared to relocate, with everything this entails, in order to make the most of their market opportunities. Mobility may also be involved in efforts to *diversify* assets across distinct markets or uses. In particular, diversification of *human* as opposed to alienable capital assets may require spatial mobility on the part of its suppliers, as for example when adjunct faculty members hold part-time teaching jobs at several college campuses.

Under the conditions of the perfectly competitive model, matching is essentially costless: appropriate exchange partners are always available (at least at the equilibrium wage rate), immediately identifiable, and instantaneously paired. As discussed in the previous chapter, costless matching implies that market actors would lose all existing or prospective trading partners should they try to alter the wage rate in a self-serving direction, and thus provides a partial foundation for the wage-taking assumption of the competitive model.

Under actual labor market conditions, in contrast, all of the just-mentioned aspects of matching may be costly. In particular, it may be difficult to identify suitable labor exchange partners, or having identified them, difficult to reach them. These costs have two potential implications.

First, matching costs raise the specter of individual market power in setting wage rates. For example, if a firm's employees find it costly to locate suitable alternative positions, the firm may be able to lower their wage rates below competitive levels without losing its work force. If both parties to a labor exchange face significant costs, then a potential bargaining problem arises out of the resulting scenario of *bilateral* market power. As explored in chapter 7, the distribution of gains from a given labor exchange may depend on who faces the greater costs of exit.

Second, the volume of exchange may be less than if matching were costless, since some might be deterred from entering the market by the prospect of these costs. For example, those who study the phenomenon of unemployment frequently encounter the "discouraged worker" syndrome, in which would-be employees have left the labor market after being frustrated in their efforts to find jobs. Relatedly, any given moment may find would-be labor market traders continuing to search for appropriate exchange partners rather than realizing the benefits of a successful pairing.

The presence of significant matching costs may therefore give rise to organizational innovations designed to ameliorate these costs and their impact on labor exchange. However, the motives for – and consequently, the direction of – organizational responses to matching costs is complicated by the dual potential impact of these costs, as just described. On one hand, a reduction in overall costs will tend to increase the volume of labor exchange and thus the overall gains from trade in labor markets. On the other, a change in the *relative* incidence of these costs will tend to alter the balance of bargaining power between the two sides of a labor transaction. The tension between these two effects is illustrated by the role of the *padrone* system of supplying labor for east coast agricultural labor markets early in the twentieth century. (See discussion box.)

THE PADRONE SYSTEM: MATCHMAKING IN AGRICULTURAL LABOR MARKETS

By the end of the nineteenth century, "truck farms" supplying fresh fruit and vegetables to large metropolitan areas had proliferated up and down the east coast of the United States. However, truck farmers encountered ever-increasing obstacles in securing an adequate labor force: the crops had to be harvested immediately when they ripened, but the work was hard, the hours were long while they lasted, and the fields were far from urban centers where labor was plentiful. And when the crops were in, there was no more need for workers. Moreover, truck farmers were not willing or able to pay high wages to attract the necessary labor.

The labor demands of east coast truck farmers, especially those in southern New Jersey, were met to some extent through the use of *padroni* or labor contractors who recruited workers, transported them to the fields, provided housing, and in most cases supervised their efforts as "row bosses" (*padrone* is an Italian word meaning "owner, boss, or master"). The padrone system was an outgrowth of the large-scale migration of southern Italians to the US in the period from 1876 to the First World War. Historian Cindy Hahamovitch notes that the original padroni were agents of US railroad and mining interests who recruited displaced Italian farm labor to work in the US for a set period of time, until Congress outlawed this practice in the mid-1880s. Latter-day padroni recruited women, children, and unemployed males from the Italian immigrant communities of large urban areas to work in the fields, typically charging them for transportation and housing out of already low wage rates.

This arrangement initially fulfilled the labor requirements of east coast truck farmers, but precariously: Hahamovitch notes that their increasing

continued

reliance on this system put padroni in an increasingly strong bargaining position, reinforced by the language barrier dividing English-speaking growers and the Italian-speaking immigrant workers recruited by the padroni. This tendency plus the improvement in employment opportunities for urban immigrants created by the First World War led to the eventual demise of the padrone system. Growers turned increasingly to government officials, first at the state and then the federal level, to help them secure workers on a broader scale less dependent on the efforts of regional labor recruiters.

Related discussion question:
1. Why might the padroni have enjoyed greater bargaining power vis-à-vis truck farmers than the individual workers they recruited? Under what conditions, if any, might individual workers have shared in the fruits of the padroni's bargaining power?

Related reference:
Cindy Hahamovitch, *The Fruits of Their Labor: Atlantic Coast Farmworkers and the Making of Migrant Poverty, 1870–1945* (Chapel Hill: University of North Carolina Press, 1997).

Negotiation

Once prospective exchange partners have been matched, they must still specify and agree to the terms on which they will exchange. This is the exchange activity of *negotiation*. Negotiation can be as simple as agreeing to a posted price for a well-defined and perfectly observable good, but in some cases, particularly in labor markets, it may involve haggling over multiple terms of exchange concerning various dimensions of a good (such as number and scheduling of labor hours, range of skills required, desired labor intensities across a menu of tasks, and conditions under which labor is to be performed), some of which are not easily specified.

The problem of negotiation becomes especially involved when anticipated gains from trade are affected by states of the world that won't be realized until after a deal is consummated, depending for example on vagaries of the weather or macroeconomic fluctuations. In this case a complete specification of the terms of exchange would require precise descriptions of each element of a possibly large set of contingencies. In some cases this may prove difficult or impossible to do, with consequences to be discussed more fully in chapter 8.

The activity of negotiation is also potentially complicated by the presence of multiple parties on one or both sides of a prospective exchange. The attainment of scale economies, for example, may dictate that firms employ a large number of workers simultaneously, in which case the firm might have to bargain with all of its workers at once. The presence of multiple transactors raises the specter of collective choice issues in the negotiation process, in addition to the more basic question of how gains from exchange are to be divided. For example, a firm's workers may have a common interest in some features of the workplace, such as location, temperature, and so on.

Under perfectly competitive conditions, of course, negotiation is a trivial exercise. This would be true even if ongoing negotiation were costly, since the assumption of wage-taking behavior effectively implies that there is nothing to negotiate over. Similarly, negotiation becomes a simple matter (translation: take it or leave it!) when wage-setting power is enjoyed by only one side of the market. However, the prospect of bilateral wage-setting power looms whenever matching costs are incurred by both buyers and sellers, and in that case negotiation costs may play a significant role in the determination of labor market outcomes. These costs may be *directly* incurred, as when parties to a bargaining dispute share in the cost of renting a neutral site in which to carry out negotiations, or *indirectly* experienced as opportunity costs, as when negotiation breakdowns delay the onset of mutually beneficial employment relationships.

As in the case of matching costs, the potential effects of negotiation costs are twofold: first, the prospect of extensive haggling may deter some labor exchange relationships from being formed, with consequent losses in total gains from trade. But second, as explored further in chapter 7, the incidence of negotiation costs influences the expected distribution of these gains. Again, the dual connotations of these costs yield correspondingly mixed incentives for organizational innovations to address them. Some labor market institutions would seem to have the primary effect of reducing the difficulties associated with hammering out given terms of labor exchange. For example, the role of labor *mediators* is essentially to facilitate discussions among negotiating parties and thus to work out solutions to potential stumbling blocks on the road to labor agreements. The role of *arbitration*, in contrast, is to provide a low-cost alternative to the negotiation process by vesting an outside party, presumably accepted by both sides of the bargaining dispute, with the power to decide on the ultimate terms of exchange.

While reducing overall negotiation costs, however, some labor market institutions may have the additional, and possibly chief, effect of changing the relative incidence of these costs between buyers and sellers, with immediate implications for the distribution of bargaining power. To anticipate a subsequent discussion, for example, some organization theorists have spoken approvingly of the benign effect on haggling costs of "internal promotion ladders," in which firms assign fixed compensation levels to given jobs. Typically not mentioned in these assessments is the unilateral power to set compensation levels consequently reserved by the firms that put these pay schedules in place.

Enforcement

Finally, *enforcement* refers to the set of activities devoted to ensuring that given terms of exchange, once negotiated, are duly fulfilled. These activities might include monitoring the execution of the negotiated terms of trade to make sure that they are carried out, and if necessary providing appropriate inducements for this execution. It may be possible that parties to an exchange can implement the terms of their agreement by themselves. In such cases the transaction is said to be *self-enforcing*. Possible strategic methods of self-enforcement are considered in chapters 6 and 8 and part III.

However, in many if not most instances of exchange the activity of enforcement relies to some extent on the power of an external agency, generally the judicial branch of the political system. The sanctity of mutually accepted terms of trade is backed up by provisions of civil law, including penalties for non-compliance with these terms. This is where the property rights discussed earlier in the chapter get their teeth: rights asserted by one party correspond to obligations owed by others, and the legal system is used to ensure these obligations are dependably carried out.

A particularly important instrument for the purpose of enforcing given terms of exchange is the *contract*. A contract is simply a specification of agreed-upon terms of exchange in a form that can be enforced by an outside agency, such as courts of law. In many cases of labor exchange, the corresponding transactions are so mundane or immediate that formal contracts are not used. One rarely writes an explicit contract in order to get one's car washed, for example. In most such cases, however, an *implicit* contract may be understood to exist for legal purposes.

Explicit or formal contracts become salient when there are many components or dimensions to a labor transaction, or if a significant period of time separates the performance of various terms of the exchange. In such cases, formally specified contracts provide a bridge between agreement and execution that increases the likelihood that the terms of the agreement will be achieved. Formal contracts may thus play an important role if production conditions are affected by multiple contingencies created by the physical, social, or economic climate in which production occurs. For example, if the gains from a given exchange can be compromised by weather conditions, then it might be useful to specify contractually what should be done in each possible type of weather emergency.

Under the conditions of the perfectly competitive model, contractual enforcement is automatic and costless. In the event that someone is accused of violating given terms of exchange, the relevant enforcement agency simply compares the outcome of the challenged transaction with the terms comprehensively and unambiguously spelled out in the contract, and then penalizes any deviation according to the relevant legal or contractual provisions. The attached penalties are presumably sufficient to deter any such deviation, and thus negotiated terms of trade are always faithfully executed in this scenario.

In practice, however, the ideal scenario of costless external enforcement based on fully specified contracts may be unattainable. For example, parties to a given labor exchange may find it difficult to specify complex terms of exchange so as to render them easily verifiable by an external agency, as when understanding such provisions requires specialized knowledge unavailable to enforcement agencies.

Alternatively, one or the other party may find it necessary to monitor certain agreed-upon actions to make sure that they are undertaken.

An extreme instance of costly enforcement arises when it is practically impossible to ensure that certain significant aspects of the labor exchange relationship affecting the potential gains from trade are implemented in a mutually satisfactory way. For example, trading partners may be unable to anticipate all of the future contingencies potentially influencing the outcome of the employment relationship, or some important aspect of the labor supplier's contribution – such as the degree of attention paid to certain complex tasks – may be simply impossible to observe or to record in a verifiable manner. In such cases the related enforcement costs are effectively infinite, and thus contracts become only an imperfect means of implementing given terms of trade. The implications of imperfect contracting are investigated at length in chapter 8.

Unsurprisingly, the presence of significant enforcement costs has implications for both the magnitude of feasible gains from labor exchange and the distribution of those gains. Perhaps most evidently, anticipation of these costs reduces the potential for gains from labor exchange by rendering some otherwise viable labor market transactions unpalatable. Less obviously, strategies of self-enforcement under imperfect contracting conditions may necessitate the redistribution of given net gains from exchange in order to achieve desired incentive effects, as in the scenario of *efficiency wages* discussed in chapter 10. (A version of this scenario is also examined near the end of the previous chapter.)

In sum, costs associated with the constituent exchange activities of matching, negotiation, and enforcement may have a powerful impact on both the scope for gains from labor exchange and the distribution of those gains between workers and firms. As discussed above, each individual form of exchange cost has the potential for both quantitative and qualitative effects on labor exchange, reducing the overall scope for mutually beneficial labor exchange, as well as altering the nature of the exchange relationship.

An important additional consequence is that the overall incidence of exchange costs may alter the content of labor transactions by rendering the market system as a whole *incomplete*. Markets are said to be *complete* if it is possible to trade any good with any person. This condition is violated if transactional obstacles preclude exchange in a particular set of goods or with a given set of trading partners. To take one example of potential relevance for labor market outcomes, many forms of insurance are not commercially available, particularly insurance against variations in labor income (including the extreme variation resulting from unemployment).

Why does this matter? Generally speaking, if market incompleteness precludes some goods from being purchased independently, workers may seek their provision in the context of employment relationships. As you'll see in part III, some theories pertaining to the structure or content of these relationships assume that employers provide their workers with partial insurance against income risk, which only makes sense if workers are unable to purchase this insurance separately at competitive rates. Another possible application is found in the provision of non-pecuniary benefits such as medical insurance as a portion of worker compensation; presumably workers would find this option appealing only if they were unable to purchase these goods at comparable rates apart from the employment relationship.

The respective consequences of matching and negotiation costs on one hand and enforcement costs on the other are investigated in the next two chapters. These costs correspondingly create incentives for organizational innovations intended to reduce the magnitude or relative incidence of exchange costs. The manifestations of such incentives, as well as the consequences for labor exchange of important forms of market incompleteness, are investigated in part III on the nature of employment relationships.

EXCHANGE COSTS AND THE STRUCTURE OF LABOR EXCHANGE

Part III of the text considers a number of phenomena that are specifically associated with exchange relationships for labor and share the feature of being difficult to explain on the basis of the perfectly competitive model of frictionless labor exchange. One particular set of regularities, considered below, provides the context in which all of the other elements of labor exchange are put in place. These have to do with the structure of employment, defined respectively in terms of the identities of and roles played by labor buyers and sellers.

The Edgeworth box representation of labor exchange presented earlier in the chapter obscures the identity of labor buyers by hiding them behind the organizational façade of "firm"-hood. But in private ownership economies, for-profit firms are owned by households, and thus, in principle at least, act on their behalf. It is therefore appropriate to look behind the organizational veil to determine what, if anything, consistently distinguishes buyers and sellers of labor.

One way to address this issue is by noting that households supply two types of productive inputs besides labor: alienable inputs, such as land, (patented) ideas, materials, tools or machines, and productive risk-bearing. The latter input, sometimes referred to as *entrepreneurship*, reflects the fact that commercial production incurs risks – in particular, the risk of losing money or even going bankrupt – for which it is impossible to purchase complete insurance. (One of the study questions at the end of the chapter asks you to ponder why this might be so.) Those households that elect to bear the uninsurable risk associated with a given commercial production venture can be thought of as the owners of the enterprise pursuing that venture. They're the ones who, as firm owners, ultimately hire the inputs used in production.

However, there is no logical or legal reason why these households need supply any input other than productive risk-bearing to the firms they own. Nor is there any economic necessity to do so, particularly under the assumptions of the perfectly competitive model. In this framework, a "firm" can suitably be thought of as a household or group of households whose preferences are somehow served by producing goods for profit. To pursue this end, the firm owners can simply buy all needed labor or non-labor inputs in competitive markets, so there's no need for the owners to supply any of the inputs themselves. If they don't have the ready cash to purchase these inputs, they can simply borrow the necessary liquidity at competitive interest rates. If durable tools or machines are needed for production, these capital goods can simply be rented.

Furthermore, within the framework of competitive theory, the only *necessary* economic difference between households that own commercial firms and those that don't is in terms of comparative aversion to risk. Given that firm ownership involves bearing uninsurable risk, households having a greater total stake in firm ownership (however that's determined) must have, other things equal, less aversion to such risks. But this could simply be a matter of idiosyncratic differences in taste.

Finally, since all inputs necessary for commercial production can, under perfectly competitive exchange conditions, be purchased in the appropriate markets, there is no reason to think that the resulting relationships between firm owners and input sellers are anything other than typical exchange relationships, fully summarized by the terms of exchange specified in the appropriate formal or informal contracts. In other words, it is presumptive that a firm's input purchases are commercial exchanges in the same way that its output sales are.

In sum, particularly under the conditions of the perfectly competitive model, there is no reason to presume that entrepreneurial households would systematically supply any other inputs to the firms they own, or that there are any systematic differences between labor buying and labor selling households other than (idiosyncratic) differences in risk preference; and no reason to think that relationships governing the purchase of labor are systematically different from relationships governing any other type of transaction. As discussed below, however, the empirical record suggests a strikingly different story: entrepreneurs systematically supply other forms of input to the firms they own, firm-owning households appear to differ systematically from those that don't, and exchange relationships governing the purchase of labor are qualitatively distinct from other types of commercial transaction. Of these remarkable empirical regularities, only the second is readily accounted for on the basis of the perfectly competitive model. The others suggest the impact of exchange costs on the structure of labor market and related transactions.

Capital- vs. labor-owned firms

In principle, firm-owning households need only supply "entrepreneurship" to their commercial production endeavors. If they wished, they might also supply some other input to the firm – land, labor, or "capital" goods such as tools and machines. But as mentioned above, there is no obvious reason, particularly under conditions of perfectly competitive exchange, to expect any systematic connection between firm ownership and any other input supply. A firm's owners might also supply it land, or labor, or capital goods, or any mixture of these, or none of them.

It is striking, then, that in the vast majority of commercial enterprises producing for profit, firm owners constitute a subset of the firm's *capital* suppliers, and thus firm ownership is defined in terms of ownership of the firm's capital assets. The most familiar case of such *capital-owned* firms is perhaps the limited liability corporation, whose owners, as stockholders, own equity shares of the firm's capital assets. But in addition, most single proprietorships and partnerships are also "capital-owned" in this sense. In all such cases, firm owners may also borrow money to cover capital costs; but as discussed below in the context of self-employed workers, their ability to do so may be limited by the extent of their own equity in the firm.

In a small minority of commercial firms, ownership is defined instead on the basis of individuals' *labor* contributions to the firm, rather than ownership of alienable capital assets. These are known as "labor-" or "worker-owned" firms. While this structure of firm ownership is relatively rare, its incidence also displays interesting regularities.

Capital-owned firms dominate in every industrial sector, with the exception of high-skill professions such as in law, medicine, or advertising. However, there are "pockets" of worker-owned enterprises in certain industries such as construction or printing, in both the US and Western Europe. Worker-owned firms are typically production enterprises characterized by relatively low capital intensity, relatively high *human* capital requirements (in terms of specialized training or education), small production scale, or low task differentiation. For example, professional legal and medical partnerships generally satisfy all of these conditions. (The third pure ownership scenario, in which firm ownership is limited to suppliers of *land*, is rarer still, to the point of invisibility.)

A possible explanation for these regularities in the structure of firm ownership, to be explored further in chapters 8 and 9, is that the presence of significant exchange costs somehow favors prospective owners who can supply their own capital assets. In this perspective, worker ownership may emerge in sectors whose production conditions render this advantage less compelling. In any case, it is difficult at best to explain the empirical incidence of firm ownership *without* some reference to costs of exchange.

Household wealth and firm ownership

While a household's decision to share in the ownership of a firm may be a matter of taste, it is also a matter of household wealth: overwhelmingly, firm ownership is concentrated among the most wealthy households. Of course, it is not surprising that more wealthy households would hold more wealth of all kinds, including wealth in the form of shares in firm ownership. Granting this, one might then expect, say, the top 10% of households in terms of overall alienable (that is, non-human capital) wealth would hold 10% of firm ownership shares.

Table 5.1 Median value of holdings for families holding each asset class (thousands of 1998 dollars)

	Bonds	Stocks	Business	Primary residence
Income (1998 dollars)				
Less than10,000	.[1]	14.0	37.5	51.0
10,000–24,999	8.4	10.0	31.1	71.9
25,000–49,999	25.0	8.0	37.5	85.0
50,000–99,999	19.0	15.0	56.0	130.0
100,000 and more	108.0	55.0	230.0	240.0
Net worth percentile:				
Bottom 25%	.[1]	0.7	3.5	40.0
25–49.9	.[1]	3.0	12.0	60.0
50–74.9	10.0	8.0	40.0	95.0
75–89.9	25.0	26.3	87.5	140.0
Top 10%	100.0	85.0	300.0	250.0

.[1] = 10 or fewer observations.
Source: 1998 Survey of Consumer Finances: Website
http://www.federalreserve.gov/pubs/oss/oss2/98/bulltables98.txt

Table 5.2 Source and mean level of income in 2000 of persons 15 years old and over ($000s)

Total income $196,957 Source	% with income from source	Mean income
Earnings	76%	$149,816
Nonfarm self-employment	6%	$12,462
Social Security	20%	$38,436
Retirement income	9%	$17,767
Interest	52%	$102,443
Dividends	20%	$39,111
Rents, royalties, estates, or trusts	6%	$11,405

Source: US Census Bureau, *Current Population Survey* (March 2001): table PINC-08; website http://ferret.bls.census.gov/macro/032001/perinc/new08_001.htm

The concentration of firm ownership is, however, considerably more skewed than this, at least in the US. Over 90% of business assets are owned by the wealthiest 10% of US households (they own as well 80% of all nonresidential real estate, 85% of all stock, and 94% of all bonds).[1] Indeed, as shown in table 5.1, on average the households that have significant positions of firm ownership are relatively affluent. Conversely, as shown in table 5.2, there is a marked inverse correlation between the level of household income and the *portion* of that income derived from labor earnings.

Although this relationship is not *necessarily* predicted by the perfectly competitive model, it is at least *consistent* with it. The distribution of firm ownership on the basis of household income or wealth might be explained on the basis of *income effects* on households' marginal choices with respect to leisure, current consumption, and degree of risk. Specifically, given the plausible assumption that a typical household's aversion to risk and forgone current consumption is decreasing in its attainable income level, then one would expect richer households to save more and bear more risk, both of which would lead them to increase their holdings of business assets more than in proportion to the increase in income. This may not be the primary reason for the connection between household income or wealth levels and firm ownership, but it is certainly consistent with the premises of the competitive model.

Employment as a distinct form of exchange

Under the assumptions of the perfectly competitive model, exchanges for labor are just like any other commercial transaction. But there is at least one clear indication of a qualitative distinction arising in labor exchanges for commercial ends, found in the contrasts between the case law governing *employment* and that governing more general *commercial* transactions. Specifically, the case law governing *employment* relations seems to allow much greater scope for the exercise of authority by employers in determining the actions of their employees.[2]

This asymmetry is manifested in two ways: first, in the duties and obligations required of employees, relative to those imposed on independent contractors, and second, in the sanctions invoked for violations of these legal responsibilities and the procedures by which violations are found to have occurred. On the first point, employees have stronger obligations of obedience and information disclosure than do independent contractors, and are furthermore held to a higher standard of behavior, including the requirement to maintain loyalty and good relations with employers. Concerning the latter point, employees may be subject to damages for failure to fulfill these obligations, and adjudication procedures in such cases are based on the presumption that the directives of employers should be followed first and questioned later, except when doing so would put employees in danger.

The distinction between employment and the status of independent contractor is also reflected in the US tax code, which presumes that remunerated services constitute employment if the actions taken by the service provider are under the direction of the receiver. Whether in case or tax law, however, these distinctions are difficult to understand in the absence of exchange costs inhibiting the use of contracts to enforce desired terms of exchange. Under perfect contracting conditions, any exercise of authority would be superfluous, since any outcome determined by the exercise of such authority in labor exchange could simply be spelled out in an appropriately specified legal contract.

DOES SUCCESSFUL SELF-EMPLOYMENT DEPEND ON PERSONAL WEALTH?

A significant portion of the labor force in market economies is self-employed at any given point, although this fraction varies considerably across countries and over time. For example, the incidence of self-employment in 1996 varied from a low of 5.4% in Luxembourg and Norway to highs of 22.8% in Turkey and 25.1% in Greece. Rates of self-employment also vary significantly across demographic groups, at least in the United States. Male self-employment rates are almost twice as high as those for female workers, and women choose different occupations and industries in which to be self-employed than do men. Those of Asian or Pacific Island extraction are over three times as likely to be self-employed as African-Americans. Self-employment rates also rise with age until the cohort older than 54, largely because entry rates exceed rates of exit from self-employment for most of the life cycle (Georellis and Wall, 2000).

Many workers consider self-employment a uniquely attractive option. Economists David Blanchflower and Andrew Oswald (1998) report survey evidence that, other things equal, self-employed workers register significantly higher levels of job and life satisfaction than other employees, even after controlling for variations in childhood psychological test scores. Blanchflower (2000) finds in survey data from several countries in the European Union an almost universally positive association between self-employment and job satisfaction.

This indication of welfare gains from self-employment is corroborated by the work of Barton Hamilton (2000), who reports that those who are self-employed for at least ten years have median earnings at least 35% below that of comparable workers employed by others. His econometric analysis rejects the hypothesis that this differential can be explained by differences in average ability between the two groups. Arguably, then, the typical self-employer is getting non-pecuniary benefits that serve to offset the substantial corresponding loss in money income.

Despite this average wage penalty on self-employment, there is evidence that many more people desire to work for themselves than exercise this option. Blanchflower also notes from survey results for eleven countries that those expressing a desire to be self-employed exceed those who enjoy this capacity several times over. In the extreme case, 63% of randomly sampled Americans surveyed in the International Social Survey Programme in 1989 responded that they would choose self-employment if given the option, although only about 9% of the workforce was self-employed at the time.

Why might there be such a dramatic disparity between the desire for self-employment and its realization? The foregoing argument suggests that

continued

limitations in personal wealth may reduce the viability of this option. Consistent with this suggestion, a number of studies have found a statistically significant impact of personal wealth on the probability of becoming self-employed or on the financial resources available to those who go into business for themselves. Evans and Jovanovic (1989) find evidence for both results, noting that entrepreneurs in their sample were apparently limited to a capital stock of no more than one and a half times their personal wealth.

However, such findings leave open the logic connecting wealth level to self-employment status: does wealth matter because of the inability of poorer entrepreneurs to secure adequate capital? Or is it because there are income effects on individual aversion to entrepreneurial risks, similar to the argument suggested earlier in the chapter? Finally, could it be that some third variable leads to both greater wealth and a higher propensity for self-employment? With respect to the latter point, for example, some studies show that children of the self-employed are more likely to work for themselves. It might be that the same logic also leads to greater family wealth.

Insight into these questions is provided by a number of studies linking *windfall* increases in wealth with the probability of entering self-employment. Blanchflower and Oswald report that receipt of an inheritance or gift increases the probability of self-employment, other things equal. They also present survey results indicating that the self-employed identify raising capital as their principal problem. Perhaps the most telling evidence on the logic connecting wealth and probability of self-employment is provided by Lindh and Ohlsson (1996), who find using Swedish data that lottery winnings increase the probability of being self-employed. This finding is significant in that it rules out the possibility of family-specific genetic or cultural factors that increase both wealth (and thus the prospects for inheritance) and the propensity for self-employment.

Investigating Finnish data, Johansson (2000) reports the complementary result that, holding wealth levels constant, home ownership significantly increases the probability of entering self-employment. This finding suggests that the need to provide *collateral* for financial loans presents a serious constraint on self-employment. The fact that the *form* of wealth affects the propensity for self-employment suggests that capital market failures rather than income effects on entrepreneurial risk aversion might best explain the economic role of wealth in this context.

Related discussion questions:
1. What are some reasons that people might pay such a large implicit wage premium to be self-employed rather than working for others? Would you pay that premium?
2. Why can't those with limited wealth who wish to be self-employed simply borrow the money necessary to finance their capital needs?

Related references:

David G. Blanchflower, "Self-Employment in OECD Countries," *Labour Economics* 7, no. 5 (September 2000): 471–505.

David G. Blanchflower and Andrew J. Oswald, "What Makes an Entrepreneur?," *Journal of Labor Economics* 16, no. 1 (January 1998): 26–60.

David S. Evans and Boyan Jovanovic, "An Estimated Model of Entrepreneurial Choice under Liquidity Constraints," *Journal of Political Economy* 97, no. 4 (August 1989): 808–27.

Yannis Georellis and Howard J. Wall, "Who Are the Self-Employed?," *Federal Reserve Bank of St. Louis Review* 82, no. 6 (November/December 2000): 15–23.

Barton H. Hamilton, "Does Entrepreneurship Pay? An Empirical Analysis of the Returns to Self-Employment," *Journal of Political Economy* 108, no. 3 (June 2000): 604–31.

Edvard Johansson, "Self-Employment and Liquidity Constraints," *Scandinavian Journal of Economics* 102, no. 1 (2000): 123–34.

Thomas Lindh and Henry Ohlsson, "Self-Employment and Windfall Gains: Evidence from the Swedish Lottery," *Economic Journal* 106, no. 439 (November 1996): 1515–26.

CONCLUSION

Like other transactions, exchanges for labor require potentially costly matching, negotiation, and enforcement activities by prospective traders. However, labor exchanges systematically exhibit certain features that are not shared by other forms of commercial transaction, suggesting that there is something about the nature of the good being exchanged that distinguishes *employment* from other forms of exchange in market economies. After a close examination of the strategic implications of specific forms of exchange costs in chapters 7 and 8, this hypothesis is taken up beginning in part III.

Study Questions

1. There is no scope for conflict over distribution of the gains from labor exchange when both parties are wage-takers. In perfectly competitive equilibrium, both are driven to the same point on the contract curve. What would determine the scope for distributional conflict – that is, the relevant length of the contract curve to be bargained over – when perfectly competitive conditions do not obtain? If possible, relate your answer to conditions in actual labor markets.

2. Supposing that perfectly competitive conditions did not obtain, what obstacles might keep parties to a given labor exchange from arriving at a point on their contract curve? If possible, relate your answer to conditions in actual employment settings.

continued

3. From your experience in labor markets, give examples of costly matching, negotiation, and enforcement activities. How did these costs affect your labor market experience?

4. Does a strong inverse correlation between household wealth and household labor supply measured in hours prove that the identity of labor buyers and sellers is ultimately determined by wealth differentials? Why or why not?

5. Imagine writing a contract for someone to come into your home (or dorm room) and do all your household chores. What would you specify in that contract? What activities would be difficult to specify? Are there activities that you would specifically want to rule out?

6. Name some goods that can typically only be obtained by entering an employment relationship. What factors might inhibit the independent provision of such goods?

7. This chapter defines *entrepreneurship* as bearing uninsurable risk associated with commercial enterprise – specifically, the risk that a venture may lose money or even go bankrupt. But why might such risks be uninsurable, if one can purchase insurance against other losses arising from mishaps such as auto accidents, theft, or residential fires? Conversely, workers generally can't acquire insurance against becoming unemployed unless provided by government. If unemployment insurance weren't available, should employees be thought of as entrepreneurs?

8. Use your personal experience to provide examples of the uses of authority in the workplace by employers. Could the actions you were directed to take have been specified in advance in an employment contract? Explain.

9. Can a person choose to be self-employed in any occupation? Give examples of occupations in which you think it would be hard to be self-employed, and explain why. Give examples of some occupations in which self-employment might be relatively easy, and explain why.

Notes

1 Nancy Folbre and the Center for Popular Economics, *The New Field Guide to the U.S. Economy* (New York: The New Press, 1995): section 1.4.
2 Scott E. Masten, "A Legal Basis for the Firm," *Journal of Law, Economics and Organization*, 4, no. 1 (Spring 1988): 181–98.

Suggestions for Further Reading

Samuel Bowles and Herbert Gintis, "The Revenge of Homo Economicus: Contested Exchange and the Revival of Political Economy," with comments by Oliver Williamson and Joseph Stiglitz, *Journal of Economic Perspectives* 7(1) (winter 1993): 83–114.

Oliver E. Williamson, *The Economic Institutions of Capitalism* (New York: The Free Press, 1985): chapters 1 and 2.

CHAPTER SIX

STRATEGIC LABOR EXCHANGE

Under the conditions of the perfectly competitive model, labor market participants don't take each other's actions explicitly into account in making economic decisions. So long as their exchange plans are fulfilled, at least, they don't need to: everything they need to know about the state of market competition is conveyed by the going wage rate. At the opposite extreme, pure monopolists or monopsonists take the exchange behavior of traders on the other side of the labor market into account when setting wages or quantities, but that behavior is summarized simply, completely, and anonymously by the relevant market supply or demand curve.

Labor market decisionmaking is not so straightforward in the alternative vision of labor exchange introduced in the previous chapter. In this perspective, participating in the labor market means locating a suitable exchange partner, negotiating mutually agreeable terms of exchange with said partner, and then making sure that all contractual terms are duly carried out. All of these activities are more or less costly, and some may be prohibitively so. For example, it may be practically impossible to foresee and contractually specify all possible contingencies affecting a given labor exchange. In this world, individuals may not be wage-takers, the total gains from exchange may vary with the wage rate, and wage rates may not adjust flexibly.

A host of empirical regularities and institutional arrangements specific to labor markets reinforce the hypothesis that the economic logic of labor exchange is more involved than the perfectly competitive model might suggest. Workers are paid on the basis of a vast array of compensation provisions, from piece rates, commissions, and bonuses to hourly wages and straight salaries.

Moreover, labor compensation is not always immediately paid in pecuniary terms; it may also come in the form of health or life insurance

continued

benefits or pension contributions. Labor negotiations are sometimes conducted by unions and industry councils and facilitated by arbitrators or mediators. The law governing employment relationships is in many ways distinct from that covering other commercial transactions.

An appropriate theoretical framework is needed to explore possible connections between the particular conditions of labor exchange and the often unique structural and behavioral features of labor markets. Broadly speaking, this framework is provided by the tools of *game theory* or, more descriptively, the theory of interactively optimizing behavior. The purpose of this chapter is to introduce the elements of game-theoretic analysis and illustrate the uses of this framework through applications to particular labor exchange scenarios arising under conditions of imperfect competition. This effort paves the way for the more focused examination of bargaining and imperfect contracting problems taken up in the next two chapters.

LABOR MARKET RELATIONS AS GAMES

Game theory concerns the study of decisionmaking in explicitly social contexts. The basic unit of analysis is a *game*, defined as a situation involving strategic interactions among participants. Specifically, a situation of strategic interaction is understood to exist for a group of people if the interests of each person are affected by the actions of others in the group, and this interdependence is known to all participants. The primary purpose of using game theory is to develop hypotheses as to how people act in such situations.

There are a number of labor market scenarios that might usefully be modeled as games. Several of these have been discussed in the preceding two chapters. Perhaps the most basic is the relationship of *bilateral monopoly* that arises when both the buyer and the seller in a given labor exchange enjoy some power to affect the wage rate. Here the strategic conflict is stark: given efficient bargaining, a higher payoff for one person implies less for the other.

A situation of bilateral strategic conflict might alternatively arise between a labor buyer and seller concerning actions by one or both parties that affect the magnitude of potential gains from labor exchange, rather than the specific division of gains between them. For example, an employer may find it difficult or impossible to stipulate worker effort levels in a way that can be effectively ensured through legal enforcement of contracts. As a consequence the employer must find some other means of inducing the desired effort levels.

Another type of strategic relationship arises when there are relatively few competitors on either side of the market. For example, in the case of *oligopsony* discussed in chapter 4, there exists a small number of firms hiring workers in a given labor market, so the wage and employment decisions of any one firm tend to have

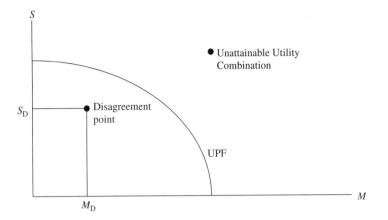

Figure 6.1   Utility possibilities frontier (UPF) with "disagreement" point.

a noticeable impact on the profitability of the others. Here the strategic conflict is not so sharp as in the setting of bilateral monopoly, in that all firms might conceivably stand to gain by colluding in their choice of wage and employment levels, rather than undercutting each other.

An even smaller degree of strategic conflict is encountered in problems of *coordination*, in which everyone has a mutual interest in undertaking a particular set of actions (for example, driving on the same side of the road), but perhaps have no immediate mechanism for ensuring that the desired harmonization of behaviors is secured. Some economists think of markets as a vast coordinating mechanism for the economic choices of self-seeking actors; this is the sense of Adam Smith's famous image of market forces as an "invisible hand" guiding individual choices.

As with the supply and demand analysis of the first two chapters, traditional game theory starts from the premise that rational agents attempt to optimize their respective objective functions. It differs from these more basic treatments in placing individual optimizing behavior in social contexts. Consequently, a useful way of thinking in general terms about the issues addressed by game theory is with the aid of a *utility possibilities frontier* (UPF for short). A UPF is defined as the locus of *maximal* utility combinations for a given set of people, in the specific sense that no one person can be made better off without making someone else worse off. As such, utility combinations on the UPF correspond to the set of *Pareto-efficient* allocations along the contract curve of an Edgeworth box representing the group's consumption possibilities.

A hypothetical UPF for two people, Mickey and Sylvia, with respectively utility levels M amd S, is illustrated in figure 6.1. Note that the UPF is downward-sloping, a necessary consequence of the restriction to Pareto-efficient utility combinations. Points inside the frontier share the property of being inefficient or *Pareto-inferior*; starting from any such point, it is always possible to make both individuals better off. Utility combinations beyond the frontier are unattainable.

In any strategic setting addressed by game theory, two issues arise. First, one might ask if participants in the game achieve a utility combination on the frontier or below it. Call this the question of *allocative efficiency* or simply *efficiency*. Second, assuming the frontier is achieved, there remains the substantive question of *which* point on the UPF is attained, that is, how the gains are divided among the players. Call this the *distributive* question. In general, then, issues of allocative efficiency and distribution arise in any strategic relationship, and the purpose of game theory is to analyze how those issues are resolved in given settings. (As a point of reference, recall that any equilibrium allocation achieved in a perfectly competitive market system is efficient, so it must correspond to some point on an economy's UPF. However, the theory makes no general prediction as to *which* point is reached on the UPF.)

There are two main approaches to addressing such questions in the literature on game theory, based on a distinction between *cooperative* and *noncooperative* games. A *cooperative* game is one for which it is *assumed* that participants can effectively commit themselves to particular actions. As a consequence of this assumption, strategic outcomes in cooperative-game settings are generally presumed to occur along the UPF rather than inside it. No such presumption informs the analysis of *noncooperative* games, understood as strategic settings in which participants do not necessarily enter into binding commitments.

Another way of framing this distinction is that in noncooperative analysis, predictions about the outcome of a game are derived from studying the specific strategic choices made by the players, while in the context of cooperative games, outcomes are not derived on this basis. Instead, the analyst posits specific conditions characterizing the game's outcome, and then considers what set of outcomes satisfy the postulated conditions. This raises an obvious question as to how one decides what conditions to impose on the game's solution. There is no single necessary answer to this, as reflected in the very wide range of solution concepts for cooperative games.

Cooperative game theory might therefore best be thought of as a convenient and perhaps intuitively justifiable shortcut in the analysis of what might prove to be very complex strategic interactions. It is with this advantage in view that the chapter's analysis begins by introducing a familiar cooperative equilibrium concept known as the *Nash Bargaining Solution*, named after its inventor, John F. Nash (the very same John Nash featured in the recent biography and movie *A Beautiful Mind*). This solution concept is potentially useful in the analysis of relationships involving bilateral monopoly power.

BARGAINING AS A COOPERATIVE GAME

Bilateral monopoly and the bargaining problem

Bilateral monopoly generically leads to a bargaining relationship because both parties to the exchange enjoy the power to influence the wage rate – or to put it

in different terms, both parties find that they cannot costlessly replace their existing trading partner. Consequently, they are to some extent stuck with each other,
and have to arrive at a mutually agreeable distribution of the prospective gains
from labor exchange.

The strategic logic of bargaining has long bedeviled economists, due to the
basic indeterminacy of relationships involving bilateral monopoly power. Consider this point in the context of figure 6.1 above. What would induce Mickey and
Sylvia to agree on any particular point on the UPF? You might be tempted to
answer that the outcome depends on their *relative* bargaining power, but then
you'd face the equally problematic task of explaining the determination of relative bargaining power, thus simply replacing one question with another.

One way to reduce the indeterminacy of the bargaining outcome is to add
some plausible structure to the economic logic of the problem by assuming that
Mickey and Sylvia have alternatives they can fall back on in the event that their
bargaining relationship breaks down. These alternatives are represented by the
utility combination labeled (S_D, M_D) in figure 6.1. With this addition, it seems
reasonable to assume that Mickey and Sylvia can guarantee themselves at least
their respective "disagreement" or fallback utility levels, and therefore would
only be willing to consider points along the UPF that lie to the "northeast" of the
utility combination (S_D, M_D). Thus, introducing these alternative payoffs plausibly reduces the scope for bargaining outcomes to this smaller segment of the
UPF.

This procedure still leaves considerable room for disagreement in bargaining,
however: other things equal, Sylvia would prefer points on the UPF further up
and to the right, while Mickey would prefer points further down and to the left.
How would their differences be resolved into a particular allocation? This is the
question considered by John Nash when he first studied the bargaining problem
over fifty years ago.

The Nash bargaining solution

Nash's *cooperative* solution concept for this problem is based on defining a bargaining environment in terms of the players involved, their attainable utility combinations as represented by the UPF, and their *disagreement point* (S_D, M_D). (Since
this is a cooperative game, it is unclear what exactly is meant by "disagreement"
in this context. In particular, it is not evident if positing the existence of such a
point is tantamount to assuming that either player could exit the relationship
voluntarily. This indeterminacy is resolved with the aid of the bargaining framework developed in the next chapter.) Given this structure, Nash listed a set of
conditions that bargaining agreements in this context might be expected to satisfy
(see the reference given at the end of the chapter for details), and derived a simple
formula entailed by these conditions.

Specifically, the *Nash Bargaining Solution* corresponds to the particular payoff
combination (S^*, M^*) on Mickey and Sylvia's UPF that maximizes the product

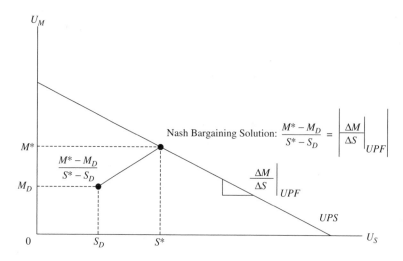

Figure 6.2 Nash bargaining solution (special case of linear UPF).

$(M - M_D)(S - S_D)$, where (S, M) are feasible utility combinations and as before (S_D, M_D) represents an exogenously given pair of "disagreement" utilities for Mickey and Sylvia. The Nash bargaining solution (mathematically derived in the appendix to this chapter) has an interesting graphical property, illustrated in figure 6.2: the ratio of the players' equilibrium payoffs, net of disagreement utilities, must be equal to the absolute value of the slope of the UPF at the equilibrium point. That is, at the Nash bargaining solution, the absolute value of the UPF's slope equals the ratio $\dfrac{M^* - M_D}{S^* - S_D}$.

This graphical condition can be manipulated to derive the following properties of the Nash bargaining solution, to be interpreted as hypotheses concerning the outcomes of labor exchange relationships characterized by bilateral monopoly power:

- *If the disagreement point does not lie on the UPF, then both players share in the gains from labor exchange*
- *If the total gains from labor exchange increase (as depicted by an outward shift in the UPF), then the equilibrium payoffs of both players increase*
- *Each player's equilibrium payoff is strictly positively related to the value of her disagreement payoff and strictly negatively related to the value of her opponent's disagreement payoff*

These are strong and potentially testable hypotheses, so Nash's cooperative-game solution provides a useful starting point for thinking about the outcomes of bargaining relationships. As discussed in the appendix to this chapter, the model can also be extended to accommodate multiple bargaining parties and differences in effective bargaining power. However, it can't be used to explain how differences in bargaining power arise.

LABOR MARKET RELATIONSHIPS AS NONCOOPERATIVE GAMES

Like all other solution concepts for cooperative games, the Nash bargaining solution assumes the attainment of efficient allocations, but doesn't explain how this is accomplished. Consequently a different approach is needed if one wants to study the logic informing social outcomes reached in strategic settings. This study is the special province of *noncooperative* game theory.

Noncooperative games in normal form

The most basic description of a noncooperative game has just three elements: the set of *players*, or participants in a given strategic interaction; a list of the possible *strategies* adopted by each player; and the set of player-specific *payoffs* associated with each possible combination of strategies. A player's *strategy* is defined as a complete representation of how he or she would play the game, contingent on the moves of the other players. Notice that a strategy is therefore different from a single "move" or action, since it may involve several moves, the specific determination of which depends on the actions taken by competing players. A *payoff*, finally, is the benefit to a player resulting from a given combination of strategies. Think of a player's payoff as a utility function defined in terms of strategy combinations rather than consumption bundles.

This most basic description of a noncooperative game, encompassing players, strategies, and payoffs, is known as the *normal* or *strategic* form of the game. This is illustrated for the scenario of a *coordination game* in figure 6.3. In this scenario there are two players, Shirley and Lee, each with two strategies, "left" and "right"; you might think of these as choices to drive on the left side of public roads (as in England or Australia) or on the right (as in the US and most other countries). All of the elements of the normal form are presented in figure 6.3: it indicates the players, their strategies, and inside the cells of the game box, the payoff pairs corresponding to each of the four possible strategy combinations (with Shirley's payoff always listed first.)

Note that two of the possible strategy combinations for this game, (left, left) and (right, right), are Pareto-efficient, while the other two are not. Furthermore, the players are indifferent between the two Pareto-efficient outcomes, since they receive the same payoffs in either case. Thus the only strategic issue is one of coordinating their strategies. Is there any reason to think this will be accomplished, based solely on the information presented in figure 6.3?

Before addressing this question, examine the normal form of another well-known noncooperative game, the so-called *prisoners' dilemma*, depicted in figure

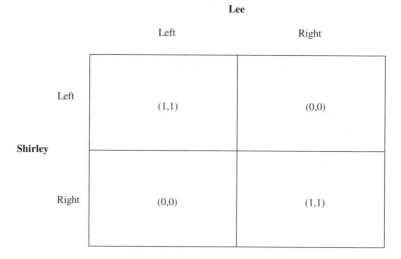

Figure 6.3 A coordination game.

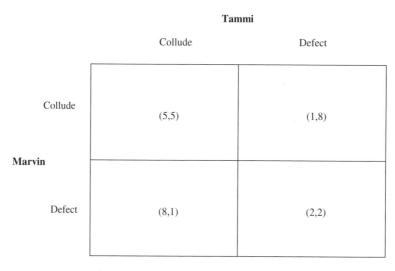

Figure 6.4 A prisoners' dilemma game.

6.4. Note that all of the elements required for the normal form are again present: the players are Marvin and Tammi, and they each have two strategies, collude and defect. The payoffs corresponding to each pair of strategies are shown in the four cells of the game box.

The basic idea of the prisoners' dilemma game is that each player has the option of acting as if to promote the common good of both players (colluding), or of defecting from this collusive arrangement. The implicit difficulty is that the players are somehow prevented from *committing* themselves to the collusive outcome. The question thus arises whether each player will freely choose to collude and thus achieve the outcome yielding the highest sum of payoffs. Mutual collusion may seem like a plausible outcome of this game, since it is clearly better for both players than mutual defection.

However, a closer look at the insidious payoff structure of the game raises some doubts about this assessment. Remember that neither player can commit to particular strategies. Therefore the danger lurks that a player may turn renegade with respect to the apparently socially desirable situation of mutual collusion. To see this, suppose that player A chooses to collude; what is the best player B can do in response? Clearly player B gets a higher payoff playing "defect" in this case. Moreover, defecting is also player B's best strategy if instead player A chooses to defect. The same conclusion holds for player A: no matter what player B chooses to do, player A can garner a higher payoff by choosing to defect. Thus, in the absence of binding commitments, it appears that mutual defection is the likely outcome of this game. This seems unfortunate, if not perverse, in that it is the sole outcome which is Pareto-inefficient.

This notion of the "likely outcome" of a noncooperative game is formalized in the solution concept known as a *Nash equilibrium*, also named for John Nash, who first advanced the concept in the early 1950s.[1] (This notion of equilibrium for *noncooperative* games should not be confused with the Nash bargaining solution, a cooperative equilibrium concept.) A strategy combination is said to constitute a *Nash equilibrium* if each player's strategy maximizes his or her payoff, *given* the strategies of all the other players. Applying this definition to the prisoners' dilemma game in figure 6.4, it should be clear that the outcome (defect, defect) is a Nash equilibrium, and (collude, collude) is not – indeed, nor are the other two strategy combinations, so (defect, defect), the uniquely Pareto-inferior outcome, is also the unique Nash equilibrium of the game, a consequence of the twin assumptions that players are strictly self-interested and unable to bind themselves to particular strategies.

Moreover, the Nash equilibrium strategies of the prisoners' dilemma game are also *dominant*, meaning that each player's strategy maximizes his or her payoff no matter what the other player does. Note, for example, that player A gets a higher payoff from defecting no matter whether B colludes *or* defects. Of course, not all Nash equilibria are also dominant-strategy equilibria. You should confirm that there are at least two Nash equilibria for the coordination game discussed earlier (left, left) and (right, right), and thus there is clearly no dominant strategy equilibrium in that case. (There is a third Nash equilibrium involving a *mixed strategy*, such that both players select each of their possible moves with positive probability, but this possibility will not be discussed further here; interested readers should consult the end-of-chapter references.)

The foregoing analysis of the prisoners' dilemma is not meant to suggest that people will necessarily act in a socially perverse manner when presented with the opportunity to gain at others' expense. In fact, it is easy to come up with empirical examples where people do just the opposite, acting to promote the general interest even when they are not encouraged by selfish considerations to do so. First, of course, if binding commitments are possible in a given strategic interaction, it might be expected that the parties involved could work out a mutually desirable solution. This is why cooperative and noncooperative games typically yield different results.

But second, there is no contradiction in suggesting that rational individuals might reject defection from a collusive outcome, even if this were inconsistent with a narrow reading of their self-interest. A rational person, for example, might sacrifice self-interest in the interest of justice or fairness. This suggests a different hypothesis about individual motives than is typically invoked in game-theoretic analysis, but nothing in the structure or definition of game theory rules this out.

DO PEOPLE RESPOND TO SOCIAL NORMS IN STRATEGIC SETTINGS?

As originally conceived, game theory was simply an extension of the theory of rational optimizing behavior to contexts involving strategic interaction. As such, it was built on an earlier framework's presumption of *self-interested* behavior narrowly construed, although this is not a defining feature of the theory. This restriction has been subject to significant challenges by the growing field of *experimental economics*.

There is now a significant amount of experimental evidence that people do not play games involving small monetary payoffs in ways consistent with the predictions of game theory based on a narrow interpretation of self-interested behavior. In "charity"/"dictator" games involving unilateral decisions over the distribution of a given sum of money (for which the optimal strategy of the "dictator" from a selfish point of view is to keep everything for oneself), players often behave altruistically (Eckel and Grossman, 1996), sharing a portion of their gains. In "ultimatum" games, in which one player proposes a particular split of a given sum and a second player either rejects or accepts the offer, with both players getting nothing if the offer is rejected, the result predicted by standard theory is that the proposer will make the smallest possible positive offer, which is immediately accepted. Experimental results confirm neither aspect of this prediction: responders routinely reject positive offers considered to be too small, and proposers typically make offers that are closer to equal distribution of the surplus than to zero (Saad and Gill, 2000).

Interestingly, game outcomes vary systematically by sex of the players, with women generally acting more generously in anonymous distribution games. There is also evidence of interesting dynamics between players in games where people play face to face, namely that men give more generously to women players than to other men. It may well be that outcomes would vary systematically along other demographic dimensions as well; unfortunately, most game subjects are college students, and experiments have not yet been widely conducted in a cross-cultural context, so these are areas that remain largely unexplored. However, there appear to be rewarding prospects for enlarging the reach and sophistication of game theory by incorporating a more nuanced theory of human behavior in strategic settings.

Related discussion questions:
1. In the ultimatum game involving the split of a hundred dollars, if A and B were both acting out of rational self-interest, what offer should A make? Would B accept it?
2. Why do you think there are gender differences in game play? Should economics take such differences into account in its theoretical models, or try to structure experiments so as to eradicate such gender differences? Would you expect differences along other demographic lines? For example? Why or why not?

Related references:
Catherine Eckel and Phillip Grossman, "Altruism in Anonymous Dictator Games," *Games and Economic Behavior* 16 (1996): 181–91.
Gad Saad and Tripat Gill, "Gender Dynamics in the Ultimatum Game: An Evolutionary Psychology Perspective," working paper, 2000.

That said, standard noncooperative game-theoretic analysis has proved useful in the study of a wide range of social outcomes. For example, the prisoners' dilemma game illustrated above has been used to explain the seemingly perverse behavior resulting in arms races, depletion of the earth's ozone layer, and the self-destruction of such immensely profitable cartels as OPEC in the 1970s. A generalized version of the prisoners' dilemma game is applied in the analysis of labor markets characterized by *oligopsony*, considered next.

Application of normal-form game analysis: oligopsony in labor markets

Recall from the discussion of chapter 4 that *oligopsony* is defined as a market characterized by the presence of a small number of buyers. An oligopsonistic labor market is thus one in which a relatively small number of firms compete for labor inputs supplied by numerous wage-taking labor sellers. The earlier discussion suggested that the outcomes achieved in oligopsonistic markets would tend to fall somewhere between perfectly competitive equilibrium and the wage and employment combination chosen by a monopsonist.

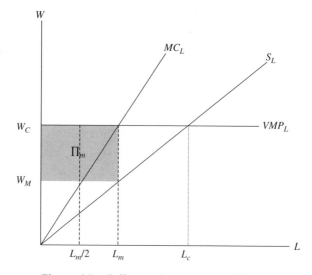

Figure 6.5 Collusive duopsony equilibrium.

The easiest way to pursue this point is in the context of *duopsony* (a market with just two buyers), in which rival firms choose optimizing *employment levels* noncooperatively. Call this the *Cournot* duopsony model, in honor of the nineteenth-century French engineer who first conceived of describing imperfectly competitive behavior in terms of strategic *quantity* choices by firms.

To motivate the Nash equilibrium of the Cournot duopsony game, first suppose that the two firms somehow collude to establish the jointly profit-maximizing level of total employment in the labor market. The question is whether the duopsonists would be able to maintain this collusive outcome in a noncooperative context. Suppose initially that the two labor buyers mimic the single wage-setting monopsony equilibrium and divide the resulting profits equally. To keep the analysis simple, assume that the firms face a horizontal VMP_L curve and a linear, upward-sloping market supply curve, as shown in figure 6.5.

The collusive outcome described above is indicated by the employment–wage rate combination (L_m, W_m). It is useful to note at this point that under the stated conditions, the monopsonistic employment level L_m is just equal to *half* of the competitive employment level L_c. Each duopsonist initially hires $L_m/2$ workers. Total consumer surplus under the collusive equilibrium is represented by the rectangle marked Π_m and each buyer receives half that surplus. This outcome would correspond to a particular *cooperative game* solution to this problem. Would this outcome also arise under *noncooperative* conditions?

To answer this, imagine that one firm (call it firm A) looks for a way to take advantage of this arrangement. Suppose initially that this firm assumes that its rival will hold to the collusive agreement and thus continue to hire half of the monopsony employment level. Given this assumption, firm A can determine the wage rate

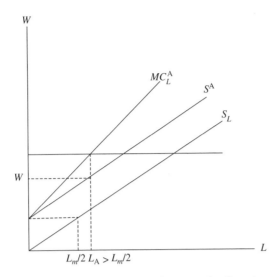

Figure 6.6 Residual supply curve for firm A.

that will result for each level of its own hiring decision, given the market supply curve and the employment level of the other firm. Firm A can thus calculate its *individual* labor supply curve as the *residual* which remains after subtracting firm B's employment level from total market quantity supplied at each wage rate, so long as the result is non-negative (since it is impossible to hire a negative quantity of labor).

Firm A's *residual supply curve* thus derived is depicted in figure 6.6, running parallel to and a horizontal distance of $L_m/2$ from the market supply curve. Suppose, therefore, that firm A chooses the quantity of labor hired to maximize its profit on the basis of this new supply curve, labeled S^A, and its constant VMP_L of hiring labor. The resulting employment level for firm A is L_A, as shown in figure 6.6. It turns out that this quantity of labor hired exceeds $L_m/2$. Since a parallel argument can be made for firm B, this result demonstrates that duopsonists will have an incentive to "cheat" on any collusive joint profit-maximization arrangement. Here, "cheating" on the collusive outcome takes the form of departures from collusive employment levels.

Since both firms have an incentive to diverge from the collusive employment level, it cannot constitute a Nash equilibrium of the corresponding noncooperative game played by the two firms. But then what is the Nash equilibrium, and how is it determined? The easiest way to see the answer to this is by constructing a *reaction function* for each firm, defined as the firm's payoff-maximizing labor choice in response to the other firm's employment choice, whatever it is. By following the method described above for constructing a firm's *residual* labor supply curve given the labor hiring choice of the other firm, you can demonstrate for yourself that each firm's reaction function is downward-sloping, so that it hires less labor, the more the other firm hires.

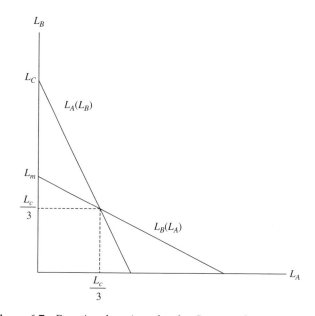

Figure 6.7 Reaction functions for the Cournot duopsony game.

The algebraic representation of the firms' reaction functions (denoted $L_A(L_B)$ and $L_B(L_A)$) is derived in the appendix to this chapter. Their visual representation is shown in figure 6.7. As you might guess, the equilibrium labor choices of the two firms are given by the intersection of the two reaction functions, since this is where each firm is doing the best it can given the choice of the other firm.

What then is the *total* Nash equilibrium employment level for the Cournot duopsony? As demonstrated in the appendix and suggested in figure 6.7, this is equal to two-thirds of the competitive outcome L_C. Since this exceeds the collusive employment level, which you'll recall is one-half of the quantity of labor exchanged under competitive equilibrium, Cournot duopsony thus clearly establishes an "intermediate case" between pure monopsony and perfect competition. By the same reasoning, the Nash equilibrium wage rate for this market lies in between the monopsony and perfectly competitive levels. Equilibrium profits per firm correspondingly fall between zero (the perfectly competitive level) and the monopsony level.

Now suppose that there are more than two labor buyers. What are the strategic implications of increasing the number of competitors in this market? It can be shown that the Nash equilibrium employment and wage rates both rise as the number of buyers increases, approaching their respective competitive values as this number gets very large. More specifically, the general conclusion yielded by the Cournot model with linear upward-sloping supply and constant VMP_L is that equilibrium employment will equal $N/(N+1)$ times the competitive employment level, where N denotes the number of labor buyers.

In sum, the general conclusion yielded by the Cournot–Nash model of oligopsony is that the degree of monopsonistic exploitation decreases as the number of competitors rises, with wage and employment tending to their respective perfectly competitive levels as the number of competing firms becomes large.

Noncooperative games in extensive form

For some analytical purposes, the normal form does not yield sufficient information about the nature of specific strategic interactions under study. This would be the case, for example, when the *sequence* in which players take action has an important bearing on the outcome of given relationships. In that case it is necessary to study the *extensive form* of the corresponding game. The extensive form of a game includes all of the elements incorporated in the normal form, plus two more: a statement of *who moves when*, illustrated by a *game tree*, and of *what each player knows* when his or her time to move comes, represented by *information sets* within the tree.

The game tree depicting the extensive form of the prisoners' dilemma game examined earlier is presented in figure 6.8. Since the prisoners' dilemma is typically understood as a simultaneous-move game, the determination of which player is shown as moving "first" is purely arbitrary. Here, player A goes "first," as indicated by the label of the initial *decision node* representing a point where some player must choose a move.

Second, since moves are made simultaneously, player B, although depicted as moving "second," really can't know the strategy chosen by player A. This uncertainty is indicated by B's *information set*, defined as the set of decision nodes among which B can't distinguish (it might thus be more appropriately called an "ignorance" set), and depicted by an oval drawn around the nodes in the set. The payoffs are as before, with the payoffs of the initial player listed first. Note a key

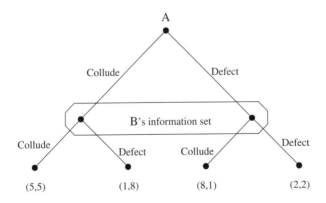

Figure 6.8   Extensive form of a prisoners' dilemma game.

feature of information sets: the player moving next must have the same available moves at each decision node in the set. If this weren't true, that player could infer the decision node by observing what moves could or could not be made.

Putting the one-shot prisoners' dilemma game in extensive form doesn't add much to an understanding of how the game is played, since the sequence of moves is obviously trivial in a simultaneous-move game. This verdict changes, however, when the game is repeatedly played by the same individuals over time. This scenario is considered next.

Application of extensive-form game analysis: self-enforcement in repeated noncooperative games

One way of thinking about the distinction between cooperative and noncooperative games is in terms of the opportunities individuals have for enforcing mutually preferred outcomes by contract. According to this perspective, a cooperative game setting is one for which commitments to mutually desired outcomes can always be costlessly enforced by contract, while a noncooperative game situation is one in which players may not have the option of signing costlessly enforceable contracts. An immediate corollary is that noncooperative games naturally arise whenever significant costs of negotiation or enforcement impede the use of formal contracts to secure desired exchange outcomes. As discussed earlier, inefficiency may be the result.

In some noncooperative settings, however, it may be possible for the participants themselves to induce "cooperative" or Pareto-efficient equilibrium outcomes by strategic means. Prospects for equilibrium *self-enforcement* of mutually preferred outcomes arise particularly in the case of games that are played repeatedly over time, creating the strategic possibility of conditioning *current* behavior on *past* outcomes of the repeated game. Players thus have the option of "rewarding" mutually beneficial behavior and "punishing" undesired outcomes.

Consider how this works in the context of the prisoners' dilemma game considered earlier in the chapter. As noted, mutual defection is the only Nash equilibrium when that game is played just once. It would by the same reasoning constitute a Nash equilibrium for a repeated version of the game, since clearly the best response of each player to the persistent defection of the other is also to choose defection in every period.

However, it is not generally the only Nash equilibrium outcome when the game is repeated a sufficient number of times. In that scenario, a player can elect in each period to reward past cooperation with continued cooperation, and to "punish" any prior defection with subsequent defection. Since any such punishment is "triggered" immediately by evidence of past defection, this option is generally known as a *trigger strategy*. A simple trigger strategy for the repeated prisoners' dilemma is *Nash reversion*, in which a player begins by colluding, continues to collude so long as the other player does, and responds to any defection from the mutually collusive outcome by defecting in return for the remainder of the game.

Faced with this strategy from an opponent in the repeated prisoners' dilemma game, a player considering defection in any period must weigh the immediate gain from defection (in terms of the payoff structure shown in figure 6.4, a payoff of 8 from unilateral defection compared to a payoff of 5 from continued cooperation) against the impending losses from eliminating the prospects for future cooperation (a payoff of 1 for the remainder of the game in place of the possibility of getting a payoff of 2 for at least some subsequent rounds of the game). The relative benefits of continued cooperation and permanent defection will depend in part on the degree to which the player *discounts* future payoffs. Other things equal, the higher the player's discount rate, the lower the cost of triggering future punishments.

Conversely, if the game is repeated a sufficient number of times and players don't discount the future too heavily, then mutual collusion for at least some repetitions of the prisoners' dilemma is consistent with equilibrium play, and the resulting Pareto improvements in outcomes are thus *self-enforced* by strategic means. However, the more efficient outcomes are not unique; in general, a large number of possible outcomes, from perpetual defection to perpetual cooperation, may be sustainable in equilibrium. Note two aspects of this result: first, the simple requirement of Nash equilibrium offers no basis for distinguishing among equilibria in terms of relative likelihood. All equilibria are equally plausible.

Second, nothing in the foregoing argument depends on representing the repeated prisoners' dilemma in *extensive* form. Exactly the same analysis could in principle be conducted with respect to the normal form of the repeated game, once appropriate allowance is made for the expanded strategic options made possible by repetition. As discussed next, the relevance of using the extensive form becomes apparent as one begins to grapple with the issues posed by the existence of multiple equilibria.

Multiple equilibria and subgame-perfect Nash equilibrium

Multiple Nash equilibria arise in a number of strategic settings in addition to the repeated-game context considered above. You saw an example of this earlier in the chapter in the case of the coordination game, in which there are at least two Nash equilibria. In such instances, the power of noncooperative game theory as a tool for yielding unambiguous behavioral hypotheses is obviously impaired. Of course, such ambiguities might simply be an innate feature of strategic human interaction, at least in some of its manifestations. Perhaps strategic behavior is to some extent unpredictable by its nature.

However, there is another possibility: perhaps Nash's proposed solution for noncooperative games, while a *necessary* condition for equilibrium in the strategic settings studied with this framework, is not sufficiently restrictive to eliminate all intuitively implausible outcomes. In that case, the appropriate way to mitigate the ambiguity associated with a multiplicity of equilibria is to tighten or "refine" the requirements for equilibrium in a given class of strategic settings. One such

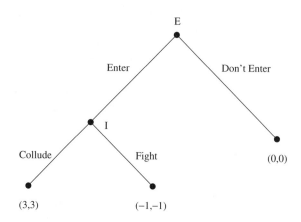

Figure 6.9   Extensive form of a market entry game.

refinement, called *subgame-perfect* Nash equilibrium, makes use of the extensive form of noncooperative games to distinguish among equilibria on the basis of strategic plausibility.

Let's first examine this approach to refining the notion of Nash equilibrium in the context of monopsony in the labor market. As discussed in chapter 4, a central question with regard to the persistence of monopsony concerns the possibility of entry by potential competitors: why don't new firms enter the labor market to take advantage of the rents enjoyed by the monopsonist? One possibility, investigated here, is that monopsonists take actions to deter potential entrants.

Consider this possibility in the context of a noncooperative "market entry" game. The game has two players, an incumbent firm and a potential entrant. The entrant (player E) moves first and has two strategies, enter or don't enter. The incumbent (player I) also has two strategies, both contingent on entry by the outsider: fight or collude. There are no information sets, so that the incumbent can clearly verify that entry has occurred before choosing a strategy. The extensive form for this game is illustrated in figure 6.9.

You should be able to ascertain that there are two Nash equilibria for this game. One equilibrium has the entrant playing "enter" and the incumbent playing "if E enters, collude;" the other involves no entry by the potential entrant, and the incumbent playing the strategy "if E enters, fight." In both cases, each player is doing the best he or she can given the strategy of the other: *if* the incumbent elects to collude when E enters, then entry is clearly preferable for the outside firm. On the other hand, *if* the incumbent elects to fight the entrant, the entrant can do no better than to stay outside the market.

However, a closer look at the game suggests that there is something problematic about the second equilibrium. To make this point clear, it is helpful to introduce the concept of a *subgame*, defined simply as a lower portion of a game tree, including associated payoffs. By definition, the entire game tree itself also constitutes a subgame. A *proper* subgame is one that is unconnected to any other by one or more information sets; the test of a proper subgame is that its extensive form also looks like a self-contained game tree, including payoffs.

Following this definition, there are three subgames in the extensive form of the prisoners' dilemma in figure 6.8, but only one proper subgame – the game itself. In contrast, there are two proper subgames of the market entry game in figure 6.9: the game itself, and the subgame that commences subsequent to entry, in which the incumbent must choose to fight or collude.

Now the problem with the second Nash equilibrium identified above can be clearly stated: it requires that the incumbent undertakes an irrational action, *given* that firm E has already entered the market. That is, *given* entry by E, fighting the entrant results in a lower payoff than simply colluding with the entrant. If it is assumed that all players are rational, and that this universal rationality is *common knowledge* among the players (a standard game-theoretic assumption), then both players in the game know that a threat by the incumbent to fight the entrant, *given entry*, is incredible – it would be like threatening to shoot oneself just to harm an opponent.

The possibility of such incredible strategies is ruled out by the condition of *subgame-perfect* equilibrium, an extension of Nash equilibrium that requires the attainment of a Nash equilibrium on *all proper subgames* of a particular game. The effect of this stricter equilibrium requirement is to rule out strategies based on future actions that would be irrational to carry out; it suggests that if everyone is rational and everyone knows it, then it cannot be credible for a player in a non-cooperative strategic environment to assert a commitment to a suboptimal future action, for exactly the same reason that players can't credibly commit themselves to non-Nash equilibrium strategies in such environments. Thus, if Nash equilibrium is a reasonable equilibrium requirement for noncooperative games, then subgame perfection appears to be a reasonable extension of that requirement to noncooperative games involving sequential moves.

Applying this logic to the market entry scenario results in elimination of one of the game's two Nash equilibria. The reason for this is that in the proper subgame resulting from entry by firm E, there is, trivially, only one Nash equilibrium, in which the incumbent colludes. Therefore, the possibility that the incumbent would fight the entrant upon entry is dismissed, and there is only one remaining equilibrium, such that firm E enters the market and the incumbent colludes. Under the specified conditions of this game, then, the unique prediction resulting from a stricter equilibrium requirement is that the incumbent can never credibly deter entry.

Subgame-perfect equilibria in repeated games

It seems reasonable to assert, at least as a general principle, that rational actors can't credibly commit themselves to irrational behavior, and yet it is tempting to think that there are circumstances that would render nominally "irrational" actions entirely rational, when framed in an appropriately broader perspective. In the context of the market entry game just discussed, the question is whether there are more general conditions under which the incumbent firm might credibly signal an intention to drive out competitors should they dare to enter its market; perhaps the stark conclusion with respect to the game described above arises due to an oversimplification of the strategic reality it is meant to capture.

Suppose, in particular, that an incumbent monopsonist faces a *series* of potential entrants over time. In this case, the game described above is effectively *repeated* rather than played out all at once. Facing the prospect of *future* challengers to its market position, might a monopsonist credibly commit to driving out initial entrants, on the basis that doing so would deter future competition?

The concept of subgame-perfect equilibrium can be used to sort out the strategic issues relevant to this question. As a reference case, suppose that the market entry game is repeated a *finite* number of times with a given string of potential entrants, and furthermore that all players know this feature of the game as well. Given this restriction, the opportunity to repeat the game a commonly known *finite* number of times is insufficient to establish a credible basis for entry-deterring behavior by the monopsonist. Why is this so?

To answer this, consider the play of the game in its last round. At this point in the game there are no future entrants to send a signal to, so the strategic situation corresponds exactly to the one-period market entry game analyzed above. And in that game, there is only one subgame-perfect equilibrium, such that the monopsonist does not deter entry.

With that result in mind, now consider the situation in the *next-to-last* play of the market entry game. The incumbent firm can't credibly commit to deterring entry in the *last* period, because deterrence is not a Nash equilibrium outcome in that period. Consequently, there is no credible signal that can be sent by deterring entry in the next-to-last period, so the payoff structure for this period is again equivalent to that for the one-shot game, and again, that game has a unique subgame-perfect equilibrium in which entry occurs. Clearly, this argument can be repeated as one moves backward toward the first period of the game. The only possible inference, therefore, is that entry-deterring behavior by the monopsonist is still not credible in any period, so long as it is commonly known that the market entry game is repeated a definite number of times.

Of course, the assumption of definite repetition is not very realistic in the context of real-world competition, since it is rare that incumbent firms would face a known number of future potential competitors. So suppose instead that the market entry game is repeated an *indefinite* number of times. Since there is no certain "last period" in this scenario, the foregoing recursive argument cannot be used to rule out the possibility of credible entry deterrence by the monopsonist, from which strategic collusion unravels as in the previous period. Consequently, the strategy "if entry occurs, always fight" may be viable even under the more restrictive equilibrium condition.

However, indefinite repetition of the market entry game does not of itself establish the possibility of credible deterrence. The reason is that, in fighting the present entry of a potential competitor, the incumbent firm is trading off *current* payoff losses (the difference between the immediate payoff to fighting and the payoff to colluding with the entrant) against expected *future* gains (if a credible deterrent is established, the incumbent needn't worry about future entry, and can enjoy a continued monopsony position). But this tradeoff would again not be credible if the firm was known to discount future payoffs heavily, so that the current losses outweighed the present value of expected future gains. Conversely, if the monopsonist is sufficiently patient, entry deterrence is consistent with subgame-perfect equilibrium for the repeated game.

Alternatively, suppose that potential entrants do not *know* that the incumbent is rational, but instead allow some positive probability that the incumbent is "irrational" in the specific sense of enjoying entry deterrence for its own sake. In this case, it can be demonstrated that entry deterrence is credible, even if the incumbent *is* rational and even if the game is *finitely* repeated, because entry deterrence in the early rounds of the game represents an "investment" in convincing potential competitors that the monopsonist *really is* irrational.

The general conclusion, then, is that entry deterrence may be credible when the market entry game is repeated and the incumbent is not too impatient, so long as repetition is indefinite or potential entrants are incompletely informed about the incumbent's true payoff function. It is important to note, though, that entry deterrence is not the only possible outcome of the repeated game, even under these conditions. Indeed, the typical consequence of repeating a one-shot game is to increase the range of possible equilibria. In particular, the outcome in which the incumbent allows entry in each round of the indefinitely repeated game also corresponds to a subgame perfect equilibrium, since this is the Nash equilibrium for the one-shot game.

The same reasoning applies to the repeated prisoners' dilemma game considered earlier. If the game is finitely repeated and players have complete information about the structure of the game, then mutual defection in every period is the only subgame-perfect equilibrium. If the game is indefinitely repeated, however, mutual collusion may be sustained as a Nash equilibrium through the use of appropriate trigger strategies (of which one option, but generally not the most effective, is that of perpetual Nash reversion). (See the appendix to this chapter for a demonstration of the role of trigger strategies in promoting collusive outcomes.) Alternatively, if players are not fully informed about their opponents' preferences, then mutual collusion may be sustainable for the initial rounds of even a finitely repeated prisoners' dilemma game.

The more general point made here is that the concept of subgame-perfect equilibrium can help sort out the strategic issues arising in games that are played out sequentially. The central idea of the equilibrium refinement is to use the greater information conveyed by the extensive form to impose a stricter notion of what constitutes credible equilibrium play on the game under study. As you can see from the examples considered above, the benefit of this procedure is that it may make it possible to sharpen predictions about the outcomes of particular games. Note this does not imply that subgame perfection is the appropriate equilibrium refinement for *all* games involving play over time. But this refinement does have the appealing feature that it takes the notion of rational, self-interested play inherent in the definition of Nash equilibrium, and extends it *across time*, such that personal commitments to subsequently irrational strategies are ruled out.

AN ECONOMIST AND A BIOLOGIST PLAY THE REPEATED PRISONERS' DILEMMA GAME; WHO WINS?

In an early experimental test of game theory's predictive power, two researchers of the RAND Corporation, Merrill Flood and Melvin Dresher, recruited a couple of professional colleagues to play the prisoners' dilemma game one hundred times in a row. With the benefit of hindsight, it is clear that their experimental design did not permit an exact test of the relevant theory, since the scenario of *repeated* games had not yet been analyzed when they staged the experiment in 1950.

Furthermore, as you can see by comparing figures 6.10 and 6.4, Flood and Dresher imposed an unusual asymmetric payoff matrix for the one-shot game. However, it is still recognizable as a prisoners' dilemma scenario, in that mutual defection is the unique Nash equilibrium, indeed a dominant-strategy equilibrium. Moreover, the experiment preserved the key noncooperative essence of the game: the players chose their strategies simultaneously in each round, and were not allowed to communicate directly with each other before or during the experiment.

Perhaps the primary value of Flood's and Dresher's experiment derives from the comments they asked the players to write in each round of play, after they had made their strategy selections but before they saw the other player's current move. These comments provide a window on the strategic considerations going through the players' minds as the repeated game unfolded, and anticipate many of the considerations discussed above. Another intriguing feature of the experiment was the identity of the players they recruited: one was an economist ("AA") and the other a biologist ("JW"). It should also be noted that the economist suffered from the asymmetry in payoffs, gaining less than the biologist from mutual cooperation and from mutual or unilateral defection.

	JW cooperates	JW defects
AA cooperates	½, 1	−1, 2
AA defects	1, −1	0, ½

Figure 6.10 Single-period payoffs in the Flood–Dresher experiment.

Before moving to the outcome of Flood's and Dresher's experiment, recall the theoretical considerations raised above. In the one-shot prisoners' dilemma (PD) game, (defect, defect) is the only Nash equilibrium, and perpetual mutual defection thus constitutes a subgame-perfect equilibrium for any version of the repeated PD game. There are multiple simple Nash equilibria for the *finitely* repeated game, involving various combinations of collusion and defection over time; however, assuming that both players are rational and self-interested, and believe the opponent to be the same, the unique subgame-perfect equilibrium dictates mutual defection in every period. Finally, a relevant consideration not raised in the previous discussion should be noted: if rational collusion is realizable in some version of the repeated PD game, it is achieved via the use of "trigger" strategies in which collusion is rewarded with continued collusion, but unilateral defection from the collusive outcome is punished by repeated rounds of defection.

How did the experiment play out? In the first round, AA defected, his written comments indicating recognition of the dominant-strategy feature of the one-shot game. Player JW, in contrast, chose collusion (and thus suffered a penalty), his short comment indicating the presumption that his opponent, if "bright," would also collude. This pattern of play was repeated in the second period, the economist registering dismay and the biologist disappointment over the first-round outcome. After that, the biologist plays defect for three consecutive periods, with the announced intention of punishing his opponent's "unwise" behavior.

Various strategy combinations are played in the next several periods, including a string of mutual defections in rounds 8–10 and a string of mutual collusion in rounds 12–15. Player JW's comments indicate his intention to play a punishing trigger strategy to induce his opponent to collude consistently, while AA's comments show him trying to discern a set temporal pattern in the biologist's order of play. A breakthrough of sorts comes in round 19, when, after 8 rounds of silence, AA wonders if his opponent is trying to "convey information" through his sequence of plays – something JW was clearly trying to do. Soon thereafter follows strings of 4, 6, and then 7 consecutive rounds of mutual collusion.

After the last string, however, AA's comments suggest that the asymmetric payoff structure, such that JW benefits the most from mutual collusion, is tainting the play of the game. Player AA complains repeatedly that JW seems unwilling to "share" payoffs by allowing him an occasional unilateral defection that is not immediately punished. This assessment is valid in the sense that JW received a 100% greater gain from each instance of successful collusion. It seems an interesting role reversal, though, that the economist ultimately worried about equity issues while the biologist seemed concerned primarily to achieve efficient outcomes.

After AA's first stated concern about the distribution of gains, mutual collusion is achieved in 39 of the remaining 51 periods. In the final round,

continued

both defected – as predicted by the theory of subgame-perfect equilibrium. Summing the payoffs across all periods without discounting, AA and JW received respective payoffs of 40 and 65. The corresponding payoff combinations for unvarying mutual defection would have been 0 and 50; for unvarying mutual collusion, 50 and 100. Thus the actual outcome was clearly Pareto-superior to the subgame-perfect equililibrium, and more egalitarian than the outcome yielded by universal defection or collusion.

What can one make of this experimental outcome? Note first that it does not evidently contradict the predictions of simple Nash equilibrium, since a large number of such equilibria exist for the *repeated* game, although only one exists for the *one-shot* game. It does contradict the implication of *subgame-perfect* equilibrium under the strict rationality and informational premises stated above, but the running comments of the players provide internal evidence that these promises were not fulfilled. In particular, the biologist showed an early commitment to the collusive outcome that is not consistent with these conditions. However, he did attempt to enforce this outcome through the use of a trigger strategy, which is consistent with the prediction for game settings in which credible collusion is possible. Finally, the result suggests that, quite apart from the dictates of rationality, strategic actors – even economists – may care about the distribution of economic gains, especially when on the disfavored end of a given distribution.

Related discussion questions:
1. Why doesn't the frequent incidence of cooperative outcomes in this game contradict the conditions of Nash equilibrium, given that mutual defection is the unique Nash equilibrium of a one-shot prisoners' dilemma? Is the outcome consistent with the stronger requirement of *subgame perfect* equilibria?
2. Get two of your friends (assuming they remain so) to play the prisoners' dilemma game repeatedly and record their thinking during each round of play, but set up the payoff structure so that payoffs are *symmetric* across the two players, unlike in the Flood–Dresher experiment. Make sure to explain the game thoroughly to them before they begin, but don't tell them how they should play the repeated game. What are the results, and are they consistent with the predictions of Nash equilibrium? Subgame-perfect equilibrium?

Related references:
Merrill M., Flood, "Some Experimental Games," Research Memorandum RM-789 (Santa Monica, CA: RAND Corporation, 1952).
William, Poundstone, *Prisoner's Dilemma* (New York: Doubleday, 1992).

CONCLUSION

Game theory provides a theoretical language and logic for dealing with social situations that feature strategic interaction. Cooperative game theory provides a convenient basis for generating potentially useful insights with respect to settings in which binding commitments are possible (such as exchanges governed by fully specifiable and costlessly enforceable contracts), but noncooperative game theory serves as the ultimate testing ground for judgments about the likely outcomes of strategic interactions, particularly when said interactions cannot be based on binding commitments. As such, noncooperative theory may be especially appropriate for the study of labor market exchanges characterized by significant costs of negotiation or enforcement. Possible applications of the theory in this direction are featured in the next two chapters.

APPENDIX TO CHAPTER 6

THE NASH BARGAINING SOLUTION

Define a bargaining game by the following ingredients: the players (Mickey and Sylvia, in the body of the chapter); a utility possibilities frontier for the players, given by a differentiable function satisfying $W(M, S) = 0$, where M and S are allocatively efficient utility combinations; and a disagreement point consisting of the respective autarkic or endowment utilities (M_D, S_D).

The *Nash Bargaining Solution* is given by the payoff combination (M^*, S^*) taken from the UPF that maximizes the product $(M - M_D) \cdot (S - S_D)$. Solving this as as the optimum of the associated Lagrangean objective function $\Lambda = (M - M_D) \cdot (S - S_D) - \lambda \cdot W(M, S)$, on the assumption that the disagreement point lies below the UPF, yields the condition that

$$\frac{M^* - M_D}{S^* - S_D} = \frac{\partial W/\partial S}{\partial W/\partial M} = \frac{dM}{dS}\bigg|_{W(M^*, S^*)=0},$$

which corresponds to the result explained in the body of the chapter and illustrated in figure 6.2.

Additional players, such as Bonnie and Clyde, can be incorporated by adding multiplicative terms $(B - B_D)$ and $(C - C_D)$ to the original objective function. Alternatively, differences in bargaining power can be incorporated by raising the respective factors to powers which sum to one, as for example in the expression $(M - M_D)^\alpha \cdot (S - S_D)^{(1-\alpha)}$, where α is a positive number between zero and one. In this case, Mickey's bargaining power is understood to increase with the value of α.

THE COURNOT DUOPSONY GAME

Imagine a labor market in which there are two labor-buying firms, A and B. For simplicity, let the VMP_L of each firm be a constant value denoted M, and let the market supply curve be an affine function, written in inverse form as $W = aL$, where $a > 0$ is a constant, W

is the market wage rate, and L is the total quantity of labor hired. Let L_i, $i = A, B$ denote the quantity of labor hired by firm i. Finally, suppose for convenience that labor is the only input.

Then firm A will choose quantity L_A to maximize

$$\Pi^A(L_A) = M \cdot L_A - a \cdot (L_A + \overline{L}_B) \cdot L_A = (M - a \cdot \overline{L}_B) \cdot L_A - a \cdot L_A^2$$

for any given value $\overline{L}_B$ of firm B's quantity of labor hired. The first-order condition for A's optimal choice is $\Pi^{A'}(L_A^*) = (M - a \cdot \overline{L}_B) - 2a \cdot L_A^* = 0$, which yields firm A's reaction function

$$L_A^* = \frac{M}{2a} - \frac{\overline{L}_B}{2}.$$

Parallel reasoning gives firm B's reaction function,

$$L_B^* = \frac{M}{2a} - \frac{\overline{L}_A}{2}.$$

Now assuming a Nash equilibrium such that each player assumes the other will choose the equilibrium quantity of labor hired, the two reaction functions establish a system of two equations in two unknowns, which can thus be solved to yield $L_A^* = L_B^* = M/3a$. The equilibrium quantity of labor hired in the market is thus $L^* = 2M/3a$ and the corresponding wage rate is $W^* = 2M/3$. The corresponding competitive employment and wage levels are respectively M/a and M, while the corresponding employment and wage levels set by a profit-maximizing monopsonist under these market conditions are respectively $M/2a$ and $M/2$.

PROSPECTS FOR COLLUSIVE BEHAVIOR IN THE INDEFINITELY REPEATED PRISONERS' DILEMMA

Consider a prisoners' dilemma game with the following normal form:

	Dave colludes	Dave defects
Sam colludes	b, b	d, a
Sam defects	a, d	c, c

where the payoff structure is such that $a > b > c > d$. It is readily confirmed that there is a unique Nash (in fact, dominant-strategy) equilibrium for the one-shot game in which both Sam and Dave defect, yielding inefficient payoffs (c, c).

Now suppose that Sam and Dave repeat this game indefinitely many times, and each of them discounts future payoffs by the fractional discount factor δ (equal to the inverse of one plus the discount *rate*). As discussed in the text of chapter 6, a new strategic possibility arises in which players can condition future moves on past outcomes. Consider in particular the *trigger strategy* in which a player chooses initially to collude, and then continues colluding in every subsequent period so long as the other player also continues to collude. Should the other player defect, however, the first player immediately defects in the next round and every subsequent repetition of the game.

Notice first that the threat to play defect forever after the other player defects is credible in the sense of subgame perfect equilibrium since, as established above, defection constitutes a dominant strategy in the one-shot game. Given that the threat is credible, the next question is whether it effectively deters defection by the other player. To see this, consider Dave's possible responses if Sam employs the trigger strategy described above. First, suppose Dave colludes in every period. Then, following the strategy, Sam perpetually colludes as well, and both players receive a present payoff value of

$$V_{col} = (b + \delta \cdot b + \delta^2 \cdot b \ldots) = b \cdot (1 + \delta + \delta^2 \ldots) = b/(1 - \delta),$$

where the ellipses indicate an infinite series.

Alternatively, suppose Dave chooses to defect in response to Sam's collusion. Then, following the trigger strategy, Sam defects in every subsequent period, and the best Dave can do in response is to defect as well. Thus Sam gets an immediate payoff of a followed by an infinite string of payoffs of c. The present payoff value to Dave of this alternative response is

$$V_{def} = a + (\delta c + \delta^2 c + \delta^3 c \ldots) = a + \delta c(1 + \delta + \delta^2 \ldots) = a + (\delta c/(1 - \delta)),$$

where again the ellipses indicate an infinite series. Clearly, it pays Dave to respond to Sam's trigger strategy with perpetual collusion so long as $V_{col} \geq V_{def}$, which can be shown with some algebraic manipulation to imply $\delta \geq (a - b)/(a - c) > 0$. In other words, perpetual collusion can be supported as a subgame perfect equilibrium for the indefinitely repeated prisoners' dilemma game so long as the discount factor for both players is sufficiently high (that is, Sam and Dave aren't too impatient).

Finally, reversion to mutual defection is not generally the most effective "punishment" for defection consistent with subgame perfect equilibrium. In general, the most effective punishment will require the defector to suffer the greater loss of playing "collude" against the other player's "defect" for some initial periods. However, in the context of labor market exchange relationships, in which "defect" might translate as "terminate the relationship," mutual defection may be the most effective feasible punishment for defection.

Study Questions

1. In a typical labor exchange, what does the UPF for that exchange represent; why is it downward-sloping; and what does the slope represent? Finally, to what points in the Edgeworth box for the labor exchange does the UPF correspond?

2. Determine the Nash Bargaining Solution for the special case in which Mickey's and Sylvia's UPF is a straight line, given by the function $U_M = 100 - U_S$. Using this solution, demonstrate that each player's equilibrium payoff is increasing in his or her own disagreement-point payoff and decreasing in that of his or her opponent. What are the equilibrium payoffs when the disagreement-point payoffs are equal? Does this make sense as a general solution to the bargaining problem? Explain.

continued

3. Suppose that firms strategically choose *wage* rather than *employment* levels in the duopsony model. Call this the *Bertrand* duopsony model to distinguish it from the quantity-setting duopsony scenario. What is the Nash equilibrium of the corresponding noncooperative game, and how does it compare to the competitive equilibrium defined under identical conditions? (Hint: what is a firm's residual labor supply if it offers the same wage as its identical competitor? A slightly higher or lower wage rate?)

4. Construct the normal and extensive forms for the noncooperative two-player simultaneous-move game of Rock, Paper, Scissors. Suppose that the winner (Rock beats Scissors, Scissors beats Paper, Paper beats Rock) receives a payoff of 1 and the loser a payoff of −1. Show that there are no pure-strategy Nash equilibria for the game. In that case, what is the optimal strategy to play in this game?

5. Construct the extensive form for the following noncooperative game. There are three players, a firm F, "Chance" C, and the firm's employee E. Player F moves first, choosing a wage rate W. The next player to move is "Chance" (player C), who chooses among increasing alternative wage offers W_0, W_1, W_2 with corresponding probabilities of a third each. The third move is taken by the employee (player E), who decides whether or not to reject the firm's wage offer and take the alternative offer provided by Chance. Let F's revenues be denoted by R, its wage offer by W, and the cost of replacing a departing employee by K. Then the firm's average or expected profit is given by the expression $\Pi = R - q \cdot K - W$, where q is defined as the probability that the employee leaves the firm to take an alternative offer.

    Demonstrate that the probability q is a decreasing function of the wage offer of the firm, written $q = Q(W)$, by working "backwards" from the choices of the player who moves last, player E. Given a pair of wage offers supplied by the Firm and Chance, which one will E choose? Use the resulting optimal decision rule to derive the probability that the employee will leave as a function of the wage offer of the firm, given the probabilistic offers of Chance. Given this result, show that the firm's *expected* net revenue, defined as $R - Q(W) \cdot K$, is *increasing* in the wage rate.

6. Consider the following normal form of a coordination game:

	Marvin chooses H	Marvin chooses L
Tammi chooses H	5, 5	0, 3
Tammi chooses L	3, 0	2, 2

This game exhibits two interesting features. The first is *positive spillovers*, defined as a situation in which a change in one player's strategy consistently increases the payoff to the other player. Note, for example, that no matter what strategy Tammi chooses, she gets a higher payoff when Marvin chooses H instead of choosing L. The second feature is *strategic complementarity*, defined as a situation in which changing one player's strategy in a certain direction increases the *marginal* payoff to the other player from changing strategies. Thus, for example, Tammi's marginal payoff from choosing H over L is higher when Marvin chooses H rather than L.

A common result in strategic settings with these two features is that there are multiple equilibria that can be ranked by the criterion of Pareto-superiority. Demonstrate that there are two pure-strategy Nash equilibria for this game, one of which is Pareto-superior to the other. Suppose that both players are extremely averse to risks of big changes in their payoffs. Why might this risk aversion lead to the selection of the Pareto-inferior equilibrium?

7. Construct a standard Edgeworth box in consumption goods. Both parties, Emily and Henry, have well-behaved indifference curves, a pair of which cross at endowment point E. If Emily is allowed to make the first *and only* suggestion for a move away from E, what should she suggest? If instead Henry is allowed to make the first *and only* suggestion for a move away from E, what should he suggest? Illustrate these two cases in your diagram. In either case, will the other person agree to the trade? Explain your reasoning.

8. Suppose that two individuals are considering whether to undertake production separately or as a team. The solo production process for each person i is given by the function $x_i = m \cdot e_i - f_i$, where m and f_i are positive constants. The team production function is given by $x = m \cdot (e_1 + e_2) - F$, where m and F are constants and e_1 and e_2 denote the respective productive efforts of the two workers. Assume x is zero for $e_i \le \dfrac{f_i}{m}$ and for $(e_1 + e_2) \le \dfrac{F}{m}$.

   (a) Graph each of the production functions. What is the marginal product of effort in each case? Under what condition is it *technically efficient* to produce x via team production rather than autarkic production (i.e., to have the two individuals produce as a team)?

   (b) Suppose each individual has a utility function of the form $U_i = y_i - e_i^2$, where y_i is person i's income (that is, the portion of output that goes to that person). Suppose each person chooses e_i to maximize his or her utility. Find the optimal level of effort and utility if each person produces for herself or himself using the autarkic production process. [Hint: the marginal cost of effort for each person is $2e_i$]

   (c) Now consider team production. Suppose that individual efforts are unobservable, so that individual payment can only be based on team output, and suppose in particular that $y_i = \dfrac{x}{2}$. Find the Nash equilibrium level of effort and utility per person given: (i) team production; (ii) this payment rule; and (iii) the utility functions given above. Under what conditions can both individuals achieve higher utilities via autarkic production than via technically superior team production? Interpret these conditions.

Note

1   Since Nash's work essentially formalized a notion first considered by the French econ-
    omist Augustin Cournot in the early 1800s, this concept is sometimes also referred to
    as *Cournot–Nash* equilibrium. We use the simpler term, while pausing here to com-
    memorate Cournot's anticipation of game theory almost 100 years before its formal
    invention. Nash's work earned him the 1995 Nobel Memorial Prize in Economics,
    shared with fellow game theorists Reinhard Selten and John Harsanyi.

Suggestions for Further Reading

Avinash Dixit and Susan Skeath, *Games of Strategy* (New York: W.W. Norton & Co.,
    1999).
Robert Gibbons, *Game Theory for Applied Economists* (Princeton, NJ: Princeton Uni-
    versity Press, 1992).

CHAPTER 7

BARGAINING IN LABOR EXCHANGE

Bargaining scenarios arise under conditions of bilateral monopoly, when both parties to an exchange enjoy wage-setting power. It might be tempting to take this condition literally, so that bargaining behavior is understood to determine wage levels only for those rare cases in which a monopoly union faces a pure monopsony. By this reading, the relevance of bargaining analysis is limited to instances of centralized wage bargaining or bargaining by public sector unions.

At least for certain analytical purposes, this temptation should probably be avoided. As discussed in chapter 6, bilateral monopoly is more appropriately thought of as a matter of degree, arising whenever both parties to a given exchange face difficulties in locating suitable alternative exchange partners. This will typically be the case in labor markets if both firms and workers typically incur some form of matching costs, which appears to be a reasonable description of actual labor market conditions.

The purpose of this chapter is to develop a bargaining theory of wage determination for scenarios in which some degree of bilateral monopoly exists. After a discussion of possible sources of bilateral labor market power, the chapter's argument turns to a theoretical exploration of the determinants of relative bargaining power and the consequences of this power. Two key themes are developed: first, the impact of alternative exchange opportunities on the distribution of bargaining payoffs within a given labor transaction depend on whether exit is voluntarily chosen or externally imposed. In the latter case, captured by the cooperative Nash bargaining solution discussed in the previous chapter, outside payoffs always affect bargaining outcomes. In the former case, "outside" payoffs only affect bargaining outcomes if they are sufficiently high, and therefore credible. The second theme, applicable in the event that outside payoffs

continued

don't dictate bargaining outcomes, is that these outcomes are determined by the relative incidence of negotiation costs across the bargainers.

The bargaining model developed in this chapter will provide a foundation for the text's subsequent investigations of a wide range of labor market phenomena, including union wage effects, labor market segmentation, involuntary unemployment, and the connection between unemployment and wage inflation.

EXCHANGE COSTS AND BILATERAL MARKET POWER

Matching costs and bilateral monopoly

As discussed in chapter 5, the institution of exchange requires three sorts of activity: matching, negotiation, and enforcement. Exchange activities, like production activities, are typically costly, but exchange costs are distinct from production costs in having the capacity to alter the strategic nature of given exchange relations. In the present context, this general principle translates into the following two-part hypothesis: first, mutually incurred matching costs give rise to bilateral monopoly conditions, and second, given these conditions, bargaining outcomes are determined in part by the incidence of both matching and negotiation costs.

Recall that *matching* refers to the problem of identifying and pairing with suitable exchange partners, noting that this includes the possibility of separation from less-suitable partners. Broadly speaking, labor market transactions give rise to two sources of matching costs, *search* and *exit*. Consider each in turn. First, before negotiations in a prospective transaction can commence, suitable exchange parties must be identified and paired. But market participants may have to expend considerable time, effort, and money in searching for suitable partners, especially in populous or geographically dispersed markets. Time spent in searching for suitable partners is costly of itself if searchers have impatient preferences or limited resources to live on as search proceeds. Search may also involve direct costs of transportation, advertising, and screening potential exchange partners.

Once a prospective employment pairing has been identified, effective search may also involve spatial relocation of market participants. This is particularly relevant to labor market exchanges, for which the inalienable nature of labor inputs implies that workers must be physically present where their work is to be performed. Successful matching may therefore require that workers are able to locate wherever the desired jobs are. The most obvious examples of spatial mobility are immigration, where labor suppliers change countries in order to avail themselves of desired employment opportunities, and geographical relocation of production facilities by firms.

Alternatively, if existing labor exchange relationships prove unsatisfactory, traders may face direct or indirect costs specifically associated with *exiting* particular relationships after they've been established. Direct costs of exit arise if there are legal or procedural requirements for terminating given employment relationships. A potentially important source of indirect exit costs in employment relationships involves the loss of employee skills that are specific to the relationship. For example, members of a firm's incumbent labor force may acquire knowledge of production methods that are unique to the firm, or simply learn over time how to operate more effectively in the firm's "corporate culture." In the event of a termination, the employer loses because of the time or resources required to impart these skills to replacements, while employees lose because the skills are not transferable to new positions.

A second source of indirect exit costs arises when employers cannot directly observe the capabilities of prospective employees, and thus must make inferences based on ancillary information. In this case, leaving an existing job may send a negative signal to other employers about the revenue productivity of departing workers, since the separation may have been driven by unsatisfactory job performance. Exiting employees may thus find it harder to locate a position, even if this inference were false.

Whether flowing from the demands of job search or specific to the process of leaving existing relationships, mutually incurred matching costs create a situation of bilateral monopoly. This is the case because each party to a given labor transaction gains some power to influence the terms of exchange to the extent that the other party cannot easily locate an alternative exchange partner. How this bilateral market power translates into bargaining outcomes depends, at least in part, on one more consideration: the costs incurred by traders in negotiating the terms of labor exchange.

Strategic implications of negotiation costs

Once prospective exchange partners have been matched, they must still negotiate the terms on which an exchange will take place. In doing so they may incur *negotiation costs* of various forms. The magnitude and configuration of these costs have two distinct implications for the bargaining relationship.

First, high negotiation costs may create a situation of bilateral monopoly subsequent to the commencement of a given labor exchange, whether or not bilateral wage-setting power initially existed. This possibility arises when it is extremely difficult or time-consuming to determine and contractually specify all the matters and contingencies potentially affecting the gains to be had from a given exchange relationship. For example, the mutual benefits realized in a prospective labor exchange may hinge on an overwhelmingly large number of contingencies which would be extremely costly to identify and spell out in advance.

In the extreme, parties to a transaction may simply be unable to anticipate the full range of contingencies or other element relevant to exchange. In this case, the marginal cost of determining these aspects of an exchange can be said to become virtually infinite beyond some point. This has the same interpretation as when marginal production costs become infinite: it indicates that the desired activity can't be conducted.

The inability to determine and contractually specify all relevant contingencies in advance may mean that scenarios arise after an exchange relationship has been initiated for which the distribution of gains has not been determined. For example, automobile producers may find that a key supplier has gone out of business, making it necessary to locate another, untested source of supply. If both the firm and its labor force face costs of exiting, then the gains from exchange specific to that scenario must be determined through bargaining.

This leads to the second potential impact of negotiation costs, concerning the relative willingness of exchange partners to engage in haggling over the terms of trade. The actual process of bargaining tends to be stressful, takes time, and may incur direct costs as well. If the parties to a labor exchange are not equally willing to incur these costs, they will likely have implications for ultimate bargaining outcomes. For example, the bargaining partner with more impatient preferences may be induced to settle for a smaller share of a given economic pie in order to avoid the time costs of protracted haggling. This consequence of negotiation costs is explored more extensively in the next section.

THE IMPACT OF MATCHING AND NEGOTIATION COSTS ON BARGAINING OUTCOMES

The theoretical problem

It seems intuitive that the incidence and magnitude of matching and negotiation costs should play a significant role in the determination of bargaining outcomes. For a long time, however, economists found it very difficult to translate this intuition into a coherent and tractable theory. The nature of the analytical challenge can be illustrated via reference to two distinct game-theoretic approaches to the bargaining problem.

A cooperative-game approach, in the specific form of the Nash bargaining solution, was previously discussed in chapter 6. This solution has the appealing feature of yielding (generally) unique predictions that arguably bear some intuitive force. As noted in the earlier discussion, however, there are at least two related problems with using this approach as the basis for studying bargaining conflicts in labor exchange. First, since the Nash cooperative solution is derived from a set of axioms rather than from an analysis of optimal strategy choices in a concretely specified negotiation process, it is not clear how the "disagreement point" payoffs are to be understood. As explained below, they cannot be plausibly interpreted as the payoffs resulting from settings in which bargainers can freely choose to exit the relationship.

Second, and for similar reasons, it is not clear how the incidence of negotiation costs affects bargaining positions in the cooperative bargaining framework. As

demonstrated in the appendix to chapter 6, it is possible to incorporate the possibility of unequal bargaining positions in the Nash bargaining model, but the economic basis for such asymmetries cannot be explained by the theory. This raises
the question of whether the Nash bargaining solution might be understood as the
equilibrium outcome of a suitably specified *noncooperative* bargaining game, in
which players make offers and counteroffers until agreement is realized as part
of the players' Nash equilibrium strategies. Examples of such games are considered further below.

The problem with this approach is that it does not yield definite predictions
about the division of gains from exchange. To the contrary, if bargaining outcomes
can be represented as points along a continuous utility possibilities frontier (UPF)
defined for the bargaining relationship under study, then there is generally a
continuum of equally valid Nash equilibrium outcomes, any one of which is sup-
portable by the following strategies: one player insists on a certain minimum
payoff whenever making an offer, and rejects any counteroffers yielding a payoff
below the minimum. The other player accepts any offer that yields the total
surplus to be shared net of the minimum payoff demanded by the first player, so
long as this sum is at least as big as the second player's "disagreement" payoff
(assuming this option could be freely chosen at any point).

There is an evident objection to this result. Suppose that the second player finds
the minimum payoff demanded by the first excessive, and thus consistently
refuses to accept it. At some point, wouldn't it pay the first player to moderate
his or her demand, rather than holding to an offer that is never accepted? Consideration of this possibility leads one to question the credibility of some range of
payoff demands by each player. However, incorporating such matters into the
analysis of bargaining requires a refinement of the equilibrium condition imposed
on the noncooperative bargaining game.

This is the basis of the analytical approach taken by game theorist Ariel Rubinstein in his path-breaking treatment of the bargaining problem.[1] Rubinstein's
strategic bargaining approach yields the Nash bargaining solution as a special case,
but can also be wielded to generate plausible and potentially testable hypotheses
about bargaining outcomes for a wide range of alternative conditions. In particular, this approach makes it possible to study the effects of negotiation and matching costs on bargaining outcomes.

The basic idea behind the framework proposed by Rubinstein is to model the
bargaining problem as an extensive-form noncooperative game that takes place
in real time. This entails specifying the structure of the bargaining process and the
payoff functions of the bargainers, including in particular the marginal costs to
them of continued bargaining. The signature feature of this approach is to limit
attention to *subgame-perfect* bargaining strategies, thus dismissing strategies that
could not be credibly maintained by fully informed rational players. Given this
restriction, it is possible in many cases to establish the existence of unique and
intuitively appealing outcomes for given bargaining environments, and to do so
in a way that makes explicit the connection between these outcomes and the incidence of exchange costs.

The basic framework

Imagine that two parties, Ludwig and Karla, are contemplating an employment relationship that yields total gains V. Before production begins, Ludwig and Karla must bargain to determine the distribution of these gains, and they agree to bind themselves to any agreement reached through negotiation. Each player cares only about his or her share of the surplus. Let X represent Ludwig's share of the surplus if agreement is reached; consequently $V - X$ is the share going to Karla.

Assume that the bargaining process consists of the players taking turns in making and responding to offers, beginning, let's say, with Ludwig. In any given round, the player whose turn it is makes an offer, to which the other player responds with acceptance or rejection. If the offer is accepted, bargaining ceases immediately and the surplus is distributed according to the accepted offer. If the offer is rejected, bargaining resumes in the next round with a counteroffer from the player who rejected the previous proposal. Bargaining continues until agreement is reached.

Although this is rarely likely to be the case in practice, it is useful to begin by assuming that both players are fully informed about all aspects of the game, including each other's payoff functions. The consequences of allowing for imperfect or asymmetric information are considered after the basic bargaining model is fully analyzed.

A detail of the simple bargaining game just described is illustrated in figure 7.1. Note that the possibility of exiting the relationship has not yet been incorporated.

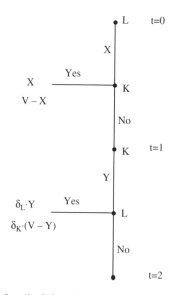

Figure 7.1   A detail of the alternating-offers bargaining game.

In the present context, this is equivalent to assuming that the common value of the players' exit options is zero.

Particular solutions to the bargaining problem are determined by specifying the players' costs of negotiation – that is, of making and responding to offers – and their opportunities for terminating the bargaining relationship. Several alternative bargaining scenarios are addressed in the following discussion. In each case, there is a *unique* bargaining equilibrium involving immediate acceptance of an initial offer, driven by the requirement that players choose only those strategies that are optimal to carry out *at each stage* of the bargaining game, given the future payoffs determined by equilibrium strategies. This is the sense underlying the condition of *subgame-perfect equilibrium* described in the previous chapter.

The simple "voice" model with discounting and no exit options

Now assume that both players are impatient, so that bargaining payoffs received today are valued more highly than identical shares accrued in the future. Ludwig's and Karla's impatient time preferences are indicated by the respective fractional discount factors δ_L and δ_K. Thus, for example, the present value to Ludwig of a bargaining payoff of X tomorrow is equal to X times δ_L, the present value of a payoff received two periods from now is X times the square of δ_L, etc. In order to focus on the consequences of negotiation costs for bargaining outcomes, maintain for the time being the assumption that neither player can exit the relationship.

Given impatient preferences, each player incurs a cost by rejecting a current offer. Rejection puts off payday for at least an additional period and thus reduces the present value of any given division of the surplus. Consequently, in assessing an existing offer each player must weigh the immediate offer against the eventual payoff that could be achieved through continued bargaining, allowing for the utility costs of delay.

The unique solution flowing from the stipulation of subgame-perfect equilibrium can be illustrated in terms of the players' *bargaining reaction functions*. Each bargainer's reaction function shows the *minimum* share that can credibly be offered in a current round to the opponent, given the latter's expectation of (discounted) future payoffs derived from subsequent equilibrium play. In other words, each reaction function shows the amount that must be offered in a current period to render a bargaining opponent *just indifferent* between the current offer and the present value of expected future payoffs. Label the bargaining reaction functions for Ludwig and Karla as B_L and B_K, respectively.

To construct the reaction functions, call X the share that Ludwig proposes for himself when making an offer, and call Y the share that Karla proposes for Ludwig. Then, for example, if X is the share that Ludwig can credibly demand for himself in the *next* round of bargaining, his expected value of continued bargaining in the *present* round is the discounted value of X, or δ_L times X, and that is thus the minimum payoff Y that Karla must offer him.

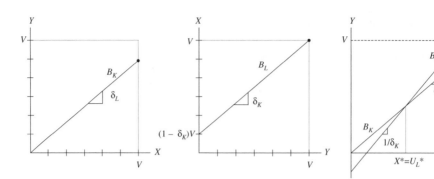

Figure 7.2(a) Karla's bargaining reaction function B_K.

Figure 7.2(b) Ludwig's bargaining reaction function B_L.

Figure 7.2(c) Rubinstein bargaining equilibrium with discounting and no exit options.

A similar logic holds in constructing the bargaining reaction function for Ludwig, noting that if Karla credibly expects to offer Y in the next round, she will receive the net surplus $V - Y$, and thus has in the *present* round an expected payoff from continued bargaining equal to δ_K times $V - Y$. Ludwig must thus choose an offer X in the present round so that that Karla's share $V - X$ is just equal to her expected payoff from continued bargaining.

The bargaining reaction functions just described are illustrated in figure 7.2, panels a and b. In each case they depict a relationship between offers X and Y. Note that the axes are reversed going from panel A to panel B; this is because Karla takes Ludwig's *future* offer X as given in deciding on her *current* offer, with the reverse holding for Ludwig.

An increased value of δ_L, signalling *more* patient preferences on Ludwig's part, rotates Karla's bargaining reaction function upward from the origin: since Ludwig suffers less from waiting for a later payoff, Karla must offer him a larger payoff when she initiates the bargaining round. This effect is shown in figure 7.2a.

For similar reasons, an increase in δ_K, indicating that Karla discounts future payoffs *less* heavily, rotates Ludwig's bargaining reaction function *downward*, keeping the right-hand side intercept constant. Since Karla is more patient in evaluating *future* payoffs, Ludwig must demand *less* X in any round of bargaining that he initiates. (Remember that Karla receives the surplus V *net* of Ludwig's proposal for his share; this also explains the different axes of rotation for the two bargaining reaction functions.)

The unique bargaining equilibrium is illustrated by superimposing the two reaction functions, as shown in figure 7.2c. (The algebraic solution for this bargaining scenario is derived in the appendix to this chapter.) The intersection of the two reaction functions establishes equilibrium payoffs because, at that point, each player's expected future payoff is based on an offer that the other player is just willing to accept. The value of X at the point of intersection, labelled X^*, indicates Ludwig's equilibrium bargaining payoff, which he secures by proposing X^* in the first round of bargaining, an offer that is immediately and optimally accepted by Karla. Karla's equilibrium bargaining payoff is thus the remainder, equal to $V - X^*$.

The unique bargaining solution exhibits two key characteristics. First, as you can infer from the foregoing discussion, each player's equilibrium payoff *increases* with the level of his or her own discount factor, and *decreases* with the level of his or her *opponent's* discount factor. This result should be intuitively appealing: it says, in effect, that your bargaining payoffs are lower if your negotiation costs rise or those of your opponent fall.

The second feature of equilibrium payoffs seems less intuitively compelling, at least at first glance. Suppose that the two players have *identical* discount factors equal to some common fraction δ. You might be tempted to say that they therefore receive equal bargaining payoffs (each garnering just half of the surplus), but such is not the case: the player who goes first receives a premium that is declining with the level of the common discount factor.

However, it is not hard to see the logical basis for this asymmetry. If players are both impatient, even if equally so, delays in reaching agreement matter, and the player who goes first gains a corresponding bargaining advantage thereby. The advantage diminishes, however, the less that delays matter to the players, so that the players' equilibrium payoffs both approach $V/2$ as the value of the common discount factor approaches one (i.e., as players become more patient).

The foregoing argument shows how negotiation costs, interpreted in a particular way, can be translated into a unique and arguably intuitive bargaining outcome. This is not the only way of representing costs of voice in the strategic bargaining framework, but it offers a good sense of how the analysis works. Other specifications of voice costs are considered in the appendix.

The next step in the analysis is to assess the role of matching costs in determining bargaining outcomes. Two scenarios are considered: in the first, exit is an option freely elected by the player responding to a current offer; in the latter, outside payoffs are only received as the consequence of an *externally* imposed breakdown in the bargaining relationship. Contrasting the two scenarios will lend insight to the strategic sense of the Nash bargaining solution discussed earlier.

Voluntary exit with discounting

In actual labor market negotiations, it is generally possible for exchange partners to terminate the relationship at any point. To accommodate this possibility, the basic bargaining game with discounting is now augmented by allowing each player to respond to a standing offer by either rejecting it and making a counteroffer, as before, or leaving the relationship. Correspondingly, let A_L and A_K denote the respective alternative or exit payoffs for L and K. The timing of exit options is illustrated in the portion of the bargaining game illustrated in figure 7.3.

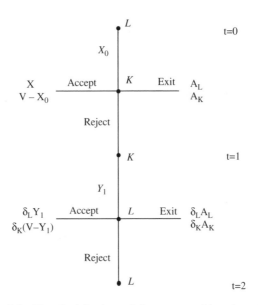

Figure 7.3 Detail of the bargaining game with exit options.

Assuming that both of the outside payoffs can be denominated in monetary terms, the surplus V generated by the employment relationship must be at least as great as the sum of outside payoffs, or else both players would not be willing to enter the relationship. Refer to this restriction as the *viability* condition for bargaining with outside options. The following analysis assumes that the surplus *strictly* exceeds this sum, so as to allow scope for non-trivial bargaining conflict. A scenario of perfectly competitive exchange results if the viability condition holds with equality.

Note that these exit options give each player a choice between two prospective payoffs: the utility from exit versus the expected utility derived from making a counteroffer in the following round of bargaining. An optimizing player will naturally choose the higher of the two payoffs. Since the value of outside payoffs does not vary with the strategies chosen by the players, the exit option puts a constant "floor" on the bargaining outcomes each player is willing to accept.

This "floor" shows up in an evident way in the bargaining reaction functions, as shown in figures 7.4a and 7.4b. The horizontal portion of Karla's reaction function is set by the value of Ludwig's outside payoff A_L; thus Karla can never make an offer lower than this payoff and expect Ludwig to accept it. Similarly, Karla's outside payoff A_K puts a "ceiling" on the share X that Ludwig can credibly pose for himself: if he demands more than $V - A_K$, leaving Karla less than the value of her outside opportunity, she can always do better by leaving.

As before, the unique equilibrium for this bargaining scenario can be determined graphically by superimposing the two reaction functions in the same diagram. This is shown in figure 7.4c. The value X^* selected by this intersection

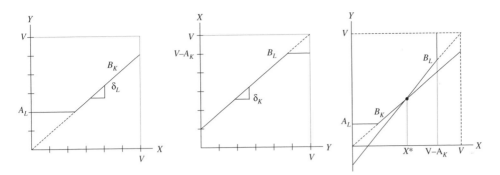

Figure 7.4(a) Karla's bargaining reaction function with discounting and exit option.

Figure 7.4(b) Ludwig's bargaining reaction function with discounting and exit option.

Figure 7.4(c) Rubinstein bargaining equilibrium with discounting and exit options.

still represents the equilibrium payoff to the player who goes first, which by assumption is Ludwig.

What difference does the introduction of exit options make to the equilibrium bargaining payoffs? Seemingly none at all, given the scenario illustrated in figure 7.4c: since L and K's bargaining reaction curves still intersect within their respective diagonal regions, the equilibrium payoffs are the same as in the absence of exit options with positive payoffs!

What's going on? The key to the puzzle is that figure 7.4 is drawn on the assumption that the outside options of L and K are both *low* relative to the surplus to be shared, and thus relative to the payoff each player would receive if outside options weren't present. If instead the magnitude of A_L were relatively high (adjusting A_K as necessary to ensure that the viability condition is met), then the horizontal segment of Karla's bargaining reaction function correspondingly shifts upward. If this segment were pushed up far enough, it would intersect Ludwig's reaction function at a higher point and thus yield a new solution featuring a higher payoff to Ludwig.

Alternatively, if Karla's exit payoff A_K were increased (while correspondingly reducing A_L as necessary to maintain the viability condition), the result is to shift the vertical portion of Ludwig's bargaining reaction function B_L to the left in figure 7.4c. If this segment were pushed in far enough, it would intersect B_K at a lower point and thus create a new solution featuring a lower payoff to Ludwig.

The easiest way to summarize the impact of exit options in the Rubinstein bargaining game is in the context of the special case that the discount factors of both players are "almost" one, which is to say that players are sufficiently patient that their costs of negotiation are virtually zero. This scenario has the added advantage of allowing a direct comparison to the Nash solution, which in effect ignores the impact of negotiation costs.

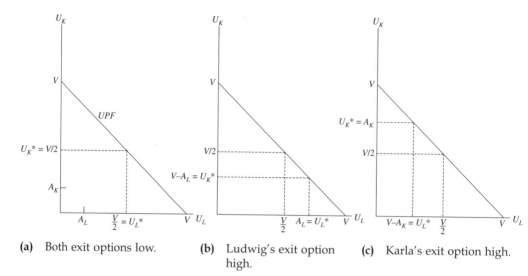

(a) Both exit options low.   **(b)** Ludwig's exit option   **(c)** Karla's exit option high.
                                        high.

Figure 7.5 Summary of bargaining equilibria with exit options and virtually zero voice costs.

The three possible equilibrium scenarios consistent with the viability condition are illustrated in figure 7.5. First, in the case that the outside options are "relatively low" (that is, each of the exit payoffs is smaller than half of the total surplus), both players just receive half of the value added, $V/2$, as shown in figure 7.5a. This is the same outcome as in the case with no exit options at all.

Second, if either player has a "relatively high" outside option (that is, an exit payoff higher than half of the surplus), then that player just receives the value of his or her outside option, while the other player gets whatever is left over (which necessarily exceeds that player's exit payoff, given the strong version of the viability condition assumed above). These cases are depicted respectively in panels (b) and (c) of figure 7.5.

In sum, exit options only affect equilibrium payoffs if they are sufficiently high relative to the total gains from trade, in which case the player with the high outside option just receives the value of his or her exit payoff. The intuition behind this result is that threats to exit the bargaining relationship must be *credible*, according to the dictates of subgame-perfect equilibrium. But since a player with low outside options can guarantee a higher payoff simply through the credible imposition of bargaining costs on his or her opponent, no additional leverage can credibly be gained by threatening to exit.

This point can be dramatized with the following illustration. Suppose two players who otherwise face protracted unemployment somehow come to negotiate over a large sum of money. If their bargaining costs are virtually zero, the foregoing analysis of the bargaining game with zero outside options indicates that their payoffs will each be equal to half of the total pie, and half of a large sum is still a large sum. The results stated above indicate that a player gains no extra bargaining muscle if he or she suddenly receives the prospect of employment in a job that is just barely an improvement over being unemployed, since the threat to exit to a low-paying job rather than stay and enjoy half of the large surplus is not credible to the other player.

It is interesting to note the significant difference between the prediction of the strategic bargaining model with voluntary exit and the Nash bargaining solution discussed in chapter 6. The values of outside payoffs *always* influence bargaining outcomes in the Nash solution, while in the Rubinstein solution exit options only influence the outcome if they are sufficiently high relative to the surplus to be divided. As indicated by the ensuing discussion of the second "exit" scenario, the Nash bargaining solution corresponds to a setting in which there is an *exogenously imposed* chance of breakdown in bargaining, and either exit cannot be freely chosen by the players or the exit options are too low to constitute credible threats in the bargaining process.

HOW DO OUTSIDE OPTIONS AFFECT ACTUAL BARGAINING PAYOFFS?

Strategic bargaining analysis offers a very different assessment of the impact of outside payoffs than that suggested by the Nash bargaining solution. In the latter, variations in "disagreement" payoffs *always* affect equilibrium payoffs at the margin, while in the Rubinstein bargaining game with discounting and voluntary exit, an outside payoff can only affect bargaining outcomes if it is sufficiently high relative to the surplus to be divided. Which hypothesis is borne out in practice?

There are two types of evidence that address this question, the first coming from the literature on economic experiments. Binmore, Shaked, and Sutton (1989) describe one such experiment that they conducted, for which 120 social science students were recruited at the London School of Economics. Students who had studied game theory or bargaining models were excluded from the study. Participants were then paired anonymously, and put into separate rooms, each with a computer through which to play the game. £7 (about $10) was to be divided if the pair could agree on the division. Player 1 had no outside option, while Player 2 had an outside option of either £0 (10 pairs), £2, or £4 (25 pairs each). The pairs alternated offers, starting with Player 1, and the discount factor was 0.9.

The prediction from the Rubinstein model is that in the case where the outside option is greater than half of the surplus, Player 2 will receive an amount equal to the outside option; in the other cases, the players will split the amount. This prediction received some support from the experiments, with Player 2 receiving a higher proportion (close to the predicted 57%) in those games with the high outside option, but with equal splitting occurring much of the time in the games where the outside option was low.

continued

However, another prediction from the model, namely that players would never play beyond a first offer, was not well-supported; many games lasted for more than three rounds, and one game lasted for ten rounds. This could be because the model's assumption of complete information about the game's payoff structure and the consequences of alternative strategies could not be unambiguously replicated in the experimental environment.

The second bit of evidence is derived from econometric analysis of empirical data. Economist Pasquale Scaramozzino (1991) studied a panel of over 200 manufacturing firms in the United Kingdom for the period 1972–82. Scaramozzino divides observations into bargaining regimes based on an assessment as to whether employers' or workers' outside options were binding, if either, and then considered whether wage outcomes over this time period could be explained in terms of the predictions of the Rubinstein bargaining model.

His empirical test produced evidence that was broadly consistent with the Rubinstein hypothesis: first, the estimated structure of wage determination varied significantly across the three outside option regimes (employer option binding, employee option binding, neither binding). Second, per capita industry profits were found to affect wages only in the "neither binding" regime, consistent with the Rubinstein prediction that the bargaining surplus is shared when neither outside option binds. Third, observed wage levels were affected by average wages in the industry only in the two "outside option binding" regimes, consistent with the idea that outside options don't matter if they're relatively low, and that industry wages affect both employers' alternative profit opportunities and employees' alternative job prospects. However, Scaramozzino's empirical results also suggest that changes in industry unemployment levels affect equilibrium wages in both the "employer option binding" and "neither option binding" regimes, inconsistent with the notion that bargaining payoffs are unaffected by relatively low outside options.

Related discussion questions:
1. Try running the outside option game on a couple of your friends (seat them in separate rooms and convey offers back and forth so that the game is anonymous). What happened? Did the results support or contradict Rubinstein's predictions?
2. Why don't people always act in accordance with economic theory? Give at least two explanations.

Related references:
Ken Binmore, Avner Shaked, and John Sutton, "An Outside Option Experiment," *Quarterly Journal of Economics* 104, no. 4 (November 1989): 753–70.
Pasquale Scaramozzino, "Bargaining with Outside Options: Wages and Employment in UK Manufacturing," *Economic Journal* 101, no. 405 (March 1991): 331–42.

Before turning to the second "outside payoffs" scenario, consider the link between these theoretical results and the chapter's earlier discussion about mobility costs. The point of the analysis was to show how *relative* costs of negotiation and mobility influence bargaining outcomes, given that a situation of bilateral monopoly is created by *absolute* levels of mobility cost. To see this connection more clearly, note that each player's exit payoff is inversely related to his or her costs of exiting the relationship. Thus, high exit costs imply a low exit payoff, other things equal. For example, suppose that Karla's outside option is just equal to the surplus minus the cost of searching for a replacement exchange partner, or $V - C$. Then if C is less than $V/2$, her equilibrium payoff is $V - C$, and her partner just receives the cost of replacing him, or C.

Alternatively, if both players' mobility costs are sufficiently high, equilibrium payoffs in the Rubinstein bargaining model are determined solely by negotiation costs, represented here by the rates at which the players discount future payoffs. As discussed in the earlier bargaining scenario, the equilibrium is then such that each player's bargaining payoff is inversely related to the level of his own costs of voice, and directly related to the level of his opponents' bargaining costs.

Involuntary termination of the bargaining relationship

To illustrate by way of contrast the role of voluntary exit in bargaining, turn now to the case in which negotiations can only be terminated by some *exogenously given* random process. It is certainly unrealistic to suppose that bargaining partners can't voluntarily terminate their relationship; but as discussed below, this is not a critical flaw, in that the results of this model can be seamlessly combined with those of the scenario with voluntary exit. In any case, it is certainly plausible to imagine that exchange relationships might be shut down by random events, such as unexpected changes in the legal environment, the eruption of violent international conflict, or abrupt alterations in the personal circumstances of one or both of the parties.

Correspondingly, assume now that there is some unvarying probability P that the bargaining relationship will break down after each period in which agreement is not reached. This implies, of course, that bargaining continues after each round of disagreement with probability $(1 - P)$. If bargaining terminates, the exchange partners receive their respective outside payoffs A_L and A_K. To keep the analysis as simple as possible, imagine further that there are no costs of continued bargaining other than that related to the persistent chance that the bargaining relationship will be terminated against the will of the participants.

The reaction functions for this version of the strategic bargaining model are illustrated in panels (a) and (b) of figure 7.6. Notice two key differences from their counterparts in the voluntary exit scenario depicted in figure 7.4: first, there are no "kinks" in the present reaction functions, so if outside options affect equilibrium payoffs in *any* case, they must do so in *every* possible case; second, outside options determine the *vertical intercepts* of the respective reaction functions, so that

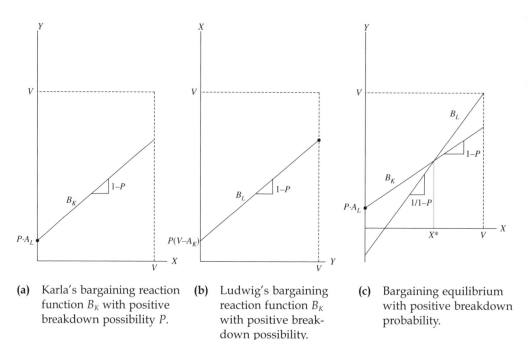

(a) Karla's bargaining reaction function B_K with positive breakdown possibility P.

(b) Ludwig's bargaining reaction function B_K with positive breakdown possibility.

(c) Bargaining equilibrium with positive breakdown probability.

Figure 7.6 Bargaining with fixed probability of termination.

each player's reaction function shifts upward with an increase in his or her outside payoff.

As ever, the equilibrium payoff to Ludwig (the player who initiates bargaining) is established by the intersection of the two reaction functions once they are superimposed, indicated by the point X^* on the horizontal axis of figure 7.6c. Karla just receives the residual net of the equilibrium payoff to Ludwig, or $V - X^*$. In light of the above, the unique prediction of this scenario is that the magnitude of outside payoffs *always* influences bargaining outcomes: other things equal, a player's equilibrium bargaining share is increasing in her outside payoff and decreasing in her opponent's outside payoff.

To emphasize how this conception of outside payoffs affects bargaining outcomes, let's consider a special case of this scenario in which the termination probability P is allowed to approach very close to zero. It is easy to demonstrate (see the appendix to this chapter) that in this case the equilibrium payoff to Ludwig approaches the value $X_0 = (V + A_L - A_K)/2$; Karla receives $V - X^* = (V - A_L + A_K)/2$. These are just the payoffs corresponding to the Nash bargaining solution for the cooperative game with total surplus V and "disagreement" payoffs A_L and A_K.

The strategic foundation of the Nash bargaining solution is now clear: it characterizes an exchange environment in which termination of bargaining is exogenously imposed (with a minutely small probability) rather than voluntarily chosen (and bargaining costs associated with discounting future payoffs are virtually zero). This is the basic reason why outside payoffs influence equilibrium in a different way in this solution than in the strategic bargaining scenario with voluntary exit. Knowledge of both scenarios is analytically useful, since as a practical matter a bargaining relationship can be terminated either voluntarily or involuntarily.

The outcomes of the two scenarios can be combined in a single bargaining model. This synthetic model would show that changes in outside payoffs affect both players' bargaining outcomes in the manner described just above if the value of both options is less than half of the surplus to be bargained over; otherwise, given the viability condition, the payoff of one player is equal to the value of his or her outside option, and the other player gets the residual.

OTHER BARGAINING SCENARIOS

The chapter's purpose thus far has been to identify the sources of bilateral market power, and more specifically to indicate the basic determinants of wage-setting power in given labor exchange relationships. Consequently, the argument has focused on very simple bargaining scenarios that ignore a number of practical complications arising in actual market settings. However, a number of these complications can be analyzed using extensions of the basic framework studied in this chapter. Three such extensions are briefly discussed here: bargaining with more than two players, with incomplete information, and with additional strategic options. Some of these extensions are studied further in conjunction with substantive issues raised in later chapters.

A modification of particular empirical relevance to the study of employment relationships deals with the case in which there are multiple bargainers on one side or the other of the bargaining table, as when a single firm owner bargains with the members of the firm's workforce. In this more complicated case bargaining remains essentially *bilateral* in that workers negotiate either collectively or individually with the single buyer, rather than with each other. This is sometimes referred to as a scenario of monopoly/oligopoly bargaining.

As explored further in chapter 12, it is possible to generate unique and intuitively appealing predictions by applying the strategic bargaining model to this more complicated setting. Qualitatively speaking, the key difference from the more basic setting of bilateral monopoly lies in the strategic options newly available to the "monopoly" side of the bargaining table. For example, the monopolist may be able to replace a single member of the oligopoly in the bargaining relationship, rather than exiting the entire relationship to seek a new team of bargaining opponents. Other things equal, the power of individual replacement increases the monopolist's bargaining payoffs by reducing its exit costs. As discussed further in chapter 12, this insight helps to explain why the ability to bargain *collectively* strengthens the bargaining position of workers in a given firm's labor force.

The analysis gets a bit more involved in the case of *multilateral* rather than bilateral bargaining, as when members of a large production team bargain over the fruits of their coordinated labor inputs. In this case the practice of rotating offers among players from round to round yields a multiplicity of equilibrium distributions so long as bargainers do not discount future payoffs too severely and exit payoffs are not too high. In other words, the collective choice yielded by bargaining may be indeterminate.

A second extension to the basic bargaining framework addresses the impact of *incomplete information*. In the language of game theory, this refers to a situation in which players are not fully apprised of each other's available strategies or payoff functions when they assess alternative strategies. Applied to the context of bilateral bargaining, this may mean that at least one of the players is unaware of the other's bargaining cost or outside payoffs.

In the presence of incomplete information, a player's bargaining offer has two strategic functions: first, as before, to propose a distribution of the available pie; second, and uniquely, to elicit information about the other player's unknown characteristics. Given the maintained assumption of credible equilibrium behavior, the latter function is accomplished by eliciting informative signals about the other player's true characteristics through the choice of bargaining responses. For example, a player with a very high outside option might reject an offer that could not be credibly refused by a player with poor alternatives.

Because of the additional strategic problem of eliciting information, equilibrium in strategic bargaining games with incomplete information typically involves the possibility of delay in reaching agreement, implying expected payoffs which may be Pareto-inferior to those obtained under conditions of complete information. Delay may result due to the unavoidable possibility that a player with certain characteristics rejects an initial offer. The possibility of equilibrium disagreement for some initial rounds of bargaining is not unique to games with incomplete information, however; it could also arise in scenarios in which players are completely informed but multiple equilibria exist. One such scenario arises in the case of *fixed* bargaining costs that you are asked to explore in one of the study questions at the end of the chapter.

Another basis for multiple equilibria arises in the third extension of the basic model. This involves the addition of a new strategic option to the bargaining game beyond making and responding to offers and deciding to exit. Of particular relevance to the study of employment relationships is the option to "strike" against employers or "lockout" employees.

Either form of this option implies that players can elect *not to produce* and yet to continue within the bargaining relationship. Failure to produce means that the potential gains from labor exchange are at best delayed. As suggested above, adding this option creates the possibility of multiple equilibria that are equally plausible in terms of the criterion of credible or subgame-perfect behavior. This scenario is studied further in chapter 12 on representation of collective employee interests in the workplace.

CONCLUSION

The ideal labor market model corresponds to a world with large numbers of potential buyers and sellers and free entry and exit into markets for every type of labor service. There is no scope for the exercise of market power in this world. In contrast, one or both sides of the labor market may enjoy wage-setting power when finding alternative exchange partners is costly.

High costs of matching potential exchange partners necessarily limits the scope for mutually beneficial exchange. Beyond this, however, the significance of matching costs has primarily to do with the *distribution* of net gains from trade rather than their potential magnitude. Absent informational problems of the sort discussed in the next chapter, one typically would expect outcomes "along the contract curve" that are dictated by the relative bargaining power of exchange partners. The exception to this is when bargaining parties have more options than simply to exit or continue bargaining.

Besides establishing a theoretical framework for use in subsequent analysis of various labor market phenomena, the foregoing analysis also suggests a central theme: the impact of potential "outside" payoffs on bargaining outcomes depends critically on whether these alternatives are freely available to the bargainers. If so, then the value of outside options affects equilibrium payoffs only if one or the other is sufficiently high relative to the surplus to be shared. If this is not the case, then the equilibrium division of gains from exchange is generally determined by the relative incidence of negotiation costs.

APPENDIX TO CHAPTER 7

DERIVATION OF THE RUBINSTEIN BARGAINING EQUILIBRIUM WITH DISCOUNTING AND NO EXIT OPTIONS

Statement of the problem

Suppose there are two players, K and L, who bargain over the distribution of a surplus $V > 0$. In any current period each player cares only about income, and discounts future payments by a factor δ_i per period, where δ_i is a positive fraction. The utility to player i of a bargaining share s_i received τ periods from the present is thus equal to $\delta_i^\tau \cdot s_i$.

Bargaining occurs over time, beginning in period $t = 0$ and continuing in periods $t = 1$, $2, 3, \ldots$, until agreement is reached. In each period, one player makes an offer and the other either accepts or rejects the offer. Players alternate in making offers, beginning with L's offer in period 0. If an offer is accepted, bargaining immediately concludes and the surplus V is distributed according to the accepted offer. Any player who rejects an offer makes a counter-offer in the following period.

The solution concept adopted is that of *subgame-perfect equilibrium*, which implies that players are restricted to Nash equilibrium strategies *on each subgame* of the bargaining game, meaning that at each decision node players are assumed to adopt only those strategies which maximize their (expected) utility given others' strategies.

Derivation of equilibrium payoffs for the game with discounting and no exit options

The argument follows the recursive proof technique developed by Avner Shaked and John Sutton.[2] The first critical step in deriving equilibrium payoffs for this game is to note that the *structure* of the game is recursive, meaning that the pattern of available moves and countermoves repeats itself every two periods (since in principle bargaining may go on forever). For example, player L makes an offer and player K responds with acceptance and rejection in periods 0, 2, 4, . . .

The significance of this for the solution is that any equilibrium defined at $t = 0$ must also be an equilibrium for the game beginning at period $t = 2$, since the subsequent game trees are identical (that is, alternating offers going on forever, beginning with L's offer). Therefore, assume for the sake of argument that an equilibrium exists, and define m as the *minimum* equilibrium payoff for player L. Then m must also be the minimum equilibrium payoff for L at $t = 2$.

Now move backward in time to period $t = 1$. Since player L can expect to receive a payoff of at least m a period later, and discounts future payoffs by δ_L, player K must offer L *at least* $\delta_L \cdot m$ in period 1 in order to gain acceptance of the offer. This means that K can expect to receive a payoff of *at most* $V - \delta_L \cdot m$ in period 1.

Now move backward in time once more to period $t = 0$. Since player K can expect a payoff of *at most* $V - \delta_L \cdot m$ in period 1 and discounts future payoffs by δ_K per period, player L must offer K *at most* $\delta_K \cdot (V - \delta_L \cdot m)$ in order to gain acceptance of the offer. This implies that L can expect a payoff of *at least* $V - \delta_K \cdot (V - \delta_L \cdot m)$ in period 0. But then by definition this is the minimum payoff L can expect in equilibrium for the game, and so equals m. Thus we have a single equation in a single unknown, $m = V - \delta_K \cdot (V - \delta_L \cdot m)$, which simplifies to

$$m = \frac{(1-\delta_K) \cdot V}{1 - \delta_L \cdot \delta_K}.$$

Now redefine m as the *maximum* equilibrium payoff for player L in the bargaining game, and go through the previous steps in order, replacing the phrase "at least" with "at most" and the phrase "at most" with "at least." The upshot of this is that $m = \frac{(1-\delta_K) \cdot V}{1 - \delta_L \cdot \delta_K}$ is also the *maximum* equilibrium payoff for L, implying that if an equilibrium exists, it generates unique payoffs. It is easy to show that equilibrium strategies supporting this payoff exist, such that in each bargaining round player i offers player j a bargaining share of $\frac{\delta_j \cdot (1-\delta_i) \cdot V}{1 - \delta_i \cdot \delta_j}$, and player j accepts any bargaining share at least as high as this offer. The respective equilibrium payoffs to L and K are thus $x^* = \frac{(1-\delta_K) \cdot V}{1 - \delta_L \cdot \delta_K}$ and $V - x^* = \frac{\delta_K \cdot (1-\delta_L) \cdot V}{1 - \delta_L \cdot \delta_K}$, which implies that each player's bargaining share increases as her own discount factor increases or that of her partner decreases.

Study Questions

1. In the strategic bargaining framework represented by the Rubinstein model, why is it the case that bargaining payoffs generally depend on relative negotiation costs (represented, for example, by relative discount factors)? Why is it the case that changes in the value of outside payoffs don't always affect bargaining outcomes, as in the Nash Bargaining Solution?

2. In the specific context of real-world wage bargaining between employers and individual employees, what labor market conditions correspond to the respective scenarios in which the employee's outside option is relatively high, the employer's outside option is relatively high, and neither's outside option is high relative to the equilibrium bargaining payoff that would obtain when both parties' exit options are valued at zero?

3. Consider a version of the bargaining problem between K and L with respective fixed bargaining costs C_K and C_L per period and no discounting. What might be examples of fixed bargaining costs? Suppose that both players have outside options with payoffs of zero, and that they are bargaining over surplus V.

   (a) Derive and separately graph the B_K and B_L functions for this bargaining problem.

   (b) Illustrate the conditions of bargaining equilibrium for the case in which $C_K = C_L$. How would you describe the nature of these conditions? By what process do you suppose bargaining equilbrium would be determined in this situation?

4. Consider a version of the bargaining problem between K and L in which there are no discount factors or fixed bargaining costs, but rather a fixed probability $1 - q$ between 0 and 1 that the bargaining relationship will dissolve after each period in which agreement is not reached, forcing K and L to receive their respective outside options a_K and a_L with that probability. [Note that this means that bargaining will continue into the period after each disagreement with probability q.]

   (a) Suppose person K initiates bargaining. Construct and graph the B_K and B_L functions for this version of the bargaining problem, and indicate the corresponding equilibrium payoffs to K and L.

   (b) In this case, how does equilibrium respond to changes in the values of the outside options? Are equilibrium payoffs always responsive to these changes?

   (c) Suppose that the probability q is very close to 1. What happens to the equilibrium payoff to K? [Hints: the term $(1 - q^2)$ factors into $(1 - q) \cdot (1 + q)$, and you'll know you're on the right track if you can cancel lots of terms before moving q close to 1.]

   (d) Comparing this result to that for the standard alternating-offers bargaining relationship with outside options, what is apparently necessary to guarantee that equilibrium payoffs are always influenced by the level of outside payoffs?

Notes

1   Ariel Rubinstein, "Perfect Equilibrium in a Bargaining Model," *Econometrica* 50, no. 1 (January 1982): 97–109.
2   Avner Shaked and John Sutton, "Involuntary Unemployment as a Perfect Equilibrium in a Bargaining Model," *Econometrica* 52, no. 6 (November 1984): 1351–64.

Suggestions for Further Reading

Avinash Dixit and Susan Skeath, *Games of Strategy* (New York: W.W. Norton, 1999): chapter 16, "Bargaining."
Martin Osborne and Ariel Rubinstein, *Bargaining in Markets* (San Diego: Academic Press, 1990).

CHAPTER EIGHT

IMPERFECT CONTRACTING
IN LABOR EXCHANGE

Exchanges involving paid labor are potentially very complex transactions. As discussed in previous chapters, the labor input into a given production process can vary along a number of dimensions, including number of workers, hours per worker, effort or intensity per hour, and skill level. Additionally, if multiple workers are engaged in the same production process, their efforts must somehow be effectively coordinated.

Furthermore, the inalienability of labor from the labor supplier implies that various workplace conditions, such as location, comfort, and job safety are salient to the transaction. Moreover, numerous uncertainties or contingencies may affect the process of production, so that a different configuration of labor inputs is needed for each possible contingency. Finally, there may be a significant passage of time from when a worker is engaged, the desired work is actually performed, and the worker is duly compensated.

The institution of legally enforceable contracting facilitates exchanges characterized by such complications. The terms of exchange agreed upon by transacting parties are spelled out in contractual language in such a way that it is possible for third parties, typically agents of the judicial system, to ensure that they are carried out by levying penalties for any observed transgressions of the contracted agreement. Enforceable contracts thus help to ensure traders that their intentions upon entering into given transactions are reliably implemented. For example, well-chosen contractual language may deter a trading partner from using an unanticipated contingency as an excuse not to deliver or pay for a particular service.

Given the multiple issues and concerns potentially arising in exchanges for labor, one might expect that contracts governing these transactions are correspondingly detailed. But to the contrary, contracts governing employment transactions are often relatively simple. Even where these contracts

continued

are lengthy, as in some collective bargaining agreements, a number of matters that are presumably salient to the relationship, such as workers' effort levels or the specific tasks to be performed under alternative contingencies, are not spelled out in the contract.

This chapter examines the seeming paradox that key aspects of potentially complex labor exchanges are generally not covered by associated labor contracts. The core argument builds on the premise that in such cases contracts with the necessary level of detail are prohibitively costly to specify and enforce. The chief implication of this scenario is that transaction costs of this sort reduce the feasible gains from labor exchange, thus creating incentives for organizational responses to minimize or redistribute the losses associated with imperfect contracting arrangements. This theme is explored in more depth in the next several chapters of the text.

TRANSACTION COSTS AND CONTRACTUAL FAILURES

The model of perfectly competitive labor markets effectively assumes that all exchange activities are virtually costless. Under this assumption, labor transactions are understood to be governed by contracts in which all possible contingencies have been anticipated and all aspects of the labor input have been determined and spelled out in clear contractual language. Furthermore, contractual stipulations are enforced by external agencies at no cost to the transactors.

Of course, this vision of "frictionless" transactions never perfectly obtains in practice, although it may serve as a useful simplification for many analytical purposes. In reality, exchange, like production or any other activity, incurs direct and opportunity costs. This chapter considers two possible manifestations of such costs. The first is *contractual incompleteness*, in which contingencies affecting the eventual realization of gains from exchange are not fully covered by the labor contract. In the second scenario, imperfect contracting results from asymmetrically held information about key features of the labor exchange such as the level of work effort.

As you read, keep in mind that enforcement costs need not actually be incurred to influence labor market outcomes. Just as an input might not be used in a given production process when it becomes too expensive, so may the use of a particular contract enforcement device be foregone in anticipation of its cost. An extreme instance of this is when the costs of particular enforcement activities are essentially infinite, which is to say that the objective in question is virtually impossible. The result is perhaps that no enforcement costs at all are actually incurred – and no attempt is made to achieve the costly enforcement objective, either.

Specification, verification, and incomplete labor contracts

Imagine a situation in which the outcome of a production relationship depends on a number of contingencies relating to such things as the weather, vagaries in the timeliness or quality of externally supplied materials, changes in macroeconomic conditions, and so on. Even if participants in the production process were unboundedly rational, so that each of them could, without strain or error, anticipate all possible contingencies and their respective implications for how production should be carried out, it might be extremely expensive and time-consuming to spell out these considerations contractually in such a way that the terms of exchange could be effectively enforced by outside parties. As a consequence, rational exchange partners may elect to forego articulating the terms of trade under every possible contingency. This problem is compounded if parties to the transaction are instead only boundedly rational, such that even conceiving of all relevant contingencies is difficult if not virtually impossible.

In light of these difficulties, parties to the transaction may choose, or perhaps even be compelled, to forego specifying the terms of exchange under each possible contingency. The resulting contract is said to be *incomplete*. Contracts can be incomplete either through omitting to identify relevant contingencies or by failing to specify the obligations and benefits of the exchange partners under each possible contingency. The key test of contractual incompleteness as defined here lies in the possibility of specifying the terms and conditions of exchange in such a way that failure to achieve them can be verified by an external enforcement agency. Contracts are deemed complete so long as all matters affecting the potential gains from trade that are observable to the trading parties can also be verified by the appropriate external enforcement agency, and rendered incomplete to the extent that this condition does not hold.

As noted, non-verifiability may result because the sheer number of potential contingencies makes it prohibitively expensive to write a complete contract. Another possibility is that intended outcomes are not readily describable in ways that would satisfy the rules of evidence in a judicial proceeding. This would be the case, for example, when specialized expertise is required to recognize that a given contractual stipulation has been violated. Without spending considerable time and money to acquire that expertise, the judicial body could not then reliably assess if contractual terms stipulating a given quality were violated.

It is particularly difficult to write verifiable contractual language to cover cases in which desired outcomes are a function of the suitability or aptness of a given labor input rather than its quantity measured along a given dimension. For example, one advantage in hiring workers with advanced skill or experience in a particular activity is that they know what to do when something unexpected happens. But it might then be difficult to convince a court that workers failed to "do the right thing" unless the court had acquired the specialized ability to determine what exactly the right thing to do was under the given circumstances.

Note that the issue of verifiability concerns the information available to the external enforcement agency, not to the parties of the transaction. In particular, outcomes of a given exchange relationship may be fully known to all transacting parties and yet not verifiable by the enforcement body. As a consequence, exchange outcomes desired by the transactors must be in some sense self-enforcing to be feasible, since the outside agency can't enforce what it can't see.

THE PROS AND CONS OF WORKING WITH FRIENDS AND RELATIVES

One method of solving some of the problems related to imperfect contracting might be to hire people that you interact with in other settings. Why would this work? One possibility is that you could use the threat of negative interactions in the other setting to induce good behavior in the work setting. For example, if your domestic partner appears to be shirking at work, you shirk at home in retaliation (or just sulk around the house and make their home life generally less pleasant). In part because your partner knows you can do this, they avoid shirking. Indeed, a large proportion of small businesses in all countries involve people related by blood or marriage, although not necessarily or primarily for this reason.

Another possibility is to hire people that interact in other settings. New York City entrepreneur Charlie Kim, who hired large numbers of friends – and friends of friends – to work at his marketing firm NextJump Inc., reasoned that "employees would feel more comfortable and be more productive working with people whom they already knew. After all, they wouldn't want to let their friends down by not delivering on responsibilities" (Silverman, 2001).

One drawback to this plan is that if things go badly at work, the effect may be compounded through the effect of personal interactions. As the company's personnel director pointed out: "You have a group of five, six, 10 people – all best friends, who all went to school together. If one gets disillusioned it affects the rest of the people in that group." Particularly if you have to fire one or more of them; when Mr Kim downsized his company during the Internet start-up slump of early 2000 and began firing employees, other employees quit to follow their friends out of the company. When Mr Kim began hiring again, he hired a professional headhunter.

Related discussion question:
1. List some specific pros and cons related to working with family members. Do the same for working with friends (i.e., people one knows before one starts working with them). Do the items on your lists relate to specific theoretical concepts discussed so far in the text? If not, how could they be incorporated into this theoretical framework?

Related reference:
Rachel Emma Silverman, "For Charlie Kim, Company of Friends Proves a Lonely Place," *Wall Street Journal*, February 1, 2001: A1; A6.

Observability and asymmetric information

An alternative, and in some sense more severe, contracting problem exists when exchange partners are not equally informed of all conditions relevant to their transaction. This problem typically arises when one party has private information that is difficult or impossible for the other party to elicit. This situation is referred to as one of *contracting under asymmetric information.*

The economic literature on this subject distinguishes two forms of asymmetric information, hidden *action* and hidden *state*. In the former case, one agent chooses an action or set of actions that affects the magnitude of gains from exchange and is at least partially invisible to the other exchange parties. The distinct economic significance of asymmetric information in this form lies in the fact that the hidden item is a matter of choice to one of the transacting parties. This implies that hidden action settings generically give rise to problems of *incentive provision*, since it is necessarily difficult to provide incentives for actions that ultimately can't be observed by one of the traders, let alone verified by an external enforcement agency.

In the context of labor market exchanges, the most obvious source of hidden action problems is the choice of work effort or intensity. Exertion is often as much a mental state as it is a physical one. For example, a worker may be standing still while thinking vigorously about how to overcome some obstacle to productivity. Conversely, a worker might give the appearance of being busy or engaged while actually attempting to do very little. Thus it may be difficult for an observer to infer precisely the true level of work effort from casual observation.

In the case of hidden *state*, one party to a transaction knows something about a condition affecting potential gains from exchange that is not visible to the other trader. Here the invisible element is not a matter of choice, but rather a significant characteristic of one of the traders or of the environment within which the exchange is carried out. What matters in this case is when the informed party first observes the state or condition hidden from the other trader.

A plausible scenario of hidden state relevant to the specific context of labor exchange concerns the relevant abilities or skills of prospective employees. It may be extremely difficult for an employer to ascertain if a worker possesses the particular set of capabilities required for a given position without actually seeing how the worker undertakes the corresponding tasks. Here the primary strategic issue is not one of providing incentives to selected trading partners, but rather making sure that partners with the desired characteristics are selected.

In either case of contracting under asymmetric information, the ignorant party may benefit from efforts to learn what the other party knows. In the case of hidden effort, for example, a firm may elect to monitor or supervise the work of its employees in order to get a better idea of how hard they're working. Even if the information thus garnered is imperfect, the employer might be able to tie penalties or rewards to the monitoring signal so as to increase work effort.

Supervision might also play a role in the case of hidden state, if the situation of asymmetric information arises subsequent to the initiation of an exchange. In this case, supervisors might be used to acquire information about the hidden conditions affecting production. One example of this is when workers acquire specific information about a production process via "learning by doing." By observing how workers produce, supervisors might be able to infer what it is that workers learn as they gain familiarity with given production techniques and relationships.

Suppose in contrast that the hidden state concerns a quality of the worker that precedes a given labor market transaction, such as the worker's skill in a certain production activity. In this case the labor buyer might wish to invest resources in screening potential employees for the hidden quality. This screening may take the form of a written test, a "tryout," or a probationary period in which the prospective employee's effectiveness is assessed. The benefit to the employer of screening may go beyond its efficacy in distinguishing hidden worker qualities; for example, knowing of an employer's screening efforts may discourage workers without the desired qualities from applying for jobs in the first place.

The next step in the analysis is to consider how each of these contractual imperfections, incompleteness and contracting under asymmetric information, affects the scope for realization of gains from labor exchange. The scenario of incomplete contracting is examined first.

LABOR EXCHANGE UNDER INCOMPLETE CONTRACTS

The basic setting

Imagine that three people, named Paula, Pete, and Marty, enter into an agreement to produce lemon trees. The agreement is struck at time 0 and includes a statement of how the expected gains from production are to be distributed among the three parties. Production of lemon trees occurs at a later time, say period 2. In between, at period 1, one of several possible contingencies affecting future productivity is realized and observed by all parties.

If, despite their visibility to all parties to the transaction, the potential contingencies cannot be specified in a verifiable way, then a situation of contractual incompleteness exists. This raises two related problems for the transaction. First, since the implications of each contingency have not been spelled out, the obligations of each party relevant to the realized production conditions must be determined after the fact. Second, distribution of the anticipated gains from production under the realized contingency may also be at issue. As mentioned earlier, one or more parties to the agreement may wish to renegotiate the initial terms of exchange.

Why should this matter? That is, if Paula, Pete, and Marty can exercise bargaining power *subsequent* to the realization of a particular contingency, presumably they could also exercise that power *prior* to its realization if contracts were, contrary to hypothesis, complete. Why is it necessarily worse to have bargaining with respect to specific contingencies occur later in the relationship rather than at the beginning?

Generally speaking, a logically adequate response to this question must have two parts.

First, the average or expected value of bargaining outcomes under individual production contingencies must be different from the bargaining outcome that would be generated up front under complete contracting, but before any particular contingency is realized. Second, the eventual bargaining outcome anticipated under incomplete contracting arrangements must be somehow undesirable, for example because it adversely affects the commitments individuals are willing to make in the initial period covered by the agreement. A plausible scenario relevant to labor market transactions in which these problems arise is considered next.

Asset specificity and quasi-rents

As suggested above, some initial commitments might be necessary to make a particular production venture a reality. Suppose that for at least one input supplier, say Paula, the required commitment is an investment that improves her productivity, but only in the production relationship shared with Pete and Marty. Such investments, and the assets they create, are said to be *relationship-specific*. Suppose in this case that the investment in question is in human capital rather than an alienable productive asset.

There are a number of reasons why human capital investments might exhibit some degree of relationship-specificity. First, productivity may depend in some way on the idiosyncratic social relationships among the co-producers; for example, some workers' effectiveness may depend on their ability to maneuver in the particular "corporate culture" of the firm. Second, a given production process may use a patented technique that demands special skills. Third, production may involve a uniquely demanding relationship with the buyers of the output.

By definition, relationship-specific investments increase the attainable surplus within a given production relationship, but nowhere else. In the language of the strategic bargaining theory studied in chapter 7, relationship-specific investments increase the value added by the relationship, but do not correspondingly increase the value of outside options. They therefore create *quasi-rents*, defined as returns to a factor supplier that exceed the level necessary to retain that factor in its current use. Quasi-rents must be distinguished from economic *rents*, defined as returns to a factor in excess of the level required to attract its supply to a given occupation.

What's the difference? Rents are determined relative to the payment just necessary to secure *entry* of a factor supplier to a given occupation, while quasi-rents are determined relative to the payment just necessary to deter *exit* of the factor supplier from a current occupation. In the present case of relationship-specific investments, the difference between the two is created by the initial costs to factor suppliers of making these investments. Once these costs are incurred, they are sunk, and cannot then affect the relative benefits of maintaining or leaving the relationship.

The fact that costs of relationship-specific investments are eventually sunk does not mean that factor suppliers don't care about them, of course. Before making such investments, input suppliers naturally wish to ensure that their costs will be covered. This is where the problem of contractual incompleteness re-enters the picture. If achievement of the desired investments is for some reason not verifiable by external enforcement agencies, then factor suppliers cannot contractually guarantee recompense for their costs, and thus might not be willing to undertake the investments in the first place.

Renegotiation and the "holdup" problem

Return to the scenario in which Paula, Pete, and Marty enter into a production agreement, this time with the modification that Paula can make a relationship-specific human capital investment that increases her productivity. Some provision for Paula to recoup her investment costs might correspondingly be included in the initial agreement. Suppose, however, that all payments must be drawn from the realized value of the final output.

But now suppose in addition that Paula's investment is not verifiable, perhaps because the costs are purely psychic and there is thus no way for a court to determine that Paula incurred them. Alternatively, perhaps Paula's expenditures are verifiable, but not the relevance or usefulness of these expenditures. The contract among Paula, Pete, and Mary is thus necessarily incomplete.

This creates a problem insofar as Paula's chances of recouping her investment costs are correspondingly endangered. The bargaining analysis of the previous chapter suggests the nature of the problem: once the investment has been made, it is a sunk cost and does not factor into the net surplus to be bargained over. Moreover, Paula's exit options are not improved by the investment because it is relationship-specific. Therefore, Pete and Marty can "hold up" Paula by credibly bargaining away the portion of the surplus that might otherwise go toward compensating her investment costs. If Paula is rational and can anticipate the "holdup" problem, she may decide not to undertake the investment in the first place, and the gains from the production relationship are thus reduced.

Consider the following numerical example.[1] Suppose that the total expected return (net of all input costs except those from Paula's human capital investment) from Paula, Pete, and Marty's production relationship is 120 if Paula does not make the investment and 240 if she does. Paula's investment cost is 60. Clearly it is socially desirable for her to undertake the investment, other things equal, since it yields a net gain of 60 for the group.

But now suppose that Paula's investment is not verifiable, and therefore its remuneration is not ensurable by contract. Suppose further that returns from the production relationship are determined by bargaining among the three individuals. To keep things simple, assume that payoffs are given by the Nash bargaining solution, and that each actor's outside payoff is zero.

If Paula does not make the investment, the total return of 120 is split evenly three ways, so that each player receives a net payoff of 40. If Paula makes the relationship-specific investment at a cost of 60, it becomes a sunk cost, and the quasi-rent to be bargained over is 240. With outside payoffs identically zero, the Nash bargaining solution has each player receiving a share of 80, so that Paula's net payoff is 20. Consequently, in this example, she loses 20 by electing to make the investment, despite the fact that it increases total net payoffs for the group. Thus, Paula's optimal choice would be to forgo undertaking the investment.

Note that this negative outcome depends on the condition that all three participants in the agreement have equal bargaining power. If it were somehow the case that one party, say Pete, could be limited to just his input cost (so that he has no claim on the surplus), then once Paula makes the investment, she and Marty split the 240, yielding Paula a net return of 60 and thus making it worth her while to undertake the investment. The social costs of contractual incompleteness thus depend in part on the determinants of bargaining power over quasi-rents.

LABOR EXCHANGE UNDER ASYMMETRIC INFORMATION

Now consider the problem of contracting for labor services under asymmetric information. In this scenario, ignorance about key conditions affecting the gains from exchange extends beyond the external agency to one or more parties to the transaction. Recall that there are two possible forms of this asymmetry involving hidden characteristics and hidden actions. These are examined in turn before moving to a more in-depth exploration of the problem of incentive provision.

Adverse selection and moral hazard

In the scenario of hidden state, a condition or characteristic known by one party to the exchange is unobservable by others. This asymmetry can arise prior to the exchange agreement or subsequent to it. If the information asymmetry pertains to a prior condition, the possibility arises that the terms of the contract will influence the characteristics of the set of agents who seek an exchange relationship. This phenomenon is sometimes referred to as *adverse selection*.

Consider the following example. A firm wishes to engage workers with certain characteristics: perhaps the firm prefers employees who show evidence of being highly productive in a particular enterprise, or who are likely to remain in the relationship for an extended period. The problem is that the buyer cannot costlessly observe the characteristics sought.

But is this really a problem? Even if the characteristics are unobservable, the buyer might still request that only workers with the desired qualities apply for the position being offered, and then construct a job description and compensation package that is sufficiently attractive for workers with the desired profile. A difficulty arises, however, if the resulting offer is even more attractive to workers who don't have the characteristics being sought. In that case, the offer might be expected to attract an applicant pool that is heavily weighted with candidates the buyer would rather avoid, but cannot distinguish from the desired candidates. The offer has thus resulted in an "adverse selection" of applicants from the larger population.

A classic example of adverse selection arises in insurance markets. Suppose a competitive insurance company offers complete insurance against risk for risk-averse agents. The company's problem is that there are two types of potential customer, those with a high propensity for the loss being insured against, and those with a lower propensity to incur this loss. In principle, the company could offer separate policies for the two risk classes, with less attractive terms being offered to high-risk insurees. A difficulty arises if the insurer can't distinguish the two customer types, because the high-risk agents will always prefer the terms offered to the low-risk customers. But if they buy insurance meant for low-risk customers, the company can't offer as desirable a policy to the low-risk customers, leading to an inefficient equilibrium in the insurance market.

The key question in the presence of adverse selection is whether a contract can be designed which effectively separates agents with different hidden types, so that agents from each class only select contracts intended for their type. Under some conditions, the desired separating equilibrium can be achieved simply through judicious selection of the alternative contractual terms offered to different types, although this may come at some social cost, resulting in an equilibrium that is strictly *second-best* from an efficiency standpoint.

In the insurance market scenario, for example, insurance contracts could perhaps be designed so that those who identify themselves as having low accident propensity are made to bear some of the risk, rather than receiving full insurance. High-risk customers might avoid this contract in favor of one in which they're completely insured (albeit with a higher insurance premium), because they face a higher chance of incurring the loss that is now incompletely insured. Thus, the proffered policy options "separate" the two types, but at the cost of inefficient insurance provisions to the low-risk customers.

In the contrasting case of hidden action, the indicated information asymmetry cannot precede the exchange relationship, because it concerns a choice taken by one of the trading partners after the relationship has begun. Because this choice is by assumption hidden from the other exchange partners, they cannot use contractual means to tie rewards and penalties directly to the action chosen by the informed party. Consequently, the latter may choose a suboptimal action or set of actions, creating a situation of *moral hazard*.

The key issue in the case of hidden action is thus the provision of appropriate incentives to the agent with private information. In the context of labor exchanges, as indicated earlier, a relevant case of this asymmetry arises when workers choose effort levels that are not visible to their employers. In such cases, the fact that effort is not directly observable does not necessarily rule out efficient exchange outcomes. The remainder of the chapter examines possible additional conditions under which hidden effort might negatively influence the outcome of labor exchange.

Imagine an exchange relationship in which the employee's work effort is completely invisible to the buyer of labor services. This scenario is sometimes referred to as the *principal–agent* problem, since the "principal" or employer faces a problem in getting the "agent" or employee to pursue his or her objectives. As a point of reference, a principal–agent setting is first constructed to illustrate that invisible effort is not a problem of itself. Two distinct scenarios are then identified in which effort unobservability affects the scope for realizing gains from exchange.

Labor exchange with unobservable effort: a reference case

Imagine a situation in which a prospective buyer of labor services named Rose wishes to hire a single worker named Jack from a competitive labor market. This implies that Jack is a *utility-taker*, meaning that he will accept any labor contract which ensures a payoff that on average is at least equal to that available from his employment alternatives.

Let X represent the monetary value of the output generated by Jack's effort, and let Y represent the pecuniary compensation to Jack for producing the desired output. Suppose that Rose cares only about profit, so that her utility is represented by a profit function, which to keep things simple will be specified as simply the value of output minus compensation, or $X - Y$.

Now suppose that output X increases linearly with Jack's labor effort. This implies in turn that Rose's profit is increasing in labor effort and decreasing in the payment to Jack, with a constant marginal rate of substitution just equal to the marginal productivity of Jack's effort, assumed to be a constant value M. Rose's isoprofit map is illustrated in figure 8.1a. Note that Rose's profits increase as effort increases and payment to Jack decreases.

Now examine Jack's payoff from employment given that he likes income but dislikes providing work effort, other things equal. Let E represent Jack's work effort. For simplicity, assume that Jack's preferences over effort and income are summarized by a utility function with the property that Jack's marginal rate of substitution between compensation and effort is everywhere just equal to E, his work effort (see the appendix to this chapter). This implies that Jack's indifference curves are parallel and each increasing in slope as effort increases, as shown in figure 8.1b. As illustrated, Jack's utility level increases as you move across indifference curves up and to the left in the figure. Also assume for simplicity that Jack's competitively determined utility level, indicated by the indifference curve going through the origin, is just equal to zero.

Now let's imagine that Rose wants to write a contract for labor effort and compensation so as to maximize her profit subject to the condition that Jack just receives the competitive level of utility. To analyze this problem, superimpose Rose's isoprofit map on Jack's indifference map, creating an Edgeworth box in effort/payment combinations. The result is shown in figure 8.1c.

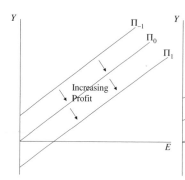

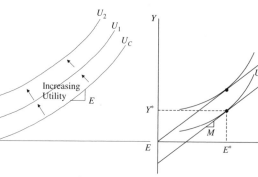

Figure 8.1(a) Rose's isoprofit map over Jack's effort and compensation levels.

Figure 8.1(b) Jack's indifference map over effort and compensation bundles.

Figure 8.1(c) Profit-maximizing effort and compensation levels given competitive utility U_c.

For reasons that should be by now familiar, the profit-maximizing contract terms are determined by a point of tangency between Rose's highest attainable indifference curve and Jack's competitive-level indifference curve. Since tangency means that the slopes of the two curves are equal, profit maximization implies that $E^* = M$, that is, Jack's optimal effort is just equal to his marginal product of effort (this is a special result of the particular choice of Jack's utility function, not a general implication of the asymmetric information scenario).

The corresponding compensation level, Y^*, just guarantees Jack his competitive utility level of zero, given his effort of E^*. If Jack's effort were fully observable, Rose could achieve this first-best outcome simply by stipulating that Jack is to be paid Y^* if and only if he performs labor effort E^*. This is also the outcome obtained under perfectly competitive market conditions.

But now suppose instead that Rose is unable to observe Jack's effort level, and thus cannot stipulate effort in a labor contract. Does this affect Rose's ability to induce the profit-maximizing combination of work effort and compensation derived above? The answer is no: since output and effort are perfectly correlated via the production function, Rose can achieve precisely the same outcome by making Jack's compensation contingent on output rather than on effort level.

This result is indicated in figure 8.2, depicting precisely the same production and payoff conditions as above, the only exception being that payoffs are represented in terms of output and pay rather than work effort and pay. Note that the common slope of Rose's isoprofit curves is equal to one. The optimal output X^* is thus exactly the output that results when Jack chooses E^*. What's more, Rose need not even stipulate output levels in order to achieve the profit-maximizing

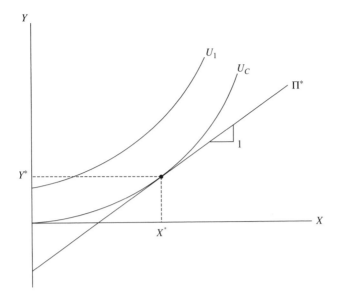

Figure 8.2 Profit-maximizing output and compensation levels given competitive utility U_c.

outcome shown in figure 8.1c. Rose can induce Jack to perform the profit-maximizing level of work effort simply by offering him a compensation schedule in which Jack's pay increases with output.

A particularly simple and empirically relevant compensation scheme is one in which Jack receives a fixed payment of B (thought of as "base rate" or "hourly wage" defined independently of output level) and a constant "piece rate" or payment per unit of output equal to P. This translates into a "budget line" for Jack with a constant slope equal to the piece rate, as depicted in figure 8.3. Jack then chooses output to maximize his utility along this line.

By choosing a piece rate equal to one (which means that Jack receives his entire marginal product), Rose can ensure that Jack will choose exactly the profit-maximizing level of output without having to specify that output contractually. Rose can then set the fixed portion of Jack's compensation schedule to ensure that he receives no more than the competitive level of utility when choosing the profit-maximizing output. (The fact that the fixed payment is negative in this example is an artifact of setting Jack's competitively-determined utility at zero.) Note that the optimal compensation schedule simply overlays Rose's optimal isoprofit curve.

Now complicate the foregoing scenario by assuming that output X is *stochastic*, which is to say that it depends both on Jack's effort input and on the realization of a random variable. For example, the level of output might be influenced

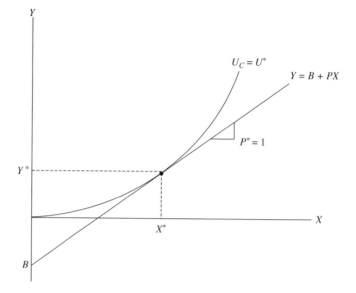

Figure 8.3 Efficient piece rate scheme induces profit-maximizing output and compensation.

by weather conditions as well as Jack's effort. In this case, if Rose cannot determine the realization of the random variable before production takes place, then it is impossible for her to stipulate by contract the level of output Jack must produce. Nor can she any longer reliably infer Jack's effort from his output level, since the random element in production implies that high effort could yield low output and vice versa. However, she can still offer to pay Jack according to the affine payment scheme introduced above, with the key difference that Jack's pay will now be stochastic as well, since the output level on which it is based is assumed to be random for any given work effort chosen by Jack.

How does this new dimension of randomness affect Rose's ability to secure profit-maximizing levels of work effort and compensation? Not at all, so long as Jack is *risk-neutral*, which is to say that he is indifferent between receiving a risky payment and the expected value or probability-weighted mean value of that payment. The only difference would be that Jack is paid Y^* *on average*, rather than in every possible state of the random element in production.

The upshot of this analytical exercise is that the invisibility of work effort to employers does not *of itself* pose any fundamental obstacle to the achievement of profit-maximizing outcomes. This is true even if output were stochastically determined, so long as the worker whose effort is to be elicited is risk-neutral. Thus, if hidden effort is to pose a problem for labor exchange, it must combine with other complications. Two such complicating factors are considered next.

Worker risk aversion and insurance-incentive tradeoffs

Now suppose that Jack dislikes the prospect of risky income. A simple way of representing this assumption is to suppose that, holding Jack's *average* income constant, his utility declines at a constant rate with increases in the *variance* of his income, understood as a measure of the degree of riskiness in output. Let V represent the variance of income and R represent Jack's constant marginal *dis*utility of risk measured in this way.

This new specification leaves unaffected Jack's marginal rate of substitution between effort (or *average* output) and average income, but negatively affects his absolute level of utility to the extent he is made to bear risk. The significance of this indicated in figure 8.4. On the assumption that output is risky and the piece rate equals one, Jack bears undesirable risk and must therefore be compensated via a higher fixed payment in order to achieve his competitive utility level. But this higher fixed payment for Jack's services necessarily cuts into Rose's expected profits, resulting in attainment of a lower profit level than that realized in the absence of production risk.

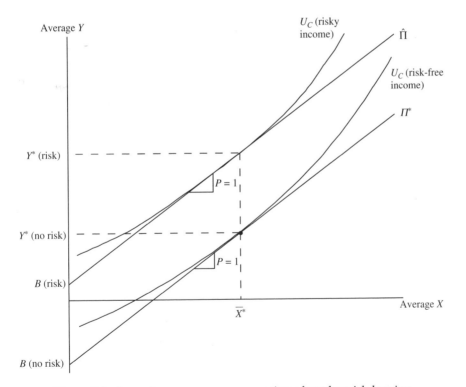

Figure 8.4 Impact on average compensation of worker risk-bearing.

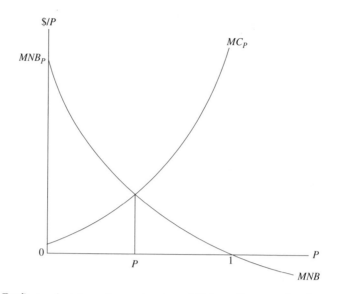

Figure 8.5 Profit-maximizing piece rate given hidden effort, production risk, and risk-averse workers.

Clearly, then, Rose has an incentive to avoid making Jack bear any risk. The obvious way to do this is make Jack's pay entirely independent of output risk, which, given Rose's inability to observe Jack's effort level, can only be accomplished by giving Jack a fixed salary. In doing so, Rose effectively "insures" Jack against production risk. But in doing so, she also ensures that Jack has no incentive to perform the effort level that maximizes expected profits, since his pay no longer increases on average with his work effort.

Rose thus faces a sort of microeconomic Catch-22: if she makes Jack bear the full production risk in his payment, he will choose the profit-maximizing effort level, but Rose will lose profits compared to the reference case constructed above because she must compensate Jack for bearing production risks. If on the other hand Rose avoids imposing any risk on Jack, since she can't stipulate effort levels in the contract, Jack consequently has no incentive to work, and Rose's expected profits suffer once again. What's Rose to do?

In the absence of organizational responses of the sort considered in part III of the text, the best Rose can do is to modify the piece rate she pays so as to optimally trade off the insurance and incentive effects of pay. The desire to insure Jack against risk argues in favor of a lower piece rate, while the desire to give efficient incentives pulls in the direction of a higher piece rate.

The nature of the tradeoffs faced by Rose is illustrated in figure 8.5. The marginal net benefit of the piece rate (MNB_P) corresponds to the net marginal profitability of the work incentives flowing from the piece rate P, while the marginal cost of the piece rate (MC_P) corresponds to the marginal loss in profit

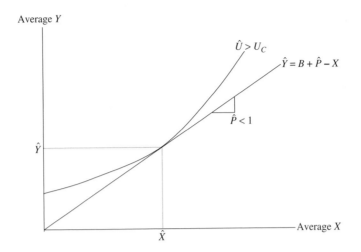

Figure 8.6   Second-best compensation and output given binding compensation floor.

Rose incurs by compensating Jack for higher risk. Familiar reasoning suggests that Rose will consequently choose the level P* that just equates the marginal net benefit and marginal cost of the piece rate.

It can be shown that under the stated conditions the profit-maximizing piece rate increases with the worker's marginal productivity M and decreases with the worker's risk aversion R or the degree of output risk (measured by the variance V) (see appendix). It also follows that the profit-maximizing piece rate under these conditions is less than one, and thus smaller than the optimal value conditions of certainty or zero risk aversion.

A special version of the risk-aversion model that has significant empirical relevance is one in which Jack's compensation level can never fall below a certain level, say zero, no matter what the value of the random element in production. This is equivalent to assuming that Jack has extreme aversion to risks involving negative income. Practically speaking, it corresponds to a scenario in which limited wealth and capital market failures imply that Jack can't afford to pay any monetary penalties from low output.

This was never an issue in the certainty version of the model, despite the fact that Jack received a negative fixed payment. The negative portion of his compensation scheme is offset by the earnings guaranteed by the piece rate. However, with stochastic output, the possibility arises that the piece rate component of pay might be too low to offset other losses. If the constraint is binding, its effect is correspondingly to push up the fixed payment that Rose must offer to Jack. This is illustrated in figure 8.6.

As in the more general version of the risk aversion model, the impact of a compensation "floor" is to drive the equilibrium piece rate away from its profit-maximizing level in the reference case. If the constraint is not too stringent, the optimal piece rate will again be less than one, indicating that Jack is induced to perform inefficiently low effort. A unique result of this version of the model, as depicted in figure 8.6, is that Jack receives a level of utility in excess of his competitively-determined best alternative. A corollary of these results is that if the compensation floor were in fact compelled by Jack's limited wealth, Rose would strictly prefer that Jack were more wealthy – so long as she was not the one providing Jack the additional means.

In this first departure from the reference case, it has been established that effort unobservability significantly affects the outcome of labor exchange when workers are risk averse. In this event the firm must trade off the insurance and incentive properties of pay, leading to potentially testable hypotheses about the connection between risk and risk aversion measures to the magnitude of the piece rate. Notice also that in this scenario the equilibrium contract is based to some extent on (random) output, rather than on the worker's effort level.

Given that this departure from the reference case leads to a loss in expected profits, the model suggests that labor buyers facing this scenario have some incentive to expend resources on monitoring worker effort in order to diminish the reliance of compensation on risky output. A somewhat different role for monitoring arises in the case that more than worker effort is hidden, as assumed in the final scenario of asymmetric information in the labor exchange.

Hidden effort plus hidden productivity

As mentioned earlier, hidden effort is of itself insufficient to compel a departure from the labor exchange and production conditions that would obtain under full information. The fact of hidden effort must combine with some other factor to make a qualitative difference in exchange outcomes. In the scenario just studied, that element was worker risk aversion combined with stochastic output. In the case now under consideration, the worker acquires information about production conditions that is unavailable to the employer.

Assume once again that output depends just on Jack's effort E and his marginal productivity M. However, and this is the key modification in the incentive problem under study, M can take on one of two values, low (M_l) or high (M_h), and *only Jack* learns the true value of M after production has commenced. A possible interpretation of this is that Jack "learns the ropes" by directly engaging in the production process, so only he acquires the relevant information.

Suppose further that Jack's productivity is specific to this relationship, so that the level of utility he can obtain elsewhere is unaffected by the ultimate value of M. In addition, to promote comparison to the previous versions of the model, assume that Rose is limited to payment schemes which vary linearly with output (the "fixed payment plus piece rate" scheme considered earlier). Finally, assume that the payment to Jack must assure him the competitive level of utility for each possible value of M. This makes sense because Jack can always quit if, given his private information, he knows he can do better elsewhere under the payment scheme Rose offers.

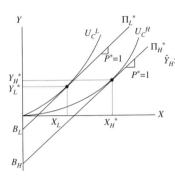

Figure 8.7(a) Profit-maximizing productivity-specific compensation and output.

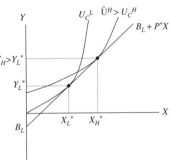

Figure 8.7(b) "Naïve" equilibrium when employer selects efficient payment scheme based on worker's report.

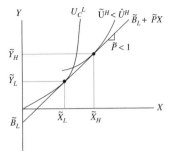

Figure 8.7(c) Second-best profit-maximizing compensation scheme given worker's private information.

What sort of contract should Rose offer Jack in order to maximize her profits? If, contrary to hypothesis, she learned the value of M at the same time Jack did, she could simply tailor Jack's compensation "budget line" to his productivity level, offering a "low" output–compensation pair if M_l obtains and a "high" output–compensation pair if Jack's true productivity is M_h. This outcome is shown in figure 8.7a. Note that the optimal value of the piece rate is one, just as in the reference case considered earlier.

Given the assumption that Rose *doesn't* observe the true value of M, how might she proceed? One possibility is that she simply asks Jack to reveal his productivity and offers him a linear compensation scheme that ensures his competitive utility, *given* his reported level of productivity, yielding the contingent outcomes shown in figure 8.7a. However, there is an obvious problem with this procedure.

Since only Jack observes the value of M, he has a choice of what to tell Rose. And as illustrated in figure 8.7b, if Jack in fact enjoyed the high level of productivity, he could make himself strictly better off by reporting that he had low productivity, and thus receiving the "low-productivity" budget line. He then produces the "high" output along this line and enjoys a correspondingly higher level of pay. The reason for Jack's utility bonus is his high productivity, which makes it relatively easy to earn an economic rent. Since Jack thus always produces along the "low-productivity" budget line, no matter what the value of his true productivity, Rose can expect less average profits than if she could anticipate learning Jack's productivity as well.

It is tempting to infer from this that Rose's problem would be ameliorated if the production relationship with Jack were repeated over time. Since Jack always produces a "high" output when he enjoys high productivity, no matter which budget line he's on, one might imagine that Rose could find out his true productivity after just one period, and then return to the outcome shown in figure 8.7a, where Jack earns no economic rent and Rose thus maximizes profit.

The problem with this reasoning is that if Jack is rational he anticipates this outcome as well, and thus has an incentive to hide his information in the first round of production by producing the same output as if he faced M_l. If he does this, Rose cannot then infer Jack's true productivity level. Thus, repeating the relationship over time does not eliminate the basic incentive problem.

Putting aside possible organizational responses in which Rose monitors Jack (discussed further in the next chapter), what might she do to reduce the rents she pays and thus increase profits? In the general case, her optimal response is to reduce the piece rate she offers Jack, as shown in figure 8.7c. This has two consequences. First, it induces Jack to produce an inefficiently low level of output, no matter what productivity level he enjoys. However, the profit reduction due to this inefficiency is more than offset by the reduction in economic rent Rose pays to Jack.

Even with this optimal response to asymmetric information, however, Rose earns less profit on average than she could expect if she also learned Jack's private information before production takes place. Consequently, as in the previous scenario, this setting implies that firms have an incentive to monitor their workers. However, in the present context monitoring is useful to the employer if *either* worker effort *or* worker productivity is revealed. Either way, the employer can achieve the profit level enjoyed in the reference case (net of monitoring costs, at any rate).

For this reason, the scenario just studied is probably the closest to the conditions that prompted the "scientific management" phenomenon discussed in the adjoining discussion box. Scientific management featured the use of "time-and-motion" studies designed to determine the *connection* between a given amount of worker effort and maximal output – in other words, worker productivity, not just worker effort. Clearly, Taylorist methods would have been unnecessary if employers knew *either* the productivity or the effort levels of their employees. The results just described help explain why employers had a financial incentive to explore these methods.

The model also suggests why workers often fought the use of Taylorist methods. In this setting, workers' private information guarantees them economic rents. Once this information asymmetry is eliminated, employers have no incentive to pay these rents, and can instead limit workers to their competitively determined payoffs.

This line of reasoning creates a puzzle that is encountered in different contexts later in the text. Given that otherwise competitive workers entering production relationships characterized by this information scenario can expect economic rents, why don't employers simply extract these rents *up front* by charging an employment fee equal to the expected value of the rents? Workers drawn from competitive labor markets would still be willing to take the job so long as the fees were set to ensure them payoffs equal to their next best alternative.

There are a number of possible resolutions of the puzzle. One is that wealth constraints generally bar workers from paying such fees. A more involved explanation, but one in the spirit of the analysis of this chapter, is that a parallel incentive problem on the part of employers arises in cases where such fees are demanded. This possibility is considered later in the text.

"SCIENTIFIC MANAGEMENT": INCENTIVE AND HOLDUP PROBLEMS IN US INDUSTRY

Beginning in the late nineteenth century, a mechanical engineer named Frederick W. Taylor proposed a new system of structuring and supervising manufacturing processes that he called "scientific management" and came to be known to social scientists as "Taylorism." Taylor's efforts were motivated by his desire to eradicate "the great loss which the whole country is suffering through inefficiency" (Taylor, 1911) – inefficiency that resulted, in his estimation, from "systematic soldiering," or efforts by workers to produce less than the maximum output consistent with given technical conditions. Taylor argued that elimination of soldiering would redound to the benefit of all, ensuring higher profits for employers and higher wages for employees.

Taylor traced the failure of "ordinary" management methods to two roots: first, that workers knew much more about the production processes being managed than did their foremen and supervisors, and used this informational advantage to keep managers from discovering that they routinely expended less efficient levels of labor effort; and second, that this practice was individually rational, in that workers were not provided with "special incentives" to exceed the average amount of work being done.

Taylor's proposed solution to what he saw as an epidemic of soldiering had four key elements:

1) *Specialization in the conception and execution of production tasks* Taylor argued that leaving both the conception and execution of work to employees was inefficient, and thus called for a division of labor in which management assumed complete responsibility for the structuring of work, including the tasks to be done as well as the manner and order in which they were accomplished; workers were made responsible only for executing the orders of management.

2) *"Scientific" study of the connection between labor input and output* Since employees knew the technical details of their work much better than their managers did, Taylor argued, any "tricks of the trade" learned by individual employees were not effectively utilized to raise productivity. To address this problem, Taylor instituted the use of "motion and time studies" in which the execution of given production tasks was minutely studied and timed with a stopwatch, with a view to identifying and eliminating unnecessary or inefficient motions. Based on these studies, methods of structuring and executing production tasks were developed with the goal of promoting maximum sustainable productivity.

continued

3) *Minute task specialization based on employee characteristics* A key component of Taylor's system involved matching observed employee characteristics to task requirements. As an example, for the menial but physically demanding task of lifting "pig iron," Taylor's system called for a man that is "so stupid and so phlegmatic that he more nearly resembles in his mental make-up the ox than any other type. The man who is mentally alert and intelligent is for this very reason entirely unsuited to what would, for him, be the grinding monotony of work of this character. Therefore, the workman who is best suited to handling pig iron . . . is so stupid that . . . he must consequently be trained by a man more intelligent than himself."

4) *Strong pecuniary work incentives* The final key component of Taylor's antidote for soldiering was giving workers guaranteed bonuses for working at the more intense levels dictated by his system. He insisted that incentive pay increases had to be both significant and *permanent*, so that workers would never fear having their pay per unit of output cut once their true productivity was discovered and output increased.

Taylor's concerns on this point proved to be well-founded. Employers, eager to capture the quasi-rents accruing to workers by virtue of their private information about productivity conditions, often violated the *quid pro quo* Taylor insisted on by cutting piece rates once this information was uncovered by time and motion studies. This is a particular version of the "holdup" problem discussed in the body of the chapter, in which workers' power to secure quasi-rents from improved productivity depended primarily on their privately held information about production conditions. As a consequence, despite Taylor's insistence that there was no fundamental conflict of interest between employers and employees concerning the expenditure of work effort, efforts by individual firms to institute his system of "scientific" management met with consistent and vociferous opposition by workers. This opposition played a role in the eventual discontinuation of Taylor's system.

Related discussion questions:
1. What are the potential advantages to employers of specializing in the conception and organization of production, while having workers specialize in its execution? Under what conditions would this be an inefficient way to organize production?
2. Under what conditions might employers have been deterred from cutting piece rates once they learned workers' true productivity levels? Why might these conditions not have been universal?

Related references:
Frederick W. Taylor, *Principles of Scientific Management* (New York: Harper, 1911).
Harry Braverman, *Labor and Monopoly Capital* (New York: Monthly Review Press, 1974).

CONCLUSION

This chapter concludes the general investigation of strategic issues that arise in labor market transactions when exchange activities are costly. The next step in the argument is to consider possible organizational responses to these strategic conflicts and how such responses relate to observed institutions of labor exchange. Doing so will lead us back to questions first posed in chapter 5: why might employment transactions involve relationships of *authority*, and why is it generally the case that profit-seeking firms are owned by capital suppliers rather than workers or entrepreneurs making no other input contributions? While the present chapter does not resolve these questions, it does at least suggest where one might begin to look for answers to them.

APPENDIX TO CHAPTER 8

THE PROBLEM OF HIDDEN EFFORT

Reference case

Suppose there are two agents, Rose and Jack. Rose hires Jack to produce output for compensation Y. Rose cares only about profit Π, given as the difference between the monetary value of output X and compensation Y. Thus, Rose's isoprofit curves are determined by the expression $\Pi = X - Y$, for given values of Π.

Assume that the production function takes the simple form $X = M \cdot E$, where E is Jack's work effort and M is the marginal productivity of effort. Rose's profit function can then be written as $\Pi = M \cdot E - Y$, and her marginal rate of substitution between effort and compensation is thus equal to M. Rewriting the profit function as $Y = M \cdot E - \Pi$ for a given level of profit, it is readily seen that Rose's isoprofit curves drawn in (E, Y) space are parallel straight lines with slope M.

Now suppose that Jack's utility over income and effort combinations is given by the function:

$$U = Y - \frac{E^2}{2}.$$

The slope of a representative indifference curve in (E, Y) space is given by:

$$\frac{MU_E}{MU_Y} = \frac{E}{1} = E.$$

Let Jack's "outside" or reservation utility be zero, implying that $Y = E^2/2$ at all points along the corresponding indifference curve.

To find the profit-maximizing effort level consistent with Jack receiving his reservation utility level, substitute $Y = E^2/2$ into Rose's profit function, take the first derivative with respect to E, and set the result equal to zero. Letting E^* denote the solution candidate, this procedure yields $M - E^* = 0$, or $E^* = M$. Since the second derivative of the profit function with respect to effort is negative, second-order conditions for a maximum are also satisfied, so this is indeed the solution. Now substitute backward to find the corresponding levels of compensation and profit,

$$Y* = \Pi* = \frac{M^2}{2}.$$

Rather than specifying the level of output and compensation, Rose can achieve the same outcome by offering Jack a compensation scheme of the form $Y = B + P \cdot X$, where B is the fixed component of pay and P is the "piece rate" per unit of output. To see this, plug this expression for Y into Jack's utility function, differentiate the result and set the derivative equal to zero. Letting $E*$ again represent the solution candidate, the first-order condition implies $PM = E*$ (the second-order condition for a maximum is always satisfied). This corresponds to the profit-maximizing effort level if $P = 1$.

To find the profit-maximizing level of the fixed payment, plug $P*M = E* = M$ back into Jack's utility function and set it equal to 0, his reservation utility level. This yields $B* = -(M^2/2)$. It is easily seen that this yields the values of $Y*$ and $\Pi*$ derived above.

Now add the condition that production is stochastic. Specifically, write the production function as $X = M \cdot E + Z$, where Z is a random variable with mean 0 and variance V. Consequently, the *expected value* of output is just $\overline{X} = M \cdot E + \overline{Z} = M \cdot E$, the same as the production function in the deterministic case just studied. Similarly, the expected value of the linear compensation scheme is just $\overline{Y} = B + M \cdot \overline{X} = B + M \cdot E$. Thus, the analysis goes through exactly as before, with expected values of output and compensation replacing the deterministic values expressed in the previous case.

Hidden effort with stochastic output and risk-averse worker

Maintaining the assumption that output is stochastic, now add the condition that Jack is averse to risk. This is captured by rewriting his utility function in the form $U = \overline{Y} - R \cdot V_Y - (E^2/2)$, where R is a measure of Jack's risk aversion and V_Y is the variance of Jack's compensation. Given the linear payment scheme introduced above, it is readily shown that $V_Y = P^2 \cdot V$, where V is the variance of the random element Z. Thus Jack's utility function can be rewritten as:

$$U = B + P \cdot M \cdot E - R \cdot P^2 \cdot V - \frac{E^2}{2}.$$

To find Jack's utility-maximizing effort level for any given value of the piece rate, differentiate the utility function with respect to E and set the derivative equal to zero, yielding as before $P \cdot M = E*$. To find the profit-maximizing value of B, plug this expression for $E*$ back into the utility function and set the result equal to zero, Jack's reservation utility level. This yields:

$$B* = R \cdot P^2 \cdot V - \frac{P^2 \cdot M^2}{2}.$$

Since Rose is still assumed to be risk-neutral, her payoff from labor exchange is given by expected profit $\overline{\Pi} = \overline{X} - \overline{Y}$. Plugging in the form of the compensation scheme and the optimized values of effort and fixed payment gives expected profit as a function of only one choice variable, the piece rate; in reduced form, the expected profit function is:

$$\overline{\Pi} = M^2 \cdot P - P^2 \cdot \left(R \cdot V + \frac{M^2}{2} \right).$$

Taking the first-order condition of this expression with respect to P yields a candidate value $P^* = M^2 / (M^2 + 2R \cdot V)$. From this we can infer the following:

- if there is no risk ($V = 0$) or the agent is risk-neutral ($R = 0$), the piece rate equals one, just as in the reference case;
- however, if the agent is risk-averse and production is stochastic, the optimal piece rate is less than one, so the worker is induced to provide lower effort than in the base case;
- and furthermore, the optimal piece rate is increasing in the agent's marginal productivity and declining in both the level of risk and the agent's risk aversion.

Study Questions

1. Give some examples of assets (for example, labor skills) that are *specific* to a given employer or firm. What keeps these assets from being productive in other contexts?

2. Suppose that it is desirable for employees to develop certain firm-specific skills at some personal cost. As a practical matter, why might it be difficult to write complete contracts ensuring that employees would be compensated for undertaking such investments?

3. For each of the following principal–agent scenarios in which a risk-neutral principal knows the production function but can't observe the agent's effort, explain how the principal would induce the agent to perform the efficient (that is, expected profit-maximizing) effort level, consistent with the agent receiving his or her reservation utility. Then give an empirical illustration of that incentive arrangement (not necessarily in labor markets).

    (a) The agent is risk-averse and the agent's output is an increasing, non-stochastic function of the agent's effort level.

    (b) The agent is risk-neutral and output is an increasing, stochastic function of the agent's effort.

    (c) The agent is risk-averse and output is a stochastic function of the agent's effort in which the lowest possible output level is finite, strictly increasing in the agent's effort level, and has a strictly positive probability of occurring.

4. A risk-neutral firm owner K hires a risk-averse worker Λ in a situation where net revenues of the firm are fixed and higher in state-of-the-world

continued

one than in state-of-the-world two. The probability of the high-revenue state is q, $0 < q < 1$. Suppose that the firm must receive the "competitive" level of average profit Λ, Π_0.

(a) Illustrate the equilibrium wage contract between K and Λ, indicating slopes of the relevant indifference curves. Is the equilibrium Pareto efficient? Explain.

(b) Suppose that the worker's effort is perfectly observable and fixed, so that there is no effort incentive problem. However, the worker can be one of two types or quality levels, H or L, associated respectively with the probabilities of the high-revenue and low-revenue states of the world, q_H and q_L, where $q_H > q_L$. Suppose that the firm can observe the worker's type upon hiring the worker. Illustrate the equilibrium wage contract it would offer the worker in each case, labelling the appropriate utility levels and slopes. [Hint: remember the firm always has to make competitive profits. Which type of worker can it afford to pay more?]

(c) Suppose instead that the firm can't observe the worker's type upon hiring the worker. Could the firm simply ask the worker which type s/he is and pay the corresponding wage contract illustrated in (b)? Explain. Illustrate the pair of wage contracts, one for each possible type of worker, that would induce each type of worker to tell the truth and guarantee the firm competitive average profits in each case. Are the resulting contracts both Pareto-efficient?

Note

1   Taken from Oliver Hart and John Moore, "Property Rights and the Nature of the Firm," *Journal of Political Economy* 98, no. 6 (December 1990): 1119–58.

Suggestions for Further Reading

Oliver Hart, *Firms, Contracts and Financial Structure* (Oxford: Oxford University Press, 1995).

Bernard Salanié, *The Economics of Contracts: A Primer* (Cambridge, MA: MIT Press, 1998).

Oliver E. Williamson, *The Economic Institutions of Capitalism* (New York: The Free Press, 1985).

PART THREE

THE EMPLOYMENT RELATIONSHIP

Under the various scenarios of imperfect contracting considered in the previous chapter, buyers and sellers in labor markets cannot secure desired exchange outcomes through the use of fully specifiable and costlessly enforceable contracts. Thus, for example, buyers may prefer specific levels of work effort that can't be stipulated by contract because effort is to some extent unobservable, and workers may prefer to work under production conditions that are not easily rendered intelligible to external enforcement officials. In that case, one or both parties have a potential incentive to supplement given contract terms with direct oversight of production activities or use ownership of productive assets as a strategic substitute for missing contract language. Thus is born the unique exchange relationship of *employment*, pursued in the institutional context of *firms*.

Chapter 9 considers the nature of employment relationships, understood to involve the exercise of *authority* in production decisions by owners of productive assets who are distinct from the workers who use those assets. The chapter also examines the strategic considerations that inform the structure of firm ownership. Although organizational innovations to correct or sidestep contracting failures can potentially benefit all parties to labor exchange, the distribution of these gains may be open to contest. Thus, every employment relationship might best be thought of as a potential arena for both cooperation and conflict.

The remaining chapters consider various aspects of the employment relationship and their corresponding patterns of cooperation and conflict. Chapter 10 examines the strategic use of compensation schemes to motivate worker effort, noting the scope for disagreements over the use of these devices. Chapter 11 studies consequences of the tension between the scope for mutual gains from long-term employment relationships and the exter-

continued

nalities created by labor market competition, posing *internal labor markets* as a strategic response to this tension. Job matching, on-the-job training, and long-term provision of effort incentives and earnings insurance are featured aspects of employment continuity.

Finally, chapter 12 considers the two faces of worker representation in the workplace. On one hand, the effects of collective bargaining arrangements are primarily distributional, in that they improve the negotiating position of employees vis-à-vis firms, but they may have positive or negative efficiency consequences as well. On the other hand, institutions to ensure worker participation in production decisions might be expected to have positive allocational effects, but could also have systematic implications for the distribution of gains from the employment relationship.

CHAPTER NINE

THE NATURE OF THE EMPLOYMENT RELATIONSHIP

This chapter begins the process of weaving together the analytical threads set out in the preceding chapters. The first strand, advanced in chapter 5, identified possible forms and sources of transaction costs and noted marked regularities in the structure of firm ownership and the legal treatment of employment relationships that are difficult to explain using the perfectly competitive model of labor markets. The second strand, put forward in chapter 6, introduced a theoretical language for discussing the strategic interactions that might be expected to arise when exchange is not frictionless. The final thread, presented in the previous chapter, suggested how significant transaction costs might limit the attainable gains from labor exchange, creating incentives for organizational responses to such transactional failures.

Bringing these lines of analysis together, this chapter attempts to understand the employment relationship as an institutional response to the strategic features of labor exchange resulting from the presence of significant transaction costs. It addresses two interrelated aspects of this response: the nature of employment as an authority relationship, and the role of firm ownership as a strategic substitute for transactional failures in markets for labor or complementary goods. Under such conditions, organizational innovations generally raise both efficiency and distributional concerns. As a result, firms, and the employment relationships established under their auspices, might be viewed with equal plausibility as *governance structures* erected to sidestep wasteful transactional difficulties, or as *arenas of conflict* in which workers and owners clash over the distribution of gains from labor exchange and the exercise of decision-making power with respect to the process of production. Or as some irreducible mixture of both. What scenario best describes actual labor exchanges can only be determined by assessing the evidence in light of the competing theoretical possibilities.

FIRMS AND EMPLOYMENT RELATIONSHIPS

The nature of the firm

Any comprehensive analysis of employment relationships must lead us sooner or later to a discussion of the nature and behavior of firms. This is not true simply as a matter of definition; for example, households may hire employees, and certain firms don't have any employees, at least in the conventional sense of the term. However, the connection between firms and employment relationships is sufficiently strong that it is most useful to commence an analysis of the employment relationship by defining what a "firm" is.

For the purposes of labor market analysis, one might reasonably define a *firm* as a commercial enterprise (that is, one that produces goods or services for sale) with either or both of the following characteristics: (1) the set of people who *own* the enterprise's alienable productive assets is not identical to the set of people who *use* these assets to produce the enterprise's output; (2) the enterprise is characterized by formal relations of *hierarchy* in which one set of actors *oversees* or *directs* the work of others. By this definition, for example, a *producer cooperative*, in which the productive assets of the enterprise are owned by (a subset of) its workers, constitutes a firm so long as it either hires some non-owner workers or has some worker-owners overseeing the efforts of others (see the related discussion box). In contrast, a *limited liability corporation* satisfies the definition redundantly, since a stockholder needn't work for the corporation whose shares she holds, and hierarchy is a standard feature of corporate organization charts.

THE MYSTERY OF MONDRAGON

A commercial enterprise in which all workers are also co-owners counts as a firm by the above definition so long as some worker-owners are supervised by others. Robust examples of this type of firm are provided by the *Mondragon* cooperatives centered in the Basque region of Spain. Springing from a single producer's cooperative with just five workers in 1954, the Mondragon cooperatives have grown dramatically into a network of 150 member cooperatives with a total of 42,000 employees under the auspices of an umbrella organization called the "Mondragon Cooperative Corporation" (MCC). Since the late 1950s, Mondragon cooperatives have received financing from their own "central bank," the Caja Laboral Popular (CLP), which also closely monitors the financial accounts of member cooperatives (Dow, 2003).

The "cooperative" aspects of Mondragon's production arrangements are reinforced by many aspects of the organization's structure. Prospective members are carefully screened and impressed with the ethos of cooperative behavior. New members must pay a significant entry fee which goes toward financing investment expenses and helps to encourage long-term commitments, since the fee is not refundable. Organizational rules limit wage disparities between workers and managers, and although these restrictions have been relaxed, it remains the case that managers make less than in comparable positions in capital-owned firms. Membership shares are not tradeable, and there is limited scope for employment of non-members.

Despite these differences, production processes in Mondragon cooperatives are not organized much differently than in standard capital-owned firms. The degree and structure of hierarchy is about the same (other than the fact that workers have more say in removing managers), and production tasks are organized in much the same way as elsewhere.

The "mystery" of the Mondragon cooperatives, apart from their continued success and growth despite the unusual entry costs and absence of unusual production conditions, lies in their notable differences from the average profile for worker-owned firms (discussed later in the chapter). First, Mondragon cooperatives are on average an order of magnitude larger (hundreds rather than tens of employees) than their worker-owned counterparts elsewhere in Western Europe (Ben-Ner, 1988). They are also more likely to feature relatively high physical capital intensity and/or relatively low skill intensity. And unlike other producer cooperatives, they are less likely to be transformed into standard capitalist firms through investor buyout.

If the Mondragon cooperatives provide a model for the successful implementation of worker-owned commercial production, it is not a model that has been imitated elsewhere. That's part of the mystery.

Related discussion questions:
1. Is it surprising that production in Mondragon cooperatives is organized in much the same way as in capital-owned firms producing similar goods? Wouldn't worker-owners presumably want to allow scope for more interesting work or less intense supervision of their work efforts?
2. Why might having their own bank make it possible for Mondragon cooperatives to pursue more capital-intensive production lines? Wouldn't outside banks provide the necessary financing if the intended production lines were shown to be profitable?

Related references:
Avner Ben-Ner, "Comparative Empirical Observations on Worker-Owned and Capitalist Firms," *International Journal of Industrial Organization* 6, no. 1 (March 1988): 7–31.
Gregory K. Dow, *Governing the Firm: Workers' Control in Theory and Practice* (Cambridge: Cambridge University Press, 2003).

Note that firms are not distinguished from households solely by virtue of being commercial enterprises. Thus, by this reading, deciding to produce a good or service for sale is not tantamount to deciding to become a firm. To qualify as a firm under the present definition, a commercial enterprise must *also* engage workers who use its productive assets without sharing in their ownership, or else have some members directing or overseeing the work of other members. An important implication of this definition is that a firm corresponds to a set of social relationships, so there can be no one-person firms in this context.

The nature of the employment relationship

This chapter is primarily concerned with a particular set of transactions that occur routinely in firms, called *employment relationships*. *Employment* is defined here as an economic relationship characterized by *both* conditions (1) and (2) of the preceding definition of the firm. Specifically, an *employee* is someone who is engaged to perform productive activities overseen or directed by others, using productive assets owned by others. An *employer* is either the set of owners of the enterprise's productive assets or agents of the owners who hire employees and oversee and dictate the conditions of their work.

Notice that on the basis of this definition, it is possible both for households to have employees, and for firms *not* to have employees. However, as a descriptive matter most people that fit the definition work for firms, and the discussion in the remainder of the chapter presumes that this is the general case. Note also that employees are not simply agents who transact to engage in production activities: if you hire a plumber to unclog your kitchen drain, for example, the plumber does not thereby become your *employee*, since it is not required (and, as a general rule, not desired) that you oversee the plumber's efforts.

This definition is consistent with the distinctions drawn in Anglo-American case and statutary law between *employment* contracts and more general *commercial* contracts. For example, case law recognizes the right of employers to dictate the conditions under which their employees work, while independent contractors are held legally responsible for the *results* they promise, rather than the means by which these results are generated. Furthermore, the rights of employers to *terminate* given employment relationships are consistent with the notion that employees do not share ownership of the employer's productive assets. More specific distinctions between employment and commercial contracts, where relevant, will be discussed below.

The next task is to consider possible economic reasons for the existence of firms and employment relationships, as well as for why the two phenomena are so closely connected. The common demoninator in these explanations is the existence of transaction costs that create imperfect contracting conditions.

PRODUCTION HIERARCHIES AND AUTHORITY IN THE WORKPLACE

In addition to and in contrast with the essentially horizontal relationship of exchange, whose parties have symmetric economic roles, employment is characterized by "vertical" social structures of hierarchy within firms, as suggested by the pyramiding lines and boxes of corporate organization charts. Hierarchy implies an asymmetric relationship in which superiors exercise powers or choices that are not extended to subordinates. Firm-level hierarchies are thus sometimes referred to as "authority relations." This section considers possible economic bases and consequences of authority relations occurring within the workplace.

The degree of hierarchy in firms, as measured by the average ratio of supervisory and other non-production personnel to total nonagricultural employment, varies significantly across countries. For example, in 1989 this ratio was 2.6% in Sweden, 3.9% in Germany, 4.2% in Japan, 6.8% in Norway, and about 13% in the United States and Canada. In the US at least, this ratio has also been increasing steadily over time, both absolutely and relative to other countries such as Germany, and Japan, and Sweden, until the early 1990s.[1] Since that time, the degree of hierarchy in the US has shown indications of falling significantly. These comparisons prompt the following questions: what determines the existence and extent of hierarchy in firms? Why might the degree of hierarchy vary across countries and over time?

From a microeconomic standpoint, supervisory personnel in the upper echelons of workplace hierarchy perform one or both of two tasks: *direction* and *coordination* of work to be done, and *monitoring* and *assessment* of work that has been performed. The fundamental question to be asked is why these tasks, understood as distinct from the labor required for production, must be done via hierarchical relationships; why can't they be accomplished by production workers themselves, perhaps as guided by appropriately delineated contracts?

This is not an idle question. One can easily imagine conditions in which the coordination of various services does not entail direct oversight of production activities by the person for whom the services are performed. For example, a person moving into a new home may need her furniture moved, her utilities connected, and new telephones installed by a certain date. Yet she needn't dictate how the movers arrange the furniture in their truck or the route that they take in transporting it to the new location; the manner in which water, electrical, or gas services are started up or reconnected; or the way in which the new telephones are put in service.

This is not to say that the new homeowner or tenant would *never* exercise a coordinating function in the provision of such services. Examples of when this might occur are highly suggestive of the possible economic logic of authority relations. For example, a homeowner might want to oversee the unloading of the furniture, both to guard against possible physical damage to the residence and to direct where the furniture is placed. It's not hard to imagine situations in which neither of these concerns can be effectively addressed by means of externally enforced contracts: in the first case, it might be difficult to establish the cause of any visible damage to the residential structure, and in the second case, the resident might not know where the furniture should be placed until it arrives inside the home.

To explain the logic of production hierarchies, then, it is necessary to consider difficulties in contracting that might prompt the direct oversight and coordination of productive activity. Two distinct motivations for hierarchy stemming from different types of enforcement costs encountered in labor exchange are considered next.

Incomplete contracts and the "authority relation"

Chapter 8 considered a scenario of labor exchange in which the ultimate gains from trade are determined in part by contingencies that are not realized until production is under way. For example, the level, quality, cost, or timing of production may depend on vagaries of weather, human error, or unplanned adverse events, such as equipment breakdowns. To use the phrasing of Ronald Coase, an early and important contributor to the economic theory of the firm, conditions such as these make the price system itself expensive to use as a basis for determining the exact terms of exchange (see the reference at the end of the chapter). In this case, transaction costs stem from trying to anticipate all possible contingencies affecting the exchange relationship. The contingencies may be too numerous or complex to spell out precisely, or it may simply be impossible for parties to a transaction to anticipate all the events that might conceivably influence subsequent gains from the relationship.

In this case, Coase argued, it may be less costly to substitute direct coordination of production activity by an entrepreneur for "coordination by the price system," in which the allocation of production activity is guided solely by price signals channeled through the appropriate contract language. This substitution gives rise to an authority relation, and thus to a firm if the purpose of the relationship is commercial in nature, in that someone must take on the task of dictating what is to be done subsequent to the realization of any given contingency.

Contractual incompleteness is clearly necessary for an authority relation to arise in this context; otherwise, the desired contingent actions could simply be dictated via externally enforceable contracts. However, the motivation to set up an authority relation in this case does not depend on the existence of market power, so this phenomenon is ignored for the sake of simplicity. Furthermore, in Coase's depiction, incentive provision need not be an issue, since the worker may be indifferent among the productive activities dictated by alternative contingencies. Therefore incentive issues resulting from imperfect contracting are initially sidestepped as well.

To see why it might be too costly to use a set of contractual prices to coordinate production activities, consider a version of the principal–agent relationship

Table 9.1 Cost of a complete-state contingent contract

Number of cost and performance levels	Number of tasks			
	2	5	10	15
2	$0.16	$10	$10,000	$10 million
3	$0.81	$600	$35 million	$2 trillion
4	$2.56	$10,000	$11 billion	$11,000 trillion
5	$6.25	$100,000	$1 trillion	$10 million trillion

Note: Cost of a contract clause: 1 cent.
Source: W. Bentley MacLeod and Daniel Parent, "Job Characteristics, Wages, and the Employment Contract," *Federal Reserve Bank of St. Louis Review* 81, no. 3 (May/June 1999): table 3. Reprinted with permission.

introduced in chapter 8 in which agent performs up to T distinct tasks. Suppose further that the level of each task depends on the realization of S possible states of the world affecting that particular activity. Thus, for example, weather conditions might affect tasks undertaken out of doors, while randomness in supply schedules may affect tasks making intensive use of intermediate goods. Assume finally that there is some small cost, say a penny, incurred for each additional clause that must be written to create a complete contract covering the labor exchange.

In this case, it is easily shown that the required number of clauses in a complete contract increases *exponentially* in the number of tasks the agent undertakes. Even with a small per-unit cost, this implies that contractual completeness quickly becomes exorbitantly expensive as jobs become more complex and multifaceted. Table 9.1 illustrates the explosive impact of increasing the number of tasks on the costs of writing a complete contract at only a penny per clause. Costs become prohibitive for only ten tasks and a moderate number of contingencies.

It is not hard to come up with cases in which workers must perform a large number of distinct tasks. For example, team production often requires members of the labor team to work in separate subgroups for given amounts of time. Thus a "task" could be defined in this context as a production activity undertaken with a given subset of team members.

To illustrate this, suppose that there are N members of a team, and for simplicity let's imagine that members only work together in subgroups of two. Thus, for example, worker 1 must spend a certain amount of time with worker 2, with worker 3, worker 4, and so on. Consequently, there are one-half N times $N - 1$, or $(N^2 - N)/2$, possible worker pairings. Treating each pairing as a separate task, this number is ten or higher for production teams as small as five!

In light of the foregoing, it is at least plausible to suppose that production conditions routinely encountered in modern economies give rise to extremely daunting contracting problems if governed solely by a decentralized system of prices. However, contracting costs can be significantly reduced if production is instead governed by an "authority relation" in which a designated coordinator assigns production tasks once the specific contingency affecting production has been determined. Because task levels are assigned after the relevant contingency has been realized, the authority only needs to make assignments equal to the number of tasks.

Note that the story just summarized doesn't indicate *who* should take the role of production coordination, much less require that the coordinating function rests ultimately with the owner of the firm's alienable productive assets. For example, it might be possible for workers themselves to take turns directing the production process. Indeed, rotation of managerial and "line" production tasks is a common feature in worker-owned firms. Thus, this analysis cannot be used to provide a theory of firm ownership.

A necessary condition for this story to work in practice is that the coordinators, whoever they are, must have sufficient knowledge about production technology, worker characteristics, and the realization of possible random elements to guide productive activities effectively. This is not a trivial assumption, as there is no automatic conduit in the authority relation by which knowledge acquired by workers in the process of production is conveyed up to the central coordinator.

A second necessary condition for this account of the authority relation to hold is that fundamental disagreements over the terms of the labor exchange are somehow avoided once particular production-related contingencies are realized. This problem was sidestepped initially by assuming that workers were indifferent among production tasks and conditions; however, nothing guarantees this outcome in general. Some contingencies – such as the tardy delivery of crucial parts for a manufacturing process, for example – might require employees to work longer, more quickly, or under greater stress. It seems reasonable that in such cases workers would insist on some form of compensation for the additional demands placed upon them.

Assuming that the legal system is directly or indirectly responsive to systematic difficulties encountered in contracting, the factors just discussed may help to explain some of the key differences drawn in case law between employment and other commercial transactions. Speaking to the problem of information flows in systems of central coordination, the law governing employment contracts vests employees with a greater duty than independent contractors to disclose relevant information to the employer. The law also limits the extent to which employees can use their privately-held information about production conditions for personal gain.

Respecting the possibility that disagreements over assignments and working conditions arise subsequent to the beginning of production, case law uniquely assigns to employees a duty to obey all "reasonable" rules, orders, or instructions of the employer. The law thus establishes a presumption for direction of work tasks by employers rather than their determination by the mutual consent of employers and employees or by the unilateral will of the latter. This presumption is backed up by court decisions supporting the right of employers to seek monetary damages for failure to obey this presumption. Even when workers are collectively represented by labor unions, the presumption established by law is that, so long as employee health or safety is not evidently jeopardized, employer commands should be followed first and challenged if necessary through grievance procedures after the fact.

Note that these legal guidelines leave considerable scope for distributional conflict within the authority relation, especially if it is costly for employers to use the court system to enforce their exercise of authority in the workplace. First, workers may gain from selective disclosure of production-related information, and it is necessarily difficult to establish that privately held information has not been divulged. Second, what constitutes "reasonable" rules or commands, or the conditions under which following such rules endangers the personal safety of workers, may routinely be a matter of controversy.

The considerations raised here thus suggest that distributional and efficiency-related concerns are both integral to the employment relationship understood as involving the exercise of authority under incomplete contracts. On one hand, employers may exercise authority primarily to avoid costs associated with using the price mechanism; if so, then everyone in the employment relationship stands to gain. On the other hand, as discussed further below, there is considerable scope for employers to use their powers to garner a larger share of the gains from the labor exchange. Since it is difficult to rule out either possibility absolutely, both possibilities must in general be allowed for in the empirical study of employment relationships.

Incentive costs and the role of monitoring

A second basis for hierarchy stems from contracting difficulties due to asymmetric information about worker effort or productivity. Take, for example, the case in which the level of labor effort cannot be inferred directly from the output of a given production process, due perhaps to some random element in production. As demonstrated in the preceding chapter, this can create costly dilemmas for individuals seeking to purchase labor services in an otherwise competitive market.

In the scenario involving risky production with risk-averse workers, entrepreneurs have to trade off the insurance aspects of pay against the need to provide work incentives to labor suppliers, inducing inefficient effort relative to a setting of full information. Alternatively, in the scenario in which both the worker's effort and true productivity level are hidden from the employer, the provision of appropriate incentives may dictate that the employer pays a rent to high-productivity workers and induces low-productivity workers to operate at an efficiently low level of effort.

The upshot of these scenarios is that employers have an incentive to monitor workers so as to mitigate the costly tradeoffs resulting from their inability to infer labor effort from output levels. Although one would expect monitoring itself to be a costly activity, both in time and effort, it enables the strategic option of linking compensation to the monitoring signal rather than to output, and thus of providing incentives without exposing workers to the full extent of production risk.

An early version of this argument was posed by economist Frank Knight, who viewed hierarchy in firms as a consequence of realizing gains from comparative advantages in dealing with production uncertainty. In his formulation, some individuals have relative strengths in dealing with uncertainty, either through superior ability in making good decisions in the face of the unknown, or on the basis of experiencing less utility loss from the risks they impose.

In Knight's story, these individuals become entrepreneurs and bear the full brunt of production uncertainty, guaranteeing the workers they hire complete income insurance against this risk. However, for reasons just reviewed, provision of full insurance to workers impairs their work incentives, at least under standard assumptions about motivation. Therefore entrepreneurs must combine insurance with direct oversight of the production process to ensure efficient work effort.

Economists Armen Alchian and Harold Demsetz have more recently posed a complementary aspect of Knight's story (see the related reference at the end of the chapter). Since monitoring itself presumably takes effort, a question arises as to who will "monitor the monitor," that is, ensure that the monitor performs efficiently? This turns out to be an old question: *quis custodiet ipsos custodes* is how the question was stated in the heyday of the Roman empire.

Alchian's and Demsetz's answer to this venerable question is that the monitor (or the "head" monitor, if there are multiple levels of hierarchy) is induced to undertake the necessary effort by receiving the *residual* income induced in part by her monitoring efforts, net of payments to the monitored factors. Examine this argument more closely.

Suppose the monitor is risk-neutral, as in Knight's original story, and cares only about average profit and the cost of undertaking supervisory effort S. The monitor's utility is thus given by net profit, equal to gross profit Π minus monitoring cost C, where both are understood as functions of S. Suppose in this scenario that gross profits are risky because of some random element in production, but that the monitor is risk-neutral, and thus only cares about *average* profit $\overline{\Pi}$.

By now-familiar reasoning, maximization of average net profit implies that the monitor will choose the level of monitoring effort S^* which equates marginal expected profit generated by monitoring, denoted $M\overline{\Pi}_S$, to the marginal cost of this level of effort, MC_S. This result is illustrated in figure 9.1. Note that if the marginal cost of supervision were always zero, then the optimal level of monitoring would be where marginal expected profit is equal to zero, the result obtained under perfectly competitive market conditions.

Note further that under imperfect contracting conditions, marginal profitability depends on other factors besides the level of monitoring effort. Based on the previous chapter's analysis of work incentives in the presence of production risk and risk-averse workers, it can be assumed that the marginal expected profitability of monitoring increases (shifts upward) with the level of production risk and the degree of worker risk aversion, since these factors complicate the use of simple piece rate schemes to maximize average profits.

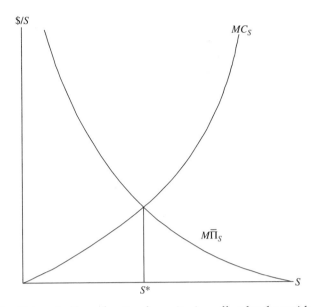

Figure 9.1 Determination of optimal monitoring effort by the residual claimant.

The Alchian and Demsetz argument is also significant in that it offers a possible explanation for the fact that firm owners typically bear risks associated with the firm's income stream. However, note that there is no *necessary* connection in their story between firm ownership and risk-bearing in this sense; for example, owners could exercise their property rights by assigning the residual income to a monitor who is not an owner. Thus, for example, it would be possible for workers to be monitored by another worker who elects to receive the residual income after subtracting fixed payments to owners and the other labor suppliers.

Thus, although the monitoring argument at this stage cannot be used to explain patterns of firm ownership (a phenomenon considered in more detail in the next section), it offers a potential explanation of why firms are organized hierarchically and why the monitors at the top of the hierarchy might bear some income risks. The complementary analysis of how monitoring signals are incorporated into worker compensation schemes is left for the next chapter.

The argument has thus far proceeded as though monitoring mattered only on efficiency grounds. However, as in the case of the authority relationship, monitoring may also have an impact on the *distribution* of gains from labor exchange. This is most readily seen in light of the scenario, examined in the previous chapter, in which wealth-constrained workers hold private information about both their effort levels and the firm-specific productivity of those efforts.

Recall that in this case workers can expect a rent in the event that their firm-specific productivity is high. Correspondingly, the employer might be able to reduce or eliminate this rent by monitoring workers to discover their true level of productivity. In the case considered in the previous chapter, if Rose could learn *either* Jack's productivity *or* his actual effort expended, she could determine which scenario actually obtains (since a high-productivity Jack obviously needs less effort to produce a given output than does his low-productivity alter ego), and thus assign Jack the payment scheme that limits him to his competitive utility level.

Unlike in the earlier versions of the monitoring problem, there is scope for intra-firm conflict over the nature and degree of monitoring when economic rents are at stake. This observation helps to explain why workers do not always welcome intensified monitoring with open arms.

Recall in this connection workers' historical opposition to the "scientific management" schemes of Frederick W. Taylor and his followers. If, as Taylor suggested, the sole effect of this system were to improve efficiency, then workers could be made strictly better off through its adoption, and thus would have no basis for opposition.

FIRM OWNERSHIP

Employment has been defined in this chapter as a hierarchical relationship in which the work of non-firm owners is supervised by firm owners or their agents. Having identified possible reasons for hierarchical relations to develop within firms, the analysis now addresses the microeconomic logic of firm ownership and its connection to the nature of employment. The related issue can be stated as a two-part question: first, why should the allocation of firm ownership rights matter at all? And second, given that it does matter, why is ownership status typically linked to supplying capital rather than labor services to a firm? Furthermore, given the answer to the latter question, why is it that labor-owned firms prevail in some forms of production?

Note that the issue raised in the second part of the question is why workers don't generally share in firm ownership on the basis of their *labor* contributions. Thus, the judgment that most firms are capital-owned is not altered by the possibility that employees own equity shares through their pension funds or stock option plans. The key point here is that stockholding employees can still be fired or laid off *as workers* even if they remain as part-*owners* of the firm's alienable assets.

There are thus two empirical aspects of firm ownership that require explanation. The first concerns the marked predominance of capital-based firm ownership. No worker-owned firms at all exist in most industrial classifications, and no classifications are dominated by worker-owned firms, with the stark exception noted below.

The second salient fact about firm ownership is that where worker ownership does occur, it tends to concentrate in industries or sectors with certain characteristics, including a relatively small scale of production, relatively low task differentiation among worker-owners (as in the taxicab cooperatives in San Francisco, in which most owners are drivers), relatively high *human* capital requirements, and, despite occasional important exceptions, relatively low capital intensity of production techniques. In Western Europe, particularly Italy and France, the largest concentration of worker ownership is in construction.[2] In the US, worker-owned firms in the form of professional partnerships predominate in high-skill services such as law, accounting, architecture, engineering, management consulting, advertising, and medicine, although the incidence of capital-ownership has been increasing in these fields.[3]

For present purposes, the significance of these patterns is twofold. First, they suggest that firm ownership is not incidental: it matters who owns firms, or these regularities in the pattern of ownership would presumably not arise. But ownership can only matter in a world of incomplete contracts, since otherwise parties to labor exchange could secure all the *relational* benefits associated with ownership simply by making the appropriate contractual stipulations.

Second, the fact that ownership status is so often correlated to the nature of the input supplied to the firm suggests that there is a qualitative difference between supplying financial or physical capital and human capital assets to a production relationship under conditions of imperfect contracting. Thus the related analytical task is to consider how any such distinction achieves strategic significance in a world of contracting failures, and the implications of this link.

Three possible theoretical connections are considered here, again distinguished according to the source of contractual failure. Note in light of the foregoing discussion that any viable theory of firm ownership must satisfy a double burden. It must be capable of explaining not only why worker ownership is on average rare, but also why it thrives in particular sectors.

Firm ownership and appropriation of firm-specific quasi-rents

One possible account of firm ownership is based explicitly on the problem of contractual incompleteness emphasized in Ronald Coase's analysis of the nature of the firm. Consider a scenario in which some input suppliers to a particular production relationship must make costly investments in assets whose productivity is linked to that specific firm. For example, one firm may hold a patent for a production process which requires specialized machines or labor skills. Alternatively, firms may have unique "corporate cultures" in which workers must exert effort to learn in order to perform effectively. The key issue is that the productivity gains yielded by such costly investments cannot readily be transferred to any other production relationship.

As explained in the previous chapter, the presence of costly firm-specific investments gives rise to *quasi-rents*, that is, economic returns which exceed the sum of outside payoffs available to firm members. Quasi-rents arise because investment costs become *sunk* once incurred, and thus do not inform rational decisions to leave or remain in the production relationship.

The existence of firm-specific assets thus raises the issue of whether investors in these assets can expect to recoup the costs of making the necessary investments, since they cannot re-employ these assets as productively elsewhere. This does not pose a problem in a world of complete contracts, as investors can in that scenario simply stipulate the compensation required for given commitments of their effort, time, or money. If significant enforcement costs of the sort described in the previous chapter preclude such stipulations, however, then these actors must seek alternative mechanisms for ensuring a return on their investments.

One such mechanism is the bargaining status conferred by firm ownership. A concomitant of the rights of voice guaranteed by ownership is its protection against being replaced: you can't fire a co-owner of firm assets. Anyone who can't be replaced must be negotiated with, and by virtue of this can exercise bargaining power in making claims on the gains from production, thus ensuring a return on investments in firm-specific assets.

This point can be illustrated in the context of the previous chapter's "Paula, Pete, and Marty" scenario involving incomplete contracts. Recall that Paula could not expect to recoup the marginal cost of a socially optimal firm-specific human capital investment so long as all three players bargained over the quasi-rents, but that the investment was worth her while if she could split the resulting surplus with just one other player, say Marty. The distribution of bargaining power among participants in the production relationship is thus crucial for the optimality of the outcome when costly investments are unverifiable, and the key question is how this condition informs the allocation of ownership rights in commercial enterprises.

Suppose that bargaining takes place after production but before the good is delivered to a consumer; in any event there is no way to prevent a participant from re-opening negotiations at this stage. Both the Nash bargaining solution and the strategic bargaining model with outside options imply that individuals who can be eliminated from the relationship at no cost to the surplus have no effective bargaining power. Sadly, once production has taken place, Paula has no bargaining power by virtue of her firm-specific investment, because her entire contribution to the relationship is at that point a sunk cost: the value of output is the same whether or not she remains in the relationship once production has taken place.

At this stage, participants can only derive bargaining power from one of two sources: first, their continued presence is uniquely necessary to realize the full market value of the output, or second, they have ownership rights and thus cannot be dismissed. As an example of the former condition, if the product has positive market value only if consumed by Marty, then Marty has bargaining power as well. Absent such a condition, Paula enjoys bargaining power, and is thus ensured of a return on her investment, only if she has an ownership claim on the firm's product.

Note further that unless Pete's presence is also necessary for realizing the maximal value of output – that is, unless he makes a firm-specific investment, has a unique ability to make effective use of this investment, or places a uniquely high value on the resulting output – it would be better if he were *not* an owner, and thus not given the ability to dilute the surplus flowing back to Paula. The foregoing arguments thus identify who should and who should not be an owner:

Paula, with her firm-specific investments, should be an owner; Pete, without specially valuable skills, actions, or tastes, should *not* be an owner; and it is a matter of indifference whether Marty, with a unique willingness to pay for the product, should be an owner, since Marty thereby enjoys bargaining power in any case.

This observation translates into a positive theory of firm ownership if supplemented by the assumption that equilibrium in the market for firm ownership is efficient in the sense just indicated. As explained below, this is a very strong assumption, but it is a useful starting point for the analysis of firm ownership patterns.

The theory yields two types of prediction. First, as illustrated by the example given above, it identifies who will and who will not have ownership rights in a given firm under given conditions. Second, it implies that all complementary assets should be owned *together*, that is, by the same set of owners. If they weren't, then gaining the benefits of productive complementarity would require bargaining with more individuals, and thus potentially diluting incentives for productive investment. Suppose, for example, that production required the use of computer hardware and software, both of which require firm-specific investments to use (say, because they have been customized for uses idiosyncratic to a given firm). Then the theory implies that, other things equal, both hardware and software should be owned by the same set of people.[4]

A potential limitation in the explanatory power of the theory stems from its assumption that all who "should" share in firm ownership can afford to purchase control rights. Chapter 4 discussed contrary evidence that labor suppliers may routinely face binding capital constraints due to lack of wealth and capital market imperfections. This is a potentially compelling reason why worker ownership of firms is less prevalent than this theoretical approach might otherwise predict.

Firm ownership and the structure of work incentives

An alternative theory of firm ownership flows from the problem of providing incentives when work effort is imperfectly observable. As with the preceding argument, the key theoretical challenge is to explain the need for given allocations of control rights in the firm, rather than simply for appropriate contract language governing the relevant aspects of labor exchange.

To illustrate this point, recall the problem of "who monitors the monitor" discussed in the section on production hierarchies. In the resolution of this problem supplied explicitly by Alchian and Demsetz and implicitly by Knight, the "head monitor" is motivated to provide the optimal supervisory effort by receiving the firm's residual income flowing, in part, from this effort. The difficulty posed at the end of that discussion concerned the plausible case in which the realized level of residual income is *negative*.

This difficulty gains salience if the candidate for head monitor has no personal wealth with which to cover the shortfall, because then he or she can't credibly promise to bear the residual whatever it may turn out to be. The earlier

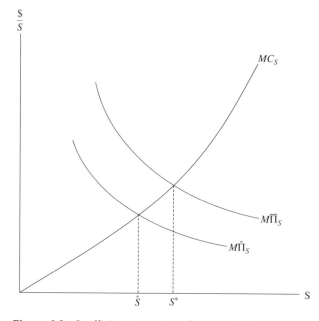

Figure 9.2   Inefficient incentives for a wealthless monitor.

discussion raised the possibility that the monitor could borrow to cover any short-fall, noting that in that case the wealthless monitor would still receive zero net income in the event of that profits are negative, since he or she cannot be made to bear income losses. The loss would instead be borne by the lender, who does so in return for a promised interest payment in the event that net firm income is positive.

The significance of this can be seen in light of figure 9.1 above. Efficient mon-itoring incentives require that the monitor receive the expected marginal profit from her monitoring efforts, net of a fixed interest payment. Given the possibility of negative residual income, however, the wealthless monitor can only repay the loan when residual income is positive. This implies that the monitor won't receive the full marginal profit of monitoring, since higher monitoring raises the proba-bility that the interest payment must be paid. Consequently, the monitor chooses an efficiently low level of monitoring intensity.

This result is depicted in figure 9.2. Here a "net marginal profitability" curve $M\hat{\Pi}_S$ is depicted which is strictly lower than the "full" marginal expected prof-itability of supervisory effort, indicated as in figure 9.1 by the curve labelled $M\overline{\Pi}_S$. As explained above, the reason for this difference is that, for a wealthless monitor, higher supervisory effort increases the probability of paying the full interest rate R, thus partially offsetting the profit incentive to do more monitor-ing. The result, as depicted in figure 9.2, is an inefficiently low supervision level $\hat{S} < S^*$.

This outcome must necessarily be viewed with alarm by the capital supplier who loans the monitor the wherewithal to cover negative residual income. Lower monitoring effort implies less total labor effort in production, and thus *increases* the chance of zero or negative profits – that is, the probability that the monitor cannot repay the loan. Furthermore, the problem can't be solved simply by increasing the interest rate charged to the monitor, since this further decreases the marginal benefit of effort to the monitor and thus induces even lower monitoring intensity.

The upshot of this is that the only way for the lender to ensure optimal monitoring incentives is to take over production directly and become the head supervisor. But this suggests that those with personal wealth – physical and financial capital suppliers – will tend to be firm owners, since only they will have the individual wherewithal to bear losses and thus avoid the incentive problem faced by would-be monitors with no personal wealth.

This argument is logically coherent as far as it goes, but it only accounts for the allocation of residual income rights, not for the allocation of control rights in firms' physical assets. For example, a team of workers who collectively own a set of alienable productive assets could solve the monitoring incentive problem just described by hiring a wealthy monitor and vesting him or her with residual income rights. Thus, an additional condition must be adduced to account for systematic patterns in the allocation of control rights in firms.

One such condition arises if effective supervision depends on *the structure of workplace tasks* as well as monitoring intensity. For example, a given level of monitoring effort might be more productive if a set of production tasks is linked in a given time sequence, or performed in a common, easily overseeable area. These issues are treated more thoroughly in next chapter's discussion of the *multi-task* version of the principal–agent problem.

For now, it suffices simply to raise the possibility that monitoring intensity and workplace structure have complementary incentive effects on work effort, and that contracts are *incomplete* with respect to such structures. For example, a sufficiently detailed description of task sequence may be too technical for agents of the legal system to interpret accurately. In this event, the head monitor may need to exercise control rights in the use or adaptation of physical productive assets in order to ensure that the optimal monitoring conditions are put in place.

This theory does a better job than the previous one of explaining why firm owners typically are capital suppliers, and why these owners enjoy *both* residual income and control rights. Capital suppliers require residual income rights to ensure optimal monitoring incentives, and require control rights to help ensure that optimal monitoring conditions are established.

Moreover, the theory is also consistent with the uneven incidence of worker ownership where it does arise. Small-scale production processes may face a lesser danger of incurring large random losses, thus reducing the scope for creating the perverse incentives described above. Small-scale enterprises may also be better able to sustain cooperative labor effort via the appropriate trigger strategies in an ongoing production relationship.

A key defect of the theory is that it has a difficult time accounting for the prevalence of partnerships and limited liability corporations, since in these cases, monitoring incentives are diluted by free-rider problems among multiple owners, and, in the case of corporations, by the very limits on downside risk that firm ownership is supposed to avoid in this perspective. If the structure of monitoring incentives is the key determinant of firm ownership, one would expect these forms to be superceded by single-owner proprietorships.

Firm ownership and collective decision making

The foregoing arguments take for granted that prospective firm owners are unanimous with respect to the intended purpose of production – presumably, profit maximization. This is a legitimate assumption when all relevant markets are perfectly competitive, but becomes problematic when markets are imperfectly competitive or incomplete. In the absence of non-market means of securing unanimity with respect to production goals, groups of would-be owners face potentially knotty problems in achieving consensus regarding collective choices.

Recall here the observation made in chapter 2 with respect to the objectives typically attributed to firms in economic theory. The objective of profit maximization does not *necessarily* correspond to the interests of firm-owning households, and in fact typically does *not* follow from the basic assumption that households seek to maximize utility subject to constraint. An additional condition is consequently required to ensure that firm-owning households unanimously endorse the objective of profit maximization. One such condition is that markets are *complete*, meaning that it is possible for a person to exchange any good with any other person. If markets are complete, then firm-owning households can always fulfill their consumption objectives independently of the *particular* input and output choices of the firms they own, and are thus only interested in the profit streams they generate.

If, to the contrary, markets are incomplete, then prospective firm owners have a potential interest in the specific production activities of firms, not just the profits that result from these activities. Given heterogeneous preferences, these interests may lead to fundamental disagreements over the production objectives of firms. With respect to the question of firm ownership, the relevant question is whether the intrinsic features of physical or financial capital and human capital inputs have any consequences for the ability of the respective input suppliers to achieve agreement over collective production goals. If this were so, then it is possible that observed patterns of firm ownership can be explained on the basis of differential costs of collective decision making.

There are two significant differences between physical (or financial) and human capital that may pertain to the ability to achieve consensus over production objectives. The first has to do with comparative capacities for accumulation of the relevant asset by a single input supplier. There is no obvious limit to the financial wealth that can be amassed by a single individual (consider Microsoft's chairman

Bill Gates), while there are practical limits to how much "capacity to labor" can be embodied in one person. For example, large-scale production processes requiring large numbers of workers may yet be financed by a single capital supplier.

The significance of this is that a capital supplier is presumably more often in a position to achieve unanimity by virtue of being the only person, or at least the majority voter, determining the firm's production goals. For example, a corporate shareholder with over 50% of a firm's common stock (equities with voting rights attached) will always be able to determine the outcome of votes on company policy. Practically speaking, even strong minority holdings are often sufficient to force certain outcomes.

The second potential difference between human and alienable capital assets that impinge on the collective choice problem is more subtle, having to do with the comparative mobility of labor and capital suppliers. Think specifically in terms of the comparison between embodied or human capital and *financial* capital, that is, wealth that can be held in the form of various financial instruments such as stocks and bonds. Compared to human capital, financial capital incurs significantly lower mobility costs in moving among firms.

A possible consequence of this differential in mobility costs is that markets for ownership shares in capitalist firms (equities) are more likely to be *competitive* in a specific sense than markets for membership in worker-owned firms. The specific sense is that competition among potential *buyers* eliminates the possibility of accruing consumer surplus from purchasing ownership shares. The reason for this assessment was suggested in chapter 4: if a firm is small relative to the number of potential buyers of its goods, even if it has no other close competitors, then it can sell as much as it wants at a *given* price. If the firm also has monopoly status because it offers a unique combination of firm-specific consumption goods (say, combinations of risk and average income), this price is the *maximum* the market will bear, leaving no scope for consumer surplus.

This implies in turn that potential firm owners would not have any basis for disagreement about the particular configuration of firm-specific consumption goods, since they get no net utility from these in any case. Thus the only remaining motive for firm ownership is the universal desire to maximize the value of the firm, that is, maximize the flow of expected future profits. Consequently, the superior mobility of financial relative to human capital suggests that capital-owned firms are presumptively more likely than worker-owners to reach consensus on a particular objective for the firm, specifically that of wealth maximization.[5]

A corollary of this result is that worker cooperatives, whose owners might not easily achieve unanimity with respective to an alternative set of firm objectives, might be relatively prone to buyouts by groups of investors who presumably share the objective of wealth maximization. However, the converse does not hold: capital-owned firms would not be subject to buyouts by their employees unless the latter had sufficiently unified interests in taking over the firm. Furthermore, employees can also pursue their interests within a firm through collective bargaining, possibly obviating the need to buy out the firm to ensure these interests are met.

There is some evidence that problems of collective decision making are relevant for the determination of ownership structure. For example, case studies of the taxicab cooperatives in San Francisco and the plywood cooperatives in Oregon lend partial support to this hypothesis by suggesting that worker-owned enterprises typically incur significant costs of collective decision making.[6] More extensive evidence supporting this hypothesis would require a comparative study with capital-owned enterprises of similar size, but existing data indicate that the issue of collective decision making is not irrelevant.

This theoretical approach potentially accounts for the predominance of capital ownership. It may also explain the concentrated incidence of worker ownership where it arises. Recall that worker-owned firms tend to congregate in sectors characterized by relatively small production scale and low task differentiation. Small-scale production has reduced scope for potential disagreements as there are fewer workers among whom disagreement could occur. Low task differentiation serves to diminish potential preference differences among workers by ensuring that they share more or less the same experiences in production.

The three theories summarized above share a common feature: they all illustrate the potential strategic significance of firm ownership under conditions of contractual or market incompleteness, thus giving some basis for understanding why patterns of firm ownership are apparently not purely random in modern industrial exchange economies. They also suggest that intrinsic differences in human and alienable capital assets may help to explain why firms are typically owned by suppliers of the latter, who may have non-trivial interests in excluding suppliers of the former from ownership status. The last task in this chapter is to draw these threads together to indicate their implications for the nature of the employment relationship.

CONCLUSION: WHAT IT MEANS TO BE AN EMPLOYEE

The analysis of the preceding two sections indicates that the employment relationship is characterized by two asymmetries between buyers and sellers of labor services that are both the consequence of contractual imperfections. The first is that labor suppliers are subject to oversight of their work effort in a hierarchical production relationship. The second is that labor suppliers typically do not share in the ownership of the alienable physical assets used in this relationship, at least not by virtue of their status as workers. Furthermore, these two features might be intertwined, because the need to provide effective monitoring incentives for profit maximization may imply that owners must have some personal wealth.

These conclusions are broadly consistent with the distinctions made in common law between *employment* and *commercial* contracts. The chief unique feature of the law pertaining to employment relations is that the employer is given the right to oversee and dictate the work *process* undertaken by employees, rather than simply the *outcomes* of that process as in a purely commercial contracting relationship. The analysis suggests that employers' interest in overseeing the labor process itself stems from some form of contractual incompleteness that makes it difficult or impossible to stipulate desired outcomes before production occurs.

In addition, employment law provides somewhat broader grounds than commercial law for *terminating* a relationship, including employee indolence, dishonesty, disloyalty, or disrespect, even if these are not shown to affect the substantial performance of the desired production services. The broader scope allowed for worker dismissal suggests the importance of restructuring the scope of ownership status. In a world of incomplete contracts, detrimental employee characteristics might be feared to have an effect on productive outcomes which might perhaps not be observable or verifiable by external enforcement agencies. Thus, there is some connection at least between the microeconomic implications of contract incompleteness and the legal structures governing employment relationships in the real world. Employment relationships, in other words, are a unique phenomenon deserving careful study.

Study Questions

1. What distinguishes an *employment* relationship from one of simple *contracting* for labor services? What conditions might give rise to an employment relationship? Explain.
2. What is a firm? What are its distinguishing characteristics? What is the connection between firms and employment relationships? Can you have one without the other?
3. Under what conditions is it reasonable to assume that a firm's owners wish to maximize profits? Under what conditions would that not be the case? If not, what would firms want to do instead, and why? What implications might this have for a firm's relationship with its employees?
4. Summarize the theories of firm ownership discussed in this chapter. Do they necessarily suggest that firm owners will typically be capital suppliers, and if so, why? What problems arise in applying these theories to explain the ownership of modern limited liability corporations?
5. According to the theory of firm ownership based on provision of efficient monitoring incentives, capital suppliers will want to become firm owners to avoid losses that result when they loan money to workers/supervisors who can't afford to repay the loan when production revenues are low. Why can't these lenders recoup their expected losses on average by simply raising the interest rate that workers/supervisors must pay when production revenues are sufficiently high?
6. According to Frank Knight's theory of the firm, relatively risk-averse people become employees and input suppliers to firms, while relatively risk-neutral people become employers and oversee the efforts of

continued

employees while guaranteeing them a certain income. Suppose that, for *given* levels of wealth from whatever source, individuals all have the same basic risk preferences. Under this assumption, in Knight's account, why would financial capitalists rather than human capitalists tend to become employers?

7. In accounts of real-world industrial settings corresponding to the "Jack and Rose" problem described in this chapter, workers sometimes collude to keep employers from learning their productivity levels through the strategic use of piece rates. However, these collusive arrangements were sometimes disrupted by employees very near to retirement, who generated high rates of output and thus signaled workers' productive capacities. Why might this pattern have occurred?

8. Consider an exchange between an employer and a worker in which the employer's preferences are summarized by the profit function $\pi = x - y$, where x is the dollar value of the worker's output and y is the employer's payment to the worker. The worker's preferences over output and pay are given by $U = y - \frac{x^2}{\theta}$, where θ is a parameter representing the worker's productivity in this particular exchange. The worker's productivity can take one of two values, $\theta = 1$ ("low") or $\theta = 2$ ("high").

   (a) Suppose the worker must receive a competitively-determined level of utility $\overline{U} = 0$. Illustrate the worker's indifference curve corresponding to this level of utility for each possible value of θ (label these respectively $\overline{U}_L$ and $\overline{U}_H$). What is the slope of each indifference curve at any given level of x? [Hint: $MU_x = -(2x/\theta)$.] In which direction is the worker's utility unambiguously increasing?

   (b) Graph the employer's profit-maximizing isoprofit curves associated with each value of θ and indicate the corresponding profit-maximizing values of y and x in each case. What is the slope of the isoprofit curve? In what direction is profit unambiguously increasing? Which value of worker productivity would the employer prefer?

   (c) Suppose that both the employer and the worker learn the true value of θ before the worker begins production. Show that the employer can induce the worker to produce the corresponding profit-maximizing level of output through the appropriate choice of a linear payment scheme $y = \alpha + \beta x$, where α is fixed pay or salary and β is the piece rate. Indicate the profit-maximizing values of α and β for each possible value of productivity.

   (d) Now suppose the worker, but *not* the employer learns the true value of θ before production begins, and suppose the employer chooses one of the forms of the linear payment scheme considered in (c) based on the worker's representation of the value of θ. If acting selfishly, will the worker always be willing to report the true value of θ?

(e) In light of your answer to (d), what form of the payment scheme is likely to maximize the employer's average profit, if s/he considers the two values of θ to be equally probable? [Remember the worker must be guaranteed at least $\overline{U}$ in any case.]

9. Consider an employment relationship in which production is risky, workers are risk-averse, and the firm pays the workers according to a linear payment scheme of the form $y = \alpha + \beta x$.

(a) Illustrate and explain the factors which determine the profit-maximizing value of the piece rate β. Explain why the profit-maximizing value of the piece rate will generally be insufficient to induce the efficient level of worker effort.

(b) Suppose that output is non-stochastic (no random element in production), but a function of *team* rather than *individual* effort. Show that workers in the team can be induced to provide efficient effort through the appropriate linear payment scheme based on team effort. What might preclude such a payment scheme from being practical?

(c) Given your answers to (a) and (b), there is a potential economic role for monitoring. Why might the achievement of efficient monitoring require that the "head monitor" also own the firm? Explain.

(d) Given your answer to (c), why might we expect to find a greater incidence of worker-owned firms in markets with relatively *labor*- (as opposed to capital-) intensive production?

Notes

1 David M. Gordon, *Fat and Mean: The Corporate Squeeze of Working Americans and the Myth of Managerial "Downsizing"* (New York: The Free Press, 1996): 43–8. As Gordon recognizes, these data must be read guardedly, in part because they include both public and private sector employment, and in part because they don't control for sectoral weights. Thus, it might be that the US and Canada post such high percentages because they have a relatively large incidence of "high-supervision" occupations. Gordon's reading of the data suggests this is not entirely the case, however.

2 Avner Ben-Ner, "Comparative Empirical Observations on Worker-Owned and Capitalist Firms," *International Journal of Industrial Organization* 6, no. 1 (March 1988): 7–31.

3 Henry Hansmann, *The Ownership of Enterprise* (Cambridge, MA: The Belknap Press, 1996).

4 The theory also yields a range of additional predictions about asset ownership. See Oliver Hart and John Moore, "Property Rights and the Nature of the Firm," *Journal of Political Economy* 98, no. 6 (December 1990): 1119–58.

5 Gregory K. Dow, *Governing the Firm: Workers' Control in Theory and Practice* (Cambridge, UK: Cambridge University Press, 2003): 202–4.

6   Lee Benham and Philip Keefer, "Voting in Firms: The Role of Agenda Control, Size and Voter Homogeneity," *Economic Inquiry* 29 (October 1991): 706–19.

Suggestions for Further Reading

Margaret M. Blair, *Ownership and Control*: *Rethinking Corporate Governance for the Twenty-First Century* (Washington, DC: Brookings Institution, 1995).

Gregory K. Dow, *Governing the Firm*: *Workers' Control in Theory and Practice* (Cambridge, UK: Cambridge University Press, 2003).

Henry Hansmann, *The Ownership of Enterprise* (Cambridge, MA: Belknap Press, 1996).

CHAPTER TEN

EMPLOYEE COMPENSATION AND INCENTIVE PROVISION

If all market transactions were mediated by perfect contracting arrangements, one would expect to see worker compensation explicitly linked to the specific services to be rendered, possibly modified by contingencies, such as might arise from severe weather events or supply disruptions, that affect production outcomes. In this scenario, workers are compensated on pre-arranged terms that are closely tied to verifiable conditions under which they might produce.

However, methods of worker compensation don't generally take this form. In the dominant case of wages and salaries, workers are respectively paid by the hour or simply according to job title, with no explicit basis in amount of work done or output produced. Where pay is tied in some way to performance, it is usually either linked to given measures of individual output, as in the case of piece rates, commissions, and gratuities, or based on supervisory assessments of overall performance, as in the case of bonus clauses or promotion ladders. Thus, it needs to be explained why compensation schemes are simpler and yet more variable in form across establishments than predicted by a model of frictionless exchange in perfectly competitive labor markets.

It is not simply the *existence* of these phenomena that calls for explanation; it is also the case that their incidence varies dramatically across economies and over time. For example, there has been a significant decline over the last century in industrial reliance on piece rates and other forms of payment by performance to motivate and direct work effort, although this trend has shown some signs of reversal in recent years.

This chapter attempts to sort out the relevant issues and identify explanations for variations in the form of employee compensation. As indicated, contractual imperfections are a necessary starting point for any attempt to

continued

account for these phenomena in microeconomic terms. The central theme of the analysis is that compensation structures are chosen by firms to respond to given departures from perfect contracting conditions, possibly as constrained by the protests of workers who oppose possible redistributional effects of imposing these provisions.

After a review of the empirical incidence of compensation structures, the analysis begins by returning to the problem of incentive provision under asymmetric information first discussed in chapter 8. The new step in the argument is to factor in the possibility that employers can gain some information about employee performance by monitoring their production activities. This possibility raises the question of how profit-seeking employers would incorporate monitoring signals into compensation arrangements with workers, possibly in conjunction with organizational innovations that increase the scope for effective supervision of work effort. The theoretical discussion is followed by a review of empirical studies on firms' choice of compensation methods. These results might best be described as highly suggestive but generally not conclusive.

EMPIRICAL INCIDENCE OF COMPENSATION STRUCTURES

Firms have employed a remarkably wide array of schemes for compensating their workers, ranging from the apparent simplicity of hourly wages or salaries to more or less complex systems involving piece rates, individual and group bonuses, commissions, gratuities, profit sharing, and promotion ladders. At the most basic level, compensation schemes can be divided into those that provide explicit work incentives, such as piece rates, profit sharing, or bonuses, and those that don't, such as hourly wages or salaries.

However, it will prove useful for some analytical purposes to refine this distinction somewhat. Consequently, the taxonomy invoked here distinguishes among schemes in which no explicit work incentives are provided (hourly wages or salaries); payment based solely on some measure of output, such as piece rates, commissions, or profit sharing; and compensation or promotions based on supervisory assessments of performance (possibly including some measure of output).

Data on compensation structures show striking variations in the form of pay. First, there are significant differences in compensation method across industries and occupations. For example, US chemical, manufacturing, and processing industries such as paints, industrial chemicals, and plastics make very little use of piece rates, while textiles and clothing manufacturing sectors such as shirt-making and cotton and wool textiles make relatively heavy use of performance-based pay. Across occupations, while wages and salaries are by far the most prevalent forms of pay, some occupations (e.g., engineers and science technicians) report no income paid on the basis of piece rates, while other occupations (e.g., about a third of US precision machine operators) report that some portion of their income takes this form.

Second, there are systematic differences in forms of compensation by worker characteristics. For example, women are more likely to be paid by the piece than are men, but US male managers and professionals are more likely to have pay contingent on job performance (e.g., bonuses).[1]

Notably, there has been a dramatic shift away from piece rates in most developed countries. For example, about 80% of US manufacturing employees were paid via piece rates in the 1920s, but less than 14% were paid by this method in the 1980s. US industry-level data show a significant decline in the use of incentive pay over a roughly ten-year period from the mid-1960s to the mid-1970s. Similarly, payment solely by the piece in Sweden has fallen from about 48% of the blue-collar labor force to less than 10% as of the late 1980s. However, there has recently been increased reliance on bonuses as opposed to strict salary or wage provision among US firms, as well as renewed interest in piece rate payment schemes in some industries.

SUPERVISION AND COMPENSATION STRUCTURES

In chapter 8, it was explained how asymmetric information about worker effort levels might force firms to make costly tradeoffs between incentive provision and other goals such as insuring workers against production risks. In light of these tradeoffs, firm owners have an incentive to increase their information about labor effort by investing in workplace supervision. This section of the chapter explores factors influencing how firms incorporate monitoring signals in determining how to compensate their workers.

Informative monitoring signals and efficient incentives

Information generated by supervision of work effort offers the possibility of increasing the gains from labor exchange by reducing compensation risk or more finely tuning incentives. To see the possible efficiency gains from monitoring, return to the case considered in chapter 8 involving the relationship between a risk-neutral employer, Rose, and Jack, a worker hired from a competitive labor market. Suppose as before that Jack's effort is not freely observable by Rose, and furthermore that it can't be inferred from output because production is affected by random and unmeasurable events. Thus, if Jack is to be given material work incentives, Rose must base his pay on *stochastic* output, determined by both random and non-random components.

This creates a problem for Rose if Jack is averse to risk. Rose must then either compensate him for the risk he faces or make compensation independent of output, thereby eliminating work incentives. As discussed in chapter 8, Rose's optimal choice involves a tradeoff between the two goals, such that Jack is pro-vided with some incentives at the cost of bearing some risk. Rose thus incurs a cost in the form of a risk premium paid to assure Jack his competitive utility level.

Now bring the possibility that Rose monitors Jack's work into the picture. Presumably Rose incurs opportunity costs of time and energy in doing so, but in return she may acquire information about Jack's work effort apart from the noisy signal given by output. So long as the monitoring signal is *informative* about Jack's effort, it is possible for Rose to use this signal to reduce Jack's risk, sharpen his incentives, or both, by incorporating it into the payment scheme.

What does it mean for a monitoring signal to be *informative*? As discussed in chapter 8, it may be difficult if not impossible to determine precisely a worker's labor effort from outward appearances, because effort or intensity has a mental as well as a physical component. However, there may be external manifestations that, although not perfectly indicative of productive activity, do provide relevant information. For example, the sales of a floor assistant in a retail establishment may not always depend on how quickly he or she offers to help a new customer, but the latter may well provide some information on the likelihood of making a sale. In that event the employer could gain from this aspect of employee perfor-mance in the determination of pay.

To see how the inclusion of informative monitoring signals might improve the efficiency of labor exchange, return to the contracting scenario from chapter 8 in which Jack's utility depends on both the mean and variance of his income. It was shown there that if Rose paid Jack via a piece rate scheme, the size of the piece rate is inversely proportional to the variance of output. But now imagine instead that Rose can base her payment to Jack on a signal which has the same mean as the frequency distribution of output, for a given effort input by Jack, but a smaller variance. Then Rose could increase the piece rate and thus provide stronger work incentives without making Jack bear more risk, thus increasing the overall gains from labor exchange.

Monitoring signals may thus be informative, and potentially increase efficiency, even if they are to some degree noisy and workers are risk-averse. The general implication of this line of reasoning is that employers who find it cost-effective to monitor workers would want to incorporate all possible signals in the compen-sation scheme, including output. Consequently, the theory predicts that firms using supervision would typically employ schemes that link compensation to supervisory assessments of worker effort and productivity.

There are some important caveats to this conclusion. First, if specific monitor-ing signals are costly to obtain, then employers may not choose to generate them even if they are informative. Thus, compensation schemes are likely to be corre-spondingly simpler – based solely on measures of output, for example – in set-tings where monitoring is extremely difficult. For example, where efficient output calls for a great deal of worker autonomy and independent judgments about pro-duction activities, one might expect, other things equal, to find less reliance on monitoring signals. Two additional problems are considered next at greater length.

WHY TIP?

> I do not know why people leave anonymous tips in restaurants, and the fact that I leave them myself in no way alleviates my sense of mystery (Steven E. Landsburg, *The Armchair Economist*, 1993, p. 19).

A number of occupations (e.g., food servers, cabdrivers, hairdressers, bell-hops) in many countries routinely receive a substantial proportion of their pay in the form of tips. The foregoing discussion gives an apparent ratio-nale for this procedure: it delegates responsibilities for monitoring employee effort to customers, who are potentially in a better position than managers to observe the true extent and results of employee behavior. In principle, better-performing employees would be rewarded with bigger tips and therefore higher pay. But this delegation also creates an economic puzzle: assuming that customers want to minimize the cost of dining out, other things equal, why don't they "free ride" on the tipping of others, thus reduc-ing the effectiveness of this delegation? In particular, why do customers who plan never to return to given establishments still tip?

There are other puzzling aspects of tipping. The average size of tips is influenced by factors that do not appear directly related to employee per-formance. Research shows that in the US, putting a "smiley face" on the bill increases tips for female servers, but cuts them for male servers. Credit-card customers tip more lavishly than cash customers (Grimes, 1999).

Moreover, the use of tips to improve performance becomes problematic, at least from the standpoint of firm owners, when employees can act in ways that increase their tip income at the cost of profits. For example, waiters may recommend dishes that have lower profit margins, thereby ingratiating themselves with the customer (Paules, 1991). This is an instance of the *multi-task* incentive problem discussed next in the chapter.

Related discussion questions:
1. William Grimes (1999) writes: "It is well documented that [restaurant] tip size decreases with the size of the party . . . single diners leave an average tip of 19.7 percent. That number drops to 6.9 percent for two people, 15.2 percent for three, 14.9 percent for four and 13.2 percent for five." How might this phenomenon be explained on economic grounds?
2. Restaurant staffs often pool tips, allocating them across pool members based on job type (waiters gaining more than buspersons, seaters, som-meliers, etc.) and hours worked. What are the pros and cons of a pooling system, from the point of view of the pool participants? From the point of view of customers?

Related references:
William Grimes, "The Tip: A Reward, but for Whom?," *The New York Times*, Febru-ary 3, 1999.
Greta Foff Paules, *Dishing It Out: Power and Resistance among Waitresses in a New Jersey Restaurant* (Philadelphia, PA: Temple University Press, 1991).

Task complexity and the scope of monitoring

The analysis of incentive provision in employment relationships given asymmetric information has so far been premised on the assumption that workers' unseen effort varies along a single dimension, loosely thought of as "intensity." This is unlikely to be the typical case. In most workplace settings, one might expect that profitability is affected by the particular *set* of work activities chosen as well as the total degree of effort put forth.

It is easy to imagine realistic examples of this scenario. Employers might be concerned with the effort devoted to the quantity of current output, but also with the efforts devoted to the product's quality, rate of completion, or presentation to potential customers. The employer might also wish workers to spend time at teaching production techniques to new colleagues, making themselves available to answer customer questions, or conveying information about shopfloor conditions to supervisory personnel. Employers may be concerned as well about how workers treat the machinery in producing output, since the firm's value at any point depends in part on the condition of these assets. Front office personnel may be expected to greet visitors in addition to performing clerical tasks. Et cetera. The many-sided incentive puzzle that arises in such cases is called the *multi-task principal–agent problem*.

The multi-task version of the principal–agent model introduces a new element to the incentive problem faced by employers when employee work efforts are difficult to determine. If the different dimensions of work effort are substitutes from the standpoint of workers' utility, then increasing pecuniary incentives for one dimension of activity will have the side effect of diminishing *relative* incentives with respect to the other dimensions, ignoring possible income effects on effort choice. The problem is exactly analogous to the effect of changing relative prices on individual consumption choices, discussed back in chapter 1.

This suggests that employers would in principle want to provide direct incentives for all dimensions of worker effort that affect profitability, rather than just for total effort. Correspondingly, employers would wish to receive signals for the whole range of worker activities, rather than just a few dimensions of that effort. If, to the contrary, monitoring signals are limited in scope, a new aspect of the incentive problem emerges.

To see this, recall the case of hidden effort with stochastic output as a point of reference. Suppose for simplicity that Jack is risk-neutral and can borrow as necessary to cover income deficits. Then, by reasoning discussed in chapter 8, Rose can in this scenario costlessly elicit the profit-maximizing effort from Jack simply by charging him a fixed "up-front" fee and letting him keep his entire *marginal* product.

However, this strategy may not work in the multi-task version of the incentive problem. Suppose that the employer cannot generate monitoring signals corresponding to all possible dimensions of work effort. In the Rose and Jack scenario, for example, suppose that Rose can measure Jack's output but not the *quality* of

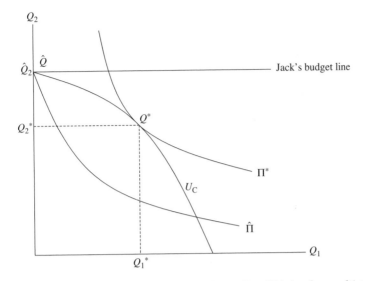

Figure 10.1 Consequence of unobservable work quality (Q_1) in the multi-task principal–agent problem.

his output. If both dimensions matter for Rose's bottom line, and efforts toward promoting quantity and quality are substitutes in Jack's view, then she might not want to give him full incentives to increase quantity, since this may reduce or eliminate his desire to assure the quality of the product.

Rose's problem is illustrated in figure 10.1. This graph presents a sample of Jack's indifference curves and Rose's isoprofit curves defined over combinations of quality Q_1 and quantity Q_2. Consistent with the analysis of chapter 8, assume that Jack dislikes producing higher levels of quantity and quality (since this requires greater effort) and that Rose gains from higher levels of both. As usual, it's assumed that Rose's and Jack's preferences over alternative bundles are convex.

Denote the utility of Jack's next best employment alternative by U_c. Then the profit-maximizing effort combination consistent with Jack receiving this level of utility is at the point marked Q^* in figure 10.1. Of course, Rose can't stipulate this outcome by contract, because she cannot observe Jack's efforts toward promoting quality.

In the scenario discussed in chapter 8, however, Rose could construct a "budget line" for Jack that would induce him to *select* the profit-maximizing point. Can that be done here? The answer is no: since Rose has no signal, not even a noisy one, about Jack's effort in promoting quality, there is no way for her to attach a positive price to this effort. She can only reward increases in quantity, which she can observe with more or less precision.

Consequently, the only budget line she could construct for Jack would have a slope of zero, that is, the ratio of the (zero) price for quality efforts to the (positive) price for quantity efforts. It's left to you to confirm that no horizontal budget line can be drawn in figure 10.1 that would induce Jack voluntarily to select point Q^*. The best Rose could therefore expect to achieve is point $\hat{Q}$, corresponding to a lower level of profit $\hat{\Pi}$ than she could achieve under conditions of full information. Notice that this point involves *no* effort from Jack toward promoting quality.

Now suppose, contrary to the situation shown in figure 10.1, that achieving positive levels of profit requires strictly positive levels of both quantity and quality (what would Rose's isoprofit curves look like in this case?). Then Rose would not want to provide Jack with *any* direct incentives linked to quantity, since this would mean that he would devote no effort at all toward quality. Since Jack is assumed to dislike undertaking effort, this would imply that Jack makes no effort at all.

The only way Rose could expect positive profits in this scenario is if Jack preferred doing some level of effort to doing nothing at all (to stave off boredom, perhaps, or out of intrinsic interest in the work involved). Then Rose's optimal strategy is to offer Jack a level of fixed income just sufficient to ensure him his competitive level of utility, and give no targeted incentives whatsoever for the quantity of output, even though she can monitor his efforts in that direction.

Thus, the multi-task version of the principal–agent problem suggests an additional reason why employers might not offer targeted performance incentives in the compensation packages they offer to employees, even when monitoring signals are available for some aspects of employee performance. If potential signals are not comprehensive in the dimensions of profitable work effort, improving incentives along some dimensions may weaken incentives along others. In that case the best thing to do might be to let workers determine their own effort allocations.

Multi-task incentives and job design

The inability to provide efficient work incentives obviously has a negative impact on expected profitability. Consequently, when incentive problems persist, employers have a strong interest in adopting organizational innovations to overcome the related obstacles. In the scenario of multi-task incentive problems, for example, employers may wish to structure tasks so as to minimize the number of workers for whom it is counterproductive to provide with high-powered incentives. Thus, *job design* might generally be thought of as an intrinsic component of employers' strategies for providing work incentives to their workers.

Consider this possibility in the context of the multi-task agency problem described earlier. Suppose as before that a worker chooses levels of multiple production tasks, rather than simply undifferentiated "effort," and that all of these tasks are more or less imperfectly observed by the employer. The firm then faces the more complex incentive problem of inducing the most profitable *array* of production tasks by its workers. As discussed above, this problem gets especially thorny if some dimensions of worker activity are difficult or impossible to observe.

For example, early in the twentieth century US firms encountered this difficulty when attempting to implement "Taylorist" management strategies to accelerate production rates. A frequent aftereffect of these efforts was that machines broke down at much higher rates. Naturally differences of opinion arose as to the cause of these breakdowns, with workers insisting that they were being made to run the machines too fast and management consultants insisting with equal fervor that the workers were sabotaging the machines in order to discredit the consultants' proposals. The point is that the firm's owners could not be sure which story was true, and thus had to be concerned with the nature and severity of the tradeoff between the intended speed of operations and the rate of unanticipated mechanical downtime.

Consequently, firms in such settings will typically have an incentive to structure production activity so as to limit the scope for this unfavorable outcome. Two implications of this analysis are of particular relevance. First, if employees can freely choose among work-related and non-work related tasks, firms will have a clear incentive to structure the workplace so as to limit the latter options, in order to minimize the need to provide incentives for the strictly work-related tasks.

This consideration may have formed part of the historical basis for the replacement of "proto-industrial" work organization by the factory system. Proto-industrial production, typified by the "putting-out" system in England, generally took place in rural workers' homes, with capital suppliers providing raw materials and direct incentives in the form of piece rates. Historical accounts of this transition suggest that capitalists faced a number of incentive problems, including embezzling and the inability to increase production rapidly in response to growing international demand, which were not completely solved through the use of piece rates.

By bringing workers into the factory and away from their homes, in contrast, capitalists were able (according to this theory) to restrict the range of activities available to the workforce, and thus arguably to focus efforts more narrowly on profit-yielding activities. That incentive difficulties rather than technological improvements prompted the move to factories may help to explain why proto-industrial forms of production continued alongside the factory system well into the nineteenth century (and still thrive today in many developing countries).

Turning from the historical record to contemporary experience, the theory of multi-task incentives provides potential explanations for the incidence of employment arrangements involving "telecommuting," in which employees are allowed to work in their homes, and "contracting out," in which tasks previously reserved for employees are assigned to independent contractors. The theory predicts that these cases would only arise when the work-related activities of telecommuters and outside contractors are sufficiently observable that it is unnecessary to require their physical presence at the workplace.

A second implication of the theory for workplace organization is that it is profitable to have workers specialize in different bundles of tasks, even in the absence of comparative advantages or technically driven increasing returns. In particular, employers gain by assigning relatively observable and unobservable tasks respectively to separate workers. If a worker cannot profitably be given "high-powered" incentives to the extent she or he performs unobservable tasks, it is best from the employer's standpoint to minimize the number of workers for whom this is true.

FROM TAYLORISM TO FORDISM TO . . . TOYOTAISM?

Dramatic changes in the organization of work over the past century or so, particularly in manufacturing enterprises, suggest that workplace design is best understood as a dynamic response to the combined dictates of consumer demand, technical progress, and employee incentive provision. As discussed in chapter 8, Frederick Taylor's system of "scientific management" confronted craft-based production methods in which workers enjoyed consistent informational advantages relative to firm owners and overseers. To counter the "systematic soldiering" he saw as a byproduct of this situation, Taylor's system called for increased managerial control of production technology and work procedures, extensive task specialization, and the use of high-powered individual incentive schemes such as piece rates.

"Fordism," so named in honor of the assembly-line methods favored by Henry Ford, can be seen as the logical outgrowth of Taylorist management philosophy and rapidly growing market demand for manufactured goods. Fordist methods combined the hierarchical control structure and detailed task specialization of Taylorism with the use of specialized, single-use machinery favoring mass production of standardized goods. Compensation schemes tied to individual output became less useful as increased mechanization of production helped regulate the pace of work and diminished the connection between individual effort and total output, reflected in dramatic reductions in the incidence of piece-rate compensation through the middle portion of the twentieth century. Ford himself may have paid "efficiency wages" to attract and motivate employees for monotonous assembly-line work (Raff and Summers, 1987).

The 1980s saw the emergence of new work structures sacrificing large-scale production of standardized goods to promote responsiveness to rapidly changing market demands for highly customized products. These new methods of flexible or "lean" production, traceable in part to innovations adopted decades earlier by the Toyota automobile firm in Japan (Rubery and Grimshaw, 2003, p. 55), featured greater employee involvement in shopfloor decision making with corresponding reductions in levels of managerial hierarchy. Increased reliance on employee teamwork has been combined with sharply reduced task specialization, so that employees are called upon to undertake multiple tasks and continuously update their skills. Increased employee discretion and responsibility, combined with the increased use of information technology making it possible for firms to keep close tabs on team output, favored the increased use of group-based incentive schemes, such as profit sharing.

Economists Assar Lindbeck and Dennis J. Snower (2001) review evidence suggesting the dramatic expansion and pervasive use of these new production methods since the 1980s. As will be discussed in chapter 19, these changes may have also had an impact on how labor markets function, with implications for wage determination and prevailing unemployment levels.

Related discussion questions:

1. What conditions of "lean production" might have made it possible for firms to dispense with some layers of supervisory hierarchy? Wouldn't reduced task specialization imply that workers were *harder* to monitor, rather than easier?

2. Are "Toyotaist" production techniques likely to have any systematic implications for the degree of bargaining power enjoyed by incumbent workers? Explain.

3. The new "lean" production methods feature small-batch, customized production runs in place of the large-scale production of standardized goods that characterized "Fordist" production. What economic developments might have prompted this change?

Related references:

Assar Lindbeck and Dennis J. Snower, "Centralized Bargaining and Reorganized Work: Are They Compatible?," *European Economic Review* 45 (2001): 1851–75.

Daniel M. G. Raff and Lawrence H. Summers, "Did Henry Ford Pay Efficiency Wages?," *Journal of Labor Economics* 5, no. 4 (October 1987): part 2, S57–S86.

Jill Rubery and Damian Grimshaw, *The Organization of Employment: An International Perspective* (New York: Palgrave MacMillan, 2003).

Verifiability of monitoring and bilateral moral hazard

The analysis of supervision and compensation has to this point assumed that any signals generated by monitoring are verifiable by external enforcement agencies. If this is not the case, then a new incentive problem arises: employers may under this condition be tempted to increase their profits by misrepresenting the information gleaned from supervision of work effort. To flesh out this point with an example, recall from the previous chapter the hypothesis that motivating optimal supervisory effort might require paying residual profits to the "head" monitor. But if this were done, supervisors stand to gain by reporting that workers "shirk" even when they don't, since any income not paid to workers becomes part of the residual. Such self-serving behavior would obviously threaten the efficiency gains made possible by monitoring in settings with asymmetric information. Thus, the inability to verify monitoring signals gives rise to a *bilateral* incentive problem.

What can be done to counter the firms' incentives to misrepresent unverifiable monitoring signals? The trick is somehow to maintain the positive incentive properties of monitoring while ensuring that the monitor doesn't benefit from distorting information. Since work effort and the content of monitoring signals are both unverifiable in this scenario, any solution to the resulting bilateral incentive problem must be *self-enforcing*. How might this be accomplished?

The key to this puzzle lies in the strategic use of *dismissals* or *quits* to enforce desired outcomes. For example, suppose that an employer can only respond to evidence of insufficient work effort in the *current* production period by dismissing the offending workers at the end of the period, *after* they've been paid. Imposing this penalty yields no direct gain to the employer, other things equal, and thus creates no incentive to misrepresent information gleaned from monitoring of work effort. However, workers may be effectively induced to provide the desired effort level by fear of losing their jobs if caught shirking.

Alternatively, and by parallel reasoning, if *current* compensation were tied to the monitoring signal reported by the employer, then workers might effectively deter strategic misrepresentation of the signal by threatening to quit their jobs after the current production period. If this is effective, then it is strategically possible for employers to provide incentives through the provision of *bonuses* to workers observed working sufficiently hard.

If the workers' threat to quit is insufficient to deter moral hazard on the part of the employer, the conditions stated above may lead to the payment of *efficiency wages* by firms in order to motivate employee effort. The economic logic of this incentive device is examined next.

Efficiency wages

Given the conditions of bilateral moral hazard discussed above, employers can credibly motivate worker effort only by offering a wage premium and threatening to fire any workers who are found shirking. Since the incentive effect of the firing threat is greater the higher the wage premium, the wage rate determines not only the marginal cost of labor hired, but also the net revenue productivity of labor. The *efficiency wage* is defined as the level of compensation that maximizes the firm's (expected) profits, *given* that the net revenue productivity of labor is a function of the wage rate. The modifier "efficiency" is thus something of a misnomer, as nothing guarantees that wage levels chosen by firms are efficient in the standard sense of Pareto-optimality. To the contrary, the wage rate chosen under these conditions by profit-maximizing firms may be inefficiently low.

There are other potential grounds for paying efficiency wages besides the provision of effort incentives. As mentioned in chapter 4, efficiency wages might be paid in developing economies because the productivity of impoverished workers depends on the amount of food they can afford to consume. Raising wages above the competitive level allows workers to secure enough nutrition to sustain higher levels of productivity.

Alternatively, the level of compensation may influence both labor productivity and labor cost by reducing worker turnover. (Study question 5 for chapter 6 addressed this scenario.) When turnover is costly, workers' decisions to change jobs may impose significant negative externalities on their employers, either directly by necessitating costly search for new employees or indirectly by removing firm-specific skills that are not immediately replaceable. In either case, employers have a potential incentive to offer wage premia in order to reduce the turnover rate.

Another way in which wage levels might influence average productivity is if they affect the average quality of the applicant pool for a given job, rather than the net revenue productivity of any given applicant. While less-productive workers would presumably be willing to work for either low or high wages (and thus to join a given firm's applicant pool in any case), higher-productivity workers may only apply for jobs which promise a sufficiently high rate of pay. Thus, a higher wage offer by the firm might raise the average quality of the applicant pool. Contractual imperfections play an essential role in this account, since if worker characteristics were directly observable then presumably firms could specify exactly the levels of worker quality they're willing to pay for, given existing wage rates.

The efficiency wage hypothesis will be explored further in subsequent discussions of internal labor markets and involuntary unemployment. For now, focus on the effort-based version of the efficiency wage hypothesis in the presence of bilateral moral hazard. Putting the pieces introduced above together, one arrives at a picture of the employment relationship in which employers use supervision to link pay more closely to effort, but do so subject to the restriction that penalties for observed shirking take the form of dismissing shirkers only in the period after that in which shirking has been detected.

As indicated earlier, an immediate consequence of this restriction is that workers must earn quasi-rents in employment relationships characterized by effort-related efficiency wages. Since employers cannot threaten to lower current-period pay and credibly ensure truthful representation of monitoring signals, workers must be deterred from choosing unprofitably low effort by the prospect of continuing to enjoy higher payoffs than they could hope to secure if they left their current position. Consequently, the wage rate must be higher than the strictly competitive level.

Will this higher wage ensure pure rents to workers rather than just quasi-rents after being hired? That is, can they anticipate a strictly higher than competitive level of utility before joining the firm? This depends on the ability of employers to extract any rents from otherwise competitive workers "up front" by charging employment fees equal to the amount of the rent enjoyed by workers subsequent to being hired. If workers are hired in competitive labor markets, they would in principle be willing to accept the firm's offer, including the fee, so long as they can anticipate an expected present value of payoff at least equal to what they could earn in other positions.

However, the ability of firms to use employment fees in this way requires very stringent informational conditions that are inconsistent with the scenario under study. Specifically, given that monitoring signals are nonverifiable, firms have an incentive to overstate employee shirking and fire incumbent workers so they can collect employment fees from their replacements. Consequently, if payment of efficiency wages is an optimal response to bilateral moral hazard conditions, then the resulting rents could not in general be siphoned off with employment fees.

What determines the wage level paid in this scenario, and thus the magnitude of economic rents transferred? A careful theoretical response to this question requires construction of an economic model incorporating the considerations discussed above. An overview of the indicated analysis is given here, with the corresponding technical details presented in the appendix to this chapter.

As suggested by the foregoing discussion, there are three primary ingredients of this efficiency wage model: the need to motivate workers with material incentives, the determination of pay on the basis of noisy monitoring signals rather than output, and critically, the bilateral incentive problem that results when monitoring signals are unverifiable. The level of the efficiency wage is then determined by workers' outside options, given in turn by the unemployment rate and income from unemployment insurance or income maintenance programs.

As demonstrated in the appendix, the efficiency wage model of effort incentives yields the following hypotheses:

- unless left to perform a minimal, "incentive-free" level of effort, workers paid an efficiency wage receive a quasi-rent (and also a rent if employment fees are infeasible);
- the level of the efficiency wage is increasing in the value of the transfer payment the worker receives when unemployed, and decreasing in the unemployment rate (since a larger transfer payment raises and a higher unemployment rate lowers the expected payoff associated with dismissal), other things equal;
- other things equal, the efficiency wage is decreasing in the likelihood that a worker is caught when shirking (and thus increasing in the level of monitoring intensity), implying in turn that monitoring intensity and the wage rate are substitutes in motivating worker effort.

Empirical evidence with respect to the hypothesis that workers are paid efficiency wages is examined later in the chapter.

Supervision and distributional conflict

Under a number of scenarios, the nature and extent of asymmetric information can have implications for the distribution of gains from labor exchange as well as for efficiency. This is clearly the case in the context of efficiency wages, for example: if employers can't credibly charge initial employment fees, then they won't be able to siphon off the rents subsequently provided in the form of efficiency wage premia. For another example, it was shown in chapter 8 that information asymmetries may give rise to quasi-rents when workers face wealth constraints or have private information about their firm-specific productivity. As before, quasi-rents translate into economic rents if employers are unable to charge offsetting employment fees.

Under such conditions, monitoring efforts devoted to eliminating the information asymmetry would also have the effect of threatening worker quasi-rents or rents. In this case, unlike in the case where only efficiency concerns are at stake, one would expect systematic worker opposition to the introduction of heightened monitoring activity. Conflicts might also arise over the content of given monitoring signals. If monitoring is imperfect and not equally observable by supervisors and employees, there may be sharp disagreements with regard to firms' decisions to penalize individual workers observed to provide inadequate effort.

To take an instance from US industrial history discussed earlier in the text, conflict over the distribution of information-based rents is a plausible explanation for worker opposition to "Taylorist" or "scientific management" schemes introduced by firms in the late nineteenth and early twentieth centuries. A frequent complaint of employers in this era was that workers colluded to restrict work effort, a practice known as "systematic soldiering."[2] A major part of employers' motivation for the use of "time and motion studies" and close supervision of the details of the labor process was to determine the true link between work intensity and output, and thus to break up workers' informational monopoly regarding certain key aspects of production conditions.

Furthermore, as Taylor himself acknowledged with some frustration, employers frequently yielded to the temptation to use their newly acquired information to "cut the piece rate" and thus reduce the (quasi-) rents paid to their workers. Indeed, worker opposition is usually cited as one of the key factors prompting the decline of "scientific management" in US manufacturing.

Let's bring the theoretical discussion to a close by drawing together the different threads of the argument. The basic result is that employers may gain from supervising work production activities when work effort is not costlessly inferable from output levels and workers are risk averse or wealth-constrained. If monitoring is cost effective, employers would then presumably desire to use all informative signals in structuring incentives for their workers. Exceptions to this rule arise when (1) agents perform multiple tasks and monitoring signals are not correspondingly comprehensive in scope; (2) monitoring signals are not verifiable by external enforcement agencies; or (3) workers oppose monitoring on redistributional grounds when used to address situations of hidden effort combined with private information.

These theoretical considerations can be linked back to the three-part taxonomy of compensation structures introduced near the beginning of the chapter by using them to identify hypothetical scenarios under which each compensation form is most likely to flourish. This exercise yields the following predictions:

- Output-based compensation schemes such as piece rates or commissions are most likely to be used when work effort is difficult to observe directly but yields verifiable indicators of performance that are not significantly distorted by random noise factors. For example, commissions paid to new car sales personnel fit these conditions, especially if misrepresentation of product information or peremptory treatment of hesitant buyers can be controlled via feedback provided by customer complaints to management. A special case of output-based schemes is simple fees for services rendered, such as charges for office visits to physicians, which is the presumptive case as well under perfect contracting conditions. Use of these schemes is presumptively associated with risk premia for the corresponding risk borne by employees.

- Compensation based on supervisory assessments of performance is most likely when individual effort is not easily connected to output, as in the case of team production, and with little cost monitoring yields informative signals that can be verified using the rules of evidence applied by the relevant enforcement body. An example might be the use of tangible albeit indirect performance indicators (punctuality, unexcused absenteeism, meeting attendance, rate of assignment completion) in evaluating a middle manager's case for raises or promotion.

- Where compensation schemes feature no direct incentive provisions, as in the case of hourly wages, incentives may be provided indirectly through the threat of termination. These schemes are most likely to be found when worker efforts are not easily connected to verifiable individual performance indicators, these indicators are incomplete, or workers oppose the use of these indicators for procedural or distributional reasons. Alternatively, these schemes might be used when the profit-relevant dimensions of effort are easily regulated, as for instance by setting the speed of an assembly line.

The next section considers how these predictions fare in light of available evidence.

THE CHOICE OF COMPENSATION SCHEME

As much as for any other topic in labor economics, empirical analysis of the role of compensation has involved a race between the supply of relevant data and the evidential demands of an ever-evolving theory. Virtually all studies on this topic lament the paucity of data, even as evident progress is made in accounting for the use and effects of alternative payment schemes. It is not hard to understand why data are hard to come by when imperfect information is at the heart of the phenomena under investigation. In the final analysis, empirical findings to date should be taken as suggestive rather than as establishing clear-cut support for the choice-theoretic analysis of compensation forms. Some of the key findings are summarized below.

The incentive effects of compensation

The core hypothesis of the theory summarized above is that the choice of compensation scheme is driven by the need to provide incentives under conditions of asymmetric information. It should immediately be added that this hypothesis is not at odds with the pervasiveness of compensation based on hourly wages or salary, even though these forms provide no direct effort incentives. One possibility consistent with the core hypothesis is that wages or salary constitute the "fixed" or "income insurance" component of pay, which is combined with other incentive provisions such as bonuses, profit sharing, or promotion ladders.

A number of studies have found evidence for the incentive properties of piece rates and other performance-linked payment schemes. For example, Eric Seiler (1984) compared the mean and variance of incomes for otherwise similar employees working under "incentive pay" (including piece rates, commissions, and bonuses) and "time rate" (hourly wage) regimes. He found that employees working under the former regime faced both higher mean and higher dispersion of income relative to hourly wage workers, and attributed the difference in means to both incentive effects and risk premia.[3] These results were corroborated in a subsequent study using more recent data.[4]

Firm's choice of compensation scheme

The core hypothesis here is that employers choose among competing payment schemes on the basis of their relative costs and benefits, given the informational, technical, and market conditions they face. Thus, for example, extreme randomness in output makes the use of piece rates relatively costly when workers are risk averse. The problem researchers face in testing this hypothesis is that they rarely have direct measures of these costs and benefits, and thus must make use of proxies to represent the conditions identified by theory.

For instance, direct measures of the cost of monitoring effort are typically not available, so labor economists have made use of proxies such as firm size (measured by number of employees), arguing that the more employees in a firm, the harder it is to track the efforts of any one employee. On the basis of this postulate, the prediction is that larger firms will tend to make less use of payment schemes that rely on monitoring signals, and rely more on output-based schemes. Evidence in support of this prediction was found in US data by Charles Brown (1990)[5] and Australian data by Robert Drago and John Heywood (1995).[6]

Relatedly, Bentley MacLeod and Daniel Parent (1999) find that the use of commissions becomes more likely relative to salary or bonus schemes in jobs that involve significant worker autonomy.[7] This is consistent with the predictions discussed above if it is difficult to assess the effort of employees who enjoy a good deal of flexibility in approaching their work. Similarly, they find that piece rate jobs are associated with more worker autonomy and fewer tasks performed relative to hourly paid jobs, and that the number of tasks seems to be associated with use of relatively incomplete contracts.[8]

Another central prediction of the theory is that payment schemes based on a single dimension of performance (commissions, for example) become less desirable the more multi-faceted are the tasks to be undertaken by employees. Brown finds strong evidence for this in data on US workers who were asked about various job characteristics that relate to task complexity. Providing somewhat less clear support for this argument, MacLeod and Parent (1999) find evidence that piece rates and commissions are less likely to be used in jobs that involve taking several distinct actions in finishing a "complete task."

Seemingly counter to the basic prediction, however, MacLeod and Parent find that the likelihood of piece rates relative to hourly wages, and commissions relative to salary or bonuses, *increases* with jobs that are described as involving a "variety" of tasks. Adding a new element to the theoretical story, they suggest that this is so because the increased variety of tasks makes it more likely that workers can make "opportunistic" use of unexpected contingencies. The model they construct to capture this phenomenon uniquely predicts that bonuses become more desirable as the *local* unemployment rate increases, and they find clear evidence for this prediction.

Brown finds that the use of hourly wage or salary schemes increases relative to those that depend on monitoring signals other than output, the higher the percentage of unionized workers in an establishment. This is consistent with the argument that monitoring signals create scope for distributional conflict, assuming that workers are better able to pursue their distributional concerns when unionized. Interestingly, though, neither Brown nor Drago and Heywood find any impact of union density on the use of output-based schemes like piece rates.

While these empirical results suggest the relevance of microeconomic analysis in explaining the incidence of alternative compensation schemes, this is clearly an area of labor economics in which more empirical work needs to be done. This is particularly so in light of unsystematic evidence pointing to a recent trend of increasing reliance on performance-based pay. If this trend in fact exists, it would be interesting to explore the economic logic that drives it.

DO FIRMS PAY EFFICIENCY WAGES?

One of the difficulties in testing for the presence of efficiency wages is that one or more of the theory's predictions are also consistent with other models of wage determination based on the effects of bargaining power or the payment of "compensating differentials" for undesirable working conditions. For example, both the cooperative Nash bargaining model and the effort-based efficiency wage model predict that wage rates vary inversely with the unemployment rate and reflect the payment of economic rents.

A second problem in testing the model stems from the possibility of missing or poorly measured explanatory variables in the statistical test. The most obvious example of this is seen with respect to the effort-based efficiency wage model: if employers can't generate verifiable signals of work effort, as presumed by the theory, then it seems unlikely that economists would be able to measure effort more accurately. Thus, it might be that seemingly above-equilibrium wage rates simply reflect offsetting compensation for higher effort or other unobserved job disamenities.

Finally, a third problem arises in distinguishing among alternative versions of the efficiency wage hypothesis. As noted earlier, efficiency wages might also be paid to increase the quality of a firm's employee applicant pool, reduce turnover, or improve general morale. These alternative models yield overlapping but not identical predictions.

For example, a number of labor economists have found evidence of large and persistent wage differentials across industries that cannot readily be accounted for in terms of the competitive labor market hypothesis. This evidence also suggests that wage rates in high-pay industries vary directly with profit rates and extend to *all* employees in the industry, not just those whose work is presumably difficult to monitor. These results are not predicted by standard effort incentive versions of the efficiency wage model, although they are consistent with a model based on the morale-building effects of wage premiums.

A number of studies have dealt directly with one or more of these problems. Carl Campbell (1993) tests for the presence of efficiency wage effects on turnover and worker productivity using firm-level survey data from 1980. He finds that wage rates vary directly with unit turnover costs and inversely with the unemployment rate, as predicted by the turnover-reduction version of the efficiency wage hypothesis. His results suggest, however, that turnover effects are probably supplemented by direct productivity effects of wage premiums. Finally, he explains the universality of high wages in industries found to pay wage premiums by possible complementarities of worker effort with the productivity of highly-skilled workers.

Peter Cappelli and Keith Chauvin (1991) examine data from a multi-plant manufacturing firm to discern an inverse relationship between plant-level wage premiums and the frequency of disciplinary dismissals, understood as a measure of worker "shirking." Although no equilibrium shirking occurs in either the compensating differential or the simple efficiency wage model, some equilibrium shirking will arise in an efficiency wage context if workers are assumed to have heterogeneous preferences and firms only seek to eliminate shirking of the average worker. The use of plant-level data from the same firm allows Cappelli and Chauvin to control indirectly for other unobservable influences on the wage level.

The authors find strong support for the hypothesis that wages vary directly with effort, as indicated by the relative absence of dismissals. They

continued

are also able to rule out the possibility that this relationship arises from the impact of wage rates on the quality of the labor applicant pool, since they find no relationship between dismissals and wage rates *at the time of hire*. The authors caution, though, against drawing conclusions on the evidence of a single, albeit large, firm.

Noting that a long-run correlation between wages and effort is consistent with efficiency wage, bargaining, and compensating differential models of wage determination, Stephen Machin and Alan Manning (1992) note that only the first model predicts a positive link between current productivity and expected *future* wages. On the basis of this distinction, they find strong evidence for the efficiency wage model in firms with low union density, but for the bargaining model of wage determination in firms with high union density. This suggests that the additional wage-setting power wielded in collective bargaining overwhelms possible incentive effects of the wage rate.

Not all investigators find evidence for the existence of efficiency wages. Given uneven findings and the difficulties noted above, it cannot be said that the efficiency wage hypothesis has been strongly confirmed, but nor can it be ruled out on the basis of existing evidence.

Related discussion questions:
1. What variables are predicted to affect wage levels under the conditions of the efficiency wage model but not under perfectly competitive labor market conditions?
2. What data would be needed to determine whether higher wages reduce turnover, as suggested by Carl Campbell, or lower turnover leads to higher wages, say by increasing firm-specific experience?

Related references:
Carl M. Campbell, III, "Do Firms Pay Efficiency Wages? Evidence with Data at the Firm Level," *Journal of Labor Economics* 11, no. 3 (July 1993): 442–70.
Peter Cappelli and Keith Chauvin, "An Interplant Test of the Efficiency Wage Hypothesis," *Quarterly Journal of Economics* 106, no. 3 (August 1991): 769–88.
Stephen Machin and Alan Manning, "Testing Dynamic Models of Worker Effort," *Journal of Labor Economics* 10, no. 3 (July 1992): 288–305.

CONCLUSION

Presumably, all employers have the option of responding to the hidden-action incentive problem by allowing workers to choose their own levels of effort and then paying a wage rate that ensures them the competitive level of utility when their desired effort level is expended. Assuming that employees would choose to work at all, this scenario would correspond closely to that generated by the ideal market model: workers would be wage-takers, the wage rate would be equated to marginal revenue product of labor time, and the labor market would clear in equilibrium.

It is at least equally presumptive that most employers prefer higher levels of effort than would be freely chosen by workers in the absence of any pecuniary inducements. The argument and evidence covered in this chapter suggest that this is the primary reason for the wide array of payment schemes observed in practice. Under a number of plausible scenarios, however, adoption of these schemes implies departures from the exchange outcomes predicted by the ideal labor market model. Long-term employment relationships may dominate spot-market labor exchanges, distributional conflicts may arise routinely in the workplace, and otherwise competitive workers may enjoy economic rents.

Consequences for the nature and operation of labor markets are potentially wide-ranging. In particular, employers' profit-maximizing responses to informational problems of the sort considered in this chapter might create involuntary unemployment, qualitatively distinct labor market segments, and opportunities for efficiency-enhancing governmental interventions in the operation of labor markets. These phenomena and their roots in the issues considered here are discussed in parts IV and V of the text.

APPENDIX TO CHAPTER 10

CONTINGENT RENEWAL AND THE EFFICIENCY WAGE

Imagine a scenario in which bilateral incentive problems prevent the credible use of incentive schemes linking current pay to current output. Consequently, employers must oversee the production process and induce effort through threats of dismissal, *given* a particular level of compensation. Here, a simple model is developed to derive the optimizing level of the "efficiency wage" paid to workers.

Set-up

Worker utility: $U = y - c(e)$, where y is worker income, e is worker effort, and $c(e)$ is the utility cost of effort to the worker, with $c' > 0$, $c'' > 0$ for all $e \geq 0$.

Payment scheme: $y = w$, a fixed wage per production period (due to firms' inability to use team bonuses or piece rates)

δ = the worker's discount factor (a positive fraction reflecting the worker's time preference)

v = the present value to the worker of continued employment with a given firm, measured at the beginning of a new period of employment

z = the present value to the worker of being newly unemployed, measured at the beginning of a new period of (un)employment

u = the unemployment rate (a positive fraction)

s = the intensity with which the employer supervises the worker

$q(e, s)$ = the probability that the worker is found *not* to be shirking, as a function of effort and monitoring intensity; it is assumed that q is increasing and strictly concave in e, and that increasing s reduces the "noise" in the monitoring signal of effort.

The structure of the employment relationship is such that the worker is paid a wage in each period that he or she is employed; if caught expending low effort (which occurs with probability q), he or she is dismissed beginning the *next* period; otherwise the worker continues to be employed.

There are three analytical steps in deriving the efficiency wage:

1. *Incentive condition*

For given levels of z and w, v, and s chosen by the firm, the worker chooses effort level $e \geq 0$ to maximize $U = w - c(e) + \delta \left(q(e,s) \cdot v + (1 - q(e,s)) \cdot z \right)$, with the first-order necessary condition

$$\delta q_e(e^*, s) \cdot (v - z) - c'(e^*) = 0 \tag{10.1}$$

for $e^* > 0$ (which is assumed), where $q_e(e^*,s)$ represents the partial derivative of probability q with respect to effort level e, evaluated for given supervision s and the utility-maximizing level of effort e^*. Satisfaction of second-order conditions for this interior optimum is also assumed.

2. *Derivation of $(v - z)$*

Immediately upon being unemployed, the worker receives a welfare or unemployment compensation benefit b. In the next period, either he or she finds a new job, assumed to occur with a probability equal to one minus the unemployment rate, and receives v, or fails to find a job, (which occurs with probability u) and re-encounters the same situation in the next period. Therefore, $z = b + \delta \cdot (u \cdot z + (1 - u) \cdot v)$.

If market conditions do not change over time, the worker's utility-maximizing effort and the firm's profit-maximizing wage and supervision policy will remain the same, so that $v = w - c(e^*) + \delta(q(e^*,s) \cdot v + (1 - q(e^*,s))z)$. Differencing the expressions for v and z yields, after some rearrangement,

$$v - z = \frac{w - c(e^*) - b}{1 + \delta \cdot (1 - q - u)}, \tag{10.2}$$

which is then substituted into expression (10.1). Given satisfaction of strict second-order conditions, there exists an implicit function $e^* = e(w,s,u,b,\delta)$ which locally satisfies equation (10.1) as an identity. Comparative statics for the implicit function $e^* = e(w,s,u,b,\delta)$ can be derived by differentiating with respect to the indicated parameters. Using either procedure, it can be shown that utility-maximizing effort is increasing in w, s, u, and δ, and decreasing in b.

3. *Derivation of the efficiency wage*

For convenience, rewrite the worker's effort function as $e(w,s)$, and suppose the employer chooses the wage rate w, monitoring intensity s, and labor hours l to maximize profit, given by:

$$\Pi = p \cdot f(e(w, s) \cdot l) - w \cdot l - p_s \cdot s \tag{10.3}$$

where p is output price and p_s is the unit price of monitoring services (ignoring for simplicity's sake the problem of providing incentives for monitoring effort). The associated first-order conditions for an interior solution to the employer's problem are:

$$\Pi_l = p \cdot f'(e^* \cdot l^*) \cdot e^* - w = 0; \tag{10.4a}$$

$$\Pi_w = p \cdot f'(e^* \cdot w^*) \cdot e_w \cdot l^* - l = 0; \tag{10.4b}$$

$$\Pi_s = p \cdot f'(e^* \cdot l^*) \cdot e_s \cdot l^* - p = 0. \tag{10.4c}$$

Equations (10.4a) and (10.4b) can be combined to yield:

$$\eta_{ew} = \frac{w^* \cdot e_w}{e^*} = 1, \tag{10.5}$$

where η_{ew} is the wage elasticity of the effort function. In a similar manner, equations (10.4a) and (10.4c) imply:

$$\eta_{es} = \frac{s^* \cdot e_s}{e^*} = \frac{p_s \cdot s^*}{w^* \cdot l^*}, \tag{10.6}$$

where η_{es} is the elasticity of utility-maximizing effort with respect to monitoring intensity.

The corollary that the efficiency wage is determined independently of output market conditions depends on the assumption that effort and labor hours enter only multiplicatively into the production function. If this is not the case, conditions (10.5) and (10.6) won't hold in general, and the value of the efficiency wage will typically depend on output market conditions.

Study Questions

1. One study discussed in the chapter found that workers who are paid piece rates on average receive higher *total* compensation. Does this follow simply from the proposition that piece rates create more powerful work incentives?

2. How would you explain the dramatic fall in the use of piece rates in manufacturing enterprises over most of the twentieth century?

3. In the simple principal–agent problem discussed in chapter 8, worker compensation might not vary significantly with output due to high degrees of worker risk aversion. What *additional* reason for not having compensation vary significantly with output would arise in the *multi-task* version of the principal–agent problem?

4. In the efficiency wage model based on worker effort, workers' *current-period* compensation doesn't depend on information yielded by monitoring; instead, workers who are found shirking are dismissed *after* the current period of production is finished. How does this result follow from the problem of *bilateral* moral hazard resulting when monitoring signals are unverifiable?

5. Give intuitive explanations for why the level of the efficiency wage is increasing with welfare or unemployment compensation payments but decreasing with the unemployment rate and monitoring intensity.

Notes

1 Keith W. Chauvin and Ronald A. Ash, "Gender Earnings Differentials in Total Pay, Base Pay, and Contingent Pay," *Industrial and Labor Relations Review* 47, no. 4 (July 1994): 634–49.

2 Stanley Mathewson, *Restriction of Output by Unorganized Workers* (New York: The Viking Press, 1931).

3 Eric Seiler, "Piece Rate vs. Time Rate: The Effect of Incentives on Earnings," *Review of Economics and Statistics* 66, no. 3 (August 1984): 363–76.

4 Daniel J. B. Mitchell, David Lewin, and Edward E. Lawler III, "Alternative Pay Systems, Firm Performance, and Productivity," in Alan S. Blinder (ed.), *Paying for Productivity: A Look at the Evidence* (Washington, DC: The Brookings Institution, 1990): 15–94.

5 Charles Brown, "Firms' Choice of Method of Pay," *Industrial and Labor Relations Review* 43, no. 3, special issue (February 1990): 165–82.

6 Robert Drago and John S. Heywood, "The Choice of Payment Schemes: Australian Establishment Data," *Industrial Relations* 34, no. 4 (October 1995): 507–31.

7 W. Bentley MacLeod and Daniel Parent, "Job Characteristics, Wages, and the Employment Contract," *Federal Reserve Bank of St. Louis Review* (May/June 1999): 3–27.

8 W. Bentley MacLeod and Daniel Parent, "Job Characteristics and the Form of Compensation," Working Paper (January 1998).

Suggestions for Further Reading

"Do Compensation Policies Matter?," *Industrial & Labor Relations Review* 43, no. 3 (February 1990): special issue. Contains numerous articles addressing the empirical question of whether variation in compensation policies appears to generate different outcomes.

Canice Prendergast, "The Provision of Incentives in Firms," *Journal of Economic Literature* 37, no. 1 (March 1999): 7–63. Provides an overview of the empirical and theoretical literature.

CHAPTER ELEVEN

EMPLOYMENT CONTINUITY AND INTERNAL LABOR MARKETS

Employment relationships, once formed, often last for a remarkably long time: years, decades, sometimes for workers' entire careers. Continuous employment within given firms for some period is in fact the norm rather than the exception, although turnover rates vary dramatically across labor markets. In general terms, prolonged labor market attachments can be explained as a method of economizing on *employment adjustment* costs, incurred whenever a firm changes the size of its workforce or a worker changes employment status. These costs are consistent with the operation of perfectly competitive markets so long as labor allocation in the resulting long-term transactions is governed by essentially costless means of external or strategic enforcement.

If this is not the case, or if employment adjustment costs coincide with some other form of exchange frictions, then long-term job attachments may be accompanied by phenomena that are not readily explained on the basis of the model of perfectly competitive markets. Of particular empirical relevance in this regard are instances in which firms provide *training* or *earnings insurance* to workers in addition to compensation and workplace amenities. These provisions may be accompanied by administrative rules and procedures for hiring, pay increases, promotion, and termination that are relatively impervious to changes in external market conditions or yield unexpected temporal profiles in wages or employment. Evidence of such phenomena, anomalous from the standpoint of the competitive model, has prompted the hypothesis that allocation of labor in long-lived employment relationships is governed by *internal labor markets* exhibiting a distinctive economic logic and dynamic.

This chapter investigates the economic logic of employment continuity. Following a brief review of empirical regularities with respect to this

continued

phenomenon, the concept of an "internal" labor market is defined and its core hypothesized features identified. This leads to a discussion of alternative explanations for employment tenure and their potential implications for other aspects of labor exchange. The core argument of the chapter is that employment continuity may be associated with exchange frictions generating *ex post* market power, contracting failures, market incompleteness, or some combination of the three. Administrative rules, promotion ladders, seniority protections, and other putative features of internal labor markets might therefore be understood as strategic responses to these exchange conditions.

JOB STABILITY AND INTERNAL LABOR MARKETS

Empirical incidence of job continuity

Overall, there is a strong degree of attachment between given employers and employees. Although consistent and comprehensive data are hard to come by, the average stint of employment at incumbent firms for currently employed workers in member countries of the Organization for Economic Cooperation and Development (OECD) is between nine and ten years. The corresponding *median* job spell across OECD countries is somewhat smaller, about six years, indicating that the distribution of job spells is asymmetric, with a relatively "fat tail" representing a disproportionate number of long-term job spells.

These averages mask significant variations across countries, industries, and employee characteristics. First, there are significant international differences in average job duration among developed economies, as indicated in table 11.1 for a subset of the thirty countries of the OECD. Note that the United States is at the bottom of the scale, with average job tenure of 6.7 years, three years below the group average. Not reported in this 1999 data set is at least one country, Japan, noted for its long-term employment attachments (see related discussion box).

National averages have also changed over time. This is in some instances due to variations in macroeconomic performance, as with Japan in the 1990s. However, this is not always the case. In the 1990s, a boom period for the US, there were indications of significant changes in firm hiring practices that tended to reduce overall job stability, especially for more senior workers. Heavier reliance on "outsourcing" of work and workers, as well as many well-publicized instances of "downsizing" and mass layoffs by major corporations, pointed to a reduction in the average span employees spent with given firms. A number of econometric studies was devoted to gauging the magnitude of this trend, if in fact a trend existed. A comprehensive review of such studies, most of which investigated patterns of job attachment and separation well into the mid-1990s, found consistent evidence of

Table 11.1 Average job duration, selected OECD countries, 1999[1]

Country	Average job tenure (in years)
Australia	6.9
Austria	10.6
Belgium	11.7
Canada	8.1
Denmark	8.5
Finland	10.1
France	11.2
Germany	10.3
Greece	13.3
Ireland	9.4
Italy	12.1
Luxembourg	10.9
Netherlands	9.6
Portugal	11.8
Spain	10.1
Sweden	11.5
Switzerland	9.4
United Kingdom	8.3
United States	6.7

[1] Data refer to employees, except for Canada and Australia where they refer to all persons in employment. Data are from 1999, except Australia and United States (2000), Canada (1998), and Austria (1995).
Source: OECD, *Employment Outlook* (June 2001): 119, table 3.B.3.

reduced job stability in US labor markets, although indications of the likely causes or persistence of these changes were not identified.[1]

Second, there are significant differences in average job tenure across industries and employers. Goods-producing industries tend to feature greater average job tenure than service industries, with particularly high levels of average tenure in mining, utilities, and some types of manufacture, and particularly low levels of average tenure in wholesale and retail trade. Average tenure is systematically higher at large firms (1,000 employees or more) than at small ones (100 employees or less). Moreover, at least in the US, there is some evidence that large firms bucked the 1990s trend toward reduced job attachments. For a sample of firms employing a thousand or more workers, one study found evidence that mean job tenure and the percentage of employees with at least ten years on the job had both *increased* over the 1990s.[2] When downsizing occurred in these firms, layoffs primarily affected the most junior employees.

Third, there are consistent and significant variations in average tenure by worker characteristics. Average tenure increases with employee age, and male workers routinely experience longer average job attachments than female workers. Table 11.2 indicates sizeable differences in tenure between employed

Table 11.2   Percentage of employed US workers in job for ten years or more, by age group and gender, 1973 and 2000

	1973[1]	2000[2]	Change
All workers, by age			
25–34	6.6	8.3	1.7
35–44	28.8	31.1	2.3
45–54	45.1	46.7	1.6
55–64	54.6	53.1	−1.5
Men			
25–34	7.5	9.3	1.8
35–44	35.6	34.8	−0.8
45–54	53.7	50.1	−3.6
55–64	60.3	53.3	−7.0
Women			
25–34	5.0	7.3	2.3
35–44	17.3	27.0	9.7
45–54	31.0	43.3	12.3
55–64	45.1	53.1	8.0

Sources:
[1] US Department of Commerce, Bureau of the Census, *Current Population Survey, Mobility Supplement* (January 1973).
[2] *Statistical Abstract of the United States* (2001): 378, table 588. Data are for employed wage and salary workers 16 years old and over.

male and female workers of comparable age, with men having substantially higher probabilities of long-term job attachment. However, this differential is changing over time, as average tenure may be rising among women as it falls for male workers.

THE DEMISE OF JAPAN'S "LIFETIME EMPLOYMENT" SYSTEM?

On average, Japanese workers enjoy much greater job security than their counterparts in other OECD countries, particularly the US. Median job tenure for male Japanese workers was 10.1 years in 1990, compared to 3.5 years for male workers in the US. While about one in five Japanese workers has been employed continuously by the same firm for at least twenty years, only one in twelve American workers has reached that milestone (Brown et al., 1997, p. 30). Japanese workers are also much more likely to receive training than their American counterparts, especially in the first year of employment.

Japan's lifetime employment system, an integral feature of its industrial reorganization after the Second World War, and further expanded in the mid-1950s, is in part reinforced by court rulings that restrict employers' ability to dismiss workers without substantial evidence that such actions are both reasonable and "socially appropriate" (Brown *et al.*, p. 39). However, there are important qualifications to the provision of "lifetime" employment security in Japan: retirement from long-term positions is mandatory at a relatively early age (55 to 60), and workers must accept transfers and job changes within their companies, even if this involves relocation and personal hardship. Furthermore, only "core" jobs, involving white-collar workers and blue-collar laborers in large firms and constituting between 50 and 65% of total employment, feature lifetime security provisions. Finally, opportunities for long-term employment attachments are much fewer for women than men; in 1990, average tenure for female Japanese workers was 4.8 years, less than half the figure for their male counterparts.

The feasibility of Japan's lifetime employment system depends vitally on the country's commitment to macroeconomic and trade policies that minimize the unemployment rate. Consequently, the system has been sorely tested by Japan's long-term economic woes beginning in the early 1990s. However, in a recent study of Japanese employment trends, Takao Kato (2001) found that employment continuity has been successfully maintained for core positions, with the brunt of downsizing in response to the recession being borne by younger workers, women, and middle-age employees with short tenure.

Related discussion question:
Might the differences in US and Japanese employment systems be usefully ascribed to *cultural* differences between the two countries? What considerations would tend to favor "cultural" over "economic" explanations of these differences, and vice versa?

Related references:
Clair Brown, Yoshifumi Nakata, Michael Reich, and Lloyd Ulman, *Work and Pay in the United States and Japan* (New York: Oxford University Press, 1997).
Takao Kato, "The End of Lifetime Employment in Japan?: Evidence from National Surveys and Field Research," *Journal of the Japanese and International Economies* 15 (2001): 489–514.

The internal labor markets hypothesis

Labor economists whose work defined the first era of the discipline argued that supply and demand analysis was insufficient to capture many of the key institutional features of real-world labor exchange. Case studies conducted by this first generation of labor economists suggested in particular that the allocation of labor within many firms was determined by administrative rules and procedures that were largely unaffected by changes in external economic conditions. These allocative systems came to be known by the term *internal labor markets.*

The following characteristics are generally associated with this designation. First and foremost, internal labor markets (ILMs for short) feature long-term employment relationships in which seniority brings some form of protection against layoffs. Moreover, although there is continuing debate on the magnitude of this effect, there is some evidence of increasing returns to seniority for workers in long-term positions, even after controlling for experience and other human capital variables. Second, job openings in pre-set "promotion ladders" are filled from within the firm except for designated, low-level "ports of entry" for which workers are hired from external markets. Third, wage and employment levels are largely impervious to changes in macroeconomic or labor market conditions.

The existence of ILMs is suggested in part by the presence of significant wage dispersion *within* industries, even after controlling for observable differences in human capital and workplace conditions. One study found that occupational status and establishment identity alone accounted for over 90% of wage variations among blue-collar workers, with enterprise wage differentials registering a similar magnitude relative to wage variations *across* industries.[3] The presence of ILMs is also suggested by evidence of positive returns to seniority within firms, controlling econometrically for observed productivity measures.[4]

These findings shouldn't be taken as *proving* the existence of ILMs, as the observed wage variations might alternatively be explained by unobserved differences in human capital or working conditions. The key question is whether these and related phenomena, such as the observed temporal structure of wages in long-term employment relationships, can be accounted for satisfactorily on the basis of the perfectly competitive model.

Any theory put forward to account for these phenomena would need to satisfy two additional conditions. First, since not all establishments exhibit the features of internal labor markets, the theory must provide a basis for determining when these features emerge and when they don't. As discussed further in chapter 16, many researchers associate the incidence of internal labor markets closely with the distinction between "primary" and "secondary" labor markets, based in part on consistent differences in labor turnover rates. Second, while phenomena suggestive of ILMs are strongly associated with unionization (at least in the US economy), they are not strictly dependent on workers having union status.

Job stability and employment adjustment costs

What accounts for the pervasive incidence of long-term employment relationships? The key point to note with respect to this question is that employment attachment innately involves a two-sided puzzle. Given freedom of contract, the persistence of a given employment relationship implies that at least one party to the relationship gains, and neither party loses, by establishing a long-term association. Further, wherever indentured servitude is illegal, the corresponding presumption is that workers *strictly* prefer job stability, other things equal, while employers at least do not suffer by ensuring it. Thus, when employment relationships persist one must ask why *both* firms and workers choose to maintain them. Once employment stability has been theoretically accounted for, the question then becomes whether the corresponding model of employment relations can address other empirical features of these relationships as well.

Generally speaking, employment continuity can be thought of as an economic response to the existence of *employment adjustment costs*, that is, costs associated with changing a given worker's employment status vis-à-vis a given firm. These costs might be incurred either in initiating an employment relationship or in terminating one. They might be borne by firms or workers or both. Finally, they might be explicit or indirect. In any case, their presence creates incentives to establish long-term relationships to avoid these costs.

What are the possible sources of employment adjustment costs? Assuming the existence of perfectly competitive markets (and thus of perfect contracting conditions and complete markets), these would be limited to conditions that arise subsequent to the initiation of given employment relationships, rather than inhibiting the initial formation of these relationships. Otherwise, the costs in question would tend to undermine the conditions for perfectly competitive exchange.

One example of employment adjustment costs in a perfectly competitive environment arises in the case of *quasi-fixed* labor costs. As discussed in chapter 2, quasi-fixed labor costs vary with the number of employees hired rather than the number of hours they work. Anticipating these costs, a firm wishing to expand production is not indifferent between hiring more workers and using its incumbent force more extensively. Thus it would prefer, other things equal, to establish a long-term relationship with its incumbent workers, with provisions made for variation of work hours according to economic conditions. In the absence of significant exchange costs, these provisions can be made without compromising perfectly competitive market conditions. The corresponding contracts are written to ensure that both parties receive expected payoffs at least equal to their respective best alternative options.

Employment adjustment costs may, however, be associated with other forms of exchange cost that undermine the attainment of perfectly competitive exchange conditions. In that case, long-term employment relationships may feature additional characteristics that are not implied by the competitive model, or are even inconsistent with it. The key analytical question is, again, whether the empirical regularities associated with continuous employment attachments can be satisfactorily accounted for on the grounds of the competitive model alone.

This chapter examines three basic scenarios involving long-term employment that are central to the function of labor markets. The first, and in some ways the simplest, is based on the premise that labor productivity is *match-specific*: good matches of employers and employees yield mutually desirable outcomes, bad matches otherwise. The second scenario features the role of *on-the-job training* in multi-period employment relations and its connection to the *transferability* of training benefits. The third approach starts from the premise that market incompleteness leads workers to seek insurance from their employers against random income fluctuations. The corresponding theory of *implicit contracts* suggests that firms respond to this demand by offering wages that are at least downwardly rigid and giving at least partial protection against layoffs. Since the provision of earnings insurance requires that workers stay with their incumbent firms, this approach suggests a theory of employment continuity as well.

As indicated in previous chapters, provisions for insurance against labor income risk may also create incentive problems when work effort is imperfectly observable. Such conditions imply the need to combine earnings insurance with appropriate work incentives. In this framework, employment continuity can arise from the demands of incentive provision either as a way to minimize workers' exposure to income risk or in response to the strategic obstacles posed by the problem of *bilateral* moral hazard (discussed in the previous chapter). Consequently, the phenomena of income insurance and intertemporal incentives are considered together.

Matching and job tenure

Lasting employment attachments may result from difficulties associated with achieving good employment matches in markets populated by heterogeneous firms and workers. Specifically, suppose that a worker's productivity depends in part on achieving a harmonious match with a suitable employer. For example, workers may be heterogeneous in the sense of possessing idiosyncratic combinations of skills that are effectively exercised only in particular environments.

Of itself, this heterogeneity bears no special implications for the longevity of employment attachments. For instance, suppose mutually suited firms and workers could costlessly sort themselves into distinct and otherwise competitive markets, and their respective qualities were commonly known. Then there would be no more reason for long-term employment relationships in these markets than in a single labor market inhabited by homogeneous buyers and sellers. Therefore, to generate a story about job tenure, this heterogeneity must be combined with some form of matching or mobility costs. Suppose, therefore, that worker or employer types are not generally observable, and that the suitability of a given match can only be determined after workers have been in a particular employment relationship for some period of time. A corollary of this assumption is that would-be exchange partners have no ability to *signal* their types to each other (as in the case of signaling based on formal educational attainment, discussed in chapter 14). For simplicity, suppose that there are only two possible types of match, good and bad, and that all market participants somehow know the *proportions* of types in the market as a whole.

Assume finally that other than being unable to determine the qualities of their prospective exchange partners, labor market participants incur no matching costs, so that everyone takes the going market wage rate, whatever it is, as given. Against this backdrop, consider the optimization problem of an employer search-

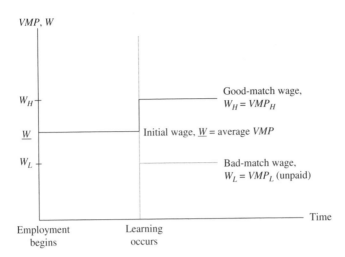

Figure 11.1 Temporal wage profiles given job matching under uncertainty.

ing for a suitable labor force. An employer will seek to hire workers up to the point where the expected marginal benefit flowing from a new hire just equals the marginal cost of the last-hired employee, which in turn just equals the market wage rate.

Generalizing this optimization rule to all the firms hiring workers in this market, aggregate demand for new workers must be based on the *average* value marginal product to be expected from well- and poorly-matched workers, since employers can't tell workers apart beforehand. The equilibrium wage rate is the same for all workers and is determined in the standard way by the intersection of supply and demand. The resulting initial wage rate $\underline{W}$ is shown in figure 11.1.

However, after an initial match, one of two things happens. In the less desirable case, a paired firm and worker discover they have made a bad match, so that the employee's match-specific VMP_L is below the going wage rate. Since both the employer and the employee thus have better *average* market options elsewhere, they agree to terminate the relationship at that point. Alternatively, in the mutually preferred case, the paired exchange partners discover that the match is a good one, and therefore that the returns from maintaining the match are greater than can be expected elsewhere. A situation of bilateral monopoly consequently arises, and thus the distribution of the gains is determined by bargaining. In general, the wage rate W_H paid to well-matched workers will rise, as shown in figure 11.1. (Study question 3 has you consider how strategic bargaining considerations would inform the degree of wage increase.)

Thus, this scenario of matching under conditions of incomplete information yields a theory of job attachment and returns to seniority, such that workers who remain with firms are initially paid less than their value marginal product, and then paid it in all subsequent periods. Note, therefore, that this theory doesn't explain why wages would *continue* to rise thereafter. Yet the data on individual wage profiles suggest that wages do continue to increase with tenure. Thus the theoretical scenario would need further augmentation in order to yield progressively increasing wages. For example, the viability of a match may be a matter of degree rather than kind, and the closeness of a particular match might only be revealed in increments over time.

There is some evidence for the relevance of the matching hypothesis. Indirect support for the matching thesis comes, for example, from a study of the effects of "old boy networks" on job matches.[5] If these networks provide relevant information about the quality of job applicants, they would reduce the need to increase wages subsequent to the creation of a favorable job match. Consistent with this hypothesis, the authors found evidence that workers hired through these networks received higher initial salaries and experienced both lower subsequent wage growth and longer average job tenure than those hired outside the network.

ON-THE-JOB TRAINING AND INTERTEMPORAL WAGE STRUCTURE

Prevalence of on-the-job training

Provision of job-relevant skills to employees, often referred to as *on-the-job training* (OJT), is a common, although not universal, feature of employment relationships. However, data limitations make it difficult to pin down the exact incidence of OJT and how this incidence varies across countries. For the same reason, international comparisons are made on the basis of *formal* training programs, rather than *informal* training conveyed by peer demonstrations and the like.

Available data suggest significant national differences in the average incidence of OJT among employees and in its temporal incidence with respect to workers' tenure with given firms. On the first point, for example, data from 1989–91 indicate that the average incidence of OJT across tenure levels was over 75% of employment in Japan, followed in descending order by Finland, Australia, Norway, the Netherlands, and the United States, which only breaks the 25% mark for workers with over 20 years of job tenure.[6]

There are also sharp differences across these countries in the timing of formal training: whereas Japanese companies train almost 80% of new employees in their first year on the job, no other economy's firms train more than 28% of new hires in a comparable period, and again US firms post the lowest figure at 8.4%. Partly as a consequence, the US experiences the sharpest rate of increase in OJT with the level of employee tenure, the incidence of formal OJT more than tripling to 26.2% for employees with at least 20 years on the job.

Cross-national data also suggest that the provision of OJT varies significantly by firm size.[7] The variation along this dimension is particularly dramatic among US firms: while 96% of firms with a thousand or more workers provide OJT, only 15% of firms with fewer than five employees do so. For the US, the incidence of formal training also varies by sector, with higher levels of OJT in manufacturing and public administration and comparatively low levels in wholesale and retail trade. Finally, unionization is associated with a 40% increase in the average incidence of formal OJT.[8]

On-the-job training and asset complementarity

Human capital theory suggests an analogy between OJT and firm investments in alienable capital stock (e.g., machines, buildings, and patentable ideas) to increase labor productivity. The analogy holds insofar as OJT represents a planned trade-off of immediate costs for prospective future gains. In that light, both forms of investment raise the same question: why does it matter whether the firm itself undertakes the desired investment (as in the case of OJT), rather than simply purchasing capital services flowing from investments made by others (as would be the case if the firm simply hired workers trained elsewhere rather than undertaking OJT)?

A possible answer, discussed below, is based on the *complementarity* of training with the alienable assets used in given production processes. Complementarity implies that OJT is cheaper or yields greater benefits than training received elsewhere. The issue of asset complementarity also arose in chapter 9's discussion of theories of firm ownership. The general prediction of the relevant theory is that asset complementarities have implications for the structure of firm ownership under imperfect contracting conditions, in that complementary productive assets should optimally be owned by the same agents when contracts are incomplete.

This creates a potential difficulty for the analogy between alienable and human capital when labor exchanges are governed by incomplete contracts. If the illegality of indentured servitude precludes ownership of workers by firms, and worker wealth constraints, combined with capital market imperfections (or some other form of market failure), obstructs ownership of firms by workers, then asset complementarities creating incentives for OJT cannot be strategically accommodated by common ownership of assets. A key consequence of this is that workers or firms may opt to sever the relationship after the costs of OJT have been incurred but before the benefits have been mutually realized. As discussed in the following section, this implies that the willingness to undertake OJT, and the intertemporal structure of the employment relationship in which OJT occurs, depend on the degree of *transferability* of these benefits.

To establish a point of theoretical reference, leave aside for a moment the question of why firms undertake OJT at all, and imagine a scenario in which a profit-seeking firm must decide not only how many workers to hire, but also how much to train them. Given the temporal aspect of investments in training, such that costs are borne now in anticipation of benefits to be realized later, the relevant measure of profit in this scenario is given by the difference between the discounted *present values* of revenue and cost streams. In general, both of these magnitudes depend on chosen quantities of labor hired L and training per worker T, as well as the

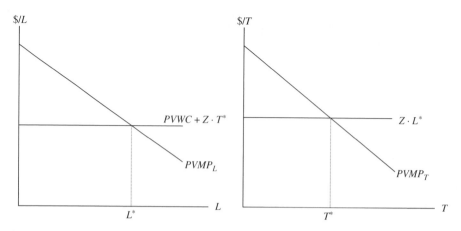

Figure 11.2(a) Optimal employment of
workers to be trained.

Figure 11.2(b) Optimal provision of OJT.

fractional factor δ by which both firms and employees are assumed to discount future costs and benefits.

Next, assume that training imposes a constant unit cost Z per worker and that training only occurs in the initial period of the employment relationship. Suppose in addition that the firm can hire as many identical workers as it wishes for any wage stream with the market-determined present value PVW_C, representing the opportunity cost of supplying labor to this firm over the horizon of the relationship. Finally, assume for the sake of argument that the firm's shutdown condition is satisfied, so that it wishes to hire and train a strictly positive number of employees.

Given these assumptions, the profit-maximizing firm will hire workers up to the point where the present values of the value marginal product of trained labor and its marginal cost are equated, or $PVMP_L = PVW_C + Z \cdot T^*$, where T^* represents the optimal level of OJT per employee and $PVMP_L$ is understood to depend on both T^* and optimal employment level L^*. Similarly, profit maximization implies that the firm will equate the present values of the value marginal product and marginal costs of *training*, denoted $PVMP_T = Z \cdot L^*$. These results, depicted in panels (a) and (b) of figure 11.2, also reflect *efficient* provision of employment and OJT, as the marginal social costs and benefits of employing trained workers are also equated given these conditions.

To capture the relevant features of the temporal structure of the corresponding employment relationship, it is analytically sufficient to focus on the scenario in which the relationship is just two periods long, beginning with period one. Given this further simplification, the first marginal condition above can be written as $VMP_L^1 + \delta \cdot VMP_L^2 = W_1 + \delta \cdot W_2 + Z \cdot T^*$, where the discounted wage stream $W_1 + \delta \cdot W_2$ is set equal to the market-determined value of PVW_C. In this representation, the returns to OJT show up in the relative size of VMP_2, the marginal employee's revenue productivity after being trained. The costs of training show up in two places, the direct cost of training Z and the indirect cost in lost production while the marginal employee undergoes training in the first period, reflected in the diminution of VMP_1 relative to the marginal employee's revenue productivity when not undergoing training.

Notice that this optimization condition says nothing about the relative values of wages in the two periods, and thus offers no prediction about the temporal structure of wages over the course of a given employment relationship. Relatedly, it does not indicate who *ultimately* bears the cost of training. While these costs might *nominally* be borne by the firm, they can effectively be shifted to the worker by reducing the value of first-period wages correspondingly. Note finally that this outcome doesn't reveal which side of the relationship gains on balance from the availability of training. (As an exercise, you might try to illustrate perfectly competitive scenarios in which the absolute gains from training flow respectively to only labor buyers or sellers.)

Whatever the temporal structure of wages, attainment of this efficiency condition is potentially jeopardized by the fact that the productive assets affected by OJT investments are owned by separate parties, the firm and the workers who receive training. In the absence of indentured servitude, efficient incentives for OJT are compromised if there is some positive probability that one or the other party leaves the relationship after training has occurred, reducing the firm's expected marginal returns from training (the expected value of VMP_L^2 declines) or the wage received by trained workers (the next-best market wage is below the value of W_2 offered by the firm). Given the threat of termination, parties to the labor exchange will have less incentive to bear the costs of training, and will thus tend to underinvest in workers' human capital.

This possibility poses no real obstacle to the attainment of efficient OJT given perfect contracting conditions, however. Under this ideal scenario, parties to transactions in which OJT occurs can protect against losses from undesired separations by stipulating contractually that the departing party reimburse the other for any losses resulting from termination of the relationship after training has occurred but before the benefits of training have been mutually realized. For example, if the firm ultimately bears the cost of training, it can require that departing workers pay for this cost as well as the forgone benefits of training to the firm.

For reasons to be explored presently, such ideal contracting conditions may not be attainable in practice. But before examining possible reasons for this, note that even with perfectly competitive exchange conditions, firms are, under the scenario described above, at best indifferent between hiring workers and training them and hiring workers who receive the optimal level of training elsewhere. To see this, suppose workers undertake the costs of training themselves at a separate institution while working for the firm. Presumably, they receive a lower wage in the first period commensurate with the lower productivity while undergoing training. Under competitive supply conditions, they must then receive a compensating wage differential for their training costs, so that the equilibrium discounted wage stream for the two periods, denoted PVW_T, must satisfy the condition $PVW_T = PVW_C + Z \cdot T^*$. It should be clear from the foregoing analysis that profit-maximizing firms facing this discounted wage stream will again choose to hire L^* workers, each with T^* level of training.

Thus, even under (or rather *particularly* under) perfectly competitive exchange conditions, profit-maximizing commercial firms have no net incentive to provide OJT, so long as the desired levels and qualities of training can be provided by other agencies (vocational schools, for example) at identical costs. For firms to have a positive direct or indirect incentive to provide OJT, there must consequently exist some form of *complementarity* between training and the firm's alienable productive assets, as noted above. A simple case of this complementarity arises if employees can economize on transportation costs by receiving their training at the workplace. More subtly, complementarity exists if relevant production techniques are most effectively conveyed through demonstrations by the firm's own managers or incumbent employees using its own equipment.

Whatever the source, the existence of such complementarities implies that firms can provide more cost-effective training to their own employees, making it possible to raise wages or profits or both. This provides a possible theoretical basis, consistent with the operation of perfectly competitive markets, for the empirical incidence of OJT. The caveat made earlier still applies, however: the corresponding theory makes no prediction whatsoever about the temporal structure of wages or the responsiveness of this structure to market conditions. To address these and related phenomena, it is necessary in addition to posit the existence of significant enforcement costs and resulting contractual incompleteness.

Incomplete employment contracts and the transferability of training benefits

The ideal contracting conditions presumed in the perfectly competitive model of labor markets are unlikely to obtain in practice with respect to the allocation of OJT. While contractual provisions requiring departing workers to pay for the costs of their training are not unheard of, these provisions are in any case much rarer than the incidence of OJT. There are several possible reasons for this. First, the successful acquisition by workers of skills imparted by OJT may not be verifiable by external enforcement agencies. Consequently, these agencies could not effectively adjudicate a situation in which a firm fires an incumbent worker for nonperformance and then demands reimbursement for training costs. Second and relatedly, other possible grounds for dismissing workers, such as inadequate work effort, may be similarly unverifiable. Third, it may be difficult to verify if firms have actually provided the skills sought by workers, or if they are of the form or quality advertised by employers.

Suppose, therefore, that labor transactions involving OJT are governed by contracts that do not specify the terms of trade for all possible contingencies, particularly those in which one or both parties terminates the relationship after the training period. Under such conditions, the intertemporal structure of wages and the corresponding incidence of training costs will generally depend on the *transferability* of skills imparted by training. Skills are transferable to the extent that they can be gainfully employed at firms other than those at which the skills were acquired. Transferable skills can be "poached" by outside firms offering trained workers wage inducements to change jobs, thus reducing incumbent firms' incentives to undertake OJT.

Broadly speaking, there are two obstacles to transferability. The first is technological: by their nature, some skills are *specific* to the firm at which they're acquired, as for instance when they are relevant only to the particular production process used by a given firm. In contrast, skills are said to be *general* if they lack any element of firm-specificity. Basic literacy and numeracy are examples of general skills because their usefulness is not limited to a single employer. Second, the transferability of skills may be inhibited by imperfectly competitive labor market conditions. For example, an incumbent firm's monopsony power is reflected in the fact that members of its labor force cannot readily gain access to comparable alternative employment.

To see the implications of transferability for the temporal structure of wages under imperfect contracting conditions, suppose initially that contractual incompleteness is limited to the firm's inability to demand reimbursement for costs and forgone benefits of training in the event that workers elect to change jobs after participating in OJT. Consequently, firms can assure newly hired workers that their wage stream just equals their opportunity cost PVW_C, no matter what the temporal structure of wages offered by the firm, but cannot impose any costs on workers who depart after receiving OJT. As a point of reference, first consider the polar case in which the skills acquired through OJT are *completely* transferable. This implies that the skills imparted by OJT are general rather than firm-specific, and that trained workers face no obstacles to using their newly acquired skills to equally good effect at other firms.

Consider the implications of this scenario in light of the profit-maximization condition $VMP_L^1 + \delta \cdot VMP_L^2 = W_1 + \delta \cdot W_2 + Z \cdot T^*$. Under the specified conditions, workers can command a wage rate equal to VMP_L^2 in the competitive labor market once they've been trained, so that firms providing OJT must set $W_2 = VMP_L^2$ to keep trained workers from leaving. Substituting this into the profit-maximization condition yields the implication that $W_1 = VMP_L^1 - Z \cdot T^*$, which is to say that, in this case, workers will pay for the full direct and indirect costs of training through lower wages in the initial period of employment. This suggests in turn an upward-sloping temporal wage structure, illustrated in figure 11.3, such that workers are paid less than their value marginal product in the initial period and exactly their value marginal product in the latter period.

Now suppose instead that the skills imparted by OJT are completely firm-specific, so that the marginal revenue productivity of trained workers outside of their incumbent firms is the same as before they were hired and trained. Denote this initial level of revenue productivity by VMP_L^0, noting that it satisfies the relationship $VMP_L^1 < VMP_L^0 < VMP_L^2$ if, as assumed earlier, there are both benefits from

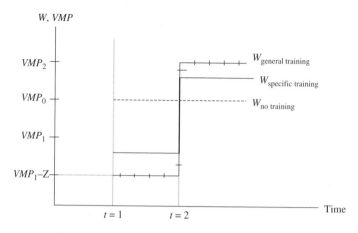

Figure 11.3 Temporal wage profiles under alternative training scenarios.

OJT and indirect costs from forgone production while workers undergo training. Under competitive market conditions, workers would command the wage rate $W_0 = VMP_L^0$ upon leaving a firm in which firm-specific OJT was provided.

What are the implications of this scenario for the temporal structure of wages? The key point here is that the provision of firm-specific OJT creates *quasi-rents* in the final period of the relationship, so the question becomes how these quasi-rents are to be distributed. Supposing that a given firm is free to set wages however it wants so long as it guarantees workers the present value of their competitive wage stream PVW_C, it will want to set the wage in period two above workers' alternative wage rate in order to ensure that they remain with the firm after receiving OJT. By the same reasoning, incumbent workers will want the firm to receive some of the quasi-rents in order to secure its interest in maintaining the relationship.

These arguments taken together yield the prediction that second-period wages will be set such that $VMP_L^0 < W_2 < VMP_L^2$. This implies in turn that $W_1 > VMP_L^1 - Z \cdot T^*$, which is to say that firms and workers share the cost of OJT in the case of firm-specific human capital. This outcome, also illustrated in figure 11.3, suggests that firm-specific OJT corresponds to a smaller intertemporal wage gradient than in the case of OJT involving purely general skills.

Note that an argument exactly parallel to the preceding one can be made for the scenario in which the transferability of skills acquired through OJT is limited by the monopsony power of incumbent firms rather than the specificity of skills imparted by training. For example, suppose workers receive training in general skills but face exit costs if they leave, with the consequence that the value of their outside payoff falls strictly below VMP_L^2. In that case, the same considerations as above suggest that workers will receive a wage somewhat above their best alternative in period two, and share the cost of training with employers in period one. Thus, the general prediction yielded by the foregoing arguments is that contractual incompleteness yields an upward-sloping temporal wage profile associated with the provision of OJT, such that the gradient of that profile is positively correlated with the transferability of skills thus acquired.

As a final nuance to the theoretical argument, suppose that the degree of contractual incompleteness is such that firms are unable credibly to guarantee workers what wages they will receive in the future. This means that, rather than having workers bear part of the costs of training in the initial period, firms must offer a wage rate at least equal to their alternative market payoff $W_0 = VMP_L^0$. This yields two new implications when combined with the foregoing arguments. First, since workers must still be paid a wage rate exceeding VMP_L^0 in period 2 whatever the transferability of their skills, the optimal temporal wage profile offered by the firm is still upward sloping, albeit less so than in the two preceding cases due to the lower bound imposed on first-period wages. In this case, $W_1 = VMP_L^0$ and W_2 is somewhat higher

Second, and consequently, this imperfection raises firms' marginal cost of hiring labor to be trained, and thus reduces their willingness to provide OJT. Generally speaking, the increase in marginal cost, and consequent negative impact on incentives to provide OJT, depends on the relative bargaining power of firms and workers. Since the second-period wage can't be stipulated by contract, it will in general be determined by negotiation between firms and workers. As you're invited to explore in study question 6 at the end of the chapter, this insight may yield additional predictions about the intertemporal structure of wages associated with OJT under conditions of incomplete contracting.

Empirical determinants and effects of on-the-job training

The empirical incidence and effects of OJT have received extensive scrutiny by labor economists. This literature is too vast to summarize conveniently, but it may be instructive to consider a few studies specifically addressing some of the issues raised in the foregoing analysis. First, with respect to the human capital interpretation of the basis for providing training of any sort, Bartel (1994, 1995) finds evidence that OJT increases worker productivity.[9] She also finds a consistent connection between training and wage growth, consistent with the hypothesis that OJT arrangements are governed by incomplete contracts with respect to the temporal profile of wages. Similarly, a 1992 survey by the US Small Business Administration found that each additional month of on-the-job training leads to a subsequent increase of 6.5 cents in hourly wages.[10]

Acemoglu and Pischke (1999) summarize a large body of evidence that firms engage in, and pay for, general training, consistent with the notion that even general skills may have limited transferability due to imperfectly competitive labor market conditions.[11] One study of general training provided free by temporary help agencies (Autor, 2000) speaks to the role of input complementarities in the provision of OJT, noting that these agencies use workers' response to general skills training to elicit private information about their abilities.[12]

Relatedly, at least one study raises doubts with respect to the hypothesis that general training leads to steeper wage gradients than does specific training.[13] Moreover, the authors find no evidence for the claim that generally trained workers receive lower wages in the training period, suggesting the existence of contractual imperfections that limit firms' ability to credibly commit to specific future wage premiums.

INCOME INSURANCE AND INTERTEMPORAL INCENTIVE PROVISION

Market incompleteness and implicit contracts for earnings insurance

Under perfectly competitive exchange conditions, risk-averse workers could minimize their exposure to random income fluctuations by diversifying their human capital portfolios – that is, working at a variety of jobs – and purchasing insurance against non-systemic risk. If income risks are systemic, say as the result of universal macroeconomic fluctuations, or because enforcement and diversification costs limit the scope for risk mitigation, risk-avoiding workers will have an incentive to seek income "insurance" from firm owners with superior prospects for portfolio diversification. Since employers can only provide this insurance if their employees remain with the firm, this provides a potential explanation for long-term employment attachments as well as the relative invariability of the terms of employment for incumbent workers.

Since explicit agreements to insure against earnings risk are rarely seen, these provisions are described as being provided through self-enforcing *implicit contracts* between workers and firms. Implicit contract theory was initially developed to explain why wages in long-term employment relationships are often invariant to macroeconomic fluctuations. As such, it has applications to the analysis of unemployment, and will therefore be discussed in further detail in chapter 18. For now, the key issues are its implications for the continuity of employment relationships and the logic of wage determination within these transactions.

Insofar as it deals with the phenomenon of earnings insurance, implicit contract theory overlaps with the analysis of principal–agent relationships, discussed in chapter 8. There are, however, at least two key differences in the two approaches. First, while principal–agent theory explicitly assumes that the terms of exchange are governed by externally enforceable contracts, the informal status of these terms in the other theory implies that these terms must be *strategically* enforced by the parties to labor transactions. The theory itself, however, does not incorporate an explanation of how this is done.

The self-enforcement aspect of implicit contracts for earnings insurance raises an issue discussed earlier in connection with the provision of OJT. Presumably workers are always free to leave given employment relationships if they can secure better terms elsewhere. Therefore, implicit contracts could not force incumbent workers to accept wages below available market alternatives. When this feature is built into the analysis, the theory predicts that wages are downwardly rigid but upwardly flexible. This asymmetry is not a feature of the standard principal–agent model because it posits a one-period relationship in which compensation follows the realization of some observable but noisy signal of effort, such as output or revenue.

The second key difference in the two approaches is that principal–agent theory explicitly considers the implications of compensation insurance for work incentives, while implicit contract theory ignores this tradeoff. This is logically defensible so long as one assumes there are sufficiently informative signals about work effort, so that the provision of income insurance can be premised on the credible threat of immediate dismissal for shirking. However, if contractual imperfections extend to enforcement difficulties with respect to work effort, then a complete analysis of income insurance in employment must consider its implications for work incentives.

One hypothesis concerning the provision of income insurance and work incentives in long-term employment relationships, the *efficiency wage* model, was examined in detail in the previous chapter and its appendix. Its implications for the responsiveness of employment levels in these relationships to external economic variations are discussed below. But before addressing these issues, first consider an alternative theory that is in some sense a more immediate extension of the implicit contract framework. This alternative approach features the use of upward-sloping wage profiles and *promotion ladders* to induce work effort.

Increasing wage profiles and promotion ladders

Suppose, therefore, that implicit contracts providing workers with income insurance also impair effort incentives, other things equal. To address the incentive problem, employers may acquire noisy signals of worker effort by monitoring the labor process. These signals are used to induce work effort by threatening workers who are caught shirking with termination. However, workers cannot be made to pay up-front employment fees or bonds due to verifiability and bilateral moral hazard problems. All these assumptions, of course, are consistent with the efficiency wage scenario discussed in the previous chapter.

An alternative hypothesis, suggested by economist Edward Lazear, is that firms respond to this incentive problem by providing employees with a wage profile that increases over time.[14] According to this hypothesis, employees are paid less than their value marginal product initially, but then are eventually paid a wage that exceeds their net marginal contributions to revenue. Given this compensation structure, workers avoid shirking so as to gain access to the higher payoffs later in their careers. If possible, rising wage profiles are combined with mandatory retirement to reduce the efficiency losses from workers extending their careers despite depreciating human capital in order to gain access to the higher late-career wages. This hypothesis is illustrated in figure 11.4.

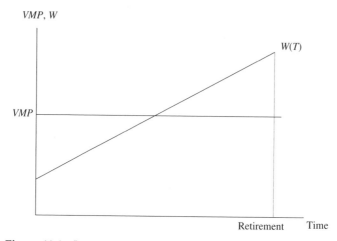

Figure 11.4 Incentive provision with upward-sloping wage profile.

Lazear's model differs from the efficiency wage model in two other key respects. First, and critically, he assumes that employers can credibly commit to the long-term wage structure and to accurate representation of monitoring signals even though doing otherwise would permit replacing high-wage workers with less-paid ones. As discussed in the previous chapter, this assumption makes economic sense only if monitoring signals are verifiable by external enforcement agencies, or, failing that, employer moral hazard in reporting monitoring signals can be deterred by workers through the strategic use of quits. This possibility is not analyzed in the model.

Second, given this assumption, the equilibrium wage profile in Lazear's framework clears the labor market, unlike the excess-supply equilibrium characteristic in efficiency wage models. Consequently, workers do not earn rents as a result of the incentive problem associated with earnings insurance provisions, and there is no involuntary unemployment in equilibrium. This model does, however, imply features consistent with the internal labor markets hypothesis, the first being that internal wage structures are invariant to contemporary economic fluctuations.

In addition, the equilibrium wage profile features increasing returns to seniority. The theory thus offers a potential explanation for the existence of *seniority rules* with respect to promotion and layoff decisions. Since under Lazear's theory workers are eventually paid in excess of the competitive wage, firms have the incentive to replace them with lower-priced labor of equal productivity. Seniority rules, which require that workers be targeted for layoff in increasing order of seniority, inhibit employers from acting on this desire and thus help preserve the incentive property of upward-sloping wage profiles.

One problem with this hypothesis is that the promise of *eventual* wage premia may be insufficient to deter shirking in the *early* stages of workers' careers if they discount future payoffs sufficiently heavily. Other things equal, efficiency wages, which penalize shirking immediately, would be more profitable under such conditions.[15]

Suppose, however, that the production process features multiple tasks, such that workers' productivity levels in these tasks are directly correlated with the difficulty of monitoring efforts expended in performance of these tasks. In that case, it may be more profitable for the firm to assign newer workers to low-productivity, easy-to-monitor tasks, eliminating the scope for early-career shirking.[16] While the resulting equilibrium is inefficient, since workers initially work below their true productivity levels, the corresponding wage profile is market-clearing.

A key feature of this equilibrium scenario is the presence of *promotion ladders* in which pay increases are accompanied by movements of more senior workers from lower- to higher-productivity tasks. In this interpretation, "port of entry" jobs in internal labor markets are those for which monitoring is relatively easy and thus shirking relatively easy to deter. As workers move up the rungs of a firm's promotion ladder, jobs become progressively harder to monitor, but the negative incentive consequences of this are counterbalanced by the upward wage profile.

In sum, the model of deferred compensation as an incentive device provides two key predictions. First, it uniquely provides an explanation for returns to seniority, such that the temporal wage profiles for workers in long-term employment relationships have a steeper gradient than the time path of their productivity increases. Evidence for this outcome is discussed by Abraham and Medoff (1985).[17] A version of the theory allowing for the existence of multiple tasks differentiated by productivity and monitoring difficulty also offers a potential explanation for the existence of promotion ladders in these relationships, reflecting a strictly second-best wage policy that nonetheless still clears the labor market, unlike in the efficiency wage scenario.

Lazear's hypothesis has an additional implication with ramifications for recent legislation in the US banning mandatory retirement provisions in employment contracts (e.g., for professors). According to Lazear's story, workers are encouraged by the promise of future supra-competitive wages to work hard, but they are thereby also encouraged to stay on the job longer than they might if paid commensurate with their true productivity. Mandatory retirement provisions solve this problem by forcing workers to leave at a certain age.

If mandatory retirement is prohibited, upward-sloping wage profiles must represent a less desirable incentive instrument to employers, so one would expect either less frequent reliance on this instrument, or smaller wage gradients over time, in response to the legislation. There is some evidence that this has been the case: after the legislation banning mandatory retirement, a significant number of firms altered their compensation policies, perhaps to reduce the rents that would otherwise have to be paid to older workers who have longer than anticipated careers.

THE NATURE OF EMPLOYMENT CONTINUITY: WHY DOES IT MATTER?

This chapter has presented two visions of the economic logic underlying long-term attachments between firms and workers. In one vision, these attachments are the consequence of efforts to economize on various forms of employment adjustment costs, consistent with the operation of perfectly competitive labor markets. According to a strict reading of this perspective, these attachments are mediated by explicit long-term contracts. A slight variant on this reading allows for the possibility of functionally equivalent "implicit" contracts, enforced by strategic means.

By this first vision, rigidities in the terms of long-term labor exchange that some economists associate with the operation of internal labor markets are more appropriately understood as contractually guaranteed terms arrived at through otherwise prosaic exchange relationships in perfectly competitive *external* labor markets. This would be the implication, for example, of implicit insurance contract models, or of optimal OJT provision in which the future wage stream is guaranteed by implicit or explicit contractual provisions. Were this the case, these provisions would be impervious to variations in the degree of labor or product market competition; for instance, risk-averse workers would still demand earnings insurance from employers even if the latter faced increased competition from foreign suppliers.

At least two studies have found evidence inconsistent with this assessment. Economist Marianne Bertrand (1999) reasoned that if the terms of exchange in long-term employment relationships featuring income insurance were governed by explicit contracts or their functionally equivalent implicit counterparts, then these terms would be determined by market conditions at the beginning of the employment relationship, rather than by variable market conditions after the long-term conditions of labor exchange were already arrived at and written into contracts. Studying data for US workers, she found econometric evidence to the contrary on both counts: using exchange rates to reflect degrees of import competition, she found evidence that increased output market competition *increased* the sensitivity of individual wages to current unemployment conditions, consistent with the operation of spot labor markets, and *decreased* the sensitivity of individual wages to unemployment conditions at the time of initial employment, contrary to the hypothesis of long-term income insurance via explicit or implicit contracts.[18]

Taking a slightly different approach to the same issue, Sandra Cannon *et al.* (2000) inferred from their analysis of US firm-level data that increased competition was associated with *increased* variation (or "decompression") of wages *within* establishments, suggesting increased responsiveness to spot market conditions for different types of workers, and *reduced* variation in wages for given workers *across* establishments, consistent with the notion that firms were increasingly responding to a common set of conditions.[19]

These preliminary econometric results can't be taken as definitive, but they do point to the second major vision of long-term employment attachments discussed in this chapter. In this alternative, employment adjustment costs are accompanied, or perhaps generated, by exchange costs that create imperfectly competitive labor market conditions. If so, then the operation of internal labor markets may reflect something more than simply the manifestation of long-term contracts. But why does this matter? Whatever the departures from perfectly competitive conditions in the labor market, isn't it always socially desirable to have more rather than less competition in labor or product markets?

The answer to the latter question may be decidedly in the negative when labor market imperfections transform employment relationships into noncooperative games characterized by *positive spillovers*, defined as a situation in which increasing the level of one actor's contribution to the relationship consistently increases the payoffs enjoyed by the *other* party (or parties) to the employment relationship (see study question 6 at the end of chapter 6). The existence of positive spillovers establishes scope for the existence of *coordination failures* (arising when positive spillovers are combined with *strategic complementarity*, defined as a setting in which increasing one actor's contribution to a relationship increases the other parties' *marginal benefit* from increasing their contribution) and *prisoners' dilemma* conflicts in labor market exchange.

Under such conditions, increased competition in either labor or product markets may *reduce* the scope for efficient cooperation between workers and firms by disrupting the incentives to establish long-term employment relationships when these are mutually beneficial. Generally speaking, increased competition in the labor market may transform a coordination game with multiple, Pareto-rankable equilibria into a prisoners' dilemma game in which the Pareto-inferior outcome is the sole equilibrium. Alternatively, increased product market competition may either reduce the gains from coordination or the scope for enforcing cooperative outcomes through the use of trigger strategies.

CONCLUSION

This chapter investigates two distinct scenarios in which noncooperative strategic settings with positive spillovers might arise. First, in the case of OJT based on asset complementarities, positive spillovers result from commitments to long-term employment relationships, allowing workers and firms to internalize the gains from these spillovers. If enforcement costs preclude the use of contracts to secure the mutually desirable terms of long-term relationships, a noncooperative setting results. In this setting, increased competition in the labor market may transform a coordination game in which mutual commitment to a long-term relationship with high levels of training is a Pareto-superior equilibrium into a prisoners' dilemma game by eliminating the condition of strategic complementarity.

For example, increased competition on the buyers' side of the market increases the prospects for alternative employments to "poach" the freshly trained employees of an incumbent firm, thus getting the benefits of their training without sharing in the costs, and increasing the prospects for a Pareto-inferior outcome characterized by less long-lived relationships and less training. Note that in this case there is no scope for using trigger strategies to enforce cooperative outcomes; since workers only need to acquire given skills once, the prisoners' dilemma game isn't repeated.

In contrast, there is a repeated prisoners' dilemma aspect to the scenario in which income insurance is accompanied by a bilateral moral hazard problem in which worker effort is imperfectly observable and monitoring signals are non-verifiable. In this case, the respective strategy choices for workers and firms are such that workers can choose either low or high labor effort, and firms can choose either to not bother with costly monitoring and misrepresent their (nonexistent) monitoring signals, or to undertake costly monitoring and report the results truthfully. If this relationship were played just once, then it is readily seen that the only equilibrium involves a combination of low effort from the employee and no monitoring from the firm.

As discussed in chapter 6 and its appendix, however, the Pareto-superior strategy combination of hard work combined with truthful monitoring is attainable as a subgame-perfect equilibrium strategy in the case that the relationship is indefinitely repeated. As demonstrated in the appendix to chapter 6, however, the scope for enforcing cooperative outcomes depends on the relative gains from cooperation. Increased product market cooperation reduces these gains, other things equal, by reducing the rents flowing to cooperating firms and workers. Alternatively, increased labor market competition also negatively affects the prospects for long-term cooperation by increasing the payoffs to one or both players from exiting the relationship, reducing the "punishment" value of the trigger strategy.

In sum, if "internal labor markets" represent a strategic response to labor exchange characterized by imperfect contracting and positive spillovers, then it is not generally the case that increased labor or product market competition unambiguously improves economic welfare. To the contrary, it is then necessary to balance the gains and costs of increased competition. In this connection, it is significant that economies featuring high levels of job tenure and training also have provisions to limit the scope of labor market competition (e.g., job security or layoff notification laws, incentives to avoid dismissals, or centralized bargaining) and, in some cases, product market competition (e.g., through informal trade barriers).

Study Questions

1. What is meant by an *internal labor market* (ILM), and what are possible grounds for thinking that allocations in ILMs are qualitatively different from those that obtain in *external* markets?
2. What is an *employment adjustment cost*? Give examples of such costs arising respectively from competitive and imperfectly competitive labor market conditions.

3. Use the Rubinstein bargaining model to yield predictions as to how the quasi-rents resulting from a good job match are divided between the firm and the worker. In particular, under what conditions, if any, would one or the other actor receive all the quasi-rents? Finally, under what conditions would the return to job tenure (the increase in wages for workers who elect to remain with incumbent firms) be the highest?

4. What does it mean for productive assets to be *complementary*, and why is asset complementarity relevant to firms' decisions to provide on-the-job training (OJT)? Finally, what is the connection, if any, between *asset* complementarity and *strategic* complementarity?

5. What is meant by the *transferability* of benefits from OJT? What is the difference between *firm-specific* and *general* human capital, and how does this distinction relate to the condition of transferability? How does this distinction affect the temporal structure of wages in labor markets characterized by incomplete contracts?

6. In the scenario with OJT in firm-specific skills and incomplete contracting with respect to the wage stream, suppose that wages in the post-training period are determined by strategic bargaining with exit options. Derive the equilibrium wage stream for each possible equilibrium scenario in the strategic bargaining model.

7. Ask five people (of any age over 18, preferably not currently economics majors): *Why do wages rise with job tenure?* (You can give some context before asking the question and define the terms "wages" and/or "job tenure" if they don't understand, but don't provide them with any further discussion of labor economics other than assuring them that it is in fact generally the case that they rise if they are skeptical.) Characterize and categorize their answers. Review the various explanations for the phenomenon presented in this chapter. Do the answers given fit into the explanation categories discussed in this chapter? If so, into which one(s)? If not, how would you characterize those answers that do not fit?

8. How might honest monitoring be strategically enforced in Lazear's model of incentive provision through upward-sloping wage profiles? What would keep firms from dismissing workers once they begin being paid a wage higher than their value marginal product?

9. Using the following normal form to represent an employment relationship characterized by positive spillovers (such that payoffs *a* and *d* are both greater than one), explain how (a) increased competition in the *labor* market might eliminate strategic complementarity and thus change the strategic setting from a coordination game to a one-shot prisoners' dilemma; (b) increased competition in the *product* market reduces the scope for self-enforcement of cooperative behavior in the case of an indefinitely repeated prisoners' game setting.

	Buffy chooses H	Buffy chooses L
Spike chooses H	A, a	0, d
Spike chooses L	D, 0	1, 1

Notes

1   David Neumark, "Changes in Job Stability and Job Security: A Collective Effort to Untangle, Reconcile and Interpret the Evidence," in David Neumark (ed.) *On the Job: Is Long-term Unemployment a Thing of the Past?* (New York: Russell Sage Foundation, 2000): 1–27.

2   Steven G. Allen, Robert L. Clark and Sylvester J. Schieber, "Has Job Security Vanished in Large Corporations?," NBER Working Paper No. 6966 (February 1999).

3   Erica L. Groshen, "Sources of Intra-Industry Wage Dispersion: How Much Do Employers Matter?," *Quarterly Journal of Economics* 106, no. 3 (August 1991): 869–84.

4   For example, Erling Barth, "Firm-Specific Seniority and Wages," *Journal of Labor Economics* 15, no. 3 (July 1997): part 1, 495–506. There is ongoing disagreement about the extent of returns to seniority, however. For example, after controlling for possible specification and measurement biases, Joseph Altonji and Nicolas Williams find grounds for sharp downward revision in estimated returns to seniority. Joseph G. Altonji and Nicolas Williams, "Do Wages Rise with Job Seniority?," NBER Working Paper No. 6010 (April 1997).

5   Curtis J. Simon and John T. Warner, "Matchmaker, Matchmaker: The Effect of Old Boy Networks on Job Match Quality, Earnings, and Tenure," *Journal of Labor Economics* 10, no. 3 (July 1992): 306–30.

6   OECD, *Employment Outlook* (July 1993): chapter 4: "Enterprise Tenure, Labour Turnover, and Skill Training," table 4.8, p. 138.

7   OECD, op. cit.: 139–42.

8   Peter Cappelli, Laurie Bassi, Harry Katz, David Knoke, Paul Osterman, and Michael Useem, *Change at Work* (New York: Oxford University Press, 1997): table 4.2.

9   Ann P. Bartel, "Productivity Gains from the Implementation of Employee Training Programs," *Industrial Relations* 33, no. 4 (October 1994): 411–25; "Training, Wage Growth, and Job Performance: Evidence from a Company Database," *Journal of Labor Economics* 13, no. 3 (July 1995): 401–25.

10 John M. Barron, Mark C. Berger, and Dan A. Black, *On-the-Job Training* (Kalamazoo, MI: W.E. Upjohn Institute for Employment Research, 1997).

11 Daron Acemoglu and Jorn-Steffen Pischke, "Beyond Becker: Training in Imperfect Labour Markets," *Economic Journal* 109, no. 453 (February 1999): F112–42.

12 David H. Autor, "Why Do Temporary Help Firms Provide Free General Skills Training?," National Bureau of Economic Research Working Paper No. 7637 (April 2000).

13 Barron, Berger, and Black, *loc. cit.*

14 Edward P. Lazear, "Why Is There Mandatory Retirement?," *Journal of Political Economy* 87, no. 6 (December 1979): 1261–84; "Agency, Earnings Profiles, Productivity, and Hours Restrictions," *American Economic Review* 71, no. 4 (September 1981): 606–20.

15 George A. Akerlof and Laurence F. Katz, "Do Deferred Wages Eliminate the Need for Involuntary Unemployment as a Worker Discipline Device?," in Yoram Weiss and Gideon Fishelson (eds) *Advances in the Theory and Measurement of Unemployment* (London: Macmillan Press, 1990): 172–203.

16 Kevin M. Murphy and Robert H. Topel, "Efficiency Wages Reconsidered: Theory and Evidence," in Yoram Weiss and Gideon Fishelson (eds) *Advances in the Theory and Measurement of Unemployment* (London: Macmillan Press, 1990): 204–40.

17 Katherine G. Abraham and James L. Medoff, "Length of Service and Promotions in Union and Nonunion Work Groups," *Industrial & Labor Relations Review* 38, no. 3 (April 1985): 408–20.

18 Marianne Bertrand, "From the Invisible Handshake to the Invisible Hand? How Import Competition Changes the Employment Relationship," NBER Working Paper No. 6900 (January 1999).

19 Sandra A. Cannon, Bruce C. Fallick, Michael Lettau, and Raven Saks, "Has Compensation Become More Flexible?," Federal Reserve Board Finance and Economics Discussion Paper 2000/27 (April 2000).

Suggestions For Further Reading

Alison L. Booth and Dennis J. Snower (eds), *Acquiring Skills: Market Failures, Their Symptoms and Policy Responses* (Cambridge, UK: Cambridge University Press, 1996).
Paul Osterman (ed.), *Internal Labor Markets* (Cambridge, MA: The MIT Press, 1984).

CHAPTER TWELVE

EMPLOYEE REPRESENTATION
IN THE WORKPLACE

The idea of representing collective employee interests in the workplace has no evident place in the context of perfectly competitive markets. On one hand, there are no truly *collective* worker interests in given employment relationships under such conditions (other than a collective interest in raising the wage rate), since each competitive worker can fully pursue his or her individual economic interests simply by choosing the optimal feasible bundle of workplace and household consumption goods. On the other hand, representation could have no effect, since the choice of workplace conditions is entirely driven by competitive forces and implemented via comprehensive and costlessly enforceable contracts. These assessments are nicely summarized in economist Abba Lerner's comment that the domain of neoclassical economic analysis is the set of "solved political problems."

However, the microeconomic conditions that give rise to the employment relationship as a unique transactional form also tend to infuse it with an essentially political character. That is, contractual difficulties of the sort studied in the last three chapters create a setting in which issues involving power and distribution, rule-making and adjudication, and the determination of collective interests routinely arise in labor market transactions. Under such conditions, political rights concerning such matters as representation of collective interests gain significance.

At the same time, employment clearly remains an economic relationship involving the allocation of scarce resources in the context of market competition. The salience of political rights is thus modified by the ability of workers to "vote with their feet" in seeking alternative employment.

This combination of political and economic characteristics makes the issue of employee representation in the workplace both analytically interesting and potentially controversial: some labor economists emphasize the role of "exit" to other market opportunities in shaping the terms of labor exchange, while others give positive and normative priority to the role of "voice" within given employment relationships in shaping those terms.

This chapter explores features of the labor exchange that infuse it with political as well as economic features. To understand the nature and impact of worker representation in the employment relationship, it will be necessary to analyze how exchange costs affect the scope for exit and voice in determining employment outcomes, and to consider related strategic issues that arise under imperfect contracting conditions. This analysis is then used to help understand the specific labor exchange institutions of *unions* and *works councils*, the two organizational forms that have most commonly served as vehicles for employee representation in the workplace.

EXCHANGE COSTS AND POTENTIAL ROLES FOR WORKER REPRESENTATION

In effect, there are no costs associated with the key activities of exchange – matching, negotiation, and enforcement of terms of trade – in perfectly competitive markets. Additionally supposing the presence of a large number of potential competitors on both sides of the market, the absence of matching costs implies that terms of labor exchange are determined by impersonal conditions of supply and demand, rather than negotiated on a relationship-specific basis. These terms can then be securely implemented via fully specified, externally enforced contractual provisions, at no cost to the transactors. There is thus no obvious role for representing collective employee interests in the workplace.

This conclusion may be altered fundamentally when exchange activities are costly. This section of the chapter presents a detailed look at the potential functions of worker representation in the employment relationship under imperfect market conditions. This analysis is then applied in the subsequent discussion of the most prevalent institutions of employee representation.

Exit and negotiation costs under collective bargaining

A basic economic conflict arises when both parties to the employment relationship enjoy some power to influence wage levels. This clash generally takes the form of wage bargaining between employers and their employees. Bilateral wage-setting power may arise simply because there are few potential competitors on both sides of the market, perhaps due to collusion among would-be competitors. For example, a single firm may represent the demand side of a given labor market, and all workers in that market may belong to a single union.

However, firm-level bargaining conflicts can also arise in otherwise competitive market settings when there are mutually incurred costs of *exiting* given employment relationships. As you saw in previous chapters, these costs can arise directly from difficulties in seeking or training new exchange partners, or indirectly through the loss of firm-specific investments in human or physical capital. In this case quasi-rents emerge because there are dividends attainable within the relationship that cannot be achieved outside it, once exit costs are netted out.

Firm-level economic conflicts of this sort can be studied using the Rubinstein or Nash bargaining models. In the present context the Rubinstein bargaining model with exit options seems most appropriate, since workers can presumably quit unsatisfactory employment relationships, just as firms can elect to replace incumbent workers. The specific issue to be addressed here concerns the impact of *collective* bargaining by workers on distributional outcomes within the firm. The key point to be developed is that the distribution of rents or quasi-rents within firms may be significantly altered simply by the fact that members of a firm's labor force bargain collectively rather than individually. This is so for at least two reasons: collective bargaining rights tend to reduce the value of employers' exit options and to increase their costs of continued negotiation.

Begin with the former point. At first glance, firm owners and workers enjoy the same property rights within the employment relationship, suggesting that negotiations over the gains from labor exchange are generally joined on a level playing field. In particular, both parties possess the freedom of contract and the right to select their trading partners.

However, this formal symmetry in the property rights of capital and labor suppliers may not translate into strategically equivalent bargaining positions in the labor exchange. The main reason for this is that in exercising their property rights, multiple joint owners of a given firm's capital assets can generally appoint an agent to represent their collective interests in negotiations with employees. For example, the interests of a corporation's shareholders are represented in contract negotiations with workers by its management. This tactic ensures that employees cannot use a bargaining strategy of "divide and conquer" by playing individual firm owners against each other. But workers in that firm do not typically enjoy a parallel advantage simply by virtue of their respective property rights in their human capital; in the absence of explicit collective bargaining rights, employers can wield the threat of dismissing individual workers to gain a strategic advantage in negotiating the terms of exchange for labor services.

The significance of this asymmetry can be seen with the aid of the Rubinstein bargaining game with exit options discussed in chapter 7. As explained there, if the cost of replacing individual employees is small, the firm just receives a payoff that approximates the value of its outside option. Correspondingly, each employee receives a payoff which just exceeds her outside wage by the amount it costs the firm to replace her.

How would this outcome be altered by a requirement that firms bargain collectively with its workers? Effective collective bargaining rights prohibit a firm from replacing individual workers in the process of wage negotiations; it must

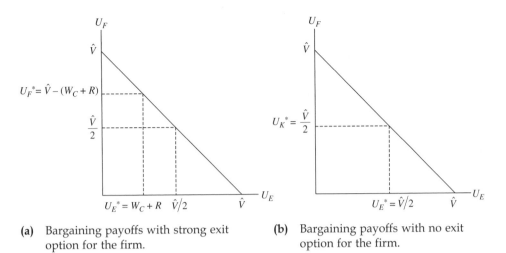

(a) Bargaining payoffs with strong exit option for the firm.

(b) Bargaining payoffs with no exit option for the firm.

Figure 12.1 Solution cases for the bilateral Rubinstein bargaining game under individual and collective bargaining conditions.

either bargain with or replace its incumbent workforce as a group. The impact of this restriction can be illustrated with the aid of figure 12.1.

As a back story for this figure, imagine that a firm with N identical employees (where N is at least equal to two) produces a value added of $V > 0$. The distribution of V is determined by strategic bargaining between the firm owner (or a group of owners assumed to act as a single agent) and the N incumbent workers. Against this backdrop, consider the bilateral bargaining relationship between the firm owner F and a representative employee E, such that the two actors bargain over a net surplus $\hat{V}$ defined as the value added V net of the *equilibrium* wages paid to the $(N-1)$ other incumbent workers, assuming $\hat{V} > 0$. Suppose finally that the firm owner and representative employee bargain sequentially as depicted in the Rubinstein game with exit options considered in chapter 7, and assume for simplicity that discount rates are very small.

Now consider a scenario in which the firm owner enjoys a relatively strong outside option in bargaining bilaterally with a representative employee, equal to the net surplus $\hat{V}$ minus the sum of the competitive wage rate W_C and a small replacement cost R. Then, as mentioned just above, the firm's equilibrium payoff in this bilateral game is just equal to $\hat{V} - W_C - R$, and the representative employee just receives a payoff of $U_E{}^* = W_C + R$, as shown in figure 12.1(a). Since all workers are identical, this must also be the equilibrium payoff to each employee, so the firm owner receives an equilibrium payoff equal to $U_F{}^* = V - N \cdot (W_C + R)$.

But now suppose instead that the incumbent employees are covered by a collective bargaining arrangement that bars the firm from replacing individual employees in the negotiation process. In that case, the firm has no exit option in the bilateral bargaining game with a representative employee. Assuming for the moment that the firm does not exercise its option of replacing the entire incumbent labor force, the resulting bilateral equilibrium is as shown in figure 12.1(b), with each player receiving half of the net surplus $\hat{V}$. Adding the plausible stipulation that identical workers receive the same payoffs in equilibrium, one can show with a bit of algebra that each employee would then receive $\tilde{U}_E = V/(N+1)$ in the equilibrium for the entire bargaining relationship, which strictly exceeds U_E^* given the initial assumption that the value of the firm's outside option in the absence of collective bargaining is relatively high. This implies in turn that the firm owner's payoff, also equal to $V/(N+1)$, is strictly less than that obtained on the basis of individualistic bargaining.

Will the firm owner settle for this payoff? It depends on the cost of exercising its remaining option to replace the firm's entire incumbent labor force. If there are diseconomies of scale in replacing incumbent workers, so that the cost of replacing an incumbent workforce of size N is greater than N times the cost of replacing any individual worker, then the firm cannot credibly threaten to exit the existing employment relationship, and the equilibrium is as described above. Such diseconomies might arise, for example, if the firm must move its entire production operation to a new location in order to gain access to a workforce not covered by collective bargaining laws, or because costs of confusion, delay, and loss of "insider knowledge" associated with replacing *all* incumbents are disproportionately severe.

The first theoretical result, then, is that collective bargaining arrangements increase the wages of a firm's incumbent labor force by eliminating the firm's option of replacing individual workers during bargaining, so long as there is a net surplus to be shared, low cost of replacing individual workers, and increasing average costs of replacing incumbents. But as noted earlier, there is a second potential impact of collective bargaining on wages, arising from the ability of incumbent workers to coordinate work stoppages – that is, to *strike*.

To appreciate this, note that up to this point it has always been assumed that participants in sequential bargaining do not receive their payoffs until negotiations are *completed*. In the context of an employment relationship, this is tantamount to assuming that workers always withhold their productive activity – or what amounts to the same thing, firm owners always "lock out" employees from the workplace – until the terms of employment are fully agreed upon. But this need not be the case, and indeed does not occur in many real-life bargaining situations. For example, some unions bargain subject to a "no-strike" clause that prohibits coordinated work stoppages by employees. Furthermore, employees in collective bargaining units that enjoy the right to strike don't always elect to exercise this right during wage negotiations.

The theoretical significance of strategic work stoppages can be illustrated using the bargaining reaction functions introduced back in chapter 7. For the sake of simplicity, and continuity with the analysis presented in that chapter, assume that there are just two bargainers, a firm owner F and an employee E, each of whom discounts future payoffs by the fractional factor δ per period. Their employment relationship yields an added value of V per period. Again for simplicity, assume

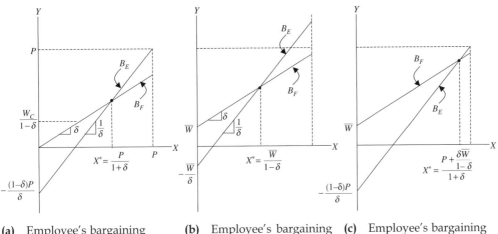

(a) Employee's bargaining payoff with strikes after every period of non-agreement.

(b) Employee's bargaining payoff with no strikes.

(c) Employee's bargaining payoff with strikes only after firm's rejection of employee's offer.

Figure 12.2 Bargaining consequences of the power to strike.

that the production relationship, once begun, lasts forever, so that the present value of the stream of value added once production begins is $P = V/(1 - \delta)$, and also posit that once agreement is reached, the negotiated bargaining shares hold for the remainder of the relationship.

Let's start with the familiar case of sequential bargaining with discounting and no exit options, this time with the proviso that this corresponds to an employment setting in which the worker elects to strike in *every* bargaining period that fails to yield agreement. This outcome is illustrated by the intersection of bargaining reaction functions B_F and B_E in figure 12.2(a), and resembles the bargaining equilibrium shown in figure 7.2(c), the only differences being that the players have a common discount factor and bargain over P rather than V. The equilibrium payoff to worker E, who is assumed to initiate bargaining, is thus $U_E^* = P/(1 + \delta) = V/(1 - \delta^2)$. Note this outcome is unchanged if the employee were to have an outside option with present value $W_c/(1 - \delta)$, so long as the competitive wage W_c is small relative to V.

Now contrast this outcome with two alternative scenarios, one in which the employee does not enjoy the right to strike, and one in which the employee has this right and exercises it strategically to maximize his or her equilibrium payoff. The first scenario, then, is one in which production occurs in each period even if bargaining has not been successfully concluded. Therefore imagine that *in each period* in which agreement is not yet reached, the employee receives a "default" wage of $\overline{W}$ and the employer gets the remainder, $V - \overline{W}$. Otherwise, bargaining proceeds as before.

How does this modification change the bargaining reaction functions? First, it should be intuitively clear that the cost to E of rejecting an offer from F and thus continuing negotiations is smaller, since the employee now receives an immediate payoff of $\overline{W}$ before making a counteroffer. By the logic explained in chapter 7, this causes F's bargaining reaction function B_F to shift upward by the amount $\overline{W}$. Taken alone, this would cause E's equilibrium payoff to increase. By parallel reasoning, however, E's bargaining reaction function B_E also shifts upward by the amount $(V - \overline{W})/\delta$, since the employer's cost of rejecting a standing offer also declines. This pushes E's equilibrium payoff back downward.

What is the net effect of these changes? The new equilibrium, illustrated in figure 12.2(b), is such that the employee receives a payoff of $\overline{W}/(1 - \delta)$, tantamount to receiving the default wage in every future period. To appreciate the significance of this, suppose that the default wage just equals the competitive wage W_c. Then, lacking the power to strike, the employee just receives the competitive wage rate forever after!

This stark result would be modified slightly if there were distinct costs of continued bargaining – for example, a fixed cost C incurred by each player for each additional round of bargaining. In that case it could be shown that the employee receives an increment over the default wage equal to a fraction of this fixed cost. But supposing this cost to be small relative to the value added by production, the basic conclusion remains the same: absent the power to strike, the employee doesn't enjoy significant bargaining power, even if future payoffs are discounted. This result carries over to the case of multiple workers engaged in collective bargaining, although the latter arrangement may still increase wages by restricting employers' exit options.

Finally, suppose that employee E enjoys the right to strike, and exercises this right *strategically* to maximize the equilibrium wage. It should be clear from the two preceding cases that the employee's bargaining position can be improved by electing to strike after the *firm* rejects an offer, but not after the employee rejects an offer by the firm. This selective work stoppage strategy implies that only the firm's reaction function B_F shifts up, leading to an unambiguous increase in E's equilibrium payoff relative to the scenario in which the employee strikes in every period that agreement is not reached. This can be seen by comparing the outcomes in figures 12.2(b) and 12.2(c). Furthermore, electing to strike only in periods that the firm rejects an offer is in fact the wage-maximizing strategy.

The foregoing argument demonstrates a second key theoretical result concerning the impact of collective bargaining arrangements on equilibrium wages: assuming that quasi-rents exist, the right to strike increases employee payoffs, and the magnitude of this increase depends on the extent to which employees are able to exercise this right strategically. Of course, an exactly symmetric result obtains concerning the impact of "lockouts" imposed by employers, but the point is that firm owners generally enjoy this power in any case, while the capacity to strike may depend on the explicit grant of collective bargaining rights to employees.

Joint consumption of employment amenities

The foregoing analysis was constructed on the assumption that all employees want the same thing from an employment relationship: higher wages. While this certainly makes sense, in most cases there are a number of other aspects of employment besides the level of monetary compensation that employees care about. For example, a typical employee may also be concerned about the variability of compensation in response to market conditions, the level of job safety, the geographical proximity of the job site, the average temperature, noisiness, and ambient air quality in the office or factory, the provision of in-kind benefits, the availability of vending machines or rest areas, and so on. If employment-related amenities are costly to provide, then tradeoffs must be made in determining the particular mix of such goods to be offered by given firms. What if employees disagree as to how these tradeoffs should be made?

This is not a problem if markets sufficiently approximate the perfectly competitive ideal. For example, if all of the various non-pecuniary amenities of employment could be traded in any amount (that is, markets are sufficiently complete) at a commonly available set of prices (that is, markets are sufficiently competitive), then the standard marginal conditions of optimization analysis would imply that all employees for a given firm would have the same marginal rate of substitution across the amenities it provides, so that no basis for collective disagreement could arise. To put this point another way, individual workers would face identical price ratios but different budget constraints for these goods. As a result, employees in a given firm can focus on the common goal of raising compensation, consistent with the analysis in the previous section.

But there are at least two reasons why ideal market conditions might not be attainable in the allocation of workplace amenities. First, some goods, like the temperature or noise levels in a factory, are by their nature jointly consumed by everyone who works in the factory, and thus can't be individually adjusted at the margin. Second, the presence of significant transaction costs may imply that some amenities cannot be effectively traded, rendering markets incomplete. If, in addition, mobility costs preclude workers from fine-tuning their consumption of employment related goods by holding a "portfolio" of part-time jobs, then all employees for a given firm face choices along the same budget line, albeit with widely different marginal rates of substitution with respect to the employment-related amenities offered by the firm. For example, employees may not be able to buy individual health insurance policies at the same rates as are available in employer-provided group plans, and if they choose the latter they may all be required to sign up for the same plan.

What role for collective worker representation, if any, is suggested by this possibility? To answer this question, it is necessary to compare the respective choices among bundles of employment-related goods that would be made by a profit-maximizing employer and by the workers in a given collective bargaining unit or a representative appointed by them. To simplify this comparison, begin by assum-

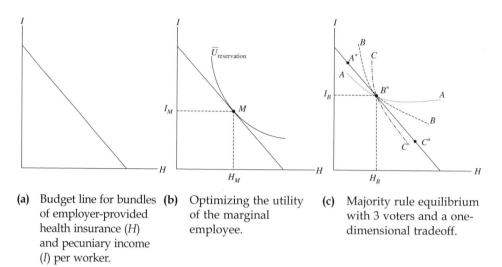

(a) Budget line for bundles of employer-provided health insurance (*H*) and pecuniary income (*I*) per worker.

(b) Optimizing the utility of the marginal employee.

(c) Majority rule equilibrium with 3 voters and a one-dimensional tradeoff.

Figure 12.3   Choice of compensation structure by profit-maximizing firm and collectively bargaining employees.

ing that there are just two such goods, say, the level of pecuniary compensation and the provision of health insurance through an employer-specific group plan, and that the monetary value of total worker compensation, including in-kind benefits, has already been determined. These assumptions suggest that all employees of a given firm face the budget line illustrated in figure 12.3(a).

First consider what point along this budget line would be chosen by a profit-maximizing employer. To determine this, recall that profit maximization implies, on one hand, minimization of input costs, and on the other, the hiring of a given input up to the point of equating its marginal revenue productivity and marginal cost. Putting these two implications together in the present context implies that a profit-seeking employer would choose the compensation structure that reflects the preferences of the *marginal* employee, that is the worker (or set of workers) who is just indifferent between working for the firm or not. This outcome is illustrated at point M in figure 12.3(b). If the firm did not do this, then it must either pay marginal employees more or do without their labor services, leading in either case to lower profit.

Now consider the collective choice of presumably heterogeneous workers in the firm's labor force, assuming, plausibly enough, that this choice is to be determined by majority rule. It is not difficult to see that any choice consistent with this voting rule must optimize the utility of the worker with *median* preferences, with equal numbers of workers wanting to move respectively up and down the budget frontier and thus cancelling out each others' votes. If the preferences of this median voter were not satisfied at a given point on the budget line, then necessarily a majority of workers would favor moving away from that point, so that it could not constitute an equilibrium subject to the majority voting rule.

The median voter equilibrium is illustrated in figure 12.3(c) for the simple case in which there are just three workers with differing marginal rates of substitution between pecuniary and in-kind compensation. At the equilibrium allocation, worker A has a relatively flat marginal rate of substitution and would thus prefer a greater proportion of pecuniary compensation (say at point A*), while worker C has a relatively steep marginal rate of substitution and would thus prefer a smaller proportion of pecuniary compensation (say at point C*). Only worker B is fully satisfied, since the selected allocation B* maximizes her utility subject to the constraint that the total dollar value of compensation is fixed.

Could the choices of the firm's marginal and median-preference workers ever be identical? Perhaps, but this outcome could in general only be assured by very special market conditions. One such scenario is that workers can sort themselves across firms so precisely that in equilibrium all employees of a given firm have identical preferences, and are thus *all* "median" voters. A second possibility is that all employees are just indifferent between working for the firm or not, and thus equally "marginal." Outside of these highly restrictive scenarios, however, the choices of median and marginal employees will differ, implying that most of a profit-maximizing firm's employees would generically prefer to alter its selection of workplace goods.

The foregoing analysis would be significantly complicated if there were more than just two costly employment-related goods to decide among (say, workers cared about the degree of job safety in addition to wage and benefit levels). As you'll be invited to demonstrate in one of the end-of-chapter study questions, a "median voter" may not even exist in such settings, so that it is difficult to say, even in principle, what bundle would be chosen collectively by workers. However, it is unlikely that adding this additional degree of complexity would cause the choices of the firm and its workers to overlap, so that the foregoing conclusion about the potential role of worker representation would presumably be maintained.

Worker representation in rule enforcement

Another way in which worker representation might affect turnover and related issues in the employment relationship arises from the enforcement of rules imposed by firms to promote work incentives. In this context, the role of worker representation is similar to that which arises in the defense of individuals accused of crimes in judicial proceedings. Relatedly, workers might use representatives to pursue complaints with firm actions in much the same way that suits are brought to address violations of civil law. In both cases, semi-judicial procedures within the firm serve as substitutes for court proceedings in settling disputes.

In the US, workers not covered by collective bargaining agreements authorized by the Wagner Act of 1935 are employed "at will," which is to say that in principle they can be fired by their employers for any or no reason. Although this principle has been subject to various modifications and challenges, for instance due to developments in legal remedies for discrimination, it is still a basic tenet of employment law. This means, for example, that firms are free to use the threat of firing to spur greater work effort from their employees, or to maintain workplace discipline in other ways that are judged to affect the interests of firm owners.

One instance of this incentive device is provided in the efficiency wage model discussed in chapters 10 and 11. In this scenario, workers are threatened with firing if they are observed by supervisors to expend less than some stipulated level of effort. The key here is that the exercise of the firing threat depends on the testimony of supervisors, without any external check on the reliability of supervisors' observations or interpretations of worker actions. There is the possibility, as in all uncertain events, that in this situation workers might be faced with dismissal on the basis of inaccurate information or non-work related motives of particular supervisors.

Under the Wagner Act, in contrast, workers covered by collective bargaining agreements can only be fired "for cause," that is, some basis that is accepted or negotiated as legitimate by parties to the agreement. This stipulation discourages firms from using firing to increase their bargaining power via the strategic logic discussed earlier. Under this provision, workers can challenge attempts to fire or otherwise penalize them for alleged misdeeds. A standard framework for pursuing these challenges is the "grievance procedure" in collective bargaining arrangements, which may be entirely internal to a given firm's governance structure or else end up in externally provided arbitration or mediation proceedings.

Representation in enforcement proceedings has at least two consequences for workers' welfare in the employment relationship. First, representation may reduce the probability of unjustified firings or other penalties. These can arise for two reasons: on one hand, when observations of worker effort are noisy, there is always some probability that supervisors will make "Type II" statistical errors in which they judge that inadequate work has been done even when it hasn't. In this case a grievance procedure might be used to bring contrary evidence concerning the charge that a worker has shirked. On the other hand, supervisors may have personal reasons for dismissing or otherwise penalizing subordinates which do not represent the interests of firm owners, let alone workers. The requirement to show cause before imposing given penalties may alone be sufficient to deter this type of supervisory misconduct.

Second, although the phenomenon is not typically incorporated in economic models, workers may place an intrinsic value on being treated fairly by employers. In this case workers may favor representation in quasi-judicial proceedings in the workplace because it reduces the chance that their concerns will be dealt with in an arbitrary fashion. On this point, there is some evidence from industrial history that workers care about issues of fairness in employment relationships, to the extent that they are willing to expend economic resources (say, by striking in protest of particular actions) to battle what they perceive to be arbitrary or unfair treatment.

Worker participation in firm-level decision making

Institutions of worker representation may also be important in ensuring that employees' views are taken into account in firm-level decisions. For example, workers may gain special insights into the logic of problems arising in production that are not available to managers who are a step or more removed from the shop floor. Participatory decision making may help increase the chance that these insights are conveyed to the firm's management.

But why is a formal structure needed to guarantee that workers' views are heard? Wouldn't it necessarily be in a firm's interest to elicit relevant information from employees before making crucial production decisions? There are at least two reasons why this conclusion is not assured.

First, managers may have personal motives not to consult workers in reaching decisions. They may feel that they are better trained to acquire and assess the relevance of information than their workers, or may have an egotistic stake in autonomous decision making, feeling that to allow worker participation is to reduce managerial control over the workplace. In this case a formal structure of worker participation ensures that any such arbitrary motives are overcome.

Second, workers may not volunteer relevant information if they see no immediate reward in doing so and have no long-term commitment to an employment relationship in which their views might regularly be sought. In this event, forms of worker representation that reduce turnover or the prospects of improper dismissal can bolster incentives for workers to share information.

Forums for eliciting workers' views on production matters do not in and of themselves ensure that these views will be acted upon. For that reason it may also be desirable to include workers in the process of making production decisions, an arrangement known as *codetermination*. In Germany, for example, it is legally mandated that establishments over a certain size must formally include workers in decision making processes.

Institutions of worker representation may also facilitate the flow of information from managers to workers. In many cases management has special access to information that can help workers assess the legitimacy of particular decisions. For example, management may be better informed than workers about market conditions for the firm's product that provide the economic rationale for layoffs or additional hires.

Again the question arises as to why formal institutions of worker involvement are required. Why can't owners or managers simply convey the relevant information to the firm's workers as necessary? The key issue here is the credibility of information thus transmitted, given the potential for firm-side moral hazard. For example, a firm may have a bargaining interest in convincing its workers that economic times are bad in order to induce them to accept lower wages. In such cases a formal mechanism may be needed to ensure that the firm isn't opportunistically misrepresenting information.

One way to do this is to guarantee workers access to the firm's accounting data. If workers or their representatives can always verify a firm's true financial picture, the potential for misinformation is eliminated. The downside, from the firm's point of view, is that workers are thereby given a corresponding bargaining advantage when the market for the firm's product is favorable: if this information is reliably available to workers as well, they can use it to insist on higher wages in good economic times.

The foregoing argument suggests that exchange costs that give rise to employment relationships may also create a role for representation of collective worker interests in production. This representation may have both distributional and efficiency consequences, which may help explain why formal structures of worker representation in capitalist economies are most robust when their existence is legally guaranteed. Where not, opposition by firm owners or managers may threaten their long-term viability.

Of all the formal organizational forms that might be used to implement worker representation, two have played a particularly important role in developed economies: trade unions and works councils. Their incidence, however, is neither universal nor constant over time. Works councils, which ensure workers a voice in firm-level decision making, are prevalent in Western Europe but uncommon elsewhere. While unions are a typical feature of most market economies, they do not enjoy the same legal status in all cases, and partly for this reason flourish in some countries even as union membership declines in others. The United States, in particular, has seen a dramatic decline in union membership since the 1950s. The next step in the analysis is to consider how the theoretical issues discussed above are manifested with respect to these institutions.

THE (ELUSIVE) BENEFITS OF EMPLOYEE PARTICIPATION

A large and growing empirical literature in economics supports the idea that worker participation in production is beneficial, but there is little or no consensus on the nature, extent, or determinants of these benefits. Surveying extant studies on the topic, David Levine and Laura D'Andrea Tyson (1989) find consistent support for the hypothesis that participation yields positive but small contributions to productivity, especially when it involves substantive worker decision making rights with respect to shop-floor issues, and almost no evidence of negative effects from participation. The evidence also leads them to conclude that participation is most likely to succeed if supported by an industrial relations system that features sharing of productivity gains, long-term employment relationships, significant group cohesion, and guaranteed individual rights of workers.

Analyzing data from a survey of forty firms, Michael Conte and Jan Svejnar (1990) find econometric evidence for significant positive effects on productivity from worker participation and from unionization, but caution against drawing general conclusions from their results without replication for a bigger, more scientifically constructed sample. A key problem in this regard is controlling for selection biases, in which the correlation between participation and productivity springs from some third, unmeasured factor rather than any causal connection between the two variables.

In recognition of this problem, Peter Cappelli and David Neumark (2001) construct a large panel data set that includes measures before and after firms' adoption of "high-performance" work practices vesting greater decision-making power in employees. They find at best weak econometric evidence for the existence of positive net efficiency, but positive effects on workers' gains. They conclude that high-performance work practices increase the compensation received by workers without necessarily reducing the profitability or competitiveness of firms.

These results are consistent with the findings of Freeman *et al.*, who assess the gains from employee involvement programs to both firms and employees. They find no consistent evidence of productivity improvements from worker participation, but consistently strong improvements in measures of employee well-being. However, the authors echo earlier cautions about the possibility of selection biases in the results.

Virtually every student of worker participation programs emphasizes that any benefits that are to be had do not come automatically, but require an environment of trust and cooperation between workers and management. The relevance of these caveats can be seen clearly in the experience of A. O. Smith's automobile frame plant in Milwaukee, Wisconsin. Faced with high defect rates and low worker morale, management attempted, with limited results, to institute limited employee involvement (EI) programs in the early 1980s. A more broad-based commitment to these practices took six years to develop, but yielded dramatic gains upon implementation, with a doubling of productivity growth rates and a dramatic reduction in defect rates the following year.

Success ultimately depended on the active cooperation of management and the several unions representing the plant's workforce, prompted at least in part by the growing fear of lost sales and jobs. Workers were organized into teams and given real decision-making authority, including the power to revise procedures established by the company's engineers. Concurrently, the ratio of foremen to production workers fell from 1 in 10 to 1 in 34 over a two-year period. Both sides note that despite the evident benefits, the changes did not constitute a cure-all for conflicts between management and labor.

Related discussion questions:
1. Given the repeatedly documented gains to employee involvement, why do managers often oppose attempts by workers to gain a systematic

continued

voice in firm decision making? Conversely, what might explain why labor unions are often opposed to employers' introduction of worker participation programs?

2. What policies might promote the likelihood that firms adopt and accrue significant gains in productivity or employee well-being from participatory work practices?

Related references:

Peter Cappelli and David Neumark, "Do 'High-Performance' Work Practices Improve Establishment-Level Outcomes?," *Industrial and Labor Relations Review* 54 (July 2001): pp. 737–84.

Michael A. Conte and Jan Svejnar, "The Effects of Worker Participation in Management, Profits, and Ownership of Assets on Enterprise Performance," in Katharine Abraham and Robert McKersie (eds) *New Developments in the Labor Market: Toward a New Institutional Paradigm* (Cambridge, MA: The MIT Press, 1990).

Richard B. Freeman, Morris B. Kleiner, and Cheri Ostroff, "The Anatomy of Employee Involvement and Its Effects on Firms and Workers," NBER Working Paper No. 8050 (December 2000).

David I. Levine and Laura D'Andrea Tyson, "Participation, Productivity, and the Firm's Environment," in Alan S. Blinder (ed.) *Paying for Productivity: A Look at the Evidence* (Washington, DC: The Brookings Institution, 1989): 183–237.

UNIONS, COLLECTIVE BARGAINING, AND ADJUDICATION OF WORKPLACE DISPUTES

Labor unions are organizations that represent the collective interests of workers in relations with their employers. In particular, unions act as agents for workers in *adversarial* relations involving wage determination or prosecution of alleged acts of misconduct by employers or employees. Union representation of worker interests is typically given "teeth" via legislated rights to bargain collectively, to enforce procedures for hearing worker grievances, and to strike.

The introduction of a union armed with legally ensured collective bargaining powers changes the structure of a given employment relationship in two primary ways. First, as mentioned earlier in the chapter, it creates a formal symmetry in the bargaining relationship between owners and employees. Even if there are multiple owners of an enterprise, their property rights enable them to appoint a single management agent to represent their common interests, making it difficult or impossible for workers to use "divide and conquer" strategies to gain the upper hand in negotiations over compensation and working conditions. The same advantage does not automatically flow to a firm's labor force on the strength of individual workers' property rights, and can only be guaranteed by the power to bargain collectively.

Second, as generally structured, collective bargaining rights modify the traditional property rights of firm owners by limiting their power to exclude others from

Table 12.1   Union density, OECD countries, 1995

Country	Unionization rates	Country	Unionization rates
Australia	35.2%	Italy	44.1%
Austria	41.2%	Japan	24.0%
Belgium	51.9%	Luxembourg	43.4%
Canada	37.4%	Netherlands	25.6%
Czech Republic	42.8%	Norway	57.7%
Denmark	80.1%	Portugal	25.6%
Finland	79.3%	Spain	18.6%
France	9.1%	Sweden	91.1%
Germany	28.9%	Switzerland	22.5%
Greece	24.3%	United Kingdom	32.9%
Ireland	48.9%	United States	14.2%

Source: ILO, *World Labour Report* 1997–98: table 1.2. Data are from 1995, except Denmark, Italy, Spain, Sweden, and Switzerland (1994), Ireland and Canada (1993).

the use of given assets. When workers are covered by a formal collective bargaining arrangement, employers must generally show cause before they are able to dismiss workers, and unions have the power to contest dismissals and other penalties.

Given the power of unions to act on behalf of workers in adversarial proceedings, it is no surprise that both firm owners and managers typically oppose unionization, and will often take actions to deter this outcome if it is not mandatory. Historically, these actions have ranged from threats and acts of violence against union organizers, to (dis-)information campaigns about putative negative effects of unions, to attempts to weaken the demand for unionization by providing better wages and working conditions.

As a result of this opposition, the incidence of unionization depends at least in part on the strength of legal and social support for unions, suggesting that it may vary dramatically across economies and over time. The magnitude of this variation is suggested by the data presented in tables 12.1 and 12.2. Table 12.1 indicates the unionized portion of the labor force in a number of industrialized countries, while table 12.2 shows the time trend in unionization for a more select group of countries. The latter table suggests a general downward trend in percentage of labor force unionized, with the steepest decline occurring in the United States.

The primarily adversarial nature of union representation suggests that the main effects of unionization are likely to be with respect to the distribution of the value added in production between firm owners and employees. However, firm-level unionization may have positive or negative efficiency effects as well. On the negative side, standard market theory likens unions to monopolies and suggests that monopoly wage-setting, and efforts to buttress wage-setting power (for instance, by making it more difficult for firms to relocate production facilities), reduce net social welfare. These conclusions are generally drawn on the assumption that the affected labor markets otherwise at least approximate ideal exchange conditions.

Table 12.2 Time trends in unionization, selected countries, 1955–95 (union membership as an approximate percentage of wage and salary earners)

Country	1955	1965	1975	1985	1995
Austria	60	60	67	51	41
Belgium	60	60	70	52	52
Canada	30	28	35	37	37[1]
Denmark	60	62	70	78	80[2]
Germany (FRG)	38	36	39	35	29[1]
Netherlands	44	41	42	29	26
Norway	62	63	61	56	58
Sweden	62	68	80	84	91[2]
United States	32	28	25	18	14

[1] Data from 1993.
[2] Data from 1994.
Source:
OECD, *Labour Force Statistics*, for 1955–75 data, and ILO, *World Labour Report* 1997–98: table 1.2, for 1985–95 data.

If this is not the case, then there is scope for unionization to have strictly positive efficiency effects. Theoretical bases for this possibility have been established in the previous chapter and earlier in this chapter. Given imperfect contracting conditions leading to the creation of quasi-rents, it was argued in the previous chapter that firm owners may have the incentive to alter the conditions of production to promote their bargaining position with respect to this surplus, even if this results in less total additional value being produced. If unionization provides a countervailing power to offset this tendency (for instance, by bargaining over working conditions or size of the labor force), then such inefficient production choices might be forestalled.

The argument earlier in the present chapter indicated a number of ways in which the collective interests of workers might be promoted by union representation. For example, the interests of the average or median worker might be better served by collective bargaining when market imperfections produce workplace-level public goods. Alternatively, representation of workers in quasi-judicial proceedings within firms may restrain what could appear as the arbitrary exercise of power by employers, leading to an increase in worker morale. The degree to which such efficiency gains are registered is, of course, an empirical rather than a theoretical issue.

The available evidence suggests that unionization does indeed have both distributional and efficiency consequences, increasing the share of production surplus going to workers while in many cases increasing the magnitude of total gains from the employment relationship. The key areas of impact that have been studied extensively involve union effects on wage and compensation levels, inequality of compensation among unionized employees, the composition of pay in terms of pecuniary and in-kind income, turnover rates, and productivity. The evidence on each of these effects is reviewed in turn.

While the general prediction of the formal bargaining analysis presented earlier is that union status raises total worker compensation, a number of difficulties must be addressed in measuring the actual wage effect of firm-level collective bargaining. First, firm-level wage effects based on the obstruction of "divide and conquer" strategies by employers must be distinguished from market-level effects that result when an entire industry is unionized.

At the firm level, the scope for wage gains from collective bargaining is limited by the cost to firms of replacing the entire unionized workforce, say by moving a plant to a different region or country. Thus, it should be expected that wage gains flowing solely from firm-level unionization are smaller than those that result from market- or economy-wide unionization, and are likely to vary significantly with market and technological conditions.

Second, in isolating the effect of firm-level union status on wages it is necessary to control statistically for such confounding features as variations in worker quality. For example, if workers with *initially* high marginal productivity are also more likely to join unions, then estimates of union wage effects that fail to control for this correlation will be biased upward. Furthermore, differences in worker quality may prove difficult to measure in practice. Similarly, firm characteristics must be taken into account, since there is some correlation between a firm's size and the union status of its workforce, and large firms have been found to pay higher wages on average, even without unionization.

Third, as mentioned earlier, non-union firms may offer better wages and working conditions in order to discourage their workers from voting for union representation. Although this "threat effect" on the job offers of non-union firms is a benefit to both unionized and non-unionized workers its direct effect is to bias downward the statistical measure of union effects on wages and working conditions.

An overview of studies that attempt to account for these difficulties suggests two main conclusions. The first is that estimates of the wage effect, while generally positive, vary significantly from industry to industry, supporting the suggestion above that firm-level wage effects will depend significantly on specific labor market conditions. In particular, unionization is found to have a greater effect in industries whose profits have been historically bolstered or protected from competition by regulation, such as air travel and trucking. Second, there is considerable disagreement on the average union effect on wages, with estimates ranging from 10 to 15% up to 25%.[1]

A second potential impact of union status is on wage inequality. A couple of theoretical considerations come into play here. First, as suggested by the bargaining model developed earlier, unionization replaces bargaining positions based on costs of replacing individual workers with a collectively enjoyed bargaining position based on the cost of replacing an entire labor force. One might therefore expect, other things equal, that workers who are relatively difficult for firms to replace, for instance because of sizable investments in firm-specific skills or tight conditions in their respective markets, gain less from union status than their less initially-advantaged counterparts.

Second, collective bargaining may bring to light a "democratic" interest in more nearly equalized wages. Recall in this connection that democratic voting will, where possible, reflect the interests of the "median" voter. Furthermore, to the extent that wages of all workers are raised above their respective competitive levels, it is possible to condense a firm's wage structure without necessarily inducing high-wage workers to leave.

Consistent with these notions, the available evidence suggests that union status has a significant moderating effect on wage inequality, even when attention is restricted to firm-level effects. Wage gains, as predicted, are greater for those who are less skilled and less well paid in the absence of a union. Consistent with such findings, an econometric study by labor economist Richard Freeman attributes a significant portion of the increase in US male earnings inequality during the 1980s to the precipitous fall in union membership over the same period.[2]

Relatedly, union status is also found consistently to raise the share of labor income received in "fringe benefits" or in-kind compensation, such as health and life insurance, employer pension contributions, and paid vacations. This is particularly the case for the US, where these benefits are less extensively guaranteed by law. This can be seen as reflecting the same collective choice considerations as discussed above, at least if it can be assumed that the median voter–worker cares about in-kind pay.[3]

Union status has also been found to have a significant impact on the *total* gains to be had from the employment relationship, not just the distribution of those gains. One key effect is on the rate of worker turnover. In assessing this impact, however, it is necessary to disentangle it from the effect of unions on total compensation. One would expect workers who are paid more to quit less, but this doesn't imply a net efficiency gain, especially since firms would presumably take the rate of turnover into account in setting wages in the absence of collective bargaining. Furthermore, a correlation between union status and turnover may simply reflect the fact that workers with poorer market alternatives are more likely to be unionized.

A number of studies have shown, however, that union status reduces worker turnover rates dramatically, even when controlling both for the level of total labor compensation and a measure of the market alternatives available to workers. This result is especially remarkable in light of the theoretical prediction, discussed above, that median-voter decision making might be expected to lead, other things equal, to an increase in turnover relative to the outcomes selected by profit-maximizing firms.

Labor economists Richard Freeman and James Medoff find, for example, that controlling for these other factors, union membership reduces the average probability that a worker quits by 31 to 65% and thus increases the average tenure of a worker with a given employer by 23 to 32%. Moreover, they estimate that the lower turnover attributable to union membership corresponds to a 1 to 2% reduction in employers' costs, and that the welfare gain to workers – independent of bargaining effects of the total compensation level – is equivalent to a 40% wage increase.[4]

Estimates of the direct impact of unionization on worker productivity are more controversial than those for turnover or bargaining effects on total compensation. This is true for a number of reasons: first, because estimated productivity effects of unionization vary widely across industries, from negative to positive values; second, because it is difficult to isolate cases in which unions contribute to productivity in some positive way, as opposed to simply acting as a drag on profits which forces management to increase efficiency in order to compete; and third, as in other studies of union effects, one must control for biases that emerge because more productive workers might be more likely to be in unions.

It appears that unionization often increases productivity significantly, both directly and via reduced turnover, but rarely to an extent that offsets the impact of collective bargaining effects on the profit levels of unionized firms, and possibly at the cost of efficiency losses from strikes, lockouts, or work slowdowns. Thus it could be that unions increase the size of the "pie" to be shared between firm owners and workers, yet the share of that larger pie going to firm owners is sufficiently smaller that total profits fall in most or all cases. This would explain why management opposes unionization of its workforce, often strenuously, even in the presence of strongly positive productivity effects.

This conclusion might lead you to ask why the best of both worlds could not be secured through the appropriate cooperative arrangements. These might be structured to enhance the efficiency gains from collective worker representation while minimizing losses from work stoppages. But this reasoning leads back to the problem of imperfect contracting studied throughout this part of the text, in that it may be difficult or impossible to ensure that only the "good" or "mutually beneficial" aspects of unionization follow an organizing drive. If this claim is valid, then the "bad" must be taken with the "good," and it is a matter of social judgment whether the allocational and distributional benefits outweigh such negative effects as production losses from strikes, inflexible work rules, or work slowdowns.

WORKS COUNCILS AND EMPLOYEE PARTICIPATION

Works council is the commonly used term for a firm- or plant-level employee representation body that is primarily designed to promote worker participation in firm decisions, rather than to advance worker interests which conflict with those of the employer. Correspondingly, works councils have as a historical matter rarely been accorded the right to strike or to bargain directly for wages and working conditions. Rather, works councils have been designed first and foremost to facilitate the essentially non-adversarial aspects of employee interests, including transmission of information and representation of collective preferences over bundles of workplace public goods made available by firms.

Works councils are primarily encountered in the economies of Western Europe, where their existence is assured as a matter of law along with union representation. They are occasionally approximated on a voluntary basis in countries outside Western Europe; for example, the "consultation committees" of Japan are closely related to works councils in form and function, as are Canadian occupational safety and health monitoring committees.

Although the functions of works councils and their kin are primarily partici-patory and non-adversarial, they may often wield some degree of redistributive power as well. For example, works councils could implicitly threaten to withhold vital information, or create delays in giving feedback on proposed managerial decisions, as a way of securing greater levels of employee compensation or more favorable working conditions. Because of this, the legal status of works councils potentially matters in the same sense that it does for unions – profit-seeking employers are likely to give inefficiently low autonomy to works councils.

This prediction is consistent with US experience with voluntary works councils, which were also referred to as "employee representation plans" or "company unions." US firms, mostly large corporations, experimented widely with these plans over the decade from roughly 1918 to 1928. Inclusion in company unions went from almost zero workers in 1917 to almost half a million employees in 1919, to a peak of 1.5 million workers by 1928. However, US workers were almost never guar-anteed the right to participate in firm-level decisions or gain access to company accounts, with the result that these plans were never actively supported by employ-ees, and died out completely with the passage of the Wagner Act in 1935.

In the Western European model, the representative nature of works councils is assured by regular democratic elections of works councilors. Employers are typ-ically required by law to consult with their councils before implementing any deci-sion affecting worker interests, although they are not typically bound to follow the council's suggestions. An important exception is the case of Germany, where works councils are accorded legal *codetermination* rights in decision making.

Important additional functions served by European works councils include the transmission of information from employers to employees and monitoring of compliance with occupational safety and health regulations. In the former case, employers may use works councils as a device to convey "bad news" to workers in a credible manner; for example, councils may be asked to confirm the need for layoffs on the basis of weak demand for the firm's products. In the latter case, works councils may help to ensure adherence to legislated safety and health codes, while in some cases suggesting improved methods for meeting these requirements.

Case studies of experience with works councils suggest that management learns to work more effectively with councils over time, and as a consequence to include them more fully in decision making. Consequently, although there are efficiency costs associated with the formation of works councils, these appear to dissipate over time. On the other hand, there is significant evidence to suggest that regular employee participation in workplace decisions yields productivity gains (see the previous discussion box).

CONCLUSION

This chapter has explored how market imperfections might create a role for employee representation, whether in the adversarial context of collective bar-gaining and rule adjudication or the primarily cooperative context of worker participation in firm-level decision making. This exploration has given rise to two fundamental questions: first, are the effects of collective representation of worker interests purely redistributive? Second, to the extent they are not, can the potential social benefits of worker representation be realized through purely voluntary arrangements between firms and employees exercising their respective property rights?

If either of these questions is answered in the affirmative, then clearly government interventions to support institutions of worker representation must be justified on other than Pareto-utilitarian grounds. There are a number of ways this might be done; in particular, if the depiction of employment relationships as being to some extent political in character has any validity, then one might legitimately argue for guarantees of worker representation on the basis of normative theories of individual rights, even in the absence of demonstrable scope for general welfare gains from such interventions.

However, on the basis of arguments and evidence suggested in this chapter, one might conclude that affirming both questions simultaneously is problematic at best, and in any case constitutes an empirical rather than a theoretical matter. Admitting the same sorts of transactional imperfections that give rise to firms and employment relationships, the event that legislative or constitutional guarantees of employee representation in the workplace might improve total gains from production relationships cannot be ruled out *a priori*, and furthermore there is significant evidence that government-mandated forms of worker representation in the status quo contribute positively to economic efficiency.

Study Questions

1. Use the Rubinstein bargaining model with negligible discounting to answer the following questions concerning the theoretical impact of collective bargaining:
    (a) Under what conditions, if any, would a shift from individualistic to collective bargaining *not* be expected to increase the equilibrium payoffs of workers in a firm's labor force?
    (b) Suppose that the value added by a firm's production activities is an increasing and concave function of the size of its labor force, written $V(N)$. What would be the size of a profit-maximizing firm's labor force if it could hire workers at the competitive wage rate W_c? What would be the profit-maximizing size of the labor force given the collective bargaining equilibrium discussed in the text? Are these results different? How so?
2. In what sense are collective bargaining and worker ownership of firms substitute responses to the problem of collective choice in the employment relationship? What factors might help determine which option workers would choose as the basis for making such collective choices in the workplace?

continued

3. Some studies suggest that there is more likely to be a positive relationship between industry profits and average industry wages when workers are unionized. Is this consistent with the implications of the collective bargaining model discussed in the text? Explain.

4. Recall the strategic bargaining relationship between a firm owner and a single employee with a common fractional discount factor, exit options valued at zero, and no capacity to strike on the part of the worker. Suppose the default wage in the case of disagreement is W_c. Show the impact on the bargaining reaction functions and the equilibrium payoff to the employee when both players incur a fixed bargaining cost C in every new round of bargaining, assuming that the employee begins the bargaining process.

5. Consider a collective choice problem for a firm's three-worker labor force to which the firm offers alternative bundles of three employment-related public goods. Let the budget set for these three goods be represented by a triangle in three dimensions (the obvious extension of a budget line drawn in two dimensions). Show that a "median voter" equilibrium need not exist on this budget plane. How would the respective preferred points of the three workers have to line up in order for such an equilibrium to exist?

Notes

1 The classic reference for this literature is H. Gregg Lewis, *Union Relative Wage Effects: A Survey* (Chicago, IL: University of Chicago Press, 1986), which updates and expands upon his earlier book, *Unionism and Relative Wages in the United States: An Empirical Inquiry* (Chicago, IL: University of Chicago Press, 1963). Additional work has been done in this area subsequently, but this range likely still contains certainly the upper bound on union wage effects.

2 Richard B. Freeman, "How Much Has De-Unionization Contributed to the Rise in Male Earnings Inequality?," in Sheldon Danziger and Peter Gottschalk (eds) *Uneven Tides: Rising Inequality in America* (New York: Russell Sage Foundation, 1993).

3 Note, however, that granting the role of collective voice in this regard does not answer the standard microeconomic conundrum: why would rational actors *ever* choose in-kind compensation over equal dollar amounts of income in monetary form, since the former must necessarily limit workers' choice in spending their income?

4 Richard B. Freeman and James L. Medoff, *What Do Unions Do?* (New York: Basic Books, 1984).

Suggestions for Further Reading

Richard B. Freeman and James L. Medoff, *What Do Unions Do?* (New York: Basic Books, 1984).

Barry T. Hirsch and John T. Addison, *The Economic Analysis of Unions: New Approaches and Evidence* (Boston: Allen & Unwin, 1986).

Joel Rogers and Wolfgang Streeck, "Workplace Representation Overseas: The Works Councils Story," in Richard B. Freeman (ed.) *Working Under Different Rules* (New York: Russell Sage Foundation, 1993).

PART IV

LABOR MARKET DIVISIONS

With partial exceptions in chapters 3 and 4, the labor market analysis of parts I through III generally proceeded as though there were but a single undifferentiated market for labor. This simplification is useful for isolating the implications of particular assumptions about market structure, and for making conditional predictions and value judgments with respect to particular types of labor. But for many of the most important topics in labor economics, the key issue is that workers and firms face very different labor market experiences and outcomes.

This idea is captured by the notion of labor market *divisions*, defined as any basis on which groups of labor market participants face systematically different opportunities and outcomes. Each of the chapters in this part of the text considers one fundamental basis for such a division. The first two chapters consider divisions consistent with the operation of perfectly competitive labor markets, while allowing for the consequences of departures from competitive conditions. Chapter 13 examines the allocation of workplace characteristics such as job safety, and assesses the scope for *compensating wage differentials* corresponding to the incidence of workplace risks and other disamenities. Chapter 14 studies the impact of individual ability and formal schooling decisions on labor market outcomes, primarily contrasting the implications of *human capital* and *signaling* theories respecting these relationships.

The latter two chapters address labor market phenomena that may or may not be consistent with the scenario of perfectly competitive labor markets. Discrimination against workers from given demographic groups, the subject of chapter 15, may take the form of a compensating differential under competitive conditions (and as such, it poses no insult to social welfare defined in terms of economic efficiency), but has less benign impli-

continued

cations given various forms of exchange costs. Wage variations within and across industries, the focus of chapter 16, may simply reflect unobserved differences in human capital, or be the manifestation of systematic *segmentation* of labor markets that channels otherwise identical workers into good and bad jobs.

Keep your antennae up for lines of analytical continuity across parts III and IV of the text. Exchange conditions that inform the structure of employment relationships also influence labor market divisions and resulting differences in the labor market opportunities enjoyed by workers. The factors giving rise to internal labor markets within firms, for example, may also distribute firms across dual labor markets or affect the allocation of workplace risks.

CHAPTER THIRTEEN

WAGES AND WORKING CONDITIONS

Some jobs are nastier or more dangerous than others. Some require people to work in mine shafts sunk deep underground, on scaffolding high above the ground, or amidst toxic materials, while others are pursued in pleasant settings far removed from everyday hazards. This chapter inquires into the allocation of such workplace characteristics, in both positive and normative terms: how are working conditions determined in labor markets, and are the resulting allocations desirable?

At first glance, the latter question may seem absurd. Isn't it obvious that the preferred market outcome is always to have nicer working conditions, especially if that means fewer job-related illnesses or accidents? If all other related considerations are held equal, the answer is clearly yes. But what if more amenable working conditions can only be obtained at the cost of other desired outcomes, such as shorter hours or higher pay? To put the same question in positive rather than normative terms, if given the chance, would workers in a given enterprise always vote to accept lower average pay in order to secure lower risks of job-related accident or illness?

To answer the positive aspects of this question in specific circumstances, one would need to know such things as what information workers have when they make choices about wages and working conditions, and what their effective options are when they choose job conditions. If workers are informed about their options, it is plausible to imagine that they would under some circumstances accept higher average pay in return for bearing less desirable working conditions. This suggests a theory of *compensating differentials* in labor income corresponding to given employment dis-amenities. Pursuing this hypothesis, one might then ask if compensating differentials are in fact paid, and if they reflect socially desirable outcomes.

continued

The corresponding theoretical issue concerns the market conditions under which working conditions are allocated. One would expect compensating wage differentials for workplace disamenities to arise under perfectly competitive exchange conditions, and under these conditions the resulting allocation is efficient. However, as explained in this chapter, there is a number of reasons why wage compensation for workplace disamenities might shrink or disappear in the presence of significant exchange costs. In the latter scenario, there may be scope for efficiency-improving government interventions to promote job safety or other workplace goods.

Both possibilities must be kept in mind when evaluating the connection between working conditions and wage levels. While there is a growing body of econometric evidence for the hypothesis that compensation is paid for undesirable working conditions, there are important inconsistencies in the empirical record, suggesting that either the available data or the assumptions underlying the compensating differential model are problematic. Before considering these alternatives, the chapter begins with a brief overview of the data on a particularly important aspect of working conditions relating to worker health and safety levels.

WORKPLACE RISKS AND WAGE DIFFERENTIALS

The incidence of workplace risks

Workplace risks are of two types: injuries from specific events on the job, including accidents and acts of violence, and work-related illnesses such as cancer or respiratory disease. By nature, it is harder to quantify illnesses due to workplace conditions, so there are necessarily ongoing disagreements as to their magnitude. Subject to this caveat, the International Labor Organization (ILO) estimates that there were two and a quarter million work-related fatalities worldwide in 2002, about 15% of which were due to accidents and acts of violence. Estimated shares of accidents and violent deaths in total fatalities vary considerably by global region, with developed economies displaying considerably higher likelihoods of fatality due to illness.[1]

In the United States, there were at least 200,000 job-related deaths from traumatic injuries in the period 1972–2001, according to data from the Bureau of Labor Statistics. This may be an underestimate due to reliance on industry self-reporting. However, fatality rates have been generally falling since the BLS began recording them in the early 1970s (save for a spike in 2001 due to the terrorist attacks on New York's World Trade Center, which killed 2,886 workers).[2] Total fatalities, on the other hand, show some cyclical variation, increasing by 400 from

1992 to 1994 before resuming a declining trend. Excluding the effects of the 9/11 attacks, about 5,900 workers died from work-related injuries in 2001.

The incidence of US work-related injury fatalities by cause, industry, and occupation follows stable patterns. The three primary causes of work-related fatal injuries are, in declining order, highway accidents, homicides, and falls. Fatality *rates* per 100,000 workers are highest in mining; agriculture, forestry and fishing; and construction, while the largest number of *total* fatalities in private industry occurred in construction. In declining order of fatality rate, the riskiest occupations are construction, farm-related work, and truck driving.

There are striking differences in the incidence of work-related fatalities by worker characteristic. Relative to employment, self-employed workers experience over three times the fatality rates of wage and salary workers, while female workers have a fatality rate that is one-tenth that for male workers. The incidence of fatalities relative to employment tends to increase with age, and is higher for Hispanics and Asians than for white and African-American workers.[3]

There were a total of 5.2 million private non-fatal work-related injuries and illnesses reported in the US for 2001, about half of which involved lost work days. The corresponding incidence rate was 5.7 per 100 equivalent full-time workers, which is also a part of a decades-long declining trend and is the lowest rate recorded by the Bureau of Labor Statistics since occupational safety data were first compiled in 1973.[4] Non-fatal injuries were higher in goods-producing than in service industries, with the highest rates experienced in manufacturing; construction; and agriculture, forestry and fishing, in declining order.

A hedonic model of compensating wage differentials

Let's take a closer look at the microeconomic logic of allocating occupational risk in labor markets, beginning with the scenario of perfectly competitive exchange. The analytical horizon will then be broadened to consider departures from this framework. The goal in each case is to determine implications of given market conditions for both observed market outcomes and appropriate government policies with respect to occupational risks.

The approach developed here is called a *hedonic* model of wage determination in that wage differentials are understood to arise from workers' psychic assessments of alternative workplace characteristics. Since workers' pleasures and pains can't be directly observed, the theory yields instead a hypothetical relationship between wages and potentially observable working conditions given perfectly competitive market conditions. Begin the analysis with a simple scenario in which there are just two dimensions of choice, the wage rate W to be paid to workers and the magnitude of safety measures S taken by a firm. Other aspects of labor choice such as the length of the workday are held constant or assumed to be always at their respective equilibrium levels. Given these simplifying assumptions one can define a typical worker's occupational preferences in terms of a utility

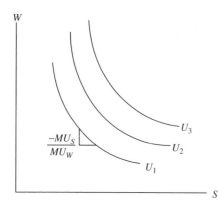

Figure 13.1(a) Worker's indifference map over wage and safety levels.

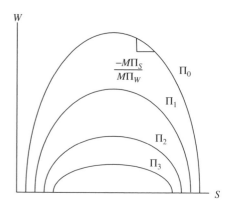

Figure 13.1(b) Firm's isoprofit map over wage and safety levels.

function in the two goods, denoted $U = u(S, W)$, with corresponding positive marginal utilities MU_W and MU_S.

These preferences can be represented by the worker's indifference map over wage and safety combinations. As shown in figure 13.1(a), a given indifference curve for the worker will have a negative slope equal to $-MU_S/MU_W$, where as always the ratio of marginal utilities expresses the worker's marginal rate of substitution between the goods. Note that under standard assumptions about preferences, the worker's utility increases across indifference curves "to the northeast," and each indifference curve is convex relative to the origin.

In parallel fashion, the profit level of a representative firm can be defined in terms of the two variables, indicated by the profit function $\Pi = \pi(S, W)$. Under perfectly competitive exchange conditions, the marginal profitability of increasing wages is negative, so that $M\Pi_W < 0$. However, it is not necessarily the case that the marginal profitability of increasing safety expenditures, denoted $M\Pi_S$, is *always* negative. For example, paying some attention to safety may initially increase profits by reducing the cost of replacing injured workers.

Assume, however, that there are diminishing and eventually negative marginal returns to profit from increased safety measures, implying that isoprofit curves eventually slope downward, as shown in figure 13.1(b). The slope of any isoprofit curve at a given point is just equal to $-M\Pi_S/M\Pi_W$, which becomes negative once $M\Pi_S$ does. The ratio of the marginal profitabilities (without the negative sign) indicates the firm's marginal rate of substituting wages for safety measures. The standard assumption of diminishing marginal rate of substitution implies that each isoprofit curve is concave relative to the horizontal axis.

Now suppose that large numbers of heterogeneous workers and firms participate in the labor market. Specifically, assume that workers are distinguished by their marginal rates of substitution between wages and safety, with more "risk

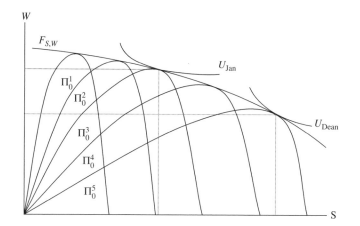

Figure 13.2   Wage–safety frontier under ideal market conditions.

averse" workers having relatively *steep* indifference curves drawn through any given (S, W) combination (signifying that their marginal utility of safety is high relative to their marginal utility of income), while less risk-averse workers have relatively *flat* indifference curves evaluated at the same point in the graph.

Similarly, assume that firms operate in different industries, distinguished by the different marginal rates of substitution between wages and safety made possible by the production technologies employed in the respective industries. This implies that the isoprofit curves of firms from different industries will have unequal slopes when evaluated at a particular combination of safety measures and wage rates. A relatively steep slope thus implies that it is very costly for a firm to increase safety measures, relative to the marginal cost of increasing the wage rate.

Finally, suppose that all firms operate in perfectly competitive output markets, which is to say that competition drives equilibrium profits for firms in all markets to their normal levels, assumed to be the same value, denoted Π_0, for all markets. On the basis of this framework, let's now examine the allocation of wage rates and safety levels across workers and industries that would arise in perfectly competitive equilibrium.

As a first step, note that under ideal market conditions firms are in effect driven by competitive pressures to maximize the well-being of their workers, subject to the condition that they must achieve the normal rate of profit. Consequently, the graphical analysis can be simplified by replacing the set of normal-profit isoprofit curves for the several industries with a *wage–safety frontier*, representing the allocatively efficient combination of wage rates and safety levels made possible by the existing array of technology and market conditions. If there is a sufficiently large number of industries and the technological differences between them are sufficiently small, this frontier can be approximated by a smooth curve, such as that labeled $F_{S,W}$ in figure 13.2. Every point on this frontier represents a particular combination of wage rates and safety measures for firms in a particular industry earning just the normal rate of profit Π_0.

Individual workers choose their respective utility-maximizing allocations along the wage–safety frontier. To focus the argument, consider the optimizing choices of two hypothetical workers, Jan and Dean, with different attitudes toward risk. Suppose that Dean is relatively more risk-averse and so has a relatively steeper indifference curve at any given point in figure 13.2. The result is that Jan will choose a point further up the wage–safety frontier than Dean, corresponding to a higher wage rate and a higher degree of risk (that is, a lower level of investment in safety measures), as shown in the diagram.

This reasoning establishes a theoretical basis for the emergence of compensating wage differentials in competitive labor markets. Higher wages are paid to workers incurring higher risks, with the wage premium being paid to workers who are relatively *less* risk averse. This may sound paradoxical until it is understood that only these workers are willing to face the higher risk in the first place. In any case, compensating differentials are a reflection of the underlying heterogeneity in preferences, endowments, and production technologies.

Note that under this scenario, equilibrium wage premia do not "compensate" for higher risks in the sense of rendering workers indifferent between adjacent combinations of wage and safety levels. To the contrary, workers with convex preferences would generally be strictly worse off at any wage and safety bundles other than the ones they respectively chose. Workers are thus "compensated" in that they're at least as well off at selected wage/safety combinations than at any viable market alternatives featuring greater levels of safety.

Positive and normative implications of the theory

The hedonic wage model constructed above generates a potentially testable inverse relationship between wage rates and workplace characteristics, in this case those corresponding to safety measures taken by the firm. Furthermore, the resulting wage differential paid for greater risk is a *necessary* consequence of the model under the stated assumptions. But it must be remembered that this is a *ceteris paribus* relationship, understood to obtain only when all other factors affecting wage levels are held constant, either by hypothesis or by empirical test design.

To see the significance of this qualification, consider the impact of allowing other factors consistent with the operation of perfectly competitive markets to vary. Suppose, for example, that workers may have two different levels of training, T_1 and T_2. As discussed in chapter 11, training increases workers' marginal productivity. In the present context, this implies that firms employing more highly trained workers can afford both higher wage rates and greater safety measures. This suggests in turn that workers with more training face a more favorable wage–safety frontier than their less-skilled counterparts, as illustrated in figure 13.3.

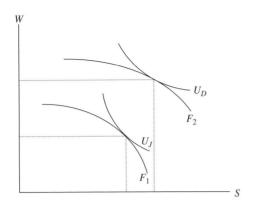

Figure 13.3   Different wage–safety frontiers generated by unequal training.

Note that the prediction of a compensating wage differential for greater work-place risk obtains along each frontier. However, it will not necessarily hold *across* frontiers; nor should it be expected to, since more than one variable changes in moving across frontiers. Thus, empirical tests of the compensating differential hypothesis must control for any such confounding factors.

Consider, for example, the situation depicted in figure 13.4(a), showing a hypo-thetical scatter plot of data points linking wage rates and safety measures enjoyed by five individuals. If you were to draw the straight line in this diagram which best summarizes the deterministic relationship between wages and workplace risk suggested by these data (the basic goal of statistical linear regression analysis), the apparent choice would be *upward*-sloping, indicating that workers demand wage premiums for working under safer conditions! An alternative interpretation is rep-resented in figure 13.4(b), which suggests that the anomalous result stems from trying to infer the shape of a *single* frontier from data derived from *multiple* frontiers.

The key question facing empirical researchers concerns the choice of variables to control for statistically in testing the hypothesis of compensating wage differ-entials. According to the theory of perfectly competitive labor markets, there are primarily two sets of variables to control for: those that raise both the revenue productivity and supply price of labor services, and those that are the conse-quences of government interventions in an otherwise ideally functioning market. In the former case, for example, one would want to control for innate worker ability and job-related skills acquired through general education, training, and experience. With respect to the latter phenomena, researchers would want to control for the effects of government policies directly or indirectly affecting actual tradeoffs between wages and safety measures, such as collective bargaining rights, wage controls, or job safety regulations.

If labor exchange conditions do not correspond to the perfectly competitive sce-nario, however, one might expect additional factors to influence the connection

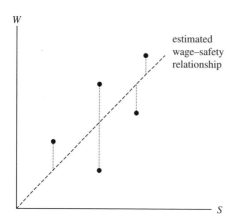

Figure 13.4(a) Estimated wage–safety relationship.

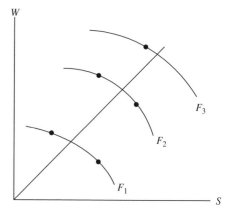

Figure 13.4(b) True wage–safety relationships.

between job safety and wage rates. These factors are discussed in more detail below, but it should be clear that the incidence and degree of mobility and transaction costs may strongly affect labor market outcomes. To the extent this were true it is necessary to control for factors influencing the configuration of these costs in order to get unbiased estimates of wage differentials for workplace risk and other disamenities. These issues arise again in the chapter's subsequent discussion of empirical research on workplace characteristics and compensating differentials.

The present analysis of compensating wage differentials in perfectly competitive markets is concluded with a discussion of the effects of government policies with respect to workplace safety. To facilitate this analysis, refer to the situation depicted in figure 13.5, which reproduces the equilibrium setting involving two hypothetical workers, Jan and Dean. Label their equilibrium choices of safety measures in the workplace as S_J and S_D, respectively.

Now suppose the government introduces a regulation mandating minimum safety measures of $\underline{S}$ in all firms, where $\underline{S}$ falls somewhere between S_J and S_D. If the regulation is universally obeyed, Jan will be guaranteed a safer working environment, while Dean's wages and working conditions are unaffected. Is Jan made better off thereby?

As can be seen in figure 13.5, the answer is clearly in the negative. It is true that Jan receives the benefits of increased safety measures $\underline{S}$, but they come at a cost. In order to maintain a normal rate of profit, the affected firms must lower the wage rate they offer in combination with the mandated level of safety. However, since Jan's initial allocation of income and safety is Pareto-efficient, the effect of this non-incremental shift in safety measures is a net loss in utility, indicating by the lower indifference curve attained by Jan at the regulated equilibrium $(\underline{S}, \underline{W})$.

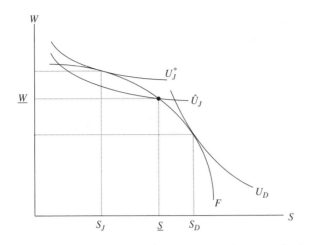

Figure 13.5 Equilibrium consequences of minimum safety standards in ideal labor markets.

As in other cases of government intervention in perfectly competitive markets, safety regulations on market outcomes cannot be expected to increase social welfare.

Alternatively, suppose the government imposes a system of *worker's compensation*, to be financed by firms according to their safety records, in which employees are paid *after the fact* for injuries received or illnesses contracted on the job. Under the conditions of perfect competition specified above, the expected costs of the system must subtract, dollar for dollar, from the wage rates firms are able to pay workers. As a consequence, up-front wage differentials decrease the more compensation is paid. The only thing that changes is the *incidence* of compensation, after the fact; whereas all workers in riskier jobs receive the wage premium in the absence of the worker's compensation system, only those workers who actually sustain injuries or illnesses receive payments under the latter arrangement. However, *expected* utilities attained at the point of labor exchange are not, and can't be, altered.

Note that the foregoing judgment abstracts completely from purely distributional considerations. For example, suppose that Jan's relatively high marginal utility of income relative to safety, and thus his choice of relatively riskier working conditions results from being in poverty. While it is true that he would be strictly better off if he could command bother greater wages and greater safety, given his position in a competitive labor market he is nonetheless made even worse off by the safety regulation, since he is thereby forced by market conditions to a lower wage.

This normative assessment depends, of course, on the assumption of perfectly competitive exchange conditions, implying that Jan is fully informed about labor market alternatives and exchange costs are virtually zero. It does not necessarily follow, however, that *any* departure from ideal market conditions will establish grounds for government safety regulations or other interventions. This point is illustrated in the following examination of alternative departures from perfectly competitive exchange conditions and their respective consequences.

MARKET POWER AND THE ALLOCATION OF WORKPLACE CHARACTERISTICS

The next step in the analysis is to investigate the allocation of workplace conditions and wages in the presence of market imperfections. The effects of labor market power are considered first, followed in the next section by scenarios of imperfect contracting due to prohibitive costs of enforcing given terms of labor exchange.

Market power and compensating wage differentials

The existence of wage-setting power in labor markets doesn't necessarily imply either the elimination of compensating wage differentials, other things equal, or inefficient allocation of workplace conditions. Rather, market power primarily affects the distribution of costs and benefits associated with workplace disamenities. For inefficiency also to emerge, market power must be accompanied by some form of transaction cost that inhibits contractual or strategic enforcement of mutually beneficial terms of labor exchange. These points are developed below for the specific case of labor market monopsony.

To facilitate the analysis, consider employment transactions between two heterogeneous workers, Jan and Dean, and a single firm that offers a wide range of wage and safety combinations (perhaps because it produces a number of different products using multiple plants). Maintain the previous assumptions about preferences for wages and safety measures on the part of firms and workers. Given these assumptions, it is possible to draw an Edgeworth box representing the possible terms of labor exchange between the firm and Jan and Dean, respectively. This is illustrated in figure 13.6, which also shows the separate contract curves in wage and safety bundles for the two workers.

If the existence of market power favoring labor buyers or sellers is the *only* departure from perfectly competitive exchange conditions, then all individuals remain fully informed about market alternatives and it is possible to write binding contracts covering all aspects of a mutually agreeable employment transaction. Then any such transaction would most plausibly occur on the *contract curve* between the firm and a given worker.

Suppose, for example, that by virtue of its monopsony status the firm enjoys some extranormal level of profit Π_M. Then, as indicated in figure 13.6, compensating wage differentials for workplace risk will still arise for workers employed by this monopsonist, so long as they can choose different combinations of wages

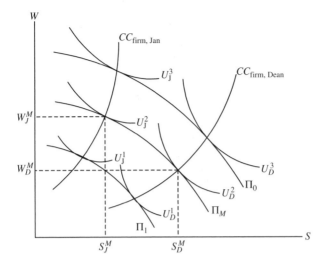

Figure 13.6 Compensating differential paid by a firm with monopsony power.

and safety along the corresponding isoprofit curve (say, by selecting a particular plant at which to work). In the scenario depicted by the figure, the equilibrium bundles for Jan and Dean are respectively (S_J^m, W_J^m) and (S_D^m, W_D^m). These contracts lie on the respective contract curves for the two workers, and ensure as in the competitive scenario that Jan receives a wage premium for incurring greater workplace risk.

The resulting exchanges are efficient, although they represent strictly lower combinations of wage and safety for each worker than would obtain under perfect competition. (And the possible draconian nature of the redistribution in such scenarios, such that higher monopsony profits are gained at the expense of higher rates of worker injury, illness, or death, should not be ignored. See the discussion box on this issue.) Thus, although there are potential economic grounds for government intervention to eliminate the monopsony, there is once again no scope for efficiency-improving safety regulations. Any such restrictions must force tradeoffs of income for safety that, given the conditions of this scenario, workers would otherwise not choose to make.

The presence of monopsony power does, however, potentially raise a new problem for researchers attempting to ascertain the payment of compensating wage differentials. The problem arises when monopsony exists only in certain labor markets, establishing a different pattern of relative wages than would occur under perfect competition. If the effect of monopsony is to lower wages in jobs characterized by relatively high workplace disamenities, it would tend to obliterate wage differentials that would obtain under universally competitive conditions.

For example, suppose that jobs in market A are safer than jobs in market B, but monopsony power in the latter market ensures uniformly higher wages paid to workers in the safer jobs of market A. As a result, if monopsony effects were not taken into account, one would observe a strictly positive relationship between wage rates and undesirable job characteristics, apparently contradicting the compensating differential hypothesis. Thus, one must control econometrically for the effects of market power when seeking evidence of compensation for workplace risk.

Conversely, the effects of labor market power could be to create the appearance of a compensating differential for workplace disamenities even if none would otherwise obtain. For example, suppose for some reason (explored further below) wage premia are not paid for existing differences in workplace risk. If firms featuring higher levels of risk are also unionized, then they might pay higher wages than low-risk firms – but as the result of the union's wage setting power, not due to market-generated differentials for workplace risk. Once again, it would be necessary to control for the effects of market power in order to discern the true incidence of compensating wage differentials.

Market power and workplace-level public goods

The existence of monopsony power is not a random event. As discussed in chapter 5, market power arises when people incur matching costs in pairing with suitable exchange partners. Monopsony power, then, arises to some degree when workers face search or mobility costs in moving among potential jobs. This possibility (or one in which the monopsonist has but a single plant) conflicts with a key assumption of the foregoing argument, to the effect that workers can freely sort themselves across a monopsonist's individual plants in order to secure constrainedly optimal tradeoffs between safety and income.

This restriction matters because workplace conditions may take on the aspect of *public* goods or bads within individual work sites, meaning that they would unavoidably affect all employees operating in the same working environment. This outcome is particularly likely in the case of job safety, since workplace hazards are rarely limited to specific employees at a job site. For example, the provision of a smoke alarm system would ensure that everyone within hearing of the alarms would be alerted to the danger of a fire. The "publicness" of job safety raises issues both for the definition and the attainment of efficient allocations of workplace characteristics when workers can't freely sort themselves according to relative safety preferences.

In the case of a public good, Pareto-efficient allocation requires the equalization of the firm's marginal rate of transformation with the *sum* of marginal rates of substitution of individuals affected by the public good. This modification is dictated by the fact that, if any one person consumes a public good, then all members of the relevant "public" also consume the same level of the good. To translate this idea into the theoretical framework developed above, imagine the wage–safety frontier for a given firm as the tradeoff between job safety and total wages at a given workplace. The efficient allocation along this frontier would then occur at

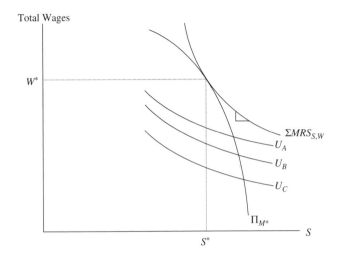

Figure 13.7   Allocation of optimal "public" workplace safety.

the point of tangency with the relevant "social" indifference curve reflecting the sum of individual marginal rates of substitution of income for safety among the firm's employees, as depicted in figure 13.7.

Attainment of this modified efficiency condition poses no problem if workers can choose among alternative working environments based on complete information about workplace conditions. Given sufficient degrees of choice, this would result in unanimity within each self-selected labor force concerning the desired tradeoff between compensation and job safety. However, if workers' range of choice is restricted by monopsony conditions or limited information about workplace alternatives, then situations can arise in which workers at a given firm or plant have heterogeneous preferences with respect to income and safety tradeoffs.

Again, this need not preclude attainment of efficient allocations so long as workers can express their collective interests with respect to the tradeoff between income and safety. But suppose that workers do not bargain collectively over wages and working conditions, and the monopsonist chooses a single wage rate and safety level to maximize its profits. This scenario is a simple extension of the single-wage-setting monopsony case examined in chapter 4. The new element to the model is that labor suppliers are assumed, as above, to have varying marginal rates of substitution between wages and safety.

Given these conditions, the market behavior of competitive labor sellers can be represented by a labor supply curve for which safety level is a shift variable: other things equal, higher safety shifts the market supply curve to the right. For any given number of workers hired by the monopsonist, this relationship between wage rates and safety levels corresponds to a downward-sloping "demand curve" for safety, showing what levels of workplace safety employers would require at each wage rate in order to work for the monopsonist. This demand curve is

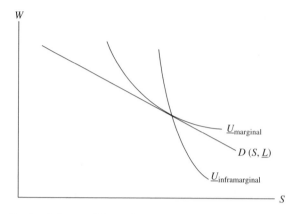

Figure 13.8(a) Derived demand for safety by monopsonist's incumbent labor force $\underline{L}$.

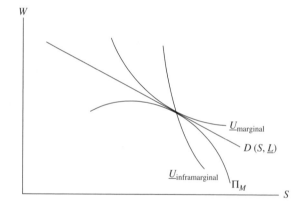

Figure 13.8(b) Profit-maximizing safety level for a single-wage-setting monopsonist.

illustrated in figure 13.8(a). As indicated, the demand curve has the key feature of being tangent at each point to the indifference curve of the *marginal* worker, that is, the worker who is just indifferent to participation in this labor market at the wage and safety combination corresponding to the point of tangency. In contrast, the marginal rates of substitution for all *inframarginal* workers, those who receive some producer surplus at that point, are all higher, as shown.

A profit-maximizing monopsonist will choose the point on the safety demand curve that is just tangent to its highest attainable isoprofit curve Π_M, as shown in figure 13.8(b). Thus, in maximizing profits, the monopsonist selects a wage and safety combination that is efficient only with respect to the preferences of the marginal employee. By the Pareto-optimality condition for public goods discussed above, the safety level chosen by the monopsonist is therefore inefficiently low, since it ignores the preferences of all its inframarginal employees.

In this scenario, there is a potential role for efficiency-improving government interventions in labor markets. One alternative is for the government to impose effective minimum safety standards. It's left to you to illustrate how this policy might improve on the allocation of income and workplace conditions achieved in the market. Another alternative is to promote workers' ability to bargain collectively, which would tend to increase the ability of inframarginal workers to express their preferences. This aspect of collective bargaining is discussed in more detail in the previous chapter. Finally, if it is not possible simply to eliminate the monopsony, the government might at least mitigate the degree of monopsony power by policies to improve worker mobility in the labor market.

THE IMPACT OF MONOPSONY ON JOB SAFETY

The foregoing argument suggests two potentially conflicting effects of monopsony power on safety. On one hand, increased monopsony reduces the range of alternative safety and wage combinations for workers to choose among, reducing their ability to make optimal tradeoffs of job safety for income. On the other hand, absent perfect wage discrimination, increased monopsony power tends to reduce the number of workers hired. If, as suggested in the text, monopsonists respond to the relative safety preferences of the marginal worker and inframarginal workers prefer great safety, then reduced employment will correspond, other things equal, to greater safety provision by profit-maximizing firms with monopsony power. In this context, the connection between job safety and the degree of monopsony power is an empirical issue.

The empirical connection is investigated by Shulamit Kahn (1991) using data for nonunionized coal mining companies in Kentucky, a particularly likely scenario for monopsony given the specialized skills of coal miners and their strong attachment to the region. Measuring the degree of monopsony power by the number of mines within a ten-mile drive, Kahn finds consistent evidence for the hypothesis that increased monopsony power leads to increased accident rates.

In a three-part exposé, reporters David Barstow and Lowell Bergman (2003) give a harrowing account of the consequences for worker safety of firm behavior consistent with the exercise of monopsony power in pipe manufacturing. The reported stratagems used to acquire and exercise this power included: purchase of troubled companies in economically declining regions where workers had few alternative employment opportunities; immediate layoffs subsequent to takeover while maintaining or increasing existing rates of production, requiring speedup and lengthening of work

continued

shifts for the remaining employees; sharp cutbacks on safety personnel, maintenance and cleanup crews, safety equipment and training, and even relief workers (so that employees were routinely denied timely restroom breaks); incentive pay to supervisors for increasing output, with no corresponding incentives for maintaining safety standards; disincentives for workers to report injuries, in the form of "disciplinary actions" for "careless behavior," leading to eventual dismissal, and "modified duties" for injured workers in the form of unpleasant tasks overseen by domineering supervisors; requirements that workers receive care only from company-approved doctors, given incentives to minimize workers' compensation costs; disregard of government safety regulations; efforts to obstruct and mislead safety inspectors, including the communication of fictitious or altered data; and the exercise of political clout to ward off criminal investigation and prosecution. As Barstow and Bergman report, these behaviors translated into high levels of profit and rates of injury and illness well ahead of already-high industry averages.

Related discussion questions:
1. What factors would determine the relative cost-effectiveness, with respect to increasing worker safety, of policies to reduce monopsony power and minimum safety regulations?
2. In the case of the pipe manufacturing firm reported in the *New York Times*, the practices listed above were initiated by the firm after it bought out existing plants. If the labor markets where these plants existed were perfectly competitive, would the post-takeover plant safety levels necessarily have stayed the same? If not, what would have happened instead?

Related references:
David Barstow and Lowell Bergman, "At a Texas Foundry, An Indifference to Life," *New York Times*, January 8, 2003: A1, A18–19; "A Family's Fortune, a Legacy of Blood and Tears," *ibid.*, January 9, 2003: A1, A20–A21; "Deaths on the Job, Slaps on the Wrist," *ibid.*, January 10, 2003: A1, A16–A17.
Shulamit Kahn, "Does Employer Monopsony Power Increase Occupational Accidents? The Case of Kentucky Coal Mines," NBER Working Paper No. 3897 (November 1991).

Insider power and observed wage differentials

Alternatively, suppose that *workers* enjoy wage-setting power in labor markets by virtue of the cost to employers of replacing them, possibly reinforced by collective bargaining rights. In general, this will result in higher than competitive-level wage rates, and consequently, given the presence of such *insider* power, labor economists seeking to ascertain the presence of compensating wage differentials for workplace disamenities would need to take this into account. This obstacle might present itself in two forms. In one scenario, parallel to that arising in the presence of monopsony power, the incidence of monopoly power may tend to offset compensating wage differentials that would otherwise obtain. This tendency would be exacerbated to the extent that monopoly power created conditions of excess supply that created supply spillover effects in markets with less safe jobs. Consequently, researchers would need to control for variations in insider power in order to detect compensating wage differentials.

The alternative scenario presents greater potential difficulties for assessing the empirical extent of wage compensation for workplace disamenities. In this case, the presence of insider power is strongly correlated with the incidence of workplace risks, so that jobs in which workplace risks are relatively high are also jobs in which workers enjoy wage-setting power. In that case, it would be difficult for researchers to distinguish the independent effects of wage-setting power and workplace disamenities, since the two tend to arise together. Keep this scenario in mind when reading the chapter's subsequent discussion of the related empirical literature on compensating wage differentials.

IMPERFECT CONTRACTING AND THE ALLOCATION OF WORKPLACE CHARACTERISTICS

In the scenarios just considered, inefficiency did not result from the existence of market power itself. For example, it was implicitly the limited information of the monopsonist concerning the preferences of its employees that kept it from providing an efficient level of safety consistent with maximizing its profits. This suggests that the fundamental problem yielding inefficient workplace safety levels stems from contracting failures due to significant transaction costs.

Moreover, in the specific context of assessing alternative policy responses to given market imperfections, the relevant issue is not simply whether contracting failures exist, but whether policy interventions might be able to improve on the resulting market outcomes. For example, suppose that compensating wage differentials for safety fail to arise because workers don't have information about safety risks at alternative employment sites. Even supposing that government agents were somehow better informed about market risks than market participants and politically inclined to improve labor market performance, it's not clear why, in the absence of monopsony, the government couldn't induce efficient market outcomes by simply releasing the relevant information to workers. In light of these considerations, this section considers two scenarios in which contracting failures create a potential role for beneficial policy interventions.

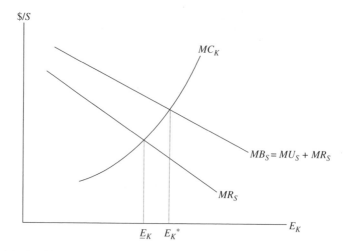

Figure 13.9   Inefficient incentives for safety provision with bilateral moral hazard.

Bilateral moral hazard in safety production

One form of contracting failure with implications for government policies respecting workplace safety arises when job safety levels are the joint product of unobservable or unverifiable efforts of both workers and employers. If payoffs to these parties can consequently only be conditioned on observed safety levels rather than respective efforts devoted to improving safety, then private contracting arrangements may be insufficient to generate efficient outcomes. This creates a potential role for government policies to change the feasible configuration of incentives.

To see the economic logic involved, imagine a simple scenario in which a firm hires a single employee. Suppose that the level of safety in the workplace, denoted S, positively affects both worker utility $U(S)$ and firm revenues $R(S)$ (by reducing production downtime and lost person-hours of specifically trained workers, say), and is a function of the efforts of both the firm and the employee, denoted respectively E_K and E_L. Assume that the worker's utility can be represented by monetary units, so that the gross social benefit of safety for this labor exchange is given by the sum of employee utility and firm revenues. The worker's payment for work effort not related to safety, which enters positively in worker utility but negatively in firm profits, is assumed to cancel out in this sum.

In addition, each actor has a private cost of expending effort toward safety, given respectively by the functions $C^K(E_K)$ and $C^L(E_L)$. Again assuming that these can be measured in pecuniary terms, the net social benefit of safety is represented by the sum of benefits $U(S) + R(S)$ minus the sum of effort costs $C^K(E_K) + C^L(E_L)$. Given this specification, the *efficient* level of effort for each actor is given by the intersection of that actor's marginal effort cost and the marginal social benefit curve. This condition is illustrated for the case of the firm's efficient effort level in figure 13.9.

As shown, the firm's efficient effort level E_K^* equates its marginal cost of effort to its *total* marginal benefit, the sum of marginal revenue and the worker's marginal utility of safety.

If it were possible to write enforceable contract terms governing respective safety contributions, the firm and worker could readily achieve these efficiency conditions by specifying the desired effort levels in the contract, accompanied by suitable penalties for failures to meet these terms. But suppose that the actors can't contract on their individual efforts, but only on safety levels that are the joint product of their efforts. In this case, it is not generally possible to achieve efficient safety provision by contractual means, at least if the employment relationship lasts for only a single period. The reason is that the inability to contract on individual safety efforts creates an unavoidable externality with respect to each actor's effort choice, such that each actor receives less than the full marginal benefit of any contribution to total safety.

Other things equal, the firm or worker will only consider private benefits and costs of efforts. For example, a profit-maximizing firm would elect a safety effort level that equates its marginal effort cost with marginal revenues, rather than the sum of marginal revenue and the employee's marginal utility of safety. As shown in figure 13.9, this will result in the firm contributing an efficiently low level of safety effort (denoted $\underline{E}_K$), with a parallel result holding for the worker's effort choice. This problem cannot be solved by reallocations of the revenue generated by production, since any such reallocation could only be based on total safety levels, and thus any increase in payment accruing to one actor would mean a reduction in payment, and consequently a further attenuation of effort incentives, to the other.

How might the inefficiency resulting from this contracting failure be addressed? One strategic possibility arises in the case that the relationship is repeated indefinitely over time. In that case, efficient effort combinations can be supported as a subgame-perfect equilibrium of the corresponding repeated game through the use of credible trigger strategies (discussed in chapter 6 and its appendix), so long as the firm and employee don't discount future payoffs too heavily. A possible trigger strategy, although not necessarily the most effective, would involve choosing efficient effort levels in each period of the relationship until a sub-par safety level is observed, after which the relationship is terminated immediately.

A second possibility that does not require a long-term employment relationship is for the government to fine one or both actors for safety levels that fall below the efficient level. Doing so eliminates the zero-sum aspect of pecuniary inducements that the two actors give each other. For example, if the firm is fined for failure to reach the efficient safety level, this causes a reduction in its profits that doesn't result in an automatic increase in payment to the employee. The firm could then induce the employee to provide the optimal level of safety through the appropriate incentive scheme, since its own efficient incentives could still be ensured by the externally imposed government sanctions.

Contracting failures and safety training

A related source of inefficiency arises if the attainment of optimal safety levels within an employment relationship requires that workers be trained in appropriate safety techniques, a particular form of human capital investment in which training costs are incurred initially in order to avoid lost person-hours and production downtime later on. As discussed in chapter 11, certain forms of contracting failure may create inefficient incentives for firms to invest in on-the-job training. For example, if the firm is unable to commit credibly to the payment of future wage premiums to trained workers, then in the case of general safety training it will not be able to make workers bear the full costs in this training, with a negative impact on total training. Alternatively, the firm has reduced incentives to provide training if there is some exogenously given probability that workers will leave after receiving training, creating a positive externality with respect to the firm's incentives to provide safety training.

As in the case of bilateral moral hazard, government safety regulations accompanied with financial sanctions could improve incentives by compelling the firm to internalize the externalities involved. For example, fines for safety violations could offset the reduction in safety incentives due to worker turnover. Of course, as in the scenario discussed above, the government would need to have adequate information on firm safety levels in order for the sanctions to have the desired effect; but at least there is no necessity that the government be better informed than market participants for safety regulations to have a beneficial effect.

EVIDENCE CONCERNING THE WAGE COMPENSATION HYPOTHESIS

The notion that workers are paid a wage premium for workplace disamenities has a long standing in the economics literature, dating back at least to the publication of Adam Smith's *Wealth of Nations* in 1776. The topic has also received a great deal of attention in more recent and econometrically oriented research in labor economics. Despite this, there remains a good deal of controversy about the range, prevalence, and magnitude of compensating wage differentials for unpleasant or dangerous job characteristics. Increasingly sophisticated empirical tests have provided evidence both for and against the hypothesis that compensating differentials are typically paid.

Serious econometric testing of the wage compensation hypothesis began in the early 1970s. Reviewing this early work in a 1980 article, labor economist Charles Brown found that some empirical support for the hypothesis had been established, but with an uncomfortable number of exceptions in which no evidence of a compensating differential had been found.[5] In another survey article published at about the same time, Robert Smith concluded that evidence for the existence of compensating differentials was inconclusive except for the risk of fatal injury.[6]

There are three possible explanations for the inconsistency of the results. The first is that the hypothesis simply fails to hold in some number of cases. This is clearly at least a logical possibility. For example, compensating differentials may fail to arise even in otherwise competitive markets, given high worker turnover (making it difficult for workers to ascertain the true characteristics of jobs) or low income (leading workers to favor income to the evident exclusion of other goods).

However, there are other possible reasons for the inconsistent empirical record. The second possibility is that inconsistencies stem from unreliable data; the corresponding *measurement error* could imply that estimates of the impact of given explanatory variables were biased up- or downward, either creating spurious evidence of compensation when none took place, or failing to discern it where it existed.

A particular problem in this regard arises with respect to data on workplace risks faced by workers. The direct method of acquiring these data through worker surveys may be plagued by intentional or accidental mis-reporting of actual workplace hazards. The more frequently used procedure of imputing industry averages for accident risk faces the obvious problem that individual risks may vary widely from the mean.

A final possibility is that the tests were marred by the omission of relevant explanatory variables in the regression equation. As discussed above, failure to control for the possibility that workers operate along different wage–safety frontiers may lead to spurious inferences of systematic relationships (or the lack thereof) between wages and workplace characteristics.

There are two types of variable that need to be controlled for in assessing the wage compensation hypothesis. The first concerns *individual* characteristics that may be difficult to observe, such as variations in individual effort or ability that can shift the wage–safety frontier. The second type of variable concerns *market conditions* that can also influence the wage–safety frontier. These would include factors that affect market power or the ability of market participants to write complete employment contracts.

The latter two problems must first be addressed before any sound conclusions can be drawn about the presence or absence of compensating differentials in real-world labor markets. Empirical work subsequent to Brown's and Smith's surveys has been geared to addressing one or both difficulties in the econometric tests, with varying results.

An interesting attempt to deal with both problems was undertaken in a study using data on Swedish workers.[7] The study considered a fixed set of workers whose experiences were recorded over time. To mitigate the problem of misreporting in survey data, the researchers used workers' reports on *changes* in working conditions rather than absolute *levels*, reasoning that any reporting bias, intended or otherwise, would thus cancel out. The researchers found statistically significant positive wage differentials for six characteristics out of sixteen presumptively unpleasant or dangerous workplace characteristics, with the rest being insignificant or (in one case) significant and negative. This is more compelling support than previously attained for the wage compensation hypothesis.

This study, however, did not control for potentially relevant market conditions other than the level of unemployment. Other work has suggested that three such conditions, market turnover, union status, and industry, may have a particularly strong bearing on the existence and magnitude of observed differentials. For example, labor turnover rates matter because it may take some time on the job for workers to learn about workplace characteristics such as risk levels. As a result, compensating differentials may not be paid in markets where average tenure at any given firm is low. One study compared observed responsiveness to workplace risk by workers having more or less than 3 years' standing in given jobs.[8] The researchers found that employees with longer than 3 years' tenure were more likely to take job conditions into account in their decisions.

A number of studies have found a puzzling dichotomy in the estimated responses to risk of unionized and nonunionized workers. The estimated wage differential for *fatal* accidents is typically much higher for unionized workers than for their nonunion counterparts, with the latter sometimes found to receive *negative* compensation for facing fatal accident risks! Moreover, the situation is reversed for non-fatal accident risk: unionized workers have been found to receive small or even negative compensation for such risks, while the estimated differential for nonunionized workers is typically positive, although not always statistically significant.

Although it's not surprising that unionized workers, presumably enjoying market power, would receive *different* levels of compensation for given risks than their nominally more competitive counterparts, it is not at all clear why there would be *systematic* differences in the level of compensation, especially in this dichotomous form. With respect to compensation for fatal accidents, two explanations for the union premium emerge from our earlier discussion: first, if safety is a normal good, more highly-paid union workers will have a higher marginal rate of substitution of safety for income, and thus would require greater compensation for a given increase in risk. Second, a similar result would emerge if unions are more responsive to *median* worker preferences, and these are based on higher average income or tenure than the *marginal* worker in given firms. Neither of these explanations account for the findings of negative compensation to nonunionized workers for fatal accident risks, however.

With respect to the absence of a union premium for non-fatal accident risks, it has been suggested that the anomaly results because unionized workers receive part of their compensation for accidents in the form of more time off work rather than greater pay. The reasoning here is that union power allows workers to take the extra time off after being injured without facing the threat of losing their jobs. But again, this doesn't account for the cases in which nonunionized workers are found to receive statistically insignificant compensation for non-fatal accident risks.

Perhaps the most dramatic challenge to the relevance of the wage compensation hypothesis comes from studies that control for the industry in which employees work. The basic problem stems from the fact that there is a high correlation between industries that pay high wages on average, and those that have high

accident rates. Of the US industries that pay relatively high wages, including manufacturing, mining, transportation/communications/public utilities, and construction, the latter three are also characterized by relatively high accident rates.

The problem for the compensation hypothesis arises because the first phenomenon may have no connection to the second. A number of studies have found
systematic inter-industry wage differentials, both in the US and in other industrialized countries, that have no readily apparent connection to variables relevant
to the ideal market model of employment outcomes. (This issue is discussed in
more detail in chapter 16.) Consequently, it may be that putatively compensating
wage differentials are simply an artifact of the reality that high-wage industries
typically also happen to be high-risk industries, with no intrinsic connection
between the two.

At least four recent studies have lent weight to this possibility. In each case, the
goal was to test for the presence of compensating differentials after first controlling for the industry in which members of the sample were employed. In all cases,
the inclusion of industry controls dramatically reduced the estimates of wage
compensation, and sometimes rendered them statistically insignificant. In one
study, no estimates for compensating differentials remained statistically significant after controlling for industry status.[9] A follow-up study found that after controlling for industry status only two estimates were statistically significant: a
positive premium paid to unionized workers for fatal risks, and *negative* compensation to nonunionized workers for non-fatal risk.[10]

While more empirical work needs to be done to sort out the effects of industry
status on the payment of wage compensation for risks, these studies suggest a
fundamental dichotomy with respect to the payment of differentials, such that
workers with high income, job tenure, and union protection (highly correlated
conditions) tend reliably to receive compensation, while nonunionized workers
with low income and high rates of job turnover do not. If valid, this dichotomy
suggests a fundamental *segmentation* of labor markets, a phenomenon to be discussed further in the chapters to follow.

CONCLUSION

Do labor markets allocate workplace disamenities, including risks of occupational
injury or illness, appropriately? The theory of compensating wage differentials
answers this question in a way that may seem surprising, initially even counter-
intuitive, to non-economists. Just as standard economic theory would not suggest
that all harmful pollutants should be eliminated, it doesn't imply that jobs should
be outlawed just because they're dangerous. In the same way that informed individuals might be granted the right and responsibility to determine their self-
exposure to risks outside of the workplace, in competitive markets these individuals might be presumed to make rational tradeoffs between risk and income. The
hypothesized result, as explained in the body of the chapter, is wage compensation for workplace disamenities.

However, the presence of wage premiums for dangerous jobs does not of itself imply that workers are fully compensated for the risks they face. The incidence of monopsony power resulting from worker mobility costs, for example, may prevent workers from exacting full compensation for undesirable work characteristics. Conversely, the inability of labor economists to discern wage differentials does not of itself prove they are not paid, given the possibility of inadequate data or improper statistical test design.

Ultimately, the fundamental issue for policy purposes is not the presence or absence of observed wage compensation, but whether there is any scope for beneficial government interventions with respect to job safety. Generally speaking, this scope is created by contracting failures with respect to the provision of working conditions and not, for example, the presence of labor market power, although there might be compelling reasons to eliminate this power on alternative grounds.

Study Questions

1. Define a *compensating wage differential*. What conditions must exist to give rise to a compensating differential under competitive labor market conditions? If perfectly competitive labor market conditions do not hold, do observed wage differences necessarily reflect full hedonic compensation for workplace risks? Under what conditions would wage differentials for unsafe working conditions *not* arise even under the conditions of the hedonic wage model?
2. Illustrate and explain the impact of government interventions in the form of minimum safety regulations and after-the-fact worker's compensation for job-related injury and illness under conditions of perfect competition and wage-discriminating monopsony. Under what market conditions, if any, might these interventions be expected to improve social welfare?
3. Suppose that job safety conditions are a workplace-level public good and a firm's employees have heterogeneous preferences with respect to the tradeoff of income for safety. What is the likely impact if these workers are allowed to bargain collectively with the firm?
4. Other things equal, why might protections of senior workers against layoff improve the allocation of safety in given employment relationships?

Notes

1   ILO InFocus Programme on Safety and Health at Work and the Environment, "Global Estimates of Fatalities Caused by Work-Related Diseases and Occupational Accidents, 2002." Website: http://www.ilo.org/safework.

2   Bureau of Labor Statistics, US Department of Labor, "National Census of Fatal Occupational Injuries in 2001," news release, September 25, 2002. Web address: http://stats.bls.gov/iif/oshcfoi1.htm.

3   Bureau of Labor Statistics, Department of Labor, "National Census of Fatal Occupational Injuries in 2000," news release, August 14, 2001. Web address: http://stats.bls.gov/oshhome.htm.

4   Bureau of Labor Statistics, Department of Labor, "Workplace Injuries and Illnesses in 2001," news release, December 19, 2002. Web address: http://www.bls.gov/iif/home.htm.

5   Charles Brown, "Equalizing Differences in the Labor Market," *Quarterly Journal of Economics* 94, no. 1 (February 1980): 113–34.

6   Robert S. Smith, "Compensating Wage Differentials and Public Policy: A Review," *Industrial and Labor Relations Review* 32, no. 3 (April 1979): 339–52.

7   Greg J. Duncan and Bertil Holmlund, "Was Adam Smith Right After All? Another Test of the Theory of Compensating Wage Differentials," *Journal of Labor Economics* 1, no. 4 (October 1983): 366–79.

8   W. Kip Viscusi and Michael J. Moore, "Worker Learning and Compensating Differentials," *Industrial and Labor Relations Review* 45, no. 1 (October 1991): 80–96.

9   J. Paul Leigh, "Compensating Wages, Value of a Statistical Life, and Inter-industry Differentials," *Journal of Environmental Economics and Management* 28, no. 1 (January 1995): 83–97.

10 Peter Dorman and Paul Hagstrom, "Wage Compensation for Dangerous Work Revisited," *Industrial and Labor Relations Review* 52, no. 1 (October 1998): 116–35.

Suggestions for Further Reading

Peter Dorman, *Markets and Mortality: Economics, Dangerous Work, and the Value of Human Life* (Cambridge: Cambridge University Press, 1996).

Michael J. Moore and W. Kip Viscusi, *Compensation Mechanisms for Job Risks: Wages, Workers' Compensation, and Product Liability* (Princeton: Princeton University Press, 1990).

CHAPTER FOURTEEN

EDUCATION AND ABILITY

In his classic treatise *The Wealth of Nations*, published over two hundred years ago, Adam Smith compared the acquisition of occupational skills to investments in physical capital stock:

> When any expensive machine is erected, the extraordinary work to be per-formed by it before it is worn out, it must be expected, will replace the capital laid out upon it, with at least the ordinary profits. A man educated at the expense of much labor and time to any of those employments which require extraordinary dexterity and skill, may be compared to one of those expensive machines. The work which he learns to perform, it must be expected, over and above the usual wages of common labor, will replace to him the whole expense of his education, with at least the ordinary profits of an equally valu-able capital.[1]

In this vision, an individual's capacity for productive labor is an asset that can be augmented through costly investments in education and training. Unlike intermediate inputs such as tools and machines, however, *human capital* assets are inseparable from their suppliers.

Human capital theory, the modern elaboration on Smith's simple theme, posits that education and training raise wages by increasing the revenue productivity of workers who gain job-relevant skills thereby. This basic hypothesis offers a potential microeconomic explanation for the strong and consistent correlation between years of formal schooling and individual labor income, and posits human capital investments as a potential source of macroeconomic growth and economic development. The theory yields potentially testable explanations for such seemingly disparate phenomena as the aggregate distribution of earned income, the temporal structure of savings, and the lifetime trajectory of individual labor incomes. In large part due to its power to generate hypotheses respecting a wide range of labor market outcomes, human capital theory provides the analytical core of most work in contemporary labor economics.

The basic elements of human capital theory were introduced in chapter 3 and then applied to the analysis of on-the-job training in chapter 11. The present chapter fleshes out the theory by considering factors that affect households' opportunities and decisions with respect to formal schooling, and the economic consequences of these decisions. As in chapter 3, the theory and its primary implications are studied in the context of perfectly competitive labor markets.

The conception of education as a remunerative investment in human capital doesn't require the assumption that labor markets are perfectly competitive, but departures from ideal market conditions may modify or weaken the logical chain connecting formal schooling to labor productivity to wage levels. Two such scenarios are considered in this chapter. First, if employers have incomplete information about worker characteristics affecting productivity, they may use educational attainment as a basis for screening prospective employees. An implication of educational screening is that wage rates increase with formal schooling levels even if the latter make no contribution to workers' human capital.

Second, if exchange frictions obstruct market-clearing wage adjustments (as in the efficiency wage scenarios examined in chapters 10 and 11), then resulting mobility barriers may induce systematic differentials in returns to schooling. Persistent differentials, if they exist, suggest a theory of "dual" or "segmented" labor markets at odds with standard human capital analysis. Possible bases and implications of labor market segmentation are investigated in chapter 16.

FORMAL SCHOOLING AND WAGE LEVELS

The basic assumption of human capital theory with respect to educational choice is that the acquisition of formal schooling is costly and yields returns in the form of higher revenue productivity in the workplace. Assuming that individual workers bear at least some of the costs of their education, these conditions ensure that more highly educated workers are paid a compensating wage differential under competitive labor market conditions. This elemental prediction of human capital theory was advanced in chapter 3.

This implication is corroborated by simple correlations between individual educational attainment and labor income. On average, people with more years of formal schooling earn higher wage rates. Table 14.1 provides numerical detail on this relationship between educational attainment and annual income for a sample of full-time US workers from 1999, separately for women and men.

Table 14.1 Median annual income of year-round, full-time US workers 25 years old and over, by educational attainment and sex, 1999

Educational attainment	Male	Female
Less than 9th grade	$20,429	$15,098
9th to 12th grade, no diploma	$25,035	$17,015
High school graduate	$33,184	$23,061
Some college, no degree	$39,221	$27,757
Associate degree	$41,638	$30,919
Bachelor's degree	$52,985	$37,993
Master's degree	$66,243	$48,097
Professional degree	$100,000	$59,904
Doctorate degree	$81,687	$60,079

Source: Digest of Education Statistics (2001): table 382; website: http://nces.ed.gov/pubs2002/digest2001/tables/XLS/Tab382.xls. Data are in constant 1999 dollars.

The average impact of years of schooling on hourly earnings has been increasing since the 1970s. In 1975, aggregating over all years of educational attainment, employed men in the US labor force earned just over 6% more in average hourly wages for each extra year of formal education, while employed women received an increment of just under 8% on average for each extra year. The corresponding percentage increases respectively for men and women are both just over 8% in 1985, and exceeded 10% in 1995. Apparently, the positive impact of education on earnings has increased substantially over this period.

Disaggregating the data by level of educational attainment reveals a startling dichotomy underlying the increasing average return to education. Over the 25 years from 1973 to 1997, while average hourly earnings significantly increased for those with a college or more advanced degree, real hourly wages on average *fell* for workers in the US labor force with less than a college degree. Moreover, these changes are not unique to the US economy. Data from OECD countries for roughly the same period show increasing returns in average hourly earnings to additional formal schooling, and a similar dichotomy in the real hourly earnings paths between those who have and those who lack at least a college degree.

Viewed through the lens of human capital theory, the divergent wage trends for workers with different educational attainments indicate a shift in the balance of supply and demand for skills imparted in college and beyond, relative to that for skills acquired in lower levels of education. Specifically, the demand for college degree-bearing workers increased, while that for workers without a degree remained stagnant or fell, and the relevant supply curves have not (yet?) adjusted to the new wage differentials. This scenario is illustrated in figure 14.1.

If this diagnosis is correct, it prompts an immediate question as to the causes of the shift in relative demand. Why might the demand for college-trained workers have increased and that for less-educated workers fallen? There are at

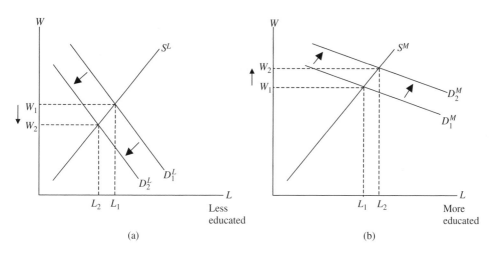

Figure 14.1 Effects of opposite demand shifts for less- and more-educated workers.

least two possible explanations based on the dramatic changes in the global economy over the past quarter-century or so. First, there has been a substantial increase in the volume of international trade in this period, raising the possibility that emerging patterns of specialization have favored highly skilled workers to the detriment of their less-educated counterparts. Second, the dynamic path of technical innovations – spurred, for example, by the remarkable development and diffusion of computer technology – may have fundamentally altered the structure of demand for labor skills. These competing explanations are explored further below.

A parallel question with respect to the human capital interpretation of wage trends concerns the behavior of labor supply. Granting that the relative demand for college-educated workers has increased, why hasn't relative supply shifted in response? Presumably the increased wage differential favoring workers with greater schooling would prompt individuals to acquire more education; they might plausibly even have done this in *anticipation* of future demand changes. To assess the response of skilled labor supply to changing wage patterns, it is necessary to understand the economic logic of educational choices. This issue is taken up in the next section.

However, at least three features of the empirical relationship between schooling and wages offer potential challenges to the human capital interpretation of wage trends. One concerns the disproportionate impact of certain levels of educational attainment on wages. In table 14.1, note the relatively large jumps corresponding to completion of high school and of a standard four-year bachelor's degree program.

Abrupt jumps in average hourly earnings for workers with a high school or college degree, compared to their respective counterparts with one less year of

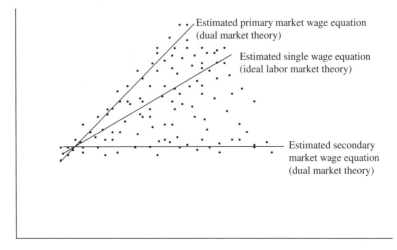

Figure 14.2   Hypothetical scatter plot given dual labor markets.

schooling, suggest that labor markets attach special significance to the attainment of particular educational milestones. But why should this be the case? If education matters because it creates job-relevant skills, it's at best not obvious why particular stages of schooling should *consistently* accrue a premium. These irregularities therefore suggest the existence of "credential" or "diploma" effects, meaning that attainment of the relevant credential somehow has a greater impact on subsequent income than the incremental skills acquired in attaining the credential. Possible economic grounds for the existence of diploma effects are considered later in the chapter.

A second problematic feature involves the degree of wage dispersion *within* groups defined by educational attainment. Not only has wage inequality *across* schooling levels increased since the 1970s, but the variance in wage rates for *each* level of schooling has increased as well. Although increased dispersion by educational level does not necessarily contradict the assumption that labor markets are perfectly competitive, it does raise a question as to why mobility across labor markets doesn't tend to eliminate within-group wage variations, or at least maintain them at given levels.

Third, while there is a strong and consistent correlation between formal schooling and wage levels for all labor suppliers, a focus on the overall relationship may obscure systematic differences in the wage–schooling nexus among subsets of workers. Some economists have argued, for example, that the empirical connection between schooling and wage levels for US workers is better represented by *two* regression lines, one of which has zero slope. This hypothesis is illustrated in figure 14.2.

This possibility sharpens the question raised above about mobility conditions in labor markets. If the hypothesis of a "dual" relationship between schooling and wages is valid, why don't workers receiving no returns on costly educational investments simply move to markets in which these investments are rewarded? Keep the questions raised here in mind as you work your way through the arguments and evidence presented in this chapter.

FORMAL EDUCATION AS HUMAN CAPITAL INVESTMENT

Workers enter the full-time labor force with very different levels of educational attainment. Some idea of the diversity of educational backgrounds for labor suppliers in the US economy is given by table 14.2, which represents the US labor force by years of formal schooling for two years, 1995 and 2000. Note that just within the indicated span of five years the distribution has shifted in the direction of greater average educational attainment.

What explains the wide differences among workers in formal schooling? Of course, mandatory school attendance laws put a more or less pervasive floor on educational attainments. In the US, for example, it is typically the case that children are required by law to attend school until age sixteen. But beyond such legally mandated minimums, a person's level of schooling is largely a matter of choice subject to constraints of ability and means.

A basic model of educational choice

Begin the analysis of educational choices by letting the variable S denote the extent of post-mandatory schooling and then defining $R(S)$, $C(S)$ respectively as the total returns and total costs of schooling. To keep the analysis as simple as possible, ignore the prospect of risky returns to educational investments and focus only on pecuniary costs and benefits of education. Returns to schooling then consist of the discounted lifetime earnings associated with a given level of post-mandatory education, while the cost of schooling includes direct costs of educational services, plus the opportunity costs of purchasing these services in lieu of the best alter-

Table 14.2 Educational attainment of the civilian non-institutional US population 25 to 64 years of age, 1995 and 2000

Educational attainment	1995	2000
Less than a high school diploma	10.8	9.8
High school graduates, no college	33.1	31.8
Less than a bachelor's degree	27.8	27.9
College graduates	28.3	30.4

Source: *Statistical Abstract of the United States* (2001): 369 (table 571).

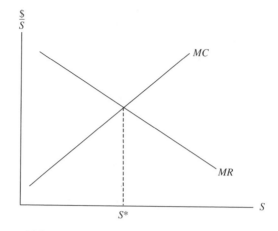

Figure 14.3   Determination of individual schooling choices.

native investment and forgoing full-time employment at the best available wage rate.

Other things equal, an optimizing household will choose the level of education that maximizes the positive difference between benefits and costs of elective education. Under the simplifying assumptions stated above, the standard postulate of optimizing behavior yields the prediction that each person will choose the level of post-mandatory schooling that equates the *marginal* returns and costs of education. This outcome is illustrated in figure 14.3. The downward slope of the MR curve reflects the standard assumption of diminishing marginal returns. The upward slope of the MC curve can be interpreted as reflecting either the use of more costly inputs for higher levels of education or a rising opportunity cost of forgoing full-time employment.

The next step in the analysis is to introduce factors that might induce variations in educational choices among households. One possibility that has received a great deal of attention in the economic literature on education and labor market outcomes has to do with the effects of individual differences in innate *ability*. The conception of innate ability, and especially the idea that it is a quality measurable along a single dimension, is a controversial issue. An alternative view insists that ability can vary along a number of dimensions, such as spatial, mathematical, creative, neuro-motor, and expressive aptitudes, that need not be strongly correlated.

There is a related controversy as to the appropriate measure of innate ability. This is clearly a problem if ability is understood to have many dimensions: which dimensions should be measured, and if more than one, how should the distinct measures be weighed relative to each other? However, even if ability could be defined along a single dimension, there might remain the problem of measuring individual positions along that dimension accurately. For example, studies have revealed cultural or ethnic biases in some standardized tests of basic aptitude.

For present purposes, the first controversy can be sidestepped by defining ability functionally as individual characteristics that are revenue-productive in given labor markets. Of course, these characteristics need not truly represent "ability" in the standard interpretation of the term, but may rather include such attributes as punctuality or perseverance. Furthermore, these traits may not be accurately reflected in ability measures available to economic researchers. For example, one study found that the individual traits most reliably reflected in supervisory ratings were orientation to following rules, dependability, and internalization of firm goals. It seems at least questionable that these characteristics are strongly correlated with more presumptive measures of "ability" such as scores on standard aptitude and IQ tests.[2]

Putting aside the measurement issue for the time being, the immediate issue concerns the role of ability differences in the model of educational choice depicted in figure 14.3. The most plausible consequence, in view of the manner in which "ability" has been defined, is that the marginal returns to education curve is a function of ability, in the sense that higher ability (however measured) shifts the MR curve upward. That is, more able people are presumed to make "better use" of each additional year of schooling in terms of market payoffs.

It is possible that individual ability also affects the marginal cost curve, but the direction of net impact is less clear. On one hand, the opportunity cost of forgoing full-time employment is presumably higher for individuals with greater ability. On the other, it is possible that more able people incur lower direct marginal costs of schooling, for instance because they need to consume fewer educational inputs to achieve given skills. However, in either case the cost effects are felt only in the relatively few years that a person pursues formal schooling, while the returns are accrued over a lifetime. Thus it is reasonable to suppose that the impact of ability on cost is swamped by its effects on returns, and thus can be ignored for the sake of simplicity.

Let a representative individual's innate ability be denoted by A. The implications of introducing ability as a variable in the basic model are shown in figure 14.4, indicating that greater ability corresponds to higher marginal returns at each level of schooling (represented by the shift from $MR_1 = MR(A_1)$ to $MR_2 = MR(A_2)$). Two predictions result from this representation: first, other things equal, individuals with higher ability choose higher levels of education. Thus, for a given marginal cost curve, individuals with ability level A_1 choose S_1 years of schooling, while those with higher ability level A_2 choose $S_2 > S_1$.

To grasp the second implication of variable ability for educational choice, note that the area under the marginal return curve up to a given level of schooling corresponds to the *total* returns associated with that level of schooling. With that in mind, note with respect to figure 14.4 that the area under MR_2 up to the corresponding schooling choice S_2 exceeds the area under MR_1 up to point S_1 for two distinct reasons: first, because more able workers choose more schooling, and

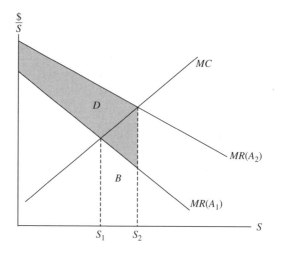

Figure 14.4 Impact of individual ability on schooling choices.

second, because more able workers receive higher marginal returns for *each level* of schooling.

Consequently, for the difference in total returns to schooling between A_1 and A_2 workers, area B is the portion of the difference attributable solely to the additional schooling ($S_2 - S_1$), holding ability level fixed at A_1, while area D is the difference in returns attributable to the fact that A_2 workers have higher ability. This result implies that empirical estimates of the marginal return to schooling which fail to control for ability will tend to *overstate* the incremental contribution of education to income.

A second variable affecting individual educational choices is the *quality* of education received. Denote the level of educational quality by Q. A given quantity of education is understood to exhibit higher quality if it increases market returns, other things equal. That is, higher Q, like higher ability, shifts the marginal return curve upward, other things equal.

It is plausible to assume that higher quality educational inputs cost more, so that higher quality is associated with higher marginal cost of schooling as well. For reasons similar to those explained above, it is reasonable to suppose that the revenue effect swamps the effect on marginal cost of increased quality, and thus to ignore the latter for the sake of simplification.

The consequences of increased educational quality are thus essentially the same as for increased personal ability: consumption of higher-quality schooling is typically associated with the purchase of higher levels of schooling, and the return to each additional unit of schooling is higher than for lower-quality educational inputs. Again, a necessary corollary is that failure to control for educational quality implies that the incremental returns to *quantity* of schooling would be overstated in statistical studies.

Capital market failures and formal schooling choices

The theoretical story constructed so far is consistent with the universal operation of perfectly competitive markets. There are, however, potentially significant ramifications for personal educational choices if capital markets are imperfect. These imperfections can have an impact on labor markets even if the latter markets are themselves perfectly competitive.

There are two reasons why investors in *human* capital might be particularly likely to encounter credit market imperfections. First, it may be difficult for lenders to ascertain that resources are being used effectively for skill acquisition (as opposed, say, to purely consumption-oriented educational choices), or that skills once acquired are remuneratively employed. Informational constraints of this sort may lead to moral hazard problems with respect to the use of loans for educational purposes.

Second, recall from chapter 9's discussion concerning the determinants of firm ownership that one remedy for moral hazard imperfections lies in the ability to provide *collateral* for risky loans. But offering one's *human* capital as collateral is not a viable option, given its inalienable nature (and the illegality of indentured servitude). Workers thus cannot secure educational loans by promising to give up their acquired skills for sale in the event of loan default.

Credit market imperfections may take either of two forms. First, lenders may require a higher rate of interest than would prevail under ideal market conditions, thus reducing the quantity demanded of educational loans. Second, and more severely, lenders may *ration* credit, implying that some economically desirable loans cannot be arranged at any interest rate. In either case, the marginal cost of educational finance will depend on family wealth available for investment in skill acquisition. Thus, to reflect capital market imperfections, marginal cost of schooling is represented as a function of family resources, denoted by the letter F.

The consequences for human capital acquisition of credit market imperfections are depicted in figure 14.5. Here a higher level of family wealth, $F_2 > F_1$, leads to a *lower* level of marginal cost for each level of schooling, other things equal. The most immediate implication is that binding credit market imperfections reduce the amount invested in education by raising the marginal cost of this investment above that which would obtain under ideal conditions. As a corollary, workers from families with less personal wealth can also anticipate having lower lifetime income, other things equal. If Pareto-optimal conditions would have been achieved under ideal credit market conditions, then credit market imperfections lead to suboptimal investments in human capital.

The final implication to note concerns the association between level of educational attainment and observed *marginal* returns from education. Other things equal, variations in family resources F will shift the marginal cost curve up and down along a given marginal return curve, leading to an *inverse* relationship between years of schooling and the marginal return on schooling. That is to say, once other systematic variations are controlled for, each additional year of

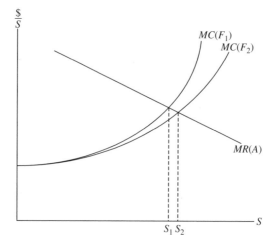

Figure 14.5 Impact of differential family wealth on individual schooling choices.

schooling is associated with a smaller increment to an individual's lifetime income.

This is the opposite of what would occur allowing ability or school quality to vary holding other systematic effects constant. If educational variations are driven primarily by differences in these variables, then one would expect a *positive* correlation between levels of educational attainment and the marginal return to schooling, with successively higher levels of education leading to correspondingly higher marginal contributions to discounted lifetime income.

FORMAL EDUCATION AS A
LABOR MARKET SIGNALING DEVICE

Credit market imperfections prompt the inclusion of a new explanatory variable, family income or wealth, in the analysis of personal schooling choices, but don't challenge the fundamental postulates of human capital theory concerning the relationship between education and income. In contrast, informational asymmetries with respect to individual ability may alter the basic economic logic connecting individual ability, schooling levels, and labor income. In particular, under such conditions educational attainment may serve as a *signal* of unobservable individual ability, in addition to, or perhaps even instead of, reflecting the acquisition of additional skills.

The theory of formal schooling as a signaling mechanism can be constructed as follows. First, suppose for the sake of argument that schooling makes no independent contribution to labor productivity (total or marginal), which is instead determined solely by individual ability (however that might be defined). In this case, prospective employers have no *direct* interest in the educational attainment

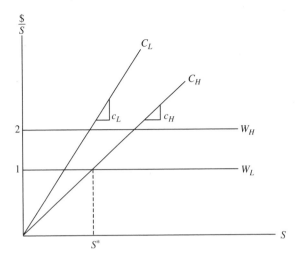

Figure 14.6 Sorting equilibrium in individuals' choice of schooling.

of workers, and under perfectly competitive conditions, would be unwilling to pay a wage premium to workers with more schooling.

But now assume in addition that individual ability levels are both invisible to employers and inversely correlated with the cost of schooling. Employers would like to know the ability of potential employees, since other things equal more capable employees contribute more to the bottom line, but can't distinguish among labor suppliers on the basis of ability. They might, however, be able to *infer* a worker's ability from his or her choice of educational attainment, assuming that the labor market has attained a *sorting equilibrium* (to be defined presently).

This point can be illustrated with the aid of figure 14.6, which depicts two possible wage levels, $W_L = 1$ and $W_H = 2$, relative to possible schooling levels S chosen by a given worker. Interpret these respectively as the discounted lifetime labor incomes obtained under competitive labor market conditions for workers of low and high innate ability. These are drawn as horizontal lines since formal schooling does not contribute directly to a worker's value marginal productivity by assumption, contrary to the basic premise of human capital theory. Under competitive conditions, employers would thus pay low-ability workers W_L and high-ability workers W_H in equilibrium.

The assumption that schooling costs are inversely related to ability is reflected in the educational cost curves C_L and C_H. Their respective slopes, denoted c_L and c_H, satisfy $c_L > c_H$, indicating that low-ability workers incur higher marginal costs of schooling. These curves also reflect the absence of credit market imperfections; otherwise, as in figure 14.5, costs of educational financing would presumably depend on family wealth.

Now consider the optimization problem faced by employers in deciding which workers to hire. By assumption, firms cannot directly distinguish workers by ability. If they let prospective employees announce their ability levels and select their own wage levels accordingly, self-interest would prompt all workers to claim greater abilities and thus secure the higher wage, whatever their true ability levels. Alternatively, employers could elect to pay every worker a wage corresponding to the *average* value marginal product of the two types of worker, as in the matching model studied in chapter 11. This stratagem would cause low-ability workers to be overpaid and high-ability workers to be underpaid relative to their respective competitive wages. Clearly, then, both employers and high-ability workers have an incentive to alter this wage *pooling* arrangement if they can.

Under the conditions depicted in figure 14.6, high-ability workers can signal their true productivity by their schooling choices. To see this, suppose that employers require some minimum educational level $\underline{S}$ of any worker seeking the wage stream W_H. Assuming as before that workers choose the schooling level that yields the highest net return, they will undertake at least that minimum schooling level only so long as its net return, W_H minus the cost of acquiring $\underline{S}$, exceeds W_L (since schooling has no investment value unless it secures the higher wage, those who choose not to attain the minimum will not acquire any extra schooling). Conversely, a worker will elect not to achieve $\underline{S}$, and thus to receive W_L, if the inequality is reversed.

Define a *signaling equilibrium* as a level of schooling S^* which achieves the double condition that workers will select it, and thus receive the higher wage rate, *if and only if* they have high ability (this is also called a "separating equilibrium," since it entails that different worker types are treated differently). If this condition is met, then employers can unerringly infer workers' ability levels from their schooling choices. Under the assumptions discussed above, the minimum equilibrium schooling level satisfies the condition $W_H - W_L = c_H \cdot S^*$, since at this point high-ability workers are just indifferent between meeting the educational requirement and not doing so, while low-ability workers would be made strictly worse off by meeting the requirement.

If a signaling equilibrium is achieved, then higher-ability workers receive higher wages, just as under perfectly competitive labor market conditions. But note crucially that the necessity of signaling implies a positive correlation between schooling and labor income, just as predicted by human capital theory. This is despite the assumption, in sharp contrast to the basic postulate of that theory, that education does not provide employment-relevant skills!

An additional implication of the signaling model is the presence of *credential* or *diploma* effects on wages, reflected in abrupt increases in labor income associated with attainment of particular educational plateaus such as completion of high school or a bachelor's degree. The discussion earlier in the chapter indicated possible evidence for the existence of such effects. In the signaling model, diploma effects arise due to the informational features of particular educational milestones. The existence of multiple such milestones, consistent with the data reviewed earlier, would be predicted by a richer version of the model with more than two possible ability levels.

Schooling requirements may seem like a relatively expensive and indirect way for employers to ascertain worker quality. The theory of education as a sorting mechanism has thus been criticized on the grounds that employers could presumably find more cost-effective ways of distinguishing workers by ability. However, this criticism may not be as compelling as it first seems.

First, unlike with more direct tests of worker ability, employers incur no direct costs in using worker educational attainments for sorting purposes. Second, it may be difficult or impossible to test reliably for affective characteristics, such as punctuality or persistence, that manifest themselves over a long period of time.

On the other hand, employers may have means other than testing to screen for desired worker characteristics. For example, suppose employers prefer workers with a lower propensity to quit, other things equal. One way of attracting employees with this characteristic is to offer a low initial wage coupled with the promise of substantial wage increases over time, as in the Lazear model of temporal incentive provision studied in chapter 11. Workers who do not expect to remain long with given employers would find such offers relatively unattractive, while non-quitters could be sufficiently compensated for the initially low wage.

Thus, while there is a certain plausibility to the educational screening hypothesis, it does not follow necessarily from the condition that employers can't directly observe ability levels of prospective employees. Consequently, the connection between schooling levels and wage levels is ultimately an empirical issue. The next task is thus to assess the empirical evidence linking schooling and labor income. Findings on this question may provide clues to the explanation for recent dramatic changes in the wage structure of developed economies, discussed above.

EVIDENCE ON THE SCHOOLING–INCOME NEXUS

Distinguishing ability and schooling effects on labor income

The wage trends examined earlier in the chapter suggest that formal education has a positive effect on labor income and that this effect has become more powerful over the past two and a half decades, leading to an increasing disparity in the incomes of high school- and college-educated workers. But the subsequent theoretical analysis yields the caution that schooling decisions are affected by variations in individual ability and family background, so that at least part of the correlation between schooling and income might be accounted for by other explanatory factors. For example, in the pure version of the signaling model considered above, *all* of the correspondence between education and income can be explained by unobserved productivity differences among workers. Consequently, the independent effect of individual ability on labor income must somehow be isolated in order to make any meaningful assessment of the labor market impact of schooling.

THE BELL CURVE CONTROVERSY

The task of controlling for the independent effect of individual ability on labor income has gained increased salience subsequent to the publication in 1996 of a controversial book, *The Bell Curve*. Authors Richard Herrnstein and Charles Murray argue that most of the observed variation in economic success can be explained by genetically transmitted differences in intelligence. On this basis they assert that there is little scope for increasing the economic prospects of those with low inherited ability by giving them more education.

While scientists from a number of disciplines responded vigorously to these claims (cf. Fischer *et al.*, 1996 and Devlin *et al.*, 1997), economists focused in particular on the asserted link between cognitive ability and wage differentials, as well as the authors' claim that wage variations across race and gender are due primarily to differences in cognitive ability. Both of these claims are rejected by the data (Cawley *et al.*, 1999). Ability is evidently rewarded unequally in the labor market, as workers of the same measured ability but of different race and gender receive different wages. Also, measured cognitive ability explains only a small percentage of wage variance – only between 1% and 3% (Cawley *et al.*, 1996). Hence both the positive claims made in *The Bell Curve* and the policy recommendations based on those claims appear unreasonable.

Related discussion questions:
1. Why doesn't cognitive ability matter more in determining wages?
2. Do you think cognitive ability mattered more or less in the past for determining wages? Do you think it will matter more or less in the future?

Related references:

John Cawley, Karen Conneely, James Heckman, and Edward Vytlacil, "Measuring the Effects of Cognitive Ability," National Bureau of Economic Research Working Paper No. 5645 (1996).

John Cawley, James Heckman, and Edward Vytlacil, "Meritocracy in America: Wages within and across Occupations," *Industrial Relations* 38, no. 3 (July 1999): 250–96.

Bernie Devlin, Stephen Fienberg, Daniel Resnick, and Kathryn Roeder (eds), *Intelligence and Success: Is it All in the Genes? Scientists Respond to THE BELL CURVE* (New York: Springer Verlag, 1997).

Claude Fischer, Michael Hout, Martín Sánchez Jankowski, Samuel Lucas, Ann Swidler, and Kim Voss, *Inequality by Design: Cracking the Bell Curve Myth* (Princeton: Princeton University Press, 1996).

Richard J. Herrnstein and Charles Murray, *The Bell Curve: Intelligence and Class Structure in American Life* (New York: Simon & Schuster, 1996).

As noted earlier, the chief problem faced by researchers attempting to isolate the impact of schooling choices on labor income lies in controlling for the effects of invisible ability differences. To address this problem, labor economists have primarily relied on two strategies: first, comparing the incomes of identical twins with different levels of schooling, and second, estimating the consequences of "natural experiments" or exogenous events that influence individual schooling levels without directly affecting individual prospects for earning income.

An example of such an exogenous event is being born in the first quarter of the calendar year. Given the typical content of mandatory school attendance laws, people with first-quarter birth dates start school later and thus receive less education on average than others in their age cohort. Moreover, one would not expect a first-quarter birthday to have an *independently* negative impact on one's economic chances. Thus this event can presumably only affect lifetime income through its impact on individual education levels.

Reviewing the findings of a range of studies employing these or related research strategies, labor economists Orley Ashenfelter and Cecilia Rouse conclude that a significant impact of schooling on income generally remains even after controlling to the extent possible for ability differences.[3] The estimated rates of return to schooling they summarize range from 3 to 18%, with a median estimate of about 8 to 9%. They argue that while the inability to control for ability biases the estimate upward, errors in measuring the extent of schooling tend to bias estimates downward, with the net effect that studies controlling for both problems tend to arrive at estimates very close to those of studies that control for neither. Thus they find significant econometric evidence for the claim that formal schooling directly increases lifetime income, independent of ability.

Granting that higher educational attainment leads to more income after controlling for levels of ability, it might still be the case that ability and marginal returns from education are positively correlated, as implied by the model of educational choice developed above. Somewhat surprisingly from this theoretical standpoint, Ashenfelter and Rouse also find that rates of return to schooling do not vary with (observable) individual ability or family background. This conclusion is seemingly at odds with the hypothesis that higher ability increases the marginal return to education. One might infer from this evidence, for example, that at least the aspects of ability captured by standardized tests are not systematically rewarded in labor markets. However, this is not a necessary inference from these empirical results.

To see this, note that the impact of ability on marginal rates of return is assessed in the context of a multiple regression analysis that holds other explanatory factors constant, *including* the level of education. But if ability raises marginal returns, as assumed, one would expect that those with greater ability acquire *more* education, other things equal. Consequently, the theory of schooling choice implies that in order to observe individuals with different ability selecting the same level of education, there must be some other, unmeasured factor that reduces the marginal return of higher-ability workers. This point is illustrated in figure 14.7, which indicates the anomaly of observing the same educational choice by individuals

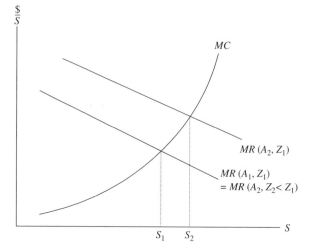

Figure 14.7 Unobserved basis for identical schooling choices by individuals with different ability levels.

of varying ability, *given* the assumption that ability raises marginal return, and assuming all other factors save one are controlled for. Note one possibility is that *unmeasurable* aspects of ability supply the offsetting factor.

Human capital vs. signaling effects of formal schooling

While it seems clear that education necessarily provides some significant contribution to earning capability (particularly via the transmission of basic literacy and numeracy), the empirical magnitude of this effect remains a source of controversy. This is due to the difficulty of separating out the human capital and signaling effects of education, especially given that signaling may occur with respect to characteristics other than purely cognitive skills.

On this point, note that the "natural experiment" and identical twin studies discussed above do not necessarily rule out educational signaling effects on wages. First, signaling theory predicts that more educated individuals receive higher wages even if formal schooling conveys no job-relevant skills, so long as employers cannot observe ability variations directly. By the same reasoning, involuntary schooling increments due to mandatory attendance laws will also be associated with higher wages, so long as employers don't take into account the effects of these laws on individual educational choices.

Second, the point of studying sets of identical twins is to control for genetically determined ability differences. But if the market rewards worker characteristics that are *acquired* outside of school rather than inherited, this experimental procedure will fail to provide the relevant controls. Note in this connection that it is difficult to explain why truly *identical* twins would choose different levels of schooling; one possibility is that acquired but unmeasurable ability differences create the divergence. Even if ability levels were fully accounted for by this procedure, note further that employers would still wish to use education as a sorting mechanism in paying one twin so long as they don't have information on the wage paid to the other twin. Consequently, twin studies do not rule out the possibility of educational signaling effects on wages.

Moreover, researchers have uncovered a number of direct indications of substantial sorting effects in the link between education and income. One such indication, mentioned earlier in the chapter, is the apparent "diploma effect" of reaching particular educational plateaus, such as a high school or college degree. For example, one study estimated the following wage changes associated with completion of different schooling levels: 11th grade, 0.7%, 12th grade (i.e. senior year of high school) 8.6%, 15th grade (junior year of college) −4.9%, 16th grade (typically senior year of a 4-year college program) 17.6%.

Second, many studies have failed to find a statistically significant link between *courses taken* or *achievement test scores* and lifetime income, holding years of education and other observable factors constant. Absence of the former link challenges the notion that schooling raises lifetime income by virtue of the marketable skills imparted; if more coursework doesn't increase income, what is the basis of skill transmission? The inconsistent statistical association of achievement test scores and labor income, on the other hand, questions the claim that *cognitive skill transmission* is the basis for the relationship between schooling and income.

Third, recall the evidence reviewed in chapter 11 concerning the wage effects of on-the-job training. Contrary to the predictions of the human capital model, one study found that this training affected subsequent wage growth only if accompanied by a probationary period. This raises the possibility that the observed wage growth was a product of the employer's ability to assess worker ability rather than from any direct productivity effect of training.

Returns to quality of schooling

Thus, despite extensive evidence linking the *quantity* of schooling to labor income, it is not as yet clear to what degree this connection is explained by the human capital hypothesis. What about the labor market effects of schooling *quality*? The human capital model also predicts that higher-quality schooling should raise lifetime income.

At least two difficulties are encountered in investigating the evidence for this prediction. First, just as in the case of quantity of schooling, school quality is potentially endogenously determined by ability, meaning that workers might signal their superior abilities partly on the basis of the quality of educational institutions they attend. If this were the case, correlations between quality and income may simply mask the underlying effects of differential ability. Second is the problem of defining what is meant by educational quality. When can it be said that one source of education is better than others in a sense relevant to determination of labor income?

Economists Dominic Brewer, Eric Eide, and Ronald Ehrenberg address the latter question by considering the economic returns to attendance at "elite" private colleges, a status identified by a popularly available college guide.[4] After controlling for the possible endogeneity of school quality choices, Brewer *et al.* find a significant premium flowing from attendance at elite private institutions, with a smaller return to attendance at middle-rated institutions. They also find some evidence of a premium paid for attendance at elite public universities. Their evidence does not identify exactly what it is about such institutions (the style of education, the level and quality of inputs provided per student, or the alumni networks associated with these institutions, or the like) that generates the wage premium.

This evidence raises a question about the social optimality of admission policies at elite institutions. Their elite status suggests the existence of potential barriers to consumers *and* producers from entering markets for the type of education these institutions provide. In particular, one might ask whether it is socially desirable to determine admissions on the basis of standardized measures such as the Scholastic Aptitude Test (SAT). The social optimality of private educational decisions is discussed in more detail below.

Family background and formal schooling choices

What are the effects of family wealth on educational choices? There is clearly a strong positive correlation between socio-economic status and educational level. But is this association due to financial constraints or other factors? The model of schooling choice developed above predicts that, given imperfect credit markets, those with more limited financial resources face higher marginal costs of education and thus choose less schooling for given levels of ability. But it also predicts an inverse relationship between level of schooling and marginal return for schooling, for given levels of education.

Summarizing the results of a number of earlier studies, George Psacharopoulos finds generally declining marginal returns to schooling in both developing and developed countries, with higher overall returns in the former.[5] These results are consistent with the premise that financial constraints influence individual schooling choices. On the basis of the model considered earlier, one would only expect to see an inverse relationship between schooling and marginal returns *on average* if financial constraints vary more widely across the labor force than do variations in ability and family background.

This conclusion, however, is seemingly contradicted by recent wage trends in the US and elsewhere, which indicate a *rising* premium to college and more advanced degrees relative to a high school education. In order to assess the extent of this inconsistency, one must return to the underlying explanation for these trends in light of the theory developed above. At least three phenomena require explanations: rising wage inequality *across* educational cohorts, rising wage inequality *within* educational cohorts, and an inverse relationship between unemployment rates and educational levels.

Widening wage differentials by educational level

With respect to the growing wage disparity among workers with different educational backgrounds, the favored explanation on the grounds of human capital theory concerns the impact of recent patterns of technical change on the relative demand for skills acquired after high school. This hypothesis argues that *skill-biased* technical change (SBTC), rather than international trade, has increased the demand for skilled workers while reducing that for the unskilled, thus accounting for growing wage inequality across educational levels on the hypothesis that education imparts job-relevant skills.

The chief evidence for the SBTC hypothesis is twofold: first, the relative demand shifts between skilled and unskilled labor are *pervasive* across the developed countries (and, based on more limited evidence, many developing economies as well), rather than *asymmetric* depending on individual countries' particular directions of trade specialization. Second, the demand shifts tend to occur in the same industries in different countries. These patterns are buttressed by qualitative evidence concerning the diffusion of computer microprocessor technology in given industries.

There are ambiguities in the evidential support for the SBTC hypothesis, however. For example, with respect to the Canadian experience, Paul Beaudry and David Green identify wage trends that are inconsistent with the predicted effects of skill-based technical change, and see instead a worsening of the labor market position of younger workers relative to earlier age cohorts, resulting in both smaller starting wages and smaller rewards to experience.[6] They also find a divergence in wage trends by gender, with male workers experiencing greater reductions in the return to experience. On the basis of these results, Beaudry and Green call for further research into explanations based on changes in relative labor supply or in labor market institutions.

Granting that SBTC has caused widening wage disparities *across* worker education levels, why is it also the case that wage inequality is increasing among workers with the *same* educational backgrounds? If skill is more highly rewarded and formal schooling imparts skills valued by markets, shouldn't all workers with the same schooling benefit alike from skill premia?

Not necessarily. Even if formal education imparts job-relevant skills, the correlation between schooling and skill levels need not be perfect. Indeed, given variations in individual ability, upbringing, and family wealth, we should presumptively expect just the opposite. If labor markets truly reward skill rather than the level of education, we should thus expect disparities in individual returns to schooling.

The key issue in this case concerns the dramatic *increase* in wage dispersion within educational cohorts, accounting by one estimate for two-thirds of the increasing wage and labor income inequality in the US since 1970. Within the rubric of human capital theory, one might look for "supply-side" or "demand-side" explanations for the increased variance in returns to education.

Caroline Hoxby and Bridget Terry pursue a supply-side explanation for rising wage inequality among US workers with some college education.[7] They argue first that there has been growing demographic diversity in the set of people receiving some college education, and second, that there has been a rising return to basic aptitude (as opposed to acquired skills). Finally, they posit that there has been increasing segregation by aptitude among colleges, with aptitude differences among students narrowing on average at any given college. They conclude from their empirical analysis that these changes account for about 70% of the increased wage dispersion among workers having at least some college background.

In contrast, labor economist Daron Acemoglu offers a demand-side account of recent wage trends based on the premise that the *skill composition* of jobs is endogenous, modified by prospective employers in response to skill-biased changes in technology or labor supply.[8] This approach is notable in that most human capital analyses take labor demand as passively dictated by technology and competitive supply conditions. In Acemoglu's account, profit-seeking firms actively shape the skill requirements of their labor forces in response to costs of search in addition to relative supply considerations.

Specifically, if the supplies of skilled and unskilled workers are relatively balanced, firms economize on search costs by offering jobs that can be performed by either high- or low-skill workers, at the cost of productivity losses from employing the less skilled. If the supply of high-skilled workers increases sufficiently (or if technical change favors the highly skilled), then it pays firms to match job requirements to skill levels. To the extent that skill and education levels are imperfectly correlated, this shift leads to an increase in wage dispersion.

An additional consequence of the model is that changing the skill composition of jobs can lead, in a dynamic context, to increasing unemployment rates for *both* skilled and unskilled workers. Acemoglu offers a range of evidence to buttress his claim that US employers have altered the skill composition of job offerings since the 1970s, with a corresponding increase in search and screening efforts in hiring decisions by firms.

Bifurcated returns to human capital

Human capital theory does not *categorically* imply that workers will earn positive returns to schooling. Some people may seek post-mandatory formal education for purely consumption-related reasons, for instance to satisfy a general hunger for knowledge. But unless they were to deliberately avoid all courses imparting skills relevant to their future careers, and then only enter labor markets in which no other workers pursued job-relevant schooling for instrumental reasons, the theory still predicts they would earn positive returns to formal educational attainment, other things equal. Human capital theory thus establishes at least a strong presumption for the prediction of universally positive returns to formal schooling.

This presumption is challenged by evidence that some workers consistently receive zero returns to formal schooling or labor market experience. This evidence has prompted some economists to argue for the existence of *segmentation* or *duality* in labor markets, such that workers in "secondary" jobs enjoy less favorable compensation and working conditions than their counterparts in "primary" jobs. For this segmentation to exist, workers in the secondary sector must face mobility barriers in their attempts to find primary-sector jobs, inconsistent with the perfectly competitive conditions assumed in the standard human capital model.

One difficulty in testing for labor market segmentation has been the absence of a firm theoretical basis for assigning workers or firms *a priori* to primary or secondary segments. In their examination of the dual labor market model, William Dickens and Kevin Lang address this problem by specifying a model that allows for two distinct wage determination equations and a third equation predicting the allocation of workers to sectors given their characteristics. They then conduct a two-step test, the first step of which is to determine whether the data are better fit by one equation or two. They find that the "single wage equation" alternative is strongly rejected.[9] They then consider whether the two-equation system thus affirmed is consistent with the market segmentation hypothesis, and find that the data are most closely fit when one of the equations displays a zero rate of return to education and *negative* returns to experience.

Evidence of duality, in which one market segment accrues significantly lower returns to formal schooling than the other, serves as a qualification rather than a fundamental rejection of human capital theory. Understanding the exact nature and significance of this challenge, however, requires an explanation as to why rates of return don't tend to be equalized over time. Possible bases for such an explanation, along with additional evidence for and against the labor market segmentation hypothesis, are considered in chapter 16.

In sum, there is substantial evidence to support the basic hypotheses of human capital theory, and the theory provides a coherent account of recent and dramatic change in the wage structure that is to a significant degree supported by available data. These data do not necessarily support the subsidiary hypothesis that labor markets are perfectly competitive, however. In particular, it remains difficult to distinguish the relative magnitudes of human capital and signaling effects.

CONCLUSION

The positive association between educational level and labor income is one of the most frequently documented relationships in empirical labor economics. As discussed in this chapter, however, there is much less certainty as to the exact basis for this connection. While it seems presumptive that labor markets require and reward certain basic skills of computation and communication, human capital considerations may not be the entire reason that more schooling is associated with higher income. This is particularly likely to be the case if labor markets are imperfect. Given asymmetric information about productive worker characteristics, for example, employers may use schooling level as a sorting mechanism in choosing among prospective employees. In this scenario, workers with more education may command higher wages even if the additional schooling contributes no additional skills whatsoever.

Not *all* jobs must reward schooling, even if education does impart remunerative skills. One could imagine cases in which automation or frequent turnover nullifies the potential benefits of a more highly educated workforce. But in that event, one would expect workers with more schooling to gravitate toward jobs that reward their training, especially if these jobs are more attractive on other grounds as well. This may not occur if transaction failures create labor market segments that keep markets for primary jobs from clearing. This hypothesis is explored in chapter 16.

Study Questions

1. Individuals with college degrees earn more on average than those without college degrees. Why might this be so?
2. An economist estimates the following equation using data from a cross-section of people in one country in one year:

$$\ln(\text{hourly earnings}) = a + b^*(\text{years of education})$$

   The economist finds that $b = 0.09$. Based on this result, he concludes that the social rate of return from an additional year of education is 9%. Discuss the problems with drawing this conclusion from the economist's findings.
3. Explain and, if possible, illustrate the differential predictions of the human capital and signaling models regarding the effects of scholarships for post-secondary education.

Notes

1 Adam Smith, *An Inquiry Into the Nature and Causes of the Wealth of Nations* (New York: The Modern Library, 1937): 101.
2 Harry J. Holzer, *What Employers Want: Job Prospects for Less-Educated Workers* (New York: Russell Sage Foundation, 1996).
3 Orley Ashenfelter and Cecilia Rouse, "Schooling, Intelligence, and Income in America: Cracks in the Bell Curve," NBER Working Paper No. 6902 (January 1999).
4 Dominic J. Brewer, Eric R. Eide, and Ronald G. Ehrenberg, "Does It Pay to Attend an Elite Private College? Cross-Cohort Evidence on the Effects of College Type on Earnings," *Journal of Human Resources* 34, no. 1 (Winter 1999): 104–23.

5 George Psacharopoulos, "Returns to Investment in Education: A Global Update," *World Development* 22, no. 9 (September 1994): 1325–43.
6 Paul Beaudry and David A. Green, "Cohort Patterns in Canadian Earnings: Assessing the Role of Skill Premia in Inequality Trends," *Canadian Journal of Economics* 33, no. 4 (November 2000): 907–36.
7 Caroline M. Hoxby and Bridget Terry, "Explaining Rising Income and Wage Inequality Among the College-Educated," NBER Working Paper No. 6873 (January 1999).
8 Daron Acemoglu, "Changes in Unemployment and Wage Inequality: An Alternative Theory and Some Evidence," NBER Working Paper No. 6658 (July 1998).
9 William T. Dickens and Kevin Lang, "A Test of Dual Labor Market Theory," *American Economic Review* 75, no. 4 (September 1985): 792–805.

Suggestion for Further Reading

Gary S. Becker, *Human Capital: A Theoretical and Empirical Analysis with Special Reference to Education*, 3rd edn (Chicago: University of Chicago Press, 1993).

CHAPTER FIFTEEN

EMPLOYEE CHARACTERISTICS AND DISCRIMINATION

In its general sense of "making distinctions," *discrimination* is not necessarily a bad thing. One may well speak approvingly of a friend's discriminating taste in music, for example, or of the ability to discriminate between right and wrong. Certain forms of discrimination with respect to other persons might also be deemed acceptable in some circumstances, as when parents discriminate among prospective caretakers on the basis of their prior experience with children.

When applied to social institutions, the term is generally used in the stronger, pejorative sense of making *illegitimate* distinctions among persons. This is the sense usually intended in discussions of discrimination on the basis of race, sex, ethnicity, sexual orientation, or other personal characteristics. The normative judgment being asserted in such cases is that individuals should not be denied equal opportunities or legal protections solely on the basis of such attributes.

This chapter is concerned with discrimination in this stronger sense as it arises in labor markets. The *prospect* of discrimination is to some extent intrinsic to labor exchange, given the inalienability of human capital: a firm cannot contract for labor services without engaging the persons doing the work, along with their particular bundles of attributes. The assessed *incidence* of discrimination depends critically on what is understood to count as illegitimately differential treatment in employment transactions. As discussed below, the standard economic definition does not count unequal wages or employment opportunities as presumptive evidence of discrimination *in the labor market* if they are based on individual differences in productivity or preferences for workplace conditions. This is true even if these differences are the result of discrimination experienced prior to entry into the affected labor markets.

Discrimination may arise in either perfectly or imperfectly competitive labor markets. The scope for discriminatory behavior is greater when labor markets are imperfectly competitive, however, since voluntary transactions among informed, self-serving actors might be expected to limit some forms of discrimination. In particular, discriminatory proclivities of individual actors need not translate into *market* discrimination given sufficient competition. It is possible, for example, that no employee experiences unequal wages, working conditions or employment opportunities even though some employers practice discriminatory hiring behavior.

Given the distinctions just introduced, it is no simple task to determine the extent of discrimination originating in labor market transactions. While few would deny categorically that market discrimination exists, there is considerable ongoing debate concerning the scope and degree of this phenomenon. A key aspect of this controversy has to do with the statistical problem of disentangling the effects of "pre-market" differences in ability, training or preference from the effects of discriminatory behavior by labor market participants.

There are corresponding disagreements concerning appropriate policy responses to labor market discrimination, including whether there should be any response at all. On the latter point, as discussed below, standard economic welfare analysis does not yield the implication that labor market discrimination is undesirable *per se*. Indeed, at least under perfectly competitive exchange conditions, labor market discrimination is economically efficient for the same reason that compensating wage differentials are. This line of reasoning would prompt economists to recommend policies to offset discrimination only when such behavior reflects inefficient outcomes and not, for example, because it is intrinsically unjust or inappropriate.

Another source of disagreement concerns the appropriate target or locus of anti-discrimination policies. Part of the motivation for distinguishing discrimination *in the labor market* from the effects of pre-market discrimination derives from the presumption that the latter should not be addressed through governmental interventions in the labor market. However, any such presumption is surely rebuttable in some cases, even on the relatively narrow grounds of economic efficiency. For example, a societal commitment to affirmative action policies may prompt employers to lobby for the elimination of discriminatory practices outside the arena of market exchange, such as in educational institutions.

DIFFERENCES IN LABOR MARKET OUTCOMES BY DEMOGRAPHIC GROUP

The chapter's analysis begins with an overview of variations in labor market experience by demographic group. Largely to keep the discussion of manageable size, the overview focuses on distinctions of race and class, and primarily as these arise in US labor markets. This should not be interpreted as downplaying other potential bases of discrimination such as age or ethnic origin, or to assume that the US experience is representative of the rest of the world.

Group differences in labor market outcomes are not necessarily due to discrimination originating *within* the labor market. However, an overview of the data on differentials across demographic groups gives an idea of where to look for evidence of labor market discrimination, and perhaps more importantly, of the different ways in which discrimination might be reflected in economic outcomes. Consequently, the following summarizes demographic variations along three dimensions of labor market experience: labor force participation and unemployment rate, wages and benefits, and occupational segregation.

In viewing these data, keep in mind the different ways in which discrimination along racial and gender lines is expressed. For example, discrimination on the basis of race is likely to result in spatial and social segregation (as found for example in the vast socioeconomic gulf between urban ghettoes and suburban enclaves), resulting in fundamentally different life experiences prior to entering the labor market. Geographic segregation and mobility costs may even imply that demographic subgroups participate in essentially separate labor markets.

Discrimination based on gender, in contrast, does not typically express itself in spatial segregation. Males and females of given racial or ethnic groups are raised in the same households, and marriages are more likely to be made within these groupings. Gender discrimination is more likely to be reflected in differences in social roles, as for instance in the unequal division of household labor with respect to child-rearing and housekeeping.

Labor force participation and unemployment rates

The *labor force participation rate* for a certain group is the percentage of working-age persons in that group who are either employed or actively seeking work. The most striking variations along this dimension are found in the comparison of male and female participation rates, both over time and across races and countries. These comparisons are indicated in tables 15.1–15.3.

Perhaps the most significant story, at least with respect to the US labor market, concerns the remarkable increase in the proportion of women entering the labor market, especially in light of the *declining* trend of male labor force participation since the end of the Second World War. These changes are indicated in table 15.1. Starting from a rate of about 35% in the decade immediately after the war, women's labor force participation has increased decade by decade thereafter to an average rate of about 60% for the period 1987–2001. For the same intervals, the participation rate for all working-age males in the US economy has declined from 86% to about 75%.

The most dramatic single aspect of the upward trend in female labor force participation is the marked increase in *married* women who are employed or actively

Table 15.1 US labor force participation rates, by sex, 1948–2001

	Women	Men
1948–56	34.5	86.0
1957–66	38.1	82.4
1967–76	44.0	79.1
1977–86	52.2	77.0
1987–96	57.8	75.7
1997–01	60.0	74.7

Source: *Economic Report of the President* (2002): table B-39; website
http://w3.access.gpo.gov/usbudget/fy2003/sheets/b39.xls

Table 15.2 US labor force participation rates by sex, all and by racial/ethnic group, 1990

	Female	Male	Male/Female
All	56.8	74.4	1.31
African-American	59.5	66.5	1.12
Asians and Pacific Islanders	60.1	75.5	1.26
American Indian	55.1	69.4	1.26
European-American	56.4	76.1	1.33
Hispanic-origin	55.9	78.0	1.41

Source: Joyce Jacobsen, *The Economics of Gender* (Malden, MA: Blackwell Publishers, 1998):
459, table 15.2. Reprinted with perimission.

seeking work. This figure went from under 5% to over 60% in the century from
1890 to the 1990s.[1] This has led in turn to a sharp rise in the number of two-earner
families.

While there is a persistent upward trend in female labor participation, women
have consistently been engaged in more part-time work than men. For the period
from 1970 to 1996, the percentage of employed women engaged in part-time work
has hovered around 25 to 27%, while the corresponding figures for men in the
same period have stayed between 9.5 and 11%.[2] In contrast, there are relatively
small differences in rates of part-time employment among white, black, and
Hispanic workers.

The role of social and cultural factors in determining the division of household
and workplace activity along gender lines is suggested by comparing participation rates across races and developed economies. As shown in table 15.2, the ratio
of male to female labor participation rates varies noticeably across racial groups
in the US economy, from a low of 1.12 (66.5% for males to 59.5% for females) for
African-Americans to a high of 1.41 (78% for males to 56% for females) for those
of Hispanic descent. There are also interesting differences across race in labor force
participation by gender. The highest participation rates for both genders are
registered by those with Asian or Pacific Island heritage (75.5% for males and

Table 15.3   Labor force participation rates by sex and male/female ratios

Country	Women	Men	Ratio Men/women
Iceland	80.6	89.5	1.11
Sweden	74.4	78.1	1.05
Denmark	73.8	84.2	1.14
Norway	71.1	82.2	1.16
United States	70.5	85.3	1.21
Finland	69.9	77.1	1.10
Canada	67.8	82.6	1.22
Switzerland	67.5	97.5	1.44
United Kingdom	66.2	84.0	1.27
New Zealand	64.9	83.9	1.29
Australia	63.4	85.2	1.34
Austria	62.1	81.0	1.30
Japan	62.1	90.6	1.46
Portugal	62.0	80.8	1.30
Germany	61.8	80.8	1.31
France	59.6	74.4	1.25
Netherlands	57.4	79.1	1.38
Luxembourg	56.5	97.2	1.72
Belgium	55.1	72.4	1.31
South Korea	52.7	76.4	1.45
Israel	51.6	69.0	1.34
Ireland	47.2	78.5	1.66
Greece	44.6	74.6	1.67
Spain	44.1	74.0	1.68
Italy	42.9	73.9	1.72

Source: Joyce Jacobsen, *The Economics of Gender* (Malden, MA: Blackwell Publishers, 1998): 346, table 10.1. Reprinted with permission.

60.1% for females). The lowest female participation rate is found among American Indians (55.1%), while the lowest rate among males is for African-Americans (66.5%).

As shown in table 15.3, labor force participation rates vary even more dramatically among countries, both in terms of absolute levels by gender and ratios of male and female rates. Among OECD countries in 1994, female labor force participation ranges from a high of over 80% in Iceland to a low of about 43% in Italy. Male/female ratios for the same year vary from 1.72 in Luxembourg to a low (indicating virtual parity in labor force participation) of 1.05 in Sweden.

The *unemployment rate* for a population is defined as the ratio of those who are jobless but actively seeking paid work to the total labor force of that population. Note that a person who performs only unpaid labor (in the home or for charitable purposes, say) is counted neither as unemployed nor as in the labor force. The

Table 15.4   US unemployment rates by sex, 1967–2001

	Women	Men
1967–76	6.5	4.8
1977–86	7.8	7.2
1987–96	6.0	6.2
1997–01	4.5	4.4

Source: *Economic Report of the President* (2002): table B-42;
website
⟨http://w3.access.gpo.gov/usbudget/fy2003/sheets/
b42.xls⟩. Data are for civilian persons ages 16 and over.

construction and interpretation of unemployment rate figures is discussed more thoroughly in chapter 18.

Just as white men in the US economy have higher participation rates than their counterparts among white women or black and Hispanic men, so too do they enjoy lower comparative unemployment rates. However, in this case the most dramatic differences are found across racial rather than gender divisions. Patterns of unemployment for US workers are indicated in table 15.4. For the 34-year period from 1967 to 2001, women's unemployment rates exceeded the corresponding men's rates by progressively smaller increments, beginning with 1.8 percentage points in 1967 and declining to a tenth of a percent in 1997. In contrast, unemployment rates for blacks are consistently more than double the corresponding white rates, while unemployment rates for Hispanic workers are consistently higher over the three decades spotlighted in the table.

There are also significant racial differences in the ratio of male to female unemployment rates. While white males face almost the same unemployment rates as white women, black and American Indian men face higher unemployment rates than their female counterparts. The interplay of race and gender in labor market outcomes thus appears to be somewhat complex, at least in terms of unemployment: gender differentiation works in opposite directions for whites, Hispanics and Asian-Americans on one hand, and blacks and American Indians on the other.

Wages and benefits

There are significant and persistent differences in wage rates across both racial and gender lines, and once again there is significant interplay between race and gender divisions. Tables 15.5, 15.6, and 15.7 show recent trends in US wage differentials by race and gender. Consider first the trends in wage ratios for male workers. As shown in table 15.5, the ratio of median wage rates for black and white men fell from just over 80% to about 77.5% in this period. In 2001, the ratio of black to white median weekly wages was about 75%, while the corresponding ratio for Hispanic workers was 63% (down from 65% in 1989).

Table 15.5 Median weekly earnings ratios of US male full-time wage and salary workers by race, 1989–2002

Year	White	Black	Hispanic origin	Black/White
1989	482	348	315	0.72
1990	497	360	322	0.72
1991	509	374	328	0.73
1992	518	380	345	0.73
1993	531	392	352	0.74
1994	547	400	343	0.73
1995	566	411	350	0.73
1996	580	412	356	0.71
1997	595	432	371	0.73
1998	615	468	390	0.76
1999	638	488	406	0.76
2000	669	503	414	0.75
2001	694	518	438	0.75

Source: *Employment and Earnings*, 1989–2002.

Table 15.6 Ratios of US female to male median weekly earnings rates, 1983–2001

Year	Male	Female	Female/Male
1983	379	252	0.66
1984	400	259	0.65
1985	406	277	0.68
1986	419	290	0.69
1987	433	303	0.70
1988	449	315	0.70
1989	468	328	0.70
1990	485	348	0.72
1991	497	368	0.74
1992	505	381	0.75
1993	514	395	0.77
1994	522	399	0.76
1995	538	406	0.75
1996	557	418	0.75
1997	579	431	0.74
1998	598	456	0.76
1999	618	473	0.77
2000	646	491	0.76
2001	672	511	0.76

Source: *Employment and Earnings*, 1984–2002. Data are for persons 16 years old and over.

Table 15.7 Ratios of US female to male median weekly earnings for full-time wage and salary workers by race, 1989–2002

Year	White	Black	Hispanic
1989	0.69	0.86	0.85
1990	0.71	0.86	0.87
1991	0.73	0.86	0.89
1992	0.75	0.88	0.88
1993	0.76	0.89	0.89
1994	0.75	0.87	0.89
1995	0.73	0.86	0.87
1996	0.74	0.88	0.89
1997	0.75	0.87	0.86
1998	0.76	0.85	0.86
1999	0.76	0.84	0.86
2000	0.75	0.85	0.88
2001	0.75	0.87	0.88

Source: *Employment and Earnings*, 1990–2002.

Over the same period, as seen in table 15.6, the ratio of female to male median weekly earnings has increased from 66% in 1983 to almost 76% in 2001. These aggregate numbers hide an interesting deviation in trend across racial lines. As seen in table 15.7, gender wage ratios for whites have risen dramatically due to a combination of rising wage rates for women and falling wage rates for men. In contrast, while the gender ratio for blacks has also risen (though not as much), average wage rates for both black women and black men have fallen over the period 1989–2001.

EARNINGS DIFFERENCES BY SEXUAL PREFERENCE

A related topic to differences in earnings by gender is differences in earnings by sexual preference. While much less data are available for studying this topic, one interesting study using US data from 1989–1991 finds that gay and bisexual male workers earned from 11 to 27% less than heterosexual male workers with equivalent experience, education, occupation, marital status, and region of residence (Badgett, 1995). The evidence was less robust regarding whether or not lesbian and bisexual women earned less than heterosexual women.

This finding regarding lower earnings is consistent with a variety of explanations (as are almost all earnings differentials between groups). An

continued

interesting question that arises in the case of sexual preference that does not tend to arise in the case of gender or race earnings differentials is whether employers, other employees, and customers are aware of one's sexual preference.

Marketing surveys often make the point that gay persons have higher household income. Badgett (2001) discusses this finding and argues that the marketing surveys may not be representative of the full gay population. This could again relate in part to whether or not people represent their sexual orientation in public, including to marketing surveyers.

Related discussion questions:
1. Why might lesbian women be less likely to differ from straight women in earnings as compared to gay and straight men?
2. Explain how it could be possible that gay households have higher income (overall and/or per household member) even if their earnings are lower.

Related references:
M. V. Lee Badgett, "The Wage Effects of Sexual Orientation Discrimination," *Industrial & Labor Relations Review* 48, no. 4 (1995): 726–39.
M. V. Lee Badgett, *Money, Myths, and Change: The Economic Lives of Lesbians and Gay Men* (Chicago: University of Chicago Press, 2001).

There are also significant differences across racial and gender groups in terms of employer-provided pensions and health care benefits. As indicated by the data presented in table 15.8, men are significantly more likely than women, and whites much more likely than blacks and Hispanics, to be covered by employer-provided health care and pension plans. From 1979 to 1996, male/female differentials in benefits received have narrowed while the corresponding disparities by race have remained the same or increased, most noticeably between whites and workers of Hispanic descent.

Occupational segregation

An alternative and potentially fruitful perspective on demographic differences in labor market experience is gained by examining the degree to which *occupations* are segregated along lines of race or gender. Here, as in the case of labor force participation, the most stark differences arise across lines of gender rather than race. Indeed, it is difficult to find examples of occupations in which the genders are truly integrated, such that the proportion of women in the occupation closely and persistently matches the proportion of women in the labor force.

Table 15.8 Pension plan, health care and health insurance coverage rates of US workers by sex and race, 2000

	Pension plan coverage[1]	Health insurance coverage[2]
Sex		
Male	46.2	65.3
Female	42.7	63.0
Race		
White	45.2	66.0
Black	42.2	54.5
Hispanic	28.3	44.7

Note: Rates are in percentages.
Source: [1] US Census Bureau, "Current Population Survey, Annual Demographic Survey, March Supplement";
website ⟨http://ferret.bls.census.gov/macro/032001/noncash/nc8_000.htm⟩.
[2] website: ⟨http://ferret.bls.census.gov/macro/032001/health/h01_001.htm⟩.

Table 15.9 US occupational sex segregation indices, all and by race, 1960–1990

	1960	1970	1980	1990
All	64	66	59	53
Whites	63	66	59	55
Nonwhites	70	64	56	50

Source: Joyce Jacobsen, *The Economics of Gender* (Malden, MA: Blackwell Publishers, 1998): 213, table 6.4. Reprinted with permission.

A useful statistic for discussing this phenomenon is a *segregation index*, used to compare changes in aggregate segregation over time and across countries and demographic groups. The most commonly used segregation index is the *Duncan dissimilarity index*, which is based on summing across all occupation categories differences in the proportional occupational representation of two demographic groups. Possible values of the index range from zero to one hundred.

One way to interpret a Duncan index number is that it shows what percentage of either group would have to switch occupations in order to achieve complete integration. For example, if the index equals 50, 50% of either group would have to switch into occupations dominated by the other group in order to achieve complete integration. Clearly, the higher the index number, the greater is the degree of segregation.

Levels and trends in US occupational segregation by gender and race are indicated in tables 15.9 and 15.10. Table 15.9 shows selected levels of occupational segregation by race for the period 1960–90. The data show that levels of occupational segregation have continually fallen for both whites and nonwhites, but remain significant (55% for whites and 50% for nonwhites) as of 1990. Women also tend

Table 15.10   US occupational race segregation indexes by sex, 1960–1990

	1960	1970	1980	1990
Men	45	38	28	24
Women	50	36	26	22

Source: Joyce Jacobsen, *The Economics of Gender* (Malden, MA: Blackwell Publishers, 1998): 215, table 6.7. Reprinted with permission.

to be relatively overrepresented in low-income occupations such as retail, non-financial services, and elementary and secondary teaching.

Historical studies of specific occupations also bring to light dramatic examples of gender switching in which virtually all-male occupations have become predominantly filled by women, typically with corresponding declines in prestige and average salary. For example, although virtually all bank tellers were men prior to the Second World War, 90% were female as of 1980.[3] Average salaries for tellers dropped significantly in this time. Cases of switching from female to male dominance within an occupation are much rarer, the most interesting instance being perhaps the occupation of delivering newborn babies.

In contrast, US occupational segregation by race has declined much more dramatically over the period 1960–90. This is shown in table 15.10, which breaks down racial segregation across occupations by sex. On average, rates of occupational segregation by race have fallen by more than half, to index values of just 24 for men and 22 for women in 1990 – less than half the degree of segregation by gender in the US economy indicated by table 15.9.

The incidence and degree of occupational segregation by gender also varies significantly across countries. Tables 15.11 and 15.12 give occupational segregation indices by country using seven occupational categories (these are thus not comparable to the US-only data reported above, which are derived using more occupational categories). Index values for industrialized countries range from a high of 45 for Luxembourg to a low of 20 for Portugal. Variations in the degree of occupational segregation are even greater among less-developed economies, ranging from highs of 62 in American Samoa and 60 in British Virgin Islands and the United Arab Emirates to lows of 12 in Sri Lanka, 5 in Ethiopia, and 3 in Burkina Faso.

Variations along a number of other dimensions of labor market experience could be examined, but those considered so far suffice to make the point that demographic groups face very different labor market experiences on average, with white and Asian-American men systematically enjoying higher wage rates and benefits and lower rates of unemployment. It's also clear that these demographic differences can vary significantly over time and across economies. It's much less obvious, however, why such demographically-based differentials persist.

Table 15.11 Occupational sex segregation indexes using seven occupational categories, industrialized countries

Country	Index
Luxembourg	45
Denmark	42
Norway	41
Ireland	41
Belgium	40
Finland	39
Germany	39
France	38
Australia	38
Canada	38
United Kingdom	37
Israel	36
Switzerland	35
New Zealand	35
Sweden	35
Netherlands	33
United States	32
Austria	32
Spain	29
Greece	27
South Korea	26
Japan	26
Portugal	20

Data are from 1998 or 1999, except Norway (1995), Switzerland (1994), Belgium (1992), Luxembourg (1991), and France (1982).
Source: ILO, *Yearbook of Labour Statistics* (1992–1996) (table 2B) and (2000) (table 2C).

This issue is the basis of fundamental and ongoing disagreements in the social and behavioral sciences. The most severe clash is between those who ascribe demographic differences (as experienced in both economic and non-economic spheres) primarily to genetic causes and those who see them as primarily the consequence of social factors. Variations in demographic differences over time and across countries tend to favor the latter mode of explanation, of course, but even allowing for these there is, as seen in the data reported above, a significant core of persistent differentials in labor market outcomes along the lines of demarcation by race and sex.

Table 15.12 Occupational sex segregation indices using seven occupational categories, developing countries

Region	Country	Index	Year
Africa:			
	Seychelles	46	1981
	South Africa	46	1991
	Nigeria	35	1986
	Cape Verde	35	1990
	Sao Tomé and Principe	32	1981
	Comoros	31	1980
	Namibia	30	1991
	Zambia	30	1980
	Zimbabwe	24	1987
	Equatorial Guinea	23	1983
	Gambia	22	1983
	Ghana	21	1984
	Sudan	20	1983
	Botswana	19	1995
	Malawi	18	1987
	Rwanda	12	1989
	Togo	12	1981
	Mauritius	10	1995
	Ethiopia	5	1995
	Burkina Faso	3	1985
Asia:			
	Brunei	42	1981
	Philippines	38	1999
	Pakistan	31	1997
	Bangladesh	27	1996
	Maldives	25	1990
	Malaysia	25	1999
	Singapore	22	1999
	India	16	1981
	Thailand	14	1999
	Indonesia	13	1990
	Macao	12	1999
	Sri Lanka	12	1995
Australasia:			
	American Samoa	62	1981
	French Polynesia	51	1988
	Niue	50	1986
	Tonga	43	1990
	New Caledonia	43	1989
	Cook Islands	38	1991
	Fiji	22	1996
Caribbean:			
	British Virgin Islands	60	1994
	Turks and Caicos	51	1980
	US Virgin Islands	50	1990

Table 15.12 *(Continued)*

Region	Country	Index	Year
	Dominica	40	1989
	St. Vincent	39	1980
	Puerto Rico	38	1999
	Bermuda	38	1997
	Caymans	37	1991
	Bahamas	37	1998
	Trinidad & Tobago	36	1998
	Haiti	35	1990
	Dominican Republic	32	1997
	Grenada	31	1988
	Dutch Antilles	28	1998
	Barbados	27	1995
Central America:			
	Belize	50	1994
	Panama	50	1999
	Honduras	44	1999
	Guatemala	41	1991
	Costa Rica	36	1998
	El Salvador	27	1998
	Mexico	22	1999
North Africa/Middle East:			
	United Arab Emirates	60	1980
	Algeria	55	1987
	Kuwait	50	1988
	Syria	49	1991
	Turkey	41	1999
	Iraq	40	1987
	Bahrain	33	1999
	Iran	30	1986
	Egypt	28	1998
	Cyprus	21	1989
	Morocco	18	1982
	Tunisia	11	1994
South America:			
	Falkland Islands	57	1991
	Suriname	57	1996
	Chile	48	1998
	Venezuela	47	1997
	Guyana	47	1980
	Paraguay	47	1994
	Uruguay	44	1999
	French Guiana	40	1982
	Ecuador	37	1994
	Brazil	33	1998
	Colombia	29	1999
	Bolivia	27	1996
	Peru	17	1999

Source: ILO, *Yearbook of Labour Statistics* (1985–96) (table 2B) and (2000) (table 2C).

ECONOMICS OF LABOR MARKET DISCRIMINATION

Defining labor market discrimination

For some analytical purposes, it is useful to isolate the consequences of discriminatory behavior originating within labor markets. In order to do this one must abstract from labor market responses to *pre-existing* personal differences that happen to fall along given demographic lines and thus would affect labor market outcomes even if labor market participants ignored racial, ethnic, or other differences. Correspondingly, define *labor market discrimination* as a situation in which labor market opportunities vary systematically along demographic lines for reasons other than differences in productivity or preferences with respect to workplace conditions. Differential opportunities could take the form of unequal wages and benefits, working conditions, or employment opportunities, or some combination of the three.

By this definition, it would not constitute an instance of discrimination *in the labor market* if workers of a certain group were paid lower wages or given fewer opportunities for employment because they had less job-relevant education or were more costly to hire. This would be true even if these conditions resulted from discrimination experienced prior to entry into the labor market. The key limitation posed by the definition is that differential labor market opportunities must arise solely from having a given demographic attribute, so that workers with the same preferences and productivity but without that attribute would confront no variations in labor market opportunities.

Discrimination in perfectly competitive labor markets

Under perfectly competitive exchange conditions, characterized by wage-taking behavior, free entry and exit, and perfect contracting, labor market outcomes are ultimately determined by preferences, technology, and the distribution of endowments. More specifically, equilibrium wages and employment in perfectly competitive labor markets correspond to the preferences of the *marginal* buyer and seller, determined respectively by technical conditions of production and household endowments. Thus, in such settings market discrimination can only arise through the preferences of market actors with respect to demographic characteristics of workers.

This observation prompts a theory of labor market discrimination based on *personal prejudice*. Economic analysis of this phenomenon was pioneered by Gary Becker, who suggested that prejudiced market actors might be thought of as having a taste for discrimination toward certain groups.[4] In Becker's interpretation, discriminatory tastes are manifested in the willingness to pay (perhaps indirectly) for the opportunity to discriminate. For example, a prejudiced employer may accept a lower profit rate in return for the privilege of refusing to hire certain workers.

Becker argues that from a theoretical standpoint it doesn't really matter whether this desire to discriminate is based on accurate assessments of "objective" criteria such as productivity or not. This isn't entirely valid, since discrimination based merely on mistaken beliefs can presumably be corrected by education. However, given the postulate of frictionless exchange, prejudice can be based only on subjective tastes rather than mistaken beliefs. This distinction gives Becker's analytical approach the same flavor as compensating differential theory, studied in chapter 13. Recall, for example, that under competitive market conditions a person who "discriminates" against risky workplace conditions ends up with a lower wage compared to someone less averse to risk. This parallel with compensating differential analysis is persued further below.

Becker's approach leaves open the potentially important question of how subjective tastes for discrimination arise in the first place. One might reasonably ask, for example, if discriminatory preferences are innate or acquired. It seems somewhat farfetched to suggest that prejudice, particularly along such socially constructed lines as nationality or religion, is genetically determined. If, to the contrary, tastes for discrimination are socially inculcated, then it might be possible to alter discriminatory behavior by influencing patterns of learning and communication.

A closely related possibility is that discriminatory behavior reflects socially imposed *constraints* on choices rather than social determination of preferences. For example, social taboos against interaction with members of certain groups may be enforced by such means as boycotts, ostracism, or even violence. Faced with such penalties, even unprejudiced individuals may choose to discriminate. In this case, they will exhibit a "derived demand" for discrimination in much the same sense that the demand for labor is derived from the desire to make profits. It may be difficult to distinguish the roles of preferences and constraints in prompting discriminatory behavior, however, making Becker's hypothesis a useful simplification for analytical purposes.

Becker argues that prejudicial behavior in labor markets might derive from any of three sources: employers, other employees, or customers for the products of workers targeted for discrimination. Let's consider each possibility in turn. The latter scenario is particularly useful in clarifying what is meant by discrimination that arises specifically in labor markets.

Suppose, therefore, that *consumers* are biased against workers who share a certain attribute – call it A. Following Becker's lead, posit that consumers have a preference for discrimination against A-workers. For the moment, assume in addition that discrimination takes the form of a strict preference for otherwise identical goods *not* produced by workers having attribute A. How would this form of prejudice manifest itself under otherwise competitive market conditions, if at all?

An immediate consequence of the scenario just constructed is that prejudiced consumers offer a lower price for goods produced even in part by A-workers. This implies in turn that the value marginal product of type-A workers in producing for these consumers is lower than for otherwise identical non-A workers laboring under the same production conditions. If firms have no choice but to serve

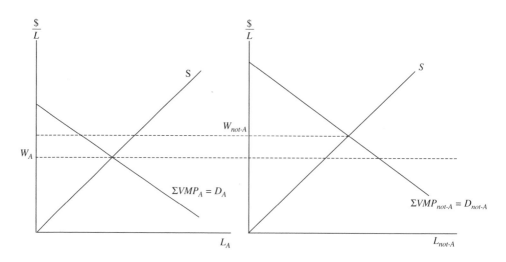

Figure 15.1 Wage differential due to consumer prejudices affecting marginal revenue productivity

prejudiced consumers, then even prejudice-free employers would have a lower derived demand for A-workers, yielding the latter a persistent wage penalty even under perfectly competitive exchange conditions. A-workers could not vie for the higher wages received by non-A workers because employers would earn less from each A-type worker hired.

This outcome is depicted in figure 15.1. This scenario meets the conditions of our definition of *market* discrimination because the wage differential would arise even if A and not-A workers had equal *physical* productivity and identical preferences for workplace conditions. Despite this, type-A workers have lower *revenue* productivity at the margin because of consumer prejudice.

Note the significance for the result shown in figure 15.1 of the assumption that *all* consumers are biased against workers with attribute A. If there were a sufficiently large contingent of unbiased consumers, then type-A workers could be used to produce for their demand without a revenue penalty to employers. The key issue here is the long-run elasticity of demand by non-prejudiced consumers, or more specifically, the number of such consumers who are able to enter the product market costlessly. If non-prejudiced buyers are costlessly available at the margin, then there is no way a wage differential could persist: unbiased consumers would bid up the price paid for goods produced by type-A workers until the basis for the wage differential is eliminated.

A similar logic highlights the significance of the manner in which discriminatory preferences are expressed. If consumers simply do not wish to relate directly to type-A workers, but do not otherwise care how goods are produced, then workers with this attribute might be employed without a revenue penalty in jobs that do not require direct contact with the buying public. If the supply of such jobs is perfectly elastic at the margin established by the market, then a discriminatory wage differential cannot persist; profit-seeking employers would hire cheaper type-A workers to perform these jobs until any such differential were erased.

A second source of market discrimination is prejudice on the part of *employees* without attribute A. In this case employers who maintain an integrated labor force would have to pay a compensating differential to their prejudiced employees, making type-A workers costlier to hire than their not-A counterparts. Employers of not-A workers would thus have a correspondingly lower demand for type-A workers.

Does this mean that type-A workers will receive lower wages or poorer employment opportunities? Not necessarily. For one thing, employee discrimination only matters in this scenario if workplaces are integrated. If market demand for the goods produced by A and not-A workers is sufficiently high, both can be hired at equal market-clearing wages in separate, completely segregated workplaces. Again, the key issue is the elasticity of entry and exit at the margin established by the labor market for type-A workers. The latter cannot persistently face a wage penalty if employers can costly segregate their labor forces, because profit-seeking firms would simply bid up the wage for the disadvantaged workers until the differential is eliminated.

Finally, consider the consequences for ideal labor market outcomes if *employers* are prejudiced. This signals a departure from the standard assumption that firm seek only to maximize profit, since prejudiced employers would be willing to sacrifice some profits in order to practice discrimination. Unlike in the standard case, then, the marginal benefit of hiring an additional worker is not necessarily given by that worker's contributions to firm revenue. As illustrated in figure 15.2, the marginal benefit to prejudiced employers of hiring type-A workers falls below their value marginal product (VMP_A). Thus, otherwise identical workers are treated differently.

To see the impact of employer prejudice on labor market outcomes, imagine dividing the labor market into submarkets for type-A and non-A workers respectively, and suppose initially that the market is populated solely by unprejudiced employers. Since these employers care only about profit maximization, given perfect mobility any wage differential between the two groups of otherwise identical workers is eliminated by competitive forces, as shown in figure 15.3a.

But now imagine adding prejudiced employers back into this setting. Since they're prejudiced, let's imagine that they hire only non-A workers, at least initially. This implies that the demand for non-A workers shifts up, other things equal, increasing the wage paid to employees without attribute A, as shown in figure 15.3b. In this setting, prejudiced employers sacrifice potential profits for the opportunity to discriminate.

This may not be an equilibrium outcome, however, given the presence of existing or potential employers who are unprejudiced. Unprejudiced employers

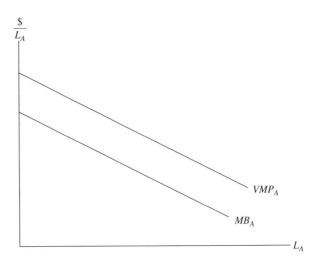

Figure 15.2   Marginal benefit of hiring type-A workers is lower than VMP_A to prejudiced employers

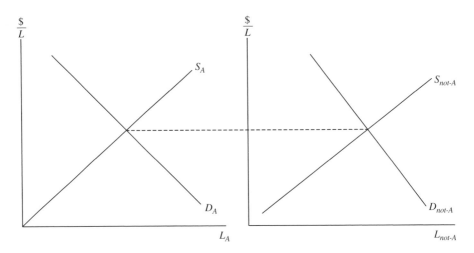

Figure 15.3(a)   Wage equalization in the absence of employer prejudice

already in the market, seeing all workers in the market as perfect substitutes, will gravitate toward the "type-A" submarket in order to take advantage of the lower wage rate. If there is a sufficiently large number of existing unprejudiced employers, the wage differential in the two submarkets will be eliminated in consequence, even though the prejudiced employers are practicing discrimination by segregating their labor forces. Equilibrium conditions will again appear as in figure 15.3a.

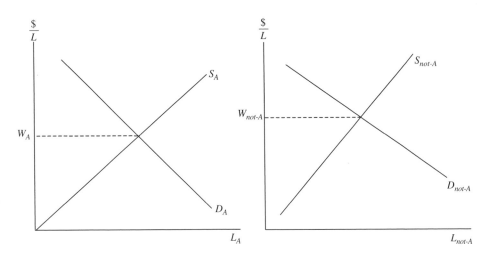

Figure 15.3(b) Wage differential due to inelastic supply of unprejudiced employers

The wage differential may be eliminated even if the number of unprejudiced employers already in the market is insufficient to eliminate the differential. This is so if there are prospective employers who are also unprejudiced. Under ideal mobility conditions, these actors could enter the market to exploit the profit opportunity caused by the wage differential, hiring the lower-paid type-A workers until the wages in the two submarkets are again equalized.

Therefore, the only way that equilibrium wage differentials can arise in response to employer prejudice is if the supply of unprejudiced employers to the type-A submarket is inelastic at the margin. In that case only prejudiced employers will be operating (and practicing complete segregation) in the non-A submarket, and by assumption these employers do not regard type-A and non-A workers as perfect substitutes. If unprejudiced employers are not available to enter the type-A market at zero cost, any remaining wage differential will not be competed away, and the equilibrium outcome will again appear as in figure 15.3(b).

THE WAGES OF BEAUTY

An interesting line of research in labor economics has considered whether there is a premium paid for good-looking employees. For instance, better-looking attorneys earn more than others, and the differential increases with years of experience (Biddle and Hamermesh, 1998). One comprehensive study using British data noted that tall men receive a pay premium, while obese women experience a pay penalty (Harper, 2000).

continued

Note that finding a beauty premium does not tell us exactly why it exists. Is it because personal beauty contributes to the bottom line, either directly or as a result of customer prejudice, or is it a characteristic for which employers are willing to discriminate (i.e., employer discrimination in the Beckerian sense), or perhaps even the expression of discrimination by fellow employees?

Related discussion questions:
1. Another study found that for a sample of Dutch advertising firms, firms with better-looking executives have higher revenues and faster growth than otherwise identical firms (Bosman *et al.*, 1997). Does this additional piece of information help determine the economic logic underpinning wage premiums for good looks?
2. Can you think of occupations in which looks have no effect on earnings?

Related references:
Jeff E. Biddle and Daniel S. Hamermesh, "Beauty, Productivity, and Discrimination: Lawyers' Looks and Lucre," *Journal of Labor Economics* 16, no. 1 (January 1998): 172–201.
Ciska M. Bosman, Gerard A. Pfann, Jeff E. Biddle, and Daniel S. Hamermesh, "Business Success and Businesses' Beauty Capital," National Bureau of Economic Research Working Paper No. 6083 (July 1997).
Barry Harper, "Beauty, Stature and the Labour Market: A British Cohort Study," *Oxford Bulletin of Economics & Statistics* 62, special issue (December 2000): 771–800

Take a moment now to register the common features of these three models of discriminatory tastes expressed in the labor market. The first feature to note is that *individual* expressions of discrimination need not translate into *market* discrimination, as this term is defined above. Even though some customers or employers (perhaps acting on behalf of their prejudiced employees) discriminate, it may still be possible that workers from the group targeted for discrimination receive the same wages and employment opportunities in equilibrium.

Second, the existence of equilibrium labor market discrimination depends on the supply elasticity of employers who are not motivated to discriminate by their own tastes or those of their customers or employees. In all three cases this elasticity depends in part on entry and exit costs (assumed to be zero under perfect competition); otherwise the conditions vary by model.

It is worth emphasizing the role of costless entry and exit on the foregoing conclusions, especially the conclusion that market discrimination need not result from individual discrimination. This assessment is easily compromised if mobility is costly. For example, suppose there are non-trivial costs of job search (a phenomenon discussed in more detail in chapters 18 and 19). In this case, the presence of a large number of discriminating employers can lower the job prospects of a type-A worker and lead to lower average wages. It might also discourage such workers from searching and thus reduce their employment prospects. Thus, the first result must be read with caution, since in practice mobility costs are seldom if ever entirely absent. In their presence, individual penchants for discrimination translate much more readily into discriminatory market outcomes.

A third common feature of the prejudice models is that any wage differential that does arise in equilibrium is *Pareto-optimal* if competitive market conditions otherwise exist. Despite the presence of discrimination, it is impossible under given supply and demand conditions to alter market outcomes so as to make some participants better off without reducing the utility of others. This is because any equilibrium discrimination reflects preferences rather than market imperfections. Thus, from the standpoint of standard economic analysis at least, *de gustibus non est disputandum* ("there's no disputing tastes"), and there is no basis *within this framework* for criticizing discriminatory behavior.

This is not to suggest, of course, that discrimination arising from the expression of prejudice in ideal labor markets is unobjectionable. It just means that there are no normative grounds within the standard framework of welfare analysis for condemning this result. The presence of such discrimination establishes legitimate grounds for looking beyond efficiency considerations in evaluating alternative economic outcomes.

Discrimination in imperfectly competitive labor markets

Consider now the scope for and possible forms of labor market discrimination under imperfectly competitive exchange conditions. As you'll see, these imperfections expand the scope for discriminatory behavior in two ways: by reducing competitive pressures on the expression of discriminatory preferences, and by accentuating differences among demographic groups that arise prior to participation in the market.

Suppose first that some labor market actors have wage-setting power. The key structural basis of this power is the presence of significant matching costs. Under these conditions, the logic of wage setting can work to compound the disadvantages of groups targeted for discrimination outside of the labor market. A second consequence of entry and exit costs is that they shield market actors earning economic rents from potential competition. If these actors are prejudiced, then they can safely "spend" some of their rents on discriminatory behavior without fear of being driven from the market, as would occur under competitive market conditions given a perfectly elastic supply of unprejudiced competitors. Thus, mobility limits allow more opportunities for the practice of discriminatory behavior.

The polar case of wage-setting power on the buyer's side is monopsony. An example of this scenario would be a "company town" in which all the local jobs are provided by a single employer. If it is costly for workers to find jobs out of the area, the firm has some freedom in setting wages, and could do so in a discriminatory way without the threat of competition. A less extreme case is that of *oligopsony*, in which there are relatively few buyers in a given labor market. So long as entry barriers into this market are significant, its employers may earn economic rents, some of which can be sacrificed for the opportunity to practice discriminatory behavior.

On the other side of the labor market, one could in principle have employee prejudices reinforced by monopoly power secured by unions. In this scenario, however, union wage-setting power could only effect an increase in market discrimination if there were some degree of integration in the absence of the union. This would only happen under conditions of *pure* (rather than *perfect*) competition in which some firms have higher costs than others; otherwise, as explained in the foregoing discussion of the perfectly competitive case, employee prejudice would be met by complete segregation of workforces.

In the scenarios of imperfect competition discussed so far, the enlarged scope for market discrimination does not stem from wage-setting power *per se*, but from the protection of discriminatory behavior from potential competition. Thus it doesn't matter for the conclusions just reached, for example, if actors with market power set a single wage or engage in perfect wage discrimination, as would occur in the absence of transaction costs or legal restrictions inhibiting this practice.

In contrast, the nature and degree of market discrimination is affected by the logic of wage-setting behavior in the case of *third-degree monopsonistic wage discrimination*, studied in chapter 4. Recall that in this scenario the monopsonist divides market supply into two submarkets according to a systematic difference in the elasticity of labor supply. A profit-maximizing monopsonist would therefore set a lower wage in the submarket with *less* elastic labor supply (as depicted in figure 4.3).

This raises a new possibility in the logic of market discrimination. In all of the preceding cases, discrimination arises through the expression of discriminatory tastes on the part of prejudiced market participants. In this case, however, wage discrimination can arise even without prejudice. This would arise in the event that labor supply elasticity varies systematically along demographic lines, due to non-market discrimination or other differences in the preferences or opportunities faced by individuals with different demographic attributes.

For example, suppose that both partners in heterosexual couples work, but for socio-cultural reasons the household location decision (and thus the determination of which labor markets to participate in) are driven by the job choices of the male partner. Other things equal, this would lead to the supply of female labor being less elastic than that for male workers, leading in turn to higher wages for male workers under a regime of monopsonistic wage discrimination.

Notice that in this case market discrimination does not arise from a response to a given attribute *per se*, but rather from an economic condition correlated with that attribute. Thus, for example, blacks in large American urban areas may face economic or racial barriers to seeking jobs outside of cities, leading to a less elastic supply of labor to inner-city labor markets. Any consequent monopsonistic wage discrimination arises from their different economic opportunities or from the effects of non-market discrimination, not from expressions of racial prejudice.

Another case in which market discrimination might arise from "pre-market" differences correlated with race is that of *bilateral* wage-setting power, in which one would expect bargaining relationships to arise. As discussed in chapter 7, economic theory suggests that bargaining outcomes are determined by two factors: outside options and personal costs of bargaining (due, for example, to impatient preferences). To the extent that conditions affecting either or both of these factors vary systematically with demographic attributes, one would expect to see discriminatory wage patterns develop. Labor market discrimination is in this case the result of economic conditions affecting relative bargaining power, rather than of prejudices against the demographic characteristic in question. However, market discrimination can exacerbate disadvantages created by differences in opportunity established outside of the market.

Enforcement costs and labor market discrimination

Labor market discrimination can also arise due to the presence of significant enforcement costs, associated for example with asymmetric information about worker skill or effort levels. Consider first a setting in which employers are unable to determine directly the productivity levels of potential employees, and thus cannot match wage rates to individual marginal productivities in a profit-maximizing fashion. More generally, suppose that workers make unequal contributions to profitability for reasons that cannot be detected in advance by employers. Besides having different levels of productivity, workers might, for example, have different probabilities of leaving and thus impose turnover costs on an employer.

Under such circumstances, visible demographic attributes may be used by employers to provide a noisy signal of invisible underlying productivity differences, resulting in a phenomenon known as *statistical discrimination*. To see how this works, suppose that while employers cannot determine individual contributions to productivity, they do have reliable information about the *average* productivity or employment cost characteristics of identifiable groups. One pertinent example of this arises in the analysis of gender-based discrimination: it is well-known that *on average* women experience more interruptions in their labor force participation than do men. Since turnover is often costly, this implies in turn that the expected profit from hiring a female worker is lower than for an observationally equivalent male.

What is true on average for a group does not, of course, necessarily apply equally to all members of the group. But if employers cannot distinguish individual variations contributing to productivity, they can improve *expected* profitability by discriminating against *all* members of the group based on its average characteristic. The incentive to do this need not reflect any innate prejudice on the part of any employer, but it has the same effect: each member of the group targeted for statistical discrimination faces lower wages and/or poorer employment prospects relative to otherwise identical workers outside the group.

It is tempting to say that no *net* discrimination has resulted from employers' inability to distinguish individual employment-relevant characteristics in this scenario, since by assumption the targeted group makes a lower average contribution to profitability. Given this assumption, *average* wages would be lower for this group even under competitive exchange conditions. However, there is an important difference: since the information asymmetry forces employers to treat all members of the targeted group alike, individual members have less incentive to break the mold by improving their appeal to potential employers. This can make initial group differences self-perpetuating in a way that would not arise in the absence of statistical discrimination.

A second issue with respect to this scenario concerns the ability of more productive members of the targeted group to *signal* their superior characteristics, as explored in the educational signaling model of chapter 14. This is a potentially compelling point. The coherence of statistical discrimination theory requires that potential screening devices are somehow too unreliable to allow individual members of the targeted group to signal their superior characteristics.

Consider two examples. First, as suggested above, female workers may be targeted for statistical discrimination because of a greater average propensity to interrupt their labor market careers, typically for the purpose of raising families. Although there is no biological necessity that women spend more total time in child-rearing activities than their male companions, it is a socially determined fact for most economies.

Yet, many women devote themselves primarily to careers, with few if any intended "stopouts." However, a woman's intention to pursue an uninterrupted career path may be difficult to signal to prospective employers. *Current* childlessness or single status is not a reliable indication of this intention, since these conditions are readily changed. And even though greater investments in career training may raise the likelihood of a woman's uninterrupted devotion to a career, it is still the case that for any given education or training level, women are more likely – again, on average – to experience interruptions in their labor force participation.

Alternatively, consider again the case in which education is the potential basis for signaling productivity differences. The informational content of the *quantity* of education received may be substantially diluted if there are significant variations in the *quality* of education. This is a serious concern especially in the US, in which there are dramatic inter- and intrastate variations in the quality of public education, and both Hispanics and African-Americans are disproportionately limited to overburdened and underfinanced inner-city schools.

A second scenario of enforcement costs promoting discrimination arises when efficiency wages are paid to provide incentives for imperfectly observable work effort. Recall from the discussion of chapter 10 that efficiency wage levels vary inversely with the value of outside employment options and the efficacy of monitoring. If these factors also vary systematically with demographic attributes, perhaps due to differential socialization patterns or the effects of pre-market discrimination, then the level of efficiency wages may vary for otherwise identical workers.

For example, suppose workers with demographic attribute A face systematically higher search costs because of locational disadvantages. These translate, other things equal, into higher costs of being fired. Therefore, they would be paid a lower efficiency wage even if they had the same productivity characteristics and preferences for workplace conditions as non-A workers with better outside options. Note that this result has the same flavor as the scenarios of third-degree wage discrimination or strategic bargaining: wage discrimination results, not from the targeted demographic attribute itself, but from a condition systematically associated with that attribute because of non-market factors.

Summary

A finding of labor market discrimination requires more than just the observation of unequal labor market opportunities along demographic lines. Any such disparities could, in principle, be accounted for by factors that differentiate members of these groups prior to their entry into the labor market. Labor market discrimination may arise even under ideal market conditions, but this requires pervasive prejudices against workers with the targeted attribute; otherwise, individual expressions of prejudice need not translate into equilibrium market differentials.

However, this conclusion is quite sensitive to market conditions, in the sense that the presence of mobility costs may significantly magnify the impact of individual acts of discrimination on market outcomes. This can occur either because discrimination increases mobility costs unequally or because mobility costs reduce the scope for competing away market differentials. In principle, discrimination can be magnified in this way by imperfectly competitive conditions on either side of the labor market.

In addition, market imperfections due to enforcement costs can induce discriminatory behavior even among purely profit-seeking actors, by investing differences in demographic attributes with strategic significance. For example, unequal employment opportunities can create systematic wage differentials between otherwise identical groups of workers through the mechanisms of imperfect wage discrimination or strategic bargaining.

EVIDENCE CONCERNING
LABOR MARKET DISCRIMINATION

Since unequal treatment of demographic groups does not of itself constitute evidence of labor market discrimination, some care must be exercised in assessing any putative empirical grounds for the existence of discrimination. Broadly speaking, three types of data have been brought to bear in discussions of discrimination: direct testimonials in legal or journalistic settings, audit studies, and econometric evidence. Each is considered in turn, along with representative empirical findings.

Direct testimony

Specific incidents of discrimination are frequently reported in a number of forums. Testimonial evidence of discrimination can be found in the popular press, in legal proceedings, and in scholarly case studies. Often in these reports the evidence of discrimination is quite blatant, as when advertisements for job openings make racial or gender preferences explicit. In a 1998 review article, Darity and Mason, for example, identify substantial racial discrimination in employment ads prior to the Civil Rights Act of 1964, which outlawed such practices.[5]

As mentioned earlier, individual expressions of prejudice need not translate into discrimination at the market level. So long as there are enough existing and potential employers without such prejudices, differentials in wages, working conditions or employment opportunities will be competed away under ideal market conditions. However, it does not take a substantial departure from ideal conditions for market discrimination to arise. Thus, evidence of the sort presented by Darity and Mason, while not sufficient of itself, might be part of a coherent body of evidence supporting a presumption of discriminatory outcomes.

Audit studies

The so-called *auditing* technique is a relatively recent approach to the investigation of discrimination in employment and other market settings in which the existence of discrimination rather than the specific terms of discriminatory exchange is at issue. In the study of discrimination in hiring, the auditing technique involves sending pairs of testers, matched as closely as possible in every observable job-relevant characteristic but differing in race or gender, out to contact prospective employers. The testers both approach employers within a short period of time, and their experiences in eliciting demonstrations of interest, follow-up interviews, or job offers are compared.

Since the testers do not actually take jobs that are offered by the employers under investigation, this method is suited specifically to uncovering discrimination in hiring rather than in pay scales or promotion policies. Presumptively, the more often that paired testers encounter differential employment opportunities, the more compelling the grounds for concluding that discrimination has occurred. As Darity and Mason report, auditing studies have consistently uncovered evidence of discrimination in hiring.

While this evidence is suggestive, and may form a vital part of a body of data supporting an assessment of discrimination, it should be viewed with some caution. As in the case of direct testimony, it should be remembered that individual acts of prejudice do not imply the existence of labor market discrimination in general. Second, the auditing technique assumes that the study designers are capable of choosing testers that match for *every* worker characteristic that may affect an employer's profitability. But it is possible that experienced employers can discern job-relevant distinctions among applicants that are invisible to the investigators.

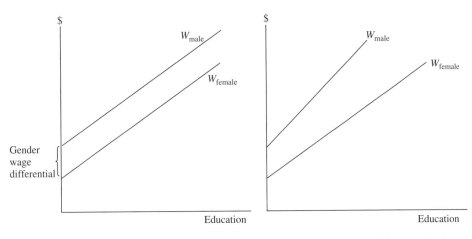

Figure 15.4(a) Constant gender-based wage differential across education levels

Figure 15.4(b) Variable gender-based wage differential across education levels

Econometric evidence

The type of evidence most frequently used by economists attempting to measure discrimination is drawn from statistical analysis using multiple regression techniques. The appeal of this evidentiary approach should be clear: since observed differentials in wages or employment opportunities can arise from market as well as non-market considerations, the unique contributions of the former must somehow be isolated. Multiple regression analysis provides a basis for making this distinction.

To see how this works, consider the problem of determining the level of market discrimination in wages, for instance by gender, using statistical analysis. Since by definition discrimination exists only if wage differentials emerge even after "holding constant" worker characteristics affecting employers' profitability, factors that might determine these characteristics must be included in the regression equation. After controlling for all potentially job-relevant worker characteristics, it can then be determined if there is a statistically significant wage differential by gender.

This differential is most easily seen when the gender differential shows up only in the constant or "vertical intercept" term of the estimated wage equation, as shown in figure 15.4a. This suggests that for any level of observable human capital variables and workplace conditions, a female worker faces the same wage penalty relative to an otherwise identical male counterpart. In this case, the degree of discrimination can be inferred simply by taking the difference of the estimated constant terms.

However, the effects of discrimination may be more complicated than this. Specifically, differential treatment by gender may imply that male and female wage regressions differ in both the constant terms *and* the coefficients on relevant control variables such as education, job market experience, or location. This situation is illustrated in figure 15.4b. In this case, the comparison of male and female wages will depend on *which* level of the control variables is chosen as the basis for comparison. In that case, how does one derive a single estimate of the level of wage discrimination?

One approach is based on the property of wage regression equations that they yield the mean group wage when evaluated at the mean values of the independent variables. One can use this property to derive estimates of mean male and female wages using the respective wage equations. These can then be compared to estimate *unadjusted* gender wage differentials from all causes.

To isolate the effects of labor market discrimination, one can derive *adjusted* gender wage differentials by calculating wage levels for *both* groups using the mean levels of the independent variables experienced by *one or the other* gender. For example, male and female wages can be calculated on the basis of the average levels of education, experience, and so on, experienced by men. Comparing the wages thus calculated holds constant the effects of job-relevant characteristics, so that any remaining differential might be viewed as resulting from market discrimination by sex. (See the appendix to this chapter for a detailed summary of this statistical procedure.)

Studies using this approach tend to find evidence of wage discrimination along both racial and gender lines, although the estimated magnitude of the latter is typically greater. Applying this method to the study of white female/white male earnings differences in the US economy yields a characteristics-adjusted ratio of 75%, compared to an unadjusted ratio of 71%.[6] This suggests that only four percentage points of the 29-point gap between the two groups can be accounted for by systematic differences in productivity and tastes – the rest, in the absence of a better explanation, might be attributable to discrimination in labor markets.

With respect to earnings differentials along racial lines, it is generally the case that more of the unadjusted difference between worker groups can be accounted for by systematic differences in characteristics (raising the possibility of greater discrimination within non-market social institutions), but even so the remaining differential typically remains large. For example, a survey of empirical studies of black male/white male earnings ratios from the 1970s revealed unadjusted wage ratios ranging from 46 to 77%, with corresponding adjusted ratios varying from 75 to 89% – a substantial revision, but not enough to rule out the possibility of significant labor market discrimination.

These findings must be interpreted with care. As with auditing studies, a finding of market discrimination depends on the presumption that the investigator has managed to control for *all* characteristics that determine worker productivity or preferences for workplace characteristics. If there are characteristics that are invisible to economists but observed and acted upon by employers, then an assessment of discriminatory behavior may be reached in error. However, the bias resulting from omitting unobserved job-relevant characteristics could work in either direction, so that the existence of discrimination might also be erroneously dismissed.

Furthermore, such econometric findings provide at best indirect evidence of discrimination because they don't offer a specific test of any particular model of discrimination. Thus, even if one were to conclude that discrimination has taken place, it cannot be determined from such data what market conditions are driving the discriminatory behavior.

POLICIES WITH RESPECT TO DISCRIMINATION

As demonstrated early in the chapter, there are large and systematic differences in how labor markets treat workers from different demographic groups. What, if anything, should societies, or governments acting as agents of social will, do about this? What one deems an appropriate policy to counter differential treatment in and out of labor markets depends on two factors: the first involves an empirical judgment as to the conditions that allow differential treatment to persist, and the second a value judgment concerning the offensiveness of such inequalities, both absolutely and relative to other ills that might be incurred in attacking them.

Let's take up the latter consideration first. One's vision of an appropriate governmental policy necessarily stems in part from a normative assessment of the fact that workers with different personal attributes face disparate economic opportunities. For example, a free-market advocate may associate no intrinsic harm with expressions of prejudice by employers or customers, arguing that these are simply exercises of free choice, while similarly assigning significant negative weight to government interventions understood to create inefficient market outcomes.

This evaluation provides part of the motivation for distinguishing discrimination *in the labor market* from that which might arise in other social arenas. It might be argued that if, say, differential wages by race were due to discriminatory practices in the public educational system, governmental policy should be directed there, and thus not "add insult to injury" by creating distortions in otherwise well-functioning labor markets.

One could, in contrast, argue that avoidance of allocative inefficiency is not a sufficient justification for differential economic treatment along lines of race, gender, or ethnicity. This judgment is reflected, for example, in *comparable worth* policies, which replace market "assessments" of revenue productivity with legislatively determined criteria for pay. Under this rubric, a worker in a female-dominated occupation might be deemed to be performing services comparable to those provided by workers in a distinct line of work performed mostly by males, and thus deserving of the same compensation, even if the market awards the two occupations unequally in the absence of such legislation.

Given a coherent set of value judgments about the absolute and relative ills of discrimination, the selection of appropriate anti-discrimination policies will also depend on an understanding of the social conditions that allow discrimination to persist. Here is where economic analysis can play a potentially useful role in guiding the formation of public policy, by indicating more or less effective strategies for combating illegitimate unequal treatment in labor markets.

For example, labor market discrimination can only persist under perfectly competitive exchange conditions given sufficiently pervasive prejudices against workers from particular demographic groups by employers, customers, or other employees. If the goal were to mitigate discrimination without distorting the allocative functions of the market, the only evident option would be investments in education designed to root out such prejudicial beliefs.

A wider range of policy weapons exists if market discrimination is associated with some departure from ideal market conditions. To take the simplest such case, imperfect competition expands the scope for indulgence in prejudicial behavior that would otherwise be driven out by competitive forces. Discriminatory market outcomes associated with such expressions of prejudice could thus presumably be eliminated through appropriate antitrust measures or other approaches to encouraging market competition.

Imperfect contracting conditions, possibly in tandem with imperfect market competition, allow scope for discriminatory behavior that is not based solely on prejudice. For example, a third-degree wage-discriminating monopsonist will pay lower wages to female workers if they are systematically less economically mobile than their male counterparts, even if the monopsonistic employer has no extra-economic bias against women. Here again, discriminatory behavior could presumably be fought by encouraging greater competition, but it could also be attacked directly – without necessarily reducing economic efficiency – simply by prohibiting the discriminatory wage-setting, inasmuch as the latter is not an expression of innate preference.

A direct prohibition of discriminatory wage-setting would be similarly effective under market conditions giving rise to efficiency wages, since here again wage disparities arise from employers' drive to maximize profits, rather than from the expression of personal prejudice.

A final policy approach to combating discriminatory market outcomes associated with imperfect contracting conditions is to mandate structures or behaviors that could be expected to offset the unequally favorable conditions, without directly banning discrimination. One such indirect approach to fighting labor market discrimination is to promote collective bargaining. As discussed in chapter 12, union bargaining tends to reduce compensation differentials among workers from different demographic groups, arguably by rendering individual differences in economic opportunity strategically moot.

A second indirect approach, and one that has received particular attention in the US, is *affirmative action*. Affirmative action policies can take several forms. In their most direct form, affirmative action requirements translate as "hiring quotas" for workers from targeted demographic groups. This is also the interpretation that has received the strongest criticism by opponents of these policies, on the basis that they create a form of "reverse discrimination" against otherwise qualified workers who don't happen to have the "favored" attributes.

More generally, however, affirmative action demands the expenditure of special efforts on the part of employers to ensure that workers of all types are represented in the pool of prospective employees. Understood as such, affirmative action policies can be a useful tool for offsetting systematic disparities in mobility and employment opportunities among workers. For example, some workers, by virtue of their social position, may not be privy to "old boy networks" or other structures for learning about and gaining access to employment opportunities. They may thus be routinely disadvantaged in gaining access to desirable jobs for which they might be otherwise well qualified. Affirmative action requirements offset such disadvantages and thus improve the prospects for matching viable workers from all backgrounds with desired jobs.

CONCLUSION

Labor economists typically define market discrimination as unequal economic treatment that is not correlated with differences in revenue productivity or tastes for workplace conditions. The key contributions of economic analysis to the understanding of this phenomenon are twofold: on one hand, the existence of a large number of prejudiced market actors is not of itself sufficient for discrimination to exist, and on the other, discrimination may arise even though no market actor bears any personal prejudices at all. The key to the existence of discrimination in both cases lies in the nature of exchange conditions.

Consequently, it is potentially important to pinpoint the exact conditions that undergird a specific finding of discrimination against workers with given attributes. A number of different explanations for discriminatory behavior have been developed in the economic literature, and in this area as in many others, theory has progressed faster than evidence; although significant evidence pointing to the existence of discrimination exists, there is far less information as to underlying causes.

This matters, in that the identification of appropriate policies to counter market discrimination depends to a large extent on determining the underlying causes of this behavior. Outright prohibitions of discriminatory practices may have significant efficiency costs in some cases, and may even be counterproductive, but in others could be expected even to improve market performance. Consequently, this is an area of the discipline in which labor economists have a potentially important role to play in helping to inform government policy.

APPENDIX TO CHAPTER 15

ESTIMATING CHARACTERISTICS-ADJUSTED WAGE RATIOS

The method which is by far the most widely used by economists for attempting to measure discrimination, either nationwide or in a more limited sphere, is statistical analysis of wage patterns. The problem is that wages and employment are determined by both labor supply and labor demand, so differences between persons are caused by a combination of factors, while discrimination is considered to operate through the demand side of the labor market. Researchers attempting to measure the amount of the wage differential attributable to demand-side discrimination try to control for supply-side factors through use of regression analysis. The unexplained amount of the wage differential is then attributed to discrimination. However, as it is difficult or even impossible to account for all supply-side factors, the unexplained portion of the wage differential can never be absolutely certified to have been caused by discrimination.

Once a particular wage equation is estimated, how is it used to discuss earnings and employment differentials? The simplest way of discussing earnings differentials is to assume that discrimination takes the form of paying men a constant amount more than women, regardless of their level of qualifications. This is equivalent to specifying that wage equations for men and women differ only in intercept, not in slope, as in figure 15.4a. This assumption makes the gender differential easy to calculate but has the disadvantage of not allowing the returns to various factors such as education and experience to vary by sex. A more general model of the way in which discrimination may operate requires estimation of separate equations by sex, which allows both the intercept and the slope of the wage equations to vary by sex, as in figure 15.4b. Then differences between, say, the coefficients on experience between the two equations can be discussed.

However, pair-by-pair comparisons of coefficients are unsatisfying, as they do not allow calculation of a summary measure with which to discuss the full effects of group differences on earnings. A common method for calculating wage differentials that controls for measurable productivity-related characteristics is to use wage regressions to create adjustments of relative earnings based on worker characteristics.[7]

There are several ways in which to make such adjustments. In comparing female and male earnings, we may want to calculate how much men would earn if they were to receive payment based on the female relationship between personal characteristics and earnings. Conversely, we may want to see how the average woman would fare relative to the average man if she were subject to the male earnings relationship.

A regression of wage W on personal characteristics can be estimated of the form $W = \sum_{}^{n} \beta X$, where X is a set of n characteristics and β is the corresponding set of n coefficients for a set of persons. Regressions have the characteristic that evaluating them at the mean for all independent variables yields the mean wage for the group. So, if separate equations are estimated for men and women, the mean wages for men and women can be calculated as:

$$\overline{W}_m = n\beta_m \overline{X}_m$$
$$\overline{W}_f = n\beta_f \overline{X}_f$$

where the subscript m denotes male values, the subscript f denotes female values, and a bar over the variable denotes the mean value for that variable.

Then the gender wage gap, G, is

$$G = \overline{W}_m - \overline{W}_f = n\beta_m \overline{X}_m - n\beta_f \overline{X}_f$$

and the unadjusted gender wage ratio, U, is

$$U = \frac{\overline{W}_f}{\overline{W}_m} = \frac{n\beta_f \overline{X}_f}{n\beta_m \overline{X}_m}$$

We can normalize the gap relative to the male wage so that it will range from 0 to 1:

$$g = \frac{G}{\overline{W}_m} = 1 - U$$

An adjusted wage ratio can be calculated in one of two ways, using either the male mean characteristics (A) or the female mean characteristics (A')

$$A = \frac{n\beta_f \overline{X}_m}{n\beta_m \overline{X}_m}$$

$$A' = \frac{n\beta_f \overline{X}_f}{n\beta_m \overline{X}_f}$$

In A, the numerator is increased relative to the unadjusted wage ratio, while in A', the denominator is reduced relative to the unadjusted wage ratio. Theoretically, there is no way to predict which will produce a larger adjustment. Also, neither method is constrained to yield a ratio less than 1; even if U is less than 1, A and/or A' may end up greater than 1, which would imply discrimination in favor of the group in the numerator of U. Then the unexplained proportion of the gap can be defined in one of several ways, either using A, as in the equation for d below; using A', as in the equation for d' below, or using a different numerator than for d, as in the equation for $d*$ below:

$$d = \frac{1-A}{1-\overline{U}} = \frac{n(\beta_m - \beta_f)\overline{X}_m}{G}$$

$$d' = \frac{1-A'}{1-U}$$

$$d* = \frac{n(\beta_m - \beta_f)\overline{X}_f}{G}$$

Inasmuch as we cannot tell whether A or A' will be larger, we cannot predict whether d or d' will be larger. However, if $\overline{X}_m > \overline{X}_f$ and $\beta_m > \beta_f$ for all n characteristics, then $d > d*$.

Study Questions

1. Why are doctors paid more than nurses? (1996 median weekly earnings in the US are $1,133 for physicians and $697 for registered nurses.) Drawing on the discussion in this chapter and the preceding chapters in this section, list at least four categories of possible reasons for this wage differential, indicating clearly the theoretical motivation for each category.
2. Consider why discrimination on the basis of race and/or sex might vary across sectors in the economy. In each of the following cases, indicate in

continued

which sector you might expect to find more discrimination (measured by a greater wage differential by race and/or sex, and/or fewer workers of the less-desired group, and/or by more worker segregation across firms), and why this might be.
   (a) worker-owned firms versus capitalist-owned firms
   (b) owner-operated firms versus manager-operated firms
   (c) nonprofit firms versus for-profit firms
   (d) the government sector versus the private sector
3. Why do women make less than men?
4. Why do minority group members make less than white men? Are these reasons likely to be different from your answers to (3)?
5. Explain and, if possible, illustrate the differential predictions of the perfectly competitive and segmented labor market models regarding the effects of comparable-worth wage policies on labor markets.
6. Explain and, if possible, illustrate the differential predictions of the perfectly competitive and segmented labor market models regarding the effects of affirmative action policies on labor markets.
7. A monopsonist has a horizontal VMP_L curve (don't worry how) and faces a straight-line upward-sloping labor supply curve.
   (a) Illustrate the equilibrium wage and quantity of labor hired for a profit-maximizing, single-wage-setting monopsonist.
   (b) Now suppose the monopsonist can separate labor supply into two distinct markets with unequally elastic straight-line supply curves. [Hint: Other things equal, the flatter supply curve, or the supply curve with the higher vertical intercept, is more elastic.] In which market will the profit-maximizing monopsonist set the higher wage?
   (c) Empirical evidence suggests that household migration decisions are driven by male labor market opportunities rather than female labor market opportunities, so the woman is often the "tied mover." Given your analysis in (b), what is the implication of this for the gender wage differential?

Notes

1 Joyce P. Jacobsen, *The Economics of Gender* (Malden, MA: Blackwell Publishers, 1998): 40, table 2.3.
2 Joyce P. Jacobsen, op. cit.: 458, table 15.1.
3 Joyce P. Jacobsen, op. cit.: 210.
4 Gary S. Becker, *The Economics of Discrimination* (Chicago: University of Chicago Press, 1957).
5 William A. Jr. Darity and Patrick L. Mason, "Evidence on Discrimination in Employment: Codes of Color, Codes of Gender," *Journal of Economic Perspectives* 12, no. 2 (Spring 1998): 63–90.

6 Joyce P. Jacobsen, op. cit.: 295, table 9.1.
7 This method was first used in the early 1970s to analyze racial and union vs. non-union wage differences, as well as gender wage differences. See Orley Ashenfelter, "Racial Discrimination and Trade Unionism," *Journal of Political Economy* 80, no. 3, part 1 (May/June 1972): 435–64; Alan Blinder, "Wage Discrimination: Reduced Form and Structural Estimates," *Journal of Human Resources* 8, no. 4 (Fall 1973): 436–55; Ronald Oaxaca, "Male–Female Differentials in Urban Labor Markets," *International Economic Review* 14, no. 3 (October 1973): 693–710; and Ronald Oaxaca, "Sex Discrimination in Wages," in Orley Ashenfelter and Albert Rees (eds) *Discrimination in Labor Markets*, (Princeton, NJ: Princeton University, 1973): 124–54.

Suggestion for Further Reading

Gary S. Becker, *The Economics of Discrimination*, 2nd edn (Chicago: University of Chicago Press, 1971).

CHAPTER SIXTEEN

EMPLOYER CHARACTERISTICS AND MARKET SEGMENTATION

If all labor markets were perfectly competitive, systematic wage variations could in principle be completely explained by differences in human capital and workplace amenities. But as noted in preceding chapters, attempts to estimate returns to human capital or compensation for unfavorable working conditions have frequently uncovered inconsistencies in these relationships that are not readily accounted for by the competitive model, such as strongly bifurcated returns to formal schooling or labor market experience. Relatedly, a number of researchers have found evidence of persistent and substantial wage differentials across industries and employers that are not accounted for by variations in observable workplace conditions or human capital variables.

How then might these differentials be explained? One possibility is that residual intra- or inter-industry wage variations simply track differences in working conditions or worker human capital that are observable to labor market participants but not to researchers. In that case, the predictions of the perfectly competitive labor market model might be borne out if only the hidden information were to be made generally known.

Another possibility, and the subject of this chapter, is that these unexplained wage differentials reflect the uneven incidence of exchange costs that create labor market imperfections resulting in worker rents. The corresponding theory of *labor market segmentation* suggests that employees in *primary sector* jobs enjoy relatively high compensation, pleasant working conditions, and job security while their less-favored counterparts in *secondary* labor markets face low wages, few or no benefits, long hours, poor or dangerous working conditions, and high turnover.

The segmentation hypothesis requires that primary sector wages do not adjust to clear the labor market. Broadly speaking, there are two distinct theoretical bases for this outcome. *Efficiency wage* models are premised on various forms of enforcement costs that lead employers to use above-market clearing wage levels to induce outcomes that cannot be achieved by contractual means. *Insider–outsider* theory, in contrast, explains supra-competitive wage levels as the result of bargaining power enjoyed by incumbent workers in certain firms or industries.

This chapter explores theoretical and empirical grounds for the labor market segmentation hypothesis. The argument begins with a review of the evidence on intra- and inter-industry wage differentials, followed by a summary of efficiency wage and insider–outsider theories and their implications for differential labor market outcomes. The results of direct and indirect tests of the segmentation hypothesis are then considered, along with relevant normative implications.

This hypothesis is the focus of significant controversy among labor economists. Some economists retain a presumption in favor of the eventual capacity of the competitive framework to explain the seemingly anomalous wage variations, in light of its theoretical coherence and past successes. Other economists argue that the empirical record compels shifting the presumption in favor of an alternative theory that incorporates relevant departures from perfectly competitive exchange conditions. Efforts to uncover further evidence in favor of one or the other position is likely to yield greater insights into the economic logic of wage determination, but not necessarily to resolve the issue to everyone's satisfaction.

WAGE DIFFERENTIALS ACROSS
EMPLOYERS AND INDUSTRIES

Casual inspection of wage data for the US and other countries suggests that some industries routinely pay more than others. These "high-wage" or "primary sector" industries are typically identified as construction, mining, durable goods manufacturing, some non-durable goods manufacturing, transportation, utilities, and FIRE (Financial, Insurance, and Real Estate). In contrast, agriculture, textiles and apparel, retail, and service industries are generally placed in the "secondary" or "low-wage" sector. However, industry may not be a perfect proxy for labor market segment. There are also significant wage variations across employers within industries, and even across individual occupations, so some "high-wage" jobs show up in "secondary" industries, albeit with a lower incidence rate.[1]

As noted in the introduction, these wage variations do not of themselves constitute a challenge to the model of perfectly competitive labor markets. The challenge arises from the persistence of these differentials even after observable variations in human capital and working condition indicators have been controlled for econometrically.[2] Observed human capital variables typically explain less than half of the total variation in wages, and adding job characteristics and union status to the regression analysis still leaves a large residue of unexplained variation. Moreover, controlling for observable working conditions and fringe benefits exacerbates the observed inter-industry differentials (Krueger and Summers, p. 268).

Patterns of inter-industry wage variation also appear to be persistent and stable over time and across national boundaries. Studying worker data from 1940 to 1980, Jean Helwege (1992) tests and rejects the hypothesis that inter-industry wage differentials reflect transitory industry-specific shocks. William Dickens and Lawrence Katz review a body of empirical work that traces the present structure of inter-industry wage differentials back to the late 1800s.[3]

A number of studies indicate also that industry wages are correlated across countries, suggesting that the same wage determination factors might be operating in different economies. Maury Gittleman and Edward Wolff find similar and stable industry wage structures across fourteen OECD countries.[4] In addition, industrialized and developing countries exhibit similar patterns of inter-industry wage differentials, although the market conditions that generate them may vary with the degree of economic development.[5]

What industry characteristics might be driving these wage differentials? That is, what factors, if any, vary systematically by industry and are significantly correlated with wages, other things equal? Answers to this question have proven difficult to nail down, in part because candidate industry variables, such as capital intensity, labor productivity, average schooling of labor force, average job tenure, percentage of workforce unionized, average firm size, and concentration ratios, are themselves highly correlated. In their own study, Dickens and Katz conclude that only the rate of profit and average education of the workforce are consistently related to industry wage rates.

The consistency and persistence of these wage variations raise the prospect that workers in primary-sector jobs earn economic rents relative to comparable employees in secondary jobs. In addition to enjoying better benefits and working conditions, primary-sector workers also experience longer average job tenure and more opportunities for promotion within firms. Why should some employers pay more than others, net of the wage effects of job characteristics and human capital? One possibility is that they really don't, but that standard measures of the latter variables don't readily allow economists to ascertain this. Exponents of this view suggest that the residual inter-employer wage differentials might be fully accounted for by unobserved variations in ability or working conditions, including individual work effort.

Before considering possible empirical grounds for this assessment, the chapter sets out an alternative framework that explains inter-industry differentials on the basis of exchange frictions that prevent some labor markets from clearing. This alternative approach suggests that labor markets are effectively "segmented" by the mobility barriers resulting from these frictions.

THE ECONOMICS OF LABOR MARKET SEGMENTATION

A satisfactory theory of labor market segmentation must meet at least three basic criteria. First, it must provide an independent and empirically assessable basis for dividing labor markets into "primary" and "secondary" segments. Merely distinguishing segments by "good" and "bad" jobs is simply tautological, and thus gives no insight into the mechanisms of wage determination that drive the hypothesized segmentation of markets. Of course, the proposed grounds should also be consistent with the premise that primary-sector jobs feature relatively high levels of pay and benefits, agreeable working conditions, and employment continuity.

Second, the theory must explain why wages in primary markets fail to adjust to market-clearing levels, allowing workers in these markets to accrue non-competitive rents. Otherwise, workers in less desirable secondary jobs could presumably enter these favored markets and compete away the rents, leaving only the differentials corresponding to variations in human capital and working conditions. The required scenario for the labor market segmentation hypothesis is analogous to that of union wage effects across unionized and non-unionized markets, illustrated in figure 4.8 in chapter 4. The graph shows two labor markets with identical market-clearing wage levels. However, the market to the left, representing the primary labor market, features a supra-competitive wage rate and excess supply. As shown, the resulting wage differential relative to the secondary market may be further widened if disappointed job-seekers in the primary sector spill over to swell the ranks of labor suppliers in the lower-wage market.

Third, the ideal theory would also be able to account for other empirical regularities associated with the existence of market segments. Two such regularities are typically featured in accounts of the segmentation hypothesis. The first is the relative security of primary-sector jobs against layoffs due to external market fluctuations. The second concerns the possible dichotomy in returns to human capital, first discussed in chapter 14, such that workers in secondary-sector jobs experience zero returns to formal schooling and perhaps even *negative* returns to labor market experience, despite their apparent similarity in economic terms to counterparts in primary-sector jobs earning strictly positive rates of return to these assets.

These criteria for a satisfactory theory of labor market segmentation are met by two distinct theoretical approaches, *efficiency wage* and *insider–outsider* models, both of which have been discussed in other contexts earlier in the text. In general terms, efficiency wages represent strategic responses of employers to enforcement costs that obstruct them from contracting directly for desired levels of work effort, employee capabilities, or employment continuity. In this scenario, wages do not adjust to market-clearing levels because doing so would eviscerate the profitable incentive effects of supra-competitive wage rates.

In contrast, insider–outsider models are based on the premise that incumbent workers derive bargaining power from the costs to firms of replacing them with new employees. Replacement costs may arise due to forgone firm-specific human capital, training requirements, search, hiring, and termination costs, or difficulties in integrating newly hired workers into an incumbent labor force. The wage-setting power thus derived may be augmented by collective bargaining arrangements, but need not depend on unions for its existence.

Both of these models predict that equilibrium wage rates exceed market-clearing levels. However, they identify different microeconomic bases for this result, and thus offer potentially testable grounds for distinguishing these accounts from each other and from the implications of the competitive market model. The following sections discuss how each model addresses the specific theoretical criteria described above. For the purposes of illustration, particular attention is given to the efficiency wage model and the Rubinstein bargaining model with costly exit.

How are market segments defined?

As discussed earlier in the chapter, although labor market segments are often described in terms of differences across industries, the corresponding divisions do not appear to be perfectly aligned: while it is clearly true that some industries offer better average compensation and working conditions than others, there are also significant intra-industry variations across employers, as well as high-paying "good" jobs found in nominally secondary industries or firms. What, then, is the independent economic logic creating labor market segments?

In the efficiency wage framework, the common starting point for identifying market segments involves production or exchange conditions that create or exacerbate contracting failures with respect to inputs valued by employers. In the effort incentive version of the model, the relevant conditions imply the existence of a bilateral moral hazard problem in which employee effort levels are imperfectly observable and supervisory monitoring signals are unverifiable. As a result, employers must induce high effort by offering wage premiums and threatening to terminate workers who are caught working at lower than expected levels of intensity.

Examples of production conditions that might be associated with the payment of efficiency wages for effort include plant size, capital intensity, team-based production, and the scope for employee multitasking. Larger plant size, in this interpretation, is associated with greater difficulties in monitoring individual workers, while the capital intensity of production increases the marginal productivity of work effort when labor and capital are complementary inputs. Team-based production processes, on the other hand, limit firms' ability to link efforts to individual output levels, and the performance of multiple tasks by employees raises the difficulty of ascertaining if they are allocating their time appropriately. (On this point, recall Frederick Taylor's insistence on minute task specialization as a component of "scientific" management; see the second discussion box in chapter 8.)

Contracting failures also drive other scenarios in which efficiency wages are theoretically paid. In the labor turnover version of the model, firms are unable to charge incumbent workers for losses associated with their departure, and so must offer wage premiums to induce them to stay in the employment relationship. By contrast, in the labor quality version of the efficiency wage model, wage premiums are offered to *new* employees to ensure a high-quality applicant pool when worker abilities are not directly observable and thus can't be stipulated by contract.

With the insider–outsider approach, segments are determined by production and exchange conditions affecting the ease with which firms can replace incumbent workers. As discussed in chapter 12, unionization tends to raise replacement costs by limiting employers' options to replace individual workers. However, unionization is not a necessary condition for the existence of replacement costs endowing incumbent workers with some degree of bargaining power. As addressed in chapter 11, incumbent workers may to some extent be shielded from market competition by firm-specific human capital investments, the costs of making good employment matches in markets with significant firm and worker heterogeneity, employer search costs, or collusive efforts of incumbent workers to obstruct the integration of new employees.

There is thus some degree of overlap among explanatory variables relevant to the two scenarios. In particular, the existence of significant costs of labor turnover increases firms' incentive to offer efficiency wages, but also increases the bargaining power of incumbent workers. Similarly, the importance of making a good employment match both creates incentives for firms to offer wage premiums to improve the applicant pool and reinforces the bargaining position of employees who provide a good fit with the firm's production needs.

Segmentation and employee rents

The essential prediction of the labor market segmentation model is that workers in the primary sector enjoy better jobs than their otherwise similar counterparts in the secondary segment. To sustain this result it is necessary to explain why equilibrium wage rates would fail to clear markets in the primary sector. Since supra-market clearing wages generically imply the existence of excess labor supply to the primary labor market, any such explanation yields a corollary hypothesis concerning worker immobility across market segments.

It is clear from previous discussions of the two models (the bargaining model in chapters 7 and 12 and the efficiency wage model in chapters 10 and 11) how supra-competitive wage rates are generated in the respective scenarios. By inference, they also suggest conditions under which wage premiums are *not* paid and thus "secondary" employment conditions obtain. Besides predicting the contingent existence of wage premiums, the theories share two necessary components: the assumption that product market rents exist to be shared with workers, and the hypothesis of contracting imperfections that preclude firms from extracting worker rents at the beginning of the employment relationship through the use of employment bonds or fees.

However, the two models differ in one important respect concerning the economic logic of wage determination in the primary sector. In most versions of the efficiency wage model, wage premiums are not influenced by the magnitude of rents enjoyed by employers; to put it another way, the model does not essentially reflect a theory of *rent-sharing*. Instead, the optimal efficiency wage level is determined, other things equal, by the magnitude of workers' payoffs outside the firm, conditioned in turn by such variables as the degree of labor market competition, search costs, the unemployment rate, and the value of leisure and home production.

A possible exception to this assessment is the *gift-exchange* version of the model, according to which workers reciprocate payment of wage premiums with above-minimum commitments of work intensity. This version of the efficiency model allows for the possibility that wage premiums – that is, the size of the appropriate "gifts" – are determined by the rents enjoyed by firms, but this is accomplished at the cost of losing other important predictive features of the model. In particular, the gift-exchange scenario does not provide an obvious basis for defining labor market segments.

In contrast, the possibility of rent-sharing is an integral feature of the insider–outsider framework. However, the connection between wage levels and employer rents depends critically on the assumed nature of the bargaining relationship. When couched in the specific context of the Rubinstein bargaining model with outside options, the presence of rent-sharing is contingent on the relative costs of exiting given employment relationships.

As explained in chapter 7 (see figure 7.5 and the related exposition), workers just receive the value of their outside payoffs when the latter are high relative to the employment surplus to be shared. In that case, the insider–outsider model shares with the efficiency wage framework the prediction that wage premiums depend on the unemployment rate and other factors affecting worker payoffs outside incumbent employment relationships. Alternatively, employers receive the value of their outside options when the latter are relatively high, with incumbent workers getting the residual. In this case, the insider–outsider model shares with the turnover version of the efficiency wage scenario the prediction that wage levels depend to some extent on the magnitude of employer turnover costs. Finally, pure rent-sharing occurs only in the case that the surplus to be shared is high relative to the outside options of both firms and workers.

The foregoing assessment is modified when the possibility of externally-imposed termination of employment relationships is added to the bargaining framework. Given this modification, the value of outside payoffs influence bargaining outcomes even when the former are relatively small, contrary to the scenario in which outside payoffs are purely elective. (See the end-of-chapter study question related to this issue.)

A key challenge to both theoretical scenarios derives from the need to explain why employees in virtually *all* occupations enlisted by a high-wage firm or industry are rewarded, not just those characterized by monitoring difficulties or high replacement costs. As mentioned above, hypothesized market segments don't divide up strictly along industry lines, but nonetheless there is a strong correlation of wages across jobs within an industry, so that, for example, clerical workers tend to share in the gains received by other employees in high-wage industries. Consequently, a satisfactory theory of market segmentation must explain the relative pervasiveness of wage premiums within primary-sector industries.

Capturing this feature of labor market duality requires an explanation of positive spillovers in wage determination. For example, one version of the efficiency wage model suggests that wage premiums affect the level of general employee morale, so that wage cuts received by a few impairs the outlook, and consequently the productivity, of the entire group. Were this the case, efficiency wage premiums would be generalized beyond just those jobs that are hard to monitor.

DOWNWARD WAGE INFLEXIBILITY IN PRIMARY AND SECONDARY JOBS

Economists have long been puzzled by evidence indicating that nominal wages – the wages actually set by firms – are downwardly inflexible, so that employers don't cut wages in recessions, contrary to the implications of simple supply and demand analysis. So Truman Bewley, although an economic theorist by trade, decided to investigate the matter directly and interviewed hundreds of business executives, consultants, labor leaders, and relevant others to find out what reasons they gave for why wages weren't cut in adverse economic times.

His main survey finding is that firms are reluctant to cut wages due to the danger of negative effects on employee morale. Coincidentally, Bewley's results corroborated and extended the findings of colleague Lloyd Reynolds nearly fifty years earlier from a case study of the New Haven labor market (Reynolds, 1951, p. 232). The possibility that wage levels affect morale is consistent with a form of efficiency wage model in which some aspect of labor input cannot be directly contracted for, but is somehow affected by employees' state of mind, influenced in turn by wage comparisons with previous periods and fellow workers. Bewley's survey also established one partial caveat to this finding: in *secondary* jobs, which he defined as short-term or part-time positions, employers were more willing to reduce wages, but then only for new hires or temporary contract workers, since this reduced the scope for demoralizing wage comparisons.

Related discussion questions:
1. Can you think of ways that employee morale has an impact on company profits? If so, why can't firms contract directly for these outcomes, rather than securing them indirectly through the impact of wages on morale?
2. The theory of rational labor market behavior implies that workers would care about *real* rather than *nominal* wages, and thus would not react negatively to nominal wage cuts if they reflected deflationary trends. Does concern over nominal wage cuts imply that workers act irrationally, and if so in what way?

Related references:
Truman F. Bewley, *Why Wages Don't Fall During a Recession* (Cambridge, MA: Harvard University Press, 1999).
Lloyd Reynolds, *The Structure of Labor Markets: Wages and Labor Mobility in Theory and Practice* (New York: Harper & Brothers, 1951).

Similarly, insider–outsider models in which incumbent workers share in the bargaining advantages yielded by significant replacement costs could be used to explain the pervasive incidence of employee rents in high-wage industries. Clearly this occurs in the case that workers are covered by collective bargaining agreements, but this is not the only possible scenario. For example, if the specificity of human capital in a given firm flows from knowing how to maneuver within its idiosyncratic "corporate culture," then all workers might gain from the corresponding costs the firm incurs in replacing incumbent employees, especially if they collude in not sharing insider secrets with new hires.

Other features of labor market segmentation

Finally, a successful theory of labor market segmentation must be able to account for other features associated with market duality. One such empirical regularity concerns the relative employment security enjoyed by primary-sector workers. This implies that employees in primary jobs are more or less impervious to layoffs occasioned by business cycle fluctuations.

The key to explaining this phenomenon is that the market imperfections associated with efficiency wages or insider bargaining power may also create a "kink" in firms' labor cost curves, leading in turn to a discontinuity in the marginal cost curve for labor inputs. Macroeconomically induced shifts in the value marginal product curve within this region of discontinuity do not prompt profit-maximizing firms to change the size of their labor force.

It is easiest to see the basis for this phenomenon using the effort-based efficiency wage model. To examine the impact of macroeconomic fluctuations in aggregate demand, augment the basic model discussed in chapter 10 by introducing an exogenously given probability λ that an individual worker is laid off, determined independently of whether he or she shirks. In this case, as demonstrated in the appendix, the efficiency wage paid by the firm is *increasing* in λ: the higher the probability of layoff, the more the firm has to pay each worker to induce high effort. The logic here is straightforward: if there is some probability that the worker will be unemployed no matter what effort level is chosen, the threat of being fired carries less bite.

Now relate a given worker's probability of being laid off to the employing firm's quantity demanded for labor in successive time periods. Let L_t represent the firm's total quantity demanded for labor in time t ("today") and L_{t+1} represent its quantity demanded for labor in the next production period ("tomorrow"). Then, assuming just for convenience that each worker in the firm's labor force faces the same probability of being laid off, a given worker's probability of layoff in period $t + 1$ can be represented as the *larger* of the numbers zero and $(L_t - L_{t+1})/L_t$.

This condition says two things at once: first, if the firm employs more workers tomorrow than it does today, then no incumbent worker faces the prospect of being laid off. Second, if the firm seeks a smaller labor force (that is, $L_t > L_{t+1}$), then

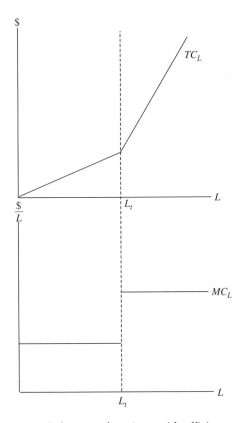

Figure 16.1   Labor cost functions with efficiency wages.

each worker faces the same positive fractional probability of layoff. Thus there is a discrete jump from zero to the layoff probability.

Given this condition and another minor simplifying assumption, the firm's labor cost function can be shown (refer again to the appendix) to have an upward "kink," as shown in figure 16.1(a). This corresponds in turn to the discontinuous marginal cost of labor curve represented in figure 16.1(b). Again, the microeconomic logic is straightforward: if the firm chooses to lay off some workers (so that $L_t > L_{t+1}$), it must raise the efficiency wage, which means that its cost *savings* from reducing unemployment are less than if the wage rate remained the same.

The implications of the efficiency wage model for the firm's hiring and firing choices are now readily seen. Suppose in the initial period t the firm's VMP_L curve intersects the higher portion of the MC_L curve at L_t, as shown in figure 16.2. Now suppose an adverse macroeconomic shock lowers the firm's VMP_L curve, as shown. So long as the reduction in the value marginal product schedule is smaller than the downward jump in marginal cost, the firm will have no incentive to change the size of its labor force. Consequently, firms subject to these employment

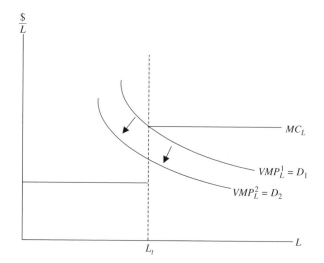

Figure 16.2   Non-responsiveness of employment to demand shifts with efficiency wages.

conditions may not respond at all to downward macroeconomic movements, and primary sector workers will accordingly enjoy some measure of job security not available to their secondary-market counterparts.

A similar conclusion flows from the Rubinstein version of the insider bargaining model given the condition that in each round of bargaining workers face a probability of layoff which is unrelated to their bargaining strategies. This would be true, for example, if firms determined their quantity demanded of labor prior to bargaining and then used a lottery after bargaining concludes to select workers for layoff. In this case, as shown in the second part of the appendix, the equilibrium wage will again be an increasing function of the probability of layoff.

Consequently, virtually the same analytical procedure as in the case of efficiency wages can be used to establish a kink in the firm's cost of labor curve, and a corresponding discontinuity in its marginal cost of labor curve. In this bargaining scenario, the reason for the discontinuity is that a worker facing an increased probability of layoff must receive a higher wage offer to induce acceptance of the offer in lieu of turning it down and taking his or her chances with a counter-offer in the next round of bargaining.

The second empirical regularity often associated with the existence of labor market segments concerns disparities in returns to human capital such that secondary-sector workers experience little or no returns to formal schooling or labor market experience. Since efficiency wage and insider–outsider models both concern wage determination within the primary market segment, neither explicitly implies this result. However, nor does either scenario contradict the possibility of divergent returns to human capital variables.

Consequently, to account for this divergence theoretically, it is only necessary to adduce reasons why secondary market conditions might not yield returns to schooling or experience. One possibility is that stereotypic secondary-sector employment involves "McJobs" in which there is little scope for the exercise of employment skills. Given this condition, the only puzzle is why workers with productive human capital assets don't secure employment in occupations that reward these assets, but this puzzle is resolved by the presence of excess supply conditions in primary-sector markets corresponding to the payment of efficiency wages or insider rents.

EVIDENCE FOR LABOR MARKET SEGMENTATION

Whether or not the evidence summarized near the beginning of the chapter can be read as establishing a presumption in favor of systematic departures from perfectly competitive labor market conditions, the inability to account for intra- and inter-industry wage differentials on the basis of observed variations in human capital factors and workplace characteristics firmly establishes the existence of an empirical puzzle in need of an explanation. If economics were a true laboratory science, the appropriate procedure for evaluating the dual labor market hypothesis would be to construct an appropriate controlled experiment to resolve the matter. However, while experimental methods are receiving increased attention in the social sciences, it is doubtful that these methods could replicate the conditions required to determine the existence of market segmentation. Consequently, here as with most other empirical issues economists have relied on increasingly sophisticated econometric methods to control statistically for confounding factors in investigating explanations for labor market phenomena.

The chief evidence marshaled in support of the market segmentation hypothesis accordingly involves econometric tests of regression models flowing from the theory or its alternative based on the model of perfectly competitive labor markets. The econometric evidence takes three forms: evidence on efficiency wages or bargaining power, evidence on duality in wage determination, and evidence on inter-industry wage differentials.

In addition, there is also a growing body of what might be called circumstantial evidence for the existence of labor market segmentation. Although sometimes econometric in nature, evidence of this sort does not arise from direct tests of the segmentation hypothesis or its chief theoretical alternative. Rather, this evidence suggests the existence of microeconomic behavior or conditions that would be difficult to explain under the hypothesis of competitive labor markets. Labor economists subsequent to the institutionalist era have typically been suspicious of this type of data, but a large body of mutually consistent circumstantial evidence can legitimately raise substantial doubts about the validity of a theory that cannot coherently account for its existence.

Econometric evidence on the segmentation hypothesis

While the empirical record reviewed earlier may strongly suggest the presence of labor market segmentation, it does not rule out the possibility that these wage differentials are driven by *unobserved* worker or workplace characteristics in a manner consistent with the operation of perfectly competitive markets. One hypothesis suggests that residual wage variations correspond to compensating differentials for unobserved and undesirable working conditions. Support for this position would require an explanation as to why most workers in high-wage firms or industries receive a wage premium; it is not obvious, for example, why office workers in a high-wage industry would be exposed to the same risks as production workers. Furthermore, this approach would have to be reconciled with the difficulty, discussed in chapter 13, of finding significant differentials paid for observed characteristics such as risk of fatal injury.

A candidate hypothesis investigated by Edward Leamer and Christopher Thornberg suggests that the wage differentials might be accounted for by variations in total effort per worker, defined as labor intensity times hours worked.[6] In this view, high wages are paid, other things equal, by competitive firms or industries in which correspondingly high levels of effort are demanded of workers. This approach can also explain the correlation of wages across occupations if it is assumed that the efforts of different types of worker are complementary inputs.

A possible illustration for this hypothesis is found in the widely known case of the Lincoln Electric Company, a producer of specialized welding equipment in Cleveland, Ohio.[7] Lincoln Electric is known for its thoroughgoing commitment to linking pay to productivity and company profits. Lincoln workers are paid well relative to the industry standard, but they also work intensely for long hours, and overtime is often mandatory.

A key problem encountered in testing this hypothesis involves the difficulty in measuring worker effort. As discussed in earlier chapters, labor intensity is often difficult for employers to observe and infer, let alone for economists studying employers' behavior. Leamer and Thornberg address this problem by using hours per worker as a proxy for total effort per worker; this is legitimate so long as intensity and hours are not perfectly inversely correlated, since this would cancel the presumed connection between wages and total work effort. The key explanatory variable for Leamer and Thornberg is the capital intensity of production. In their model, capital intensity increases effort demanded because effort and capital are complementary inputs, and increased effort increases the wage paid as a compensating differential. They argue that while the latter relationship is also predicted by efficiency wage theory, the former is not.

As noted earlier, however, the efficiency wage model doesn't rule out an increasing relationship between capital intensity and worker effort, and even suggests an alternative causal path for this connection. Other things equal, a higher efficiency wage rate leads to a higher capital/labor ratio when employers can substitute these inputs, and this will lead to higher effort as well if capital and work effort are complementary inputs. The authors note that their results are not nec-essarily inconsistent with efficiency wage theory, but argue that the robust corre-lation between wages and hours they observe does not appear to be due to insider rent sharing.

It is thus not obvious that inter-industry wage variations can be understood as merely compensating differentials with respect to worker effort. Nor is it clear that Leamer's and Thornberg's results rule out the possibility that the wage differen-tials are fully accounted for by insider rent sharing. They point out that capital intensity has a unique impact on wages even controlling for union status and industry rents, but again it could be possible that higher wages (this time due to bargaining power) increase both capital intensity and hours worked, accounting for the correlation.

The empirical difficulties in sorting out causes and effects are mirrored in the Lincoln Electric case discussed above. On one hand, workers' pay is directly linked to company profits, unlike in the efficiency wage model. Furthermore, turnover at Lincoln is quite high (with almost half of new hires leaving within three months), negating the model's supposition of long-term employment relationships as the norm. On the other hand, the ratio of applicants to hires is extremely high (75 to 1), suggesting that total pay is set high enough to allow significant selectivity in hiring. This condition is consistent with the worker quality version of the efficiency wage model, in which employers raise the wage rate above equilibrium levels to ensure high average quality in the applicant pool.

A second possibility consistent with the operation of perfectly competitive labor markets is that wage differentials across employers might be accounted for by unobserved variations in worker ability. This explanation, again, must accom-modate the evidence that workers who leave nominally primary-sector jobs typ-ically experience reductions in earnings.[8] The most obvious explanation, assuming the validity of the alternative hypothesis, is that the skills in question are industry-, firm-, or more generally, match-specific. Under this interpretation, real-ization of the highest possible marginal productivity – and thus wages – requires the right match of worker and job. But in that case, workers will correspondingly enjoy bargaining power unless firms can siphon off rents with up-front employ-ment fees or bonds.

This approach must also explain why such skill-based differentials would pervade most or all occupations within a given high-wage industry or firm. At the industry level, one might imagine that the match-specific skills of different occu-pations are complementary inputs, so that firms in these matches are willing to hire high-quality workers across the board. This is consistent with the competitive model so long as any resulting rents are competed away by free entry and exit.

It's a little more difficult to understand unexplained wage variations across employers *within* an industry on the basis of this explanation, since under perfect competition one would expect all firms in an industry to use the same inputs. Echoing this point, a study using French data has found that variations in unmea-sured worker quality might explain inter-industry wage differentials, but not the remaining variation across employers.[9] As noted in chapter 11, inter-employer differentials in the US are almost as significant as those across industries.

To accommodate inter-employer wage differentials on the basis of unmeasured labor quality differences in a model of ideal markets, it would thus be necessary to assume that labor markets are *purely* rather that *perfectly* competitive, allowing for differences in production conditions across firms. In this case, however, rents are earned in "inframarginal" firms, and one would expect rents to flow to the scarce factors, presumably the owners of the firm-specific skills.

But this suggests the existence of a dual labor market, albeit for a different reason from those considered earlier. Here, primary-market workers earn rents because they have scarce and irreproducible abilities, not because of any intrinsic market failure or imperfect competitive process. These rents are consistent with allocatively efficient outcomes, unlike in the case of efficiency wages. Also, high-wage workers would not face employment insecurity due to macroeconomic fluctuations if their supply function were inelastic at the margin.

Another body of econometric evidence speaks directly to the hypothesis of labor market duality. As first discussed in chapter 14, this evidence concerns the possibility that the empirical relationship between education and wages is best accounted for by two qualitatively distinct wage equations. To establish credible grounds for the dual market model, the latter must satisfy two conditions: first, regression results for the two-equation model must provide a significantly better "fit" of the data than does the single-equation human capital model; and second, the two equations thus estimated must be consistent with the notion of market segmentation.

The latter condition implies that wage behavior in the two sectors must be more than simply "different." It must reinforce the idea that mobility barriers prevent some workers from gaining access to strictly preferable jobs held by otherwise identical primary-sector workers. Thus this evidence, like that for inter-industry wage differentials, is subject to the critique that observed distinctions flow from as yet unmeasured compensating differentials or human capital variables.

The key hypothesized distinction between the two segments is the absence of a significant rate of return to education in the secondary sector. A number of studies have investigated this possibility over the past 20 to 30 years with varying results, although many have found empirical grounds for the segmentation hypothesis even after controlling to the extent possible for working conditions and human capital differences.

One problem with these earlier studies, as pointed out by William Dickens and Kevin Lang, is that they assume that market segmentation follows industry lines. However, there may be differentials across employers within industries, and given employers may hire both "primary" and "secondary" workers. Dickens and Lang address this problem by allowing market segment of employment to be determined probabilistically by the data, rather than assigned deterministically prior to testing the dual market model. After making this correction, they find a zero return to education and negative returns to experience in the sector identified as secondary, in contrast to positive returns for both in primary-sector jobs.[10]

Even then, evidence for a two-equation model does not necessarily support the dual market hypothesis unless primary markets show evidence of rationing jobs, consistent with the premise of mobility barriers in moving from the secondary to the primary sector. Dickens and Lang also find evidence for primary sector queuing, even after controlling for union status. This suggests that job rationing does not depend solely on the existence of collective bargaining laws and union restrictions.

The absence of statistically significant returns to education in (only) one market segment is consistent with the dual labor market hypothesis, but is not dictated by it. The key prediction is that primary jobs are persistently superior to secondary jobs due to the presence of significant mobility barriers. The next step is to consider the circumstantial evidence for the presence of these barriers and other indirect indicators of market segmentation.

Indirect evidence for segmentation

In addition to econometric tests of the dual labor market hypothesis, there is a body of less direct evidence for the existence of market segmentation. This evidence may not be the result of controlled statistical analysis or may not dispositively indicate the presence of market segments, but taken together makes a case for systematic departures from competitive exchange conditions.

First, if inter-employer wage differentials correspond to the existence of worker rents, as suggested by the dual market hypothesis, one would expect them to affect the rate of applications and quits. Several studies to date have isolated an inverse relationship between quit rates and estimated wage premiums. In addition, at least one study has found that application rates are higher for jobs in high-wage industries.[11]

Second, if market segments exist due to bargaining or efficiency wage considerations, employers in the primary sector will care about the level of their wage offers *relative* to others for similar jobs. In the Rubinstein bargaining model, employers must know this to determine the value of outside options and thus the equilibrium bargaining wage. In the efficiency wage model, outside wages will influence the incentive power of an employer's wage offer and the ability to reduce labor force turnover or attract a high-quality applicant pool. These results are at odds with the competitive model, which suggests that employers in the market for a given type of labor need only concern themselves with the signal provided by that market's wage rate – all other information is redundant. But corporate human resource officers routinely rely on wage and salary surveys to determine where they stand relative to other employers, and often make use of national rather than local wage surveys even if not searching in a nationwide labor market.[12]

Third, the presence of market segmentation due to imperfect competition or incompleteness implies that some workers will have desirable jobs for reasons not tied to ability. Survey evidence suggests that both employers and workers believe this to be the case. Howard Wial interviewed working class men in Boston who drew distinctions between "good" and "bad" jobs, and attributed employment in good jobs to fortune or personal connections rather than ability.[13] Conversely, personnel directors interviewed in 1980 by Fred Foulkes did not see high wages as paying for superior ability or skill.[14] The chief reason for paying wage premiums identified by these managers was to deter unionization of their workers.

In addition, some regression results that are difficult to explain within the framework of competitive labor markets are readily accounted for by the segmentation hypothesis. For example, Dickens and Lang note that within age cohorts, wages have risen more rapidly for blacks than for whites, despite the fact that black wages rise less rapidly for blacks than whites *within jobs*. This is puzzling under the assumption of free mobility between jobs, but perfectly consistent with the operation of mobility barriers to highly paid jobs.[15]

CAN LABOR MARKET POLICIES IMPROVE THE BALANCE OF GOOD AND BAD JOBS?

The unexplained component of intra- and inter-industry wage differentials may correspond to unobserved ability differences or, perhaps more plausibly, to compensating differentials with respect to work effort. In either scenario, these wage variations are consistent with the operation of perfectly competitive labor markets, and the subject matter of this chapter is in that interpretation best understood as an extension of chapters 13 and 14. This implies, as ever, that there is no role for welfare-improving government interventions in the labor market.

However, a compelling empirical case has not yet been made for that assessment (or for any other single model of these phenomena), and to the contrary there are a number of ancillary behaviors, such as differential job queuing, that are difficult at best to explain within the competitive framework. The alternative reading suggested by the theory of labor market segmentation is that these wage differentials reflect systematic departures from perfectly competitive conditions such that wages in the "primary" sector remain at supra-market-clearing levels, creating worker rents and excess supply for jobs in this sector and corresponding mobility restrictions for workers in relatively low-wage "secondary" jobs.

Under this scenario, market outcomes are generally not efficient and there may exist multiple, Pareto-rankable equilibria in the economy characterized by labor market segmentation, with greater and smaller ratios of primary- to secondary-sector jobs. This creates scope for welfare-improving government policies with respect to labor exchange, although of course it doesn't guarantee that actual policies will be Pareto-improving.

Economist Daron Acemoglu illustrates these ideas using a theoretical model with matching costs and incomplete contracts. Firms in this scenario are differentiated by the capital intensity of production, and sunk capital investments create exit costs for primary-sector firms, endowing their workers with bargaining power to drive up wages. Search costs reduce the ability of lower-paid secondary-sector workers to compete for these jobs.

In this framework Acemoglu considers the implications of two policy interventions, unemployment insurance and binding minimum wages, both of which tend to raise the equilibrium ratio of good to bad jobs. Unemployment insurance lowers the cost of search and allows secondary-sector workers to seek higher-wage jobs more persistently, increasing the incidence of those positions in general equilibrium. Effective wage floors have the complementary effect of reducing the profitability and equilibrium incidence of bad jobs. Both of these interventions may improve social welfare, though, as Acemoglu notes, this outcome is not guaranteed.

Related discussion question:
1. Here, capital intensity of production is associated with insider bargaining power. In the text of the chapter, it is suggested alternatively that higher capital intensity raises efficiency wage levels by increasing the productivity of (partially hidden) work effort. What sort of data might make it possible to distinguish which effect is operating in a given primary labor market?

Related reference:
Daron Acemoglu, "Good Jobs versus Bad Jobs," *Journal of Labor Economics* 19, no. 1 (January 2001): 1–21.

CONCLUSION

Over the 50-plus years that labor economics has existed as a distinct field of study, the debate on inter-employer wage differentials has come full circle. Or perhaps it would be more accurate to say that the initial debate has been rejoined at a higher level of sophistication in both the theoretical and empirical analysis of wage determination. Labor economics was initiated as a separate subdiscipline largely in response to claims that its subject matter was simply an extension of standard microeconomics. Institutionally oriented economists in the first era of the field's history rebutted this claim in part by referring to evidence of employer wage premiums.

Concern with industry and employer wage differentials was largely swept aside in light of the enormous promise of human capital theory, coupled with the construction of new large data sets that permitted more careful econometric testing of the theory's predictions. At the same time, there were insufficient microdata to allow controls for the employer-specific effects predicted by segmentation theory. Interest in this theory was briefly renewed in the second era of labor economics, but most labor economists found insufficient empirical grounds for pursuing this alternative to the human capital model.

New analytical methods and sources of data have leveled the playing field somewhat and helped usher in a new era of labor economics. Human capital analysis plays a key, perhaps a central, role in contemporary research in the field, but more extensive theoretical options and finely discriminatory data sets have widened the scope of legitimate inquiry in the discipline. This is seen perhaps most clearly in the renewed debate on dual labor markets. While deep controversies on the topic unavoidably continue, the hypothesis of labor market segmentation can no longer be easily dismissed. Indeed, it appears able to account for a wide range of phenomena that seem anomalous given the postulate of competitive labor markets.

That said, few labor economists would assert that the debate on labor market segmentation has been satisfactorily resolved. On one hand, one has the prospect of a well-understood and logically coherent theory that nonetheless appears unable to account for many of the key phenomena addressed by the segmentation hypothesis. On the other hand, while a number of models of imperfect competition exist which address one or more of these phenomena, no one existing theory has been shown to capture all of the empirical features associated with labor market segmentation. Consequently, there remains scope for fundamental advances in the understanding of how actual labor markets function.

APPENDIX TO CHAPTER 16

LAYOFF PROBABILITY AND EMPLOYMENT SECURITY

The efficiency wage model

Consider a version of the efficiency wage model presented in the appendix to chapter 10 in which each worker faces an exogenous probability λ of being laid off whether or not he or she shirks. Correspondingly, define q as the probability that a shirking worker is let go, either due to layoff or detection and firing. To keep the model simple, assume only two possible effort levels, "high" and "low," with corresponding utility costs $c_H > c_L$.

In this case, the incentive condition becomes

$$w - c_H + \delta \cdot ((1 - \lambda) \cdot v + \lambda \cdot z) \geq w - c_L + \delta \cdot ((1 - q) \cdot v + q \cdot z), \tag{16.1}$$

which just states that the agent's present value of utility from performing high effort must be at least as great, given the probabilities of layoff or firing, as the present value of utility for choosing low effort. Profit-maximizing firms will choose the lowest possible wage that induces high effort, so they will choose the wage level that satisfies (16.1) with strict *equality*. Adopting this as an assumption and simplifying yields

$$v = \frac{MC_e}{\delta \cdot (q - \lambda)} + z. \tag{16.2}$$

Now let x represent the exogenously given probability that a shirking worker is detected and fired, understood as independent of the probability that the worker is laid off. Then $q = \lambda + (1 - \lambda) \cdot x$ and thus $q - \lambda = (1 - \lambda) \cdot x$.

In equilibrium, all workers choose high effort, and thus v is equal to the left-hand side of (16.1). Substituting (16.2) into (16.1) and rearranging gives as the equilibrium efficiency wage

$$w* = \left(c_H - \frac{MC_e}{\delta \cdot x} \right) + (1 - \delta) \cdot z + \frac{MC_e}{\delta \cdot x \cdot (1 - \lambda)}. \tag{16.3}$$

Note that all terms but the last one are independent of an incumbent worker's probability of layoff λ, assuming that no one firm can affect the value of a worker's outside opportunities z.

Now consider how an incumbent worker's probability of layoff is determined and how that affects the equilibrium efficiency wage. Let n_t represent the size of the firm's incumbent labor force and n_{t+1} represent the firm's new labor force after optimally adjusting to any shifts in marginal revenue product. Then, assuming each incumbent worker faces the same probability of layoff, we can specify the probability that any one incumbent worker is laid off as

$$\lambda = \max\left\{0, \frac{n_t - n_{t+1}}{n_t}\right\}, \tag{16.4}$$

which says that the layoff probability is zero if the firm's labor force does not shrink, and equals the ratio of laid-off workers to existing incumbents otherwise.

Substituting expression (16.4) into (16.3), rearranging and simplifying, noting that the term $\dfrac{MC_e}{\delta \cdot x}$ is independent of n by assumption, we have

$$w* = a + b \cdot \max\left\{1, \frac{n_t}{n_{t+1}}\right\}, \tag{16.5}$$

where a and $b > 0$ are constants. In turn, this suggests that the cost of the firm's new labor force is wages times workers hired, or

$$C(n_{t+1}) = w* \cdot n_{t+1} = a \cdot n_{t+1} + b \cdot \max\{n_t, n_{t+1}\}. \tag{16.6}$$

Expression (16.6) gives the kinked total cost of labor curve, and the correspondingly discontinuous marginal cost curve, shown in figures 16.1(a) and 16.1(b) respectively.

The bargaining model

Results similar to (16.6) can be generated from various versions of the Rubinstein bargaining model. The bargaining model with outside options yields a conclusion most closely parallel to that of the efficiency wage model. Once again let λ denote the probability of layoff, understood as independent of bargaining strategies. Let an incumbent worker's outside option be given by w_c, understood as the competitive wage rate. The firm can hire additional workers at this wage rate, but must pay incumbent workers the equilibrium bargaining wage.

Assume that all incumbent workers have identical productivity characteristics, and consider the bargaining relationship between the firm and a representative worker. Let n_t represent the number of incumbents, and let n_{t+1} represent the firm's new labor force size in response to a macroeconomic shock. Let $\hat{V}(n)$ represent the net surplus to be bargained over between the firm and the representative worker, given a labor force size of n, and assume a common fractional discount factor represented by δ. Suppose finally that the firm suffers a firing cost of c for each incumbent let go.

The next step is to construct the bargaining reaction functions for this bargaining game. Since the representative worker faces a probability λ of being laid off subsequent to bargaining, and has an outside wage of w_c, the firm's current offer y must meet the following condition, given the worker's anticipated wage demand of x in the next period:

$$\lambda \cdot w_c + (1-\lambda) \cdot y = \max\{w_c, \delta \cdot [\lambda \cdot w_c + (1-\lambda) \cdot x]\}. \tag{16.7}$$

While the firm pays n_{t+1} workers for certain, it will only pay a *given* incumbent worker the bargaining wage with probability $(1 - \lambda)$. Therefore the worker's wage demand x must satisfy the following condition, given that the firm offers y in the next bargaining round:

$$\hat{V}(n_{t+1}) - (1-\lambda) \cdot x = \max\{\hat{V}(n_{t+1}) - w_c - c, \delta \cdot [\hat{V}(n_{t+1}) - (1-\lambda) \cdot y]\} \tag{16.8}$$

There are four potential solution cases to consider. Consider the case in which the firm's outside option is relatively high and the worker's relatively low. This implies, via (16.8), that

$$\hat{V}(n_{t+1}) - (1-\lambda) \cdot x = \hat{V}(n_{t+1}) - w_c - c, \tag{16.9}$$

which simplifies to

$$x^* = w_I^* = \frac{w_c + c}{(1-\lambda)}. \tag{16.10}$$

Given the expression for λ in (16.4), this yields expression (16.6) with $a = 0$.

Study Questions

1. What is the connection, if any, between *internal labor markets*, discussed in chapter 11, and *dual* or *segmented labor markets*, as defined in the present chapter?

2. Provide explanations based respectively on efficiency wage and insider–outsider considerations for why most employees in "primary" industries tend to receive high wages, not just those with whom monitoring or replacement costs are directly associated.

3. Suppose wage rates in the primary sector are determined by the Nash bargaining solution, where the disagreement payoff of the worker is the

secondary-sector wage and the disagreement payoff of the firm is its current profit level net of the cost of replacing the worker. Under what conditions of strategic bargaining would this result emerge, assuming that workers and firms can freely choose to terminate the bargaining relationship? Find the equilibrium wage and show the equilibrium hired in this case (algebraically and/or graphically). How do the predictions of the Nash bargaining model for wage determination in the primary sector compare to those of the Rubinstein bargaining model with voluntary exit and the effort-based efficiency wage model?

4. Suppose workers in the primary labor market are paid an efficiency wage that exceeds the market-clearing wage. Show algebraically and/or graphically the impact on equilibrium wage and labor hired of:
   a) an exogenous increase in monitoring effectiveness
   b) an increase in unemployment compensation
   c) an increase in the workers' discount factor

Notes

1 William T. Dickens and Kevin Lang, "Labor Market Segmentation Theory: Reconsidering the Evidence," NBER Working Paper No. 4087 (June 1992). On this point, recall the study by Erica Groshen on intra-industry wage differentials, cited in chapter 11.

2 See, for example, William T. Dickens and Lawrence F. Katz, "Industry Wage Differences and Industry Characteristics," in Kevin Lang and Jonathan S. Leonard (eds), *Unemployment and the Structure of Labor Markets* (Oxford: Basil Blackwell, 1987); and Alan B. Krueger and Lawrence H. Summers, "Efficiency Wages and the Inter-Industry Wage Structure," *Econometrica* 56, no. 2 (March 1988): 259–93.

3 William T. Dickens and Lawrence F. Katz, *op. cit.*

4 Maury Gittleman and Edward N. Wolff, "International Comparisons of Inter-Industry Wage Differentials," *Review of Income and Wealth* 39, no. 3 (September 1993): 295–312.

5 Erkan Erdil and İ. Hakan Yetkiner, "A Comparative Analysis of Inter-Industry Wage Differentials: Industrialized versus Developing Countries," *Applied Economics* 33, no. 13 (October 2001): 1639–48.

6 Edward E. Leamer and Christopher Thornberg, "Efforts and Wages: A New Look at the Inter-Industry Wage Differentials," NBER Working Paper No. 6626 (June 1998).

7 H. Lorne Carmichael and W. Bentley MacLeod, "Worker Cooperation and the Ratchet Effect," *Journal of Labor Economics* 18, no. 1 (January 2000): 1–19.

8 Dickens and Lang, *op. cit.*: 26.

9 John M. Abowd and Francis Kramarz, "Internal and External Labor Markets: An Analysis of Matched Longitudinal Employer–Employee Data," NBER Working Paper No. 6109 (July 1997).

10 William T. Dickens and Kevin Lang, "A Test of Dual Labor Market Theory," *American Economic Review* 75, no. 4 (September 1985): 792–805.

11 Harry J. Holzer, Lawrence F. Katz, and Alan B. Krueger, "Job Queues and Wages," *The Quarterly Journal of Economics* 106, no. 3 (August 1991): 739–68.

12 Dickens and Lang (1992), *op. cit.*: 31–2.

13   Howard Wial, "Getting a Good Job: Mobility in a Segmented Labor Market," *Industrial Relations* 30, no. 3 (Fall 1991): 396–416.

14   Fred K. Foulkes, *Personnel Policies in Large Nonunion Companies* (Englewood Cliffs, NJ: Prentice-Hall, 1980).

15   Dickens and Lang (1992), *op. cit.*: 10.

Suggestions for Further Reading

Jean Helwege, "Sectoral Shifts and Interindustry Wage Differentials," *Journal of Labor Economics* 10, no. 1 (January 1992): 55–84.

Gilles Saint-Paul, *Dual Labor Markets: A Macroeconomic Perspective* (Cambridge, MA: The MIT Press, 1996).

PART FIVE

LABOR IN THE MARKET SYSTEM

The four chapters of part IV examined labor market outcomes in comparative context, seeking to explain persistent differences in wages and labor market opportunities across individuals and industries. In the final part of the text, the focus shifts to the operation of labor markets within capitalist market economies, seeking a "big picture" with respect to the distribution of wages and the incidence of unemployment and wage inflation. While the focus shifts, the core analytical reference points stay the same. For example, transaction costs that give rise to excess labor supply in a microeconomic context may contribute to higher overall unemployment rates.

First, chapter 17 examines patterns and causes of earnings inequality related to ideal and imperfectly competitive conditions. Chapter 18 marks a shift from a general equilibrium to a macroeconomic perspective to study the nature, causes, and possible correctives to the pervasive problem of unemployment. Chapter 19 complements this analysis by placing unemployment in a dynamic context involving continuous labor market adjustments to economic shocks, with implications for the connection between unemployment rates and wage inflation.

These considerations bring the analytical path begun in part II full circle, as macroeconomic conditions not only result from the features of exchange in the presence of matching, negotiation, and enforcement costs, but at the same time establish the economic context within which labor market transactions take place. For example, macroeconomic shocks provide the unanticipated contingencies that characterize incomplete labor contracts. Vacancy and unemployment rates influence the outside options of firms and workers in bargaining.

CHAPTER SEVENTEEN

EARNINGS INEQUALITY

Preceding chapters have discussed a number of factors affecting *earnings*, that is, the income derived from employment. Some of these factors, such as race, gender, and basic aptitude, are genetically determined, while others, such as post-mandatory education, are to some extent a matter of individual choice. Still others, such as unemployment, are determined by economic or social considerations that need not reflect voluntary choices by labor market participants.

In light of all these determinants of labor income, the observation that earnings vary across individuals may not strike you as overly surprising. Indeed, it would seem more surprising if workers in market economies tended to receive the same level of income. What is striking about observed patterns of labor income inequality is rather the manner in which earnings typically vary across employees, as reflected in the characteristic shape of frequency distributions of earned income for workers in advanced market economies.

Whatever social factors drive the shape of these distributions, they don't appear to obey the same logic as the stochastic forces that give rise to the "bell-shaped curves" representing the incidence of many physical and biological phenomena. Moreover, their effects are not static. For example, the last 30 years has witnessed a dramatic increase in measured levels of earnings inequality (and inequality in incomes from all sources) in many developed economies, but especially in the United States and the United Kingdom.

There are two grounds on which given levels of income inequality might be considered cause for social concern. First, disparities in labor income gain special significance when they imply that some portion of an economy's working population falls below a socially determined minimum

continued

standard for income informally known as the "poverty line." Poverty is a matter for social concern because those who suffer it are deemed unable to afford levels of consumption understood to be minimally necessary according to some accepted standard of basic human capabilities or individual well-being.

Poverty is of course a defining element of developing economies, in which most of the world's population continues to live on the equivalent of a US dollar per day or less. But it has also proven to be a persistent feature of developed economies despite the occasional prediction that given trends in economic growth guarantee the tendential elimination of poverty. However, the incidence of poverty varies widely across developed countries, and is generally lower in countries that support policies to reduce income disparities through a combination of egalitarian social welfare measures and redistributive taxes and transfers.

Alternatively, concerns about income inequality may translate into social goals respecting *relative*, rather than *absolute*, income levels. In this assessment, income inequality matters in that there are injuries associated with *differential* access to economic goods, even if everyone in society were able to meet given minimum standards of consumption.

However, conventional utilitarian welfare analysis based on the principle of Pareto optimality does not automatically suggest norms respecting *either* absolute or relative income levels. To begin with, utility theory does not of itself establish minimal standards of individual well-being. Furthermore, according to the Pareto principle, allocations of social resources that render some individuals better off without making others worse off are unambiguously desirable, no matter what the individual circumstances of those who gain.

Conversely, the principle implies that no welfare judgment at all can be made about changes that redistribute welfare across individuals, no matter what their initial absolute or relative economic standing. Thus, unless inequality somehow creates externalities that affect everyone's welfare – a possibility considered later in the chapter – normative assessments with respect to inequality must flow from philosophical standards other than Pareto-utilitarianism. For example, theories of economic justice might yield criteria for assessing alternative distributions of income.

The present chapter first examines common features of the distribution of earnings in developed market economies and potential reasons to be concerned about income inequality. After a review of competing theories for the characteristic shape of these distributions, the chapter considers alternative measures of income inequality and uses some of these measures to assess competing explanations for the recent trend of increasing earnings inequality.

EARNINGS INEQUALITY: CONCEPTS AND MEASURES

Earnings distributions

Individual *earnings* are defined as the total income derived from employment in a given period. Although labor market compensation may take various forms, from piece rates and commissions to hourly wages to salaries, it is analytically useful to think of earnings as the product of total hours worked and the *average* compensation received per hour. However, it is not necessarily the case that the respective magnitudes of the two terms in this expression are determined by the same factors and in the same way. For example, those who chose higher levels of employment-related education may thus enjoy higher wage rates (tending to increase their earnings) yet elect to work fewer hours (tending to reduce their earnings) than those with less education.

Consequently, when comparing individual earnings levels it is best to isolate variations in one of the two terms, holding the magnitude of the other constant. For most analytical and policy-related concerns the relevant variable is the average individual wage rate. But this is not always the case, since, for example, the incidence of involuntary unemployment (and its implications for the distribution of hours worked) may be a matter of considerable normative significance. The key lesson here is that it is important to specify the precise source of earnings disparities under investigation. It is unfortunately the case that data limitations often preclude separating out the respective effects of individual variations in wages and hours worked, but the potential biases introduced by such limitations should always be kept in mind when evaluating the data.

However earnings variations might be measured, one way of representing differences in earnings within a given population is by a frequency distribution defined over possible incomes, such that each income level or range is associated with the proportion of the population receiving it. It might then be possible to discuss the nature and degree of earnings inequality in terms of the shape of the distribution or, more conveniently, statistics summarizing the information conveyed by the distribution. As you know, it is typically the case that the import of a given frequency distribution cannot be adequately summarized by a *single* summary statistic.

In the present context, it is plausible that the relevant summary statistic to start with is variance (or its square root, known as *standard deviation*), which is a summary measure of the dispersion of individual values about the mean of the distribution under study. Other things equal, distributions with higher variance tend to be more "spread out" around the mean, suggesting a greater degree of income inequality. However, variance (or some other economically appropriate measure of dispersion) is not the only interesting aspect of empirical earnings distributions pertaining to the phenomenon of inequality.

To see this point, consider the two hypothetical earnings distributions shown in figures 17.1a and 17.1b. Figure 17.1a depicts the familiar "bell-shaped" *normal*

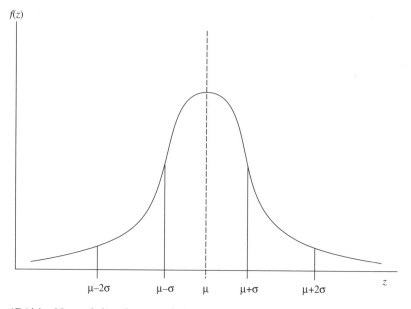

Figure 17.1(a) Normal distribution of characteristic z with mean μ and standard deviation σ.

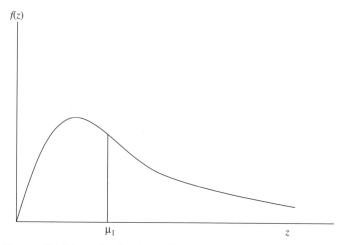

Figure 17.1(b) A "right-skewed" distribution of characteristic z.

distribution generated by the incidence of stochastic biological phenomena such as birth weight or adult height, and many physical phenomena such as variations in the width or volume of goods mass-produced by automated mechanical processes. Note that the normal distribution is *symmetric* about its mean and that the "tails" of the distribution become vanishingly small within a small number of standard deviations from the mean. These characteristics are reflected in the fact that a normal distribution can be completely described by just two summary statistics, mean and variance.

Not so the distribution depicted in figure 17.1b, which represents the characteristic shape of earnings distributions in developed economies. This distribution is *asymmetric* about its mean in the specific sense of being *skewed to the right*, so that positive deviations from the mean are larger and/or weighted with higher respective probabilities than are negative deviations. (In statistical terms, right-skewness corresponds to a positive *third* moment about the mean.) An immediate implication of the right-skewness of earnings distributions is that *mean* labor incomes exceed corresponding *median* levels. In other words, a completely egalitarian redistribution of earnings would render the median working household richer.

A second feature of real-world earnings distributions, somewhat harder to see in figure 17.1b, is the existence of "fat tails" – specifically, the distribution's right tail doesn't become vanishingly small at the same distance from the mean as in the normal distribution. In statistical language, this feature is reflected in a relatively large *fourth* moment about the mean. In practical terms, it means that the incidence of relatively *high* levels of earnings is in some sense greater than one would expect to emerge from the operation of stochastic influences.

These considerations suggest that some degree of finesse is called for in choosing appropriate summary statistics to represent the state of an economy's earnings distribution. Some of these issues are addressed in the next section's examination of some frequently used measures of income inequality and their properties. But first, the present discussion is concluded by noting certain other regularities with respect to individual variations in labor income.

At least three other common characteristics of empirical earnings disparities deserve mention. First, average earnings vary systematically and significantly across groups of workers defined by observable characteristics such as education and experience levels, occupation, and gender. Second, however, there are also substantial earnings variations *within* worker groups defined along these lines, suggesting the operation of factors invisible to economic analysts. Third, these within-group disparities tend to grow with workers' experience levels.

The fact that average earnings increase with education and experience is understandable from the standpoint of human capital theory, discussed at length in chapter 14. It is less evident, however, that human capital analysis can readily account for the other regularities in observed earnings variations. Therefore it may be necessary to incorporate particular departures from ideal market conditions in order to explain such patterns.

Measures of earnings inequality

The foregoing discussion focused on the *qualitative* features of empirically observed earnings distributions. However, for certain positive and normative purposes it is necessary to distinguish *degrees* of observed inequality, as across economies at a given point in time or for a given economy across time. Such measures, for example, would be required to give shape to theoretical claims as to determinants of the degree of inequality, or normative judgments concerning unacceptable levels of inequality.

What features would a useful measure of earnings inequality possess? It is difficult to answer this question fully without knowing the specific analytical concerns that drive a given investigation of income differentials, but speaking at a general level, three conditions seem minimally desirable. Other things equal, a desirable measure should 1) permit comparisons to be made, whatever the form of the observed distributions; 2) use information from the entire range of the distribution in representing differences in inequality (a particular form of this criterion is the *principle of transfer*, which states that an income transfer from a relatively rich to a relatively poor person should always be reflected in a reduction in measured inequality); and 3) be independent of scale, so that, for example, purely nominal changes in total income do not affect the measure, and comparisons are possible between countries with different currencies.

It is difficult to find measures that satisfy all of these conditions while still recording analytically meaningful differences in inequality. This point can be illustrated via reference to some alternative measures of income inequality that are frequently seen in the literature. In light of earlier comments about summary statistics, it would seem presumptive to start with a measure such as variance or standard deviation. But any such measure would depend on the units in which incomes were being measured, and thus violates the third criterion stated above.

Thus, the related measure used instead is the *coefficient of variation*, defined as the ratio of standard deviation to mean income. This measure is scale-free since income units in the numerator and denominator of the measure cancel out. Furthermore, as a practical matter this indicator always generates a number for comparison (given that real-world distributions, unlike some of their theoretical counterparts, always have finite variance) and makes use of all points along a given earnings distribution. Nonetheless, it may not serve as a very useful inequality measure for two reasons: it does not systematically capture variations in skewness, and since it has no necessary upper bound, the measure offers no guidance as to when measured inequality levels might be considered "very big."

Alternatively, consider an indicator such as the *concentration measure*, which gives the percentage of income received by the top $X\%$ of households ranked by income (where X is generally a number considerably less than 100). The relevance of such a measure is suggested by the right-skewed, fat-tailed aspect of empirical earnings distributions, which implies that the richest households will hold a disproportionate share of aggregate earnings. Furthermore, comparisons can always be made on the basis of this measure, and it is independent of units. However, it obviously fails the second condition, since it offers no indication of what's going on with the lower $(100 - X)$ percent of households. In particular, the principle of transfer is not met, since transfers from "medium-" to "low-"income households would not even be registered.

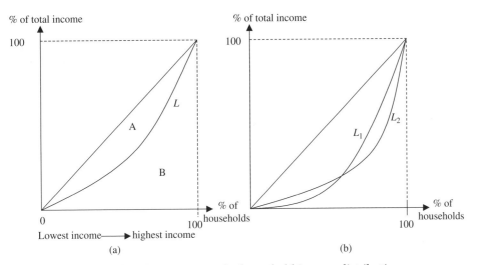

Figure 17.2   Lorenz curves for household income distribution.

A frequently used inequality measure with similar properties is the *earnings ratio*, which compares earnings levels at points relatively high and low in a given earnings distribution. For example, a typically reported earnings ratio is that given by earnings of households at the 90th percentile of the distribution relative to household earnings at the 10th decile. This has the advantage, missing in the concentration measure, of representing the lower end of a given distribution, but the corollary disadvantage of containing less information about the upper end. While the measure is unit-free and always generates a number for comparison, its failure to use information from the whole range of the distribution means that income transfers between the two reported percentiles cannot be captured.

As a final example of frequently used inequality measures, consider the well-known *Lorenz curve* and its related summary statistic, the *Gini coefficient*. To construct a Lorenz curve, imagine a pair of axes with percentage of total households, arrayed from low to high income, on the horizontal axis, and percentage of total earnings in an economy on the vertical. The Lorenz curve plots the percentage of total earnings held by successively higher proportions of the set of all households, ranging from zero to one.

The generic result of such a procedure is illustrated in figure 17.2a. The top curve, which is a straight line from the origin to the point (100,100) on the graph, serves as a reference; it represents a perfectly egalitarian distribution of labor income, such that the lowest *X* percent of households always receives *X* percent of total earnings, for every possible value of *X* between 0 and 100. The lower curve, which is the Lorenz curve itself, also goes between the origin and point (100,100) but is decidedly non-linear. It represents the actual, generically non-egalitarian, earnings distribution for a given economy. Here, the lack of perfectly equal income distribution is reflected in the fact that the lowest X percent of households ranked by income always has strictly *less* than X percent of total earnings.

The Lorenz curve offers a visual sense of the degree of income inequality in a given economy: clearly, "more bowed" curves are further away from the egalitarian reference line and thus represent unambiguously greater levels of inequality. However, consider the situation in figure 17.2b: here, two Lorenz curves cross, and as a result it's not so obvious which curve corresponds to the greater degree of inequality. The Lorenz curve, therefore, does not allow a complete ordering of alternative earnings distributions.

This problem is solved, in a sense, by the Gini coefficient. To arrive at a Gini coefficient for a Lorenz curve, take the ratio of the area in figure 17.2a marked A to the sum of the areas A and B. This is equivalent to multiplying area A by two. Since the Gini coefficient is thus simply a transformed measure of area, it can always be used in making comparisons between distributions, and the measure is unit-free.

However, it's not clear what a comparison of the corresponding Gini coefficients indicates when Lorenz curves cross. In the simplest scenario under which this occurs, there must be some target proportion of households X such that all proportions of the poorest households in one country, *up to* this target level, receive a smaller share of total earnings than do their counterparts in the other country, *and* this inequality is reversed for all proportional sets of poorest households beyond this target. In this scenario, earnings are necessarily more skewed in one country than the other, but it doesn't follow that the country with greater skewness has the higher Gini measure.

There are other, less frequently used measures of income inequality that link more closely to particular normative standards as to what constitutes objectionable patterns and degrees of income inequality. These won't be reviewed here, although if interested you are invited to pursue the topic in some of the sources listed at the end of the chapter. The next step in the argument is to link the foregoing discussion of earnings inequality to the competing visions of the labor market that have been under investigation throughout the text.

THEORIES OF EARNINGS INEQUALITY[1]

Basic considerations

As suggested in the introduction, natural variations in biological features can often be accurately represented by a normal frequency distribution. If differences in earnings could be explained via reference to natural variation in a single genetic factor in workers, for example, one might expect that earnings were also normally distributed. Indeed, one version of a result in probability theory known as the *central limit theorem* permits a stronger claim: if earnings variations were the result of a *sum* of randomly occurring factors with *independent* and *identical* probability distributions, then as the number of such factors becomes very large, the earnings distribution would approach the normal form, even if the individual factors were not themselves normally distributed. Thus a "naïve" explanation of earning variations based simply on the predicted effects of (sums of) random elements would lead one to expect "bell-shaped" distributions.

But this is evidently *not* how real-world income distributions are generated. That being the case, what's driving observed patterns of earnings variation? Unfortunately, a comprehensive answer to this question based on the existing literature would require going into a great deal of analytical and empirical detail that goes beyond the scope of this text. Instead, alternative explanations for observed earnings distributions are framed in terms of the text's fundamental distinction between perfect and imperfect labor market conditions, featuring respectively human capital analysis and theories of market outcomes under imperfect competition.

Some insight into the nature of the analytical task at hand can be garnered by thinking first in general terms about the conditions that yield skewed, fat-tailed frequency distributions. Broadly speaking, two sets of factors yield distributions with the rightward skew characteristic of earnings distributions: on one hand, factors that truncate the incidence of relatively low incomes, shrinking the lower tail of the distribution, and on the other, factors that increase the size and/or probability of positive deviations from the mean of the distribution. The latter also tend, other things equal, to contribute to the "fat-tailed" aspect of earnings distributions.

Still speaking in general terms, there are two interrelated types of phenomena that tend via the effect just described to create right-skewed, fat-tailed distributions. First, suppose that, unlike in the scenario addressed by the central limit theorem, the random factors understood to influence earnings combined *multiplicatively* rather than *additively* to determine earnings levels, causing positive variations in these factors to be *mutually reinforcing* in their effects on labor income. For example, a baseball player with excellent eyesight *and* outstanding motor skills *and* high running speed might be disproportionately more effective than a player who possesses only one of these attributes. What is the shape of the corresponding distribution in such situations?

Since the logarithm of the *product* of a set of variables just equals the *sum* of the logarithms of the variables, it follows that the central limit theorem can be applied to the latter sum if the variables are identically and independently distributed (say, according to the normal distribution). It can be shown that if the logarithm of a variable is normally distributed, then the distribution of the variable itself tends to be right-skewed, although the right tail in this case is not as long or as thick as in observed earnings distributions.

Second, the right tail of a distribution can be made to expand by assuming additionally that the random factors are *positively correlated* rather than independently distributed, implying that positive deviations from the mean in one variable tend to be associated with positive deviations in others. In terms of the baseball player example, suppose it were true that players with excellent eyesight also tended to have above-average motor skills and to run faster. Then players blessed with one

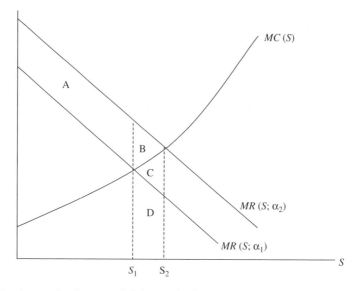

Figure 17.3 Interactive impact of ability and schooling choice on income (The income gain A due to higher ability is augmented by the gain (B+C+D) related to the correspondingly higher level of schooling chosen.)

attribute would tend to have all of them, thus raising the probability that disproportionately high baseball salaries are observed.

In sum, right-skewed distributions are generated when relatively low levels of labor income are censored and/or factors affecting earnings are interactive, and in the latter case are increasingly fat-tailed to the extent that these factors are also positively correlated with each other. Therefore, labor market phenomena that generate these conditions will tend to be associated with earnings distributions that more or less approximate those actually observed. We are thus interested in identifying theories that account for such phenomena as well as for the three additional "stylized facts" concerning the distribution of earnings across and within worker groups.

Human capital explanations for earnings inequality

First consider how the empirical regularities exhibited by earnings distributions might be accounted for on the grounds of human capital theory. Recall that this theory accounts for variations in wage levels in terms of individual differences in factors that affect a worker's revenue productivity in the workplace. These differences can be either innate, as in the case of basic aptitudes, or acquired, as with training or formal schooling.

In light of the foregoing discussion, the respective influences on earnings of these human capital elements would need to be interactive and positively correlated in order to generate observed patterns of earnings inequality. To see how this might be the case, consider figure 17.3, which replicates the basic model of individual choice for post-mandatory levels of schooling (S) first discussed in chapter 14.

In this model, a representative individual faces a given marginal cost MC of additional years of schooling and a marginal return to education function MR that depends positively on ability level α and represents the increments of later-life income associated with electing additional years of schooling. (Note that gross earnings are thus given by the area under the MR curve for any given level of education.) For a given ability level, an optimizing individual who cares only about net income would choose the level of education that equates MR and MC. For individuals with respective ability levels α_1 and α_2, these choices occur at education levels S_1 and S_2.

This basic story about educational choice establishes two relevant implications: first, the impacts of ability and schooling on earnings are interactive, such that the marginal return to ability is increasing in the level of education, and vice versa (compare, for example, the areas under the two depicted MR curves at S_1 and S_2, respectively). Furthermore, income-enhancing ability and schooling levels are positively correlated, since, other things equal, individuals with higher ability will tend to select higher levels of education. For the reasons given above, then, right-skewed wage distributions will tend to be generated by optimizing educational choices premised on variations in individual ability.

This is not the only pathway by which human capital choices might be understood to yield right-skewed earnings distributions. Skewed distributions might also be expected to emerge from optimizing training choices in perfectly competitive market conditions even when individuals have identical preferences and basic aptitudes, and under certain conditions these effects of human capital decisions on the distribution of earnings (as opposed to just wages) can be further reinforced if individual labor supply decisions are added to the story.

Alternatively, the effects of small variations in ability are potentially magnified by introducing a departure from ideal market conditions in the form of economies of scale in the provision of certain types of labor services. The "scale effects" argument is based on the observation that some markets for labor can by their nature be supplied by only a few individuals, who can therefore expect to reap disproportionate returns from slight differences in ability. Some examples: practically speaking, there can be only one chief executive officer for a large corporation, and effective decisions in that office may make very large differences in the expected returns of the corporation. Thus, slight differences in managerial ability might allow the superior performer to extract very high returns. Similarly, the most capable physicians, convincing trial lawyers, and popular musical performers might expect rewards well in excess of those who are even slightly less favored, creating a "winner-take-all" condition in markets of this sort, and corresponding right-skewness in the related wage distribution.

Thus, there are a number of ways in which human capital considerations can be made to account for the characteristic shape of earnings distributions, although this is not an inevitable implication of human capital models. In addition, the human capital approach can potentially account for some of the other stylized facts about earnings variations. Most evidently, of course, human capital theory can account for the positive association between earnings and levels of education or experience. In addition, the theory is at least not inconsistent with the existence of earnings disparities within groups defined by education or experience level; proponents of this theoretical approach would contend that these disparities, to the extent they do not simply reflect random elements, result from human capital variations that are unobservable by labor economists.

It's somewhat less obvious, however, that human capital theory can account for the fact that within-group earnings disparities tend to increase monotonically with experience. The model of educational choice tends to predict instead a U-shaped relationship, since those with the greatest ability invest the most in training early on, and thus start out their careers earning *less* income than those of their peers that started work earlier and thus accrued more work-related experience. Of course, the greater initial schooling or training levels of the more able imply that their incomes increase more rapidly, leading to greater income variations later on. In addition, human capital theory cannot readily account for systematic earnings variations by race and gender after observable human capital-related factors have been statistically controlled for.

Earnings inequality and labor market imperfections

Without necessarily contradicting the basic tenets of human capital theory, the introduction of market imperfections based on imperfect information and transaction costs can help provide a fuller account of earnings inequality that is more closely tailored to the empirical record. Introducing market imperfections also raises interesting normative issues. Whereas market outcomes are predicted to be Pareto-optimal under the ideal exchange conditions typically posited in human capital models, there is potential scope for Pareto-improving government interventions in the labor market when such imperfections exist.

The key features of earnings inequality can also be explained in terms of departures from competitive labor market conditions due to conditions of imperfect information. Most relevant here are approaches based on optimizing individual choices among earnings opportunities given such imperfections. Selection theory proceeds from the basic presumption that market actors seek the most favorable employments among competing options rather than being passively shunted into employment relations based on exogenously given individual characteristics or market processes. Of particular interest here are dynamic stories that provide for learning about market opportunities over time and job market decisions based on acquired information.

These models yield two important implications for the structure of earnings inequality: first, right-skewness of the earnings distribution is created by truncating the distribution for values of wages below a certain level. The logic underlying this result is that rational searchers refuse to accept wage offers below their reservation level, and therefore these wage levels tend not to be seen. Since selection models are not inconsistent with human capital explanations for earnings, the latter can be adduced in accounting for other regularities in earnings within this framework.

This approach does add one distinct piece to the analytical puzzle, however. Dynamic selection models allowing for information acquisition over time may also account for the positive correlation of within-group wage variation with experience, noted earlier. If individual workers' productivities cannot be distinguished early in their careers, then they will all tend to receive the same wage if workers are paid their *expected* value marginal product. Some workers subsequently learn that they are highly productive (perhaps in different pursuits) and thus move to more remunerative jobs over time. If this sorting effect is stronger than the truncation effect mentioned above, then one can expect increased variation in earnings among workers grouped, say, by education levels.

Unique additional insights into the observed pattern of earnings variations can be gained by adding worker risk aversion and imperfectly observed effort, two core features of the economic theory of insurance and incentives discussed in chapter 8. Both of these features help explain the truncation of the left-hand side of the earnings distribution (that is, the comparative paucity of relatively low earnings). First, the provision of compensation insurance to risk-averse workers by comparatively risk-neutral firms implies that unusually strong negative shocks to observed output don't translate into correspondingly low compensation. Second, the fact that insurance is typically incomplete, and thus that positive effort incentives are typically provided, implies that downward random variations in output won't be further reinforced by low effort levels.

Further insight is gained by introducing the possibility that individuals learn about their productivity levels over time. In this case a dynamic element is added to the wage insurance provided by firms: when workers are first hired, neither they nor their employers may know their true productivity levels, and thus all new workers are offered the same average wage. But as workers discover their true productivity levels over time, those with relatively high productivity become dissatisfied with receiving the average level of pay, and thus elect to leave the firm if not compensated accordingly. As in the sorting model, both the average and dispersion of wages rise with experience, but in addition the insurance element of the present approach implies that wages of relatively low-productivity workers don't subsequently fall, suggesting a truncation of the left tail of the earnings distribution relative to a situation in which this consideration doesn't arise.

Finally, the efficiency wage scenario introduced in chapter 10 suggests a possible reason why earnings vary systematically, other things equal, with such non-human capital factors as race and gender. As discussed in the discrimination chapter, efficiency wage considerations add an element similar to monopsonistic wage discrimination in the logic of earnings determination, leading for example to lower average wages for less economically mobile workers. By similar reasoning, this theory predicts that workers who face relatively high levels of unemployment (such as certain racial minorities in the US) also receive lower wages on average.

In sum, the shape of empirical earnings distributions does not of itself favor any particular theory of wage determination. However, some theories do better than others in accounting for specific regularities in earnings differentials, and it may be that the most satisfactory explanation of real-world earnings differences requires the appropriately eclectic mix of alternative theories. As you'll see later in the chapter, which theories *predominate* in any such explanation may have very significant normative ramifications.

EMPIRICAL PATTERNS AND TRENDS IN EARNINGS INEQUALITY

International variations in income inequality

While all economies tend to exhibit the same overall income distributions, the degree of inequality varies dramatically from country to country. Furthermore, there are significant differences among countries in the extent to which inequality is exacerbated in moving from earnings alone to income from all sources, or ameliorated by the redistributive effects of taxes and income transfers. Two international comparisons are of particular interest, for pre- and post-transfer income differences: differences in inequality across developed countries, and variations in measured inequality levels across countries in different stages of economic development.

First consider comparisons across developed countries – in particular, the OECD countries of North America and Europe. Table 17.1 gives Gini coefficients reflecting two distinct measures of income in these countries: *market income*, or pre-tax and transfer income from all sources, and *disposable income*, which nets taxes and transfers out of market income. The latter measure is useful because it gives a sense of the relative commitment to redistributive policies in these countries. Note the use of *market* rather than just *labor* income as the basic reference statistic. While labor income is on average about 70% of market income in developed economies, distributions of market income tend to be somewhat more dispersed and skewed than for earnings. Another caution is that the country data are from different base years.

Several patterns can be discerned from these data. First, there is a wide range of degrees of inequality across these countries, the country with the most inequality having about half again the degree of inequality of the country with the lowest Gini in each income category. Second, note that the Gini coefficient for disposable income is lower than its market income counterpart in every case, indicating that all of these countries have redistributive policies that are to some degree progressive (that is, tending to redistribute income from richer to poorer households.

Third, however, countries vary dramatically in their degrees of commitment to redistribution; for example, a decade or so ago the US was only sixth highest in

Table 17.1 Inequality in disposable and market income, OECD countries of North America and Europe

Country	Year	DPI Gini	MI Gini
Slovak Republic	1992	0.189	0.402
Czech Republic	1992	0.208	0.411
Finland	1991	0.233	0.337
Sweden	1992	0.229	0.474
Belgium	1992	0.230	0.456
Norway	1991	0.233	0.378
Luxembourg	1985	0.238	0.380
Denmark	1992	0.240	0.430
Germany	1984	0.250	0.428
Italy	1991	0.255	0.330
The Netherlands	1991	0.271	0.414
Canada	1991	0.286	0.415
Hungary	1991	0.289	0.491
Poland	1992	0.291	0.444
France	1984	0.295	0.470
United Kingdom	1986	0.304	0.488
Spain	1990	0.308	0.429
Australia	1990	0.309	0.437
Switzerland	1982	0.323	0.406
Ireland	1987	0.330	0.503
United States	1991	0.343	0.449

Source: Timothy M. Smeeding, "The International Evidence on Income Distribution in Modern Economics: Where Do We Stand?," in *Poverty and Inequality: The Political Economy of Redistribution* (Kalamazoo, MI: W.E. Upjohn Institute for Employment Research, 1997): 93. Reprinted with permission.

terms of income inequality before netting out taxes and transfers, but jumps to the top of the list in post-policy inequality, whereas Sweden, which was second-*highest* in market income inequality about ten years ago, was also second-*lowest* in disposable income inequality as measured by the Gini coefficient. That said, it's still true that there is a significant correlation between market and disposable income across these countries, indicating that redistributive policies do not, on average, significantly change the inequality rankings. With some important exceptions (such as Sweden), a country that starts out with a given level of inequality will also end up that way net of its tax and transfer policies.

The economies of Scandinavia and Northern Europe (the Netherlands and Italy being borderline cases with respect to inequality level and geography) tend to feature relatively low levels of income inequality. In cases where market income inequality is relatively high, countries in this region (particularly Sweden and Belgium) respond with strongly redistributive policies.

Next, consider variations in income inequality across both developed and relatively undeveloped economies. Making development a variable with respect to the incidence of income inequality raises a new set of considerations with respect to the logic of relative income determination. For example, developing countries typically possess political regimes that enjoy less stability, and thus perhaps less ability to enforce given redistributive policies. In addition, the lower overall level of national income in such economies may imply that there are fewer resources available to promote the income-earning capacities of the poor and undereducated.

Such considerations are reflected in the "Kuznets curve," named after the economist Simon Kuznets, who in the 1950s hypothesized an inverse U-shaped relationship between a country's level of development and its degree of income inequality.[2] This indicates that as average income increases from very low levels, it will be accompanied by an increase in inequality, while further increases past a certain, higher income threshold will tend to be associated with lower inequality.

The basis for this hypothesis can be seen in table 17.2, which shows the proportion of household income held by the top 10% of households for 41 countries grouped by income level. While once again there is considerable variation in concentration measures across countries in each income group, the respective group averages tend to support the Kuznets hypothesis.

Time trends in earnings inequality

Concerns over earnings inequality have gained salience over the past 25 to 30 due to the truly dramatic increase in inequality over this period, especially in the United States and the United Kingdom – perhaps not coincidentally, the two countries most single-mindedly devoted to "free-market," anti-"welfare state" policies. For example, from the mid-1970s to the mid-1990s, the 90/10 earnings decile ratio increased by 20% for the UK and about 16% for the US, far more than for other developed countries over the same period.[3] Focus first on the US case and then consider comparisons to the experience of other developed economies over the same period.

Over the almost three decades immediately following the Second World War, US workers enjoyed significant increases in real mean wages accompanied by relatively little change in measured earnings dispersion. The experience since that time – that is, beginning in the early 1970s – has been exactly reversed, with a historically large increase in earnings inequality combined with virtual stagnation in mean real wages. This change was accompanied, after years of decline, by a steady increase in the poverty rate (from around 11% to about 14.5%) until near the end of the 1990s, when the continuingly robust economic boom finally started bringing down the incidence of poverty.[4]

The trend toward increased earnings inequality in the US has been characterized by the following features:

Table 17.2 Percentage of household income held by the top 10% of households for 41 countries at various income levels

Country	Year	Top 10%
A. Low-Income Countries		
Bangladesh	1981–82	24.9
India	1983	26.7
Pakistan	1984–85	31.3
Ghana	1987	29.1
Sri Lanka	1985–86	43.0
Indonesia	1987	26.5
Average		30.3
B. Lower-Middle Income Countries		
Philippines	1985	32.1
Cote d'Ivoire	1986	36.3
Morocco	1984–85	25.4
Guatemala	1979–81	40.8
Botswana	1985–86	42.8
Jamaica	1988	33.4
Colombia	1988	37.1
Peru	1985	35.8
Costa Rica	1986	38.8
Poland	1987	21.0
Malaysia	1987	34.8
Brazil	1983	46.2
Average		35.4
C. Upper-Middle Income Countries		
Hungary	1983	18.7
Yugoslavia	1987	26.6
Venezuela	1987	34.2
Average		26.5
D. High-Income Economies		
Spain	1980–81	24.5
Israel	1979	23.5
Singapore	1982–83	33.5
Hong Kong	1980	31.3
New Zealand	1981–82	28.7
Australia	1985	25.8
United Kingdom	1979	23.3
Italy	1986	25.3
Belgium	1978–79	21.5
Netherlands	1983	23.0
France	1979	25.5
Canada	1987	24.1
Denmark	1981	22.3

Table 17.2   *(Continued)*

Country	Year	Top 10%
Germany, Fed. Rep.	1984	23.4
Finland	1981	21.7
Sweden	1981	20.8
United States	1985	25.0
Norway	1979	21.2
Japan	1979	22.4
Switzerland	1982	29.8
Average		24.8

Source: World Bank, *World Development Report 1990* (New York: Oxford University Press, 1990), table 30.

- *"The rich got richer and the poor got poorer"*

In the quarter century from 1947 to the early 1970s, households at all income levels shared in economic gains, such that average earnings increased in each quintile of the US distribution.[5] This pattern was reversed in rather stark terms since then, such that the increase in a household's earnings in the period from 1973 to the mid-1990s was on average strictly positively correlated with its initial income, so that households in the lower two quintiles saw their earnings *decline*, while those in the upper three quintiles enjoyed successively higher gains. The positive correlation between initial income and income gains obtained for both men and women, but unlike male workers, women in every quintile saw higher earnings over this period.

- *Increased education- and experience-based differentials*

As just suggested, inequality actually declined between men and women, primarily due to the fact that average wages for male workers fell while those of women increased slightly. In addition, labor incomes of African-Americans increased relative to workers in other racial groups until the mid-1970s, but did not continue to gain after that. In contrast to gender and race differentials, however, earnings disparities based on education and experience levels increased substantially from the late 1970s.

In the case of education-based differentials, there was a significant increase in the wage premium for college graduates beginning in 1979, after it had first fallen in the period 1963–79. Most of this increase has been driven, however, by the *decline* in earnings received by workers having a high school degree or less (20% in the period 1973–94) rather than the increase in returns to a college degree (5% over the same period). This contrast is all the more striking given that the percentage of workers with a college degree *increased* by seven percentage points, from 22 to 29%, over the period, which would have implied, other things equal, a decrease in the college wage premium on standard supply-and-demand grounds. At the same time, the wage premium attached to greater levels of work experience increased significantly from the early 1970s for both men and women, although the male differential leveled off beginning in the late 1980s.

In addition, earnings disparities driven by differences in educational attainment were reinforced by the uneven impact of employment experience. For example, from the mid-1970s to the mid-1990s, employment rates for male high school dropouts with at least 10 years' experience fell from 78.5% to 67.4%, while those for male college graduates with similar levels of experience remained constant. At the same time, employment rates for less experienced college-educated male workers increased somewhat.

- *Increased within-group inequality*

Accompanying these systematically increasing differentials has been a potentially more mystifying increase in earnings inequality *within* groups of workers defined by demographic or human capital characteristics. For male workers, in fact, more than half of the increase in earnings inequality from the 1970s to the mid-1990s is attributable to this increase in within-group differentials.

- *Increased persistence in earnings inequality*

A year-to-year increase in earnings inequality across an entire economy does not necessarily imply that any given group of workers experiences a persistent increase in earnings disparities among themselves. On one hand, increased disparities could be the result of increased *volatility* in earnings (this could potentially explain the dramatic increase in within-group inequality, for example), leading to increased random variations from year to year that nevertheless cancel out over time. Second, single-period measures of inequality will overstate the degree of disparity in *lifetime* incomes if individuals enjoy significant economic mobility over time.

Could these factors account for the change in measured US earnings inequality, suggesting that there has been much less change in *average, persistent* earnings differentials among individuals? Perhaps, but it is unlikely that this accounts for most of the trend toward increasing US inequality. There does seem to be substantially increased income volatility for individual workers over the period in question, but it is due in part to unusually wide macroeconomic fluctuations that occurred during the time span under consideration, and is not of itself sufficient to account for the measured increase in inequality.

As for economic mobility, changes in income over the life cycle can account for perhaps a third of year-to-year earnings inequality, measured for example by the 90/10 earnings decile ratio. But the key point here is that economic mobility has not *increased* over the period in question to the same degree as measured earnings inequality. Thus, even including these factors, there appears to have been a serious increase in persistent earnings inequality, a large portion of which cannot be accounted for on traditional human capital grounds.

How does the US experience with changing inequality compare with the experience of other developed economies over the same period? As mentioned above, the UK also experienced dramatically increasing earnings disparities over the same period – more than for the US, both before and after taxes and transfers are taken into account. Although not to the same extent as the US or the UK, most other OECD countries have seen a significant increase in earnings inequality. However, the US is unique even relative to the UK in the degree of its increase in within-group earnings inequality. This fact may help provide a clue to the causes of the remarkable increase in earnings disparities since the 1970s.

How might these trends in earnings inequality be explained? From the standpoint of the standard human capital framework based on competitive exchange conditions, the explanatory task is complicated by two factors: first, the dramatic increase in inequality not linked to observable differences in demographic status or skill acquisition, and second, increasing relative supplies of college-educated and female workers that imply, other things equal, changes in the respective wage premiums that are the opposite of what has been experienced, particularly in the US.

Three primary explanations have been pursued in the literature, reviewed here in increasing order of likely relevance.

1. Globalization

It is tempting to assert a link between increased earnings inequality in the US and its increased integration in world markets over the past 30 years. The volume of foreign trade as a percentage of GDP has doubled from a base of 12% in 1970. Perhaps more significantly, the share of imports from less-developed countries has increased 150% in the same period. Assuming that the US has a relative advantage in the supply of skilled workers, standard international trade analysis suggests that the US should have correspondingly increased its degree of specialization in goods produced by processes that rely primarily on skilled labor, with a correspondingly increased reliance on unskilled labor by our less-developed trading partners. This would imply in turn a relative increase to skilled labor in the United States.

There are significant problems with this line of argument, however. First, contrary to the main predictions of the theory, the increase in relative demand for skilled labor (if that's what has been driving the growth of the skill premium) has not proved to be either sector- or country-specific. There are no categories of US production for which the skill premium is shrinking, and even less-developed economies appear to be experiencing increased relative demand for skilled labor. Second, and relatedly, there has been little intersectoral mobility of unskilled workers in the US.

Third, the predicted effects of trade on relative wage levels depends only on the *existence* of US trade with less-developed countries (assuming competitive market conditions), not on its *magnitude*. But the US had established trade with these countries well before the tendency toward rising earnings inequality.

Finally, this hypothesis doesn't have much to say about the other observed trends in US earnings inequality, such as the reduced gender premium, and it speaks only indirectly to the increase in within-group inequality. For all of the above reasons, economists have not given much weight to this explanation for earnings inequality trends.

2. Changes in labor market institutions

It is provocative that while a number of developed countries have seen some increase in earnings inequality since the 1970s, this increase has been by far the most extensive in two countries, the UK and the US, that have shown a particular devotion to the pursuit of "free market" strategies in this period. It is therefore tempting to look at explanations for these countries' singular experience in terms of changes in labor market institutions that might be expected to contain wage inequality. In the US case, obvious candidates are the sharp decline in the real value of the minimum wage, the dramatic fall in the percentage of workers covered by collective bargaining agreements, and economic deregulation in the transportation and telecommunication industries.

While Congress has intermittently legislated nominal increases in the minimum wage over the last 25 or so years, these increases have not kept up with the cost of living, resulting in a significant decline in real terms as well as in relation to manufacturing wages. In addition, since 1960, the proportion of unionized workers in the US labor force has fallen by about half, with a particularly sharp decline occurring in the 1980s.[6] Finally, an unusually strong movement toward economic deregulation took place beginning with the Carter administration in the late 1970s.

None of these changes has a completely unambiguous effect on earnings inequality *in principle*. A legislated wage floor might prop up wage rates at the low end of the earnings distribution, but at the possible cost of increased unemployment for some low-wage workers. As discussed in chapters 4 and 12, one effect of collective bargaining is to reduce wage disparities among unionized workers, but it may also increase the union/non-union wage differential. Finally, deregulation occurred primarily in "high-wage" industries such as telecommunications, but not all workers in the affected industries shared equally in those gains, so deregulation could be expected to affect them disproportionately.

It does not appear that such institutional changes can explain all of the increase in US earnings inequality, but they may account for a substantial portion of it. One study suggested that as much as one-third of the increase in US wage inequality in the 1980s was attributable to changes in the degree of unionization and the real value of the minimum wage. Perhaps unsurprisingly, the effects of these changes were gender-specific, with the decline in unionization affecting primarily male wage inequality and the real decline in the legislated minimum wage having its biggest impact on female workers, who thanks to the gender wage differential are relatively overrepresented at the lower end of the wage distribution. The same study found little effect on earnings inequality due to economic deregulation.

Overall, this line of explanation for rising inequalities in labor income has been inadequately explored in the literature. For example, more work needs to be done with respect to possible links between labor market segmentation and rising within-group earnings inequality.

3.   *Skill-biased technical change*

The hypothesis that has received the most support in the economics literature posits that increased earnings inequality is due to the effects of technical innovations in production that disproportionately favor skilled workers. As with the globalization argument, it addresses the conundrum of a rising skill premium in the face of increasing relative supply of educated workers by suggesting that the increase in relative *demand* for high-skilled workers has been sufficient to swamp the supply effect. Unlike the globalization hypothesis, however, the logic of this argument does not dictate that wage effects are specific to particular sectors or countries. Since this hypothesis was discussed at length in chapter 14, it will not be rehearsed here, except to note an interesting variation on the theme in the related discussion box.

WHAT INNOVATIONS ARE DRIVING INCREASED WAGE INEQUALITY?

The chief conundrum faced by the skill-biased technical change hypothesis lay in identifying *what* technological innovations might plausibly be understood to account for the observed trends in earnings inequality. The presumptive candidate would seem to be developments in computer technology, given the widespread adoption of computer-assisted design, manufacturing, and communication systems. But it is not immediately obvious how this change alone might account for all aspects of the trends in earnings inequality over the past 30 years. For example, why would the adoption of computer-aided techniques reflect skill-*extensive* changes in techniques, resulting in rising productivity of high-skilled workers paired with *falling* productivity of unskilled workers? And how does one explain the decline in the gender wage premium given rising use of computers?

A plausible explanation advanced by economist Dennis Snower is that the computer revolution has been accompanied, and perhaps to some extent spurred, by a corresponding revolution in the organization of production. This revolution, by hypothesis, involves the use of "high-performance" production techniques that emphasize workers' ability to respond quickly and minutely to customer preferences and concerns, to interact closely with workers from other phases of production in solving problems as they arise, and to undertake a wide variety of tasks in support of the firm's overall market strategy. (See the related discussions of workplace organization in the Introduction and chapters 8 and 10.)

If this representation of changes in the organization of commercial production is accurate, it implies that a premium is placed on workers who not only have a high level of skills, but a high level of *general* capabilities in decision making, communication and teamwork, and problem solving, rather than in the execution of technique- or firm-specific tasks. If *on average* college education imparts these general skills, then this might explain the *extensive* character of technical change with respect to the demands for skilled and unskilled workers. Moreover, this explanation is at least consistent with the reduced gender premium, to the extent that female workers have shown greater average preferences for jobs that involve interaction and communication activities.

Finally, this refinement on the basic hypothesis can potentially explain the significant increase in within-group inequality if it is understood that versatility, communication skills, and thinking ability are the joint product of education and idiosyncratic (and typically unmeasured) innate abilities. Some workers, for example, may be well-educated and yet not particularly suited for jobs requiring excellent communication abilities.

Related discussion question:
How might Snower's hypothesis account for rising wage inequality *within* worker groups defined by educational level? How would it account for increased returns to *experience*?

Related reference:
Dennis J. Snower, "Causes of Changing Earnings Inequality," in *Income Inequality: Issues and Policy Options* (Kansas City Federal Reserve Bank Symposium, 1998): 69–133.

WHY DOES EARNINGS INEQUALITY MATTER?

As noted in the introduction to this chapter, the normative theory on which standard economic analysis is based does not establish presumptive grounds for believing any given level of inequality to be harmful. Utilitarianism, as modified by the Pareto principle, suggests that economic changes are socially beneficial if and only if at least one person can be benefited without making anyone worse off. Consequently, Pareto-utilitarianism provides no grounds for asserting the desirability of egalitarian redistributive policies, of themselves.

The strictures of the Pareto condition can under some conditions be relaxed by supplementing it with a *compensation principle* that sanctions economic changes creating losers as well as winners so long as it is possible for the winners to compensate the losers – whether they actually do or not – and still come out ahead. The idea here is that if such compensation were possible, then otherwise normatively ambiguous changes could be interpreted, according to this modification, as unambiguously superior.

However, this modification of the Pareto principle does not establish normative grounds for redistributive policies given perfectly competitive market conditions. According to a well-known theoretical result known as "the first fundamental welfare theorem," the equilibrium of a system of perfectly competitive and complete markets is always Pareto-optimal, so that if one assumes that market exchange (including that which takes place in labor markets) occurs under these conditions, Pareto-improving alternatives do not exist. Thus, for example, since human capital theory is generally predicated on the assumption of ideal market conditions, the market outcomes it predicts are Pareto-optimal and allow no scope for socially beneficial government interventions, let alone those with the primary effect of redistributing labor incomes.

Consequently, to construct a coherent normative case for changing given patterns of earnings inequality, one must either reject the hypothesis of ideal market exchange or else advance grounds for normative social judgments other than Pareto-utilitarianism (or some combination of both). Possible arguments of both types are explored here. In doing so, it will prove necessary to make clear how one defines "equality." This point is discussed further below. For now, assume for the sake of argument that it is possible to speak unambiguously of movements in the direction of less or greater inequality.

First consider what is involved in arguing for greater equality on Pareto-utilitarian grounds. Assuming again that competitive exchange conditions obtain, Pareto-optimality considerations could be bypassed entirely were it possible to establish one's desired income distribution "from the beginning." This notion is embodied in the theoretical result in welfare economics known as the "second fundamental welfare theorem," which asserts that any distribution of income can be supported as a perfectly competitive equilibrium relative to some given initial distribution of social resources. The corollary is that if the initial distribution were deemed inappropriate, it could be corrected with lump-sum taxes and transfers prior to the opening of markets.

Given that the economy is already up and running, this option is not available, and redistributing a *given* economic pie thus necessarily creates winners and losers, whether markets are deemed to be perfectly competitive or otherwise. Furthermore, to argue for greater income equality on Pareto-utilitarian grounds, one must overcome the conventional wisdom that there is a necessary tradeoff between equity and efficiency, such that policies to promote greater inequity can only succeed at the cost of efficiency – thus further violating the Paretian normative standard.

The conventional wisdom suggests that in pursuing greater earnings equality one must drive a wedge between individuals' productive efforts and their rewards, altering their incentives for action. And if these incentives were efficiently structured prior to the policy intervention (e.g., they were generated by competitive market conditions), then the effect of the intervention must be to introduce inefficiencies and thus *reduce* the size of the economic pie to be shared.

However, this conclusion need not hold if actual market conditions don't correspond to the ideal case of frictionless exchange. In particular, a case for greater earnings equality might potentially be made on efficiency grounds if given patterns of inequality create *negative externalities*. This can occur as the result of a number of different market failures.

One possibility is raised by the "principal–agent" theory, having to do with the provision of incentives under conditions of asymmetric information, as discussed in chapters 8–11. One implication of the theory is that efficiency losses associated with the need to expose risk-averse workers to production-related uncertainties in order to improve work incentives can be sidestepped if workers can be made to bear income *losses* in the form of up-front employment fees or penalties for avoidably severe production outcomes. But this requires in turn that workers have enough income from other sources, or wealth, to be able to absorb the income loss. If this is not the case, then certain fully efficient incentive provisions in labor exchange cannot be used. A targeted redistribution may thus allow for improved incentives without sacrificing the insurance features of employment contracts.

A related argument from a macroeconomic standpoint concerns the incidence of involuntary unemployment. Cyclical variations in unemployment have potentially significant implications for earnings inequality because the minority of workers who bear the brunt of un- or under-employment are affected greatly while the majority are unaffected, perhaps not even facing reductions in *nominal* earnings. As a consequence, presumably risk-averse workers might attach great value to macroeconomic policies designed to reduce fluctuations in the business cycle.

Arguments like the foregoing, while they assume some departures from ideal market conditions, still follow the lines of standard economic analysis by positing individually rational, optimizing economic agents whose well-being depends only on their own consumption levels. A distinct argument in favor of greater economic equality emerges by introducing the possibility that individual well-being depends on a person's *relative* status as well. This argument doesn't get much play in the economics literature, precisely because it presumes this significant departure from standard economic reasoning.

Nonetheless, a number of empirical studies suggest that social health – as reflected, for example, in national statistics on rates of illness and mortality – is inversely related to observed levels of income inequality, even after controlling for poverty levels. Such studies suggest that, even after taking account of the plausibly negative impact of poverty on personal health (discussed further in the second half of the chapter), as well as other relevant factors such as public health spending, increased income equality is statistically associated with higher rates of sickness and death.

Of course, it is not immediately apparent why this might be so, and, as mentioned, economic theory doesn't provide much guidance in this matter. One possibility is that greater income inequality creates social or psychological tensions associated with envy or reduced self-esteem that can eventually be expected to have negative physical effects. In any case, whatever the connection, these studies suggest that increased inequality can have deleterious effects on aggregate social welfare. In such a world, the Paretian presumption that increasing income is good no matter who gains has much less salience.

Relatedly, some studies find that increased income inequality results in greater political instability, holding other relevant and measurable factors statistically constant, leading to greater inefficiencies associated with corresponding increases in uncertainty and compromises of the rule of law in governing economic transactions. Here again the channel of causation falls outside the scope of standard economic reasoning, so it's hard to specify the social logic that leads to this association, but it again raises the possibility that people care about their relative as well as absolute economic status.

This leads to a third source of efficiency-based arguments for greater equality, based on dropping another standard presumption of economic theory to the effect that it is both feasible and meaningful to distinguish between "economic" and "political" phenomena. This notion is reflected, for example, in the second fundamental welfare theorem, since it suggests that political judgments about appropriate income or wealth distributions can be implemented without interfering with the operation of (competitive and complete) markets. But what if such political judgments are themselves a consequence of given economic conditions?

Consider two ways in which economic conditions can affect political decisions. First, as we discussed in the chapter on employee representation, democratic voting procedures may result under certain conditions in implementing the wishes of the median voter. Since, the asymmetry of empirically observed earnings distributions implies that the median voter earns less than the mean level of income, increased inequality under this characteristic asymmetry may imply that the median voter – and thus, the democratically determined political will – is willing to impose higher taxes to finance public goods, leading to greater distortions of incentives and lower overall levels and rates of growth.

Alternatively, in a political system such as that of the US in which "money talks" due to the disproportionate influence of lobbyists and major donors to re-election campaigns, greater inequality can result, via the resulting increased influence of special interests on the political process, in inefficiencies due to reductions in socially desirable regulations respecting the environment or protections against fraudulent behavior. The distortionary impact of greater inequality here is twofold: first, the interests of the relatively affluent may diverge correspondingly greatly from that of the median voter, and second, they enjoy greater wherewithal to influence political deliberations to their advantage.

A completely separate approach to arguing the case for greater earnings inequality can be pursued by dropping altogether the Pareto-utilitarian normative standard on which mainstream economics is premised, or more generally by augmenting this standard with principles derived from other philosophical grounds. A coherent summary of this approach won't be attempted here, other than to note that such alternative stances are generally derived from some version of the principle that social institutions should treat morally equivalent individuals equally. This raises interconnected questions as to what constitutes "moral equivalence" and "equal treatment" in this context. It proves difficult to divorce these questions from the positive distinctions raised by competing theories of income distribution.

To see this, suppose that an egalitarian norm is interpreted as requiring that everyone earns exactly the same income. Of course this would tend to deprive individuals of work incentives, since they would thus receive the same pay no matter what they did. But putting such efficiency-related questions aside, it seems difficult to insist that a principle of equal treatment *dictates* that people should not be rewarded for choosing to work harder or more intensely. And if income differentials based on unequal labor contributions are allowed, then one's normative theory must then focus on just those sources of inequality that are not morally justified. Implementing such a norm would in turn require a theory of the determinants of actual inequality as well as estimates of the empirical significance of different contributions to inequality.

For example, a compelling case might be made that individuals should not be allowed to profit from differences in innate ability, for something like the same reason that people with greater ability shouldn't be allowed to have more votes in a democratic process. But translating this normative stance into meaningful policy would require distinguishing income differentials associated with unequal innate ability levels from those generated by other causes. This task is made all the more complex given possible interactions among factors that affect earnings – as in the case, discussed above, that individuals with higher levels of ability also choose higher levels of schooling or training, other things equal.

In addition, an argument for reduced earnings differentials based on a principle of equal treatment must be prepared to demonstrate that existing disparities are not only significant, but persistent. On the former point, for example some economists have argued that differences in current income overstate differences in consumption. On the latter point, relatedly, a snapshot view of an economy depicting substantial income inequality carries much less normative weight to the extent that observed income differences primarily reflect different stages in a common life cycle of earnings, as discussed earlier in the chapter. At least two studies have suggested that, for OECD countries at least, about two-thirds of observed static earnings inequality is persistent.

In sum, alternative justifications for greater earnings equality carry different argumentative burdens. Those based on principles of equal treatment must distinguish morally relevant and irrelevant sources of earnings inequality, and also show the empirical significance of the former. In contrast, while arguments for greater equality based on Pareto optimality may not need to determine the causes of inequality, it must identify departures from the ideal market model that cause given income disparities to generate significant externalities. This implies in turn that normative and positive theories of earnings inequality cannot easily be divorced; how one judges observed levels of inequality depends to an important extent on how the latter are understood to arise.

Two sorts of policy tool can be brought to bear on the problem of earnings inequality. The desired mix of tools would depend on a particular society's goals as well as one's understanding of the primary causes of observed patterns of inequality. One set of tools attempts to address inequality by increasing the opportunities for personal advancement open to relatively low-income workers. Such policies might include measures to discourage discrimination in and out of labor markets, subsidies for investments in training and formal education, and efforts to relocate and retrain workers in declining industries or economically stagnant regions. The *primary* intended effect of such policies would be to increase the economic prospects of the relatively disadvantaged without negatively affecting those who are relatively well off. However, they might have a negative *secondary*, systemic effect on the latter group, as for instance when an increase in the relative supply of educated workers reduces the wage premium for skilled labor.

The second set of policies attacks inequality primarily by redistributing income from the relatively affluent to the relatively poor. Such policies would include progressive income and wealth taxation, income support for low-income workers, and increased unemployment compensation. While the intended effect of such policies is simply redistributive, they might also have unintended secondary effects. These are suggested, for example, by the traditional assertion of a trade-off between inequality and growth. Whether reduced capacity for economic growth is a necessary consequence of redistributive policies is, however, a matter of considerable debate.

CONCLUSION

It now seems evident that the era of steadily rising average wages combined with little change in income dispersion has been replaced by one that reverses both trends. Over the last 30 years, especially in the US, virtual stagnation in average wages has been accompanied by historic increases in earnings inequality. The corollary rise in the wage premium enjoyed by college educated workers (due more to a fall in wages enjoyed by those with a high school education or less than to a significant rise in wages for workers with college degrees) lends some credence to a human capital explanation based on extremely skill-biased patterns of technical innovation in production, but easy acceptance of this hypothesis is challenged by the dramatic increase in inequality that is not readily related to observable measures of skill or ability, combined with the puzzle of declining gender differentials.

Identification of the main causes of rising earnings inequality does not, however, immediately identify appropriate policy responses. This is so because the Pareto-utilitarian normative approach of mainstream economics is not the only relevant basis for evaluating given levels of economic inequality. An alternative egalitarian standard may justify redistributive policies even if, for example, they were to reduce total income or economic growth. Thus, an informed stance with regard to the phenomenon of (rising) earnings inequality requires an understanding not only of underlying causes, but of competing grounds for assessing the implications of these forces.

Study Questions

1. Why is it important to distinguish among *wage*, *earnings*, and *income* levels when discussing economic inequality? When might variations in the three measures not be strongly correlated?

2. In general, what explains why earnings distributions are right-skewed rather than symmetric, as in distributions of given natural characteristics such as height within a population?

3. Find data on the distribution of earnings or income across households for two different economies at similar levels of economic development and calculate the *coefficients of variation, concentration measures, earnings ratios*, and *Gini coefficients* for the two economies. Do these measures give a consistent representation of the comparative degree of inequality in the two economies? If not, what do you think caused the inconsistency?

4. One of the difficulties in arguing for an *egalitarian* normative standard to supplement or replace the standard criterion of efficiency used in economic welfare analysis has to do with the problem of specifying what economic conditions should be equalized. For example, is it meaningful to equalize real incomes if people have different medical needs, or differential social or educational handicaps? If you were to argue for an egalitarian normative standard, what norm of equality would you defend?

Notes

1   The discussion in this section is derived from Derek Neal and Sherwin Rosen, "The Theory of Earnings Distributions," in Anthony Atkinson and Francois Bourguignon (eds) *The Handbook of Earnings Distribution*, volume I (Amsterdam: North-Holland, 2000).

2   Simon Kuznets, "Economic Growth and Income Inequality," *American Economic Review* 45, no. 1 (March 1955): 1–28.

3   A.B. Atkinson, "The Distribution of Income in Industrialized Countries," *Income Inequality: Issues and Policy Options* (Jackson Hole, Wyoming: The Federal Reserve Bank of Kansas City, 1998).

4   Peter Gottschalk, "Inequality, Income Growth, and Mobility: The Basic Facts," *Journal of Economic Perspectives* 11, no. 2 (Spring 1997): 21–40.

5   Lawrence F. Katz, "Commentary: The Distribution of Income in Industrialized Countries," *Income Inequality: Issues and Policy Options* (Jackson Hole, Wyoming: The Federal Reserve Bank of Kansas City, 1998).

6   Nicole M. Fortin and Thomas Lemieux, "Institutional Changes and Rising Wage Inequality: Is There a Linkage?," *Journal of Economic Perspectives* 11, no. 2 (Spring 1997): 75–96.

Suggestions for Further Reading

Robert H. Frank and Philip J. Cook, *The Winner-Take-All Society* (New York: The Free Press, 1995).

Richard G. Wilkinson, *Unhealthy Societies: The Afflictions of Inequality* (London: Routledge, 1996).

Edward N. Wolff, *Economics of Poverty, Inequality, and Discrimination* (Cincinnati: Southwestern College Publishing, 1997).

CHAPTER EIGHTEEN

UNEMPLOYMENT

Perhaps nowhere else is the clash among competing approaches to the understanding of labor markets more in evidence than on the subject of unemployment. Alternative viewpoints are remarkably diverse and offer fundamentally different causal explanations and policy prescriptions. The key issue in the controversy, and the focus of this chapter's analysis, concerns the sense in and extent to which the condition of not having a job is voluntarily chosen.

At one extreme is the view that one's employment status is freely determined in unregulated labor markets, so that unemployment as such does not constitute an economic problem except as perpetuated by government-induced distortions of market function. The diametrically opposed position is that unemployment is the manifestation of intrinsic market failures demanding corrective governmental actions or perhaps even fundamental restructuring of the economy. Somewhere in between these polar views is the suggestion that unemployment arises primarily from the efforts of workers to improve their economic prospects. According to this theory of job search, unemployment may be a byproduct of desirable market adjustments and thus not evil *per se*, although an economy's realized unemployment rate may be excessive.

The stakes in this debate are potentially quite high. Almost all market economies have experienced periods of significant unemployment, and the magnitude of unemployment varies substantially over time, across regions, and among demographic groups. To individual workers and their families, prolonged unemployment (whatever its cause) can lead to economic hardship, diminished social standing, and even lasting physical and psychological harm. Countries languishing through periods of extensive unemployment waste their productive potential and even suffer severe

continued

social unrest. Government policymakers continually wrestle with the problem of how to balance employment goals against other political and economic concerns.

As with most of the other issues studied in this text, debates about the nature and consequences of unemployment are fueled by competing notions of how labor (and other) markets function. In the context of the perfectly competitive market model, which posits that the costs of exchange activities are negligible, unemployment cannot exist in the absence of government intervention, and in any event workers would never waste time looking for jobs that are known not to exist. This is precisely not the case under the conditions presumed by the search theory of unemployment, according to which labor market actors face significant mobility costs in locating ideal labor market matches. Alternatively, models linking involuntary unemployment to the presence of inflexible wages and prices invoke some form of market incompleteness, due for example to firms' need to motivate workers under conditions of asymmetric information.

The chapter's analysis begins by discussing how unemployment is defined and measured, and under what conditions joblessness might be considered involuntary. Next, key empirical features of unemployment in developed countries are reviewed. The new concepts are illustrated, and a familiar point of reference is established, by first constructing a simple competitive model of the aggregate labor market with and without flexible wage adjustments. This overview prepares the ground for subsequent analyses of involuntary unemployment under imperfect market conditions. Normative aspects of unemployment are taken up in the last section of the chapter. After considering the range of individual and social costs of unemployment, the chapter closes with a discussion of the scope for government intervention to reduce the incidence and costs of unemployment.

UNEMPLOYMENT CONCEPTS AND MEASURES

What is unemployment?

One might reasonably be tempted to define "unemployment" as the condition of not having a job. While this definition enjoys the advantage of simplicity, it is too broad to allow a nuanced understanding of the economic or social conditions that might create joblessness. Under this conception, for example, people would be included among the unemployed even if they were physically unable to work or, after full consideration of the available options, freely made full-time commitments to familial or academic pursuits. It is unclear why unemployment understood in this broad sense should necessarily be a matter of social concern; in any case, it is entirely consistent with the notion that markets are in competitive equilibrium.

What's missing from this simple definition is any indication concerning the *willingness* and *ability* of individuals to hold jobs. But added stipulations on these matters may not be enough to make the definition useful for immediate purposes, since presumably almost everyone could imagine being willing and able to work at a sufficiently lucrative and pleasant job, even if no such job ever existed or could plausibly be anticipated. Thus, one might begin by defining *unemployment* as a condition in which people are not currently engaged in paid labor, but are willing and able to work at jobs they believe to be currently attainable. An economy's *labor force* is then defined as the sum of employed and unemployed workers.

Accordingly, economists distinguish the state of unemployment from that of being *out of the labor force*, the difference being that households in the latter category are unable or unwilling to seek paid work given what they believe to be their available options. The term *non-employment* is used to describe the more general condition of not holding a job. A notion related to unemployment is that of *underemployment*, understood as the condition that part-time or irregularly employed workers desire to hold more stable or full-time jobs they believe to be attainable. As discussed below, recent structural changes in US labor markets may have increased the magnitude of underemployment.

The *unemployment rate*, the standard indicator of the severity of unemployment in a given economy, is defined as the ratio of unemployed workers to the total labor force, that is, to the total number of workers in the economy who are either employed or unemployed. This measure is strictly increasing in the number of unemployed workers, other things equal, and can vary in principle between zero and one. Note that the unemployment rate can go up even as the total number of employed workers increases.

The stricter economic conception of unemployment stakes a claim to greater social relevance, but at the cost of making the condition potentially more ambiguous and difficult to measure. Since by this definition the state of unemployment includes elements of volition and belief, it must somehow be determined who among the non-employed actually prefer to hold jobs they believe to exist. The problem here, as in many other areas of empirical economics, lies in determining what constitutes effective preferences and beliefs.

How is unemployment measured?

Countries generally base statistical measures of employment and unemployment on the results from household surveys. Many such surveys distinguish between the unemployed and those identified as out of the labor force on the basis of reported *job search*: a non-employed survey respondent is deemed *unemployed* only if he or she attests to seeking employment in the period under study. A further distinction is sometimes drawn between "active" search and more "passive" search activities such as scanning help-wanted ads. For example, Canada includes both "passive" and "active" job searchers among the ranks of the unemployed, while the US includes only the latter. Both countries exclude from this count those who report only that they are "waiting" for work to become available.

There may be good reasons to seek corroboration of indicated preferences for work in reports of job search activity. Engagement in search provides a credible signal about beliefs that an acceptable job exists, and that the searcher wishes to enter employment. Thus, the non-employed who search actively or passively for work may differ in economically significant ways from those who don't, whatever preferences are reported to government statisticians.

However, there are potential dangers in premising the empirical measure of unemployment on self-reported active job search. First, it may misrepresent the true magnitude of unemployment by under-counting *discouraged workers*, those who have given up on finding a job after an initial search effort. (Both Canada and the US once included discouraged workers among the ranks of the unemployed, but now count them as out of the labor force.) Second, some would-be workers may find it sufficient merely to wait for an already-identified job to become available, rather than actively searching for a new job. Indeed, some evidence suggests that workers with such "partial attachments" to the job market are more likely to transit into employment than those who do not state that they are awaiting the arrival of particular job opportunities.

On the other hand, workers might for a variety of reasons report that they are engaged in active job search even if they're not truly interested in finding a job. For example, workers might need to report engagement in active search in order to qualify for governmental unemployment insurance, or might feel that a stigma is attached to those who do not express an active desire to work.

The foregoing considerations suggest that one should read statistics about unemployment *levels* with care. However, it would still be true that unemployment statistics reliably indicate the direction and approximate magnitude of *changes* in a country's employment conditions, so long as measurement errors don't vary systematically with the unemployment rate. This is a critical difference, since changes in, say, the unemployment rate are likely to be much more meaningful than its absolute level in evaluating alternative economic theories.

When is unemployment involuntary?

The dual condition of desiring paid work and yet not having a job suggests that unemployment is not in itself desirable and is thus, for the would-be employee, an intendedly short-term condition. However, it need not follow from this that a spell of unemployment, perhaps even a lengthy one, is *involuntary*. Labor market participants might rationally choose, for example, to bypass an immediate job offer in anticipation of a future preferred alternative. The better the anticipated alternative, the longer they might reasonably spend in finding it. It is also plausible that someone might elect to quit a current job in order devote their full time and effort to finding a better one.

In light of the possibility that a state of unemployment is for at least some period freely chosen, economists typically stipulate an additional condition in defining the existence of involuntary unemployment. Generally speaking, the additional condition must be sufficient to account for the seemingly paradoxical phenomenon that potential jobs exist for which there are willing and qualified candidates who are nonetheless unable to secure them. This conclusion implies a judgment that labor markets are imperfect at no fault of those who find themselves unemployed.

A familiar definition associated with the macroeconomic theory pioneered by British economist John Maynard Keynes posits that a qualified jobless worker is involuntarily unemployed if her reservation wage, or the minimum level of pay at which she's willing to work, is lower than the going wage rate.[1] The sense in which unemployment is involuntary in this case is clear: absent some market imperfection, an employer would presumably be willing to hire the worker for at least the value of her reservation wage but less than the going wage rate.

However, the definition runs into difficulties if the "law of one price," a basic feature of ideal markets for homogeneous goods, fails to hold for labor markets under study – as will typically be the case. In that event there is no single "going wage rate" to which to compare a worker's reservation wage. To address this problem, the definition might be amended so that a jobless worker is considered involuntarily unemployed if her reservation wage is less than the *expected value* of wages received by otherwise identical employed workers.

In this context, "wage" should be understood as "discounted present pecuniary value of a job's attributes, including the actual wage rate." Thus the definition implies that workers are involuntarily unemployed if their available tradeoffs of returns to work and leisure are inferior on average to those of otherwise identical employed workers. The "involuntary" aspect of unemployment so defined is captured in the implicit assumption that rational workers would presumably not willingly choose a condition that reduces their expected level of well-being.

The amended definition has the advantage of a certain theoretical precision, but once again this gain comes at the potential cost of empirical usefulness. As discussed further below, the phenomenon actually measured as "unemployment" in economic statistics may not align very comfortably with the definitions of unemployment, voluntary or otherwise, discussed in this section. Thus in this area as in others, labor economists must be ever sensitive to the connection between available data and the conditions that they are purported to depict.

KEY EMPIRICAL FEATURES OF UNEMPLOYMENT

Next, consider some key regularities in the empirical incidence of unemployment in developed countries. These data will give some feel for the significance of unemployment as well as offering some clues as to its nature and causes.

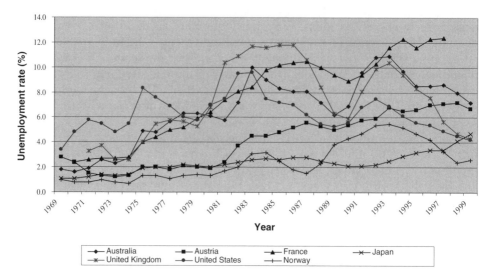

Figure 18.1 Graphs of unemployment rate series for selected OECD countries.

Incidence of unemployment over time

There are four key aspects of the temporal incidence of unemployment in developed countries. First, as illustrated in figure 18.1, national unemployment rates exhibit a broadly "cyclical" pattern, with alternating periods of high and low unemployment. Since these oscillations are of varying amplitude and length, it is not obvious whether they reflect a genuinely cyclical process with a stochastic element (as with yearly temperature variations in a temperate climate, for example) as opposed to a basically random process of change with perhaps some degree of serial correlation across years. This question is considered further in the next chapter.

Second, variations in the unemployment rate within business cycles tend to be overshadowed by variations across cycles. To the extent that temporal variation in unemployment can be described as a random process, these variations seem to reflect large probabilities of small variations with small probabilities of very large perturbations, linked to specific historical events. The skyline of unemployment trends since the late nineteenth century is dominated by a few periods of unusually high unemployment associated with severe economic downturns in the 1890s, 1930s, and early 1980s.

Third, unemployment rates exhibit some persistence over time; once high, they tend to remain high for some period. The countries of Western Europe, for example, have experienced a sustained period of unemployment since the early 1970s. A possible explanation for such persistence is that acute economic shocks have lastingly negative economic consequences.

That said, however, the fourth point to note is that unemployment rates do not seem to exhibit any consistent long-term trend. Average unemployment rates appear neither to be falling nor rising over the last hundred-plus years. Whatever economic logic gives rise to unemployment in capitalist economies, they seem to create jobs at the same long-run pace as the growth in the working-age population.

Incidence across countries

There is a great deal of co-movement in unemployment rates across developed countries. For example, all such countries suffered high unemployment rates in the "Great Depression" of the 1930s. This correlation might have been expected given the volume of international trade and capital flows. These linkages allow macroeconomic perturbations to be spread across the globe.

It is surprising, then, how much unemployment patterns may vary across economies, with countries and regions changing rankings in the severity of unemployment. Perhaps the most dramatic of these switches is seen in the relative experience of the US and the European Community (EC) since the 1950s. Average unemployment rates were consistently higher in the US than in the EC for most of the period from the mid-1950s through the mid-1970s; since the mid-1980s, however, Western European unemployment rates have consistently outstripped those of the US. Also dramatic is the relative shift in fortunes of the Japanese economy, which by US standards enjoyed remarkably low rates of unemployment from the mid-1950s. This pattern flipped in the mid-1990s, and since then the US has enjoyed consistently lower joblessness rates.

These variations in the relative incidence of joblessness across countries suggest that unemployment rates are influenced by country-specific social institutions. The superior employment picture in the US relative to the EC since the mid-1980s, for example, is sometimes ascribed to greater flexibility (and lower average compensation) in US labor markets.

SAME NATIONAL UNEMPLOYMENT RATE, DIFFERENT REGIONAL RATES

The single number of the national unemployment rate clearly cannot capture all of the differences within countries in the way that unemployment is experienced. There can be an enormous spread between regions in the local unemployment rates.

For example, in 2001 the national unemployment rate for the United States was 4.8%. Unemployment rates are also calculated for each of the 50 states, and for areas within states, including metropolitan areas. In 2001, the

continued

state-level unemployment rates ranged from a low of 3.1% in Nebraska to a high of 6.4% in Washington (and a rate of 6.5% in the District of Columbia). Among large metropolitan areas, the unemployment rates ranged from a low of 3.0% in Orange County, California, to a high of 6.9% in Miami, Florida.

Related discussion questions:
1. What kinds of things would lead to these unemployment rate differences across regions within a country?
2. Why don't unemployment rates converge within a country? In other words, why don't workers move out of areas with comparatively high unemployment rates into areas where the rates are lower? Also, why don't employers move their operations out of areas with comparatively low unemployment rates into areas where the rates are higher?

Related reference:
US Department of Commerce, *Statistical Abstract of the United States*, 2002, table nos. 565, 566.

Incidence across demographic groups

Unemployment does not strike all categories of workers equally. As shown in table 18.1, those in the US labor force under 25 years old, both male and female, have a substantially higher chance of being unemployed than their older counterparts. The table also indicates a smaller, but still consistent and significant, differential in unemployment between genders, almost always to the disadvantage of female workers.

Table 18.1 US unemployment rates by age and sex, seasonally adjusted, April 2002

Age and sex	Male	Female
16 to 24 years	13.0	11.6
16 to 19 years	18.1	15.4
16 to 17 years	19.6	19.2
18 to 19 years	17.2	12.9
20 to 24 years	10.3	9.6
25 years and over	4.8	5.0
25 to 54 years	4.9	5.1
55 years and over	4.3	3.7

Source: *Employment and Earnings* 49, no. 5 (May 2002): table A-10.

There are also significant variations in unemployment by race, although obviously patterns vary by country. In the US, blacks and Hispanics experience significantly higher rates of unemployment, especially during economic downturns, relative to whites, while workers of Asian extraction enjoy somewhat lower joblessness rates.

The biggest single difference in exposure to unemployment arises across occupations. Workers categorized as unskilled or semi-skilled experience unemployment rates that exceed those of managerial and professional workers by a factor of 4 to 5. Relatedly, the incidence of unemployment is inversely correlated with years of formal education, at least once a high-school degree or its equivalent has been achieved.

EMPLOYMENT CATEGORIES IN THE
PERFECTLY COMPETITIVE MODEL

To give an analytical context for the concepts and empirical trends discussed above, the chapter now considers how the phenomena they represent would arise in the context of perfectly competitive labor markets. Analysis of this scenario will provide a useful point of reference in thinking about the components of a logically coherent theory of involuntary unemployment.

Let's start by looking at the ideal labor market model "writ large," such that a single perfectly-functioning labor market is assumed to exist for an entire economy. This suggests that workers are homogeneous from the standpoint of prospective employers, and that all workers and firms are fully and equally capable of participating in the labor market to the extent they wish. This setup also presumes that information about job and worker characteristics is freely available to all, and that there are no costs associated with searching for a particular employment match.

This scenario is depicted in figure 18.2. Since competitive market conditions exist by assumption, all actors take wages as given, and thus their intended market behavior can be represented with aggregate labor demand and supply curves. The supply curve is assumed to turn vertical at L_{max} to suggest that there is a fixed potential labor pool for this economy. If there are no government interventions in this market, then the absence of exchange frictions implies that competition will drive the wage rate to the level that clears the market, denoted W_E.

It should be clear that workers fall into either of two employment categories in this scenario, *employed* or *out of the labor force*. The number of workers employed in equilibrium is given by L_E. The remainder, $L_{max} - L_E$, choose not to be in the labor force at this wage rate. There can thus be no unemployment in this model as the phenomenon is defined above, since no one without a job is willing to work *at the (single) prevailing wage rate*, let alone at the lower rate that the existence of additional jobs would entail, given the downward slope of the demand curve.

Of course, if some exogenous change were to cause shifts in labor supply or demand, there would be a change in the total level of employment accompanied

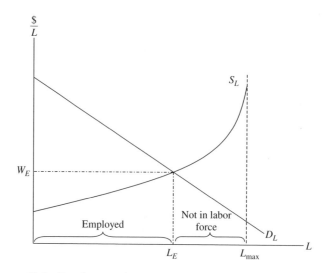

Figure 18.2 Employment status in ideal labor market equilibrium.

by a change in the equilibrium wage rate (assuming that neither curve were horizontal). But any such changes in employment would be mutually acceptable to employers and workers, since their respective willingness to hire or be hired also changes with the equilibrium wage rate. Furthermore, so long as respondents act rationally and report their status truthfully, existing governmental measures would not indicate the presence of unemployment under these hypothetical market conditions, because there is no reason to search: by assumption, job opportunities are fully known by all, and any desired job can be immediately located. Any person electing not to work at wage W_E knows for certain that no preferable job opportunities exist in the economy.

Now suppose that for some reason the wage rate is "stuck" at a level $\underline{W} > W_E$, so that the labor market fails to clear. This situation is illustrated in figure 18.3. Possible theoretical and empirical grounds for this phenomenon of "downwardly sticky" wages are discussed later in the chapter. However, under otherwise competitive exchange conditions, this wage inflexibility can only arise from government intervention in the workings of the labor market.

For now, focus on three questions: first, given inflexible wages, can unemployment be said to exist, and if so can it be considered involuntary? Second, what is the magnitude of involuntary unemployment, if it exists? And finally, would standard survey methods accurately register any such unemployment, assuming that survey respondents report truthfully?

With respect to the first question, involuntary unemployment clearly arises in this scenario. Note first that at wage $\underline{W}$ firms are only willing to hire $\underline{L}_D$ workers, leaving $L_{max} - \underline{L}_D$ workers without jobs. Of this set of non-employed households,

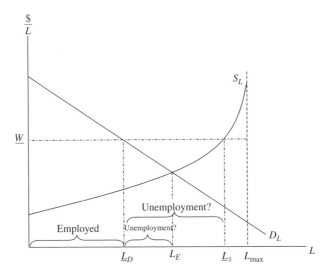

Figure 18.3 Two measures of unemployment in the perfectly competitive market model.

some are best understood as out of the labor force, since even at the higher wage $\underline{W}$ there are individuals who elect not to enter the labor market.

But not everyone is in this position. By the definition of labor supply, $\underline{L}_s$ individuals are willing and able to be employed at the going wage. Note further that if the wage rate were reduced somewhat below $\underline{W}$, more jobs would become available, and moreover there are households which would happily take these jobs at the reduced wage. The same thing could not be said at the market-clearing wage: while lowering the wage rate would increase the quantity demanded of labor, it would not elicit increased quantity supplied. Thus, involuntary unemployment exists according to the first definition advanced earlier in the chapter, and consequently the terms of the second definition are also satisfied.

With respect to the second question, the magnitude of involuntary unemployment arising in this scenario is somewhat less evident. As shown in figure 18.3, the difference between quantity supplied and quantity demanded at the prevailing wage rate, is $\Delta L = \underline{L}_s - \underline{L}_D$. It is certainly the case that this registers the difference between the number of households willing to work and those actually employed at the prevailing wage rate.

But keeping in mind the earlier stipulation that involuntarily unemployed workers be understood to desire jobs that actually exist, it's not clear that this is the appropriate measure of the magnitude of unemployment. The basic scenario constructed here doesn't make clear whether it is plausible to assume that $\underline{L}_s$ jobs exist for those who seek them. To allow this assumption, there would need to be some justification for the possibility of realizing a labor demand curve that intersects the supply curve at the point $\underline{L}_s$. Otherwise, it might be more appropriate to specify the magnitude of involuntary unemployment at $\underline{W}$ as $L_E - \underline{L}_D$.

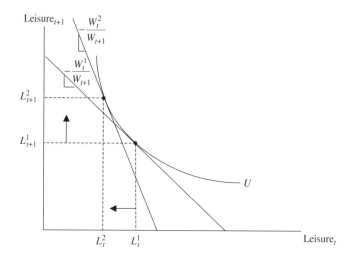

Figure 18.4   Intertemporal leisure substitution.

Finally, would standard survey methods accurately record one or the other measures of unemployment, under the stated conditions? The answer is no, so long as individuals acted rationally given their information and responded truthfully to the survey questions. Since by assumption all actors are fully informed about market conditions, there would be no reason to search for jobs that everyone knows do not exist. Nor could any non-employed individual accurately report waiting for a job to open, since there are no job openings to wait for.

The foregoing assessments do not stem simply from the one-shot nature of the model. To establish this, imagine that individuals aren't making once-and-for-all decisions about labor supply, but rather determining how to allocate their labor supply (and thus the consumption of leisure) across time. According to this version of the ideal market model, changes in the employment level in the current period reflect intertemporal substitution of labor and leisure hours in response to changes in the (expected) ratio of future to current wages. This view is reflected in figure 18.4, which depicts the response of leisure allocation in two periods to a change in relative wages. As shown, an increase in the relative value of current-period wages causes an individual to substitute leisure in the future (period $t +$ 1) for leisure in the present (period t).

However, the same distinctions as before arise in the intertemporal version of the ideal market model. If wages adjust to equate quantities supplied and demanded of labor in every period, then no unemployment of any sort exists. An adjustment in relative wages leads simply to a reallocation of labor and leisure time across periods, without creating unemployment. If currently jobless workers are simply electing to consume leisure rather than truly searching for new positions, then they do not count as unemployed. Furthermore, given honest reporting, government surveys would not register the presence of unemployment under these conditions.

A new empirical possibility arises from the multi-period version of the ideal market model, though. Since households adjust their labor and leisure allocations over time based on expected *relative* wages, it is possible to observe changes in employment levels in a given period even though that period's wage rate does not change. The magnitude of employment changes would depend on the elasticity of substitution for intertemporal leisure choices: the higher the wage elasticity of leisure demand across periods, the bigger the change in employment for a given change in relative wages. Any such changes are mutually agreed upon by the affected employers and employees, however, just as in the one-shot ideal market model.

This brief investigation of unemployment in the ideal market model yields the following conclusions. The most obvious is that involuntary unemployment cannot exist in the absence of government interference in the operation of the labor market. Some workers may not hold jobs in equilibrium, but they elect not to work given the prevailing wage rate. By the same reasoning, changes in relative wage rates across time will generically cause changes in employment in any given period, yet not give rise to unemployment.

Second, even if involuntary unemployment does arise from some unspecified government intervention, no one would be searching for paid work if the remaining conditions of the model held, since everyone would then know that jobs were not available. Thus, standard government employment surveys would not register the existence of unemployment so long as individuals reported their employment status truthfully, making it difficult to square the universal existence of positive unemployment with the presumption that ideal market conditions hold.

It's possible, of course, that unemployment survey results are biased by systematic misreporting. Proponents of the competitive market model distinguish between what people say they're doing and what, according to the theory, is actually taking place. They point out that individuals may have an incentive to claim they're searching for work even when they aren't, especially if they must appear to engage in job search in order to qualify for certain transfer payments. Granting this possibility, it's still not clear why *reported* unemployment would vary as it does across demographic groups or over time.

A third implication of the ideal market model is that there is no meaningful distinction between layoffs and quits, since employers and employees always agree about changes in employment status in response to varying (relative) wage rates. Given this, it's hard to account for the fact that quits are counter-cyclical (increasing in good times and decreasing in bad) while layoffs are pro-cyclical. This difficulty remains even granting the possibility that employees might arrange with firms to report them as laid off in order to qualify for unemployment benefits.

In sum, it is not easy to reconcile the empirical features of unemployment discussed in the previous section with the dictates of the ideal market model. If one does not assume universal misreporting by those who claim to be unemployed, then the competitive exchange model must at least be altered to account for the existence of job search by unemployed workers. However, as you'll see in the next section, altering the model in this way generically gives rise to the prediction that some form of *involuntary* unemployment occurs.

SEARCH COSTS AND UNEMPLOYMENT

Trading frictions, combined with unexpected economic contingencies that result in unplanned job separations, create a presumably short-run situation in which market participants are dissatisfied with their current economic status and seek to change it. This desire leads to a form of behavior economists call *search*. This section considers the nature of search activity undertaken by optimizing market participants. Two distinct approaches to the analysis of market search have been pursued in the literature. Since each of these approaches offer somewhat different insights into the nature and consequences of job search, both are considered here.

The mobility cost model

The most basic framework for analyzing labor market search assumes simply that mobility costs exist for all market participants. These costs can be attributed to the spatial nature of market interactions: given the inalienability of workers' power to perform labor, they must be physically present where their work is performed, and moving to where the jobs are typically takes time and money. Moreover, some degree of spatial mobility may be required just to identify potentially fruitful employment matches.

Spatial mobility costs are magnified by the existence of imperfect information about employment opportunities. Candidates for a potential labor exchange might not know of each other's whereabouts, and thus must invest scarce resources in reaching each other, even before the terms of employment can be worked out. It is typically assumed in such models that these terms are arrived at through a process of bargaining once a potential match is established.

The key assumption within this framework is that there is a given market process, summarized by a "matching function," that links the total number of searching would-be buyers and sellers to the number of successful employment matches per period. This function presumably depends in part on individual decisions as to optimal search intensity. Each individual trades off the costs of increased intensity with the benefit of an increased probability of a successful match. Equilibrium in this model occurs when each individual has chosen the personally optimal search intensity given the similarly optimizing choices of all other market participants.

Equilibria in mobility cost models generically exhibit three important features. First, assuming that labor buyers and sellers are respectively homogeneous, a

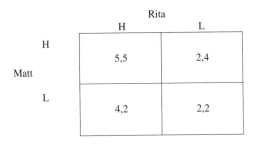

Figure 18.5   Multiple Nash equilibria in the search intensity coordination game.

uniform wage rate must result in a given equilibrium when identical actors choose identical strategies. This is because each decisionmaker on a given side of the market faces the same market conditions as every other actor when parallel strategies are pursued.

Second, equilibria in this setting are generically inefficient, in contrast to those arising under competitive market conditions. The intuition behind this result is easily seen: since each player's choice of search intensity also necessarily affects other players' prospects for entering a successful match, market choices create positive and negative externalities. For example, increased search intensity by a worker also raises the probability that prospective employers find matches, thus reducing their expected duration of search. In this case, *positive spillovers* and *strategic complementarities* are said to exist, giving rise to a macroeconomic *co-ordination game* such as the simple one illustrated in figure 18.5. In contrast, the worker's increased search reduces the prospect that other workers will achieve a match in a given period, creating a negative externality.

Third, depending on the net effect of positive and negative search externalities, the same factors that generate externalities in this scenario may also imply the existence of multiple equilibria that are unambiguously rankable on efficiency grounds. For example, as shown in figure 18.5, the H(igh search intensity) equilibrium clearly dominates the L(ow-intensity) alternative. This is intriguing because it creates a potential role for beneficial governmental intervention in the economy, as discussed later in the chapter.

The wage distribution model

Under the mobility cost framework, unemployment and job search arises in equilibrium because it takes time and scarce resources to secure a prospective employment match, even if every actor on a given side of the market can expect the same employment conditions once a successful match is achieved. However, this is not the only possible basis for persistent search by rational market actors. An alternative explanation for this phenomenon arises from the assumption that individuals face a *frequency distribution* of payoffs from job matches. It is plausible to

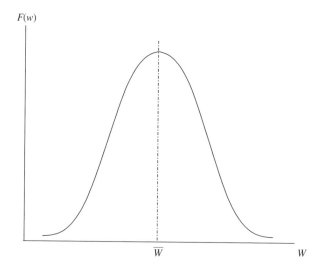

Figure 18.6   Frequency distribution of wage offers with mean $\overline{W}$.

imagine that non-uniform payoffs might arise from the assumption that prospective buyers and sellers are heterogeneous, and thus that the returns to labor exchange are match-specific.

To keep the discussion as simple as possible, let's focus just on the search problem faced by prospective employees. The basic logic of the decision problem to be discussed is the same for optimizing firms. The point of departure for this model is thus the assumption that employment-seeking workers with given productivity characteristics and workplace preferences face a *frequency distribution* of possible wage offers, with given mean $\overline{W}$, as illustrated in figure 18.6, rather than a single wage rate as in the ideal market model. A given job offer W is then understood as a single draw from this distribution, and the value of the wage offer is thus taken to be a random variable before the job hunter receives it.

Suppose for simplicity that a job-seeking worker receives a single offer per period that he or she searches. Continued search is thus fruitful in that it yields another, perhaps strictly preferable, draw from the wage distribution. However, each additional period of search is also presumed to incur at least an opportunity cost in the form of a current wage offer not taken. Suppose in addition that an unemployed worker has a "fallback" income, net of direct search costs, equal to $\underline{W}$ per period, derived from unemployment compensation and other government transfers, non-labor income, savings, or some combination of the three. To incorporate a real-world complication that will arise again in the subsequent discussion of job flows, one might also assume that a certain percentage of employed workers are laid off in each period.

Again for the sake of simplicity, assume that workers are risk-neutral and seek to maximize the expected present value of labor income. Let r be the worker's discount rate (so that a dollar received tomorrow is worth $1/(1 + r)$ dollars today). Also assume, along with the literature, that workers can only engage in job search when unemployed; the impact of relaxing this assumption is discussed after working through the basic story.

The setting just described creates a *sequential* choice problem not discussed before in this text, in which a job seeker must decide *in each period that search is continued* when to accept a current wage offer rather than continuing to seek a better one. There is no *necessary* stopping-point built into the model, so that in theory a worker could search forever if so inclined. But it won't typically make sense to do so, given that continued search both yields benefits and incurs opportunity costs. After each period of search, the representative worker must compare the current wage offer to the expected, or probability-weighted, present value of continued search. If the net expected gain from continued search exceeds the current offer, the job hunter is assumed to keep looking for an acceptable offer; otherwise the current wage offer is accepted and search is terminated.

In light of the considerations introduced above, the key to understanding the search behavior of a representative worker rests in determining the *reservation wage*, that is, the wage offer that is minimally acceptable to a prospective worker given the expected costs and benefits of continued search. The basic idea underlying the calculation of this critical magnitude is fairly straightforward: if the reservation wage is set too low, then the worker may have to settle for an inadequate offer; if it's too high, the worker may commit herself to a very long and costly search effort. The reservation wage rate is that which equates these costs and benefits at the margin.

The nature of the decision process is depicted in figure 18.7, which shows the respective expected values of stopping (denoted V_{accept}) and continued searching (denoted V_{reject}) as functions of candidate values for the reservation wage. It is intuitive that the value of stopping search and accepting the current wage offer is unambiguously increasing in the candidate wage, as shown. The value of continued search, in contrast, declines with the level of the reservation wage rate, since the searcher expects to have to wait longer to ensure receipt of higher minimally acceptable wages. The optimal reservation wage, denoted by W_R, is determined by the intersection of the two curves.

Given the process of determining the reservation wage, it is a reasonably simple matter to see how changes in underlying search conditions affect the equilibrium reservation wage. Intuitively, changes that increase the net value of continued search will increase the reservation wage, other things equal. On the basis of this observation, it can be shown that the reservation wage *increases* if the worker's fallback income goes up or if the frequency distribution shown in figure 18.6 shifts to the right (thus increasing the mean of the wage distribution), and *decreases* in response to an increase in the rate at which employed workers are laid off, in each worker's discount rate, or in the magnitude of direct search costs. The specific impact of raising the worker's fallback income from $\underline{W}_1$ to $\underline{W}_2$ is illustrated in figure 18.7.

Neither the reservation wage for a given job seeker nor its response to changing search conditions is directly observable, though of course floors on the range

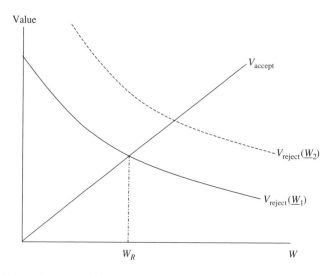

Figure 18.7 Determination of the reservation wage for optimal job search for different levels of "fallback" wage $\underline{W}$.

of acceptable wages can be inferred from offers that a searcher rejects. However, a given value of this wage translates into an expected duration of job search, making it possible in principle to test hypothesized links between search conditions (such as level of unemployment compensation) and average search duration for a large number of workers.

For a given frequency of wage offers, the theory predicts that the expected duration of job search is increasing in the magnitude of the reservation wage. Thus, for example, an increase in unemployment benefits is predicted, at least in the simple model, to lead to an increase in the reservation wage and thus the average time that a worker is willing to search for an acceptable job. This linkage may also help explain the average duration of observed employment spells, *if* it is legitimate to assume that job search is undertaken primarily by the unemployed.

SAME UNEMPLOYMENT RATES, DIFFERENT UNEMPLOYMENT DYNAMICS

The single number of the unemployment rate also cannot capture all of the differences between countries in the way that unemployment is experienced. Two systems can have equal unemployment rates, but very different average time spent in unemployment (duration) and very different flows into unemployment.

For example, from 1983 through 1997, Portugal and the United States had the same average unemployment rate (about 6.5%), but unemployment duration in Portugal was three times that of the US. The offset to this higher duration was that the flow into unemployment in Portugal was less than a third of that in the US (proportional to their labor force size) – hence equal unemployment rates with different underlying dynamics. In their study of this situation, economists Blanchard and Portugal (2001) argue that the explanation for these differences is the higher level of employment protection in Portugal relative to the US; that "high employment protection makes economies more sclerotic," but because "it affects unemployment duration and flows in opposite directions, it has an ambiguous effect on the unemployment rate."

Related discussion questions:
1. Can we say that one system, the US or Portuguese one, is *better* than the other? What are the trade-offs involved? What would be the criterion to use to decide that one is better?
2. The OECD, an international coordinating organization of developed nations, puts out many studies concerning labor patterns within its member states. It calculates an index of employment protection to compare the degree of protection across nations. What types of things do you think should be included in such an index?

Related references:
Olivier Blanchard and Pedro Portugal, "What Hides Behind an Unemployment Rate: Comparing Portuguese and U.S. Labor Markets," *American Economic Review* 91 (1), 2001: 187–207.
OECD, *The OECD Jobs Study* (Paris: OECD, 1994).

Assessing alternative explanations for job search

Labor market search by firms and workers appears to be a constant feature of modern market economies. Somewhat less evident is the primary explanation for non-trivial periods of search by unemployed workers and firms with job vacancies. Both of the theories just discussed have some claim to plausibility, since mobility costs and wide wage variations for apparently similar jobs are arguably facts of life in these economies. But which one does a better job of accounting for search behavior and providing a basis for useful policy prescriptions?

There are a number of objections to the wage distribution model of search on empirical grounds.[2]

Perhaps the biggest single strike against the wage distribution version of search theory stems from the observation that job-seeking workers rarely reject offers.

Empirical estimates of the average probability of accepting a given wage offer range from 80% to virtually 100%. This, combined with the fact that unemployment spells may last several weeks or even months, suggests that the key problem faced by unemployed workers is receiving *any* wage offer, rather than just receiving a sufficiently high one.

A second empirical problem with the wage distribution model has to do with its assumption that workers can only engage in job search while unemployed. This assumption is inconsistent with the fact that more than 50% of those who quit their jobs move into new positions without any intervening spell of unemployment. In addition, studies suggest that most people search in non-time intensive ways that are consistent with holding a job while seeking new positions.

These observations suggest that there is an important distinction to be made between job search in general and the job search engaged in by the unemployed. Those holding a current job can presumably be somewhat picky about what alternative wage offers they accept, and thus have the luxury of electing to quit only upon locating a superior alternative. In contrast, most people who are unemployed do not become so by quitting, and once unemployed may typically face the more fundamental problem of attracting any wage offer at all.

IMPERFECT CONTRACTING AND UNEMPLOYMENT

The theories just studied, although they generally predict the existence of equilibrium unemployment, share one important feature with the competitive labor market model: they both presume that wages adjust flexibly to changes in underlying market conditions. This is true even allowing for the presence of one-sided or bilateral market power when costly search occurs, though in these latter cases the equilibrium wage may not equate supply and demand as in ideal markets.

This section considers theories that build on the contrasting presumption that wages do not adjust freely to the level consistent with the incidence of market power. These theories have in common the at least implicit assumption that markets are in some way beset by contracting failures, and thus do not allow certain mutually beneficial exchanges to be realized. The polar case of this approach is that wages are completely inflexible, at least for some short-run horizon, so that labor market equilibration is achieved entirely through adjustments in employment rather than in the level of wage rates.

The discussion begins with a review of evidence for the existence of wage inflexibility, particularly in the form of downwardly rigid *nominal* wages. The next step is to summarize competing explanations for the existence of wage "stickiness" and the implications thereof for the magnitude and duration of unemployment. Finally, evidence on employer motivations for not cutting nominal wages is discussed.

Are nominal wages inflexible?

So far in this text, the analysis of labor market phenomena has ignored the possibility of changes in the general level of prices. This procedure is justifiable given the primarily microeconomic issues studied up to this point, for which variations in the price level would only constitute an additional layer of complication without adding insight. But while analyzing the macroeconomic phenomenon of unemployment, the possibility of inflating or deflating the price level must sooner or later be brought into the picture. Indeed, this issue is central to the next chapter's discussion of the Phillips curve tradeoff between unemployment and nominal wage inflation.

Once one allows for variations in the price level, it is necessary to distinguish between *nominal* and *real* wage levels. *Nominal* wages are those actually paid to workers, measured in current monetary units. *Real* wages, in contrast, represent what the wages received can actually purchase, and thus take into account variations in the price level. Thus, for example, in a period of inflating prices, nominal wages may increase while real wages remain constant or even fall. To arrive at estimates of real wages, economists use a *price index* to adjust nominal wages for inflationary or deflationary changes in the price level.

Allowing, then, for possible changes in the price level, it is necessary to distinguish inflexibility in real or nominal wages. Assuming that market actors are otherwise fully informed and rational, the theory of markets with contracting failures focuses attention on *real* wage inflexibility. The reason is basic: what rational, informed, and optimizing actors care about is what their income can actually purchase, not merely the dollar amount of wages. Thus, if economic forces preclude freely adjusting wages, we might start with the presumption that any inflexibility is in real terms.

Data from US labor markets, however, suggest that if there is inflexibility it arises in *nominal* rather than real wages, and that nominal wages are inflexible primarily in the direction of wage *reductions*. This is indicated by the "eyeball test" applied to figure 18.8, for example, which shows the frequency distribution of wage changes for non-union white males in the Panel Study of Income Dynamics (PSID).[3] Two things are striking about this distribution: first, although the mean wage change is evidently non-negative, there is a dramatic frequency "spike" at zero change in wages, indicating that this is by far the most frequent single wage event in the sample. Second, the distribution of wage changes is skewed significantly to the right, meaning that negative wage changes are considerably less frequent than positive changes. They occur, but seemingly not as much as might be expected from a purely random process generating wage changes for a random sample of workers.

Despite appearances, data such as these do not necessarily establish the existence of downward nominal wage rigidity. The first point is that nominal wage reductions are frequent, even if not to the degree suggested by a purely symmetric wage change. If nominal wage reductions happen often, then a simple wage

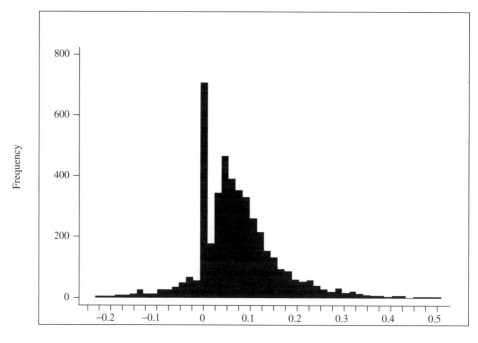

Figure 18.8 Frequency distribution of nominal wage changes, non-union white males.

Source: Joseph G. Altonji and Paul J. Devereux, "The Extent and Consequences of Downward Nominal Wage Rigidity," NBER Working Paper 7236, p. 47, July 1999. Reprinted with permission.

rigidity story can't account for the data. The major problem in settling this issue has to do with the problem of measurement error: some studies suggest that nominal wage reductions are over-reported.

Second, one might allow that the distribution of wage changes is rightward skewed, yet deny that the observed frequency distribution necessarily results from downward wage rigidity as opposed to the more general possibility of skewness in the direction of positive wage changes. There are several possible reasons that this less restrictive hypothesis is consistent with the appearances put forward by data such as in figure 18.8. For example, the true extent of nominal wage reductions might be underreported because workers faced with these cuts quit rather than accepting them. Second, the data might be explained by downward rigidity in *real* wages, which is at least easier to explain in terms of the theory of rational decision making based on sufficient information.

At this stage in the debate, the evidence seems to favor the assessment that there is partial rather than universal downward rigidity in nominal wages. The data support this conclusion with considerably more confidence than the competing hypothesis that nominal wage adjustments are completely flexible. Notice this doesn't imply that real wages might not also be inflexible; to the extent that nominal wages are downwardly rigid, though, real wage cuts can only come from an increase in the price level. But if real wages may fall, one must ask why workers or firms would care about avoiding merely nominal wage reductions. This puzzle is reconsidered after a discussion of theories of unemployment based on wage and price inflexibility.

Price vs. quantity adjustments

It is almost second nature for many students of economics, along with many economists, to associate processes of market equilibration with flexible price adjustments. There is a fundamental plausibility to the story that prices adjust toward market-clearing levels in response to excess demand or supply pressures. As discussed in chapter 4, however, wage or price flexibility need not arise under imperfectly competitive exchange conditions.

The evidence just considered surely raises some doubts about the flexibility of wage adjustments. But econometric evidence also casts a shadow on the presumption of flexible price adjustments in many non-labor markets, at least in the short run. At the level of quarterly data, for example, variations in the volume of sales are linked more strongly to changes in output and employment than to changes in wages and prices. Such data raise the possibility that short-run market equilibration occurs through adjustments in quantities as well as, or perhaps instead of, prices.

Equilibration via some combination of price and quantity adjustments may have very different implications for market function and performance. This is most easily seen in the context of a "fixed-price" scenario in which it is assumed that short-run market equilibration is accomplished *solely* through quantity adjustments in response to conditions of excess demand or supply.[4] The implications of this scenario are assessed before returning to the microeconomic basis for inflexible wages and prices.

Begin the analysis of a fixed-price economy with the aggregate labor market depicted in figure 18.9(a), in which the rigid wage rate is assumed to exceed the market-clearing level, creating a situation of involuntary unemployment. Given no other information about economic conditions, it would be natural to blame the unemployment on the excessive wage rate, and correspondingly to prescribe policies to reduce wages in order to cure unemployment. Call unemployment *classical* if it can be ameliorated by reducing the wage rate, other things equal.

Classical unemployment is the only possible outcome in an economy with just two exchanged goods, say labor and current consumption goods. In this case, since there can only be one exchange ratio in the economy (consumption goods for labor), excess supply in the labor market is necessarily tantamount to excess demand in the goods market, and reducing the wage rate would solve both problems at once. Extending this logic, a situation of classical unemployment also

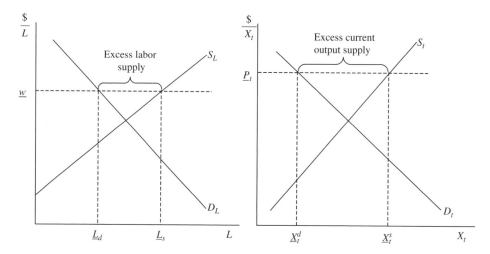

Figure 18.9   Keynesian unemployment (excess supply in labor and current goods market).

arises in a multi-good economy in which all or most goods markets experience excess demand to go with excess labor supply.

But now imagine an economy with both current and future production and consumption, and thus saving and investment. Now there are (at least) three markets (labor, current goods, and claims on future goods) and two distinct exchange ratios. Therefore, it is necessary to look at the labor and current consumption goods markets together. As before, assume the situation illustrated in figure 18.9(a), with excess supply in the labor market.

But now consider as well the situation in the market for current output, shown in figure 18.9(b). Demand for current output comes from two sources, household demand for current consumption goods and business demand for investment goods (new capital stock and inventories). As indicated, the supply curve is upward-sloping, and its level is determined by the level of the wage rate, for reasons spelled out in chapter 1. But let's complete the picture by supposing that the price for current consumption goods also exceeds its market-clearing level, so that there is excess supply in this market as well. Is it still the case in this scenario that unemployment is ameliorated by reducing the wage rate, other things equal?

To begin to answer this question, notice that the situation just constructed in the market for current output is easily recognizable from standard textbook macroeconomics as one in which actual investment exceeds desired investment. Since desired quantity supplied exceeds quantity demanded at the going price, firms are piling up excess inventories. Since by assumption the excess supply won't be eliminated automatically by price adjustments, firms must get rid of their excess inventories by reducing output.

Thus equilibrium is achieved by adjustment of "effective" supply to quantity demanded. *Once this quantity adjustment has taken place*, however, reducing the wage rate will not serve to lower the unemployment rate. To the contrary, reducing the wage rate will *increase* equilibrium. A condition of *Keynesian* rather than classical unemployment therefore emerges in this scenario, meaning that unemployment must be addressed by policies which increase aggregate demand rather than simply reducing the wage rate.

To see why this is the case, note first that since current output is already in excess supply, the rightward shift in supply induced by reducing wage costs is not helpful. It simply increases the magnitude of excess supply, other things equal. But worse, cutting the wage rate reduces workers' disposable income, and thus reduces household demand for current output. Since the demand curve determines the quantity actually exchanged, the unemployment problem is only made worse; firms must cut output still further in order to eliminate unintended investment.

The fixed-price model thus lends an important insight about the nature of unemployment in a general equilibrium setting: if prices do not immediately adjust to clear markets, then unemployment can result, and furthermore merely adjusting wage rates may exacerbate rather than improve on this market failure. While this is not a necessary outcome of the model, it would be the typical result if it is also the case that wages and prices are more rigid downward than upward, as may well be the case. But why would they be rigid at all? Possible microeconomic answers to this question are considered next.

Implicit contracts and wage rigidity

For reasons explored in chapter 8, risk-averse workers seek insurance against economic risks. Suppose, however, that markets are incomplete to the extent that workers cannot purchase insurance against variations in their labor income, perhaps because insurance companies could not prevent the resulting loss in work incentives if the level of labor income were guaranteed. Then workers might seek such protection from their less risk-averse employers.

The theory of *implicit contracts*, introduced in chapter 11, explores the implications of this for wage determination. Under the simplifying assumption that worker hours are fixed, the model predicts that the wages paid to employed workers resulting from such insurance agreements do not vary with macroeconomic fluctuations, and are thus *completely* rigid. Note, however, that this isn't the pattern of inflexibility suggested by nominal wage data. The data suggest a tendency toward downward wage rigidity, but do not suggest inflexibility in the other direction. However, as discussed in chapter 11, this problem is solved by incorporating the condition that *implicit* contract provisions need to be mutually acceptable to both parties and thus self-enforcing.

Implicit contracts that satisfy this *incentive compatibility* condition yield wage streams that are inflexible downward but not upward. The former occurs to provide workers with insurance, while the possibility of upward wage adjustments keeps workers from leaving the relationship.

The implicit contract model thus provides a logically consistent explanation for wage inflexibility, but it's not clear that it provides an equally coherent account of unemployment. In particular the model does not provide a good explanation for the empirical preponderance of unemployment due to layoffs. To see this, note that the equilibrium possibility of being laid off goes against the basic logic of the model, since risk-averse workers would presumably not want to bear the income risk associated with the prospect that they could lose their jobs. And indeed, the basic model outlined above does not necessarily predict that layoffs occur, although they might. In any case, the predicted level of layoffs is less than would be expected to arise in labor markets with flexible wages.

But this difficulty with the implicit contract approach is even more fundamental than it first appears. The possibility that any layoffs at all occur under the conditions of the basic model flows from the arbitrary assumption that hours per worker are fixed beforehand. When this assumption is dropped, the possibility of layoffs disappears entirely in equilibrium. Again, this result should not be surprising: the basic point of this approach is that workers want to ensure against income risk, and the best way to ensure this is to allow hours to vary to accommodate macroeconomic fluctuations. All that matters to workers is that total labor income, or the product of wage rate and hours per worker, is constant. But note this implies in turn that total labor income, not necessarily the wage rate, is inflexible. Thus an arguably more realistic version of the model can account for neither inflexible wages nor unemployment due to layoffs.

Other sources of wage inflexibility

It might seem to be a relatively easy matter to link wage rigidity to some form of contractual incompleteness. For example, if significant transaction costs are incurred whenever contractual terms are rewritten, firms might be loath to adjust nominal wages freely to market conditions. And indeed, the presence of such *menu costs* might help to explain why prices for certain commodities don't adjust freely. But it is less obvious that transaction costs of this sort easily explain observed patterns of wage inflexibility. In particular, it is necessary to explain why wages are inflexible downward but not upward.

One basis for this phenomenon is the version of the efficiency wage model based on employee morale. This approach presumes that workers assess their wage levels by comparing them to reference groups, and are "demoralized" in a way that affects job performance if the comparison shows them coming up short. This scenario was corroborated by the survey results of Truman Bewley, discussed in chapter 16. If his findings can be generalized, they suggest that downward nominal wage rigidity stems from market imperfections in which an aspect of work performance that cannot be contractually stipulated is influenced by employees' "states of mind." This is consistent in spirit if not in detail with the efficiency wage model, the key difference being the suggestion of Bewley's respondents that morale is tied to nominal rather than real wage cuts.

Certain of Bewley's findings were corroborated in a separate survey published in 1997 by Carl Campbell and Kunal Kamlani, who took pains to secure a representative sample of firms and to ask more targeted questions than in earlier surveys in order to promote quantification and statistical analysis of the results.[5] Asked if and why they avoided nominal wage cuts in times of high unemployment, Campbell and Kamlani's survey respondents gave the greatest support to an adverse selection argument that such wage cuts would promote quits by relatively productive workers. They also lent support to the argument, primarily favored by Bewley's interviewees, that wage cuts would affect morale and thus reduce work effort.

THE ROLE OF GOVERNMENT

This chapter has investigated a broad spectrum of aggregate labor market theories, with very different assumptions about market function and implications concerning the nature and causes of unemployment. These competing approaches correspondingly prescribe quite diverse roles for government vis-à-vis the labor market, even assuming that appropriate government policies can be fitted with some freedom to given economic conditions. This last section of the chapter summarizes the corresponding implications of actions that government might take with respect to the problem of unemployment, in increasing order or prospective government involvement in private employment relationships.

Unsurprisingly, the view dictated by the competitive market model allows no useful role for government intervention. To the contrary, government economic interventions in the form of minimum wage laws, legalized collective bargaining, and unemployment compensation are understood to distort market outcomes and thus create unemployment. According to this view, what government surveys measure as "unemployment," if not simply the consequences of such distortions, indicates instead the voluntary consumption of leisure, misrepresented perhaps because of the desire to secure unemployment benefits or avoid the stigma attached to those who don't elect to work.

Under competitive market conditions, government interventions can only reallocate the means of social welfare rather than augment them, and will generally result in Pareto-inferior outcomes. In this connection it is worth noting that even theories that identify a potential role for government intervention do not ensure that the policies actually chosen will in fact increase net welfare. Economic theories in general establish at most necessary, not sufficient, conditions for the desirability of economic interventions by the state.

In contrast to the setting of competitive markets, models of imperfect competition in labor markets (including the search model based on mobility frictions) predict suboptimal economic outcomes, and thus at least a potential role for government intervention. If the government can't take direct action to correct imperfectly competitive labor market conditions (e.g., through antitrust policies), an interesting alternative approach to improving market outcomes is suggested by the existence of externalities in this class of models. Under conditions discussed earlier in the chapter, these externalities may give rise to multiple equilibria that can be unambiguously ordered according to the criterion of Pareto-optimality. In this case, the appropriate governmental response would be to increase the prospects for attainment of the Pareto-superior equilibrium.

Take, for example, the job search scenario based on mobility frictions. If the associated externalities are on balance positive and also give rise to strategic complementarities in individual choices of search intensity, multiple inefficient but Pareto-rankable equilibria will arise. In this case the government might encourage selection of the best attainable equilibrium by subsidizing search efforts, say by offering subsidies to workers for accepting employment or to firms for hiring additional workers. These subsidies would increase the marginal benefit of generating successful job offers, and would thus efficiently promote equilibrium search intensity.

A more direct economic role for government with respect to labor markets is suggested in the scenario of downwardly inflexible nominal wages. As discussed earlier in the chapter, this scenario can give rise to either classical or Keynesian unemployment, both of which are inefficient relative to ideal market outcomes. As should be familiar to most economic students, the Keynesian outcome is not ameliorated by efforts to reduce the wage rate, but is rather most appropriately addressed by monetary or fiscal policies designed to encourage aggregate demand.

This prescription is complicated somewhat in the presence of tradeoffs between unemployment and the rate of inflation, in part because of the difficulty of ascertaining the relative economic injuries associated with the two macroeconomic pathologies. Involuntary unemployment creates wasteful underuse of productive resources while causing potentially devastating economic havoc for its victims, particularly the long-term unemployed. Unless all contracts, implicit and otherwise, are fully indexed to the rate of inflation, inflation redistributes income in a manner that especially penalizes the less affluent who live on fixed incomes, and may make prospective investors less willing to finance long-term projects that might yield uncertain and significantly devalued future returns. It is therefore important to consider the interconnection between unemployment and wage inflation, a task for the final chapter.

Study Questions

1. Define *unemployment* and distinguish it from *non-employment*. Is the existence of unemployment consistent with equilibrium in competitive labor markets?
2. Define *involuntary unemployment*. Is the existence of involuntary unemployment consistent with equilibrium in competitive labor markets?

What might explain the existence of equilibrium involuntary unemployment?

3. Should a discouraged job-seeker who has quit actively looking for employment be counted as involuntarily unemployed? Should part-time workers who desire full-time employment be considered partially involuntarily unemployed?

4. Contrast the *mobility cost* and *wage distribution* models of search unemployment. What are the key differences between them? What evidence would help determine which better accounts for the incidence of unemployment?

5. What is the distinction in macroeconomic conditions yielding *Keynesian* and *classical* unemployment?

6. Can microeconomic models such as *monopsony*, efficiency *wage*, and *insider bargaining* theories explain why involuntary unemployment might exist in equilibrium? According to these theories, what would be the impact on equilibrium wages and unemployment of an increase in aggregate demand brought about by expansionary fiscal policy?

Notes

1 John Maynard Keynes, *The General Theory of Employment, Interest and Money* (New York: Harcourt, Brace, 1936).

2 Kim B. Clark and Lawrence H. Summers, "Labor Market Dynamics and Unemployment: A Reconsideration," in Lawrence H. Summers (ed.), *Understanding Unemployment* (Cambridge, MA, and London: The MIT Press, 1990).

3 Joseph G. Altonji and Paul J. Devereux, "The Extent and Consequences of Downward Nominal Wage Rigidity," NBER Working Paper No. 7236 (July 1999).

4 The following analysis is taken from Edmond Malinvaud, *The Theory of Unemployment Reconsidered* (Oxford: Basil Blackwell, 1977).

5 Carl M. Campbell III, and Kunal S. Kamlani, "The Reasons for Wage Rigidity: Evidence from a Survey of Firms," *The Quarterly Journal of Economics* 112, no. 3 (August 1997): 759–89.

Suggestions for Further Reading

Russell W. Cooper, *Coordination Games: Complementarities and Macroeconomics* (Cambridge: Cambridge University Press, 1999).

Carl Davidson, *Recent Developments in the Theory of Involuntary Unemployment* (Kalamazoo, MI: W.E. Upjohn Institute for Employment Research, 1990).

Richard Layard, Stephen Nickell, and Richard Jackman, *Unemployment: Macroeconomic Performance and the Labour Market* (Oxford: Oxford University Press, 1991).

CHAPTER NINETEEN

LABOR MARKET DYNAMICS

Prior to the last chapter, the text's analysis of labor market phenomena has been primarily based on a framework of *static equilibrium* analysis, in that no forces for economic change have been built into the competing stories as to how these markets work. The essentially static nature of the analysis is not fundamentally altered by introducing the dimension of time, so long as individuals know the future conditions affecting their choices. Even though decisions are intertemporal, the economic context remains static if individuals can anticipate what they'll be doing at each period in their future.

Market economies, and consequently the labor markets that operate within them, are in contrast fundamentally *dynamic*, implying that conditions change over time in unforeseeable ways. In a dynamic context, individuals find that they must continually revise their plans in response to new information and contingencies. One aspect of dynamic decision making with fundamental implications for labor market outcomes is job search, discussed at length in the previous chapter.

The present chapter provides an economic context for search behavior by considering sources of dynamism in labor market exchange conditions, and possible consequences of this dynamism for the economic logic of wage and employment determination. After introducing the notion of economic *shocks* or unanticipated changes in market conditions, the chapter investigates how worker and job flows respond to these changes. In the presence of search and matching costs, desired adjustments to market shocks are not instantaneous, resulting in the symmetric conditions of unemployment and job vacancies.

Using the dynamic concept of a steady state to replace the static notion of equilibrium, the *Beveridge curve* represents the indirect connection

> between unemployment and job vacancy rates arising from costly flows. This relationship establishes a foundation for thinking of the dynamic relationship between unemployment and wage inflation, as summarized in the *Phillips curve.*

ECONOMIC SHOCKS AND LABOR MARKET SEARCH

Labor markets in flux

Labor markets are always in motion. Every year new workers enter these markets for the first time and some workers leave, often forever. Employees change jobs and employers, or temporarily cease doing paid work in order to raise families or acquire additional schooling. Firms create new positions and close down plants, laying off workers in the process.

Many of these changes are planned in advance. Most individuals anticipate entering the labor market on a full-time basis after reaching certain educational milestones, and plan on retiring at certain stages in their careers. Firms plan on hiring new employees when opening new plants or expanding existing ones.

However, in many cases labor market events aren't, and can't be, anticipated. Unanticipated economic changes, often referred to as *shocks,* impart a different type of dynamism to labor markets. In this case, market outcomes change because participants must reconsider their choices in light of new circumstances. There is thus a close connection between the notion of economic shocks and the scenario of incomplete contracts discussed in chapters 8 and 9. In the latter context, a shock is a contingency affecting the terms of labor exchange that for some reason cannot be anticipated and spelled out in enforceable contracts. This situation raises the prospect that, in the event a shock is realized, incumbent exchange partners are for some reason unable to renegotiate terms to their mutual satisfaction, and consequently one or both parties must seek new exchange partners in the relevant labor market.

If, in addition, there exist significant matching costs in the labor market, then the realization of shocks creates a new situation in which actors are in the market looking for suitable exchange partners, but have not yet found them. This is of course the phenomenon of *search* discussed in the previous chapter. But where that chapter focused solely on the implications of search behavior for unemployment, the present argument is concerned with the symmetric consequences of shocks and matching costs for unemployment and *job vacancies.* From the standpoint of the economy as a whole, it is clear that the two are interconnected; one cannot reduce unemployment, for example, unless there exist vacancies for job seekers to fill.

Before exploring the interconnected incidence of unemployment and job vacancies further, it will be useful to consider possible forms of economic shocks and their potential scope. Beginning with the former issue, natural disasters are an obvious source of economic shock. Hurricanes or floods, for example, disrupt existing exchange relationships while imposing additional costs on market actors. Technological innovations, broadly conceived, can create economic shocks, for example by rendering obsolete existing consumption goods or production processes. Sudden changes in government policy can create economic shocks, as when the central bank takes unexpected action with respect to the money supply. From the standpoint of a given open economy, policy or technological innovations of other countries can result in trade shocks in which export or import levels change suddenly.

As for the issue of scope, a shock could be limited in its effect to a particular industry or geographical region; any such change is called a *sectoral* shock. Possible examples of sectoral shocks include technical innovations that are specific to the production process used in a particular industry and extreme weather conditions that afflict a circumscribed region of a country. *Aggregate* shocks, on the other hand, affect most or all actors in a given economy, although not necessarily in the same manner. Examples of aggregate shocks include unexpected changes in a government's macroeconomic policy or sudden disruptions in the supply of an imported input used in most firms' production processes, such as occurred during the OPEC oil embargo of the early 1970s. Another possible example of an aggregate shock is when, for unclear reasons, the mutually determined expectations of investors or consumers suddenly change, creating or popping an economic "bubble."

A contemporary debate in macroeconomics pertaining to the distinction between sectoral and aggregate shocks concerns the economic basis of so-called "business cycles." This term refers to the oscillating time path of macroeconomic aggregates such as *gross domestic product* (GDP) or unemployment. Although the GDP of most market economies tends on average to grow over time, each country experiences considerable up-and-down variation around these upward trends.

Furthermore, these variations tend to be serially correlated, meaning that once an economic expansion or contraction is initiated, it tends to be continued for some time. This is what prompts the term "cycle" for what might otherwise be considered a process of purely random economic variations around a growing mean. GDP data exhibiting this "cyclical" path for several OECD countries are illustrated in figure 19.1.

It has traditionally been assumed that cyclical macroeconomic variations are explained by *aggregate* shocks affecting the investment prospects of most firms in the economy. However, recent research has given rise to the suggestion that cyclical variations are due to the cumulative effect of multiple *sectoral* shocks. A central issue in this debate concerns the heterogeneity of economic actors. The sectoral-shock view of business cycles suggests that aggregate statistics on changes in national income or the level of employment tend to hide a remarkable amount of diversity in the economic experience of individual sectors of the market system.

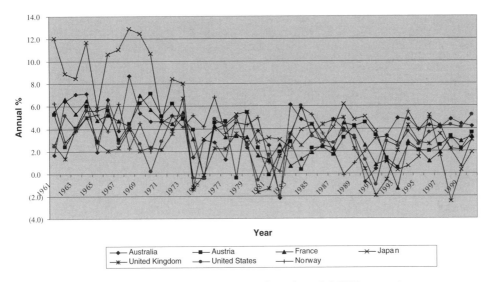

Figure 19.1   Graphs of GDP series for selected OECD countries.

This diversity shows up in the sectoral incidence of *job flows*, discussed later in the chapter.

Unemployment and job vacancies

As noted above, the possibility of labor market disequilibria induced by sectoral or aggregate economic shocks, combined with the existence of mobility costs that make adjustments to these shocks difficult, gives rise to the economic phenomenon of labor market search. Viewed respectively from the standpoints of households and firms, these conditions are manifested in the presence of *unemployed workers* and *vacant jobs*. Consider first the dynamic international incidence of unemployment.

On this point, refer back to figure 18.1 to see unemployment rate patterns over 1969–99 for several OECD countries. Note that variations in the unemployment rate exhibit the same "cyclical" pattern as the GDP measures illustrated above. Note also that while unemployment rates in Western Europe were consistently lower than those in the US through the mid-1960s, since that time the pattern has reversed and Western Europe has experienced comparatively higher unemployment rates.

An employer's counterpart to the condition of unemployment is termed a *job vacancy*, defined as an available employment position that goes unfilled. The analogy to unemployment is more apparent if the latter condition is regarded as a matter of degree, so that workers can be considered more or less *under*employed.

Vacancy rate(%)

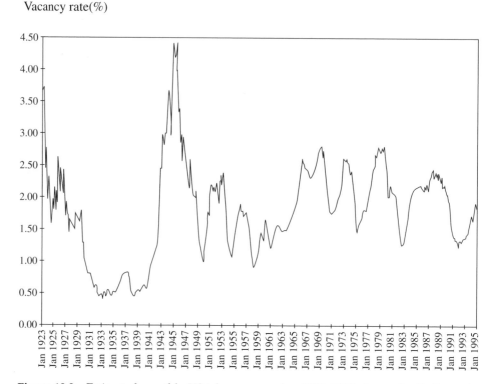

Figure 19.2   Estimated monthly US job vacancy rates, 1923–1994. *Source*: Jay L. Zagorsky "Job Vacancies in the United States: 1923 to 1994," *The Review of Economics and Statistics*, 80, no. 2 (1998): 338–45. © 1998 by the President and Fellows of Harvard College and the Massachusetts Institute of Technology. Reprinted with permission.

By the same token, employers can continue to produce while having fewer or more job vacancies. The *vacancy rate* for an economy is defined as the ratio of total vacancies to the sum of vacancies plus filled positions.

Measuring vacancy rates leads to issues similar to those encountered in calculating the unemployment rate for an economy. In particular, some basis must be established for believing that a firm has a position that it wishes to fill. For example, the fact that workers have recently quit or retired from existing positions does not itself imply that affected firms want these workers replaced; employers may to the contrary be attempting to reduce their standing labor forces through attrition. The US government does not compile vacancy rate statistics, so economists construct vacancy measures from an index of help-wanted ads in large metropolitan newspapers.

A series of estimated vacancy rates for the US for the years 1923 to 1994 is presented in figure 19.2. This series exhibits a pattern of alternating peaks and valleys similar to those seen in the time series on GDP and unemployment rates shown above. A close comparison of the unemployment and vacancy series, however, indicates that unemployment and vacancy rates move in roughly opposite directions, so that vacancy rates tend to be high when unemployment rates are low and vice versa. Why might this be so? To answer this question, it is necessary to consider the disaggregated labor market processes that influence aggregate unemployment and vacancy rates; that is, it is necessary to study the *flows* of jobs and workers.

Worker and job flows

The static supply and demand model of labor market outcomes has many uses, but the present discussion suggests that it leaves a key aspect of market reality out of the picture by ignoring the process by which employment matches are achieved. The pervasive coexistence of job vacancies and unemployment indicates that these matches are not instantaneous. In fact, even data on changes in aggregate unemployment and vacancy rates hide a significant amount of labor market activity, because they net out the large and ongoing flows *into* and *out of* these categories.

For this reason, it is potentially useful to look directly at actions taken by workers and firms that affect the magnitude of these aggregate statistics. These are represented by *worker flows* across the three categories of job market attachment (not in labor force, unemployed, and employed) and *job flows* created by firms' decisions to create or destroy employment positions. Consider each in turn.

Worker flows affect both unemployment and vacancy rates. With respect to the latter, worker decisions to quit existing jobs increase vacancies, other things equal. Concerning the former, the pool of unemployed workers in the labor market at any given time is fed by those just arriving at working age, workers re-entering the market after an extended absence, and incumbent workers who quit or were laid off and could not immediately secure alternative employment; it is depleted by successful job-seekers and "discouraged workers" who decide to quit actively searching for jobs. Thus, there are movements across the three employment categories of absence from the labor force, unemployment, and employment. These *employment flows* might be quite large even if the *net* change in total employment over time is negligible.

A sense of the disparity between gross and net employment flows is suggested by figure 19.3, which contrasts employment flows with net employment changes in the US for the years 1982–4. As you can see, net employment changed very little in these years, but gross flows into and out of employment were on average 20 times as large as net flows over this period.

In addition to studying worker movements across categories of labor market attachment, it is potentially useful to consider the creation and destruction of employment positions by firms. *Job creation* might be defined as the sum of *realized* or *intended* additions to the labor force in a given period across firms; by this definition, job creation offers some combination of reductions in unemployment

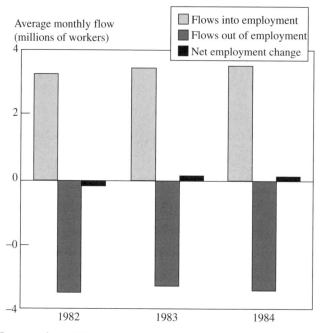

Figure 19.3   Gross and net US employment flows, 1982–1984. *Source*: Hoyt Bleakley and Jeffrey C. Fuhrer, "Shifts in the Beveridge Curve, Job Matching, and Labor Market Dynamics," *New England Economic Review*, September/October 1997: 4. Reprinted with permission.

or increases in the vacancy rate. Correspondingly, *job destruction* can be defined as the sum of *reductions* in actual or advertised jobs across all firms, so that it has the opposite effect of job creation on unemployment and vacancy rates.

The magnitude of gross job flows relative to net employment changes in modern economies is indicated in table 19.1, which shows gross and net realized job flow measures for selected developed and developing countries and sample years. Here again one can see gross flows that are typically an order of magnitude larger than net changes in employment.

Why might it be useful to study gross worker and job flows in addition to the net changes in employment and job vacancies that they induce? One reason, perhaps the most important one, is in order to get a better idea of the determinants of unemployment and vacancy rates and their persistence by studying the individual channels that feed or deplete them. For example, 50 to 60% of workers who quit their previous jobs immediately secure new employment, with the consequence that only about 10 to 15% of newly unemployed workers chose to leave their previous jobs. In contrast, job separations initiated by firms account for 50 to 60% of those unemployed, while about 25% have re-entered the labor force after a period of non-employment, and 10% are looking for their first jobs.

Table 19.1 International comparison of net and gross job flow rates (annual averages as percentages of employment)

Country	Period	Coverage	Job creation	Job destruction	Net employment growth	Job reallocation
USA	1973–88	Manufacturing	9.1	10.2	−1.1	19.4
USA	1976–85	Pennsylvania	13.3	12.5	0.8	25.8
Canada	1979–84	Manufacturing	10.6	10.0	0.6	20.5
Canada	1979–84	Tax-paying firms	11.1	9.6	1.5	20.7
France	1978–84	Private, nonfarm	11.4	12.0	−0.6	23.3
Germany	1978–88	Private	8.3	7.7	0.6	16.0
Sweden	1982–84	All employees	11.4	12.1	−0.8	23.5
Italy	1984–89	Social security[1]	9.9	10.0	−0.1	19.9
Australia	1984–85	Manufacturing	16.1	13.2	3.9	29.3
New Zealand	1987–92	Private	15.7	19.8	−4.1	35.5
Denmark	1983–89	Private	16.0	13.8	2.2	29.8
Finland	1986–91	Private	10.4	12.0	−1.6	22.4
Norway	1976–86	Manufacturing	7.1	8.4	−1.2	15.5
Colombia	1977–89	Manufacturing	13.2	13.0	0.2	26.2
Chile	1976–86	Manufacturing	13.0	13.9	−1.0	26.8
Morocco	1984–89	Manufacturing	18.6	12.1	6.5	30.7

Source: Steven J. Davis, John C. Haltiwanger, and Scott Schuh, *Job Creation and Destruction* (Massachusetts: The MIT Press, 1996), 21 (table 2.2). Reprinted with permission.
[1]Social security employees.

Contributions to unemployment by worker and job flows also vary across the business cycle. Most notably, quits are counter-cyclical and job separations are procyclical, so that the cyclical variation in unemployment rates is accounted for primarily by the latter. The cyclical pattern of unemployment is also supported by movements into and out of the labor market. Finally, at least one study of worker flows has found that the *duration* of unemployment spells varies sharply among workers who enter unemployment voluntarily (through quits), temporarily (via layoffs subject to recall), and involuntarily (through layoffs without explicit prospects for recall).

A close examination of job flows also provides useful information about the incidence of forces that generate unemployment. For example, statistics on *net* employment changes can create the impression that the forces creating business cycles affect virtually the entire economy in the same way: in recessions, firms avoid new investment and cut back their labor force, while the economic climate underlying expansions induces most firms to expand production and hire more workers. But an investigation of gross job flows suggests a very different story in which a significant number of firms expand even during recessions or destroy jobs even during economic booms. Net employment changes arise from the fact that job destruction is more cyclically volatile than job creation. This finding tends to support the hypothesis, mentioned above, that business cycles are generated by sectoral rather than economy-wide shocks.

In sum, full comprehension of labor market dynamics may demand an accounting of the several flows into and out of unemployment and job vacancies, in addition to the nature and causes of these disequilibrium phenomena. This point is underscored as we next consider the frequently shifting connection between aggregate unemployment and vacancy rates.

WAGE AND EMPLOYMENT DYNAMICS

Job matching and the Beveridge curve

The processes by which job and worker flows translate into given levels of unemployment and job vacancies are summarized in the flow chart in figure 19.4. This chart suggests why unemployment and vacancy rates can simultaneously be positive in a dynamically adjusting labor market, but can't reveal anything about possible quantitative relationships between the two magnitudes. With respect to this relationship, it was suggested earlier in the chapter that unemployment and vacancy rates are to some extent inversely correlated. Consider now possible empirical and theoretical grounds for this inverse relation.

A graph of the hypothetical relationship between unemployment and vacancy rates is called a *Beveridge curve,* after the English economist William Beveridge, who first introduced it.[1] A stylized view of the Beveridge curve is presented in figure 19.5, indicating, as suggested above, an inverse relationship between the two magnitudes: the vacancy rate for an economy is high when the unemployment rate is low, and vice versa. A plausible macroeconomic story supports this relationship: in economic booms, more firms are hiring than are laying off workers, and correspondingly the unemployment rate is low while vacancies run high. Conversely, in recessions firms are on balance cutting back their labor forces rather than looking for employees, so workers have a hard time finding employment while vacancies are relatively scarce.

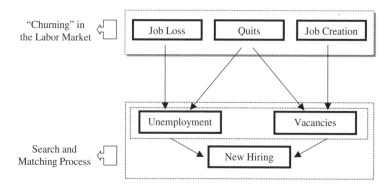

Figure 19.4   Flows into and out of unemployment and job vacancies.

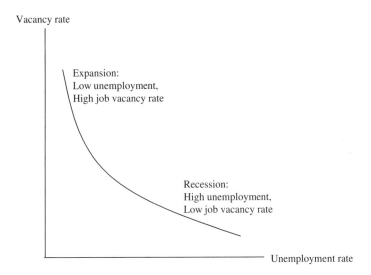

Figure 19.5 A stylized view of the Beveridge Curve.

The empirical incidence of unemployment and vacancy rates is somewhat more chaotic-looking than the simple stylized relationship presented in figure 19.5. This point is made rather dramatically in figure 19.6, which indicates the levels and movements of these two magnitudes for the US over the period 1960–98. A broadly inverse relationship between the two measures is suggested by the data series taken as a whole, but there are also transitions (such as from 1985 to 1986 or 1988 to 1989) in which unemployment and vacancy rates move in the same direction. One possibility, of course, is that in addition to (noisy) movements along a given downward-sloping Beveridge curve, there are also shifts in the entire curve that account for the seemingly anomalous cases just mentioned.

What causes movements along, or shifts in, the relationship between unemployment rates and job vacancies suggested by the Beveridge curve for a given economy? The task of constructing a theoretical story sufficient to account for the shape and movement of the Beveridge curve leads back to the earlier discussion of economic shocks. To tell this story, that discussion must be refined in two ways.[2] The first concerns the possible impacts of given shocks on the operation of the aggregate labor market. These can be labeled *cyclical* and *shift* effects, the magnitudes of which are denoted respectively by C and S.

As its label suggests, a change in C, reflecting the *cyclical effect* of an economic shock, represents a repositioning in the economy's business cycle. An increase in C represents economic expansion while a decrease indicates a decline in overall economic activity. Thus, an increase in the rate of job creation that outstrips any corresponding rise in the rate of job destruction corresponds to an increase in C.

In contrast, increasing the shift parameter S corresponds to greater reallocation of workers across jobs, without changing the aggregate supply of positions. Thus

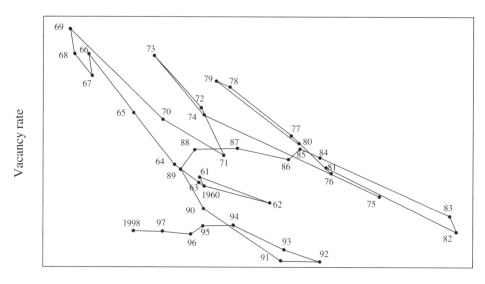

Figure 19.6 US annual unemployment and vacancy rate movements, 1960–1998. *Source*:
OECD, *Main Economic Indicators*, 1960–1998.

an increase in *S* indicates a rise in the gross rate of job creation that is *exactly
matched* by an increase in the gross rate of job destruction. In the case of decreased
S, fewer firms are either expanding and or contracting their productive operations, but the amount of potentially available jobs remains the same.

How do potential employment positions get filled? Answering this question
leads to the second refinement with respect to the impact of job flows, concerning the asymmetric nature of job separations and hires. Given the doctrine of
employment at will and the illegality of indentured servitude, either party to an
employment relationship can initiate a separation. As noted above, *quits* are at
least nominally initiated by workers, while *layoffs* are instigated by employers.
Conversely, an employment match is realized only if *both* parties to the relationship desire it.

To capture this idea, imagine that in any given period a certain percentage of
employed workers choose to quit their jobs and some other proportion of firms
decide to lay off workers, both of which actions generate flows *into* unemployment. Yet another proportion of firms elect to expand their production activities,
creating flows *into* job vacancies.

In contrast, paired flows *out of* unemployment or job vacancies are captured by
defining a *matching function* for the economy. The matching function is a simple
way of summarizing the complex process by which job and employee seekers find
each other and agree to commence employment relationships. Think of it as a sort
of production function, with the output being the number of new hires in a given

period, denoted H. Generally speaking, the form and value of the function are affected by the number of potential exchange partners, the incidence and magnitude of mobility and transaction costs, and the manner in which market participants accommodate these costs.

While one doesn't have to be facing unemployment in order to be seeking potential employment matches, the latter is the case for all unemployed workers or firms with vacant jobs according to our earlier definitions. Therefore, imagine that the number of job matches or new hires in a given period is a function of the current number of unemployed workers and vacant jobs, denoted respectively by U and V. Assume further that the matching function is increasing in each of these arguments, so that higher unemployment or vacancy levels may lead to more job matches in a given period, but never fewer. Posit finally a parameter M that represents the efficiency with which given levels of unemployment and vacancies are translated into new hires H; other things equal, increasing M leads to increased H.

Equipped with these conditions, look again at the flow chart depicted in figure 19.4. The processes in the uppermost box of the chart contribute to labor market "churning" or reallocation. Increasing S thus corresponds to an increase in quits leading to unemployment or else by equal increases in job creation and destruction. Changes in C correspond to variations in the relative magnitudes of gross flows of job creation and destruction. Paired flows out of unemployment and vacancies into new hires are captured by the matching function, and an increase in matching efficiency M leads to more hires for any given current level of unemployment and vacancies.

For simplicity, assume a fixed labor force L and a number of potential jobs K. Among other things, this makes it possible to refer interchangeably to *rates* or *levels* of unemployment and vacancies in the analysis, since increasing levels also increase rates when the respective denominators are fixed. Then, as a first step toward generating a Beveridge curve relationship on the basis of this model, determine the *steady-state* levels of unemployment U and vacancies V for given values of S, C, and M. These are defined as the levels of U and V for which their respective inflows and outflows are exactly offsetting. A steady state can thus be thought of as the analog of equilibrium for a dynamic economy.

The steady-state level of unemployment and vacancies for given market parameters can be determined by reference to two curves: the locus of (U, V) combinations such that flows into and out of unemployment are exactly equal, labeled $\Delta U = 0$, and the corresponding locus of (U, V) combinations that equate flows into and out of job vacancies, labeled $\Delta V = 0$. These two relationships are depicted in figure 19.7. The steady-state outcome for an economy given the economic conditions denoted by S, C, and M is determined by the point of intersection of the two curves, denoted (U_{ss}, V_{ss}). This point indicates the unemployment and vacancy levels at a given stage in the business cycle and for given degrees of match efficiency and market "churning."

To generate points along a given Beveridge curve or shifts therein, let one or more of the underlying parameters vary and derive the consequences. Consider

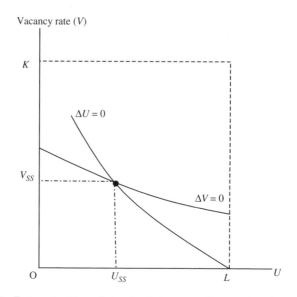

Figure 19.7   Determination of steady-state unemployment and vacancy levels.

first an increase in the parameter C, corresponding to an increase in the overall
level of economic activity. This leaves the matching function, and thus the process
of translating given levels of vacancy and unemployment, unaffected, but reduces
the net flows into unemployment for any given levels of employment. Consequently, the hiring must decline for any given value of U, and given the assumptions on the matching function, this means that the level of vacancies must decline
in order to re-establish the steady state. This implies in turn that the $\Delta U = 0$ curve
shifts *inward*.

A similar logic shows that an increase in C, say from C_0 to C_1, must shift the
$\Delta V = 0$ curve *upward*. The matching function itself is unchanged, but there is a
greater net flow into job vacancies because of the increase in economic activity.
Thus for any given level of unemployment, there must be more vacancies in order
to generate the increased job matches to offset the increased flow into vacancies.

The combination of these two effects is shown in figure 19.8. The steady-state
point for the economy as a whole has shifted up and to the left, corresponding to
an increase in vacancies and a decrease in unemployment. Here, then, is the theoretical basis for the inverse relationship between the two magnitudes originally
posited in presenting the stylized version of the Beveridge curve, and it broadly
corresponds to the intuitive argument given above to justify its hypothesized
shape. However, two additional comments should be made about the theoretical
relationship just generated.

First, remember that only shifts in *steady-state* points have been traced, that is,
hypothetical points in which job and worker flows both just balance. Of course,
nothing in a dynamic labor market will guarantee that these flows always balance,

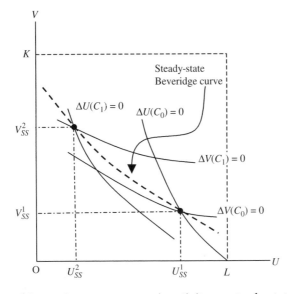

Figure 19.8 Effect of increasing macroeconomic activity on steady-state unemployment and vacancy levels.

so the indicated relationship is an approximation to the somewhat more round-about path the market would take in responding to cycle-generating economic shocks.

Second, it should be clear from the foregoing argument that the Beveridge curve doesn't have the same theoretical status as, say, market demand or supply curves, each of which summarize behavioral relationships for given sets of economic actors. The Beveridge curve is more akin to the locus of *intersections* of a series of supply and demand curves generated by a common set of changes in underlying economic conditions. This implies that the Beveridge curve corresponds to a higher level of economic abstraction than labor demand or supply curves, which presume only given preferences or technology, numbers of market participants, and optimizing, wage-taking behavior. To generate a particular Beveridge curve analytically, it is therefore necessary to make assumptions about preferences, technology, numbers of decisionmakers, and their behavior, as when deriving demand and supply functions, but also to specify how labor markets respond to economic shocks.

Imagine now an increase in S, leading to increased market churning without increasing the level of overall economic activity. This leads to increased flows into *both* unemployment and vacancies. For a given matching process, this means that in the steady state both magnitudes must be higher than before the change, shifting the point of intersection of the two curves up and outward. This outcome is depicted in figure 19.9.

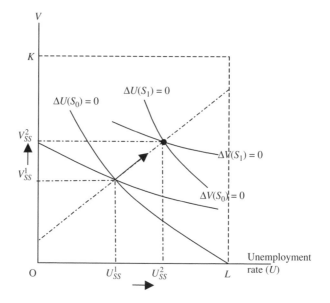

Figure 19.9 Effect of increased labor market churning on steady-state unemployment and vacancy levels.

In exactly parallel but opposing fashion, an increase in matching efficiency M increases the flows *out of* both unemployment and vacancies, without altering the respective flows into these states. Consequently, the steady-state point for the economy as a whole shifts down and inward toward the origin. In other words, changes in M or S induce inward or outward shifts in the entire Beveridge curve.

A potential basis has thus been established for understanding the empirical story presented in figure 19.6. These data are not necessarily inconsistent with the idealized Beveridge relationship; it might rather be the case that the US economy in the period studied experienced both movements along and shifts in the Beveridge curve. This suggestion is analytically coherent, but it doesn't help much in explaining what actually happened in the US economy over the indicated 38-year period to yield the data considered earlier. The following discussion box examines possible reasons for recent inward shifts in the US Beveridge curve.

WHY HAS THE US BEVERIDGE CURVE SHIFTED IN?

Examining US unemployment and vacancy rates for the period represented in figure 19.6, economists Hoyt Bleakley and Jeffrey Fuhrer (1997) identify an outward shift in the Beveridge curve for the period 1970–86 relative to the span 1960–9, and then two respective inward shifts for the periods

1987–9 and 1990–6. Their estimates of the period-specific Beveridge curves and their shifts are presented in figure 19.10. Writing four years later, Jessica Cohen, William Dickens, and Adam Posen (2001) identify two inward shifts of the US Beveridge curve in the periods 1985–9 and 1994–8 (at least).

Why have these shifts occurred? Bleakley and Fuhrer consider two factors discussed above, changes in matching efficiency and job reallocation and one, changes in labor force growth, not included in the model of labor market dynamics considered above. With respect to the latter factor, they suggest that the end of the baby boom and stabilization in the growth of women's labor force participation both reduced the flow of new and returning workers into unemployed job search, with a consequent reduction in observed unemployment rates for any given level of vacancies. They find statistically significant evidence for contributions by each of these, and suggest on the basis of simulation analysis that increases in matching efficiency account for as much as two-thirds of the inward shift in the Beveridge curve. However, they don't explore possible sources of this change in the job matching process.

Cohen, Dickens, and Posen suggest that the increase in matching efficiency has sprung from the spreading adoption of "high performance work organization (HPWO)" techniques by US businesses in response to the increased rigors of global competition. In their account, US firms reacted to market pressures for increased product turnover and reduced labor costs by relying more heavily on temporary and "outsourced" labor for tasks outside of their areas of "core competence." The latter were performed by their remaining incumbent workforces.

In addition, the new HPWO processes demanded that workers acquire higher average general skills while making shallower but more frequent investments in firm-specific human capital, associated with rapid changeover in firms' product lines. Cohen *et al.* argue further that these changes are consistent with increasing wages for generally skilled workers but reduced economic rents. They consequently identify two related bases for increased matching efficiency, and thus an inwardly-shifting Beveridge curve: first, the increased reliance on temporary and contract labor allows firms to respond more flexibly to changes in market demand, and second, the decline in economic rents means that there is less scope for unemployed workers to "queue up" for relatively desirable jobs in high-wage industries.

Related discussion questions:
1. Using the Beveridge curve model developed above, illustrate the impact of each of the changes discussed above on the position of the Beveridge curve.
2. Find data on US unemployment and vacancy rates since 1998 to see if the inward shift in the Beveridge curve detected by both groups of

continued

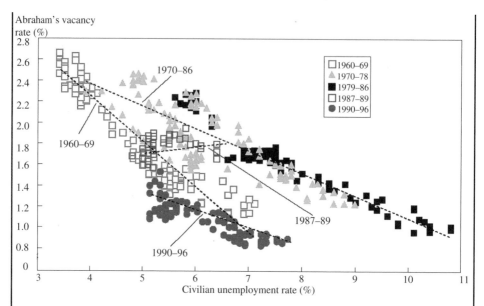

Figure 19.10 Estimated US Beveridge curve and shifts, 1960–1996. *Source*: Hoyt Bleakley and Jeffrey C. Fuhrer, "Shifts in the Beveridge Curve, Job Matching, and Labor Market Dynamics," *New England Economic Review*, September/October 1997. US Bureau of Labor Statistics; Abraham (1978); The Conference Board. Reprinted with permission.

authors has persisted. If not, what might have caused the countervailing shift?

Related references:

Hoyt Bleakley and Jeffrey C. Fuhrer, "Shifts in the Beveridge Curve, Job Matching, and Labor Market Dynamics," *New England Economic Review* 10, no. 9 (September–October 1997): 3–19.

Jessica Cohen, William T. Dickens, and Adam Posen, "Have the New Human Resource Management Practices Lowered the Sustainable Unemployment Rate?" in Alan Krueger and Robert Solow (eds) *The Roaring Nineties: Can Full Employment be Sustained?* (New York: Russell Sage Foundation, 2002).

UNEMPLOYMENT AND WAGE DYNAMICS

Labor market dynamics have so far been discussed in terms of variations in quantities exchanged, expressed in job and worker flows and the tradeoff between unemployment and vacancy rates. But as you might expect, economic changes have consequences as well for wage levels. Indeed, the basic predictions of supply

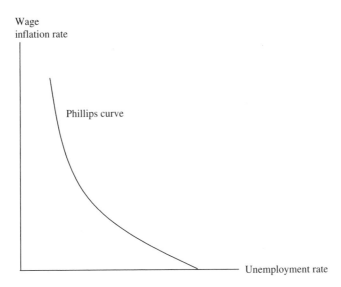

Figure 19.11   Idealized Phillips curve.

and demand theory suggest that perturbations in labor markets should in general be expressed simultaneously in wage and employment shifts.

In macroeconomic terms, the connection between wage and employment changes is often represented by a *Phillips curve*, which depicts a relationship between the unemployment rate and the *rate of change* in average *nominal* wages. (An alternative version of the Phillips curve relates unemployment to the inflation rate for other aggregate price measures, such as the consumer price index.) As conceived by British economist A.W. Phillips in the late 1960s, the hypothetical short-run relationship between these two measures is negative: other things equal, a reduction in the unemployment rate is presumed to lead to an increase in the rate of nominal wage inflation. This hypothetical relationship is depicted in figure 19.11.

The *empirical* connection between unemployment and wage inflation rates is depicted for a sampling of OECD countries for the period 1981–2000 in figure 19.12. These data seem to confirm the existence of a generally negative relationship between wage inflation and unemployment, but also suggest that the relationship is unstable, as if the Phillips curve might shift over time. In particular, a given rate of unemployment might be associated with a range of wage inflation rates.

The contrast of hypothetical and empirical connections between unemployment and wage inflation offers a forceful hint that the relationship between the two measures, if at all systematic, is a *ceteris paribus* one. Other factors evidently influence the connection between unemployment and nominal wage growth. The broader relationship is often expressed as a regression equation in which the observed rate of inflation, understood as the dependent variable, is presumed to

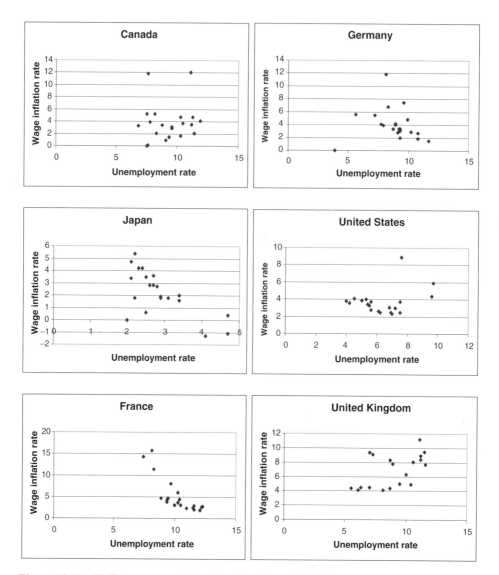

Figure 19.12   Phillips curve relationship for selected OECD countries, 1981–2000. *Source*: OECD, *Main Economic Indicators*.

vary *directly* with the expected rate of price inflation and *inversely* with the jobless rate. This is reflected in the equation $\dot{W} = f(\dot{P}_e, U)$, where $\dot{W}$ represents the rate of nominal wage inflation, $\dot{P}_e$ the expected inflation rate in the overall price level, and U the unemployment rate. Since the *expected* inflation rate is not directly observable, it is typically proxied in empirical regression analysis by the inflation rate from the previous period. Note that casting the rate of nominal wage growth as the dependent variable suggests a direction of economic causation running from unemployment to wage inflation rather than vice versa.

Related to Phillips curve analysis is the identification of a rate of unemployment for which the rate of nominal wage inflation is stable, termed the NAIRU (for Non-Accelerating Inflation Rate of Unemployment). In the above expression, this is the unemployment rate that emerges when the expected price and wage inflation rates are equated. In normative terms, the NAIRU provides a policy target for governments attempting to maintain stable macroeconomic conditions.

As specified, the broader Phillips relationship does a fairly good job of accounting for macroeconomic experience in the US, but fails to capture macroeconomic trends in Europe. To explain why this might be so, and to provide some theoretical footing for the basic Phillips hypothesis and its companion the NAIRU, it is necessary to investigate possible microeconomic foundations for the connection between unemployment and wage inflation rates. As it turns out, the Beveridge curve discussed earlier in the chapter provides a useful vehicle for thinking about these connections.

From the Beveridge curve to the wage curve

Why should any systematic relationship be expected to arise between the unemployment rate and the rate of nominal wage growth? Any theoretical account of the Phillips curve relationship must have two characteristics: it must allow for both the existence of (short-run) equilibrium unemployment and the possibility that this varies inversely with the rate of change in nominal wages. Subject to some caveats about the underlying nature of unemployment, there are at least three theoretically coherent and empirically plausible candidate explanations: competitive wages with frictional unemployment, bargaining, and efficiency wages. Each is summarized in turn.

To see the basis for these respective theoretical connections, let's begin with the simpler problem of linking variations in the unemployment rate to changes in nominal wage *levels* rather than wage *changes*. Even with this simplification the difficulty arises that most labor market theories concern the determination of *real* rather than *nominal* wages, where the former are net of changes in the aggregate price level. Since real wages are measured by the nominal wage rate divided by the price level, it is straightforward to translate predictions about real wages into hypotheses about nominal wage changes, for given values of the appropriate price index.

Next, recall the connection between aggregate labor market conditions and the unemployment rate depicted by the Beveridge curve. As discussed earlier in the chapter, this curve can be thought of as tracing out the steady-state relationship between unemployment and vacancy rates for a given size of the labor force and given processes generating new hires and job separations. Movements along a given Beveridge curve are caused by changes in aggregate labor demand, such that the unemployment rate is decreasing and the vacancy rate increasing in the level of demand. The next step in the argument is to augment this depiction of steady-state labor market outcomes by incorporating a story about wage determination.

Suppose first that all labor market participants are wage takers, so that the equilibrium wage rate is determined by the relative positions of market supply and demand, despite the exchange frictions implicit in the matching function and the existence of equilibrium unemployment and job vacancies. Under this scenario of *competitive* wage determination, an inverse relationship between the unemployment rate and the real wage rate is generated by an upward-sloping aggregate labor supply curve. This relationship is a reflection of the condition that higher aggregate labor demand leads both to low unemployment and to a position further up on an increasing labor supply function, leading to a higher wage rate. Note that it is therefore not the rate of unemployment *per se* that influences nominal wage levels, but rather the relative availability of employment opportunities for workers.

What is the economic significance of a rising aggregate supply curve? Recalling from the chapter 1 discussion of labor supply that the supply curve reflects the marginal opportunity cost to households of supplying labor, an upward slope for the aggregate curve suggests that marginal workers are characterized by successively higher reservation wage levels. By definition, a worker's reservation wage is the minimum acceptable return for supplying labor; for wages below this level, workers prefer to keep looking for jobs or else to remain outside the labor force.

The main theoretical difficulty with the competitive scenario lies in reconciling the existence of significant market frictions with wage-taking behavior by labor market participants. Rational gain-seeking market actors might instead be expected to make use of the fact that exchange partners do not have perfectly good alternatives to incumbent relationships. This presumption suggests that a bargaining model might better account for the macroeconomic phenomena summarized by the Phillips curve. For present purposes, it is sufficient to invoke the predictions of the Nash bargaining model for wage determination in the presence of varying unemployment.

As discussed in chapters 6 and 7, the Nash bargaining model predicts that a trader's equilibrium payoff is increasing in the total surplus to be shared and the value of his or her outside payoff, and decreasing in the outside payoff of the bargaining partner. Applied to the present context, this implies, other things equal, that the equilibrium wage rate is increasing in the level of labor productivity insofar as it is reflected in the value added generated in given employment relationships. The expected value of a typical worker's outside payoff is determined by his or her reservation wage and the prospects for re-employment upon being dismissed, so that equilibrium wages are again inversely related to the unemployment rate.

Finally, the existence of bargaining power may be moot if the equilibrium wage rate already exceeds the level consistent with the exercise of market power by workers. This possibility arises under the scenario of *efficiency wages*, which, as explained in chapter 10, arise under certain conditions of imperfect contracting. The focus here is on the version of the efficiency-wage scenario that concerns determination of worker effort. As detailed in chapter 10, the equilibrium wage rate is in this case once again increasing in the reservation wage level and decreasing in unemployment. The key difference from the previous two scenarios is that the equilibrium wage level bears no necessary relationship to the level of labor productivity.

Thus, with some variations in specification and underlying economic logic, the foregoing theories predict that the real wage rate varies directly with reservation wage and labor productivity levels and inversely with the unemployment rate, with respective weights to be determined empirically. The graph of the relation between unemployment and wage levels is called the *wage curve* by labor economists David Blanchflower and Andrew Oswald.[3] However, the wage curve relationship cannot be estimated directly, since reservation wage levels are not immediately observable. Instead, the reservation wage term in the predicted relationship must be replaced by an expression representing the determinants of the reservation wage.

Economists Olivier Blanchard and Lawrence Katz have suggested the plausible hypothesis that a representative worker's reservation wage is determined primarily by two factors, current-period labor productivity and *lagged-period* real wages.[4] Their reason for the latter connection is that unemployment compensation and other income supports adjust with a delay to average real wages. The former relationship is implied if the alternative uses of an unemployed person's time are influenced by general trends in productivity: for example, technical progress in commercial production may also affect home production possibilities or consumption benefits associated with leisure.

If the Blanchard–Katz hypothesis is used to modify the previously stated wage curve relationship, the resulting expression asserts that current-period real wages vary *directly* with lagged real wages and labor productivity, and *inversely* with the unemployment rate. In this context, one can define the "natural" rate of unemployment, the static analog to the NAIRU discussed earlier, as that level which emerges when current (and thus lagged) real wage levels remain stable for given levels of labor productivity. All of these variables have the virtue of being more or less directly observable; the main remaining difficulty is in specifying the current real average wage rate, since it depends on the current price level, for which data may not yet be available. Blanchflower and Oswald have devoted extensive efforts to estimating the wage curve for several countries.

Blanchflower's and Oswald's empirical strategy is to estimate the relationship using *microeconomic* data from the several regions of a given economy (for example, the 50 US states) over a given number of years.[5] This strategy allows them easily to separate out the effects of macroeconomic factors (such as productivity growth and expected inflation) that may be presumed to affect all such sub-regions more or less equally, allowing a more careful determination of the connection between unemployment and wage rates than might be permitted through the use of macroeconomic data. Using this technique, Blanchflower and Oswald study co-variations among local or regional current and lagged real wages and the unemployment rate for a panel of twelve countries.

Their chief finding is a consistent quantitative relationship between real wages and unemployment rates, such that a 10% increase in unemployment is associated with a 1% drop in the average wage rate. The striking feature of this result is its remarkable consistency across economies and time periods. This aspect of Blanchflower's and Oswald's empirical findings seems at least consistent with the Phillips curve hypothesis. However, another of their results draws this hypothesis sharply into question.

From the wage curve to the Phillips curve

To understand the criticism of the Phillips curve hypothesis implied by Blanchflower's and Oswald's second empirical finding, recall that the hypothesis asserts a direct relationship between the rate of change in *nominal* wages and the expected rate of price inflation. This can be translated into a story about real wage *levels* once the connection between real and nominal wage rates is recognized. Since the average real wage can be thought of as the ratio of nominal wages to the price level, the Phillips curve relationship can be rewritten to express a one-to-one relationship between *current* and *lagged* average real wage rates, conditioned as before by an inverse relationship between current real wages and the unemployment rate.

In Blanchflower's and Oswald's regression equations, however, the estimated coefficient on lagged real wages is always significantly less than zero, and just equals zero for the US and Great Britain. This discrepancy leads them to argue that the Phillips equation is misspecified, and moreover that the Phillips curve hypothesis itself needs to be fundamentally reconceived. It's clear in any case that an inconsistency in empirical findings needs to be resolved, since the Phillips curve specification seemingly contradicted by their microeconomic data seems at least to fit the US macroeconomic experience well.

A number of investigations of Blanchflower's and Oswald's work suggest that the source of the seeming inconsistency lies in their measurement of average wages, which fails to distinguish between variations in wage rates and variations in total labor income that may also stem from changes in hours worked. Re-analyses of their regression equations on US data using more precise measures of wage rates consistently reject their estimate of the connection between current and lagged real wages, suggesting that the true coefficient is in fact close to one, as predicted by the Phillips curve hypothesis. If this reassessment is valid, then Blanchflower and Oswald's disaggregative research strategy can be read as having provided new and empirically useful grounds for supporting the Phillips hypothesis, rather than a basis for rejecting it.

Blanchard and Katz note an important additional concomitant of this revision in Blanchflower and Oswald's empirical conclusions: affirming the one-to-one relationship between current and lagged real wages predicted by the Phillips curve hypothesis is tantamount to asserting that productivity levels have no direct impact on real wages. Again, this appears to be true for the US macroeconomic experience (consistent with the efficiency wage account of wage determination), but not for most European countries. According to Blanchard and Katz, this may explain why a "correction" term including productivity levels must be added to the European version of the Phillips curve in order to square it with the data.

And finally, what about the NAIRU? If the simple Phillips curve relationship is correct, then the minimal unemployment rate consistent with non-accelerating inflation can be defined independently of labor productivity levels. If this is the case, it seems difficult to explain the macroeconomic record of the US in the 1990s, which has shown declining levels of unemployment combined with inflation rates that are remarkably low by the standard of previous decades. If the evident shift in the NAIRU cannot be accounted for by changes in labor productivity, then by the scenarios considered above, there must have been some fundamental change in the logic of US wage determination, so that low unemployment somehow translates into significantly less upward wage pressure than in the past. This shift remains to be explained.

CONCLUSION

Capitalism is by nature a dynamic economic system. Spurred by competition, entrepreneurs are constantly seeking new products to sell and new ways of producing existing goods and services. This dynamism is transmitted to labor markets, which exhibit constant flux as employment and wage levels respond continually to changing economic conditions. Many such changes cannot be anticipated, even if they result in seemingly familiar-looking macroeconomic cycles.

Given market imperfections, economic dynamics also induce a state of disequilibrium in labor markets, at least in the long-run sense that market actors find themselves in situations they seek to change. Pervasively positive unemployment and vacancy rates are the most evident symptoms of labor market disequilibrium. Aggregate unemployment and vacancy rates are the end product of complex patterns of worker and job flows.

This chapter has explored how these flows interact to create a systematic relationship between unemployment and vacancy rates, summarized by the Beveridge curve. Market forces that determine the economy's position on a given Beveridge curve can also be understood to drive the connection between unemployment and wage inflation summarized by the Phillips curve.

Study Questions

1. What is an economic shock, and how does it relate to the scenario of incomplete contracts discussed in chapter 8? If all economic changes could be anticipated and addressed with fully specifiable and costlessly enforceable contract language, would unemployment exist?
2. Define *worker flows* and *job flows*. Which of these flows tend to increase or reduce unemployment? Which of these flows tend to increase or reduce job vacancies?
3. What does the *Beveridge curve* represent, and why is it downward-sloping? What factors would cause it to shift?
4. In their book *The Wage Curve*, Oswald and Blanchflower find an inverse relationship between wage and unemployment rates in local labor markets. What might explain this phenomenon? Is this outcome consistent with equilibrium in competitive labor markets? What would be the impact of an inward shift in the Beveridge curve on the wage curve?
5. Define the *Phillips curve*. Is it consistent with the wage curve? What would be the impact of an inward shift in the Beveridge curve on the wage curve?

Notes

1 William Beveridge. "An Analysis of Unemployment," *Economica, New Series*, 3, no. 12 (November 1936): 357–86.
2 The following model for the Beveridge curve is from Olivier J. Blanchard and Peter Diamond, "The Beveridge Curve," *Brookings Papers on Economic Activity* 1989 (1): 1–76.
3 David G. Blanchflower and Andrew J. Oswald, *The Wage Curve* (Cambridge, MA, and London: MIT Press, 1994).
4 Olivier Blanchard and Lawrence F. Katz, "Wage Dynamics: Reconciling Theory and Evidence," *American Economic Review* 89, no. 2 (May 1999): 69–74.
5 David G. Blanchflower and Andrew J. Oswald, "International Wage Curves," London School of Economics Centre for Economic Performance Discussion Paper No. 116 (February 1993).

Suggestions for Further Reading

David G. Blanchflower and Andrew J. Oswald, *The Wage Curve* (Cambridge, MA, and London: The MIT Press, 1994).
Assar Lindbeck, *Unemployment and Macroeconomics* (Cambridge, MA, and London: The MIT Press, 1994).

INDEX

Note: "n." after a page number indicates the number of a note on that page.